AF167574

Lecture Notes in Computer Science

Lecture Notes in Artificial Intelligence   16093

Founding Editor

Jörg Siekmann

Series Editors

Randy Goebel, *University of Alberta, Edmonton, AB, Canada*
Wolfgang Wahlster, *DFKI, Berlin, Germany*
Zhi-Hua Zhou, *Nanjing University, Nanjing, China*

The series Lecture Notes in Artificial Intelligence (LNAI) was established in 1988 as a topical subseries of LNCS devoted to artificial intelligence.

The series publishes state-of-the-art research results at a high level. As with the LNCS mother series, the mission of the series is to serve the international R & D community by providing an invaluable service, mainly focused on the publication of conference and workshop proceedings and postproceedings.

Giovanni Casini · Besik Dundua · Temur Kutsia

Editors

Logics in Artificial Intelligence

19th European Conference, JELIA 2025
Kutaisi, Georgia, September 1–4, 2025
Proceedings, Part I

 Springer

Editors
Giovanni Casini 🅙
CNR - ISTI
Pisa, Italy

Besik Dundua 🅙
Kutaisi International University
Kutaisi, Georgia

Temur Kutsia 🅙
Johannes Kepler University Linz
Linz, Austria

ISSN 0302-9743   ISSN 1611-3349 (electronic)
Lecture Notes in Artificial Intelligence
ISBN 978-3-032-04586-7   ISBN 978-3-032-04587-4 (eBook)
https://doi.org/10.1007/978-3-032-04587-4

LNCS Sublibrary: SL7 – Artificial Intelligence

This Springer imprint is published by the registered company Springer Nature Switzerland AG
The registered company address is: Gewerbestrasse 11, 6330 Cham, Switzerland

If disposing of this product, please recycle the paper.

Preface

These two volumes contain the proceedings of the 19th European Conference on Logics in Artificial Intelligence (JELIA 2025), held at Kutaisi International University, Kutaisi, Georgia from September 1 to 4, 2025.

The European Conference on Logics in Artificial Intelligence — Journées Européennes sur la Logique en Intelligence Artificielle (JELIA) — was first held in 1988 as a workshop, in response to the need for a European forum to discuss emerging research in this field. Since then, JELIA has been organized biennially, with its proceedings published in the Springer Lecture Notes in Artificial Intelligence (LNAI) series. Previous editions were hosted in Roscoff, France (1988); Amsterdam, The Netherlands (1990); Berlin, Germany (1992); York, UK (1994); Évora, Portugal (1996); Dagstuhl, Germany (1998); Málaga, Spain (2000); Cosenza, Italy (2002); Lisbon, Portugal (2004); Liverpool, UK (2006); Dresden, Germany (2008); Helsinki, Finland (2010); Toulouse, France (2012); Madeira, Portugal (2014); Larnaca, Cyprus (2016); Rende, Italy (2019); Klagenfurt, Austria (2021, held online due to the COVID-19 pandemic); and Dresden, Germany (2023).

The aim of JELIA is to bring together active researchers interested in all aspects of the use of logics in artificial intelligence, providing a forum to discuss current research, results, challenges, and applications of both a theoretical and practical nature. JELIA seeks to foster connections and encourage the cross-fertilization of ideas among researchers from diverse disciplines, between academia and industry, and between theoreticians and practitioners. Over the years, the conference has attracted growing interest from the scientific community, including increasing participation from researchers outside Europe. Combined with the consistently high technical quality of the contributions, JELIA has evolved into a major biennial forum and a key reference point for the discussion of logic-based approaches to artificial intelligence.

JELIA 2025 received a total of 108 submissions in two formats: 94 long and 14 short papers. Each submission was single-blindly reviewed by three members of the Program Committee. Of the 108 submissions, 44 were accepted - 39 as long papers and 5 as short papers. Among the 41 submissions declared to have a student as the lead author, 17 were accepted for inclusion in the program. All accepted papers were allocated a slot for oral presentation at the conference. This year's conference featured a Special Track on Logics for Explainable and Trustworthy AI, which focused on logic-based approaches to enhancing AI transparency, safety, and trustworthiness. Of the 108 submissions, 19 were submitted to this special track; they underwent the same rigorous review process, resulting in 4 papers being accepted and presented in a dedicated session. The conference program also included three invited talks by Natasha Alechina, Claudia d'Amato, and Andreas Herzig. The abstracts of their talks are included in these proceedings.

JELIA 2025 recognized two outstanding contributions with awards: the Best Paper Award and the Best Student Paper Award, both selected by the Program Committee for their exceptional quality. Each award was accompanied by a prize of 500 euros, generously sponsored by Springer.

We would like to express our sincere gratitude to the members of the Program Committee and the additional reviewers for their efforts in providing fair, thorough, and constructive evaluations of the submitted papers, which is essential for a successful scientific conference. Our thanks also go to all authors who submitted their work, including those whose papers were not accepted: the large number of high-quality submissions on important and timely topics made the selection process particularly competitive. We are grateful to the invited speakers for accepting our invitation and for delivering exceptional talks that greatly enriched the program. Our heartfelt thanks also go to the local organizing committee for their commitment and effort in ensuring that JELIA 2025 was a well-organized and memorable event. Finally, we wish to acknowledge the team behind EasyChair, whose conference management system was invaluable throughout the review process.

July 2025

Giovanni Casini
Besik Dundua
Temur Kutsia

Organization

General Chair

Besik Dundua   Kutaisi International University/Tbilisi State
                                University, Georgia

Program Committee Chairs

Giovanni Casini   CNR - ISTI, Italy
Temur Kutsia   Johannes Kepler University Linz, Austria

Program Committee

Sergio Abriola   Universidad de Buenos Aires, Argentina
Jose Julio Alferes   Universidade NOVA de Lisboa, Portugal
Mario Alviano   University of Calabria, Italy
Leila Amgoud   IRIT - CNRS, France
Grigoris Antoniou   Leeds Beckett University, UK
Carlos Areces   Universidad Nacional de Córdoba, Argentina
Ofer Arieli   Academic College of Tel Aviv-Yaffo, Israel
Dörthe Arndt   TU Dresden, Germany
Franz Baader   TU Dresden, Germany
Alexander Baumgartner   Universidad de O'Higgins, Chile
Peter Baumgartner   CSIRO, Australia
Salem Benferhat   CRIL - CNRS, Université d'Artois, France
Leopoldo Bertossi   SKEMA Business School Canada inc., Canada
Armin Biere   University of Freiburg, Germany
Alexander Bochman   Holon Institute of Technology, Israel
Bart Bogaerts   KU Leuven, Belgium
Richard Booth   Cardiff University, UK
Pedro Cabalar   University of Corunna, Spain
Francesco Calimeri   University of Calabria, Italy
Diego Calvanese   Free University of Bozen-Bolzano, Italy
Franco Alberto Cardillo   CNR - Institute for Computational Linguistics,
                                    Italy

David Cerna   Dynatrace Research, Austria / Czech Academy of
                               Sciences - Institute of Computer Science,
                               Czechia
Joe Collenette   University of Chester, UK
Silvano Colombo Tosatto   CSIRO, Australia
Mehdi Dastani   Utrecht University, The Netherlands
Marc Denecker   KU Leuven, Belgium
Martín Diéguez   University of Angers, France
Martin Diller   TU Dresden, Germany
Dragan Doder   Utrecht University, The Netherlands
Didier Dubois   IRIT-CNRS, France
Besik Dundua   Kutaisi International University/Tbilisi State
                               University, Georgia
Wolfgang Dvořák   TU Wien, Austria
Thomas Eiter   TU Wien, Austria
Stefan Ellmauthaler   Echo Intelligence GmbH, Austria
Esra Erdem   Sabanci University, Turkey
Santiago Escobar   Universitat Politècnica de València, Spain
Wolfgang Faber   University of Klagenfurt, Austria
Eduardo Fermé   Universidade da Madeira, Portugal
Masood Feyzbakhsh Rankooh   University of Helsinki, Finland
Johannes K. Fichte   Linköping University, Sweden
Michael Fisher   University of Manchester, UK
Tommaso Flaminio   Artificial Intelligence Research Institute, IIIA -
                               CSIC, Spain
Gerhard Friedrich   University of Klagenfurt, Austria
Maurice Funk   Universität Leipzig, Germany
Sarah Alice Gaggl   TU Dresden, Germany
Marco Garapa   Universidade da Madeira, Portugal
Tobias Geibinger   Vienna University of Technology, Austria
Alessandro Gianola   INESC-ID/Instituto Superior Técnico,
                               Universidade de Lisboa, Portugal
Laura Giordano   Università del Piemonte Orientale, Italy
Marianna Girlando   University of Amsterdam, The Netherlands
Lluis Godo   Artificial Intelligence Research Institute, IIIA -
                               CSIC, Spain
Lucía Gómez Álvarez   Inria, France
Ricardo Gonçalves   Universidade NOVA de Lisboa, Portugal
Jonas Philipp Haldimann   TU Wien, Austria; University of Cape Town and
                               CAIR, South Africa
Markus Hecher   French National Centre for Scientific Research
                               (CNRS), UMR 8188, Université d'Artois
                               (CRIL), France

Luisa Herrmann	TU Dresden, Germany
Jesse Heyninck	Open Universiteit, The Netherlands
Aaron Hunter	British Columbia Institute of Technology, Canada
Anthony Hunter	University College London, UK
Souhila Kaci	LIRMM, University of Montpellier, France
Antonis Kakas	University of Cyprus, Cyprus
Cezary Kaliszyk	University of Melbourne, Australia
Gabriele Kern-Isberner	Technische Universität Dortmund, Germany
Hiroyuki Kido	Cardiff University, UK
Matthias Knorr	Universidade NOVA de Lisboa, Portugal
Jedrzej Kołodziejski	TU Dortmund, Germany
Boris Konev	University of Liverpool, UK
Sébastien Konieczny	CRIL - CNRS, France
Roman Kontchakov	Birkbeck, University of London, UK
Markus Krötzsch	TU Dresden, Germany
Davide Lanti	Free University of Bozen-Bolzano, Italy
Joao Leite	Universidade NOVA de Lisboa, Portugal
Vladimir Lifschitz	University of Texas at Austin, USA
Anela Lolic	TU Wien, Austria
Emiliano Lorini	IRIT, France
Sanja Lukumbuzya	TU Wien, Austria
Quentin Manière	Universität Leipzig, Germany
Marco Maratea	University of Genova, Italy
Pierre Marquis	Université d'Artois, CNRS, CRIL - Institut Universitaire de France, France
Maria Vanina Martinez	Artificial Intelligence Research Institute (IIIA - CSIC), Spain
Andrea Mazzullo	Free University of Bozen-Bolzano, Italy
Arne Meier	Leibniz Universität Hannover, Germany
Thomas Meyer	University of Cape Town and CAIR, South Africa
Loizos Michael	Open University of Cyprus, Cyprus
Angelo Montanari	University of Udine, Italy
Michael Morak	University of Klagenfurt, Austria
Johannes Oetsch	Jönköping University, Sweden
Manuel Ojeda-Aciego	University of Málaga, Spain
Cem Okulmus	Paderborn University, Germany
Nicola Olivetti	LSIS, Aix-Marseille University, France
Juri Opitz	University of Zurich, Switzerland
Magdalena Ortiz	Vienna University of Technology, Austria
Stipe Pandzic	University of Milan, Italy
Nina Pardal	University of Huddersfield, UK
Pere Pardo	University of Luxembourg, Luxembourg

Xavier Parent	TU Wien, Austria
Francesco Parisi	University of Calabria, Italy
David Pearce	Universidad Politécnica de Madrid, Spain
Rafael Peñaloza	University of Milano-Bicocca, Italy
Luís Moniz Pereira	Universidade NOVA de Lisboa, Portugal
Laurent Perrussel	IRIT - Université de Toulouse, France
Ramon Pino Perez	Université d'Artois, France
Nico Potyka	Cardiff University, UK
Carlo Proietti	National Research Council of Italy (CNR) - Institute for Computational Linguistics (ILC), Italy
Antonio Rago	Imperial College London, UK
Anna Rapberger	Imperial College London, UK
Maurício Reis	Universidade da Madeira, Portugal
Francesco Ricca	University of Calabria, Italy
Aldo Ricioppo	University of Cyprus, Cyprus
Tjitze Rienstra	Maastricht University, The Netherlands
Giuliano Rosella	University of Turin, Italy
Sebastian Rudolph	TU Dresden, Germany
Mikheil Rukhaia	Tbilisi State University, Georgia
Irene Russo	CNR - Institute of Computational Linguistics, Italy
Chiaki Sakama	Wakayama University, Japan
Uli Sattler	University of Manchester, UK
Kai Sauerwald	FernUniversität in Hagen, Germany
Andrea Schaerf	University of Udine, Italy
Wolfgang Schreiner	Johannes Kepler University Linz, Austria
François Schwarzentruber	École normale supérieure de Lyon, France
Gerardo Simari	Universidad Nacional del Sur and CONICET, Argentina
Guillermo R. Simari	Universidad del Sur, Argentina
Mantas Šimkus	TU Vienna, Austria
Marija Slavkovik	University of Bergen, Norway
Umberto Straccia	CNR - ISTI, Italy
Hannes Strass	TU Dresden, Germany
Michael Thielscher	University of New South Wales, Australia
Matthias Thimm	FernUniversität in Hagen, Germany
David Toman	University of Waterloo, Canada
Anni-Yasmin Turhan	Paderborn University, Germany
Sara Ugolini	Artificial Intelligence Research Institute, IIIA - CSIC, Spain
Mauro Vallati	University of Huddersfield, UK

Leon van der Torre	University of Luxembourg, Luxembourg
Ivan Varzinczak	Université Sorbonne Paris Nord, France
Joost Vennekens	Vrije Universiteit Brussel, Belgium
Srdjan Vesic	CRIL, CNRS – Université d'Artois, France
Carlos Viegas Damásio	Universidade NOVA de Lisboa, Portugal
Miikka Vilander	Tampere University, Finland
Mateu Villaret	Universitat de Girona, Spain
Johannes P. Wallner	TU Graz, Austria
Frank Wolter	University of Liverpool, UK
Stefan Woltran	TU Wien, Austria

Organization Chair

Mikheil Rukhaia	Tbilisi State University, Georgia

Technical Chair

Nika Gagua	Kutaisi International University, Georgia

Organization Committee

Matthias Baaz	TU Wien, Austria
Mariam Gamsakhurdia	TU Wien, Austria
Revaz Grigolia	Tbilisi State University, Georgia
Lia Kurtanidze	Georgian National University, Georgia
Aleksandre Maskharashvili	University of Illinois Urbana-Champaign, USA
Konstantine Pkhakadze	GTU Research Institute for Cultural Protection and Technological Development of Georgian State Languages, Georgia
Levan Uridia	Tbilisi State University, Georgia

Additional Reviewers

Iosif Apostolakis	Pietro Galliani
Lars Bengel	Didier Galmiche
Aysu Bogatarkan	Lukas Gerlach
Cristhian Ariel David Deagustini	Maksim Gladyshev
Francesco Di Cosmo	Miika Hannula

Djordje Markovic
Oliviero Nardi
Iliana Petrova
Davide Emilio Quadrellaro
Luis Angel Rodriguez Reiners

Francisco Simoes
Daniele Theseider Dupre
Dieter Vandesande
Giovanni Varricchione
Baturay Yılmaz

Logic for Safe Reinforcement Learning

Natasha Alechina

Open University Netherlands and Flanders/Utrecht University, the Netherlands
n.a.alechina@uu.nl

Abstract. Reinforcement learning is famously about learning by trial and error, the agent getting feedback from the environment in the form of rewards. However, it is often quite difficult to specify a reward function to ensure that the learned behaviour is what the designer intended. It is also difficult to ensure that the agent's behaviour is always safe, especially when training is on- rather than offline. I will talk about using logic to provide declarative specification of desired/safe behaviours and ensuring that the learned behaviour conforms to those specifications. In particular, I will talk about how to block unsafe actions both during training and after deployment of the agent.

Tackling Semantics-Aware Machine Learning and Explanations for Knowledge Graph Refinement

Claudia d'Amato

University of Bari, Italy
claudia.damato@uniba.it

Abstract. Knowledge Graphs (KGs) are receiving increasing attention from both academia and industry, as they represent a source of graph-based structured knowledge of unprecedented dimension, to be exploited in a multitude of application domains and research fields. Despite their wide usage, it is well known that KGs suffer from incompleteness and noise, being the result of a complex building process. Significant research efforts are currently devoted to improve the coverage and quality of existing KGs via adopting numeric-based Machine Learning (ML) solutions that have proved to scale on very large KGs. They are usually grounded on the graph structure and they generally consist of series of numbers without any obvious human interpretation, thus possibly affecting the interpretability, the explainability and sometimes the trustworthiness of the results. Nevertheless, KGs may rely on expressive representation languages, e.g. RDFS and OWL (ultimately grounded on Description Logics) that are also endowed with deductive reasoning capabilities, but both expressiveness and reasoning are most of the time disregarded by the majority of the numeric methods that have been developed so far. In this talk, the role and the added value that the semantics may have for ML solutions, which include symbolic approaches, will be argued. Additionally, the importance of taking into account semantics when computing explanations for tasks such as link prediction will be addressed. Hence, the research directions on empowering ML and explanation solutions by injecting background knowledge will be presented jointly with the analysis of the most urgent issues that need to be solved.

It is Possible! Distance Semantics for Modal Belief Revision

Andreas Herzig

IRIT, CNRS, Université de Toulouse, France
herzig@irit.fr

Abstract. The belief revision literature only contains a few approaches with a modal logic basis. This talk discusses how the Alchourron-Gärdenfors-Makinson (AGM) approach to belief revision can be extended from propositional logic to modal logic S5. We propose three new rationality postulates involving the modal operator of possibility $\diamond$:

(M1) If $\varphi \wedge \diamond\mu$ is consistent, then $\varphi * \mu \vdash \diamond\varphi$.
(M2) If $\psi \wedge \diamond\mu$ is consistent, then $\varphi \vdash \psi$ implies $\varphi * \diamond\mu \vdash \psi$, for propositional μ.
(M3) If $\psi \wedge \diamond\mu$ is consistent, then $\varphi \vdash \diamond\psi$ implies $\varphi * \mu \vdash \diamond\psi$, for propositional μ.

The associated distance semantics is in terms of a lexicographic ordering that lifts the Hamming distance from a distance between valuations to a distance between pointed S5 models. Based on this account, we revisit a consequence of the AGM approach that has been much debated in knowledge representation, namely that the revisions of $p \wedge q$ and $p \wedge (p \rightarrow q)$ should be identical. We show that the problem disappears if one replaces material implication $\varphi \rightarrow \psi$ by strict implication $\varphi \succ \psi$. The latter can be expressed in modal logic as the necessity of material implication, that is, as $\square(\varphi \rightarrow \psi)$.

The talk is based on joint work with Carlos Aguilera-Ventura and Jonathan Ben-Naim and is based on our paper "Minimal Change in Modal Logic S5" (Proc. AAAI 2025) and ongoing work.

Contents – Part I

Deontic Reasoning

Description Logics and Ontological Reasoning

Higher-order and Non-classical Logics

Logic Programming and Answer Set Programming

Contents – Part II

Temporal Reasoning

Theorem Proving

Special Track: Logics for Explainable and Trustworthy AI

A Uniform Language for Safety, Robustness and Explainability

Vaishak Belle[1]([✉])[ID] and Pablo Barcelo[2][ID]

[1] University of Edinburgh, Edinburgh, UK
`vaishak@ed.ac.uk`
[2] Institute for Mathematical and Computational Engineering, Pontifical Catholic University of Chile, Santiago, Chile

Abstract. The areas of safety and robustness are key areas where communities from verification, neuro-symbolic AI, and machine learning come together. Safety and robustness are often formalized in terms of point-wise metrics: given an input point, we identify a circle or a region where certain properties hold in terms of the consistency of prediction. However, the broader goal of neuro-symbolic AI applied to machine learning correctness would ideally integrate safety and robustness conditions with explanations. Nonetheless, there is no paper that discusses these properties in a unified manner. What we consider in this paper is a new simple framework for formalizing a variety of such properties. We are able to characterize the robustness condition, safety conditions, hyper-safety conditions, counterfactual explanations, and fairness, among others. We can express these properties using simple notation for an abstract model based on a binary classifier. We hope these definitions would lead to neuro-symbolic frameworks that contribute to all of these areas jointly.

1 Introduction

The growth of machine learning (ML) systems, especially black-box models involving deep learning, across critical domains [30]—from healthcare [10] and finance to criminal justice and autonomous systems—has made urgent the need for transparent, interpretable, and accountable artificial intelligence [5]. As these models increasingly influence high-stakes decisions that directly impact human lives, the "black box" nature of AI systems has become not just a technical challenge, but an ethical imperative [8,15].

The field of Explainable AI (XAI) [18], Fairness [35], and Robustness [11] have emerged as responses to this challenge, representing an interdisciplinary effort to develop methodologies that can render machine learning models more comprehensible, trustworthy, and aligned with human values. This endeavor spans multiple dimensions: technical transparency, which involves understanding how

V. Belle—Was supported by a Royal Society University Research Fellowship. The authors thank the reviewers for helpful comments.

G. Casini et al. (Eds.): JELIA 2025, LNAI 16093, pp. 3–12, 2026.
https://doi.org/10.1007/978-3-032-04587-4_1

models arrive at specific predictions; ethical accountability, which requires ensuring that automated decisions are fair and unbiased by ensuring (say, gender) parity over predictions; and prediction consistency, which aims to make model predictions comparable across similar instances.

Existing approaches to XAI, fairness, and robustness have proliferated rapidly, generating a diverse yet distinct ecosystem of techniques. For explanations, for example, abductive explanations [23] and counterfactuals [36], along with local explanation methods like LIME and SHAP [9], have become popular. For fairness, various characterizations of individual and group fairness have emerged, such as demographic parity and counterfactual fairness, although implementing all of them in a single instance is not possible [38]. Finally, in the context of robustness [11], notions such as safety and hypersafety have also emerged [17], mostly by leveraging SMT technology [7].

However, this proliferation has also revealed a fundamental challenge: the lack of a unified theoretical framework to systematically compare, integrate, and evaluate these diverse strategies and notions. Our paper addresses this critical gap by proposing an abstract model to formalize and comprehensively compare these notions. This work is only a starting point and positions the abstract model as a potential unifying framework for distinct notions across fields. We leave open: (a) specific ways of implementing and combining definitions within a particular platform or technical framework, and (b) complexity considerations. However, it is worth noting that this abstract model has its roots in recent complexity-theoretic investigations into defining a uniform query language for explainability [2,3]. Drawing inspiration from formal logic, probabilistic reasoning, and computational learning theory, these works develop an abstract Boolean model that serves as a universal metalanguage for exploring complex XAI queries.

We reiterate that this paper primarily presents the generality of the model, but we hope it will serve as a unifying framework across fields. Our presentation is motivated by several key observations:

1. **Methodological Fragmentation**: Current trustworthy-AI research lacks a common theoretical foundation, making cross-method comparisons and knowledge integration challenging. In particular, although neuro-symbolic AI [19] offers some of the ingredients to potentially unify areas such as interpretability and fairness [13,34], there is much to be said about allowing us to put non-trivial XAI constructs, fairness and robustness in the same language.
2. **Multidimensional Complexity**: Modern ML models require explanations that simultaneously address multiple concerns—predictive accuracy, robustness, fairness, and safety.
3. **Interdisciplinary Demands**: Stakeholders from diverse domains (legal, medical, financial) require explanation techniques that are both technically rigorous and contextually meaningful.

Our approach introduces two fundamental desiderata for an ideal XAI language:

1. **Expressive Power**: The language must capture a wide range of trustworthiness (explanations, fairness, robustness) queries, enabling novel combinations

that explore relationships between model features, predictions, and underlying decision boundaries.

2. **Semantic Uniformity**: By providing a consistent mathematical framework, researchers can more effectively analyze, compare, and synthesize different methodologies.

The Boolean model we propose serves as a powerful abstraction mechanism. In particular, in this paper, we consider the following notions: (a) counterfactual explanations; (b) minimal sufficient reasons (abductive explanations); (c) fairness; (d) robustness and safety assessments; and (e) loss functions.[1]

The remainder of this paper is structured as follows. We begin by establishing the foundations, which, as one may observe, are surprisingly simple. We then systematically explore the model's applications across different domains and conclude by discussing its broader implications for responsible AI development.

2   Model

We follow the same abstract model as [2,4]. We use an abstract notion of a model of dimension n, and define it as a Boolean function $\mathcal{M} : \{0,1\}^n \to \{0,1\}$.

The input to the model is a set of features $\mathcal{X} = \{X_1, \ldots, X_n\}$ and the instances of these features are denoted using $e_1, \ldots, e_n$, respectively, where $e_i \in \{0,1\}$. So $\bar{e} = (e_1, \ldots, e_n)$ is a *complete instance* (or *full setting*) for all the features of the model. We use calligraphic letters such as $\mathcal{Y}$ to denote subsets of $\mathcal{X}$, and hence an instance $\bar{e} = (e', \ldots, e'')$ of $\mathcal{Y}$ corresponds to a *partial setting or instance* of the model. Clearly, $\mathcal{M}(\bar{e}) \in \{0,1\}$ for a complete instance $\bar{e}$. We often simply say setting to mean a full setting, and likewise, simply say instance to mean a complete instance. If $\bar{e}$ is a partial setting over $\mathcal{Y}$, we write $\bar{d} \subseteq \bar{e}$ to denote that $\bar{d}$ is the restriction of $\bar{e}$ to some $\mathcal{Z} \subseteq \mathcal{Y}$.

We focus on Boolean models for simplicity. However, since we do not focus on complexity issues or expressiveness, as in [37], most of the definitions we present in the paper can be adapted with a little effort to models of a non-Boolean nature. We also gloss over situations where the learning architecture may impose a relation between inputs (hierarchical grouping, ordering, and so on).

Weighted Model Counting. It is not hard to see that a number of existing formalisms in statistical relational learning, neuro-symbolic AI and probabilistic logical learning could be easily mapped to this Boolean model. For example, weighted model counting [12] remains a popular proposal for expressing loss functions in Neuro-symbolic AI [16,26]. Recall that the weighted model count is a computational task that extends the prototypical satisfiability problem by

---

[1] Contrasting the usefulness and significance of the Boolean model with the structural equation model [29], as used in the fairness and counterfactual reasoning literature [14,21,36], is an interesting direction for the future.

means of a weight function, and the counting of all satisfying assignments rather than obtaining a single one.

Given a formula over a propositional language and a weight function that maps the literals of the language to real numbers, we compute the weighted model count of a formula ϕ using the following expression:

$$\text{WMC}(\phi, w) = \sum_{S \models \phi} \prod_{l \in S} w(l).$$

That is, over every possible satisfying assignment S for ϕ, we consider all the literals that are true at the model S, and then multiply the weight assigned to these literals.

Given a query q and evidence e, we would compute the conditional probability of q given e using the following expression: $\Pr(q \mid e) = \text{WMC}(q \wedge e, w)/\text{WMC}(e, w)$.

Although the exact approach for using weighted model counting to define loss functions and correct the distribution of the model can vary across formalisms, as a general principle, we assume the following. Given a full setting of the features (which is the input to the neural network), one computes the classification label for these features in a supervised learning setting, for example. So therefore, we could say that given the evidence $\bar{e} = (e_1, \ldots, e_n)$, we compute the output label by letting it to be the most likely label: $C(\bar{e}) = \max_o \Pr(o \mid \bar{e})$. That is, C is assumed to be the output of the classifier, and we assume a finite set of labels $o \in O = \{o_1, \ldots, o_m\}$.

3   Formalizing Properties

3.1   Explanations

In what follows, we focus on a number of proposals of explanations and show that the above abstract model allows us to formalise these using the same meta-language. This would allow researchers in the area to infer relationships between these definitions, and leverage such relationships by adapting our proposal.

Counterfactual Explanations. Counterfactuals have a long standing history within philosophy [25], as well as within the causal modelling community [21]. When it comes to Explainable AI (XAI), they have gained significant traction in recent years, partly because there is evidence suggesting that non-technical audiences feel more comfortable interpreting such explanations in law, among other domains [36].

Furthermore, counterfactuals inherently convey a notion of "closeness" to the actual world, in the sense that they allow for detecting a set of minimal changes that can alter a model's decision. In the seminal work of Wachter et al. [36], an optimization scheme for generating counterfactuals is proposed, assuming the classifier is differentiable. In our Boolean model, differentiability, among other facets, is abstracted, of course, but based on a user-specified measure ϵ of closeness, we would capture counterfactual explanations as follows.

Definition 1 (Counterfactuals). *Given ϵ, an instance $\bar{e}$, a model $\mathcal{M}$, a counterfactual for $\bar{e}$ over $\mathcal{M}$ is an instance $\bar{e}'$ such that $\mathcal{M}(\bar{e}) \neq \mathcal{M}(\bar{e}')$ and $|\bar{e} - \bar{e}'| \leq \epsilon$.*

That is, we might use the Manhattan distance [36] or some other metric to ensure that $\bar{e}'$ is close enough (relative to ϵ) to $\bar{e}$.

So, for example, an individual might be denied a loan and the counterfactual explanation might be that an individual with the exact same profile but with twice the annual salary would be granted the loan. The metric might allow individuals of different salaries to be close enough, but individuals of different age or gender to be too far and thus would not be considered as a counterfactual.

Diverse Counterfactuals. As an extension to the work of Wachter et al. [36], Russell [31] introduces an alternative framework for generating counterfactuals in linear models. He argued that this approach not only addresses the technical limitations of the existing model, but also offers a more comprehensive method for producing "diverse" counterfactual explanations.

In the example above, we might insist that generating a counterfactual that doubles the annual salary is not feasible. So we might be willing to negotiate on other features, such as the number of monthly installments or insurance premiums. These kinds of constraints are called *diversity constraints*. Since then, there has been work on generating diverse counterfactuals in differentiable models [27] as well as multi-linear models (e.g., random forests and Bayesian networks) [28].

In our formalisation, we will assume that a constraint $\bar{c}$ is a partial setting to the features. We are then interested in a full setting $\bar{e}'$ that satisfies the constraint. That is, $\bar{c} \subseteq \bar{e}'$.

Definition 2 (Diverse counterfactuals). *Given $\mathcal{M}, \epsilon, \bar{e}$ as before, and constraint $\bar{c}$ that instantiates $\mathcal{Y} \subseteq \mathcal{X}$, find a counterfactual $\bar{e}'$ such that $\bar{c} \subseteq \bar{e}'$. That is, $\mathcal{M}(\bar{e}) \neq M(\bar{e}')$ and $|\bar{e} - \bar{e}'| \leq \epsilon$.*

Minimal Sufficient Explanations. The idea behind *sufficient reason* is to identify the subset of feature values for an instance such that no matter what values the other features would take, the decision would not change [24,32]. Since we use the same Boolean model as [2], we can capture the definition of sufficient reason and *minimal* sufficient reason. Notationally, for a partial setting $\bar{d}$ over $\mathcal{Y} \subseteq \mathcal{X}$, we write $\bar{e}_{\bar{d}}$ to denote the setting that is obtained by replacing the partial setting to $\mathcal{Y}$ in $\bar{e}$ with $\bar{d}$.

Definition 3 (Sufficient reason). *The set of features $\mathcal{Y} \subseteq \mathcal{X}$ is a sufficient reason for $\bar{e}$ over $\mathcal{M}$ iff $\mathcal{M}(\bar{e}) = \mathcal{M}(\bar{e}_{\bar{d}})$ for every partial setting $\bar{d}$ for $\mathcal{X} - \mathcal{Y}$.*

A minimal sufficient reason $\mathcal{Y}$ is then ensuring that there is no proper subset of $\mathcal{Y}$ that constitutes a sufficient reason. Minimal sufficient reasons have also been called *prime implicant* or *abductive* explanations in the literature [23].[2]

---

[2] We believe the model can be easily extended to other notions of explanations; for example, extending these formalizations to semifactual explanations as well as pref-

Definition 4 (Minimal sufficient reason). *The set of features $\mathcal{Y} \subseteq \mathcal{X}$ is a minimal sufficient reason iff: (a) $\mathcal{Y}$ is a sufficient reason, and (b) for every $\mathcal{Z} \subseteq \mathcal{Y}$ that is a sufficient reason, we have $\mathcal{Z} = \mathcal{Y}$.*

3.2   Fairness

Individual fairness states that similar individuals should be treated similarly by a model [34,35]. Formally, for two data points x_1 and x_2 that are "close" according to a predefined similarity metric $d(x_1, x_2)$, the model's predictions should also be "close". Given our definition for counterfactuals above, it should not come as a surprise that we can capture individual fairness straightforwardly. And with a Boolean model, we will suggest that the predictions need to be the same.

Definition 5 (Individual fairness). *Given any two full settings $\bar{e}, \bar{e}'$ for $\mathcal{X}$, and ϵ, if $|\bar{e} - \bar{e}'| \leq \epsilon$, we have that $M(\bar{e}) = M(\bar{e}')$.*

Group Fairness focuses on ensuring that a machine learning model provides statistically similar outcomes across different predefined demographic groups [34,35]. Usually, we declare a set of *protective attributes*, such as gender, marital status and race, over which model outcomes are to be consistent. Although there are many definitions for what kind of statistical property we might care for, in this paper we will consider demographic parity which states that the probability of a positive prediction should be the same across different instantiations of the protected attribute. Thus, we can define:

Definition 6 (Demographic parity). *Given protected features $\mathcal{Y} \subseteq \mathcal{X}$, and any instance $\bar{e}$, the model M achieves demographic parity iff $M(\bar{e}) = M(\bar{e}_{\bar{d}})$ for every partial setting $\bar{d}$ to $\mathcal{Y}$.*

3.3   Loss Functions

There is a wide range of approaches to expressing domain knowledge as logical constraints, which can then be used to train neural networks. Among the many proposals for neuro-symbolic AI, these range from probabilistic semantics, such as semantic loss [16] and DeepProbLog [26], to fuzzy regularization methods [6], among others. The crux of these contributions is determining how to back-propagate the loss of the neural network in every epoch where the constraint is falsified. Clearly, these details are not yet incorporated into this abstract model. Instead, we consider the ideal solution: a trained network that satisfies the constraint. Often, this constraint is checked against output labels (e.g., ensuring that

---

erences over explanations is a worthy direction for the future [1]. Likewise, extending the model to address *distillation* would also be interesting. Distillation is a knowledge transfer technique where a compact, more efficient model (often called the *student*) learns to predict similarly to a larger, more complex model (the *teacher*) [22]. For example, we could say that a Boolean model N is a distillation of a Boolean model M if they agree on all predictions yet N is much smaller than M, defined in some formal way.

the path suggested by the network is geometrically feasible). However, since we do not formalize the internals of the model, we simplify this account and state that a positive prediction should hold only for those variable settings that satisfy the constraint.

Along the lines of [20], let us assume a constraint is any propositional formula ϕ. Note that over a propositional language with propositions X, an instance $\bar{e}$ is an interpretation because it assigns a truth value to every proposition in X. Therefore, to check that a constraint is satisfied, we would define:

Definition 7 (Constrained predictions). *Given a propositional formula (constraint) ϕ over the variables X, we say that the model conforms to the constraint if for every instance $\bar{e}$, $M(\bar{e}) = 1$ iff $\bar{e} \models \phi$.*

3.4 Safety

We begin with robustness, where close enough instances are to be predicted similarly [11].

Definition 8 (Robustness). *Given an instance $\bar{e}$, and ϵ, we say the model M is robust with respect to $\bar{e}$ iff for every instance $\bar{e}'$ such that $|\bar{e} - \bar{e}'| \leq \epsilon$, we have $M(\bar{e}) = M(\bar{e}')$.*

Definition 9 (Global robustness). *Given ϵ, we say the model M is robust everywhere (or globally robust) iff for every pair of instances $\bar{e}, \bar{e}'$ such that $|\bar{e} - \bar{e}'| \leq \epsilon$, we have $M(\bar{e}) = M(\bar{e}')$.*

The safety property [33] generalises robustness in ensuring that a model's predictions remain within acceptable bounds, for instances that satisfy some input requirement (and not just closeness). In particular, let I be an input specification in that for every pair of complete instances $\bar{e}, \bar{e}'$, we have that $I(\bar{e}, \bar{e}') \in \{0, 1\}$. We simply write $I(\bar{e}, \bar{e}')$ to mean $I(\bar{e}, \bar{e}') = 1$.

Definition 10 (Safety). *Given instances $\bar{e}$ and $\bar{e}'$, and input specification I, we say that the model M is safe for I over $(\bar{e}, \bar{e}')$, if $I(\bar{e}, \bar{e}')$ implies that $M(\bar{e}) = M(\bar{e}')$.*

Definition 11 (Hyper safety). *Given input specification I, we say the model M is hyper-safe iff for every pair of instances $\bar{e}, \bar{e}'$ such that $I(\bar{e}, \bar{e}')$ we have $M(\bar{e}) = M(\bar{e}')$.*

4 Conclusions

Our work has introduced a simple framework for understanding and analyzing key machine learning concepts, including robustness, fairness and safety, addressing a critical need in the growing area of trustworthy AI that encompasses these notions, among others. By developing an abstract Boolean model that serves as a universal metalanguage, we have demonstrated a path toward more systematic, comprehensive views to model correctness. By allowing for a semantic unification as well as a cross-field analysis, we hope this work serves as a skeleton for introducing new techniques that bridge these areas, for at least addressing the technical dimensions of trustworthy AI. Of course, developing corresponding complexity-theoretic foundations towards a uniform query language [2] is a pertinent direction for the future.

References

1. Alfano, G., Greco, S., Mandaglio, D., Parisi, F., Shahbazian, R., Trubitsyna, I.: Even-if explanations: formal foundations, priorities and complexity. In: Proceedings of the AAAI Conference on Artificial Intelligence, vol. 39, pp. 15347–15355 (2025)
2. Arenas, M., Baez, D., Barceló, P., Pérez, J., Subercaseaux, B.: Foundations of symbolic languages for model interpretability. Adv. Neural. Inf. Process. Syst. **34**, 11690–11701 (2021)
3. Arenas, M., Barceló, P., Bustamante, D., Caraball, J., Subercaseaux, B.: A uniform language to explain decision trees. arXiv preprint arXiv:2310.11636 (2023)
4. Arenas, M., Barceló, P., Bustamente, D., Caraball, J., Subercaseaux, B..: A symbolic language for interpreting decision trees. *CoRR*, abs/2310.11636 (2023)
5. Arrieta, A.B., et al.: Explainable artificial intelligence (XAI): concepts, taxonomies, opportunities and challenges toward responsible AI. Inf. Fusion **58**, 82–115 (2020)
6. Badreddine, S., Garcez, A.D., Serafini, L., Spranger, M.: Logic tensor networks. Artif. Intell. **303**, 103649 (2022)
7. Barrett, C., Sebastiani, R., Seshia, S.A., Tinelli, C.: Satisfiability modulo theories. In: Handbook of Satisfiability, chapter 26, pp. 825–885. IOS Press (2009)
8. Belle, V.: Knowledge representation and acquisition for ethical AI: challenges and opportunities. Ethics Inf. Technol. **25**(1), 22 (2023)
9. Belle, V., Papantonis, I.: Principles and practice of explainable machine learning. Front. Big Data, 39 (2021)
10. Caruana, R., Lou, Y., Gehrke, J., Koch, P., Sturm, M., Elhadad, N.: Intelligible models for healthcare: predicting pneumonia risk and hospital 30-day readmission. In: Proceedings of the 21st ACM SIGKDD International Conference on Knowledge Discovery and Data Mining, pp. 1721–1730 (2015)
11. Casadio, M., Komendantskaya, E., Daggitt, M.L., Kokke, W., Katz, G., Amir, G., Refaeli, I.: Neural network robustness as a verification property: a principled case study. In: Shoham, S., Vizel, Y. (eds.) CAV 2022. LNCS, vol. 13371, pp. 219–231. Springer, Cham (2022). https://doi.org/10.1007/978-3-031-13185-1_11
12. Chavira, M., Darwiche, A.: On probabilistic inference by weighted model counting. Artif. Intell. **172**(6–7), 772–799 (2008)
13. Choi, Y., Dang, M., Broeck, G.V.D.: Group fairness by probabilistic modeling with latent fair decisions. arXiv preprint arXiv:2009.09031 (2020)
14. Creager, E., Madras, D., Pitassi, T., Zemel, R.: Causal modeling for fairness in dynamical systems. In: International Conference on Machine Learning, pp. 2185–2195. PMLR (2020)
15. Etzioni, A., Etzioni, O.: Incorporating ethics into artificial intelligence. J. Ethics **21**(4), 403–418 (2017)

16. Gajowniczek, K., Liang, Y., Friedman, T., Zabkowski, T., Van den Broeck, G.: Semantic and generalized entropy loss functions for semi-supervised deep learning. Entropy **22**(3), 334 (2020)

17. Gehr, T., Mirman, M., Drachsler-Cohen, D., Tsankov, P., Chaudhuri, S., Vechev, M.: Ai2: safety and robustness certification of neural networks with abstract interpretation. In: 2018 IEEE Symposium on Security and Privacy (SP), pp. 3–18. IEEE (2018)

18. Gunning, D.: Explainable artificial intelligence (XAI). Technical report, DARPA/I20 (2016)

19. Hitzler, P.: Neuro-symbolic artificial intelligence: the state of the art (2022)

20. Hoernle, N., Karampatsis, R.M., Belle, V., Gal, K.: Multiplexnet: towards fully satisfied logical constraints in neural networks. In: Proceedings of the AAAI Conference on Artificial Intelligence, vol. 36, pp. 5700–5709 (2022)

21. Hopkins, M., Pearl, J.: Causality and counterfactuals in the situation calculus. J. Log. Comput. **17**(5), 939–953 (2007)

22. Hsieh, C.-Y., et al.: Distilling step-by-step! outperforming larger language models with less training data and smaller model sizes. arXiv preprint arXiv:2305.02301 (2023)

23. Ignatiev, A., Narodytska, N., Marques-Silva, J.: Abduction-based explanations for machine learning models. In: Proceedings of the AAAI Conference on Artificial Intelligence, vol. 33, pp. 1511–1519 (2019)

24. Izza, Y., Ignatiev, A., Marques-Silva, J.: On explaining decision trees. arXiv preprint arXiv:2010.11034 (2020)

25. Lewis, D.: Counterfactual dependence and time's arrow. *Noûs*, pp. 455–476 (1979)

26. Manhaeve, R., Dumancic, S., Kimmig, A., Demeester, T., De Raedt, L.: Deepproblog: neural probabilistic logic programming. Adv. Neural Inf. Process. Syst. **31** (2018)

27. Mothilal, R.K., Sharma, A., Tan, C.: Explaining machine learning classifiers through diverse counterfactual explanations. In: Proceedings of the 2020 Conference on Fairness, Accountability, and Transparency, pp. 607–617 (2020)

28. Papantonis, I., Belle, V.: Principled diverse counterfactuals in multilinear models. arXiv preprint arXiv:2201.06467 (2022)

29. Pearl, J.: Causality. Cambridge University Press, Cambridge (2009)

30. Rudin, C.: Stop explaining black box machine learning models for high stakes decisions and use interpretable models instead. Nat. Mach. Intell. **1**(5), 206–215 (2019)

31. Russell, C.: Efficient search for diverse coherent explanations. In: Proceedings of the Conference on Fairness, Accountability, and Transparency, pp. 20–28 (2019)

32. Shih, A., Choi, A., Darwiche, A.: A symbolic approach to explaining Bayesian network classifiers. arXiv preprint arXiv:1805.03364 (2018)

33. Urban, C., Miné, A.: A review of formal methods applied to machine learning. arXiv preprint arXiv:2104.02466 (2021)

34. Varley, M., Belle, V.: Fairness in machine learning with tractable models. Knowl.-Based Syst. **215**, 106715 (2021)

35. Verma, S., Rubin, J.: Fairness definitions explained. In: 2018 IEEE/ACM International Workshop on Software Fairness (fairware), pp. 1–7. IEEE (2018)

36. Wachter, S., Mittelstadt, B., Russell, C.: Counterfactual explanations without opening the black box: automated decisions and the GDPR. Harv. JL & Tech. **31**, 841 (2017)

37. Wäldchen, S., Macdonald, J., Hauch, S., Kutyniok, G.: The computational complexity of understanding binary classifier decisions. J. Artif. Intell. Res. **70**, 351–387 (2021)
38. Xiang, A., Raji, I.D.: On the legal compatibility of fairness definitions. arXiv preprint arXiv:1912.00761 (2019)

Reinforcement Learning Meets Logic Programming: Towards Explainable AI

Luciano Caroprese[1(✉)] ⓘ, Ester Zumpano[2] ⓘ, and Domenico Ursino[3] ⓘ

[1] InGeo, University "G. d'Annunzio" of Chieti-Pescara, Pescara, Italy
luciano.caroprese@unich.it
[2] DIMES, University of Calabria, Rende, Italy
e.zumpano@dimes.unical.it
[3] Department of Information Engineering, Polytechnic University of Marche, Ancona, Italy
d.ursino@staff.univpm.it

Abstract. This paper introduces a neuro-symbolic framework designed to predict and explain subsequent facts from current observations. Facts are generated through causal relationships, which can be modeled by a set of propositional logic rules representing the domain knowledge. However, these rules remain unknown to the agent. By observing the facts, the agent constructs an approximation of them, which is then used to predict and explain new facts. The proposed framework can learn and adapt to different environments modeled by various forms of logic programs, also handling negation and recursion. Most notably, it can handle dynamic environments whose structure evolves over time. In these scenarios, the agent modifies its understanding of the environment to capture new observations, guaranteeing that its model of the domain knowledge remains up-to-date. To achieve this goal, our approach leverages the A2C (Advantage Actor-Critic) reinforcement learning algorithm. This choice allows us to integrate reinforcement learning principles into our logic framework. Through this research, we aspire to contribute to the development of explainable neuro-symbolic Artificial Intelligence systems in dynamic environments.

Keywords: Explainable AI · Reinforcement Learning · Logic Programming · neuro-symbolic system

1 Introduction

Cognitive science is an interdisciplinary field that scientifically investigates the mind, drawing insights from psychology, philosophy, neuroscience, and computer science. It explores how nervous systems encode, process, and manipulate information to produce intelligence and behavior. Artificial intelligence (AI) aims to replicate aspects of human intelligence in machines, using computational modeling and simulations to understand cognitive processes [23]. Since the 1980s, AI researchers have debated the best conceptualization of the mind: whether as

G. Casini et al. (Eds.): JELIA 2025, LNAI 16093, pp. 13–27, 2026.
https://doi.org/10.1007/978-3-032-04587-4_2

a vast network of simple neural elements (connectionism) or as a system of higher-level structures like symbols, schemes, and rules (symbolic AI). This fundamental disagreement led to a division in the AI community between two approaches: i) The *symbolic* approach, which models abstract mental functions using symbols, and ii) The *subsymbolic* approach, which focuses on the neural and associative properties of the brain. Rather than being mutually exclusive, these systems are complementary. The strengths of subsymbolic systems— such as pattern recognition and learning from experience—often address the limitations of symbolic systems, which excel at logical reasoning and explicit knowledge representation. *Subsymbolic approaches* employ neural networks that excel at processing complex data and making accurate predictions, but often lack transparency and interpretability. They provide little explanation of how outputs derive from inputs or why specific decisions are made. This opacity becomes critical in high-stakes applications—such as medical diagnosis—where understanding the rationale behind AI decisions is essential. In contrast, *symbolic approaches* use logic programming and deductive reasoning to represent and infer knowledge explicitly. While they struggle with unstructured and high-volume data, they offer distinct advantages through their ability to clearly specify semantics and various forms of inference. They support preference criteria and strong or weak constraints, while also managing ambiguous information and modeling incomplete and inconsistent knowledge. These characteristics make symbolic approaches particularly suited for explainable AI. For these reasons, recent cognitive modeling approaches have wisely begun to converge toward a *neuro-symbolic* paradigm. This approach combines symbolic and subsymbolic methods to overcome the limitations of purely symbolic or neural models while leveraging the strengths of both. By integrating the power of neural representations with the clarity of symbolic reasoning, neuro-symbolic systems aim to achieve deeper and more interpretable understanding of data. The need for this integration reflects a fundamental insight about human cognition. As researchers have recognized [12], the human brain employs two distinct modes of thinking: a fast, intuitive system specialized for pattern recognition (analogous to neural networks), and a slower, deliberative system for logical reasoning (analogous to symbolic systems). The neuro-symbolic approach represents our best attempt to replicate this dual cognitive architecture in artificial systems. This work contributes to neuro-symbolic AI by presenting a framework that leverages Reinforcement Learning to extract Propositional Programs for *explainability*. The framework implements an intelligent agent that learns cause-and-effect rules modeling relationships in observed phenomena. The agent operates by performing actions in an environment to maximize reward while learning the underlying logic program. The environment's state consists of observable facts, and the agent's actions represent hypotheses about causal connections governing the emergence of new facts. Through this process, the agent constructs and refines a predictive model of its environment. Notably, the framework handles dynamic environments whose structure evolves over time. The agent progressively adapts its domain knowledge to explain new observations.

2   Background

This section reports a brief presentation of *propositional logic* and the *A2C Reinforcement Learning algorithm*.

Propositional Logic. We refer to a *domain* $\mathcal{D} = \{\alpha_i \mid i \in [0..n-1]\}$, where α_i are *atoms* (also called *facts*), representing the simplest statements that can be *true* or *false*. A *database* s is any subset of $\mathcal{D}$. A *logic rule* r is defined as $H \leftarrow B_1 \wedge \cdots \wedge B_p \wedge not\ B_{p+1} \wedge \cdots \wedge not\ B_q$, where H and B_i, for each $i \in [1..q]$, are atoms. The atom H is called *head* of r and is denoted as $head(r)$, while the conjunction $B_1 \wedge \cdots \wedge B_p \wedge not\ B_{p+1} \wedge \cdots \wedge not\ B_q$ is called *body* of r and is denoted as $body(r)$. A *logic program* P is a set of rules. The set of all possible logic programs whose rules' atoms belong to $\mathcal{D}$ is denoted as $\mathcal{P}^{\mathcal{D}}$. A database s *entails* a conjunction $c = B_1 \wedge \cdots \wedge B_p \wedge not\ B_{p+1} \wedge \cdots \wedge not\ B_q$, denoted by $s \models c$, if $B_i \in s$, for each $i \in [1..p]$, and $B_j \notin s$, for each $j \in [p+1..q]$. Given a database s, the *immediate consequence* operator $T_P : 2^{\mathcal{D}} \mapsto 2^{\mathcal{D}}$ returns all atoms that are heads of rules in P whose body is entailed by s, that is $T_P(s) = \{head(r) \mid r \in P \wedge s \models body(r)\}$. We define the $T_P^i : 2^{\mathcal{D}} \mapsto 2^{\mathcal{D}}$ operator as: i) $T_P^0(s) = s$, and ii) $T_P^i(s) = T_P(T_P^{i-1}(s)) \cup s$. If there is i such that $T_P^i(s) = T_P^{i+1}(s)$, we say that $T_P^i(s)$ is a *fixpoint* and we denote it as $T_P^{\infty}(s)$. When the fixpoint is reached, no further atoms can be derived.

Our fixpoint definition is inspired by *inflationary semantics* [4] to reflect that facts, once occurred in the real world, cannot be retracted.

A2C Reinforcement Learning Algorithm. *Reinforcement Learning (RL)* is a paradigm within machine learning where an *agent* learns to make decisions by taking *actions* in an *environment* to maximize some notion of cumulative *reward*. Instead of receiving explicit instructions, the agent learns from the reward for its actions. This learning process follows a trial-and-error approach, wherein the agent iteratively explores the environment, taking actions in various states and observing the resulting rewards and state modifications. During this exploration, the agent learns the *policy*, which is a mapping from states to actions that maximize the long-term reward. This process can be formalized as a *Markov Decision Process (MDP)*. An MDP consists of:

- a set of *states* S, which represent the possible configurations of the environment;
- a set of *actions* A, which represent the actions that the agent can take;
- a *transition function* $T : S \times A \times S \mapsto \mathbb{R}$, that returns the probability of transitioning to state s' when taking action a in state s, that is $T(s, a, s') = p(s_{t+1} = s' \mid s_t = s, a_t = a)$, where s_{τ} (resp. a_{τ}) is the state (resp. action) at time τ;
- a *reward function* $R : S \times A \times S \mapsto \mathbb{R}$ that returns the immediate reward for each transition (s, a, s');
- a *discount factor* $\gamma \in [0..1)$, which represents the weight assigned to future rewards with respect to immediate ones.

The *value* of a state s is defined as the sum of the *discounted rewards* that an agent can obtain starting from s and then acting optimally. This value is returned by a function $V : S \mapsto \mathbb{R}$, defined as $V(s) = max_{a \in A} \sum_{s' \in S} T(s, a, s')(R(s, a, s') + \gamma \cdot V(s'))$. The *quality* of action a in a state

s is the sum of the *discounted rewards* that an agent can accumulate starting from state s, executing action a, and then acting optimally. It is returned by a function $Q : S \times A \mapsto \mathbb{R}$, defined as $Q(s,a) = \sum_{s' \in S} T(s,a,s')(R(s,a,s') + \gamma \cdot V(s'))$. Another important concept is the *advantage* of action a in a state s that quantifies the increase in rewards that can be obtained by taking action a in the state s relative to its baseline value. It is returned by a function $A : S \times A \mapsto \mathbb{R}$, defined as $A(s,a) = Q(s,a) - V(s)$. If the transition function T and the reward function R are known the quality function Q can be easily computed. Once the Q function is known, the optimal policy π just selects, for each state s, the action a having the highest quality, that is $\pi(s) = argmax_{a \in A} Q(s,a)$. However, in many real-world scenarios, T and R functions are unknown. In these cases, the quality function can be approximated by a neural network trained on the basis of the agent's experience which is acquired by exploring the environment. The algorithms based on this approach are called *value-based* algorithms. In another class of RL algorithms, a neural network is trained to output a probability distribution over all possible actions for each state. This distribution is then used to sample the action to be performed. These algorithms are known as *policy-based* algorithms. *Advantage Actor-Critic (A2C)* [16] is an algorithm within the family of *actor-critic methods*, a class of RL algorithms that use both policy-based and value-based techniques (Algorithm 1). The *Actor* refers to a neural network with parameters θ that outputs, for each state, a probability distribution over all possible actions $\pi_\theta(\cdot|s)$, which is used to select actions (the *policy*). The *Critic* is a neural network responsible for estimating the value function $V_\phi(\cdot)$, where ϕ represents its parameters. This network is used to evaluate the advantages of actions taken by the agent.

Algorithm 1 Advantage Actor-Critic (A2C) Algorithm

1: Initialize *Actor* network weights θ and *Critic* network weights ϕ randomly
2: Set discount rate γ and learning rate α
3: **for** each episode **do**
4:     Receive initial state s_0 from the *environment*
5:     **for** $t = 0, 1, 2, \ldots$ until the episode ends **do**
6:         Use *Actor* network to select action a_t based on policy $\pi_\theta(\cdot|s_t)$
7:         Execute a_t in the *environment*
8:         Observe reward r_t and new state s_{t+1}
9:         Store (s_t, a_t, r_t, s_{t+1}) in the *batch*
10:        **if** *batch* is full or episode ends **then**
11:            **for** each t from 0 to $(|batch| - 1)$ **do**
12:                Use *Critic* network to calculate $V_\phi(s_t)$ and $V_\phi(s_{t+1})$
13:                $A(s_t, a_t) = r_t + \gamma V_\phi(s_{t+1}) - V_\phi(s_t)$
14:            **end for**
15:            $L^{\text{actor}}(\theta) = -\sum_t \log(\pi_\theta(a_t|s_t)) A(s_t, a_t)$
16:            $L^{\text{critic}}(\phi) = \sum_t (r_t + \gamma V_\phi(s_{t+1}) - V_\phi(s_t))^2$
17:            $\theta = \theta - \alpha \nabla_\theta L^{\text{actor}}(\theta)$
18:            $\phi = \phi - \alpha \nabla_\phi L^{\text{critic}}(\phi)$
19:            Clear the *batch*
20:        **end if**
21:    **end for**
22: **end for**

The algorithm initializes the *Actor* and the *Critic* with random weights θ and ϕ, respectively. Then, iteratively processes episodes from the environment, within which it executes actions sampled using the current policy π_θ. For each action a_t taken in the state s_t at time t, the environment returns a reward r_t and a new state s_{t+1}, which are stored along with the current state and action in a *batch*. Once the batch is full or an episode concludes, the algorithm calculates the advantage for each state transition in the batch using the *Critic's* estimates of the current and next state values, $V_\phi(s_t)$ and $V_\phi(s_{t+1})$, respectively. The advantage, $A(s_t, a_t) = r_t + \gamma V_\phi(s_{t+1}) - V_\phi(s_t)$, measures the relative benefit of the action taken in the current state. The *Actor's* policy is updated to maximize the expected return by adjusting θ in the direction that increases the likelihood of actions with positive advantage, as reflected by the loss function $L^{\text{actor}}(\theta) = -\sum_t \log(\pi_\theta(a_t|s_t))A(s_t, a_t)$. Concurrently, the *Critic's* weights ϕ are updated to minimize the difference between the estimated state values and the computed returns, minimizing the temporal difference error through the loss function $L^{\text{critic}}(\phi) = \sum_t (r_t + \gamma V_\phi(s_{t+1}) - V_\phi(s_t))^2$. These updates leverage *gradient descent* and are modulated by a *learning rate* α, to refine both the policy and value function estimates towards optimal solutions. We chose A2C after testing other actor-critic methods (PPO and TRPO).

3   A Neuro-Symbolic Framework for Dynamic Environments

This section introduces a framework integrating *RL* with *Propositional Logic* to model the agent's interactions with the dynamic environment it explores.

3.1   Modelling the Environment and the Agent

The environment's state is a set of observable facts, while the agent's actions are hypotheses about causal relationships generating new facts. The agent builds a model to *predict* and *explain* future facts. The elements of our framework are:

- **State Representation**: The *state* of the environment at time t is the set of observable facts $s_t \in S = 2^{\mathcal{D}}$.
- **Domain Knowledge**: The *domain knowledge* is a logic program $P \in \mathcal{P}^{\mathcal{D}}$. It models the set of causal relationships that the environment applies to derive new facts from current ones. It is worth pointing out that P is unknown to the agent. The transition from state s_t to state s_{t+1} is modeled by $s_{t+1} = T_P(s_t) \cup s_t$.
- **Action as Knowledge Approximation**: An *action* a_t at any time t is an agent's approximation of the domain knowledge P, used to *predict* the future state of the environment. Thus, each action $a_t \in A = \mathcal{P}^{\mathcal{D}}$ represents a guess of the domain knowledge, leading to a predicted state $\hat{s}_{t+1} = T_{a_t}(s_t) \cup s_t$.

– **Reward Mechanism**: The *reward* r_t quantifies the accuracy of the agent's prediction and is defined as the *Jaccard similarity* between the predicted new facts $\Delta \hat{s}_{t+1} = (\hat{s}_{t+1} \backslash s_t)$ and the actual new facts $\Delta s_{t+1} = (s_{t+1} \backslash s_t)$:

$$r_t = \begin{cases} \frac{|\Delta \hat{s}_{t+1} \cap \Delta s_{t+1}|}{|\Delta \hat{s}_{t+1} \cup \Delta s_{t+1}|} & \text{if } |\Delta \hat{s}_{t+1} \cup \Delta s_{t+1}| \neq 0 \\ 1 & \text{otherwise} \end{cases}$$

This metric ranges between 0 and 1, with 1 indicating perfect prediction accuracy.

– **Episode Dynamics**: The initial state s_0 of each *episode* is randomly sampled. Therefore, a fact may occur in the environment either because it belongs to the initial state or because it is derived in the next time steps. At each time-step t the agent observes the current state s_t, selects the action a_t, and predicts the next state $\hat{s}_{t+1}$. Then, the environment moves to the next state s_{t+1}, and the agent receives the reward r_t, based on its prediction accuracy. The episode ends when a fixpoint is reached, i.e. when $s_t = s_{t+1}$.

– **Optimization Objective**: The agent's objective is to maximize the *expected sum of the discounted rewards* over an episode τ, $\mathbb{E}_\tau [\sum_t \gamma^t r_t]$, where γ is the discount factor.

Example 1. Consider a Neolithic farmer trying to understand the dynamics that will ensure a bountiful harvest by observing the events that occur (Fig. 1)[1]. The farmer notes that if "he plants seeds" (α_0) and "he waters the soil" (α_1), then "the plants begin to grow" (α_2). He then constructs an initial rule: "If I plant seeds and water the soil, plants will start growing" ($r^0 : \alpha_2 \leftarrow \alpha_0 \wedge \alpha_1$). It is the winter season, and after a while, the farmer observes a "bountiful harvest" (α_3). At this point, he constructs a new rule: "If the plants start growing, there will be a bountiful harvest" ($r^1 : \alpha_3 \leftarrow \alpha_2$). The farmer has modeled the environment's dynamics with the logic program $\{r^0, r^1\}$. Summer arrives (a new episode starts), and the farmer plants seeds and waters the soil. Applying rule r^0, he predicts that the plants will start growing. And indeed, this happens. The farmer reinforces his knowledge related to r^0, which now seems confirmed. He now predicts that after some time, he will observe a bountiful harvest, but this will not happen. He analyzes what was different compared to the previous planting and understands that it is now summer and "there is a drought" (α_4). He then updates r^1 that becomes: "If the plants start growing and there is no drought, there will be a bountiful harvest" ($r^1 : \alpha_3 \leftarrow \alpha_2 \wedge not\ \alpha_4$). The first two steps of this episode are depicted in Fig. 2.

A key feature of this framework is its ability to handle dynamic environments, where the underlying cause-and-effect rules may change over time. Our approach employs an adaptive learning process that continuously updates the agent's model based on new observations. A flexible matrix-based knowledge representation allows for dynamic modification of rules as the environment evolves.

---

[1] The image has been generated by DALL-E (https://openai.com/dall-e-3).

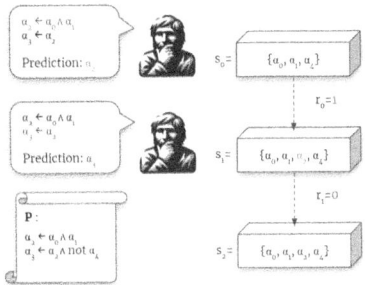

Fig. 1. The Neolithic farmer   **Fig. 2.** Second episode

Instead of discarding its entire model when faced with contradictory evidence, the agent can selectively update specific parts of its knowledge, ensuring that valuable information is retained while incorporating new insights.

3.2   Data Structures

Without loss of generality, we set the maximum number of rules that can be used to derive an atom, denoted by o.

- A *state* s is modeled by a binary vector $d_s \in \{0,1\}^n$. A fact α_i belongs to s iff $d_s[i] = 1$.
- The *domain knowledge* P is modeled by a matrix $b_P \in \{-1,0,1\}^{o \times n \times n}$. Let us consider a fact α_i and assume that it is defined by k rules $\{r^h = \alpha_i \leftarrow body(r^h) \in P \mid h \in [0..k]\}$. Then, the atom α_j occurs (not negated) in $body(r^h)$ iff $b_P[h,i,j] = 1$, and *not* α_j occurs in $body(r^h)$ iff $b_P[h,i,j] = -1$.
- An *action* a is modeled by a matrix $b_a \in \{-1,0,1\}^{o \times n \times n}$ by means of the same mapping described for P and b_P.

Example 2. Let us consider again the scenario presented in Example 1.

- In this scenario, $n = 5$. The initial state s_0 of the first episode, where the facts α_0 and α_1 are *true*, can be modeled by the vector $d_{s_0} = [1,1,0,0,0]$.
- Every fact is derived from at most one rule, thus $o = 1$. The domain knowledge $P = \{\alpha_2 \leftarrow \alpha_0 \wedge \alpha_1, \alpha_3 \leftarrow \alpha_2 \wedge not\ \alpha_4\}$ is modeled by the matrix:

$$b_P = \begin{bmatrix} \begin{bmatrix} 0 & 0 & 0 & 0 & 0 \\ 0 & 0 & 0 & 0 & 0 \\ 1 & 1 & 0 & 0 & 0 \\ 0 & 0 & 1 & 0 & -1 \\ 0 & 0 & 0 & 0 & 0 \end{bmatrix} \end{bmatrix}$$

- The action a_0 performed by the farmer in the first episode, which represents his initial guess about the domain knowledge, is modeled by the matrix:

$$b_{a_0} = \begin{bmatrix} \begin{bmatrix} 0 & 0 & 0 & 0 & 0 \\ 0 & 0 & 0 & 0 & 0 \\ 1 & 1 & 0 & 0 & 0 \\ 0 & 0 & 0 & 0 & 0 \\ 0 & 0 & 0 & 0 & 0 \end{bmatrix} \end{bmatrix}$$

It is worth noting that at the beginning of the process, the agent has no knowledge of the cause-and-effect rules governing the environment and it only guesses a set of random rules. It means that the matrix modeling these rules contains random values. As the process unfolds, the agent continuously makes hypotheses about the rules allowing it to make correct predictions. Rules that have led to accurate predictions are reinforced, while less accurate ones are weakened or discarded.

4   Implementation

The system is developed in *Python 3.10*, using *PyTorch 1.10.0* (with *CUDA 11.1* support) and the *OpenAI Stable Baselines3* library, offering a set of RL algorithm implementations (https://stable-baselines3.readthedocs.io/en/master/index.html). We use the *A2C* algorithm implementation provided by the Stable Baselines3 library and develop a custom environment using the *Gymnasium* framework. Both the Actor and the Critic networks are structured with 4 hidden layers, each including 64 neurons. The *tanh* activation function is employed across all these layers. The *rmsprop* optimization algorithm has been selected with a learning rate equal to 0.0007. In a Gymnasium environment, the STEP function advances the environment by one timestep in response to an action taken by the agent. It applies the action to the current state, computes the resultant state, evaluates the reward, and checks for the termination condition. The pseudo-code for our environment's STEP function is detailed in Algorithm 2.

Algorithm 2 Function STEP

Require: b_P, the matrix modeling the domain's logic program P
Require: d_s, the current state vector representing known facts
 1: **Input:** b_a, the action's matrix
 2: $d_{\text{before}} = d_s$
 3: $\Delta d_s = \text{FORWARD}(b_P, d_s)$
 4: $\Delta \hat{d}_s = \text{FORWARD}(b_a, d_s)$
 5: $reward = \text{COMPUTEREWARD}(\Delta d_s, \Delta \hat{d}_s)$
 6: $d_s = d_s \vee \Delta d_s$
 7: $fixpointReached = (d_{\text{before}} == d_s)$
 8: **return** $d_s, reward, fixpointReached$

The function accepts as input an action a, modeled by a matrix b_a, representing an approximation of the domain knowledge P, modeled by the matrix b_P. The state s of the environment is modeled by the binary vector d_s. The system initially backs up d_s to later determine if the environment has reached a stable condition (*fixpoint*) and the episode has to end. The function then applies both the domain's logic program, modeled by b_P, and the logic program modeled by b_a, to derive new facts Δd_s and $\Delta \hat{d}_s$, respectively. These facts represent the actual and predicted changes in the environment. They are derived by a call to the function FORWARD that implements a *immediate consequence* operator (the implementation details of this function, due to space limits, are not reported here.). It takes as input a matrix b, which models a logic program l, and a binary vector d, that represents a set of facts s. The function then outputs a binary vector that models the set of facts derived from applying l to s, that is $T_l(s)$. The reward, defined as the Jaccard similarity between the sets of facts modeled by Δd_s and $\Delta \hat{d}_s$, is computed by a call to the function COMPUTEREWARD (Algorithm 3). The Jaccard similarity is defined as the size of the intersection divided by the size of the union of two sets. When these sets are represented as binary vectors, the intersection is computed by performing a bitwise AND operation ($\wedge$) between the two vectors, and the union by performing a bitwise OR operation ($\vee$). The size of a set is obtained as the sum of the elements of its binary representation. Then, d_s is updated to include the newly inferred facts, and the function checks if a fixpoint has been reached by comparing the updated state with the previous one. The step concludes by returning the *new state*, the *reward*, and a *flag* indicating if the episode has ended.

Algorithm 3 Function COMPUTEREWARD

1: **Input**: d_1 and d_2, binary vectors that model sets of facts
2: **if** $sum(d_1 \vee d_2) \neq 0$ **then**
3:      $reward = \frac{sum(d_1 \wedge d_2)}{sum(d_1 \vee d_2)}$
4: **else**
5:      $reward = 1$
6: **end if**
7: **return** $reward$

---

5 Experiments

A series of experiments were conducted to evaluate the learning efficiency and accuracy of the agent. The aim was to assess how well the agent could learn and adapt to different environments modeled by various types of logic programs. We designed three categories of experiments:

- **Environments Modeled by Positive Logic Programs**: Experiments focus on environments that could be described by positive logic programs, without the use of negation. This setting provides a baseline for assessing the agent's learning capabilities in relatively straightforward scenarios.
- **Environments Modeled by Logic Programs with Negation**: This category explores more complex environments that require logic programs that incorporate negation to be accurately modeled.
- **Dynamic Environments**: The most challenging setting involves environments that not only include negation in their logic programs but also change over time. These dynamic environments test the agent's adaptability, highlighting its ability to dynamically alter its hypotheses about the environment's structure based on new observations.

A critical aspect to highlight is the system's ability to handle recursive logic programs, i.e. logic programs containing rules that indirectly call themselves through a chain of other rules.

5.1 Metrics

The *total reward per episode*, defined as $R = \sum_{t=1}^{T} r_t$, has not been adopted to assess the agent's performance in the experiments. Indeed, while it provides a direct reflection of the agent's performance in terms of achieving immediate objectives, it may not always offer comprehensive insights. This is because the maximum sum of rewards, equal to the episode length (reward equals 1 per step), varies depending on the initial state of the environment, which in turn affects the number of steps required to reach a fixpoint. Consequently, this metric does not account for the variability in episode lengths nor does it reflect the *explainability* aspect of our framework. Specifically, an event in the environment could be correctly predicted by the agent but attributed to an incorrect rule, indicating a *correct prediction* but an *incorrect explanation*. Instead, in the experimental evaluation, the performance of the agent is assessed by two key metrics.

- **Correctly Predicted and Explained Facts (*CPEF*%):** To address the need for evaluating the agent's ability to not only predict but also correctly explain events, we introduced a metric that calculates the percentage of events that actually occur, which was both predicted and explained correctly by the agent, focusing on the last 5% of the timesteps. This metric highlights the system's strength in integrating prediction with explainability.

$$CPEF\% = \frac{|\text{Correctly Predicted and Explained Facts}|}{|\text{Observed Facts}|} \times 100$$

- **Unobserved Predicted Facts (*UPF*%):** The second metric assesses the percentage of events that the agent predicted would occur but were not observed in the environment, focusing on the last 5% of the timesteps. This metric provides insight into the agent's tendency to overpredict or generate false positives, offering a measure of the precision of the agent's predictive model in relation to the actual dynamics of the environment.

$$UPF\% = \frac{|\text{Predicted but Not Observed Facts}|}{|\text{Predicted Facts}|} \times 100$$

5.2 Positive Programs

A *social media researcher* agent aims to discover how users become influencers by observing user histories. The unknown domain knowledge is encoded as:

$$EngagementIncrease \leftarrow CreatesQualityContent \wedge InteractsWithFollowers$$
$$BrandRecognition \leftarrow UsesPopularHashtags \wedge CollaboratesWithOtherInfluencers$$
$$FollowerGrowth \leftarrow CreatesQualityContent \wedge RegularPosts$$
$$BecomeInfluencer \leftarrow EngagementIncrease \wedge BrandRecognition \wedge FollowerGrowth$$

We report the graphs for the two metrics over $30,000$ steps and about $21,000$ episodes. At step $30,000$, *CPEF*%= 98.93% and *UPF*%= 1.89% (Figs.3 and 4).

5.3 Recursive Programs with Negation

A *Neolithic hunter* agent learns hunting dynamics through observations. The domain knowledge is modeled by the following logic program:

$$WeaponsReady \leftarrow TracksFound$$
$$WeaponsReady \leftarrow PreyApproached \wedge not\ PreyHunted$$
$$PreyApproached \leftarrow WeaponsReady$$
$$PreyHunted \leftarrow TracksFound \wedge PreyApproached$$

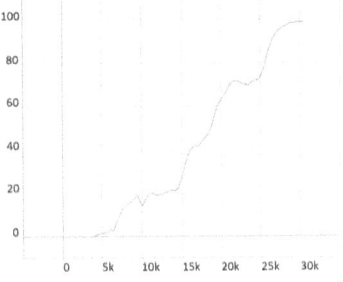

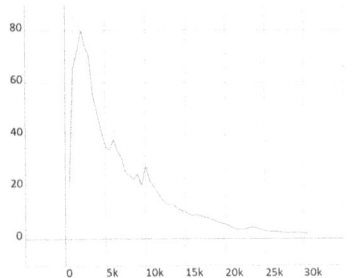

Fig. 3. *CPEF%*   **Fig. 4.** *UPF%*

The above logic program states that if the hunter has found tracks of prey (*TracksFound*), then he must prepare his weapons (*WeaponsReady*). If the hunter has successfully approached the prey (*PreyApproached*) and the prey has not yet been hunted (not *PreyHunted*), then he must prepare his weapons (*WeaponsReady*). If the hunter prepares his weapons (*WeaponsReady*), then he is approaching prey (*PreyApproached*). Finally, if the hunter has found tracks of prey (*TracksFound*), and has successfully approached the prey (*PreyApproached*), then he will successfully hunt the prey (*PreyHunted*). This logic program is particularly interesting because i) the atom *WeaponsReady* can be derived from two different rules, hence $o = 2$, ii) it contains a rule with *negation*, and iii) it is *recursive*. Figure 5 and 6 report the graphs for the two metrics over $10,000$ steps and about $5,300$ episodes. At step $10,000$, *CPEF%*$= 99.16\%$ and *UPF%* $= 2.15\%$.

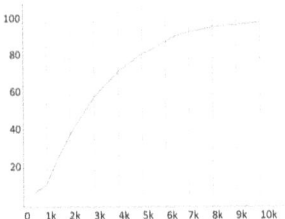

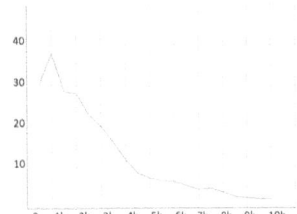

Fig. 5. *CPEF%*   **Fig. 6.** *UPF%*

5.4   Dynamic Environments

The proposed framework is designed to handle *dynamic environments*, whose structure evolves over time. In such cases, the agent adapts its model of the domain knowledge to explain new observations, ensuring its understanding remains accurate and up-to-date. Consider a *medical researcher* agent studying two new drugs, *DrugA* and *DrugB*. In the initial testing phase, the drugs are not administered to adolescents. Both drugs are indeed effective, but, if taken together, they cause side effects. The domain knowledge P_1 at this stage, which is unknown to the agent, is modeled by the rules:

$$Healing \leftarrow DrugA$$
$$Healing \leftarrow DrugB$$
$$SideEffects \leftarrow DrugA \wedge DrugB$$

In a second phase, the test is extended to include adolescents. Interestingly, the first drug has no effect on adolescents, and the simultaneous administration of the two drugs to them does not cause side effects. Therefore, in the second phase, the domain knowledge P_2 is modeled by:

$$Healing \leftarrow DrugA \wedge not\ Adolescent$$
$$Healing \leftarrow DrugB$$
$$SideEffects \leftarrow DrugA \wedge DrugB \wedge not\ Adolescent$$

In this case, $n = 5$ atoms and $o = 2$, as the fact *Healing* can be derived from two rules. We report the graphs for the two metrics over $20,000$ steps and about $14,300$ episodes. There is a transition from P_1 to P_2 at timestep $10,000$. Immediately after this timestep, a sudden collapse in the agent's predictive capabilities is observed, as its knowledge is now outdated. Following this moment, the agent restarts its learning process and, by observing new sequences of facts, reshapes its knowledge to predict and explain them. At step $20,000$, $CPEF\% = 95.73\%$ and $UPF\% = 2.27\%$ (Figs. 7 and 8).

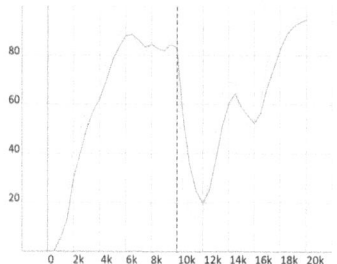

Fig. 7. *CPEF%*

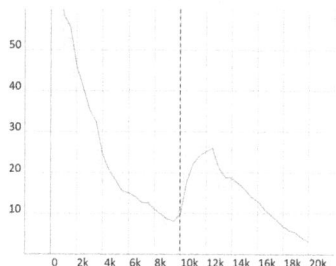

Fig. 8. *UPF%*

6   Related Works and Discussion

The survey [15] organizes XRL (Explainable Reinforcement Learning) techniques into three categories based on what they explain: *Feature Importance* (FI) includes methods that provide immediate context for individual actions, Learning Process and MDP (LPM) includes approaches that explain training effects or environment components, and Policy-Level (PL) contains techniques that summarize long-term behavioral patterns. A key distinction is between *intrinsic* interpretability (models designed to be understandable) and *post-hoc* interpretability (explanations added to existing non-interpretable models). Our framework belongs to the LPM category, specifically Model Domain Information, as LPM approaches typically learn models $\hat{T}$ that approximate the environment's transition function T and generate explanations based on $\hat{T}$. Similarly, we learn an approximation $\hat{P}$ of the causal rules that model the environment dynamics, which implicitly provides $\hat{T}$ as an approximation of T. In our framework, the environment's transition function T is modeled by an unknown logic program P, where $T(s, a, s') = 1$ iff $s' = T_P(s) \cup s$. However, our approach differs fundamentally from existing work in this category. While typical LPM methods learn transition models $\hat{T}$ for post-hoc explanation of pre-trained policies, our agent intrinsically learns propositional programs $\hat{P}$ that serve as both actions and causal explanations. Actions in our framework are hypotheses about causal relationships rather than motor commands, with the policy directly outputting interpretable rules. The agent learns to approximate the environment's deterministic causal structure through reinforcement learning on prediction accuracy, and uniquely adapts to evolving causal rules in dynamic environments. This combination of intrinsic interpretability, logic programming for causal structure learning, and dynamic environment adaptation appears novel in the XRL literature. In the majority of the proposal in the state of the art the neural-symbolic approaches operate under the assumption of pre-existing symbolic or logical knowledge - implicit structural understandings acquired during the training phase as in [3, 14], biased templates as in [6, 18, 22], or fixed hypothesis boundaries as in [7] - and concentrate on training a neural network to extract symbolic features from raw unstructured data. Some works, such as [9], use neural networks to extract propositional logic programs from input-output pairs with no negation and recursion, whereas we efficiently handle dynamic environments. Recent extensions of differentiable ILP frameworks have expanded the capabilities of the base approach in various directions: Incorporating stratified negation [13], enabling large-scale predicate invention [17], handling structured examples with function symbols [20], integrating with neural networks for unstructured data processing [2], and applying ILP to visual scene understanding [21]. However, these approaches still operate within the supervised learning paradigm with predefined templates and background knowledge. The works in [10, 19] implements logic tensor networks for deduction tasks within neural networks, while the proposed framework emphasizes interpretable cause-and-effect logic learned through reinforcement learning in dynamic environments. A new and interesting approach has been proposed in [8]. The paper presents a new differentiable model for inductive logic programming (ILP), called differentiable first-order rule learner (DFOL). DFOL generates first-order *positive* rules from relational data, focusing on matrix representations, while the proposed work focuses on propositional rules, also allowing *negation* and *recursion*, with the future goal of efficiently handling FOL programs directly. In [5], the authors present a neuro-symbolic framework that learns interpretable theories from raw sensory input using an Apperception Engine, but focuses on passive inference from pre-given sequences rather than active hypothesis testing as we do. Few works in the literature use reinforcement learning, but the spirit is completely different from our. They use

RL to enhance and existing ILP system, as in [11] or extract logic rules in a known environment, as in [1], whereas we use RL to derive logic program in a dynamic setting without any fixed environmental constraint. In the proposed framework, we currently consider propositional rules, but this is not a conceptual limitation. Indeed, FOL programs can be handled through grounding (i.e. by replacing variables with domain constants in all the possible ways). However, this approach is not practically feasible due to the exponential growth of the number of rules with respect to the domain size.

7   Final Remarks and Future Works

This work contributes to the advancement of explainable *neuro-symbolic Artificial Intelligence systems* and presents a framework that leverages Reinforcement Learning for the extraction of propositional programs to explain observations. In this framework, the agent observes the current facts and predicts the subsequent ones by providing a set of explanations for them. These facts are derived using a set of rules that model causal relationships in the underlying environment. The proposed framework is designed to handle dynamic environments, whose structure evolves over time. The versatility of the proposed framework provides a basis for developing complex reasoning capabilities, enabling the modeling of hypothetical scenarios and the exploration of their potential impacts. Its abstract and dynamic architecture enhances the model's adaptability and flexibility, allowing for the discovery of hidden causal relationships across a wide range of application domains, from *production* to *scientific research*, from *finance* to *health*. As for the future extension of this research, we plan to expand our framework to handle first-order logic and integrate an inference engine like DLV or PROLOG into its architecture.

References

1. Bueff, A., Belle, V.: Deep inductive logic programming meets reinforcement learning. In: ICLP. EPTCS, vol. 385, pp. 339–352 (2023). https://doi.org/10.4204/EPTCS.385.37
2. Cunnington, D., Law, M., Lobo, J., Russo, A.: FFNSL: feed-forward neural-symbolic learner. Mach. Learn. **112**(2), 515–569 (2023). https://doi.org/10.1007/S10994-022-06278-6
3. d'Avila Garcez, A., Broda, K., Gabbay, D.: Symbolic knowledge extraction from trained neural networks: a sound approach. Artif. Intell. **125**(1), 155–207 (2001). https://doi.org/10.1016/S0004-3702(00)00077-1
4. Denecker, M., Bruynooghe, M., Marek, V.W.: Logic programming revisited: logic programs as inductive definitions. ACM Trans. Comput. Log. **2**(4), 623–654 (2001). https://doi.org/10.1145/383779.383789
5. Evans, R., et al.: Making sense of raw input. Artif. Intell. **299**, 103521 (2021). https://doi.org/10.1016/j.artint.2021.103521,
6. Evans, R., Grefenstette, E.: Learning explanatory rules from noisy data. J. Artif. Intell. Res. **61**, 1–64 (2018). https://doi.org/10.1613/JAIR.5714,

7. França, M.V.M., Zaverucha, G., d'Avila Garcez, A.S.: Fast relational learning using bottom clause propositionalization with artificial neural networks. Mach. Learn. **94**(1), 81–104 (2014).https://doi.org/10.1007/S10994-013-5392-1,
8. Gao, K., Inoue, K., Cao, Y., Wang, H.: Learning first-order rules with differentiable logic program semantics. In: Raedt, L.D. (ed.) IJCAI, pp. 3008–3014 (2022). https://doi.org/10.24963/IJCAI.2022/417
9. Gao, K., Wang, H., Cao, Y., Inoue, K.: Learning from interpretation transition using differentiable logic programming semantics. Mach. Learn. **111**(1), 123–145 (2022). https://doi.org/10.1007/S10994-021-06058-8
10. Garcez, A., Zaverucha, G.: The connectionist inductive learning and logic programming system. Appl. Intell. **11**, 59–77 (1999). https://doi.org/10.1023/A:1008328630915
11. Isobe, T., Inoue, K.: Learning strategies of inductive logic programming using reinforcement learning. In: ILP. LNCS, vol. 14363, pp. 46–61. Springer, Cham (2023). https://doi.org/10.1007/978-3-031-49299-0_4
12. Kahneman, D.: Thinking. Fast and Slow. Farrar, Straus and Giroux, NY (2011)
13. Krishnan, G.P., Maier, F., Ramyaa, R.: Learning rules with stratified negation in differentiable ILP. In: Advances in Programming Languages and Neurosymbolic Systems Workshop (2021)
14. Lehmann, J., Bader, S., Hitzler, P.: Extracting reduced logic programs from artificial neural networks. Appl. Intell. **32**, 249–266 (2010). https://doi.org/10.1007/s10489-008-0142-y
15. Milani, S., Topin, N., Veloso, M., Fang, F.: Explainable reinforcement learning: a survey and comparative review. ACM Comput. Surv. **56** (2023). https://doi.org/10.1145/3616864
16. Mnih, V., et al.: Asynchronous methods for deep reinforcement learning. In: PMLR, vol. 48, pp. 1928–1937 (2016). https://proceedings.mlr.press/v48/mniha16.html
17. Purgal, S.J., Cerna, D.M., Kaliszyk, C.: Differentiable inductive logic programming in high-dimensional space. CoRR **abs/2208.06652** (2022). https://doi.org/10.48550/ARXIV.2208.06652
18. Rocktäschel, T., Riedel, S.: End-to-end differentiable proving (2017)
19. Serafini, L., d'Avila Garcez, A.S.: Logic tensor networks: deep learning and logical reasoning from data and knowledge. In: Besold, T.R., ag Whitney Tabor, L.C.L. (eds.) NeSy'16. CEUR Workshop Proceedings, vol. 1768 (2016). https://ceur-ws.org/Vol-1768/NESY16_paper3.pdf
20. Shindo, H., Nishino, M., Yamamoto, A.: Differentiable inductive logic programming for structured examples. In: Thirty-Fifth AAAI Conference on Artificial Intelligence, AAAI 2021, Thirty-Third Conference on Innovative Applications of Artificial Intelligence, IAAI 2021, The Eleventh Symposium on Educational Advances in Artificial Intelligence, EAAI 2021, Virtual Event, February 2-9, 2021, pp. 5034–5041. AAAI Press (2021).https://doi.org/10.1609/AAAI.V35I6.16637,
21. Shindo, H., Pfanschilling, V., Dhami, D.S., Kersting, K.: αILP: thinking visual scenes as differentiable logic programs. Mach. Learn. **112**(5), 1465–1497 (2023). https://doi.org/10.1007/S10994-023-06320-1
22. Sourek, G., Aschenbrenner, V., Zelezný, F., Schockaert, S., Kuzelka, O.: Lifted relational neural networks: efficient learning of latent relational structures. J. Artif. Intell. Res. **62**, 69–100 (2018). https://doi.org/10.1613/JAIR.1.11203
23. Sun, R.: The Cambridge Handbook of Computational Psychology, 1st edn. Cambridge University Press, Cambridge (2008). https://doi.org/10.1017/CBO9780511816772

Formal Explanations of Black-Box Ranking Functions

Francesco Chiariello[1]([✉]) [iD] and Joao Marques-Silva[2] [iD]

[1] RWTH Aachen University, Aachen, Germany
francesco.chiariello@ml.rwth-aachen.de
[2] ICREA, University of Lleida, Lleida, Spain
jpms@icrea.cat

Abstract. Ranking functions play a crucial role in supporting decision-making processes across various critical domains. Given their widespread use, coupled with the fact that these functions are often directly learned from data, it is becoming more and more important to provide explanations that make the underlying models more transparent. In this paper, we propose the first formal approach to explain ranking functions. Our approach is model-agnostic, requiring only black-box access to the ranking function. We study the formal properties of this new approach, including an analysis of the complexity of computing an explanation. To demonstrate its feasibility, we implement our approach and conduct an experimental evaluation using as a case study a neural network model for predicting breast cancer recurrence.

Keywords: Ranking · Preferences · Utility Functions · Machine Learning · Explainable Artificial Intelligence

1 Introduction

Ranking is a fundamental task in many decision-making processes, such as job recruitment, college admissions, and loan approval [57]. A critical domain is healthcare scheduling, where risk scores help prioritise hospital operations according to the urgency and severity of patient conditions. Given the significant impact that rankings have on our lives, it is therefore essential to provide clear explanations that ensure transparency, understanding, and trust. This necessity is even more pressing if we consider that such rankings are increasingly often determined by machine learning algorithms. Despite this, the problem of explaining ranking functions has often been overlooked in eXplainable AI (XAI) research, which has mainly focused on classification and regression tasks [20]. Driven by fairness concerns in machine learning, some studies have started to tackle this gap [18,45,55]. Nevertheless, these works only rely on heuristic methods, such as approximate Shapley values [36,50], which can sometimes produce misleading results for human decision-makers [23].

© The Author(s), under exclusive license to Springer Nature Switzerland AG 2026
G. Casini et al. (Eds.): JELIA 2025, LNAI 16093, pp. 28–44, 2026.
https://doi.org/10.1007/978-3-032-04587-4_3

Formal XAI (FXAI) [17,38] offers a promising alternative to heuristic methods by grounding explanations in logical definitions that enhance their interpretability. However, this research line has so far only considered classification and regression [6,39]. A naive approach to applying FXAI to ranking functions involves reducing the ranking task to binary classification. Specifically, one can construct a binary classifier that outputs 1 if and only if the ranking holds. Explaining a ranking then amounts to explaining why the classifier outputs 1. This construction was outlined by Labreuche [33], who, however, regarded it as impractical. This is because the classifier takes as input the concatenation of the vectors in the ranking, which substantially increases the dimensionality of the feature space. This higher dimensionality, in turn, negatively affects both the time needed to compute the explanations and their overall quality. Furthermore, this approach overlooks the fact that the new feature space is essentially composed of duplicates of the same features, once for each vector in the ranking.

We address the issues of previous work by introducing the first formal definitions for explanations of ranking functions. These definitions allow a feature of a vector to be part of an explanation if and only if the corresponding features in all the other vectors are also included. This results in a more natural definition, as explanations are directly defined within the original feature space. Furthermore, the reduced number of features involved makes the computation of these explanations practically feasible. We then investigate the formal properties of the proposed explanations and establish several results that support our framework, including the monotonicity of (weak) explanations. This key property allows us to cast the problem of computing an explanation of a ranking as an instance of the Minimal Set over a Monotone Predicate problem [41], which we solve using a deletion-based algorithm, akin to computing Minimal Unsatisfiable Subsets in Boolean Satisfiability [37]. Yet, our approach is *model-agnostic*, enabling its application to black-box models, whether large-scale or proprietary. We discuss the complexity of the algorithm, highlighting its greater efficiency compared to the naive approach. Finally, we provide an implementation of the approach and conduct an experimental evaluation based on the following case study, which serves as a proof of concept.

Case Study. We assume a neural network model f that estimates the probability $f(\mathbf{x}) \in \mathbb{R}$ of a patient $\mathbf{x}$ experiencing breast cancer recurrence within five years after surgery. These probabilities induce a priority ranking over patients, which can be used, for instance, to schedule medical appointments. Each patient profile is represented as a vector $\mathbf{x}$ of categorical features. While more features are considered in the experiments, we focus here on three illustrative ones: *age* (the patient's age group), *tumor-size* (the size of the tumour), and *deg-malig* (the degree of malignancy), with domain sizes of six, eleven, and three, respectively. For example, a patient profile $\mathbf{v} = (3, 8, 2)$ corresponds to an individual aged between 5059 years (category 3), with a tumour size of 4549 mm (category 8), and a malignancy degree of 2. Our goal is then to explain the ranking produced by the neural network over a given group of patients by isolating a set of features that alone account for the ranking.

The remainder of the paper is structured as follows. Section 2 provides the necessary background on formal explainability for classifiers and order theory, including an introduction to ranking functions. Section 3 defines (weak) abductive explanations for rankings and analyses their properties. Section 4 details an algorithm for computing these explanations and examines its computational complexity. Section 5 describes our case study and the experiments conducted. Section 6 reviews relevant literature. Finally, Sect. 7 concludes the paper with possible directions for future research.

2 Background

This section reviews key definitions from Formal Explainability [38] and Order Theory [48]. For a comprehensive treatment, please refer to the cited sources.

2.1 Formal Explanations of Classifiers

Let $\mathcal{F} = \{1, \dots, m\}$ denote a *feature set*, with each *feature* $i \in \mathcal{F}$ having an associated domain $\mathbb{D}_i$. These domains collectively define the *feature space* $\mathbb{F} = \mathbb{D}_1 \times \cdots \times \mathbb{D}_m$. The points $\mathbf{x} = (x_1, \dots, x_m) \in \mathbb{F}$ in the feature space are also referred to as *feature vectors*, or simply *vectors*.

We say that two vectors $\mathbf{x}, \mathbf{v} \in \mathbb{F}$, *agree* on features $\mathcal{S} \subseteq \mathcal{F}$, denoted $\mathbf{x} \sim_{\mathcal{S}} \mathbf{v}$, if $\forall i \in \mathcal{S}, x_i = v_i$. That is, when projected into the subspace defined by $\mathcal{S}$, the two vectors are indistinguishable. Note that the agreement relation $\sim_{\mathcal{S}}$ is trivially an equivalence relation on $\mathbb{F}$. We also define

$$[\mathbf{v}]_{\mathcal{S}} := [\mathbf{v}]_{\sim_{\mathcal{S}}} = \{\mathbf{x} \in \mathbb{F} \mid \mathbf{x} \sim_{\mathcal{S}} \mathbf{v}\}$$

as the equivalence class of $\mathbf{v}$ under $\sim_{\mathcal{S}}$, consisting of all points $\mathbf{x}$ that agree with $\mathbf{v}$ on $\mathcal{S}$.

Let $\mathcal{K} = \{c_1, \dots, c_K\}$ be a set of classes, and let $\kappa : \mathbb{F} \to \mathcal{K}$ be a classifier.

Definition 1 (Weak Abductive Explanation (WeakAXp)). *A set $\mathcal{S} \subseteq \mathcal{F}$ of features is a* weak abductive explanation *(or WeakAXp for short) for the explanation problem $(\kappa; \mathbf{v})$, if it holds that:*

$$\forall \mathbf{x} \in [\mathbf{v}]_{\mathcal{S}}, \ \kappa(\mathbf{x}) = \kappa(\mathbf{v}) \tag{1}$$

In other words, a WeakAXp is a set of features such that any vector $\mathbf{x}$ that agrees with $\mathbf{v}$ on those features is mapped to the same class of $\mathbf{v}$. We also write WeakAXp($\mathcal{S}$) to denote that $\mathcal{S}$ is a WeakAXp, omitting the dependence on the explanation problem to simplify the notation.

Definition 2 (Abductive Explanation (AXp)). *A set $\mathcal{S} \subseteq \mathcal{F}$ is an abductive explanation (or AXp) for the explanation problem $(\kappa; \mathbf{v})$ if $\mathcal{S}$ is a subset-minimal WeakAXp, that is,*

$$\mathsf{WeakAXp}(\mathcal{S}) \ \wedge \ \forall \mathcal{S}' \subsetneq \mathcal{S}, \neg\mathsf{WeakAXp}(\mathcal{S}') \tag{2}$$

AXps are also known as PI-explanations [51], as they correspond to the prime implicants of the classification $\kappa(\mathbf{v})$, or more precisely, the prime implicants of formula (1) when interpreted as a Boolean function over the features $\mathcal{F}$.

2.2 Order Theory

In what follows, let S be a finite set. A *preorder* $\preceq$ on S is a binary relation on S that is both reflexive and transitive. A preorder is said to be *total* if it is also strongly connected; that is, if any two elements are comparable. A total preorder is also referred to as a *ranking*. Rankings are commonly known as *preferences* in microeconomic theory [9], where they serve as models for consumer behaviour. If a ranking is also antisymmetric—thus forming a proper order—it is called a *linear order*. A preorder $\preceq_i$ on S induces an equivalence relation $\sim_i$ on S, defined by $a \sim_i b \iff a \preceq_i b \wedge b \preceq_i a$. Given two rankings $\preceq_1, \preceq_2$, the ranking $\preceq_1$ is *finer* than $\preceq_2$ if $\preceq_1 \subseteq \preceq_2$ or, equivalently, $\sim_1 \subseteq \sim_2$. Rankings are more general than linear orders in that they allow for ties, with elements being tied if they belong to the same equivalence class.

A *ranking function*, or *ranker*, (also known as *utility function* in microeconomic theory) on S is a function $f : S \to \mathbb{R}$. A ranking function f on S induces a ranking $\preceq_f$ on S, by defining $a \preceq_f b \iff f(a) \leq f(b)$. Conversely, given a ranking $\preceq$ on S, there exists a ranking function $f : S \to \mathbb{R}$ such that $\preceq$ coincides with the ranking induced by f, i.e., $\preceq = \preceq_f$. Consequently, the terms ranking and ranking function can be used interchangeably. We also blur the distinction between a ranking $\preceq$ and the rankings $\preceq_{\restriction_{S'}}$, obtained by restricting $\preceq$ to $S' \subseteq S$. Without loss of generality, one can assume the range of f to be an initial segment $\{1, \ldots, K\}$ of $\mathbb{N}$.

It is worth noting that if $(\mathcal{K}, \preceq_{\mathcal{K}})$ is linearly ordered, a classifier $\kappa : \mathbb{F} \to \mathcal{K}$ acts as a ranker on $\mathbb{F}$, inducing the ranking $\preceq_\kappa$ defined by

$$\mathbf{x} \preceq_\kappa \mathbf{x}' \iff \kappa(\mathbf{x}) \preceq_{\mathcal{K}} \kappa(\mathbf{x}') \tag{3}$$

3 Formal Explanations of Rankers

Let $\mathbb{F} = \mathbb{D}_1 \times \ldots \times \mathbb{D}_m$ be a feature space, and let $f : \mathbb{F} \to \mathbb{R}$ be a ranking function on $\mathbb{F}$. Given two feature vectors $\mathbf{v}, \mathbf{v}' \in \mathbb{F}$, such that $\mathbf{v} \preceq_f \mathbf{v}'$, i.e., $f(\mathbf{v}) \leq f(\mathbf{v}')$, we address the question: *why is $\mathbf{v}'$ ranked at least as highly as $\mathbf{v}$?* We indicate with $(f; \mathbf{v}, \mathbf{v}')$ this explanation problem.

Definition 3 (Weak Abductive Explanation (WeakAXp)). *Let $S \subseteq \mathcal{F}$ be a set of features. We say that S is a* Weak Abductive Explanation *(or WeakAXp for short) for the explanation problem $(f; \mathbf{v}, \mathbf{v}')$ if*

$$\forall (\mathbf{x}, \mathbf{x}') \in [\mathbf{v}]_S \times [\mathbf{v}']_S, \ \mathbf{x} \preceq_f \mathbf{x}' \tag{4}$$

In other words, a WeakAXp is a set S of features such that, for each pair $\mathbf{x}, \mathbf{x}' \in \mathbb{F}$ of vectors such that $\mathbf{x} \sim_S \mathbf{v}$ and $\mathbf{x}' \sim_S \mathbf{v}'$, the ranking $\mathbf{x} \preceq_f \mathbf{x}'$ is preserved. We also write WeakAXp(S) to denote that S is a WeakAXp.

The following theorem establishes the monotonicity of WeakAXps for rankers and is analogous to the corresponding result for classifiers [38].

Theorem 1 (Monotonicity of WeakAXps). *If S is a WeakAXp and $S \subseteq S''$, then S'' is also a WeakAXp.*

In practice, one can consider different rankings that vary in how finely they distinguish between alternatives. Such differences often arise from introducing tie-breaking criteria to resolve some or all ties, resulting in finer rankings derived from coarser ones. The following theorem establishes a relationship between the WeakAXps of rankers with different levels of granularity.

Theorem 2. *Let $\preceq_1$ and $\preceq_2$ be rankings on $\mathbb{F}$ such that $\preceq_1$ is finer than $\preceq_2$, i.e., $\preceq_1 \subseteq \preceq_2$. Then every WeakAXp of $\preceq_1$ is also a WeakAXp of $\preceq_2$.*

We now proceed to define abductive explanations.

Definition 4 (Abductive Explanation (AXp)). *A set $\mathcal{S} \subseteq \mathcal{F}$ is an abductive explanation (AXp) for the explanation problem $(f; \mathbf{v}, \mathbf{v}')$ if $\mathcal{S}$ is a subset-minimal WeakAXp, that is,*

$$\mathsf{WeakAXp}(\mathcal{S}) \; \wedge \; \forall \mathcal{S}' \subsetneq \mathcal{S}, \neg\mathsf{WeakAXp}(\mathcal{S}') \tag{5}$$

Observe that formula (5) is formally analogous to formula (2) for classifiers, i.e., they are syntactically equivalent. However, it is important to note that we have redefined the semantics of predicate WeakAXp in the context of rankings. Note also that, by Theorem 1, determining whether $\mathcal{S}$ is an AXp requires checking only the $|\mathcal{S}|$ maximal proper subsets $\mathcal{S}' = \mathcal{S} \setminus \{i\}$ with $i \in \mathcal{S}$, rather than all $2^{|\mathcal{S}|} - 1$ proper subsets.

The following theorem relates WeakAXps of classifiers and rankers.

Theorem 3. *Let $k : \mathbb{F} \to \mathcal{K}$ be a classifier, with $\mathcal{K}$ linearly ordered, and let $\mathbf{v}, \mathbf{v}' \in \mathbb{F}$ be two point such that $\mathbf{v} \preceq_\kappa \mathbf{v}'$. Then, if $\mathcal{S}$ is a WeakAXp for both the explanations problems $(\kappa; \mathbf{v})$ and $(\kappa; \mathbf{v}')$, then $\mathcal{S}$ is a WeakAXp also for $(\kappa; \mathbf{v}, \mathbf{v}')$.*

This follows directly from the fact that the classes of $\mathbf{x} \in [\mathbf{v}]_\mathcal{S}$ and $\mathbf{x}' \in [\mathbf{v}']_\mathcal{S}$ are fixed. The converse does not necessarily hold. In fact, formula (4) allows their classes to vary freely, as long as every $\mathbf{x}'$ is ranked at least as highly as every $\mathbf{x}$.

We began our analysis by addressing the question of why $\mathbf{v} \preceq_f \mathbf{v}'$. In fact, formula (4) can be easily adapted to the case $\mathbf{v}^{(1)} \preceq_f \ldots \preceq_f \mathbf{v}^{(n)}$. Finally, although our focus has been on AXps, contrastive explanations [26] could be adapted to the ranking setting in a similar manner.

3.1   On the Need for FXAI for Rankers

One could be tempted to explain a ranking function f by reducing such a problem to classification. One can, in fact, consider the binary classifier $\kappa_f : \mathbb{F}^2 \to \{0, 1\}$ defined by

$$\kappa_f(\mathbf{x}, \mathbf{x}') = \begin{cases} 1, & \text{if } \mathbf{x} \preceq_f \mathbf{x}', \\ 0, & \text{otherwise.} \end{cases} \tag{6}$$

Explaining why $\mathbf{v} \preceq_f \mathbf{v}'$, then reduces to explain why κ_f evaluate to 1 on the vector $(\mathbf{v}, \mathbf{v}')$ of the feature space $\mathbb{F}^2$. This approach, which we term the *naive approach* has some shortcomings. Indeed, it differs from ours in that it treats the i-th component of $\mathbf{v}$ independently from the i-th component of $\mathbf{v}'$, resulting (i) in explanations defined over the new feature set $\mathcal{F} \cup \mathcal{F}'$ obtained by adding a primed copy for each feature, and (ii) a consequently higher complexity for computing such explanations. Note also that the requirement $x_i = v_i \wedge x_i' = v_i'$ for each $i \in \mathcal{S}$, cannot be reproduced using domain constraints [19]. This is because computing an AXp involves considering a different set $\mathcal{S}$ at each step, which results in varying constraints on $\mathbf{x}$ and $\mathbf{x}'$. On the contrary, domain constraints are fixed over the feature space.

It is also useful to compare our work with approaches for explaining regression models $f : \mathbb{F} \to \mathbb{R}$, such as neural networks [28,54] and regression trees [6,8]. These methods explain a prediction $f(\mathbf{v})$ by treating all points within a circular neighbourhood of $f(\mathbf{v})$—with radius specified by a user parameter—as if they were equal to that value. In contrast, by considering the ranking induced by f rather than the exact values, our approach can handle real-valued functions without any approximation or the need for additional parameters.

3.2 On the Concept of Best Explanations

Explanation problems can admit multiple AXps, raising the question of which AXp to prefer. A natural choice is to favor smaller AXps, ideally those that are cardinality-minimal. However, computing cardinality-minimal explanations can be computationally intensive [27]. Moreover, even cardinality-minimal explanations may not be unique.

To address this, we define a score function $score : 2^{\mathcal{F}} \to \mathbb{R}$ by posing

$$score(\mathcal{S}) = \min_{(\mathbf{x},\mathbf{x}') \in [\mathbf{v}]_{\mathcal{S}} \times [\mathbf{v}']_{\mathcal{S}}} (f(\mathbf{x}') - f(\mathbf{x})). \qquad (7)$$

A set $\mathcal{S}$ is then a WeakAXp if and only if $score(\mathcal{S}) \geq 0$. We define a preference relation $\preceq$ on $2^{\mathcal{F}}$ by posing

$$\mathcal{S}_1 \preceq \mathcal{S}_2 \quad \text{iff} \quad score(\mathcal{S}_1) \leq score(\mathcal{S}_2).$$

This preference relation can then serve as a tie-breaking criterion among explanations of the same size. The concept of score is particularly meaningful when f carries significance beyond mere ranking, a common situation as demonstrated in our case study, where the ranking is based on the probabilities of breast cancer recurrence. Note also that our preference relation is defined directly by the explanation problem and therefore forms a more objective basis for identifying the best explanations, as opposed to approaches requiring the incorporation of formal models of the explainee [5].

4 Algorithms

In this section, we start by introducing a model-agnostic algorithm for verifying whether a set $\mathcal{S} \subseteq \mathcal{F}$ is a WeakAXp. We then combine it with a deletion-based

---

Algorithm 1: Verify WeakAXp.

Input: Ranker f, points $\mathbf{v}_1$, $\mathbf{v}_2$, candidate set $\mathcal{S}$, feature space $\mathbb{F}$, cache memo
Output: WeakAXp($\mathcal{S}$)

1 **Function** GenerateVectors($\mathbf{v}, \mathcal{S}, \mathbb{F}$):
2 | **foreach** $i \in \mathcal{S}$ **do**
3 | | $\mathbb{D}_i \leftarrow \{v_i\}$;
4 | **return** $\prod_{i=1}^{m} \mathbb{D}_i$ // as an iterator

5 **Function** CachedPredict($\mathbf{x}$, memo):
6 | **if** $\mathbf{x} \notin$ memo **then**
7 | | memo[$\mathbf{x}$] $\leftarrow f(\mathbf{x})$;
8 | **return** memo[$\mathbf{x}$]

9 **foreach** $\mathbf{x}_1 \in$ GenerateVectors($\mathbf{v}_1, \mathcal{S}, \mathbb{F}$) **do**
10 | $p_1 \leftarrow$ CachedPredict($\mathbf{x}_1$, memo);
11 | **foreach** $\mathbf{x}_2 \in$ GenerateVectors($\mathbf{v}_2, \mathcal{S}, \mathbb{F}$) **do**
12 | **if** $p_1 >$ CachedPredict($\mathbf{x}_2$, memo) **then**
13 | | **return false**;

14 **return true**;

---

search strategy in order to compute an AXp. Our implementation is optimised to minimise redundant calls to both the ranker and the verification procedure. While the definitions in the previous section require no assumptions about the domains $\mathbb{D}_i$, in this section we assume them to be finite.

4.1   Verification of a WeakAXp

We now describe Algorithm 1 for verifying whether a set $\mathcal{S} \subseteq \mathcal{F}$ is a WeakAXp for the explanation problem $(f, \mathbf{v}, \mathbf{v}')$. Such algorithm works by searching for a counterexample $(\mathbf{x}, \mathbf{x}') \in [\mathbf{v}]_{\mathcal{S}} \times [\mathbf{v}']_{\mathcal{S}}$ to the claim of WeakAXp($\mathcal{S}$) being true (lines 913). If no such pair is encountered, then $\mathcal{S}$ is certified as a WeakAXp (line 14). The vectors $\mathbf{x}$ are generated (lines 1–4) by fixing $x_i = v_i$ for each $i \in \mathcal{S}$ (lines 2-3), while letting x_j varying freely within the domain $\mathbb{D}_j$ for $j \in \mathcal{F} \setminus \mathcal{S}$ (analogously for $\mathbf{x}'$). This implies that the number of vectors grows exponentially with $|\mathcal{F} \setminus \mathcal{S}|$, rather than $|\mathcal{F}|$, making verification particularly efficient for large $\mathcal{S}$. Additionally, vectors are generated on-the-fly via an iterator (line 4), eliminating the need to construct the equivalence class $[\mathbf{v}]_{\mathcal{S}}$. Finally, we apply memoisation (lines 5–8) to cache predictions and avoid redundant computation, including across repeated invocations of the algorithm.

Theorem 4. *Let* $d = \max_{i \in \mathcal{F}} |\mathbb{D}_i|$. *Algorithm 1 for verifying a WeakAXp* $\mathcal{S} \subseteq \mathcal{F}$ *containing* k *of the* m *features, requires at most* $2d^{m-k}$ *calls to the function* f.

It is worth mentioning that, while Algorithm 1 systematically explores the entire feature space to guarantee correctness, its model-agnostic nature makes it naturally compatible with heuristic strategies such as random sampling to approximate the verification process—following an approach similar in spirit to that used in many popular heuristic XAI techniques [36, 46, 47].

4.2 Computing an AXp

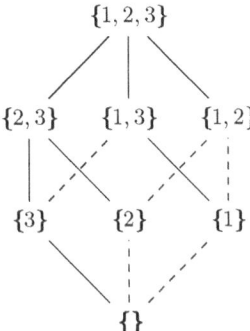

Fig. 1. Hasse diagram of the search space for $m = 3$ features. Dashed lines indicate child nodes skipped during traversal.

Algorithm 2: Deletion-based Computation of an AXp.

Input: $S \subseteq \mathcal{F}$
Output: AXp $S' \subseteq S$ or None
1   if *not* WeakAXp(S) then
2 | return None
3   $S' \leftarrow S$
4   for $i \in S$ do
5 | if WeakAXp$(S' \setminus \{i\})$ then
6 | | $S' \leftarrow S' \setminus \{i\}$
7   return S'

The monotonicity of WeakAXps, as established by Theorem 1, enables us to reformulate the problem of computing an AXp as an instance of the Minimal Set over a Monotone Predicate (MSMP) problem [41], which can be efficiently solved using the deletion-based approach presented in Algorithm 2. The basic idea is as follows. Given a WeakAXp S, the algorithm iteratively attempts to refine it by deleting one element at a time in order to find a proper subset that is still a WeakAXp. If such a deletion is possible, the algorithm proceeds with the resulting subset. This process repeats until no single element can be removed without losing the WeakAXp property, at which point the algorithm concludes that the subset is an AXp and returns it. Note that an AXp $S' \subseteq S$ exists if and only if S is a WeakAXp. Therefore, the algorithm begins by checking this condition, returning None otherwise. Note also that the feature set $\mathcal{F}$ is a WeakAXp, since we assume $\mathbf{v} \preceq_f \mathbf{v}'$, and can thus be used as the starting point of the search. This search can be viewed as a traversal of the lattice of subsets of $\mathcal{F}$, ordered by set inclusion. Figure 1 shows the Hasse diagram of this lattice for $m = 3$ features. Note how the deletion-based algorithm leverages monotonicity by testing only the maximal proper subsets. In addition, it avoids testing all such subsets by excluding the subsets $\mathcal{S}' \setminus \{i\}$, for those $i \in \mathcal{S}$ that have already been looped over. In fact, these subsets are contained in previously visited sets that were not WeakAXps and, again due to monotonicity, cannot be WeakAXps themselves. For example—referring to Fig. 1 and assuming, for illustrative purposes, the lattice is traversed by selecting features i in increasing order—if the algorithm reaches $\{1, 3\}$, it can infer that $\{3\}$ is not a WeakAXp and can therefore be skipped. This is illustrated in the figure by a dashed line. Our implementation of Algorithm 2 selects features uniformly at random to avoid biasing the returned AXps toward certain features. The algorithm returns the first AXp encountered during the traversal, not necessarily a cardinality-minimal one. However, it is worth noting that the AXps returned tend to be small in practice, as there are more paths leading to a smaller AXp than to a larger one. Also, one could run the algorithm multiple times to try to find smaller AXps. Alternatively, one could modify the algorithm to continue beyond the first AXp found.

Finally, to contextualise the efficiency of our algorithm, consider again a ranking $\mathbf{v}^{(1)} \preceq_f \ldots \preceq_f \mathbf{v}^{(n)}$ between n vectors. While Algorithm 2 has a constant query complexity with respect to n, the naive approach scales linearly. This clearly demonstrates the computational advantage of our approach compared to the naive one.

5   Case Study

The experiments were carried out using Google Colab with no hardware acceleration. The code was written in Python using TensorFlow/Keras as the deep learning framework and is available at https://github.com/fracchiariello/jelia2025.

5.1   Experimental Setup

Dataset. We use the Breast Cancer dataset from the UCI Machine Learning Repository [59], which contains real-world data about breast cancer recurrence within five years after surgery. The dataset consists of 286 instances, each with 9 categorical features and assigned to one of 2 classes. Of these instances, 201 exhibit no cancer recurrence, whereas 85 indicate its occurrence, corresponding to a recurrence rate of around 30%. Table 1 lists the feature names along with the sizes of their corresponding domains.

Problem formulation. Predicting the recurrence of breast cancer is a binary classification problem. We address it via regression, by training a neural network to predict the probability of recurrence. These probabilities then define the desired ranking over the patients. This corresponds to a pointwise approach in Learning to Rank terminology [35]. Note that one could have chosen to predict the class and then consider the classifier-induced ranking, as defined in (3). However, we prefer to work with probabilities since they are more informative, as formalised by Theorem 2, enabling us to distinguish between patients within the same class.

Dataset preparation. We denote cancer recurrence with 1 and its absence with 0. To enable the neural network to handle categorical variables, we one-hot encode them. This results in a 43-dimensional feature space, representing 299376 distinct possible patients. We then split the dataset, allocating 80% for training and 20% for testing.

Model Architecture. We consider a feedforward neural network with 3 dense layers, as shown in Table 2. The ReLU activation function is applied to the first two layers, while the output layer uses the sigmoid function, ensuring the output stays within the (0,1) range, therefore representing a probability.

Training. We train the model using the Adam optimiser and binary cross-entropy as the loss function. The trained model achieves an accuracy of 72% and an F_1 score of 53%. In comparison, a baseline model that always predicts 0 (the a priori most probable class) achieves an accuracy of 64% but an F_1 score of 0. It is important to note that the dataset is incomplete, meaning the available features do not allow for effective discrimination between the classes. Our results align with the performances reported in previous studies [14, 42]. Moreover, our primary objective is to explain the ranking induced by the model rather than optimising its performance on the machine learning task.

Table 1. Features and domains for the Breast Cancer dataset.

Feature	Name	$|\mathcal{D}_i|$
0	*age*	6
1	*menopause*	3
2	*tumor-size*	11
3	*inv-nodes*	7
4	*node-caps*	3
5	*deg-malig*	3
6	*breast*	2
7	*breast-quad*	6
8	*irradiat*	2

Table 2. Summary of the Keras model.

Layer type	Shape	Param #
Dense (ReLU)	(43, 64)	2816
Dense (ReLU)	(64, 32)	2080
Dense (sigmoid)	(32, 1)	33
Trainable params		4929
Optimizer params		9860
Total params		**14789**

5.2 Experiments

For the first experiment, we randomly sample the feature space to select 1000 pairs of feature vectors $\mathbf{v}, \mathbf{v}'$, ordering each pair such that $\mathbf{v} \preceq_f \mathbf{v}'$ to ensure the existence of AXps, with f corresponding to our neural network model. Note that the search for AXps is performed in the original feature space, as shown in Table 1, rather than in the 43-dimensional feature space of the neural network, with vectors one-hot encoded before being input into the network for processing. Table 3 reports the time required to compute the AXps. We observe that the average time increases as the size of the returned explanation decreases, consistently with Theorem 4. It is also worth noting how the support (i.e., the number of explanations for each size) varies. Specifically, the largest number of explanations corresponds to size 7, and this number gradually decreases as we move away from it. The column about the standard deviation shows that the execution time tends to vary considerably, even for explanations of the same size. This variability is expected, as execution time depends on several factors, including the specific features in the AXps, the sizes of their corresponding domains, the size of intermediate sets encountered during lattice traversal, and the time required to determine whether these sets constitute a WeakAXp. We also report in Table 4 the number of occurrences of each feature across the 1000 AXps. In this regard, it is important to recall that our implementation of Algorithm 2 selects features uniformly at random, thereby avoiding skew in the count toward any particular feature. Interestingly, the size of the tumour (*tumor-size*, feature 2) emerges as the most common feature, appearing in 957 of the 1000 AXps.

Table 3. Execution Time for computing AXps, ordered by their size.

Exp. Size	Avg Time (s)	Std Dev (s)	Support
9	2.38	0.47	49
8	5.75	3.87	236
7	14.51	12.45	393
6	37.03	36.02	259
5	95.64	70.05	62
4	314.75	0.00	1
Overall	23.01	35.88	1000

Table 4. Feature Occurrences in the AXps.

Feat.	0	1	2	3	4	5	6	7	8
Occur.	881	715	957	764	847	727	572	913	572

So far, we have examined how AXps change when varying the pairs $(\mathbf{v}, \mathbf{v}')$, gaining deeper insights into the overall structure of the feature space. We now shift our focus to analyzing the different AXps generated for a specific pair of patients, selected from the test set and reported in Table 6. For patient $\mathbf{v}'$, cancer recurrence was observed, whereas for $\mathbf{v}$, it was not. The neural network f correctly classifies these cases, assigning prediction scores $f(\mathbf{v}) = 0.08$ and $f(\mathbf{v}') = 0.97$. To generate explanations, we ran Algorithm 2 ten times: six times producing explanations of size 7 and four times of size 6, with the execution times reported in Table 5. Table 6 lists the solutions of the smaller size (with $\mathcal{S}_1$ returned twice). Given the relatively small size of the feature space, it is feasible to exhaustively verify that these solutions are indeed cardinality-minimal. Notably, all explanations agree on features 0, 2, 4, 5, and 8, differing only in the final selected feature. This brings us to the question of which explanation to prefer. To address this, we refer to the definition of the score as introduced in Equation (7). The computed scores are: $\mathcal{S}_1 = 0.305$, $\mathcal{S}_2 = 0.002$, and $\mathcal{S}_3 = 0.292$, so that $\mathcal{S}_2 \prec \mathcal{S}_3 \prec \mathcal{S}_1$. These scores can be calculated concurrently with the verification of WeakAXps by modifying Algorithm 1 to track the minimum value of $f(\mathbf{x}') - f(\mathbf{x})$ encountered. These findings not only help prioritise explanations but also suggest an implicit ranking of features based on both their occurrences across AXps and the relative scores of the explanations in which they appear: $1 \prec_f 6 \prec_f 7 \prec_f 3 \prec_f 0 \sim_f 2 \sim_f 4 \sim_f 5 \sim_f 8$.

Table 5. Execution time for computing different AXps for the same explanation problem.

Exp. Size	Avg Time (s)	Support
7	24.03	6
6	65.24	4
Overall	40.51	10

Table 6. Smallest AXps found.

$\mathcal{F}$	0	1	2	3	4	5	6	7	8
$\mathbf{v}$	2	2	3	0	1	1	1	3	0
$\mathbf{v}'$	4	0	3	3	2	2	0	2	1
$\mathcal{S}_1$	1	0	1	1	1	1	0	0	1
$\mathcal{S}_2$	1	0	1	0	1	1	1	0	1
$\mathcal{S}_3$	1	0	1	0	1	1	0	1	1

6   Related Work

FXAI has received significant attention in recent years [17,38], with approaches ranging from knowledge compilation techniques [51,52] to the use of reasoning engines (e.g., SAT, SMT or ILP solvers) [27,43]. Research has explored various dimensions, including enumeration of explanations [26], and explainability queries [4,7,22]. In addition, different types of explanations have been proposed, such as probabilistic explanations [3,31,53] and feature importance scores [34]. Techniques to efficiently navigate the feature space under constraints have also been examined [16,19,56]. Various studies focus on models with specific properties, such as monotonic classifiers [24,40]. Other research targets particular classes, such as decision trees [22,29,30] and decision lists [25], to develop practically efficient algorithms. The main challenge of formal explainability remains its ability to scale to more complex models. However, recent advancements have led to significant improvements in this area [28,54].

The problem of explaining preferences over a combinatorial structure was first studied in the domain of multi-criteria decision-making [32]. [33], for example, considers explanations for weights-based decision models. Ranking functions were then studied in [55], where the authors quantify the importance of each feature in a score-based ranker and consider other measures about stability and diversity of the ranking, useful for fairness considerations [57]. [18] proposes participation metrics to explain monotonic ranking functions, quantifying feature importance based on the analysis of the functions themself. [1] propose a framework to explain competitive rankings based on the analysis of the local impact of each feature to quantify its importance. [21] proposed an approach to explain pairwise comparisons based on Shapley values. Later [45] proposed to use Shapley values to explain score-based rankers, rather than learned pairwise comparisons. [49] uses a greedy algorithm based on Shapley values to compute counterfactual explanations for an item to reach a desired rank position, while keeping all other items fixed. Note how this is a simpler problem than the one we consider here, where we allow the features of all the items to vary.

Related research areas that consider rankings include information retrieval and recommender systems [2,13,58]. However, these studies differ considerably from the aforementioned works and the present paper, as they focus on ranking w.r.t. a given query usually expressed in natural language.

Explaining preferences has received increasing attention in Computational Social Choice to justify election outcomes [10,11,44]. However, these works typically represent candidates as atomic objects, with explanations referring to voter preferences or voting rules, rather than on specific features of the candidates. Interestingly, FXAI was recently applied in this context [15].

7   Conclusion

In this paper, we introduced the first formal definitions of explanations for ranking functions. Although applying FXAI to rankings has been considered straightforward through a reduction to classification [33], such a reduction is computationally prohibitive, limiting both research and practical use of formal explainability for rankings and preferences. By introducing definitions tailored specifically to ranking functions—resembling those for classifiers but not reducible to them—we presented the first practically feasible approach to formal explainability in the ranking setting, provided the number of features remains manageable. Our formal approach is model-agnostic, relying on querying the system, and scales linearly with the inference time of the model used to solve the specific ranking problem. We established several key properties of these definitions, including the monotonicity of WeakAXps, and demonstrated how a deletion-based algorithm can efficiently compute AXps by leveraging this property. Recognising that an explanation problem can admit multiple (cardinality-minimal) solutions, we introduce a score-based criterion to serve as a tie-breaker among such solutions. To the best of our knowledge, this is the first proposal in FXAI to introduce a preference criterion over the explanations, beyond their size, that does not rely on incorporating the preferences of the explainee. We implemented our approach and tested it on a real-world use case: a neural network model trained to predict breast cancer recurrence. Our experiments demonstrated the feasibility of the approach and highlighted the connection to the theoretical results.

On a terminological note, while we prefer the generic terms *ranking* and *ranking functions*, which also emphasise their connection to machine learning tasks, these correspond respectively to *preferences* and *utility functions* over combinatorial domains [12]. As such, the relevance of our work for AI extends beyond machine learning to encompass autonomous agents and multi-agent systems.

This paper aimed at laying down the theoretical foundations for applying FXAI to ranking functions. As a result, the challenge of efficiently computing these explanations and scaling the approach to larger problems remains an open question. Our model-agnostic approach enables the verification of explanations for black-box ranking functions. However, it is worth exploring alternative formal approaches that leverage logic-based representations of these functions, which could yield improved performance for specific classes of models. Additionally, investigating probabilistic approaches may help address the challenge posed by large numbers of features. These avenues for future research could further enhance the applicability and efficiency of FXAI in explaining ranking functions.

Acknowledgments. This work has been partially supported by the European Research Council (ERC), Grant agreement No. 885107; by the Excellence Strategy of the Federal Government and the NRW Länder, Germany; and by the Spanish Government under grant PID 2023-152814OB-I00.

References

1. Anahideh, H., Mohabbati-Kalejahi, N.: Local explanations of global rankings: insights for competitive rankings. IEEE Access **10**, 30676–30693 (2022)
2. Anand, A., Lyu, L., Idahl, M., Wang, Y., Wallat, J., Zhang, Z.: Explainable information retrieval: a survey. CoRR **abs/2211.02405** (2022)
3. Arenas, M., Barceló, P., Orth, M.A.R., Subercaseaux, B.: On computing probabilistic explanations for decision trees. In: NeurIPS (2022)
4. Audemard, G., Bellart, S., Bounia, L., Koriche, F., Lagniez, J., Marquis, P.: On the computational intelligibility of boolean classifiers. In: KR, pp. 74–86 (2021)
5. Audemard, G., Bellart, S., Bounia, L., Koriche, F., Lagniez, J., Marquis, P.: On preferred abductive explanations for decision trees and random forests. In: IJCAI, pp. 643–650. ijcai.org (2022)
6. Audemard, G., Bellart, S., Lagniez, J., Marquis, P.: Computing abductive explanations for boosted regression trees. In: IJCAI, pp. 3432–3441. ijcai.org (2023)

7. Audemard, G., Koriche, F., Marquis, P.: On tractable XAI queries based on compiled representations. In: KR, pp. 838–849 (2020)
8. Audemard, G., Lagniez, J., Marquis, P.: On the computation of contrastive explanations for boosted regression trees. In: ECAI. Frontiers in Artificial Intelligence and Applications, vol. 392, pp. 1083–1091. IOS Press (2024)
9. Barten, A.P., Böhm, V.: Consumer theory. In: Handbook of Mathematical Economics, vol. 2, pp. 381–429 (1982)
10. Boixel, A., Endriss, U.: Automated justification of collective decisions via constraint solving. In: AAMAS, pp. 168–176. International Foundation for Autonomous Agents and Multiagent Systems (2020)
11. Cailloux, O., Endriss, U.: Arguing about voting rules. In: AAMAS, pp. 287–295. ACM (2016)
12. Chevaleyre, Y., Endriss, U., Lang, J., Maudet, N.: Preference handling in combinatorial domains: from AI to social choice. AI Mag. 29(4), 37–46 (2008)
13. Chowdhury, T., Rahimi, R., Allan, J.: Rank-lime: local model-agnostic feature attribution for learning to rank. In: ICTIR, pp. 33–37. ACM (2023)
14. Clark, P., Niblett, T.: Induction in noisy domains. In: EWSL, pp. 11–30. Sigma Press, Wilmslow (1987)
15. Contet, C., Grandi, U., Mengin, J.: Abductive and contrastive explanations for scoring rules in voting. In: ECAI. Frontiers in Artificial Intelligence and Applications, vol. 392, pp. 3565–3572. IOS Press (2024)
16. Cooper, M., Amgoud, L.: Abductive explanations of classifiers under constraints: Complexity and properties. In: 26th European Conference on Artificial Intelligence (ECAI 2023), pp. à–paraître. IOS Press (2023)
17. Darwiche, A.: Logic for explainable AI. In: LICS, pp. 1–11 (2023)
18. Gale, A., Marian, A.: Explaining monotonic ranking functions. Proc. VLDB Endowment 14(4), 640–652 (2020)
19. Gorji, N., Rubin, S.: Sufficient reasons for classifier decisions in the presence of domain constraints. In: AAAI, pp. 5660–5667. AAAI Press (2022)
20. Guidotti, R., Monreale, A., Ruggieri, S., Turini, F., Giannotti, F., Pedreschi, D.: A survey of methods for explaining black box models. ACM Comput. Surv. 51(5), 1–42 (2019). https://doi.org/10.1145/3236009
21. Hu, R., Chau, S.L., Huertas, J.F., Sejdinovic, D.: Explaining preferences with Shapley values. In: NeurIPS (2022)
22. Huang, X., Izza, Y., Ignatiev, A., Marques-Silva, J.: On efficiently explaining graph-based classifiers. In: KR, pp. 356–367 (2021)
23. Huang, X., Marques-Silva, J.: On the failings of Shapley values for explainability. Int. J. Approx. Reason. 171, 1091120128 (2024)
24. Hurault, A., Marques-Silva, J.: Certified logic-based explainable AI - the case of monotonic classifiers. In: TAP. Lecture Notes in Computer Science, vol. 14066, pp. 51–67. Springer (2023)
25. Ignatiev, A., Marques-Silva, J.: SAT-based rigorous explanations for decision lists. In: Li, C.-M., Manyà, F. (eds.) SAT 2021. LNCS, vol. 12831, pp. 251–269. Springer, Cham (2021). https://doi.org/10.1007/978-3-030-80223-3_18
26. Ignatiev, A., Narodytska, N., Asher, N., Marques-Silva, J.: From contrastive to abductive explanations and back again. In: AI*IA. Lecture Notes in Computer Science, vol. 12414, pp. 335–355. Springer (2020)
27. Ignatiev, A., Narodytska, N., Marques-Silva, J.: Abduction-based explanations for machine learning models. In: AAAI, pp. 1511–1519. AAAI Press (2019)

28. Izza, Y., Huang, X., Morgado, A., Planes, J., Ignatiev, A., Marques-Silva, J.: Distance-restricted explanations: theoretical underpinnings & efficient implementation. In: KR (2024)

29. Izza, Y., Ignatiev, A., Marques-Silva, J.: On explaining decision trees. CoRR **abs/2010.11034** (2020)

30. Izza, Y., Ignatiev, A., Marques-Silva, J.: On tackling explanation redundancy in decision trees. J. Artif. Intell. Res. **75**, 261–321 (2022)

31. Izza, Y., Ignatiev, A., Narodytska, N., Cooper, M.C., Marques-Silva, J.: Provably precise, succinct and efficient explanations for decision trees. CoRR **abs/2205.09569** (2022)

32. Keeney, R.L., Raiffa, H.: Decisions With Multiple Objectives: Preferences and Value Trade-offs. Cambridge university press (1993)

33. Labreuche, C.: A general framework for explaining the results of a multi-attribute preference model. Artif. Intell. **175**(7–8), 1410–1448 (2011)

34. Letoffe, O., Huang, X., Asher, N., Marques-Silva, J.: From SHAP scores to feature importance scores. CoRR **abs/2405.11766** (2024)

35. Liu, T.: Learning to rank for information retrieval. Found. Trends Inf. Retr. **3**(3), 225–331 (2009)

36. Lundberg, S.M., Lee, S.: A unified approach to interpreting model predictions. In: NIPS, pp. 4765–4774 (2017)

37. Marques-Silva, J.: Minimal unsatisfiability: models, algorithms and applications (invited paper). In: ISMVL, pp. 9–14. IEEE Computer Society (2010)

38. Marques-Silva, J.: Logic-based explainability in machine learning. In: Reasoning Web, pp. 24–104 (2022)

39. Marques-Silva, J.: Logic-based explainability: past, present and future. In: ISoLA (4). Lecture Notes in Computer Science, vol. 15222, pp. 181–204. Springer (2024)

40. Marques-Silva, J., Gerspacher, T., Cooper, M.C., Ignatiev, A., Narodytska, N.: Explanations for monotonic classifiers. In: ICML. Proceedings of Machine Learning Research, vol. 139, pp. 7469–7479. PMLR (2021)

41. Marques-Silva, J., Janota, M., Mencía, C.: Minimal sets on propositional formulae. problems and reductions. Artif. Intell. **252**, 22–50 (2017)

42. Michalski, R.S., Mozetic, I., Hong, J., Lavrac, N.: The multi-purpose incremental learning system AQ15 and its testing application to three medical domains. In: AAAI, pp. 1041–1047. Morgan Kaufmann (1986)

43. Narodytska, N., Shrotri, A., Meel, K.S., Ignatiev, A., Marques-Silva, J.: Assessing heuristic machine learning explanations with model counting. In: Janota, M., Lynce, I. (eds.) SAT 2019. LNCS, vol. 11628, pp. 267–278. Springer, Cham (2019). https://doi.org/10.1007/978-3-030-24258-9_19

44. Peters, D., Procaccia, A.D., Psomas, A., Zhou, Z.: Explainable voting. In: NeurIPS (2020)

45. Pliatsika, V., Fonseca, J., Wang, T., Stoyanovich, J.: Sharp: explaining rankings with Shapley values. CoRR **abs/2401.16744** (2024)

46. Ribeiro, M.T., Singh, S., Guestrin, C.: "why should I trust you?": explaining the predictions of any classifier. In: KDD, pp. 1135–1144. ACM (2016)

47. Ribeiro, M.T., Singh, S., Guestrin, C.: Anchors: high-precision model-agnostic explanations. In: AAAI, pp. 1527–1535. AAAI Press (2018)

48. Rudeanu, S.: Sets and Ordered Structures. Bentham Science Publishers (2012)

49. Salimiparsa, M.: Counterfactual explanations for rankings. In: Canadian AI. Canadian Artificial Intelligence Association (2023)

50. Shapley, L.S., et al.: A value for N-person games (1953)

51. Shih, A., Choi, A., Darwiche, A.: A symbolic approach to explaining Bayesian network classifiers. In: IJCAI, pp. 5103–5111. ijcai.org (2018)
52. Shih, A., Choi, A., Darwiche, A.: Compiling Bayesian network classifiers into decision graphs. In: AAAI, pp. 7966–7974. AAAI Press (2019)
53. Wäldchen, S., MacDonald, J., Hauch, S., Kutyniok, G.: The computational complexity of understanding binary classifier decisions. J. Artif. Intell. Res. **70**, 351–387 (2021)
54. Wu, M., Wu, H., Barrett, C.W.: VeriX: towards verified explainability of deep neural networks. In: NeurIPS (2023)
55. Yang, K., Stoyanovich, J., Asudeh, A., Howe, B., Jagadish, H.V., Miklau, G.: A nutritional label for rankings. In: SIGMOD Conference, pp. 1773–1776. ACM (2018)
56. Yu, J., Ignatiev, A., Stuckey, P.J., Narodytska, N., Marques-Silva, J.: Eliminating the impossible, whatever remains must be true: on extracting and applying background knowledge in the context of formal explanations. In: AAAI, pp. 4123–4131. AAAI Press (2023)
57. Zehlike, M., Yang, K., Stoyanovich, J.: Fairness in ranking, part I: score-based ranking. ACM Comput. Surv. **55**(6), 1–36 (2023)
58. Zhang, Y., Chen, X.: Explainable recommendation: a survey and new perspectives. Found. Trends Inf. Retr. **14**(1), 1–101 (2020)
59. Zwitter, M., Soklic, M.: Breast Cancer. UCI Machine Learning Repository (1988). https://doi.org/10.24432/C51P4M

Why This and Not That? A Logic-Based Framework for Contrastive Explanations

Tobias Geibinger[1]($\boxtimes$)(iD), Reijo Jaakkola[2](iD), Antti Kuusisto[2](iD), Xinghan Liu[1](iD), and Miikka Vilander[2](iD)

[1] TU Wien, Vienna, Austria
{tobias.geibinger,xinghan.liu}@tuwien.ac.at
[2] Tampere University, Tampere, Finland
{reijo.jaakkola,antti.kuusisto}@tuni.fi

Abstract. We define several canonical problems related to contrastive explanations, each answering a question of the form "Why P but not Q?". The problems compute causes for both P and Q, explicitly comparing their differences. We investigate the basic properties of our definitions in the setting of propositional logic. We show, inter alia, that our framework captures a cardinality-minimal version of existing contrastive explanations in the literature. Furthermore, we provide an extensive analysis of the computational complexities of the problems. We also implement the problems for CNF-formulas using answer set programming and present several examples demonstrating how they work in practice.

Keywords: Explainable AI · Contrastive Explanations · Logic · Answer Set Programming

1 Introduction

The importance of explanations for decisions made by automatic classifiers has been well-established with the rise of AI methods. In this work, we investigate a category of explanations called *contrastive explanations*, which answer the question "Why P, but not Q?" These types of questions are very common in practical contexts, when an expected outcome was not obtained. It has also been argued [14] that even when not explicitly asking for one, people often prefer an explanation in the form of a comparison between the situation as it occurred in reality and a different one that could have happened.

In this work, we use a logic-based framework to formalize several problems where the task is to find contrastive explanations. Related problems have been studied previously, for example, by Darwiche [4] and Ignatiev et al. [9], where, broadly speaking, the goal is to find a *counterfactual explanation*: "Had H been true, it would have been the case that Q". In contrast to these works, solutions to our problems explicitly answer both "Why P?" and "Why not Q?" with dedicated output formulas that are required to be structurally similar. Our definitions have been partially inspired by the work of Lipton [12], where he argues that a

G. Casini et al. (Eds.): JELIA 2025, LNAI 16093, pp. 45–60, 2026.
https://doi.org/10.1007/978-3-032-04587-4_4

contrastive explanation should contrast the causes of P against the absence of corresponding causes of Q.

Our first problem, which we call the contrastive explanation problem, aims to explain why two seemingly similar entities have differing properties. For example, we might ask why two individuals with similar backgrounds were assigned different credit risk levels. An input to our problem consists of two sets of formulas S, S' along with two formulas φ, ψ such that $S \models \varphi \wedge \neg\psi$ and $S' \models \neg\varphi \wedge \psi$. The output of the problem is a minimal size triple (θ, θ', χ) of formulas, such that $\theta \wedge \chi$ explains why S implies $\varphi \wedge \neg\psi$, contrasting with $\theta' \wedge \chi$ that explains why S' implies $\neg\varphi \wedge \psi$. Formally, we require that $S \models \theta \wedge \chi \models \varphi \wedge \neg\psi$ and $S' \models \theta' \wedge \chi \models \neg\varphi \wedge \psi$. Our problem formulation naturally enforces the similarity of the two explanations, as it encourages shifting content from θ and θ' into the common formula χ. To see the intuition behind this, consider the question why A is a dog and B is a cat. Here one would not insert "cannot fly" into the differentiating formulae θ and θ', since neither A nor B can fly. On the other hand, it might be necessary to include "cannot fly" to χ, since it separates cats and dogs from, say, crows (Fig. 1).

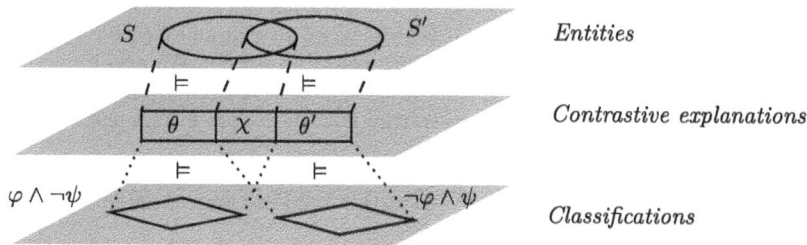

Fig. 1. Illustration of the contrastive explanation problem

Setting $S = \{\varphi \wedge \neg\psi\}$ and $S' = \{\neg\varphi \wedge \psi\}$ in the contrastive explanation problem, we obtain as a special case a problem that directly compares all the models of $\varphi \wedge \neg\psi$ with those of $\neg\varphi \wedge \psi$, giving a global contrast between the two formulas. Accordingly, we call this the global contrastive problem. We also define an alternative global problem which we call the minimal separator problem. In this problem the goal is to find a single minimal difference that suffices to separate the two input formulas.

We then move on to consider a variant of this problem where the input does not contain S' and the question we want to answer is "why does S satisfy φ but not ψ?". We formalize this problem in two distinct ways, both rooted in counterfactual reasoning. In the first problem, which we call the counterfactual contrastive explanation problem, the output is a minimal size triple (θ, θ', χ) such that $S \models \theta \wedge \chi \models \varphi \wedge \neg\psi$ and $\theta' \wedge \chi \models \neg\varphi \wedge \psi$. The second problem, called the counterfactual difference problem, is otherwise the same except that we require that $S \equiv \theta \wedge \chi$, i.e., that $\theta \wedge \chi$ defines the current state of affairs S.

Roughly speaking, in the first problem we want to find a reason for $S \models \varphi \wedge \neg\psi$ and a cause for $\neg\varphi \wedge \psi$ which are similar, while in the second problem we want to find a minimal modification to S that would guarantee that $\neg\varphi \wedge \psi$ holds.

We investigate our problems more closely in the setting of propositional logic (PL), assuming for simplicity that the output formulas are in conjunctive normal form. We first show that our definitions indeed find contrasts between the input formulas. For example, for the global contrastive explanation problem, we show that each clause C of the output formula θ is a *weak contrast* between φ and ψ, meaning φ entails C while ψ does not. We also show a link between our definitions and previous work on contrastive explanations: if the set S in the input of the counterfactual difference problem defines an assignment, then the output corresponds to a cardinality-minimal CXp [9]. As a by-product, we show that both of our counterfactual problems output partial assignments up to equivalence when presented with partial assignment inputs.

We also study the computational complexity of our problems in the case of PL. We first observe that the contrastive explanation problem, the global contrastive problem and the minimal separator problem are all Σ_2^p-complete. We then show that certain natural variants of our counterfactual problems are also Σ_2^p-complete. Finally, we provide a prototypical implementation of our problems using Answer Set Programming, which given the complexity of the underlying problems, is an adequate computation formalism [6]. We use this implementation to demonstrate how our problems work in practice via three case studies.

Related Work We now present related work on contrastive explanation within the broader context of logic-based explainable AI. It was originally for *local explanation*, namely explaining why a classifier makes a certain decision for a *given* input instance. As summarized in several works [4,9,13], local explanation answers one of the following two questions: Q1. (Why): what minimal aspects of an instance guarantee the actual decision? Q2. (Why not): what minimal changes to an instance result in a different decision? An answer to Q1 is nowadays commonly called a *sufficient reason* [5] or an AXp (short for abductive explanation) [10]. A sufficient reason is a minimal subset of its features' values s.t. changing any other feature values will not change the classification. In PL, a sufficient reason coincides with a *prime implicant* of the Boolean classifier φ which is *locally true* in the given instance. Therefore the concept was first introduced in the literature under the name PI-explanation [16]. For Barcelo et al. [2], a sufficient reason itself need not be minimal, and it is called a *minimal/minimum sufficient reason*, if it satisfies the subset-/cardinality-minimality requirement respectively. We refer to these notions as instances of *direct explanation*, for lack of a better term.

Dually, an answer to Q2 is commonly referred to as either a *contrastive explanation* (CXp) [9], a *counterfactual explanation* [17] or a *necessary reason* [4]. In all cases it is a subset-minimal part of the instance, changing the values of which results in a different classification. The duality of AXp and CXp is well-established from a logical viewpoint via minimal hitting sets [9]. Namely, an AXp is a subset-minimal intersection of every CXp of the instance and vice versa.

Similarly to before, a shift from subset-minimality to cardinality-minimality brings us to the notion of *minimum change required* by Barcelo et al. [2].

We now move from local to global explanation. Note that an explanation can be called 'global' in either *conditional* or *categorical* sense, namely either 1) it is a local explanation *if an input instance satisfies it*, or 2) it explains the whole classifier. In the former sense, the duality between AXp and CXp extends naturally to *global AXp* and *counterexamples* [13]. In propositional logic, they coincide with prime implicants and negated prime implicates. An example of a global direct explanation in the latter sense is the (shortest) prime DNF expression of Boolean classifiers [11]. However, here one cannot obtain a corresponding contrastive explanation in terms of the duality, because the contrastive explanations referred to so far are by nature localized to the actual case, viz., they are counterfactual. One must define a categorically global contrastive explanation in a genuinely global manner, which is a key contribution of our paper.

Besides the aforementioned ones, recently Bassan et al. [3] define *global sufficient reason* as the set of features which is a sufficient reason for all instances. Similarly, *global contrastive reason* is "a subset of features that may cause a misclassification for any possible input". This notion of a global contrastive explanation differs significantly from ours, which aims to describe essentially all the differences between two classifiers.

2   Preliminaries

We will formulate our various explanation problems for an arbitrary logic. For the purposes of this work, a **logic** $\mathcal{L}$ is a tuple $L = (\mathcal{F}, \vDash, \mathtt{sat})$, where $\mathcal{F}$ is a set of formulas, $\vDash \subseteq \mathcal{P}(\mathcal{F}) \times \mathcal{F}$ is a binary logical consequence relation and $\mathtt{sat} \subseteq \mathcal{F}$ is a unary satisfiability relation. Instead of $\varphi, \psi \in \mathcal{F}$ and $\{\varphi\} \vDash \psi$ we will write $\varphi, \psi \in \mathcal{L}$ and $\varphi \vDash \psi$ for simplicity. If for $S, S' \subseteq \mathcal{F}$ we have $S \vDash \psi$ for every $\psi \in S'$ and $S' \vDash \varphi$ for every $\varphi \in S$, then we say that S and S' are equivalent, denoted $S \equiv S'$. We formulate our definitions for logics $\mathcal{L}$ with classical conjunction $\wedge$ and classical negation $\neg$ with the usual semantics. These connectives are not necessary but they help to keep our definitions clean and readable.

As the logics that we consider are two-valued, the above framework works best when modeling classifiers for binary classification. To model classifiers with more than two classes, we can assign to each class c a formula φ_c which is satisfied precisely by the inputs classified as c. We call such a formula a **class formula**. This approach has been used, for example, in [4].

In addition to our very general definitions, we will also consider the important special case of propositional logic. Let τ be a set of **proposition symbols** called a **vocabulary**. The set $\mathrm{PL}[\tau]$ of formulas of **propositional logic** over τ is generated by the grammar $\varphi := \bot \mid p \mid \neg\varphi \mid \varphi \wedge \varphi \mid \varphi \vee \varphi$, where $p \in \tau$. We define $\top := \neg\bot$ as an abbreviation.

A function $s : \sigma \to \{0, 1\}$, where $\sigma \subseteq \tau$, is called a **partial τ-assignment**. When $\sigma = \tau$, we say that s is a τ-**assignment**. We often identify (partial) assignments with conjunctions of literals in the obvious way. The semantics of

$PL[\tau]$ is defined as usual, i.e., for a τ-assignment s we define $s \not\vDash \bot$ always, $s \vDash p$ if $s(p) = 1$, $s \vDash \neg\psi$ if $s \not\vDash \psi$, $s \vDash \psi \wedge \theta$ if $s \vDash \psi$ and $s \vDash \theta$, and finally $s \vDash \psi \vee \theta$ if $s \vDash \psi$ or $s \vDash \theta$. Given $S \subseteq PL[\tau]$ and a (partial) τ-assignment s, we say that S **defines** s, if $S \equiv s$. If $S = \{\varphi\}$, we write φ defines s rather than $\{\varphi\}$ defines s.

Assignments that satisfy a formula are also called its **models**. For two formulas $\varphi, \psi \in PL[\tau]$, we use the notation $\varphi \vDash \psi$ for **logical consequence**, that is $\varphi \vDash \psi$ if for all assignments s, $s \vDash \varphi$ implies $s \vDash \psi$. We extend this notation also to sets $S, T \subseteq PL[\tau]$ of formulas, defining $S \vDash T$ if $\bigwedge S \vDash \bigwedge T$.

Formulas of the form p or $\neg p$, where p is a proposition symbol, are called **literals**. The **dual** $\bar{\ell}$ of a literal ℓ is defined as $\bar{p} = \neg p$ and $\overline{\neg p} = p$. A disjunction of literals is called a **clause**. A formula $\varphi \in PL[\tau]$ is in **conjunctive normal form**, or CNF, if φ is a conjunction of clauses. We will often denote clauses as sets of literals and CNF-formulas as sets of clauses. For example, if a CNF-formula φ has the clause $\neg p \vee q$, we might write $\{\neg p, q\} \in \varphi$. We denote the set of all CNF formulas $\varphi \in PL[\tau]$ by $CNF[\tau]$.

Formula size is a key notion in our work. We do not define formula size in the general case as many different definitions could make sense depending on the logic considered. We will, however, consider the size of propositional formulas in practice so we define it here. We define the **size** of a formula $\varphi \in PL[\tau]$ simply to be number of occurences of proposition symbols. More formally, we define it recursively as follows: $\text{size}(\bot) = 0$ and $\text{size}(p) = 1$, for a proposition symbol p; $\text{size}(\neg\psi) = \text{size}(\psi)$; $\text{size}(\psi_1 \wedge \psi_2) = \text{size}(\psi_1 \vee \psi_2) = \text{size}(\psi_1) + \text{size}(\psi_2)$.

3 Generalized Contrastive Explanation

In this section we introduce several natural problems that concern contrastive explanations. We start by defining problems focused on explaining differences either between instances (objects) or between properties. After this we consider problems that deal with the problem of explaining why a given instance has a particular property. In our logic-based framework instances are represented as sets of formulas while properties correspond to single formulas.

3.1 Comparison Explanations

We begin with a problem, where we have two different instances S and S' at hand, and we want to know why one of them satisfies φ while the other satisfies ψ. In practice, the two instances could seem very similar to us, leading to the question of key differences that explain their different properties φ and ψ. Van Bouwel and Weber [19] call this question an O-contrast, also cited by Miller [14].

Definition 1. *The* **contrastive explanation problem** *is defined as follows.*
   Input: *A tuple (S, S', φ, ψ), where $S, S' \subseteq \mathcal{L}$ are finite sets and $\varphi, \psi \in \mathcal{L}$.*
   Output: *A triple (θ, θ', χ), where $\theta, \theta', \chi \in \mathcal{L}$ have the following properties.*

1. $S \vDash \theta \wedge \chi \vDash \varphi \wedge \neg\psi$ *and* $S' \vDash \theta' \wedge \chi \vDash \neg\varphi \wedge \psi$,
2. $\text{size}(\theta) + \text{size}(\theta') + \text{size}(\chi)$ *is minimal,*

3. as a secondary optimization criterion, size(χ) *is maximal.*

If no such triple exists, output error.

The output contains the contrast formulas θ and θ' as well as a shared context formula χ. *The essential part of the output are the differentiating formulas θ and θ'.* The three conditions can be motivated as follows. Condition 1 ensures that $\theta \wedge \chi$ and $\theta' \wedge \chi$ serve as explanations for why S and S' satisfy $\varphi \wedge \neg\psi$ and $\neg\varphi \wedge \psi$, respectively. Condition 2 requires these explanations to be minimal to avoid including irrelevant information. Condition 3 enforces similarity between the explanations by maximizing the common context formula χ, as it is desirable to shift content from θ and θ' into χ.

In the above definition we are asking "Why $S \models \varphi \wedge \neg\psi$ and $S' \models \neg\varphi \wedge \psi$?" as opposed to "Why $S \models \varphi$ and $S' \models \psi$?". The reason we do this is that, in accordance to Lipton [12], we allow the formulas φ and ψ to be compatible, but we seek explanations which entail that only one of them is true. We will follow this approach throughout the paper.

Example 1. We give a concrete example of Definition 1 in the case where $\mathcal{L}$ is propositional logic. Consider the propositional vocabulary $\tau = \{p, q, r\}$. Let φ be a formula of $\mathrm{PL}[\tau]$ which is satisfied by precisely those assignments which map exactly two propositional symbols to 1. Furthermore, let ψ be a formula of $\mathrm{PL}[\tau]$ which is satisfied by precisely those assignments which map exactly one propositional symbol to 1. Note that $\varphi \models \neg\psi$ and $\psi \models \neg\varphi$, whence $\varphi \wedge \neg\psi \equiv \varphi$ and $\neg\varphi \wedge \psi \equiv \psi$. Now, let $S := \{p, q, \neg r\}$ and $S' := \{p, \neg q, \neg r\}$. The following triple is a possible solution: $\theta := q$, $\theta' := \neg q$ and $\chi := p \wedge \neg r$. ∎

Consider the special case of the contrastive explanation problem, where $S = \{\varphi \wedge \neg\psi\}$ and $S' = \{\neg\varphi \wedge \psi\}$. Now we are asking for a contrast between all of the models of φ and ψ, with no limitation to a more specific locality S or S'. Thus we are asking "What is the difference between φ and ψ?" We call this case the global contrastive explanation problem and define it next separately.

Definition 2. *The **global contrastive explanation problem** is defined as follows.*

   Input: *A pair (φ, ψ), where $\varphi, \psi \in \mathcal{L}$.*
   Output: *A triple (θ, θ', χ), where $\theta, \theta', \chi \in \mathcal{L}$ have the following properties.*

1. $\theta \wedge \chi \equiv \varphi \wedge \neg\psi$ and $\theta' \wedge \chi \equiv \neg\varphi \wedge \psi$,
2. size(θ) + size(θ') + size(χ) is minimal,
3. as a secondary optimization criterion, size(χ) *is maximal.*

Example 2. Consider again the formulas φ and ψ from Example 1. Restricting our output formulas to CNF-formulas for readability, the following triple is a solution to the global contrastive explanation problem.

$$\theta := (p \vee r) \wedge (q \vee r) \wedge (p \vee q)$$
$$\theta' := (\neg p \vee \neg r) \wedge (\neg q \vee \neg r) \wedge (\neg p \vee \neg q)$$
$$\chi := (p \vee q \vee r) \wedge (\neg p \vee \neg q \vee \neg r)$$

These formulas tell us the following. First, θ says that in every model of $\varphi \wedge \neg \psi \equiv \varphi$ at least two propositional symbols are true. Secondly, θ' says that in every model of $\neg \varphi \wedge \psi \equiv \psi$ at least two propositional symbols are false. Finally, χ tells us that in models of $\varphi \vee \psi$ one propositional symbol is true and one is false. ∎

Another notion related to contrastivity is that of a separator. A separator of φ from ψ is a property that all models of φ and no models of ψ have. A separator can thus also be seen as a different answer to the question "What is the difference between φ and ψ?" The next problem asks for a minimal separator of φ from ψ.

Definition 3. *The **minimal separator problem** is defined as follows.*
    *   ***Input:** A pair (φ, ψ), where $\varphi, \psi \in \mathcal{L}$.*
    *   ***Output:** A formula $\theta \in \mathcal{L}$ such that $\varphi \models \theta$, $\psi \models \neg \theta$ and $\mathrm{size}(\theta)$ is minimal. If no such θ exists, output* error.

The global contrastive explanation problem can be seen as giving "all" separators between φ and ψ, or at least enough to achieve equivalent formulas, while the minimal separator problem only gives one minimal separator. In terms of the natural language question "What is the difference between φ and ψ?", giving all differences or a single difference could both be considered reasonable answers.

Example 3. Consider again the formulas φ, ψ in Example 1. Clearly $\varphi \models \neg \psi$. The formula $(p \vee r) \wedge (q \vee r) \wedge (p \vee q)$ is a minimal separator between φ and ψ. ∎

3.2   Counterfactual Explanations

We have seen above how the contrastive explanation problem answers the question "Why does S satisfy φ while S' satisfies ψ?" We now turn our attention to the case, where we have only one instance S at hand and we are asking about the classification of that instance. The question here is "Why does S satisfy φ and not ψ?". Van Bouwel and Weber [19] call this question a P-contrast, also cited by Miller [14]. We define two problems that modify the contrastive explanation problem in different ways to answer this question.

Our first problem is a straightforward modification of Definition 1, where we simply leave S' to be existentially quantified. The condition $S' \models \theta' \wedge \chi \models \neg \varphi \wedge \psi$ is then reduced to the form $\theta' \wedge \chi \models \neg \varphi \wedge \psi$ since S' itself is not actually needed for the output. The definition is as follows.

Definition 4. *The **counterfactual contrastive explanation problem** is defined as follows.*
    *   ***Input:** A tuple (S, φ, ψ), where $S \subseteq \mathcal{L}$ is a finite set and $\varphi, \psi \in \mathcal{L}$.*
    *   ***Output:** A triple (θ, θ', χ), where $\theta, \theta', \chi \in \mathcal{L}$ have the following properties.*

1. $S \models \theta \wedge \chi \models \varphi \wedge \neg \psi$ and $\theta' \wedge \chi \models \neg \varphi \wedge \psi$,
2. $\theta' \wedge \chi$ is satisfiable iff S is satisfiable,
3. $\mathrm{size}(\theta) + \mathrm{size}(\theta') + \mathrm{size}(\chi)$ is minimal,

4. as a secondary optimization criterion, size(χ) *is maximal.*

   If no such triple exists, output error.

The above definition places emphasis on minimal reasons for why instances satisfy properties. Another way to think about contrastive explanations is to consider minimal changes required to the input instance in order to achieve the desired outcome. This can be seen in the literature in the concept of CXp [9]. It turns out that minimal reasons for satisfaction and minimal changes to achieve satisfaction do not always coincide. This difference between reasons, or why-questions, and changes, or what-is-the-difference-questions motivates our next definition. The intuitive question here is "What is the difference between S that satisfies φ and the closest S' that instead satisfies ψ?"

Definition 5. *The **counterfactual difference problem** is defined as follows.*
   Input: *A tuple* (S, φ, ψ), *where* $S \subseteq \mathcal{L}$ *is a finite set and* $\varphi, \psi \in \mathcal{L}$.
   Output: *A triple* (θ, θ', χ), *where* $\theta, \theta', \chi \in \mathcal{L}$ *have the following properties.*

1. $S \equiv \theta \wedge \chi \vDash \varphi \wedge \neg\psi$ *and* $\theta' \wedge \chi \vDash \neg\varphi \wedge \psi$,
2. $\theta' \wedge \chi$ *is satisfiable iff* S *is satisfiable,*
3. size(θ) + size(θ') + size(χ) *is minimal,*
4. as a secondary optimization criterion, size(χ) *is maximal.*

   If no such triple exists, output error.

Remark 1. Note that for both Definitions 4 and 5, if $\psi \vDash \varphi$ and S is satisfiable, then the output is error. Here the models of ψ are included in those of φ and thus $\neg\varphi \wedge \psi$ is a contradiction. The input can be repaired by replacing φ with $\varphi \wedge \neg\psi$, since $\neg(\varphi \wedge \neg\psi) \wedge \psi \equiv \psi$. This makes the two input formulas separate and preserves the original question: "Why does S satisfy φ but not ψ?"

Example 4. Assume we have two propositional classifiers, φ and ψ, trained on some data about seabirds. The classifier φ = beak_pouch classifies a bird as a pelican if the bird has a distinctive pouch on the underside of its beak. The classifier ψ = ¬beak_pouch∧small∧((white_body∧webbed_feet)∨grey_wing) classifies a bird as a seagull if it has no beak pouch, is less than 1 m in size and either has white plumage on its body and webbed feet, or a grey wing. Note that these are not complete descriptions of these types of birds but rather classification criteria that could have been extracted from a dataset.

   Let S = {beak_pouch, ¬small, white_body, webbed_feet, ¬grey_wing} be a description of a bird. We want to know why this bird was classified as a pelican and not as a seagull. Starting with Definition 5, the output in this case is θ = beak_pouch, θ' = small, χ = (¬beak_pouch ∨ ¬small) ∧ white_body ∧ webbed_feet ∧ ¬grey_wing. We can read the solution as "This bird has a beak pouch and is large, so it's a pelican. If it had no beak pouch and was small, it would instead be a seagull." Note how all attributes of the bird are listed in the formula $\theta \wedge \chi$ even though beak_pouch suffices to classify the bird as a pelican.

The output of Definition 4 is $\theta = \texttt{beak\_pouch}$, $\theta' = \neg\texttt{beak\_pouch} \wedge \texttt{small} \wedge$ $\texttt{grey\_wing}$, $\chi = \top$. This would be read as "This bird has a beak pouch so it's a pelican. If it had no beak pouch, was small and had a grey wing, it would instead be a seagull." This time only the beak pouch is listed in $\theta \wedge \chi$ as it suffices to classify the bird as a pelican.

For another difference between the definitions, note that out of the two options provided by the classifier ψ, Definition 4 has chosen the one with the grey wing. Another option in the search space would have been $\theta = \texttt{beak\_pouch}$, $\theta' = \neg\texttt{beak\_pouch} \wedge \texttt{small}$, $\chi = \texttt{white\_body} \wedge \texttt{webbed\_feet}$. Out of these two, the grey wing option was chosen because the reasons $\theta \wedge \chi$ and $\theta' \wedge \chi$ given for why the bird was a pelican or a seagull were shorter in the first option. This illustrates the fact that Definition 4 is not concerned with minimal differences between the input and the counterfactual case, but rather minimal differences between minimal reasons for the classifications of the input and the counterfactual case. ∎

4 The Case of Propositional Logic

In this section, we investigate our problems more closely in the setting of propositional logic. We show that our problems indeed find contrasts between the inputs in a semantic sense. We also establish a formal link between our definitions and existing work on contrastive explanations. We conclude with a study of the computational complexity of our problems.

4.1 Contrasts and Likenesses

We start by defining some notions that compare two formulas φ and ψ.

Definition 6. *Let* φ, ψ, θ *be formulas of a logic* $\mathcal{L}$.

1. θ *is a **weak** (φ, ψ)-**contrast** if* $\varphi \wedge \neg\psi \models \theta$ *and* $\neg\varphi \wedge \psi \not\models \theta$.
2. θ *is a **strong** (φ, ψ)-**contrast** if* $\varphi \wedge \neg\psi \models \theta$ *and* $\neg\varphi \wedge \psi \models \neg\theta$.
3. θ *is a (φ, ψ)-**likeness** if* $\varphi \wedge \neg\psi \models \theta$ *and* $\neg\varphi \wedge \psi \models \theta$.

Strong contrasts are properties that all models of φ (or more precisely, $\varphi \wedge \neg\psi$), and none of the models of ψ, have. Weak contrasts, on the other hand, are properties that all models of, say, φ have, but not all models of ψ do. Likenesses are properties that models of both formulas have.

For global contrastive explanations, the output formulas correspond to contrasts and likenesses in a nice way. Let (θ, θ', χ) be an output of the global contrastive explanation problem (Definition 2). We have $\theta \wedge \chi \wedge \theta' \equiv \varphi \wedge \neg\psi \wedge \neg\varphi \wedge \psi \to \bot$, which means $\theta \wedge \neg\varphi \wedge \psi \to \bot$, namely $\neg\varphi \wedge \psi \to \neg\theta$, i.e. θ is always a strong (φ, ψ)-contrast. By symmetry θ' is a strong (ψ, φ)-contrast. It is also easy to see that χ is a (φ, ψ)-likeness. The following result further shows that if we assume the output formulas are in CNF, then the individual clauses of θ and θ' are all weak contrasts whereas the clauses of χ are likenesses of φ and ψ.

Theorem 1. *Let* $\varphi, \psi \in PL[\tau]$ *and let* (θ, θ', χ) *be the output of the global contrastive explanation problem with input* (φ, ψ). *Further assume that* θ, θ' *and* χ *are in* CNF. *Then* **(1)** *each clause of* θ *is a weak* (φ, ψ)-*contrast,* **(2)** *each clause of* θ' *is a weak* (ψ, φ)-*contrast, and* **(3)** *each clause of* χ *is a* (φ, ψ)-*likeness.*

Proof. Condition 2 of the problem means that it is generally more efficient in terms of formula size to list likenesses in χ rather than θ and θ'. See the full version for the proof. □

Remark 2. Minimizing $size(\theta) + size(\theta') + size(\chi)$ is not the only conceivable minimality condition for the formulas $\theta \wedge \chi$ and $\theta' \wedge \chi$. If one thinks of these as two formulas to be minimized, then another natural condition could be $size(\theta \wedge \chi) + size(\theta' \wedge \chi)$. For the global contrastive explanation problem, changing to this alternate condition would forfeit the property of Theorem 1, but gain a property, where clauses that are strong contrasts can be easily identified from the output.

We also note that the same kind of property holds for the contrastive explanation problem. The difference is that here, the contrasts are found between S and S' rather than φ and ψ.

Theorem 2. *Let* $\varphi, \psi \in PL[\tau]$ *and let* (θ, θ', χ) *be the output of the contrastive explanation problem with input* (S, S', φ, ψ). *Further assume that* θ, θ' *and* χ *are in* CNF. *Then* **(1)** *each clause of* θ *is a weak* (S, S')-*contrast,* **(2)** *each clause of* θ' *is a weak* (S', S)-*contrast, and* **(3)** *each clause of* χ *is a* (S, S')-*likeness.*

Proof. We first note that since $S \vDash \varphi \wedge \neg\psi$ and $S' \vDash \neg\varphi \wedge \psi$, we have $S \wedge \neg S' \equiv S$. Now for a clause $C \in \theta$, we have $S \vDash \theta \vDash C$ and we can use the same arguments as in the proof of Theorem 1 to prove the claim. □

Note that Theorem 2 also works for the counterfactual problems if we consider an existentially quantified S' to be implicitly present in the definitions.

4.2   Link to Existing Contrastive Explanations

In this subsection we link the counterfactual difference problem to existing notions in the literature, such as CXp. For example, we show that if the input S defines an assignment and output formulas θ, θ' and χ are given in CNF, then the output gives the minimal changes required to flip the truth values of φ and ψ. The difference from CXp is that our definition gives a cardinality-minimal solution rather than a subset-minimal one.

We start with the following theorem which shows that in the special case of the counterfactual difference problem where S defines a partial assignment, the optimal solutions also define partial assignments. Example 4 shows that in general we cannot require χ to even define a partial assignment.

Theorem 3. *Let* $\varphi, \psi \in PL[\tau]$ *and let* $S \subseteq PL[\tau]$ *define a partial assignment. Let* (θ, θ', χ) *be the output of the counterfactual difference problem* (S, φ, ψ). *Further assume that* θ, θ' *and* χ *are in* CNF. *Then* **(1)** *the formulas* θ *and* θ' *are partial assignments and* **(2)** *the formulas* $\theta \wedge \chi$ *and* $\theta' \wedge \chi$ *define partial assignments. The same also holds for the counterfactual contrastive explanation problem.*

Proof. The proofs for both problems are similar. We assume that an output (θ, θ', χ) does not satisfy the claims and then prune or move clauses to find an alternative output $(\theta_*, \theta'_*, \chi_*)$ with smaller total size that does satisfy the claims. This contradicts condition 3 of the problems. See the full version for the proof.
□

In the case where S defines a τ-assignment, we get a stronger guarantee on optimal outputs for the counterfactual difference problem.

Theorem 4. *Let $\varphi, \psi \in \text{PL}[\tau]$, let $S \subseteq \text{PL}[\tau]$ define a τ-assignment and let (θ, θ', χ) be the output of the counterfactual difference problem with input (S, φ, ψ). Further assume that θ, θ' and χ are in CNF. Now the formulas $\theta \wedge \chi$ and $\theta' \wedge \chi$ define τ-assignments.*

Proof. We know that $\theta \wedge \chi$ defines an assignment and $\theta' \wedge \chi$ defines a partial assignment. We show how a proposition missing from this partial assignment could be included with formulas that are more optimal in terms of conditions 3 and 4 of the problem. See the full version for the proof.
□

The above theorem does not hold for the counterfactual contrastive explanation problem. This is to be expected as the condition $S \vDash \theta \wedge \chi$ is not sufficient to force $\theta \wedge \chi$ to define an assignment, again highlighting the fact that the counterfactual contrastive explanation problem is concerned with comparing *reasons* for the formulas φ and ψ rather than assignments that satisfy them.

To state the last result of this section, we define the notation $s \triangle \lambda = (s \setminus \lambda) \cup \{\bar{\ell} \mid \ell \in \lambda\}$, where s and λ are viewed as sets of literals with $\lambda \subseteq s$. This result is of particular interest, as when the second input formula ψ is the negation $\neg\varphi$ of the first, the set λ of propositions to be flipped is a cardinality minimal CXp [9].

Theorem 5. *Let s be a τ-assignment and let $\varphi, \psi \in \text{PL}[\tau]$ such that $\neg\varphi \wedge \psi$ is satisfiable. Assume that $s \vDash \varphi \wedge \neg\psi$ and let (θ, θ', χ) be the output of the counterfactual difference problem for PL with input (S_s, φ, ψ). Further assume that θ, θ' and χ are in CNF. Now $\theta' \wedge \chi$ defines a τ-assignment s' such that $s' = s \triangle \lambda$ for a cardinality-minimal set λ of literals with $s \vDash \lambda$, $s \triangle \lambda \vDash \neg\varphi \wedge \psi$.*

Proof. We know from Theorem 4 that $\theta' \wedge \chi$ defines a τ-assignment s'. We show that given two candidates for s', the one with less differences compared to s is the preferred candidate due to the formula size condition 3 of the problem. See the full version for the proof.
□

4.3   Computational Complexity

We proceed to study the computational complexity of our problems for propositional logic. As per usual, we study the complexity of the related decision problems: instead of finding a minimal solution to the given problem, we want to decide whether there is a solution of size at most k, where k is part of the input.

We start with global contrastive explainability problem. Recall that in the propositional setting we require the output formulas to be CNF-formulas.

Theorem 6. *The global contrastive explanation problem is Σ_2^p-complete.*

Proof. We will give a simple reduction from the minimal formula size problem for CNF-formulas, which was proved to be Σ_2^p-complete in [18]. Let (φ, k) be an input to the latter problem. Consider the following input $(\bot, \varphi, k)$ to the global contrastive explainability problem. If (θ, θ', χ) is a witness for this input, then $\theta \equiv \bot$ and $\theta' \wedge \chi \equiv \varphi$. It is now easy to see that the output of (φ, k) is yes iff the output of $(\bot, \varphi, k)$ is yes. $\square$

For the next hardness result we use a result from [11] which states that the so-called **local explainability problem** for PL is Σ_2^p-complete. In this problem the input is a tuple (s, φ, k), where s is an assignment, such that $s \models \varphi$ and the goal is to determine whether there exist a formula ψ of PL such that $\text{size}(\psi) \leq k$ and $s \models \psi \models \varphi$. The following result demonstrates that this problem is a special case of the contrastive explainability problem and the separability problem.

Theorem 7. *Both the contrastive explanation problem and the minimal separator problem for PL are Σ_2^p-complete.*

Proof. Upper bound is clear. For the lower bounds, consider an instance (s, φ, k) of the local explainability problem. Let φ_s be a conjunction of literals which defines s. For contrastive explainability problem the hardness follows from the observation that $(\varphi_s, \bot, \varphi, \bot, k)$ is an instance of the contrastive explainability problem for which the output is yes iff the output of $(s, \varphi, k, 1)$ is yes. In the right-to-left direction we use a result from [11] which shows that if there exist a formula ψ with $\text{size}(\psi) \leq k$ and $s \models \psi \models \varphi$, then there is also one which is a conjunction of literals. For separability problem we get the hardness by considering instances of the form $(\varphi_s, \neg \varphi, k)$. $\square$

We move on to consider counterfactual contrastive and difference problems. Theorem 3 shows that if the input S defines a partial assignment, then the formulas $\theta \wedge \chi$ and $\theta' \wedge \chi$ from the output (θ, θ', χ) also define partial assignments. Thus it is natural to define the **simplified counterfactual contrastive explanation problem** and the **simplified counterfactual difference problem** by modifying Definitions 4 and 5 as follows. First, we require that S defines a partial assignment. Secondly, the output formulas θ, θ' and χ are required to be partial assignments.

Our next result shows that already the simplified problems are Σ_2^p complete. See the full version for the proof. We leave the complexity of the non-simplified problems for future work.

Theorem 8. *The simplified counterfactual contrastive explanation problem and the simplified counterfactual difference problem are Σ_2^p-complete.*

5 Implementation and Case Studies

In this section we outline our Answer Set Programming (ASP) based implementation for selected explanation problems, followed by case studies where we use it to demonstrate how our problems work on real-world instances.

Implementation. Due to the computational complexity of the considered problems, obtaining a polynomial time dedicated algorithm seems unlikely. However, the inherent complexity closely matches the one of ASP [6] and it is thus natural to implement our notions in this formalism to obtain a prototypical implementation.

We thus implemented Definitions 2, 4, and 5 in ASP. The encodings as well as a Python script for reproducing the case studies can be found online at https://github.com/tlyphed/general_contrastive_exp. Due to length constraints we cannot cover the ASP encoding in detail but we will give a brief overview.

The idea behind the encodings is to guess the output formulas θ, θ', χ as CNF and check that the required entailments and equivalences hold. Those checks are done using the *saturation technique* [6], which is an encoding method for expressing coNP problems in ASP. The criteria regarding the sizes of the formulas are then formulated using weak constraints, which essentially give preference to formulas which adhere to those criteria.

Case Studies. We used our implementation to compute contrastive explanations for decision trees that were obtained from three real-world classification datasets. The datasets that we used were Iris [7], Wine [1] and Glass [8]. We used the `scikit-learn` Python library [15] for training the classifiers. For all datasets we used 80% of the data for training and 20% for testing. To keep the learning task simple, we fine-tuned only the depth of the decision trees, selecting the smallest depth that achieved the highest accuracy on the test data.

Having trained the decision trees, we proceeded as follows. For each dataset we picked two classes c, c' at random and then used the learned decision tree $\mathcal{T}$ to form class formulas for c, c'. The propositional symbols in these class formulas correspond to pivots used by $\mathcal{T}$. We also picked a random instance from the test data that was classified as c by $\mathcal{T}$. We then ran our implementations for global contrastive explanation problem (GCE), counterfactual contrastive explanation problem (CCE) and counterfactual difference problem (CD) using the class formulas and the instance as inputs. For CCE and CD, we additionally constrained the output formulas to be partial assignments. This choice is motivated by Theorems 3 and 4, since in our case studies S (the instance) corresponds to a conjunction of literals. The results are summarized in Table 1.

We make some general remarks about Table 1. For GCE we see both simple and more complex likenesses. For example, in the case of Glass, the optimal output had no common clauses for the two class formulas. In each case we see that CCE and CD have chosen the same propositions to flip, although we know by Example 4 that this is not necessary. The CCE outputs are more informative here since they also leave out unnecessary propositions from the explanations.

Table 1. Summary of our case studies. Note that we have Booleanized the instances using the pivots learned by the corresponding decision tree.

Case	GCE	CCE	CD
dataset: Iris	$\theta : (\neg p_2 \vee p_3) \wedge (p_2 \vee p_4)$	$\theta : p_3$	$\theta : p_3$
depth: 4	$\theta' : (\neg p_2 \vee \neg p_3) \wedge (p_2 \vee \neg p_4)$	$\theta' : \neg p_3$	$\theta' : \neg p_3$
instance:	$\chi : \neg p_1$	$\chi : \neg p_1 \wedge p_2$	$\chi : \neg p_1 \wedge p_2 \wedge p_4$
$\{\neg p_1, p_2, p_3, p_4\}$			
dataset: Wine	$\theta : (p_1 \vee \neg p_4) \vee (p_1 \vee p_5)$	$\theta : p_1$	$\theta : p_1 \wedge \neg p_4$
depth: 3	$\theta' : \neg p_1 \wedge p_4$	$\theta' : \neg p_1 \wedge p_4$	$\theta' : \neg p_1 \wedge p_4$
instance:	$\chi : (\neg p_1 \vee p_3) \wedge (\neg p_1 \vee p_2)$	$\chi : p_2 \wedge p_3$	$\chi : p_2 \wedge p_3 \wedge p_5$
$\{p_1, p_2, p_3, \neg p_4, p_5\}$			
dataset: Glass	$\theta : (\neg p_1 \vee p_2) \wedge (p_1 \vee \neg p_5)$	$\theta : p_2$	$\theta : p_2 \wedge \neg p_4$
depth: 3	$\wedge(\neg p_1 \vee \neg p_3) \wedge (p_1 \vee \neg p_7)$	$\theta' : \neg p_2 \wedge p_4$	$\theta' : \neg p_2 \wedge p_4$
instance:	$\theta' : (p_1 \vee p_5) \wedge (p_1 \vee \neg p_6)$	$\chi : p_1 \wedge \neg p_3$	$\chi : p_1 \wedge \neg p_3 \wedge \neg p_5$
$\{p_1, p_2, \neg p_3, \neg p_4,$	$\wedge(\neg p_1 \vee p_4) \wedge (\neg p_1 \vee \neg p_2)$		$\wedge p_6 \wedge p_7$
$\neg p_5, p_6, p_7\}$	$\chi : \top$		

We examine the formulas in more detail for the Iris dataset. Each instance is an iris flower and the goal is to classify them into one of three species: setosa, versicolor, or virginica. We formed class formulas for versicolor and virginica. From GCE we see e.g. that the class formulas have $\neg p_1$ in common, where

$$p_1 := \text{``petal length is } \leq 2.45 \text{ cm''}.$$

So the class formulas for versicolor and virginica both agree that petal length should be more than 2.45 cm. From CCE and CD, we see that the instance $\{\neg p_1, p_2, p_3, p_4\}$ was classified as versicolor, because $p_3 \wedge \neg p_1 \wedge p_2$, where

$$p_2 := \text{``petal length is } \leq 4.75 \text{ cm''}$$

and

$$p_3 := \text{``petal width is } \leq 1.65 \text{ cm''}.$$

So the explanation is that the flower has petal length between 2.45 cm and 4.75 cm and petal width at most 1.65 cm. If the petal length had been more than 4.75 cm, the flower would have been classified as virginica.

6 Conclusion

In this work, we introduced a logic-based framework for contrastive explanations that formalizes various questions of the form "Why P but not Q?". Our framework encompasses both local and global contrastive explanations. We examined the theoretical properties of our definitions in detail in the important special case of propositional logic. Among other results, we showed that our framework subsumes a cardinality-minimal version of existing contrastive explanation approaches from [4,9]. In addition, we analyzed the computational complexity of the proposed problems and proved that, in the propositional setting, most of them are Σ_2^p-complete. Finally, we implemented our approach using Answer Set Programming and demonstrated that our problems produce useful explanations on real-world instances.

Acknowledgments. Antti Kuusisto and Miikka Vilander received funding from the Research Council of Finland projects *Explaining AI via Logic* (XAILOG) 345612 and *Theory of computational logics* 324435, 328987, 352419, 352420. Tobias Geibinger is a recipient of a DOC Fellowship of the Austrian Academy of Sciences at the Institute of Logic and Computation at the TU Wien. This work has benefited from the European Union's Horizon 2020 research and innovation programme under grant agreement No 101034440 (LogiCS@TUWien). In addition, this research was funded in part by the Austrian Science Fund (FWF) [10.55776/COE12]. The authors acknowledge TU Wien Bibliothek for financial support through its Open Access Funding Program.

The author names of this article are ordered based on alphabetical order.

References

1. Aeberhard, S., Forina, M.: Wine. UCI Machine Learning Repository (1992). https://doi.org/10.24432/C5PC7J

2. Barceló, P., Monet, M., Pérez, J., Subercaseaux, B.: Model interpretability through the lens of computational complexity. In: Advances in Neural Information Processing Systems, vol. 33, pp. 15487–15498 (2020)

3. Bassan, S., Amir, G., Katz, G.: Local vs. global interpretability: a computational complexity perspective. In: Forty-first International Conference on Machine Learning (2024)

4. Darwiche, A.: Logic for explainable AI. In: LICS, pp. 1–11 (2023). https://doi.org/10.1109/LICS56636.2023.10175757

5. Darwiche, A., Hirth, A.: On the reasons behind decisions. In: 24th European Conference on Artificial Intelligence (ECAI 2020). Frontiers in Artificial Intelligence and Applications, vol. 325, pp. 712–720. IOS Press (2020)

6. Eiter, T., Ianni, G., Krennwallner, T.: Answer set programming: a primer. In: Reasoning Web. Semantic Technologies for Information Systems. LNCS, vol. 5689, pp. 40–110. Springer (2009). https://doi.org/10.1007/978-3-642-03754-2_2

7. Fisher, R.A.: Iris. UCI Machine Learning Repository (1936). https://doi.org/10.24432/C56C76

8. German, B.: Glass Identification. UCI Machine Learning Repository (1987). https://doi.org/10.24432/C5WW2P

9. Ignatiev, A., Narodytska, N., Asher, N., Marques-Silva, J.: From contrastive to abductive explanations and back again. In: Baldoni, M., Bandini, S. (eds.) AIxIA 2020 - Advances in Artificial Intelligence - XIXth International Conference of the Italian Association for Artificial Intelligence, Virtual Event, November 25-27, 2020, Revised Selected Papers. Lecture Notes in Computer Science, vol. 12414, pp. 335–355. Springer (2020). https://doi.org/10.1007/978-3-030-77091-4_21

10. Ignatiev, A., Narodytska, N., Marques-Silva, J.: Abduction-based explanations for machine learning models. In: Proceedings of the Thirty-third AAAI Conference on Artificial Intelligence (AAAI-19), vol. 33, pp. 1511–1519 (2019)
11. Jaakkola, R., Janhunen, T., Kuusisto, A., Rankooh, M.F., Vilander, M.: Explainability via short formulas: the case of propositional logic with implementation. In: Joint Proceedings of (HYDRA 2022) and the RCRA Workshop on Experimental Evaluation of Algorithms for Solving Problems with Combinatorial Explosion. CEUR Workshop Proceedings, vol. 3281, pp. 64–77 (2022)
12. Lipton, P.: Contrastive explanation. Roy. Inst. Philos. Suppl. **27**, 247–266 (1990). https://doi.org/10.1017/S1358246100005130
13. Marques-Silva, J.: Logic-based explainability in machine learning. In: Bertossi, L.E., Xiao, G. (eds.) Reasoning Web. Causality, Explanations and Declarative Knowledge - 18th International Summer School 2022, Berlin, Germany, September 27–30, 2022, Tutorial Lectures. Lecture Notes in Computer Science, vol. 13759, pp. 24–104. Springer (2022). https://doi.org/10.1007/978-3-031-31414-8_2
14. Miller, T.: Explanation in artificial intelligence: insights from the social sciences. Artif. Intell. **267**, 1–38 (2019). https://doi.org/10.1016/j.artint.2018.07.007
15. Pedregosa, F., et al.: Scikit-learn: machine learning in Python. J. Mach. Learn. Res. **12**, 2825–2830 (2011)
16. Shih, A., Choi, A., Darwiche, A.: Formal verification of Bayesian network classifiers. In: International Conference on Probabilistic Graphical Models, pp. 427–438. PMLR (2018)
17. Stepin, I., Alonso, J.M., Catala, A., Pereira-Fariña, M.: A survey of contrastive and counterfactual explanation generation methods for explainable artificial intelligence. IEEE Access **9**, 11974–12001 (2021)
18. Umans, C.: The minimum equivalent DNF problem and shortest implicants. J. Comput. Syst. Sci. **63**(4), 597–611 (2001). https://doi.org/10.1006/jcss.2001.1775
19. Van Bouwel, J., Weber, E.: Remote causes, bad explanations? J. Theory Soc. Behav. **32**(4), 437–449 (2002). https://doi.org/10.1111/1468-5914.00197

Argumentation

On the Sensitivity of Extension Semantics to Similarity

Leila Amgoud[(⊠)]

CNRS – IRIT, Toulouse, France
amgoud@irit.fr

Abstract. This paper presents the first systematic study of how similarity between arguments affects their evaluation under extension semantics. We define a set of principles that govern how similarity should be taken into account by a semantics, and introduce a broad family of parameterized extension semantics that adhere to these principles. Each member of this family generalizes a classical extension semantics (such as preferred semantics) while disregarding redundant attacks. We identify classes of argumentation graphs in which similarity has no effect on the acceptability status of arguments, and we characterize the conditions under which a family instance either improves an argument's acceptability or coincides with the semantics it generalizes. Finally, we discuss different types of selection functions, which specify the subset of attacks to disregard.

Keywords: Argumentation · Semantics · Similarity

1 Introduction

An argumentation framework consists of a graph and a semantics. In the graph, nodes represent arguments, reflecting justifications for claims, while edges represent attacks, modeling conflicts between arguments. The semantics provides a formal method for evaluating the acceptability of each argument within the graph. Numerous semantics have been proposed (see [7] for a survey). The earliest are the extension-based semantics introduced by Dung [13], which identify sets of arguments that can be jointly accepted. More recently, gradual semantics have been introduced [10]; they assign each argument a (numerical or qualitative) value reflecting its degree of strength.

The broad spectrum of theoretical and practical applications of argumentation has brought attention to the concept of *similarity* between arguments, namely *semantical similarity*. The latter concerns the degree to which two arguments are similar in terms of their *content*-their justifications and claims. Consider the following example involving two arguments, b_1, b_2, both supporting the claim that *Paul is not a suitable candidate for the lecturer position*.

b_1: He has limited teaching experience. b_2: He taught only a few hours before.

These arguments are semantically similar as they convey the same information. Existence of similarity introduces new research questions regarding its role in argumentation frameworks. We distinguish two main roles for similarity. The first is to

© The Author(s), under exclusive license to Springer Nature Switzerland AG 2026
G. Casini et al. (Eds.): JELIA 2025, LNAI 16093, pp. 63–77, 2026.
https://doi.org/10.1007/978-3-032-04587-4_5

enhance the reliability of the information conveyed by similar arguments. In our example, this could lead to merging the two arguments into a single argument with a higher degree of trustworthiness [11]. This approach aligns with practices in belief merging, where claims supported by multiple sources are generally considered more plausible. While this approach is reasonable, its implementation in argumentation frameworks poses challenges. Similar arguments may interact differently with other arguments, so merging them would require a careful redefinition of the graph's structure.

The second role of similarity is to constrain the influence that attacks have on the strength of their targets. Within the context of gradual semantics, previous work [3,5] has shown that ignoring similarity among attackers can lead to skewed evaluations of arguments. Such inaccuracies can ultimately distort the conclusions provided by argumentation-based systems such as decision systems. These studies have developed methods for integrating similarity into existing gradual semantics. Surprisingly, there is no work in the literature on the integration of similarity into extension semantics. This paper seeks to address this gap through five main contributions:

1. It proposes three principles that extension semantics that incorporate similarity into the evaluation process should satisfy.
2. It defines a broad family of parameterized extension semantics that satisfy the proposed principles. Each member of this family is determined by two parameters: a classical extension semantics δ (e.g., grounded semantics [13]), and a selection function Δ, which identifies redundant attacks to be removed from the argumentation graph. The evaluation is then performed on the resulting subgraph using the base semantics δ. Each instance of this family is sensitive to similarity, generalizes the underlying semantics δ, and has the potential to improve its evaluations by accounting for redundancy introduced by similar arguments.
3. It shows that in *coherent graphs*-where similar arguments share the same set of attackers-similarity has no impact on argument evaluation. However, in non-coherent graphs, disregarding similarity among attackers can lead to distorted evaluations of their targets.
4. It characterizes the conditions under which a new semantics improves the acceptability status of an argument or coincides with the semantics (δ) it generalizes.
5. It discusses various strategies that can underpin the design of selection functions, offering guidance on how to systematically eliminate redundant attacks.

The paper is organized as follows: Sect. 2 introduces background, Sect. 3 defines extended argumentation graphs, and three principles that semantics would satisfy, Sect. 4 defines the novel family of parameterized semantics and analyses their properties, Sect. 5 discusses examples of selection functions, Sect. 6 recalls some related work and the last section is devoted to concluding remarks and perspectives.

2   Background

The cornerstone of argumentation theory is the notion of *argument*-a reason supporting a particular standpoint. Arguments are often interconnected through an *attack relation*, which captures the conflicts that arise between pairs of arguments. These interrelations are naturally represented in a graphical form. In this paper, we denote by Args the set of all possible arguments, by $a, b, c, \ldots$ arguments and by $r, r_1, r_2, \ldots$ attacks.

Table 1. Examples of argumentation graphs $\mathbb{G}_i = \langle \mathcal{A}_i, \mathcal{R}_i \rangle, i \in \{1, \ldots, 4\}$.

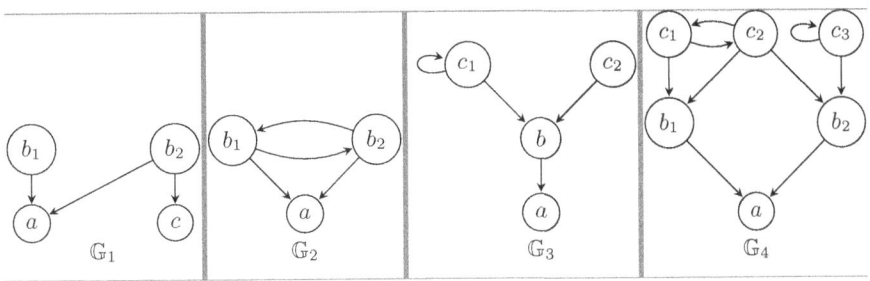

Definition 1. *An* argumentation graph *(AG) is a pair* $\mathbb{G} = \langle \mathcal{A}, \mathcal{R} \rangle$, *where* $\mathcal{A} \subseteq$ Args, $\mathcal{A} \neq \emptyset$, *and* $\mathcal{R} \subseteq \mathcal{A} \times \mathcal{A}$ *is an attack relation. Let* AG *be the set of all possible AGs.*

A pair $(b, a) \in \mathcal{R}$ is read "b attacks a". We say also that a set $\mathcal{E} \subseteq \mathcal{A}$ attacks $a \in \mathcal{A}$ if $\exists b \in \mathcal{E}$ such that $(b, a) \in \mathcal{R}$.

In the seminal paper [13], conflicts between arguments are resolved using an *extension semantics*-a formal method that defines sets of arguments that are jointly *acceptable*, with each such set referred to as an *extension*.

Definition 2. *An* extension semantics *is a function* δ *mapping every* $\mathbb{G} = \langle \mathcal{A}, \mathcal{R} \rangle \in$ AG *into* $\text{Ext}_\delta(\mathbb{G}) \subseteq \mathbb{P}(\mathcal{A})^1$. *Every member of* $\text{Ext}_\delta(\mathbb{G})$ *is called an* extension.

There are several criteria for defining extensions, thus acceptable sets, including those introduced by Dung [13] for defining his main semantics: complete (*co*), grounded (*gr*), preferred (*pr*), and stable (*st*). They are based on *conflict-freeness* and *defence*, where for $\mathcal{E} \subseteq \mathcal{A}$,

- $\mathcal{E}$ is *conflict-free* iff $\nexists a, b \in \mathcal{E}$ such that $(a, b) \in \mathcal{R}$. Else, $\mathcal{E}$ is said to be $\mathcal{R}$−*conflicting*.
- $\mathcal{E}$ *defends* $a \in \mathcal{A}$ iff $\forall b \in \mathcal{A}$ such that $(b, a) \in \mathcal{R}$, $\exists c \in \mathcal{E}$ such that $(c, b) \in \mathcal{R}$.
- $\mathcal{E}$ is *admissible* iff it is conflict-free and defends all its elements.

Let us now recall the definition of extension under the above-mentioned semantics. Let $\mathcal{E} \subseteq \mathcal{A}$ be conflict-free.

- $\mathcal{E}$ is a *complete* extension iff it defends its elements and contains all the arguments it defends.
- $\mathcal{E}$ is a *grounded* extension iff it is the subset-minimal complete extension.
- $\mathcal{E}$ is a *preferred* extension iff it is a subset-maximal complete extension.
- $\mathcal{E}$ is a *stable* extension iff for any $a \in \mathcal{A} \setminus \mathcal{E}$, $\mathcal{E}$ attacks a.

Since extension semantics may yield multiple extensions for a given argumentation graph, an *acceptability status* is assigned to each individual argument by aggregating across all extensions. In the literature (e.g., [10]), a four-valued scale $\{s, c, u, r\}$ is

---

[1] $\mathbb{P}(\mathcal{A})$ is the *powerset*, i.e., the set of all partitions of $\mathcal{A}$.

commonly used for this purpose. This scale is equipped with a total ordering $\succeq$, where $s \succ c \succ u \succ r$, and $x \succeq y$ (respectively $x \succ y$) is interpreted as "x is at least as acceptable as y" (respectively "x is strictly more acceptable than y").

Definition 3. *Let δ be an extension semantics, $\mathbb{G} = \langle \mathcal{A}, \mathcal{R} \rangle \in$ AG and $a \in \mathcal{A}$. If $\text{Ext}_\delta(\mathbb{G}) = \emptyset$, then $\text{Acc}_\delta(a, \mathbb{G}) = u$. Else:*

- $\text{Acc}_\delta(a, \mathbb{G}) = s$ *iff* $a \in \bigcap_{\mathcal{E} \in \text{Ext}_\delta(\mathbb{G})} \mathcal{E}$. *a is said to be* sceptically accepted *in $\mathbb{G}$.*
- $\text{Acc}_\delta(a, \mathbb{G}) = c$ *iff* $\exists \mathcal{E}, \mathcal{E}' \in \text{Ext}_\delta(\mathbb{G})$ *such that* $a \in \mathcal{E}$ *and* $a \notin \mathcal{E}'$. *a is said to be* credulously accepted *in $\mathbb{G}$.*
- $\text{Acc}_\delta(a, \mathbb{G}) = r$ *iff* $a \notin \bigcup_{\mathcal{E} \in \text{Ext}_\delta(\mathbb{G})} \mathcal{E}$ *and* $\exists \mathcal{E} \in \text{Ext}_\delta(\mathbb{G})$ *such that $\mathcal{E}$ attacks a. a is said to be* rejected *in $\mathbb{G}$.*
- $\text{Acc}_\delta(a, \mathbb{G}) = u$ *iff* $a \notin \bigcup_{\mathcal{E} \in \text{Ext}_\delta(\mathbb{G})} \mathcal{E}$ *and* $\nexists \mathcal{E} \in \text{Ext}_\delta(\mathbb{G})$ *such that $\mathcal{E}$ attacks a. a is said to be* undecided *in $\mathbb{G}$.*

$\text{Acc}_\delta(a, \mathbb{G})$ *denotes the* acceptability status *of the argument a in the graph $\mathbb{G}$ under the semantics δ.*

Example 1. Let us analyse the four graphs from Table 1 under preferred semantics.

- $\text{Ext}_{pr}(\mathbb{G}_1) = \{\{b_1, b_2\}\}$.
  - $\text{Acc}_{pr}(b_1, \mathbb{G}_1) = \text{Acc}_{pr}(b_2, \mathbb{G}_1) = s$,
  - $\text{Acc}_{pr}(a, \mathbb{G}_1) = \text{Acc}_{pr}(c, \mathbb{G}_1) = r$.
- $\text{Ext}_{pr}(\mathbb{G}_2) = \{\{b_1\}, \{b_2\}\}$.
  - $\text{Acc}_{pr}(b_1, \mathbb{G}_2) = \text{Acc}_{pr}(b_2, \mathbb{G}_2) = c$,
  - $\text{Acc}_{pr}(a, \mathbb{G}_2) = r$.
- $\text{Ext}_{pr}(\mathbb{G}_3) = \{\{a, c_2\}\}$.
  - $\text{Acc}_{pr}(a, \mathbb{G}_3) = \text{Acc}_{pr}(c_2, \mathbb{G}_3) = s$,
  - $\text{Acc}_{pr}(b, \mathbb{G}_3) = r$.
  - $\text{Acc}_{pr}(c_1, \mathbb{G}_3) = u$.
- $\text{Ext}_{pr}(\mathbb{G}_4) = \{\{c_1\}, \{a, c_2\}\}$.
  - $\text{Acc}_{pr}(a, \mathbb{G}_4) = \text{Acc}_{pr}(c_1, \mathbb{G}_4) = \text{Acc}_{pr}(c_2, \mathbb{G}_4) = c$,
  - $\text{Acc}_{pr}(b_1, \mathbb{G}_4) = \text{Acc}_{pr}(b_2, \mathbb{G}_4) = r$.
  - $\text{Acc}_{pr}(c_3, \mathbb{G}_4) = u$.

Below are some useful notations for the rest of the paper.

Notations: Let $\mathbb{G} = \langle \mathcal{A}, \mathcal{R} \rangle \in$ AG and $a, b \in \mathcal{A}$. Let $r \in \mathcal{R}$ such that $r = (b, a)$. The functions $\mathbf{Sc}(r)$ and $\mathbf{Tg}(r)$ return the source b and the target a of the attack r respectively. The function $\text{aAtt}(a, \mathbb{G})$ returns the set of arguments attacking a in $\mathbb{G}$. For instance, in Table 1, $\text{aAtt}(a, \mathbb{G}_1) = \{b_1, b_2\}$. The function $\text{rAtt}(a, \mathbb{G})$ returns the set of all attacks targeting a in $\mathbb{G}$. Hence, $\text{rAtt}(a, \mathbb{G}_1) = \{(b_1, a), (b_2, a)\}$. Let $X \subseteq \text{rAtt}(a, \mathbb{G})$. We define $\mathbb{G} \ominus X = \langle \mathcal{A}, \mathcal{R} \setminus X \rangle$ (i.e., the AG where the attacks in X are removed), and $\mathbb{G} \downarrow X = \langle \mathcal{A}, \mathcal{R}' \rangle$ where $\text{rAtt}(a, \mathbb{G} \downarrow X) = X$ and $\forall b \in \mathcal{A} \setminus \{a\}$, $\text{rAtt}(b, \mathbb{G} \downarrow X) = \text{rAtt}(b, \mathbb{G})$ (i.e., the AG where the set of attacks on a is X). Consider the graph $\mathbb{G}_2$ in Table 1 and the argument a. Note that $\text{rAtt}(a, \mathbb{G}_2) = \{(b_1, a), (b_2, a)\}$. For $X = \{(b_1, a)\}$, $\mathbb{G}_2 \ominus X = \langle \{a, b_1, b_2\}, \{(b_1, b_2), (b_2, b_1), (b_2, a)\} \rangle$.

It was shown in [1] that direct attacks on an argument are the primary cause of the argument's loss of strength. The author also identified the sets of attacks *necessary* and those *sufficient* to determine the status of their targets according to a given extension semantics. Specifically, a subset of attacks is considered necessary for an argument if its removal automatically leads to a change in the argument's status.

Definition 4 (Necessity). *Let δ be an extension semantics, $\mathbb{G} = \langle \mathcal{A}, \mathcal{R} \rangle \in$ AG, $a \in \mathcal{A}$ and $X \subseteq$ rAtt$(a, \mathbb{G})$. The set X is* necessary *for a iff:*

- $\text{Acc}_\delta(a, \mathbb{G}) \neq \text{Acc}_\delta(a, \mathbb{G} \ominus X)$,
- $\nexists X' \subset X$ *such that X' satisfies the above condition.*

We denote by $\text{Nec}_\delta(a, \mathbb{G})$ *the set of all necessary sets for a in $\mathbb{G}$ under δ.*

Example 1 (Cont). Let us check the necessary attacks for the argument a in each graph under preferred semantics.

$$\text{Nec}_{pr}(a, \mathbb{G}_1) = \{\{(b_1, a), (b_2, a)\}\} \qquad \text{Nec}_{pr}(a, \mathbb{G}_2) = \{\{(b_1, a)\}, \{(b_2, a)\}\}$$
$$\text{Nec}_{pr}(a, \mathbb{G}_3) = \{\{(b, a)\}\} \qquad\qquad \text{Nec}_{pr}(a, \mathbb{G}_4) = \{\{(b_2, a)\}\}$$

Remark: Note that in the graph $\mathbb{G}_4$, the attack (b_2, a) is necessary for the argument a while it emanates from a rejected argument $(\text{Acc}_{pr}(b_2, \mathbb{G}_4) = \text{r})$. Hence, a necessary attack does not necessarily come from a strong argument.

A set of attacks is sufficient for a given targeted argument if, when taken alone (i.e., removing all other attacks toward the argument), the argument gets the same status.

Definition 5 (Sufficiency). *Let δ be an extension semantics, $\mathbb{G} = \langle \mathcal{A}, \mathcal{R} \rangle \in$ AG, $a \in \mathcal{A}$, and $X \subseteq$ rAtt$(a, \mathbb{G})$. The set X is* sufficient *for a iff:*

- $\text{Acc}_\delta(a, \mathbb{G}) = \text{Acc}_\delta(a, \mathbb{G} \downarrow X)$.
- $\nexists X' \subset X$ *such that X' satisfies the above condition.*

$\text{Suff}_\delta(a, \mathbb{G})$ *is the set of all sufficient sets for a in $\mathbb{G}$ under δ.*

Example 1 (Cont). Let us check the sufficient attacks for the argument a in each graph under preferred semantics.

$$\text{Suff}_{pr}(a, \mathbb{G}_1) = \{\{(b_1, a)\}, \{(b_2, a)\}\} \qquad \text{Suff}_{pr}(a, \mathbb{G}_2) = \{\{(b_1, a), (b_2, a)\}\}$$
$$\text{Suff}_{pr}(a, \mathbb{G}_3) = \{\{(b, a)\}\} \qquad\qquad\quad \text{Suff}_{pr}(a, \mathbb{G}_4) = \{\{(b_2, a)\}\}$$

3   Extended Argumentation Graphs

In addition to an attack relation, we assume the existence of a similarity relation between arguments. This relation captures semantic similarity, that is, how closely two arguments align in terms of their content (reasons and claims). Formally, it is a binary, reflexive, and symmetric relation. It can be derived from a similarity **measure** that quantifies the **degree** of similarity between any pair of arguments (see [4, 12] for examples of measures for logical arguments). However, the raw numerical values produced by these measures are often of limited practical use, as it is unclear which value ranges genuinely indicate meaningful relatedness between arguments. A widely adopted approach in the broader similarity literature (e.g., [17]) involves applying a **threshold**, whereby objects with similarity values exceeding this threshold are deemed similar.

Definition 6. *Let* $X \subseteq$ Args. *A* similarity relation *on* X *is a* binary relation sim $\subseteq$ $X \times X$ *such that:*

- $\forall a \in X, (a,a) \in$ sim   *(Reflexivity)*
- $\forall a,b \in X, (a,b) \in$ sim *iff* $(b,a) \in$ sim   *(Symmetry)*

We define sim* $= \{(a,a) \mid a \in X\}$.

Note that due to the reflexivity property, sim* $\neq \emptyset$ and consequently, sim $\neq \emptyset$. Let us now introduce extended argumentation graphs.

Definition 7. *An* extended argumentation graph *(eAG) is a tuple* $\mathbb{E} = \langle \mathbb{G}, \text{sim} \rangle$, *where* $\mathbb{G} = \langle \mathcal{A}, \mathcal{R} \rangle \in$ AG *and* sim *is a similarity relation on* $\mathcal{A}$. *Let* eAG *be the set of all possible eAGs.*

Note that an extended graph $\langle \mathbb{G}, \text{sim}^* \rangle$ coincides with the basic graph $\mathbb{G}$ as all arguments are assumed pairwise *dissimilar*.

Extension semantics that evaluate arguments in extended argumentation graphs are functions that yield extensions, as specified in Definition 2. These extensions are then aggregated, as described in Definition 3, to derive the acceptability statuses of the arguments.

Notations: Let $\mathbb{E} = \langle \mathbb{G}, \text{sim} \rangle \in$ eAG, where $\mathbb{G} = \langle \mathcal{A}, \mathcal{R} \rangle$, $a \in \mathcal{A}$. All notations defined for simple graphs apply to extended graphs. For instance, $\text{rAtt}(a, \mathbb{E})$ is the set of attacks targeting a in $\mathbb{E}$, $\text{Ext}_\delta(\mathbb{E})$ is the set of extensions of $\mathbb{E}$ under semantics δ, and $\text{Acc}_\delta(a, \mathbb{E})$ is the acceptability status of a in $\mathbb{E}$ under δ. The function $\text{sAtt}(a, \mathbb{E})$ returns the set of attacks targeting a and whose sources are similar, that is, $\text{sAtt}(a, \mathbb{E}) = \{r \in \text{rAtt}(a, \mathbb{E}) \mid \exists r' \in \text{rAtt}(a, \mathbb{E}) \text{ s.t. } (\mathbf{Sc}(r), \mathbf{Sc}(r')) \in \text{sim}\}$.

In the extended setting, extension semantics are expected to satisfy certain key *principles*. The first is sensitivity to similarity - meaning the semantics should account for similarity whenever such information is available.

Principle 1 (Sensitivity to similarity) *An extension semantics δ is* indifferent *to similarity iff* $\forall \langle \mathbb{G}, \text{sim} \rangle \in$ eAG, $\text{Ext}_\delta(\langle \mathbb{G}, \text{sim} \rangle) = \text{Ext}_\delta(\langle \mathbb{G}, \text{sim}^* \rangle)$; *$\delta$ is said to be* sensitive *to similarity otherwise.*

The second principle addresses the question: *At which level should similarity be considered?* It posits that similarity is relevant at the level of **redundant attacks**-that is, attacks originating from similar arguments and directed at the same target. Since attacks are the primary mechanism by which arguments are weakened, disregarding redundant attacks helps prevent the target argument from being excessively diminished in strength. The principle states that when there are no similar attackers in a graph, similarity does not play a role.

Principle 2 (Neutrality) *An extension semantics δ satisfies* neutrality *iff* $\forall \langle \mathbb{G}, \text{sim} \rangle \in$ eAG *such that* $\mathbb{G} = \langle \mathcal{A}, \mathcal{R} \rangle$ *and* $\forall a \in \mathcal{A}$, $\text{sAtt}(a, \mathbb{G}) = \emptyset$, $\text{Ext}_\delta(\langle \mathbb{G}, \text{sim} \rangle) = \text{Ext}_\delta(\langle \mathbb{G}, \text{sim}^* \rangle)$.

Example 2. Consider the extended argumentation graph depicted below.

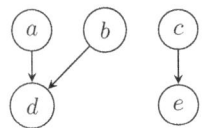

- $\text{sim} = \{(b,c),(c,b)\} \cup \text{sim}^*$.
- The principle of Neutrality implies that an extension semantics must disregard the similarity between b and c.

As a consequence of the neutrality principle, if every argument in an extended graph has at most one attacker, similarity has no effect on argument evaluation.

Property 1. Let δ be an extension semantics and $\mathbb{E} = \langle \mathbb{G}, \text{sim} \rangle$, with $\mathbb{G} = \langle \mathcal{A}, \mathcal{R} \rangle$ and $\forall a \in \mathcal{A}$, $|\text{rAtt}(a, \mathbb{E})| \leq 1$. If δ satisfies neutrality, then $\forall a \in \mathcal{A}$, $\text{Ext}_\delta(\langle \mathbb{G}, \text{sim} \rangle) = \text{Ext}_\delta(\langle \mathbb{G}, \text{sim}^* \rangle)$.

Let us now turn to situations where similarity should be considered - specifically, cases involving redundant attacks. There are two possible ways to address such redundancy: removing similar arguments or removing their attacks. However, the first approach is problematic, as it risks information loss which may result in counter-intuitive evaluations of certain arguments, as the following example illustrates.

Example 1 (Cont). Consider the extended argumentation graph $\mathbb{E}_1 = \langle \mathbb{G}_1, \text{sim}_1 \rangle$, where $\text{sim}_1 = \{(b_1, b_2), (b_2, b_1)\} \cup \text{sim}_1^*$. Suppose we remove the argument b_2 (along with all its outgoing attacks). This yields the subgraph $\mathbb{G}_{11} = \langle \{a, b_1, c\}, \{(b_1, c)\} \rangle$, which has a single preferred extension: $\{b_1, c\}$. Notice that in $\mathbb{G}_{11}$, the argument c is skeptically accepted, whereas in the original graph $\mathbb{G}_1$, it is rejected. This apparent improvement in c's status is unjustified and arises solely from the loss of critical information - specifically, the fact that c was attacked.

Removing attacks coming from similar arguments does not lead to information loss, as it only alters the set of arguments targeted by those specific attacks. Moreover, the affected arguments remain under attack, since not all attacks from similar sources are eliminated - at least one is always retained to prevent overvaluation. For example, one could remove the attack (b_2, a), ensuring that c remains rejected in the resulting subgraph, while a continues to be attacked because (b_1, a) is preserved.

The third principle concerns the impact of accounting for similarity. It asserts that removing attacks from similar sources cannot lower an argument's acceptability status. In other words, after such modifications, an argument's status in the graph can either remain the same or improve - but it will never worsen.

Principle 3 (Monotonicity) *An extension semantics δ is monotonic iff $\forall \mathbb{E} = \langle \mathbb{G}, \text{sim} \rangle \in \text{eAG}$ such that $\mathbb{G} = \langle \mathcal{A}, \mathcal{R} \rangle$, $\forall a \in \mathcal{A}$, $\text{Acc}_\delta(a, \langle \mathbb{G}, \text{sim} \rangle) \succeq \text{Acc}_\delta(a, \langle \mathbb{G}, \text{sim}^* \rangle)$.*

Property 2. If a semantics is indifferent to similarity, then it satisfies neutrality.

Complete, grounded, stable, and preferred semantics do not account for similarity. That is, for an extended argumentation graph $\mathbb{E} = \langle \mathbb{G}, \text{sim} \rangle$, applying any of these semantics produces the same extension(s) as when applied to the base graph $\mathbb{G}$, independently of the similarity relation sim. As a result, the four semantics satisfy neutrality and monotonicity in a vacuous way.

Theorem 1. *For any $\delta \in \{co, gr, st, pr\}$, the semantics δ is indifferent to similarity. It also satisfies neutrality and monotonicity.*

4   Parameterized Extension Semantics

In this section, we introduce a family of parameterized extension semantics that are sensitive to similarity and generalize the four classic semantics defined in [13]. Each instance in this family is defined by two parameters: a *base extension semantics* δ (e.g., preferred) and a *selection function* λ. It proceeds in three main steps:

1. Given an extended argumentation graph $\mathbb{E} = \langle \mathbb{G}, \text{sim} \rangle$, where $\mathbb{G} = \langle \mathcal{A}, \mathcal{R} \rangle$, it begins by removing all redundant attacks, keeping only one representative for each. This step may produce several subgraphs $\mathbb{G}_1, \ldots, \mathbb{G}_n \in \text{AG}$, where each $\mathbb{G}_i = \langle \mathcal{A}, \mathcal{R}_i \rangle$ with $\mathcal{R}_i \subseteq \mathcal{R}$, representing possible contractions of the original graph $\mathbb{G}$. For example, consider $\mathbb{E}_1 = \langle \mathbb{G}_1, \text{sim}_1 \rangle$, where $\mathbb{G}_1$ is the graph depicted below. If $\text{sim}_1 = \{(b_1, b_2)\} \cup \text{sim}_1^*$, then the argument a receives two redundant attacks, (b_1, a) and (b_2, a). As a result, two subgraphs ($\mathbb{G}_{11}$ and $\mathbb{G}_{12}$) are generated: each retains one of these two attacks along with (b_2, c).

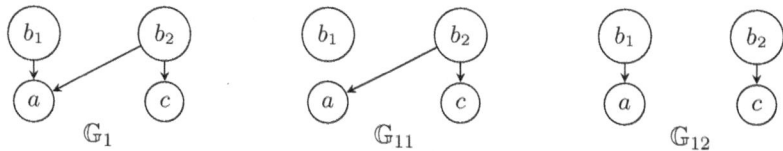

2. The selection function Δ selects **one** from the generated subgraphs $\mathbb{G}_1, \ldots, \mathbb{G}_n$. In the example, it selects either $\mathbb{G}_{11}$ or $\mathbb{G}_{12}$.
3. Arguments of the selected subgraph are evaluated using the base semantics δ. In the above example, both subgraphs have a single preferred extension $\{b_1, b_2\}$. Hence, the argument a remains rejected even after removal of redundancy.

Before defining the family of semantics, we introduce four notions. The first is the concept of an **equivalence class of attacks**, which groups together redundant attacks.

Definition 8. *Let $\mathbb{E} = \langle \mathbb{G}, \text{sim} \rangle \in \text{eAG}$ with $\mathbb{G} = \langle \mathcal{A}, \mathcal{R} \rangle$. A set $X \subseteq \mathcal{R}$ is an equivalence class iff:*

- *$\forall r, r' \in X, (\mathbf{Sc}(r), \mathbf{Sc}(r')) \in \text{sim}$ and $\mathbf{Tg}(r) = \mathbf{Tg}(r')$,*
- *$\nexists X' \supset X$ which satisfies the above condition.*

$\text{Equiv}(\mathbb{E})$ *denotes the set of all equivalent classes in $\mathbb{E}$.*

Example 1 (Cont). Consider $\mathbb{E}_1 = \langle \mathbb{G}_1, \text{sim}_1 \rangle$.

- Let $\text{sim}_1 = \text{sim}_1^*$. Then, $\text{Equiv}(\mathbb{E}_1) = \{E_1, E_2, E_3\}$, where $E_1 = \{(b_1, a)\}$, $E_2 = \{(b_2, a)\}$, and $E_3 = \{(b_2, c)\}$.

– Let $\mathtt{sim}_1 = \{(b_1, b_2), (b_2, b_1)\} \cup \mathtt{sim}_1^*$. Then, $\mathrm{Equiv}(\mathbb{E}_1) = \{E_3, E_4\}$, $E_4 = \{(b_1, a), (b_2, a)\}$.

Note that every attack belongs to a *single* equivalence class. Indeed, equivalence classes are pairwise disjoint and form a partition of the whole set of attacks.

Proposition 1. *Let* $\mathbb{E} = \langle \mathbb{G}, \mathtt{sim} \rangle \in \mathtt{eAG}$ *with* $\mathbb{G} = \langle \mathcal{A}, \mathcal{R} \rangle$.

– *For all* $X, Y \in \mathrm{Equiv}(\mathbb{E})$, $X \cap Y = \emptyset$,
– $\mathcal{R} = \bigcup_{X \in \mathrm{Equiv}(\mathbb{E})} X$,
– *If* $\mathtt{sim} = \mathtt{sim}^*$, *then* $\mathrm{Equiv}(\mathbb{E}) = \{\{r\} \mid r \in \mathcal{R}\}$,
– $|\mathrm{Equiv}(\mathbb{E})| \le |\mathcal{R}|$,
– $\emptyset \in \mathrm{Equiv}(\mathbb{E})$ *iff* $\mathcal{R} = \emptyset$.

The second key concept is that of a **set of representatives**, which selects exactly one attack from each equivalence class.

Definition 9. *Let* $\mathbb{E} = \langle \mathbb{G}, \mathtt{sim} \rangle \in \mathtt{eAG}$, *with* $\mathbb{G} = \langle \mathcal{A}, \mathcal{R} \rangle$, *and* $X \subseteq \mathcal{R}$. *We say that* X *is a set of* representatives *in* $\mathbb{E}$ *iff* $|X| = |\mathrm{Equiv}(\mathbb{E})|$ *and* $\forall Y \in \mathrm{Equiv}(\mathbb{E})$, $X \cap Y \ne \emptyset$. *Let* $\mathbf{Rep}(\mathbb{E})$ *contain all sets of representatives of* $\mathbb{E}$.

Example 1 (Cont). Consider again $\mathbb{E}_1 = \langle \mathbb{G}_1, \mathtt{sim}_1 \rangle$.

– If $\mathtt{sim}_1 = \mathtt{sim}_1^*$, then $\mathbf{Rep}(\mathbb{E}_1) = \{X_0\}$ where $X_0 = \{(b_1, a), (b_2, a), (b_2, c)\}$.
– If $\mathtt{sim}_1 = \{(b_1, b_2), (b_2, b_1)\} \cup \mathtt{sim}_1^*$, then $\mathbf{Rep}(\mathbb{E}_1) = \{X_1, X_2\}$ where:
  • $X_1 = \{(b_1, a), (b_2, c)\}$,
  • $X_2 = \{(b_2, a), (b_2, c)\}$.

It is clear that a set of representatives contains exactly one attack among redundant ones. Furthermore, when a graph is free of redundancy, then it has a single set of representatives, which is the whole set of attacks.

Proposition 2. *Let* $\mathbb{E} = \langle \mathbb{G}, \mathtt{sim} \rangle \in \mathtt{eAG}$ *with* $\mathbb{G} = \langle \mathcal{A}, \mathcal{R} \rangle$.

– *If* $\mathtt{sim} = \mathtt{sim}^*$, *then* $\mathbf{Rep}(\mathbb{E}) = \{\mathcal{R}\}$.
– $\forall X \in \mathbf{Rep}(\mathbb{E})$, $\nexists r, r' \in X$ *such that* $(\mathbf{Sc}(r), \mathbf{Sc}(r')) \in \mathtt{sim}$ *and* $\mathbf{Tg}(r) = \mathbf{Tg}(r')$.

The third notion is the **contraction** of an extended argumentation graph. A contraction is a subgraph whose attacks form a set of representatives, and whose admissible sets remain conflict-free with respect to the original attack relation. This latter condition ensures that no argument and its attackers can be jointly acceptable.

Definition 10. *Let* $\mathbb{E} = \langle \mathbb{G}, \mathtt{sim} \rangle \in \mathtt{eAG}$, *with* $\mathbb{G} = \langle \mathcal{A}, \mathcal{R} \rangle$, *and* $\mathbb{G}' = \langle \mathcal{A}', \mathcal{R}' \rangle \in \mathtt{AG}$. *We say that* $\mathbb{G}'$ *is a* contraction *of* $\mathbb{E}$ *iff* $\mathcal{A}' = \mathcal{A}$, $\mathcal{R}' \in \mathbf{Rep}(\mathbb{E})$, *and* $\nexists E \subseteq \mathcal{A}'$ *such that* E *is admissible in* $\mathbb{G}'$ *and* $\mathcal{R}$−*conflicting. Let* $\mathtt{Ctr}(\mathbb{E})$ *be the set of all possible contractions of* $\mathbb{E}$.

Example 1 (Cont). Consider $\mathbb{E}_1 = \langle \mathbb{G}_1, \mathtt{sim}_1 \rangle$ and $\mathbb{E}_2 = \langle \mathbb{G}_2, \mathtt{sim}_2 \rangle$, where $\mathbb{G}_1$ and $\mathbb{G}_2$ are depicted in Table 1. Assume that $\mathtt{sim}_i = \{(b_1, b_2), (b_2, b_1)\} \cup \mathtt{sim}_i^*$, with $i \in \{1, 2\}$.

- $\mathtt{Ctr}(\mathbb{E}_1) = \{\mathbb{G}_{11}, \mathbb{G}_{12}\}$, where $\mathbb{G}_{11} = \mathbb{G}_1 \ominus \{(b_1, a)\}$ and $\mathbb{G}_{12} = \mathbb{G}_1 \ominus \{(b_2, a)\}$.
- $\mathtt{Ctr}(\mathbb{E}_2) = \emptyset$ since both subgraphs $\mathbb{G}_2 \ominus \{(b_i, a)\}$ contain an admissible set $\{a, b_i\}$, which is not conflict-free wrt the initial attack relation $\mathcal{R}_2$.

The example shows that an extended argumentation graph may sometimes have no contractions. This occurs when all subgraphs built from $\mathbf{Rep}(\mathbb{E})$ yield $\mathcal{R}$-conflicting admissible sets. Conversely, a graph may have as many contractions as there are sets of representatives. Notably, when the similarity relation is $\mathtt{sim}^*$, the graph has exactly one contraction - namely, the base graph itself.

Proposition 3. *Let* $\mathbb{E} = \langle \mathbb{G}, \mathtt{sim} \rangle \in \mathtt{eAG}$.

- $0 \leq |\mathtt{Ctr}(\mathbb{E})| \leq |\mathbf{Rep}(\mathbb{E})|$,
- *If* $\mathtt{sim} = \mathtt{sim}^*$, *then* $\mathtt{Ctr}(\mathbb{E}) = \{\mathbb{G}\}$.

The last notion is that of **selection function**, which chooses one argumentation graph among a collection of graphs.

Definition 11. *A selection function is a mapping* $\Delta : \mathtt{AG}^n \rightarrow \mathtt{AG}$, $n \geq 1$, *such that* $\Delta(x_1, \ldots, x_n) \in \{x_1, \ldots, x_n\}$.

We are now ready to define the **parameterized extended extension semantics**, denoted by Δ^δ, where δ serves as the *base semantics* and Δ acts as the *selection function*. An extended semantics Δ^δ qualifies as an extension semantics (Definition 2). The term extended refers to the fact that it generalizes and builds upon δ.

Definition 12. *Let* δ *be an extension semantics and* Δ *a selection function. An* extended semantics Δ^δ *maps every* $\mathbb{E} = \langle \mathbb{G}, \mathtt{sim} \rangle \in \mathtt{eAG}$, $\mathbb{G} = \langle \mathcal{A}, \mathcal{R} \rangle$, *to a set of extensions:*
$$\mathtt{Ext}_{\Delta^\delta}(\mathbb{E}) = \begin{cases} \mathtt{Ext}_\delta(\mathbb{G}) & if \quad \mathtt{Ctr}(\mathbb{E}) = \emptyset \\ \mathtt{Ext}_\delta(\Delta(\mathbb{G}_1, \ldots, \mathbb{G}_k)) & else, \quad where \ \{\mathbb{G}_1, \ldots, \mathbb{G}_k\} = \mathtt{Ctr}(\mathbb{E}). \end{cases}$$
The acceptability status of any argument $a \in \mathcal{A}$ *under* Δ^δ *is:*
$$\mathtt{Acc}_{\Delta^\delta}(a, \mathbb{E}) = \begin{cases} \mathtt{Acc}_\delta(a, \mathbb{G}) & if \quad \mathtt{Ctr}(\mathbb{E}) = \emptyset \\ \mathtt{Acc}_\delta(a, \Delta(\mathbb{G}_1, \ldots, \mathbb{G}_k)) & else, \quad where \ \{\mathbb{G}_1, \ldots, \mathbb{G}_k\} = \mathtt{Ctr}(\mathbb{E}). \end{cases}$$

Note that when an extended argumentation graph has no contraction, any parameterized extended semantics defaults to the evaluation provided by its base semantics δ on the graph $\mathbb{G}$. Recall that the absence of contractions arises when all subgraphs contain at least one $\mathcal{R}$-conflicting admissible set. Selecting one of these subgraphs would lead to counterintuitive outcomes - for example, inferring the claims of the arguments $A = \langle \{x\}, x \rangle$ and $B = \langle \{\neg x, \neg x \rightarrow y\}, y \rangle$, even though A attacks B. Indeed, if x is accepted as true, then y cannot validly follow from the premises of B.

Extended semantics strike a **balance** between accounting for similarity - to avoid the undervaluation of arguments due to redundant attacks - and ensuring rational evaluations. The idea is to leverage similarity only when doing so does not introduce counterintuitive outcomes due to the structure of the graph.

Example 1 (Cont). Let $\delta = pr$ and consider the four extended graphs $\mathbb{E}_i = \langle \mathbb{G}_i, \mathrm{sim}_i \rangle$.

- Let $\mathrm{sim}_1 = \{(b_1, b_2), (b_2, b_1)\} \cup \mathrm{sim}_1^*$. Then, $\mathrm{Ctr}(\mathbb{E}_1) = \{\mathbb{G}_{11}, \mathbb{G}_{12}\}$. Any selection function Δ may choose either $\mathbb{G}_{11}$ or $\mathbb{G}_{12}$. Both contractions have $\{b_1, b_2\}$ as the preferred extension. Thus, $\forall x \in \mathcal{A}_1$, $\mathrm{Acc}_{\Delta^{pr}}(x, \mathbb{E}_1) = \mathrm{Acc}_{pr}(x, \mathbb{G}_1)$.
- Let $\mathrm{sim}_2 = \{(b_1, b_2), (b_2, b_1)\} \cup \mathrm{sim}_2^*$. Then, $\mathrm{Ctr}(\mathbb{E}_1) = \emptyset$. Hence, $\forall x \in \mathcal{A}_1$, $\mathrm{Acc}_{\Delta^{pr}}(x, \mathbb{E}_1) = \mathrm{Acc}_{pr}(x, \mathbb{G}_1)$.
- Let $\mathrm{sim}_3 = \{(c_1, c_2), (c_2, c_1)\} \cup \mathrm{sim}_3^*$. Note that $\mathrm{Ctr}(\mathbb{E}_3) = \{\mathbb{G}_{31}, \mathbb{G}_{32}\}$, where $\mathbb{G}_{31} = \mathbb{G}_3 \ominus \{(c_1, b)\}$ and $\mathbb{G}_{32} = \mathbb{G}_3 \ominus \{(c_2, b)\}$. Note also that $\mathrm{Ext}_{pr}(\mathbb{G}_{31}) = \{\{a, c_2\}\}$ and $\mathrm{Ext}_{pr}(\mathbb{G}_{32}) = \{\{c_2\}\}$.
  - If $\Delta(\mathrm{Ctr}(\mathbb{E}_3)) = \mathbb{G}_{31}$, then $\forall x \in \mathcal{A}_3$, $\mathrm{Acc}_{\Delta^{pr}}(x, \mathbb{E}_3) = \mathrm{Acc}_{pr}(x, \mathbb{G}_3)$.
  - If $\Delta(\mathrm{Ctr}(\mathbb{E}_3)) = \mathbb{G}_{32}$, then $\mathrm{Acc}_{\Delta^{pr}}(a, \mathbb{E}_3) = \mathrm{Acc}_{\Delta^{pr}}(b, \mathbb{E}_3) = \mathrm{u}$. Notice that the status of b improves as it is rejected in $\mathbb{G}_3$. As a consequence, the status of a deteriorates.
- Let $\mathrm{sim}_4 = \{(b_1, b_2), (b_2, b_1)\} \cup \mathrm{sim}_4^*$. Then, $\mathrm{Ctr}(\mathbb{E}_4) = \{\mathbb{G}_{41}, \mathbb{G}_{42}\}$, where $\mathbb{G}_{41} = \mathbb{G}_4 \ominus \{(b_1, a)\}$ and $\mathbb{G}_{42} = \mathbb{G}_4 \ominus \{(b_2, a)\}$. Note also that $\mathrm{Ext}_{pr}(\mathbb{G}_{41}) = \{\{c_1\}, \{a, c_2\}\}$ and $\mathrm{Ext}_{pr}(\mathbb{G}_{42}) = \{\{a, c_1\}, \{a, c_2\}\}$.
  - If $\Delta(\mathrm{Ctr}(\mathbb{E}_4)) = \mathbb{G}_{41}$, then $\forall x \in \mathcal{A}_4$, $\mathrm{Acc}_{\Delta^{pr}}(x, \mathbb{E}_4) = \mathrm{Acc}_{pr}(x, \mathbb{G}_4)$.
  - If $\Delta(\mathrm{Ctr}(\mathbb{E}_4)) = \mathbb{G}_{42}$, then $\mathrm{Acc}_{\Delta^{pr}}(a, \mathbb{E}_4) = \mathrm{s}$. The status of a is improved due to the removal of redundancy: $\mathrm{Acc}_{\Delta^{pr}}(a, \mathbb{E}_4) \succ \mathrm{Acc}_{pr}(a, \mathbb{G}_4) = \mathrm{c}$.

We show that the extended extension semantics satisfy the three proposed principles. In particular, monotonicity and sensitivity to similarity are guaranteed when the base semantics is any of Dung's standard semantics [13].

Theorem 2. *Let Δ^δ be an extended extension semantics.*

- *Δ^δ satisfies neutrality.*
- *If $\delta \in \{co, gr, pr, st\}$, then Δ^δ satisfies sensitivity to similarity and monotonicity.*

Every instance in the family generalizes its base semantics, as they coincide in cases with no similarity, in graphs without redundant attacks, or when each argument has at most one attacker.

Theorem 3. *Let Δ^δ be an extended semantics, $\mathbb{E} = \langle \mathbb{G}, \mathrm{sim} \rangle \in \mathrm{eAG}$, with $\mathbb{G} = \langle \mathcal{A}, \mathcal{R} \rangle$. If at least one of the following conditions holds:*

- $\mathrm{sim} = \mathrm{sim}^*$,
- $\forall a \in \mathcal{A}$, $\mathrm{sAtt}(a, \mathbb{G}) = \emptyset$,
- $\forall a \in \mathcal{A}$, $|\mathrm{rAtt}(a, \mathbb{G})| \le 1$,

then $\mathrm{Ext}_{\Delta^\delta}(\mathbb{E}) = \mathrm{Ext}_\delta(\mathbb{G})$.

Extended extension semantics coincide also with their base semantics in the case of *coherent* extended argumentation graphs-that is, graphs in which similar arguments have exactly the same set of attackers. In $\mathbb{E}_1 = \langle \mathbb{G}_1, \mathrm{sim}_1 \rangle$, if $(b_1, b_2) \in \mathrm{sim}_1$, then $\mathbb{E}_1$ is not coherent as b_1 and b_2 do not have identical sets of attackers.

Definition 13. *Let* $\mathbb{E} = \langle \mathbb{G}, \mathrm{sim} \rangle \in \mathrm{eAG}$ *with* $\mathbb{G} = \langle \mathcal{A}, \mathcal{R} \rangle$. $\mathbb{E}$ *is* coherent *iff* $\forall a, b \in \mathcal{A}$, *if* $(a, b) \in \mathrm{sim}$, *then* $\{\mathbf{Sc}(r) \mid r \in \mathrm{rAtt}(a, \mathbb{G})\} = \{\mathbf{Sc}(r') \mid r' \in \mathrm{rAtt}(b, \mathbb{G})\}$.

We next show that extended semantics based on complete, stable, preferred, or grounded semantics are indifferent to similarity in coherent graphs. Such graphs always admit contractions, and moreover, all contractions yield the same extensions, which coincide with those of the base graph.

Theorem 4. *Let* Δ^δ *be an extended semantics, with* $\delta \in \{co, gr, pr, st\}$, *and* $\mathbb{E} = \langle \mathbb{G}, \mathrm{sim} \rangle \in \mathrm{eAG}$, *with* $\mathbb{G} = \langle \mathcal{A}, \mathcal{R} \rangle$. *If* $\mathbb{E}$ *is coherent, then the following hold.*

- $\mathrm{Ctr}(\mathbb{E}) = \{\langle \mathcal{A}, \mathcal{R}' \rangle \in \mathrm{AG} \mid \mathcal{R}' \in \mathbf{Rep}(\mathbb{E})\}$,
- *For any* $\mathbb{G}' \in \mathrm{Ctr}(\mathbb{E})$, $\mathrm{Ext}_\delta(\mathbb{G}') = \mathrm{Ext}_\delta(\mathbb{G})$.

We now investigate how the acceptability status of an argument changes when moving from a base extension semantics $\delta \in \{co, gr, pr, st\}$ to its corresponding extended semantics Δ^δ. We focus on cases where similarity influences the evaluation-specifically, when **contractions do exist**. The first result establishes that an argument retains the same status under both semantics if and only if the set of attacks preserved by the contraction selected by Δ contains a **sufficient set** under δ.

Theorem 5. *Let* Δ^δ *be an extended semantics, with* $\delta \in \{co, gr, pr, st\}$, $\mathbb{E} = \langle \mathbb{G}, \mathrm{sim} \rangle \in \mathrm{eAG}$, $\mathbb{G} = \langle \mathcal{A}, \mathcal{R} \rangle$, $\Delta(\mathrm{Ctr}(\mathbb{E})) = \langle \mathcal{A}, \mathcal{R}' \rangle$, $a \in \mathcal{A}$ *s.t* $\mathrm{sim} \subseteq \mathrm{aAtt}(a, \mathbb{G}) \times \mathrm{aAtt}(a, \mathbb{G})$.

$$\mathrm{Acc}_{\Delta^\delta}(a, \mathbb{E}) = \mathrm{Acc}_\delta(a, \mathbb{G}) \quad \textit{iff} \quad \exists S \subseteq \mathcal{R}' \textit{ such that } S \in \mathrm{Suff}_\delta(a, \mathbb{G}).$$

Example 1 (Cont). Recall that $\mathrm{Suff}_{pr}(a, \mathbb{G}_1) = \{\{(b_1, a)\}, \{(b_2, a)\}\}$. Hence, each of the two contractions $\mathbb{G}_{11}, \mathbb{G}_{12}$ of $\mathbb{E}_1 = \langle \mathbb{G}_1, \mathrm{sim}_1 \rangle$ keeps one sufficient set, which explains why the two corresponding extended semantics reject a as in $\mathbb{G}_1$. For $\mathbb{E}_3 = \langle \mathbb{G}_3, \mathrm{sim}_3 \rangle$, $\mathrm{Suff}_{pr}(b, \mathbb{G}_3) = \{\{(c_2, b)\}\}$. Hence, the contraction $\mathbb{G}_{31}$ keeps the attack (c_2, b) leading a stable status for b.

The second result characterizes the conditions under which the acceptability status of an argument changes. It shows that such a change occurs if and only if a **necessary set** under δ is among the attacks removed by the contraction selected by Δ.

Theorem 6. *Let* Δ^δ *be an extended semantics, with* $\delta \in \{co, gr, pr, st\}$, $\mathbb{E} = \langle \mathbb{G}, \mathrm{sim} \rangle \in \mathrm{eAG}$, $\mathbb{G} = \langle \mathcal{A}, \mathcal{R} \rangle$, $\Delta(\mathrm{Ctr}(\mathbb{E})) = \langle \mathcal{A}, \mathcal{R}' \rangle$, $a \in \mathcal{A}$ *s.t* $\mathrm{sim} \subseteq \mathrm{aAtt}(a, \mathbb{G}) \times \mathrm{aAtt}(a, \mathbb{G})$.

$$\mathrm{Acc}_{\Delta^\delta}(a, \mathbb{E}) \succ \mathrm{Acc}_\delta(a, \mathbb{G}) \quad \textit{iff} \quad \exists S \in \mathrm{Nec}_\delta(a, \mathbb{G}) \textit{ such that } S \cap \mathcal{R}' = \emptyset.$$

Example 1 (Cont). Recall that $\mathrm{Nec}_{pr}(b, \mathbb{G}_3) = \{\{(c_2, b)\}\}$. The contraction $\mathbb{G}_{32}$ of $\mathbb{E}_3 = \langle \mathbb{G}_3, \mathrm{sim}_3 \rangle$ removes the necessary attack (c_2, b), leading a status change for b.

5   Selection Functions

The key idea behind the novel semantics Δ^δ is to retain only one attack among a set of redundant ones. The function Δ selects which attacks to keep. In what follows, we present three families of **strategies** that Δ may follow. All of them begin by evaluating arguments in the initial graph under the base semantics δ.

Strategies based on the status of arguments: These strategies remove redundant attacks depending on the acceptability status of their sources. The idea is to eliminate attacks originating from either: i) the weakest attackers, or ii) the strongest ones. Consider the graph $\mathbb{G}_3$, where $(c_1, c_2) \in \text{sim}_3$. Note that $\text{Acc}_{pr}(c_2, \mathbb{G}_3) = s \succ \text{Acc}_{pr}(c_1, \mathbb{G}_3) = u$. Removing the weakest ($c_1$) results in the same status of b and thus for a. However, discarding the strongest (c_2) leads to an improved status for b (passing from rejected to undecided). In the graph $\mathbb{G}_4$, both b_1, b_2 are rejected under preferred semantics. Thus, this strategy allows to choose any of the two attacks.

Strategies Based on Types of Attacks: These strategies consider the type of attack, rather than the status of its source. They assume the following hierarchy of importance: necessary ¿ sufficient ¿ dummy, where a dummy attack is an attack that has no impact on its target [1]. A reasonable strategy would remove the weakest available set of redundant attacks. In $\mathbb{G}_4$, the attack (b_1, a) is dummy, while (b_2, a) is necessary. Therefore, Δ would preserve the necessary attack and remove the dummy one.

Mixed Strategies: Mixed strategies combine the previous two approaches. They first identify the weakest sets of redundant attacks based on their type, then refine the choice by comparing the status of their sources.

6   Related Work

Despite its importance and notable influence on the evaluation of arguments-and consequently, on the outcomes of argumentation-based systems-the notion of similarity has received relatively limited attention within the argumentation community. Existing research addressing this concept can be broadly categorized into three main areas.

The first category focuses on *measuring similarity* between arguments. This includes studies on logical arguments [2,4,6,8,12] and textual arguments [15,16,18].

The second category investigates how similarity can be used to *modify the structure of an argumentation graph* before applying any semantics. A representative example is [9], where similarity is employed as a pre-processing step to alter the graph's relational structure. Specifically, this work prevents attack relations between similar arguments. Consider for instance the graph $\mathbb{G}_2$ in Table 1 and assume that $\text{sim}_2 = \text{sim}_2^* \cup \{(b_1, b_2), (b_2, b_1)\}$. The approach in [8,9] starts by removing the two attacks between the arguments b_1 and b_2, then evaluates the resulting sub-graph using any extension-based semantics. Thus, it does not remove the **redundant attacks**, namely the two targeting the argument a. Consequently, it violates the Neutrality principle but satisfies the Sensitivity to Similarity principle, due to the removal of attacks between similar arguments.

The third category explores how to incorporate similarity directly into the *semantics*. Two works- [3,5]-have addressed this challenge. These studies focus on gradual semantics in abstract argumentation. They propose a set of desirable properties and offer mechanisms for extending existing gradual semantics to respect similarity while satisfying those properties. However, these approaches do not consider extension-based semantics, which are the focus of our work. It is also important to highlight that the aforementioned studies are grounded in a specific class of gradual semantics that satisfy the equivalence property-i.e., the acceptability status of an argument is determined solely by the statuses of its direct attackers. In contrast, extension semantics do not satisfy this property, which necessitates a fundamentally different approach. Accordingly, our work introduces a novel method for integrating similarity into extension semantics.

Some works in the literature have studied *incomplete* argumentation graphs, where there is uncertainty regarding the presence of certain arguments and/or attacks (e.g., [14]). To evaluate arguments under such uncertainty, a widely adopted approach involves completing the graph by adding the uncertain elements, resulting in multiple possible completions. These completions are then aggregated to determine the status of each argument. While our parameterized semantics compute contractions, the objectives are fundamentally different. In the case of similarity, the issue is not uncertainty but redundancy-specifically, the presence of similar attacks-which should be minimized as much as possible. Each contraction in our framework corresponds to an alternative, similarity-aware solution.

7   Conclusion

We presented the first study on the impact of similarity between arguments on their evaluation under extension semantics. We introduced a set of principles that extension semantics should satisfy in the presence of similarity, and proposed a family of semantics that adhere to them. Furthermore, we identified structural conditions-specifically, coherent versus non-coherent graphs-that determine whether similarity can be safely ignored or must be taken into account. We identified also the conditions under which similarity affects the acceptability status of arguments, and when it does not.

This work lends itself to a number of developments in order to improve its generality and the compromise rational evaluation/removal of redundancy of the semantics. The idea is to develop a principled framework for selection functions. Another line of research consists of investigating alternative methods for addressing similarity, including the merging of similar arguments into a single argument.

Acknowledgments. This work was funded by the French program AI Cluster ANR-23-IACL-0002.

References

1. Amgoud, L.: Post-hoc explanation of extension semantics. In: 27th European Conference on Artificial Intelligence, ECAI, volume 392 of Frontiers in Artificial Intelligence and Applications, pp. 3276–3283. IOS Press (2024)

2. Amgoud, L., Besnard, P., Vesic, S.: Equivalence in logic-based argumentation. J. Appl. Non-Classical Logics **24**(3), 181–208 (2014)
3. Amgoud, L., Bonzon, E., Delobelle, J., Doder, D., Konieczny, S., Maudet, N.: Gradual semantics accounting for similarity between arguments. In: Proceedings of the Sixteenth International Conference on Principles of Knowledge Representation and Reasoning KR, pp. 88–97 (2018)
4. Amgoud, L., David, V.: Measuring similarity between logical arguments. In: Proceedings of the Sixteenth International Conference on Principles of Knowledge Representation and Reasoning KR, pp. 98–107 (2018)
5. Amgoud, L., David, V.: A general setting for gradual semantics dealing with similarity. In: 35th AAAI Conference On Artificial Intelligence (AAAI) (2021)
6. Amgoud, L., David, V., Doder, D.: Similarity measures between arguments revisited. In: Kern-Isberner, G., Ognjanović, Z. (eds.) ECSQARU 2019. LNCS (LNAI), vol. 11726, pp. 3–13. Springer, Cham (2019). https://doi.org/10.1007/978-3-030-29765-7_1
7. Baroni, P., Gabbay, D., Giacomin, M., Van der Torre, L. (eds.): Handbook of Formal Argumentation, Vol. 1. College Publications (2018)
8. Budan, P., Martinez, V., Budan, M., Simari, G.: Introducing analogy in abstract argumentation. In: Workshop on Weighted Logics for Artificial Intelligence (2015)
9. Budan, P.D., et al.: Similarity notions in bipolar abstract argumentation. Argument Comput. 11(1-2), 103–149 (2020)
10. Cayrol, C., Lagasquie-Schiex, M.-C.: Graduality in argumentation. J. Artif. Intell. Res. **23**, 245–297 (2005)
11. da Costa Pereira, C., Tettamanzi, A., Villata, S.: Changing one's mind: Erase or rewind? In: IJCAI'11, pp. 164–171 (2011)
12. David, V., Delobelle, J., Mailly, J.G.: Similarity measures between order-sorted logical arguments. In: 17èmes Journées d'Intelligence Artificielle Fondamentale, JIAF, pp. 8–19 (2023)
13. Phan Minh Dung: On the acceptability of arguments and its fundamental role in non-monotonic reasoning, logic programming and n-person games. Artif. Intell. **77**, 321–357 (1995)
14. Fazzinga, B., Flesca, S., Furfaro, F.: Revisiting the notion of extension over incomplete abstract argumentation frameworks. In: Proceedings of the Twenty-Ninth International Joint Conference on Artificial Intelligence, IJCAI, pp. 1712–1718 (2020)
15. Konat, B., Budzynska, K., Saint-Dizier, P.: Rephrase in argument structure. In: Foundations of the Language of Argumentation – the workshop at the 6th International Conference on Computational Models of Argument (COMMA 2016), pp. 32–39 (2016)
16. Misra, A., Ecker, B., Walker, M.A.: Measuring the similarity of sentential arguments in dialogue. In: Proceedings of the 17th Annual Meeting of the Special Interest Group on Discourse and Dialogue, SIGDIAL-2016, pp. 276–287 (2016)
17. Rekabsaz, N., Lupu, M., Hanbury, A.: Exploration of a threshold for similarity based on uncertainty in word embedding. In: Advances in Information Retrieval, pp. 396–409 (2017)
18. Stein, B.: Report of dagstuhl seminar debating technologies. Technical report, Report of Dagstuhl Seminar Debating Technologies (2016)

SCC-Recursiveness in Infinite Argumentation

Uri Andrews[1]([✉])[iD] and Luca San Mauro[2][iD]

[1] University of Wiscosin–Madison, Madison, WI 53706, USA
andrews@math.wisc.edu
[2] University of Bari, Bari, Italy
lucafrancesco.sanmauro@uniba.it
http://math.wisc.edu/~andrews, https://www.lucasanmauro.com/

Abstract. Argumentation frameworks (AFs) are a foundational tool in artificial intelligence for modeling structured reasoning and conflict. SCC-recursiveness is a well-known design principle in which the evaluation of arguments is decomposed according to the strongly connected components (SCCs) of the attack graph, proceeding recursively from "higher" to "lower" components. While SCC-recursive semantics such as *cf2* and *stg2* have proven effective for finite AFs, Baumann and Spanring showed the failure of SCC-recursive semantics to generalize reliably to infinite AFs due to issues with well-foundedness.

We propose two approaches to extending SCC-recursiveness to the infinite setting. We systematically evaluate these semantics using Baroni and Giacomin's established criteria, showing in particular that directionality fails in general. We then examine these semantics' behavior in finitary frameworks, where we find some of our semantics satisfy directionality. These results advance the theory of infinite argumentation and lay the groundwork for reasoning systems capable of handling unbounded or evolving domains.

Keywords: infinite argumentation · SCC-recursiveness · cf2 · stg2

1 Introduction

Formal argumentation is a major research area in artificial intelligence that models reasoning and debate by representing arguments and their interactions in a structured form. A foundational concept is that of *Argumentation Framework* (AF), where arguments are treated as abstract elements and their conflicts are captured by a binary attack relation, denoted $a \rightarrowtail b$, indicating that accepting argument a provides a reason to reject argument b. Dung [14] introduced several

© The Author(s), under exclusive license to Springer Nature Switzerland AG 2026
G. Casini et al. (Eds.): JELIA 2025, LNAI 16093, pp. 78–94, 2026.
https://doi.org/10.1007/978-3-032-04587-4_6

semantics—that is, formal criteria to identify acceptable collections of arguments called *extensions*—to accomodate various reasoning contexts. A known challenge in Dung's approach arises in scenarios involving odd-length cycles: e.g., $a \rightarrowtail b \rightarrowtail c \rightarrowtail a$, which can lead to counterintuitive outcomes. Baroni and Giacomin [6] proposed the *cf2* semantics which yields more intuitive results in the presence of such cycles. This idea was further developed by Baroni, Giacomin, and Guida [9] into a general framework of *SCC-recursiveness*, where the acceptability of arguments is determined recursively based on the structure of the *strongly connected components* (SCCs) of the argumentation framework's attack graph. These approaches have proven particularly successful for finite argumentation frameworks.

Infinite AFs, where an infinite number of arguments is considered, are important because many real-world domains involve potentially unbounded or dynamically generated arguments. Such arguments may arise from, e.g., inductive definitions, logical deductions, recursive structures, or ongoing information streams. In recent years, interest in infinite AFs has grown (see, e.g., [5,10,12,13,20]); our previous work contributes to this line of research by exploring the computational complexity of natural reasoning problems in infinite AFs (see [1,2]). More broadly, the study of infinite AFs often involves analyzing the limiting behavior of semantics—understanding which properties persist in unbounded contexts and designing algorithms that converge toward correct conclusions about infinite frameworks.

Baumann and Spanring [11] identified a fundamental issue with SCC-recursiveness, particularly in the context of *cf2* and *stg2* semantics, when applied to infinite AFs. Specifically, in the infinite setting, the recursive definition may be ill-founded, rendering the semantics themselves not well-defined. Consequently, Baroni and Giacomin's semantics—despite their naturalness and elegance in the finite case—do not reliably extend to the infinite domain.

In this paper, we propose two solutions to address this problem. The first approach involves extending the recursion *transfinitely*, which we see (Remark 2 below) is equivalent to alternative characterizations previously proposed by Gaggl and Woltran [19] and Dvořák and Gaggl [16] in the finite setting. The second approach is to introduce two new semantics, which we term *cf1.5* and *stg1.5* (Definition 7). These are defined by modifying the standard definitions of *cf2* and *stg2* by preserving the initial notion of strongly connected components throughout the recursive process, rather than redefining them at each step.

We analyze these new semantics in light of the evaluation criteria proposed by Baroni and Giacomin [7], identifying in each case exactly which of these criteria are preserved in the infinite setting (Table 1). Additionally, we use our semantics to revisit the question raised by Baumann and Spanring [10] concerning whether every *finitary* AF—that is, an AF in which each argument is attacked by only finitely many others—necessarily admits a *cf2* or *stg2* extension. Finally, we provide a deeper exploration of the finitary case, proving that *cf1.5* and *stg1.5* are, in general, more well-behaved than the transfinite extensions of *cf2* or *stg2* (Table 2).

2 Background

2.1 Logic Background

Recall that the ordinals extend the counting numbers into the infinite. We will use the following fundamental properties of the collection of ordinals:

- The collection of ordinals is linearly ordered, and every non-empty subset of the collection of ordinals has a least element.

A well-ordering is order of an ordinal. That is, it is a linear order so that every non-empty subset has a least element. Recall that the ordinal ω is the least infinite ordinal. Also recall that every ordinal α is either the successor of another ordinal β, i.e., $\alpha = \beta + 1$, or is a limit ordinal, i.e., $\alpha = sup(Y)$, which is the supremum of the ordinals in the set Y. The ordinal ω is the first limit ordinal, and is the supremum of the finite ordinals, i.e., the natural numbers.

We let $\mathbb{N}^{<\mathbb{N}}$ represent the collection of *strings*, i.e., finite sequences, of natural numbers and $\mathbb{N}^{\mathbb{N}}$ represent infinite sequences of natural numbers. A string $\sigma \in \mathbb{N}^{<\mathbb{N}}$ is a *prefix* of a string $\tau \in \mathbb{N}^{<\mathbb{N}}$ or of a sequence $\tau \in \mathbb{N}^{\mathbb{N}}$, written $\sigma \preceq \tau$, if there is some $\rho \in \mathbb{N}^{<\mathbb{N}}$ or $\rho \in \mathbb{N}^{\mathbb{N}}$ so that $\tau = \sigma^\frown \rho$, i.e, τ is the concatenation of σ with ρ. Two strings σ and τ are comparable if $\sigma \preceq \tau$ or $\tau \preceq \sigma$. A *tree* is a subset of $\mathbb{N}^{<\mathbb{N}}$ which is closed under prefixes. A *path* π through a tree T is an element of $\mathbb{N}^{\mathbb{N}}$ so that every prefix of π is in T. Note that since our trees may be infinitely branching, even trees which contain arbitrarily long strings (i.e., are of infinite *height*) may not have paths. Consider for example, the tree containing the empty string and all strings $i^\frown \sigma$ where the length of σ is $\leq i$.

Finally, the proofs of Theorems 4 and 5 will employ the compactness theorem for propositional logic [17, §XI.4, Theorem 4.5]. That is, a theory T of propositional logic is consistent if and only if every finite subset of T is consistent.

2.2 Argumentation Theoretic Background

We briefly review some key concepts of Dung-style argumentation theory (for an overview of this area, we refer the reader to the surveys [8,15]).

An *argumentation framework* (AF) $\mathcal{F}$ is a pair $(A_\mathcal{F}, R_\mathcal{F})$ consisting of a set $A_\mathcal{F}$ of arguments and an attack relation $R_\mathcal{F} \subseteq A_\mathcal{F} \times A_\mathcal{F}$. If some argument a attacks some argument b, we often write $a \rightarrowtail b$ instead of $(a, b) \in R_\mathcal{F}$. Collections of arguments $S \subseteq A_\mathcal{F}$ are called *extensions*. For any extension S, denote by $\mathcal{F} \restriction_S$ the sub-framework of $\mathcal{F}$ with respect to S: i.e., $\mathcal{F} \restriction_S = (A_\mathcal{F} \cap S, R_\mathcal{F} \cap (S \times S))$.

For an extension S, the symbols S^+ and S^- denote, respectively, the arguments that S attacks and the arguments that attack S:

$$S^+ = \{x : (\exists y \in S)(y \rightarrowtail x)\}; S^- = \{x : (\exists y \in S)(x \rightarrowtail y)\}.$$

S *defends* an argument a, if any argument that attacks a is attacked by some argument in S (i.e., $\{a\}^- \subseteq S^+$). The *range* $S^\oplus$ of S as $S \cup S^+$. The *characteristic function* of $\mathcal{F}$ is the mapping $f_{\mathcal{F}}$ which sends subsets of $A_{\mathcal{F}}$ to subsets of $A_{\mathcal{F}}$ via $f_{\mathcal{F}}(S) := \{x : x \text{ is defended by } S\}$. Most AFs investigated in this paper are infinite. An AF $\mathcal{F}$ is *finitary* if $\{x\}^-$ is finite for all $x \in A_{\mathcal{F}}$.

A *semantics* σ assigns to every AF $\mathcal{F}$ a set of extensions $\sigma(\mathcal{F})$ which are deemed as acceptable. Several semantics have been proposed and analyzed. Four prominent semantics are relevant here: conflict-free, grounded, naive, stage (abbreviated by cf, gr, na, stg, respectively). First, denote by $cf(\mathcal{F})$ the collection of extensions of $\mathcal{F}$ which are *conflict-free*: i.e., $S \in cf(\mathcal{F})$ iff $a \not\rightarrowtail b$, for all $a, b \in S$. Then, for $S \in cf(\mathcal{F})$,

- $S \in na(\mathcal{F})$ iff there is no $T \in cf(\mathcal{F})$ with $T \supsetneq S$;
- $S \in gr(\mathcal{F})$ iff $S = f_F(S)$ and there is no $T \subsetneq S$ with $T = f_F(T)$;
- $S \in stg(\mathcal{F})$ iff there is no $T \in cf(\mathcal{F})$ with $S^\oplus \subsetneq T^\oplus$.

We recall that for each AF $\mathcal{F}$, the grounded semantics yields a unique extension, which is the least fixed-point of the characteristic function $f_{\mathcal{F}}$. Observe that every stage extension is naive.

Finally, we give the recursive definition of $cf2$ and $stg2$ semantics——the main objects of study in this paper—which are based on the graph-theoretic notion of strongly connected component.

Definition 1. *For an AF $\mathcal{F}$, the* strongly connected component *of $a \in A_{\mathcal{F}}$, written* $\mathrm{SCC}(a)$ *is the set of arguments $b \in A_{\mathcal{F}}$ so that there exists a directed path from a to b (i.e., a sequence $c_0 \rightarrowtail c_1 \rightarrowtail c_2 \ldots \rightarrowtail c_n$ so that $c_0 = a$ and $c_n = b$) and there exists a directed path from b to a.*

We denote by $\mathrm{SCC}(\mathcal{F})$ the strongly connected components of $\mathcal{F}$; note that $\mathrm{SCC}(\mathcal{F})$ is a partition of A_F. In particular, $b \in \mathrm{SCC}(a)$ iff $a \in \mathrm{SCC}(b)$.

An important feature of the decomposition of an AF into strongly connected components is that the resulting graph—where each SCC is treated as a single node—is acyclic; in other words, the attack relation induces a partial order over the SCCs. The SCC-recursive schema (see Baroni, Giacomin, and Guida [9]) employs this property to define a recursive procedure that incrementally builds extensions by processing the SCCs in accordance with their partial order. In Definition 2, $D_S(\mathrm{SCC}(b))$ is the set of elements in the strongly connected component of b that are not invalidated by an argument in S belonging to an SCC that precedes $\mathrm{SCC}(b)$ in the partial order.

Definition 2. *For $X, S \subseteq A_{\mathcal{F}}$, we let*

$$D_S(X) = \{b \in X : (\exists a \in S \smallsetminus X)(a \rightarrowtail b)\}.$$

The formal definition of the *cf2* semantics is as follows:

Definition 3 (Baroni-Giacomin [6]). *Let $\mathcal{F} = (A_{\mathcal{F}}, R_{\mathcal{F}})$ be an AF and $S \subseteq A_{\mathcal{F}}$. Then, $S \in cf2(\mathcal{F})$ iff:*

- $|\mathrm{SCC}(\mathcal{F})| = 1$ *and $S \in na(F)$;*
- *or, for each $X \in \mathrm{SCC}(\mathcal{F})$, $(S \cap X) \in cf2(\mathcal{F} \restriction_{X \smallsetminus D_S(X)})$.*

Dvořák and Gaggl give the *stg2* semantics similarly by using the *stg* semantics in place of the *na* semantics:

Definition 4 (Dvořák-Gaggl [16]). *Let $\mathcal{F} = (A_{\mathcal{F}}, R_{\mathcal{F}})$ and let $S \subseteq A_{\mathcal{F}}$. Then, $S \in stg2(\mathcal{F})$ iff:*

- $|\mathrm{SCC}(\mathcal{F})| = 1$ *and $S \in stg(F)$;*
- *or, for each $X \in \mathrm{SCC}(\mathcal{F})$, $(S \cap X) \in stg2(\mathcal{F} \restriction_{X \smallsetminus D_S(X)})$.*

For finite AFs, the above definitions are well-defined—that is, the recursion always terminates—since, if $\mathcal{F}$ has more than one strongly connected component, then $|X \smallsetminus D_S(X)| < |A_F|$. In contrast, the situation becomes more delicate in the infinite setting, as illustrated by the following example.

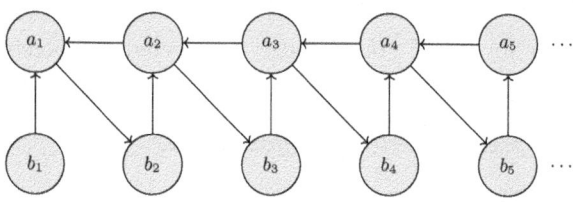

Fig. 1. An example from [11] of an infinite AF where the *cf2* and *stg2* semantics are not well-defined.

Example 1 (Baumann-Spanring [11]). The example in Fig. 1 illustrates an AF $\mathcal{F}$ for which the notion of a *cf2* or *stg2* extension is *not* well-defined. For concreteness, we consider the case of *cf2* (the case of *stg2* is analogous). Observe that $\mathcal{F}$ consists of two strongly connected components: $\{b_1\}$ and $A_{\mathcal{F}} \smallsetminus \{b_1\}$. Now, let $B = \{b_i : i \in \mathbb{N}\}$. By definition,

$$B \in cf2 \Leftrightarrow B \smallsetminus \{b_1\} \in cf2(\mathcal{F} \restriction_{A_{\mathcal{F}} \smallsetminus \{b_1, a_1\}}).$$

The restricted framework $\mathcal{F}\restriction_{A_{\mathcal{F}}\setminus\{b_1,a_1\}}$ again contains only two strongly connected components, one of which is the singleton $\{b_2\}$. Iterating this process, we repeatedly remove pairs b_i and a_i from the frameworks. However, we never reach a stage where only a single strongly connected component remains. As a result, the recursion underlying the definition of *cf2* does not terminate, and such a semantics is not well-defined for $\mathcal{F}$.

3 SCC-Recursiveness in the Infinite Setting

In this section, we propose two novel approaches to extending the concept of SCC-recursive semantics to the infinite setting. The first approach relaxes the requirement that the recursion must terminate after finitely many steps, instead allowing the process to continue transfinitely along the ordinals.

3.1 Use Transfinite Recursion

We begin by inductively defining the strongly connected component of an element $a \in A_{\mathcal{F}}$ at ordinal stages.

Definition 5. *Let $\mathcal{F}$ be an AF and let $S \subseteq A_{\mathcal{F}}$. For $a \in A_{\mathcal{F}}$ and all ordinals α, define $C_S^\alpha(a)$ inductively as follows:*

- $C_S^0(a) = \mathrm{SCC}(a)$;
- $C_S^{\alpha+1}(a)$ *is the strongly connected component of a in $C_S^\alpha(a) \setminus D_S(C_S^\alpha(a))$;*
- *finally, for limit ordinals λ, $C_S^\lambda(a)$ is the strongly connected component of a in $\bigcap_{\alpha<\lambda} C_S^\alpha(a)$.*

For $a \in A_{\mathcal{F}}$ and $S \subseteq A_{\mathcal{F}}$, we let the component ordinal of a over S, written $\alpha_S(a)$, be the least α so that either $a \notin C_S^\alpha(a)$ or $C_S^{\alpha+1}(a) = C_S^\alpha(a)$.

We are now ready to define the semantics that extend *cf2* and *stg2* transfinitely; we denote these by *tfcf2* and *tfstg2*, respectively.

Definition 6. *Let $\mathcal{F} = (A_{\mathcal{F}}, R_{\mathcal{F}})$ and let $S \in cf(\mathcal{F})$. Then,*

- $S \in tfcf2(\mathcal{F})$ *iff, for each $a \in \mathcal{F}$, either $a \notin C_S^{\alpha_S(a)}(a)$ or $S \cap C_S^{\alpha_S(a)}(a)$ is a naive extension of $\mathcal{F}\restriction_{C_S^{\alpha_S(a)}(a)}$;*
- $S \in tfstg2(\mathcal{F})$ *iff, for each $a \in \mathcal{F}$, either $a \notin C_S^{\alpha_S(a)}(a)$ or $S \cap C_S^{\alpha_S(a)}(a)$ is a stage extension of $\mathcal{F}\restriction_{C_S^{\alpha_S(a)}(a)}$.*

Remark 1. Following the same pattern but using the semantics σ instead of naive or stage, one may define, for any base semantics σ, a new semantics *tfσ2* which transfinitely extends the SCC-recursive semantics σ2. However, in this paper we restrict our attention to the specific cases of *tfcf2* and *tfstg2*.[1]

Observe that in the example from Fig. 1, $\{b_i : i \in \mathbb{N}\}$ is both a *tfcf2* and a *tfstg2* extension. For each argument b_i, at the ordinal $\alpha = i$, its strongly connected component stabilizes to the singleton $\{b_i\}$, and the restriction of B to this component forms a naive and a stage extension, respectively. Similarly, for each argument a_i, at the ordinal $i + 1$, we see that $a_i \notin C_B^{i+1}(a_i)$, and thus it is correctly excluded from the extension.

Remark 2. Gaggl and Woltran [19, Theorem 3.11], as well as Dvořák and Gaggl [16, Proposition 3.2], provided alternative characterizations of the *cf2* and *stg2* semantics in the finite setting. Their approach is based on the least fixed point of an operator $\Delta_{\mathcal{F},S}$. Notably, the existence of this least fixed point does not depend on the finiteness of the argumentation framework. In fact, it turns out that their characterizations, if considered in the infinite setting, are equivalent to the definition of the *tfcf2* and *tfstg2* semantics given in this paper. A proof of this equivalence is provided in Appendix A of the extended version of this paper [4].

One downside of working with *tfcf2* and *tfstg2* is that, for countable AFs $\mathcal{F}$, there may be $a \in \mathcal{F}$ and $S \subseteq A_{\mathcal{F}}$ whose component ordinal $\alpha_S(a)$ is an arbitrarily large countable ordinal. See Appendix B of the extended version of this paper [4] for an example of a finitary AF with high component ordinal $\alpha_S(a)$.

Remark 3. Although working with arbitrarily large countable ordinals may seem challenging, we stress that this is not fundamentally worse than the situation for the grounded extension, which can likewise require a transfinite number of steps—potentially up to any countable ordinal—to stabilize (see Andrews-San Mauro [3]). However, an important distinction arises in the finitary case: for finitary AFs, the grounded extension is found after ω steps [14, Theorem 47], whereas the ordinal values $\alpha_S(x)$ associated with the transfinite extensions of the SCC-recursive semantics can be arbitrarily large *also* in the finitary setting.

We conclude this subsection with showing that, whenever *cf2* and *stg2* are well-defined, they coincide with their transfinite counterparts (proof in Appendix B of the extended version [4]):

---

[1] We note with this general definition, *tfcf2* should be called *tfna2*, but we choose to follow the standard terminology from the finite setting.

Theorem 1. *Let $\mathcal{F}$ be an AF and $S \subseteq A_{\mathcal{F}}$. Suppose that whether or not S is a cf2-extension is well-defined. Then S is a cf2-extension if and only if S is a tfcf2-extension. Similarly, suppose that whether or not S is a stg2-extension is well-defined. Then S is an stg2-extension if and only if S is a tfstg2-extension.*

3.2 SCC-Prioritization Instead of Recursion

We now propose a second approach that retains some of the benefits of SCC-recursiveness, while avoiding the need for transfinite recursion. This method is characterized by evaluating strongly connected components as they appear in the original framework $\mathcal{F}$, without further subdividing a component X in response to attacks from arguments in S that lie outside of X.

Definition 7. *Let $\mathcal{F} = (A_{\mathcal{F}}, R_{\mathcal{F}})$ and let $S \in cf(\mathcal{F})$. Then,*

- $S \in cf1.5(\mathcal{F})$ *iff, for each* $X \in \mathrm{SCC}(\mathcal{F})$, $S \cap X$ *is a naive extension in* $\mathcal{F}\restriction_{X \smallsetminus D_S(X)}$;
- $S \in stg1.5(\mathcal{F})$ *iff, for each* $X \in \mathrm{SCC}(\mathcal{F})$, $S \cap X$ *is a stage extension in* $\mathcal{F}\restriction_{X \smallsetminus D_S(X)}$.

Remark 4. Note that, given any semantics σ, one could similarly define the semantics $\sigma1.5$, by simply saying that $S \in \sigma1.5(\mathcal{F})$ iff, for each $X \in \mathrm{SCC}(\mathcal{F})$, $S \cap X$ is a σ-extension in $\mathcal{F}\restriction_{X \smallsetminus D_S(X)}$.

As a first test of our proposed semantics, we briefly revisit Examples 4–6 from Baroni and Giacomin [6], where the authors highlight certain undesirable behaviors exhibited by the preferred and grounded semantics on argumentation frameworks containing odd-length cycles. In particular, they observe that the preferred semantics treats odd and even cycles differently—an asymmetry which is regarded as problematic. For each of these examples, it is straightforward to check that $cf2(\mathcal{F}) = cf1.5(\mathcal{F}) = stg1.5(\mathcal{F})$, indicating that our semantics avoid some of the undesirable behaviors of the preferred and grounded semantics.

Example 7 from the same paper—reproduced here as Fig. 2—reveals a distinction between $cf2$ and $cf1.5$; however, in this example, $stg1.5$ continues to align with both $cf2$ and $stg2$.

Similarly, consider a finite variant of the argumentation framework depicted in Fig. 1; for instance, $\mathcal{F}\restriction_{\{a_i, b_i \,:\, i \leq 4\}}$. In this case, the set $\{b_1, a_2, a_4\}$ is a $cf1.5$ extension, but not a $cf2$ extension. As before, the unique $cf2$ extension, and likewise the unique $stg1.5$ extension, is $\{b_i : i \leq 4\}$.

Thus, considering motivating examples, $cf1.5$ and $stg1.5$ appear to be promising candidates for well-defined semantics that preserve some of the key advantages of SCC-recursiveness, while avoiding the complexity of deep transfinite recursion. In the next section, we critically examine the trade-offs involved in adopting these semantics—alongside with $tfcf2$ and $tfstg2$—for reasoning in the infinite setting.

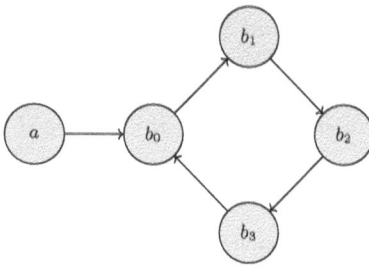

Fig. 2. An example of a finite AF $\mathcal{F}$, where the semantics $cf2$ and $cf1.5$ differ. Specifically, $cf2(\mathcal{F}) = \{\{a, b_1, b_3\}\}$, while $cf1.5(\mathcal{F}) = \{\{a, b_1, b_3\}, \{a, b_2\}\}$; however, note that $stg1.5(\mathcal{F}) = stg2(\mathcal{F}) = cf2(\mathcal{F})$.

4   Properties of These Semantics

To clarify the relative advantages of the semantics under consideration, we adopt the following naive-based evaluation criteria introduced by Baroni and Giacomin [7]:

Definition 8. *A semantics σ satisfies:*

- **I-maximality criterion** *if, for each AF $\mathcal{F}$ and for each $S_1, S_2 \in \sigma(\mathcal{F})$, $S_1 \subseteq S_2$ implies $S_1 = S_2$;*
- **Reinstatement criterion** *if, for each AF $\mathcal{F}$ and for each $S \in \sigma(\mathcal{F})$, if S defends some argument a, then $a \in S$;*
- **Weak reinstatement criterion** *if, for each AF $\mathcal{F}$ and for each $S \in \sigma(\mathcal{F})$, S contains the grounded extension of $\mathcal{F}$;*
- **CF-reinstatement criterion** *if, for each AF $\mathcal{F}$ and for each $S \in \sigma(\mathcal{F})$, whenever S defends a and $S \cup \{a\}$ is conflict-free, then $a \in S$;*
- **Directionality criterion** *if, for each AF $\mathcal{F}$ and $U \subseteq A_{\mathcal{F}}$ which is not attacked from outside U, $\sigma(\mathcal{F} \restriction_U) = \{S \cap U : S \in \sigma(\mathcal{F})\}$.*

Baroni and Giacomin [7, Proposition 63] show that in the finite setting, $cf2$ satisfies the properties of elementary and weak skepticism adequacy, which we now define. We will examine below which variants of $cf2$ or $stg2$ satisfy these conditions in the infinite setting.

Definition 9. *Let τ_1 and τ_2 be two sets of extensions of an AF $\mathcal{F}$. Then:*

- *The **elementary skepticism relation**, denoted $\tau_1 \preceq_{\cap}^{E} \tau_2$, holds iff*

$$\bigcap_{S_1 \in \tau_1} S_1 \subseteq \bigcap_{S_2 \in \tau_2} S_2;$$

- *The **weak skepticism relation**, denoted $\tau_1 \preceq_W^E \tau_2$, holds iff $(\forall S_2 \in \tau_2 \exists S_1 \in \tau_1)(S_1 \subseteq S_2)$.*

Definition 10. *For $\mathcal{F} = (A_{\mathcal{F}}, R_{\mathcal{F}})$, let $conf(\mathcal{F})$ be the set of conflicting pairs in $\mathcal{F}$: i.e., $conf(\mathcal{F}) = \{(x, y) \mid (x, y) \in R \text{ or } (y, x) \in R\}$. Next, let σ be a semantics:*

- *For each of the skepticism relations $\preceq$, we say that σ is $\preceq$-**skepticism adequate**, if $\mathcal{F} = (A_F, R_{\mathcal{F}})$ and $\mathcal{G} = (A_{\mathcal{G}}, R_{\mathcal{G}})$ with $R_{\mathcal{F}} \supseteq R_{\mathcal{G}}$ and $conf(F) = conf(G)$ implies that $\sigma(\mathcal{F}) \preceq \sigma(\mathcal{G})$.*

Table 1 summarizes which of the considered semantics satisfy each of the evaluation criteria discussed above. The proofs of these results are provided in Appendix C of the extended version [4].

Table 1. Summary of which semantics satisfy each of the evaluation criteria. Entries marked with Y* indicate cases where the criterion may be satisfied vacuously due to the semantics being undefined in some instances. For example, while every *cf2*-extension contains the grounded extension, it is possible for no *cf2*-extensions to exist, meaning that arguments in the grounded extension could fail to be credulously *cf2* accepted. Results for the naive and stage semantics are from [18].

	na	cf2	stg	stg2	tfcf2	cf1.5	tfstg2	stg1.5
Well-defined	Y	N	Y	N	Y	Y	Y	Y
I-maximality	Y	Y	Y	Y	Y	Y	Y	Y
Reinstatement	N	N	N	N	N	N	N	N
Weak reinstatement	N	Y*	N	Y*	Y	N	Y	N
CF-reinstatement	Y	Y	Y	Y	Y	Y	Y	Y
Directionality	N	N	N	N	N	N	N	N
$\preceq_{\cap}^E$-sk. ad.	Y	N	N	N	Y	Y	N	N
$\preceq_{w}^E$-sk. ad.	Y	N	N	N	Y	Y	N	N

We regard directionality as a core desideratum for both the *cf2* and *stg2* semantics; however, every version of these semantics fails to satisfy directionality in general.

Example 2. Let Σ be the following collection of semantics: *cf2*, *tfcf2*, *cf1.5*, *stg2*, *tfstg2*, and *stg2*. Consider the AF $\mathcal{F}$ with argument set $A_{\mathcal{F}} := \{a_i : i \in \mathbb{N}\}$, and attacks defined by $a_i \rightarrowtail a_j$ if and only if $i > j$. It is straightforward to verify that, for $\sigma \in \Sigma$, $\mathcal{F}$ has no σ-extension.

Now, let $\mathcal{G}$ be the framework obtained by extending $\mathcal{F}$ with two additional arguments x and y, which attack each other, and where $x \rightarrowtail a_i$, for all $i \in \mathbb{N}$. In $\mathcal{G}$, the only σ-extension for any $\sigma \in \Sigma$ is $\{x\}$. However, in the subframework $\mathcal{G} \restriction_{\{x,y\}}$, we have $\sigma(\mathcal{G} \restriction_{\{x,y\}}) = \{\{x\}, \{y\}\}$. Since $\{x, y\}$ is not attacked by any other argument in $\mathcal{F}$, we deduce that the directionality criterion fails for all the semantics in Σ.

In the next section, we will observe a different situation when restricting attention to finitary AFs.

5   The Finitary Case

We view the failure of directionality shown in Example 2 as a significant concern for the robustness of the semantics in question. The failure of directionality in $\mathcal{G}$ is an immediate consequence of the failure of existence of a σ-extension in $\mathcal{F}$, where each argument has infinitely many attackers. This observation naturally leads us to revisit a conjecture posed by Baumann and Spanring [10, Conjecture 1] which asserts, when $\mathcal{F}$ is finitary, the $cf2$ and $stg2$ semantics should always admit at least one extension. This conjecture predates the authors' later discovery that these semantics are not well-defined in the general infinite setting. Now that we have introduced two distinct reformulations of $cf2$ and $stg2$ capable of handling infinite frameworks, we are in a position to re-examine this conjecture through the lens of our proposed semantics.

Definition 11. *For a semantics σ,*

- *σ satisfies **finitary existence** if, whenever $\mathcal{F}$ is a finitary AF, then there exists some $S \in \sigma(\mathcal{F})$;*
- *σ satisfies **finitary directionality** if, whenever $\mathcal{F}$ is finitary and $U \subseteq A_{\mathcal{F}}$ is not attacked from outside U, $\sigma(\mathcal{F} \restriction_U) = \{S \cap U : S \in \sigma(\mathcal{F})\}$.*

Table 2. Summary of results on finitary existence and directionality for the semantics under consideration.

	na	cf2	stg	stg2	tfcf2	cf1.5	tfstg2	stg1.5
Finitary existence	Y	N	Y	N	?	Y	N	Y
Finitary directionality	N	N	N	N	?	Y	N	Y

Table 2 summarizes our results on this topic. We begin by examining the property of finitary existence. Example 1 demonstrates that there exists a finitary argumentation framework that admits neither a $cf2$ nor a $stg2$-extension, hence the semantics $cf2$ and $stg2$ do not satisfy finitary existence. This is due to the fact that these semantics are not well-definened in that setting; in fact, the AF from Example 1 does have an $tfcf2$ and $tfstg2$ extension—specifically, $\{b_i : i \in \mathbb{N}\}$. Nonetheless, we now show that not every finitary AF has an $tfstg2$ extension.

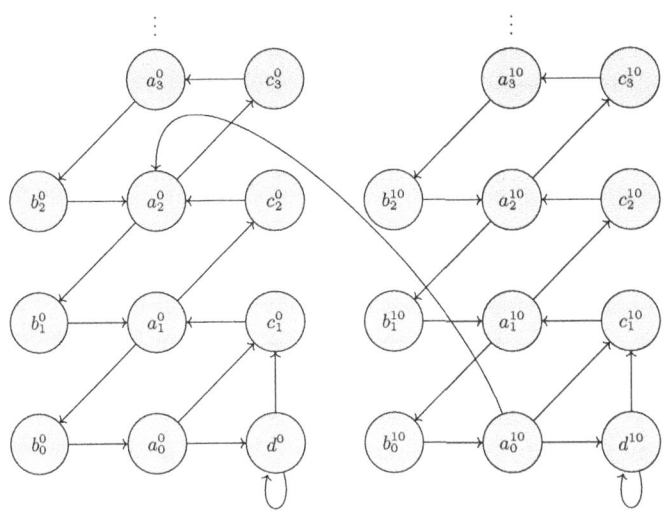

Fig. 3. Fragment of a finitary AF encoding a tree $T \supset \{0, 10\}$ in its strongly connected components. We assume that the string 10 is the second string in the enumeration of all strings that are longer than the string 0 and incomparable with it.

Theorem 2. *There is a finitary AF with no tfstg2 extension.*

Proof. Let $T \subseteq \mathbb{N}^{<\mathbb{N}}$ be a tree of infinite height with no path. We construct a finitary AF consisting of infinitely many strongly connected components, indexed by $\sigma \in T$. For each σ, the component X_σ contains the arguments: $\{a_i^\sigma : i \in \mathbb{N}\} \cup \{b_i^\sigma : i \in \mathbb{N}\} \cup \{c_i^\sigma : i \geq 1\} \cup \{d^\sigma\}$. The attack relations within X_σ are defined as follows (see Fig. 3):
For $i \in \mathbb{N}$,

- $a_i^\sigma \rightarrowtail c_{i+1}^\sigma \rightarrowtail a_{i+1}^\sigma \rightarrowtail b_i^\sigma \rightarrowtail a_i^\sigma$;
- $a_0^\sigma \rightarrowtail d^\sigma \rightarrowtail c_1^\sigma$;
- $d^\sigma \rightarrowtail d^\sigma$.

We define the full AF $\mathcal{F}$ with argument set $A_\mathcal{F} = \bigcup_{\sigma \in T} X_\sigma$. Now, for each $\sigma \in T$, fix an enumeration $(\tau_i)_{i \in \mathbb{N}}$ of all strings $\tau \in T$ longer than σ and so $\sigma \not\preceq \tau$. We then let $a_0^{\tau_i} \rightarrowtail a_i^\sigma$.

We argue that $\mathcal{F}$ has no *tfstg2* extension. Towards a contradiction, suppose that S were such an *tfstg2* extension.

First, observe that a *stg*-extension of a component X_σ must include a_0^σ. Indeed, the set $Z = \{a_i^\sigma : i \in \mathbb{N}\}$ forms a stage extension with $Z^\oplus = X_\sigma$, and the only way to include $d \in Z^\oplus$ is for a stage extension Z is to include a_0^σ. It follows that for every σ, S must contain some a_0^τ where τ has length $\geq |\sigma|$.

Next, suppose that σ is shorter than τ and both a_0^σ and a_0^τ are in S. It must be that $\sigma \preceq \tau$, as otherwise a_0^σ would attack some a_i^σ which would make b_{i-1}^σ be in its own connected component. Since it is unattacked from S, because $a_i^\sigma \notin S$, this implies that $b_{i-1}^\sigma \in S$. This in turn attacks a_{i-1}^σ, and so on, until we see a_0^σ is attacked by $b_0^\sigma \in S$, yielding a contradiction. Thus, there are arbitrarily long σ so that $a_0^\sigma \in S$, and these are comparable. This implies that T has a path, which is a contradiction.   □

Theorem 3. *The semantics cf2, stg2, and tfstg2 do not satisfy finitary directionality.*

Proof. We reason as in Example 2. Let $\sigma \in \{cf2, stg2, tfstg2\}$; each of these semantics fail to satisfy finitary existence. Now, let $\mathcal{F}$ be a finitary AF which does not have a σ-extension. Let G add two arguments x, y which attack each other and such that, for all $z \in \mathcal{F}$, $x \rightarrowtail z$. Then, G is finitary, yet fails directionality since $\{y\}$ is in $\sigma(G \upharpoonright_{\{x,y\}})$ but the only σ-extension of G is $\{x\}$.   □

We now turn to proving that both *cf1.5* and *stg1.5* satisfy finitary existence and also finitary directionality. The core idea behind both arguments is the same: we exploit the compactness theorem for propositional logic to find an extension which is *cf1.5* or *stg1.5*. The main challenge is that the space of choices used to construct a *cf1.5* or *stg1.5* extension may involve *infinitely many choices*, which obstruct compactness. Indeed, if Z is infinite, then $P_i \leftrightarrow (\bigwedge_{j \in Z} \neg P_j)$ is not a propositional formula and not subject to the compactness theorem. For instance, suppose that $\mathcal{F}$ consists of a single strongly connected component. To build a naive extension, for each argument x, we must either include x in S, or some y which is in conflict with x. However, there may be infinitely many y's with $x \rightarrowtail y$.

A natural idea would be to restrict attention to sets S such that every argument is either in S or is attacked by some element of S, thereby reducing the formulas describing the condition to a finite set of choices. Unfortunately, such an extension cannot be found in general—for example, no naive extension of a 3-cycle satisfies it.

Our strategy, therefore, is to define a restricted class of potential *cf1.5* or *stg1.5* extensions which is broad enough to guarantee that every finite AF admits an extension in this subclass, yet narrow enough to ensure that the corresponding space of choices is compact.

Lemma 1. *If $\mathcal{F}$ is a finitary AF, then there exists a well-ordering $<$ of $A_{\mathcal{F}}$ such that each argument a attacks only finitely many arguments b with $b < a$.*

Proof. Fix any enumeration $A_{\mathcal{F}} = \{a_\gamma \mid \gamma < \kappa\}$ of order type an ordinal κ. We build another ordering $A_{\mathcal{F}} = \{b_\gamma \mid \gamma < \kappa\}$ out of this one. For each ordinal β, we define γ_β to be least so that $a_{\gamma_\beta} \notin \{b_\alpha \mid \alpha < \beta\}$.

We let $b_0 = a_0$. We then let $b_1, \ldots, b_k$ be all the attackers of a_0. Next, we let $b_{k+1} = a_{\gamma_{k+1}}$. We then let $b_{k+2}, \ldots, b_\ell$ be all the attackers of any b_m with $m \le k+1$. Continuing as such, we see that if x attacks y, then x appears in our enumeration b_α at most finitely much after y.   □

Theorem 4. *If $\mathcal{F}$ is a finitary AF, there exists a cf1.5 extension in $\mathcal{F}$.*

Proof. By Lemma 1, we may assume that $A_\mathcal{F}$ is well-ordered in such a way that each element attacks at most finitely many before it. For any $a \in A_\mathcal{F}$, define $B(a)$ to be the finite set $\{x \in \mathrm{SCC}(a) : x < a$ and $a \rightarrowtail x\}$. We define an extension S to be a *greedy cf1.5 extension* if $S \in cf(\mathcal{F})$ and every element $a \in A_\mathcal{F}$ is either in S, or is attacked by an element of S, or there exists an argument in $S \cap B(a)$.

We now define a propositional theory associated with $\mathcal{F}$. For each $a \in A_\mathcal{F}$, introduce a propositional variable P_a. Define a theory T_0 consisting of the following formulas: For each $a \in A_\mathcal{F}$ with $a \not\rightarrowtail a$,

$$P_a \leftrightarrow \Big(\bigwedge_{b \rightarrowtail a} \neg P_b \land \bigwedge_{b \in B(a)} \neg P_b \Big).$$

Let T_1 be the theory that says for each $a \rightarrowtail b$, $\neg(P_a \land P_b)$. Finally, let $T = T_0 \cup T_1$.

Note that T is a propositional theory: in particular, since each argument in F has only finitely many attackers, each conjuction in the above formulas is finite.

To apply the compactness theorem for propositional logic, we must show that every finite subset T' of T is consistent. Fix T' a finite subset of T. Let X be the finite set of arguments a so that P_a appears in T'. We now argue that the framework $F \restriction_X$ has a greedy *cf1.5* extension. This can be shown by starting with an initial strongly connected component Y and using a greedy algorithm to find a naive extension:

-   Take the first element of Y (using the order on $\mathcal{F}$) and put it into S unless it attacks itself;
-   Continuing taking successive elements of Y and put them into S unless they attack themselves or are in conflict with the elements previously put into S;
-   Once finished with Y, we then proceed to another strongly connected component which is initial among the remaining strongly connected components.

As such, we can build a greedy *cf1.5* extension of $F|_X$. We note that this satisfies the formulas of T'. By compactness, T is consistent.

Let π be a model of T. Then define S by letting a be in S iff π makes P_a true. We observe that S is a greedy *cf1.5* extension of F, and is thus a *cf1.5* extension of F.   □

A similar, albeit more involved, argument shows that the *stg1.5* semantics satisfies finitary existence (see Appendix D of the extended version [4]).

Theorem 5. *If $\mathcal{F}$ is a finitary AF, then it has an stg1.5-extension.*

The following theorem does not follow immediately from finitary existence, but rather requires a new argument, in the *stg1.5* case requiring another application of propositional compactness (see Appendix D of the extended version [4]).

Theorem 6. *The semantics cf1.5, stg1.5 satisfy finitary directionality.*

6   Discussion

The results presented in this paper contribute to the broader understanding of argumentation in infinite domains, a setting of increasing relevance for AI systems that must operate over unbounded or dynamically evolving data. Our two proposed approaches—the transfinite extension of SCC-recursive semantics and the introduction of the *cf1.5* and *stg1.5* semantics—highlight different design trade-offs when generalizing well-understood concepts from the finite case.

The transfinite extensions provide a principled way to salvage the recursive methodology of *cf2* and *stg2* in the infinite setting, aligning closely with known alternative characterizations. However, our analysis reveals that these extensions can suffer from foundational issues, particularly around directionality and existence, in infinite frameworks.

By contrast, the *cf1.5* and *stg1.5* semantics preserve the original SCC structure throughout the evaluation process. This approach avoids the need for transfinite recursion. Notably, in finitary AFs, *cf1.5* and *stg1.5* demonstrate superior adherence to the key evaluation criteria of directionality and existence, suggesting that they may serve as more robust alternatives for infinite argumentation reasoning tasks in practice.

Going forward, one promising direction is to study algorithmic properties and complexity results for the newly introduced semantics, particularly in the context of incremental or streaming argumentation systems. Additionally, we left open the question of finitary existence and directionality for the *tfcf2* semantics.

In sum, our work advances the theoretical foundations of infinite argumentation and provides practical tools for constructing semantics that remain meaningful in the presence of infinite interaction structures.

Acknowledgement. This work was supported by the the National Science Foundation under Grant DMS-2348792. San Mauro is a member of INDAM-GNSAGA.

Disclosure of Interests. The authors have no competing interests to declare that are relevant to the content of this article.

References

1. Andrews, U., San Mauro, L.: On computational problems for infinite argumentation frameworks: Hardness of finding acceptable extensions. In: Proceedings of the 10th Workshop on Formal and Cognitive Reasoning (FCR-2024). CEUR Workshop Proceedings (2024), https://ceur-ws.org/Vol-3763/paper4.pdf

2. Andrews, U., San Mauro, L.: On computational problems for infinite argumentation frameworks: the complexity of finding acceptable extensions. In: Proceedings of the 22nd International Workshop on Nonmonotonic Reasoning (NMR-2024). CEUR Workshop Proceedings (2024)
3. Andrews, U., San Mauro, L.: On the complexity of the grounded semantics for infinite argumentation frameworks. In: Theoretical Aspects of Rationality & Knowledge (TARK) (2025)
4. Andrews, U., San Mauro, L.: SCC-recursiveness in infinite argumentation (extended version) (2025), https://arxiv.org/abs/2507.06852
5. Baroni, P., Cerutti, F., Dunne, P.E., Giacomin, M.: Computing with infinite argumentation frameworks: the case of AFRAs. In: Theorie and Applications of Formal Argumentation: First International Workshop, TAFA 2011. Barcelona, Spain, 16–17 July 2011, pp. 197–214. Springer (2012)
6. Baroni, P., Giacomin, M.: Solving semantic problems with odd-length cycles in argumentation. In: Nielsen, T.D., Zhang, N.L. (eds.) Symbolic and Quantitative Approaches to Reasoning with Uncertainty, pp. 440–451. Springer, Berlin, Heidelberg (2003)
7. Baroni, P., Giacomin, M.: On principle-based evaluation of extension-based argumentation semantics. Artif. Intell. **171**(10), 675–700 (2007). https://doi.org/10.1016/j.artint.2007.04.004, https://www.sciencedirect.com/science/article/pii/S0004370207000744, argumentation in Artificial Intelligence
8. Baroni, P., Giacomin, M.: Semantics of abstract argument systems. Argum. Artif. Intell. 25–44 (2009)
9. Baroni, P., Giacomin, M., Guida, G.: SCC-recursiveness: a general schema for argumentation semantics. Artif. Intell. **168**(1), 162–210 (2005) https://doi.org/10.1016/j.artint.2005.05.006, https://www.sciencedirect.com/science/article/pii/S0004370205000962
10. Baumann, R., Spanring, C.: Infinite argumentation frameworks: on the existence and uniqueness of extensions. In: Advances in Knowledge Representation, Logic Programming, and Abstract Argumentation: Essays Dedicated to Gerhard Brewka on the Occasion of his 60th Birthday, pp. 281–295. Springer (2015)
11. Baumann, R., Spanring, C.: A study of unrestricted abstract argumentation frameworks. In: Sierra, C. (ed.) Proceedings of the Twenty-Sixth International Joint Conference on Artificial Intelligence, IJCAI 2017, Melbourne, Australia, 19–25 August 2017, pp. 807–813. ijcai.org (2017). https://doi.org/10.24963/IJCAI.2017/112
12. Bistarelli, S., Santini, F.: Weighted argumentation. J. Appl. Logics **8**(6), 1589–1621 (2021)
13. Caminada, M., Oren, N.: Grounded semantics and infinitary argumentation frameworks. In: Proceedings of the 26th Benelux Conference on Artificial Intelligence, pp. 25–32. BNAIC (2014)
14. Dung, P.M.: On the acceptability of arguments and its fundamental role in nonmonotonic reasoning, logic programming and n-person games. Artif. Intell. **77**(2), 321–357 (1995)
15. Dunne, P.E., Wooldridge, M.: Complexity of abstract argumentation. Argum. Artif. Intell. 85–104 (2009)
16. Dvořák, W., Gaggl, S.A.: Stage semantics and the SCC-recursive schema for argumentation semantics. J. Log. Comput. **26**(4), 1149–1202 (2014). https://doi.org/10.1093/logcom/exu006
17. Ebbinghaus, H.D., Flum, J., Thomas, W.: Mathematical logic, graduate texts in mathematics, vol. 291. Springer, Cham, third edn. ([2021] ©2021). https://doi.org/10.1007/978-3-030-73839-6

18. Gaggl, S.A.: A Comprehensive analysis of the cf2 argumentation semantics: from characterization to implementation. Ph.D. thesis, TU Wien (2013)
19. Gaggl, S.A., Woltran, S.: The cf2 argumentation semantics revisited. J. Log. Comput. **23**(5), 925–949 (2012). https://doi.org/10.1093/logcom/exs011
20. Verheij, B.: Deflog: on the logical interpretation of prima facie justified assumptions. J. Log. Comput. **13**(3), 319–346 (2003)

Completing Structured Arguments in Assumption-Based Argumentation

Andrei Popescu[ID] and Johannes P. Wallner[(✉)][ID]

Graz University of Technology, Graz, Austria
{andrei.popescu,johannes.p.wallner}@tugraz.at

Abstract. In their daily use arguments are usually not completely enunciated. That is, we often rely on implicit parts, for example, unstated premises, sometimes referred to as enthymemes. Completions of partially stated arguments can favor knowledge engineering processes, where the workload of an engineer can be reduced by suggesting such completions. In this work, we focus on an integral aspect of completing arguments: valid argument structure of a completion. We phrase our results in the formal model of assumption-based argumentation (ABA). Based on an alternative characterization of tree-based arguments in ABA, we provide a declarative approach to compute completions of partial arguments in answer set programming (ASP), including the possibility of preferential reasoning in completions. We empirically evaluate a resulting prototype.

1 Introduction

Reasoning with uncertainty and evolving scenarios is a central aspiration in the design of intelligent systems. Computational argumentation [4,23] is a paradigm for non-monotonic reasoning that resolves conflicting and possibly incomplete information, with several heterogeneous application avenues [3] such as in legal reasoning [36] and medical reasoning [14,17].

Key to several such applications are approaches commonly referred to as structured argumentation [6,16,24,28,31,34]. In these approaches arguments are instantiated from possibly conflicting knowledge bases, and relations between such arguments are identified, such as one argument countering another. Based on the arguments and their relations, argumentation semantics lead to finding rational argumentative conclusions [11,12].

In a recent fraud detection application by the Dutch National Police [35], arguments are constructed both in support of and against a citizen's claim of being a fraud victim. In such applications of computational argumentation, the construction of adequate knowledge bases is essential. This process, especially when it involves the construction of rules, is usually subsumed under the term "knowledge engineering". Here, experienced persons distill their knowledge of domains, processes, and further thoughts into knowledge bases. Knowledge engineering encompasses various aspects [39], including, in computational argumentation, the design of rules that make up arguments. For instance, in the

© The Author(s), under exclusive license to Springer Nature Switzerland AG 2026
G. Casini et al. (Eds.): JELIA 2025, LNAI 16093, pp. 95–111, 2026.
https://doi.org/10.1007/978-3-032-04587-4_7

fraud detection example application, a knowledge engineer might decide that there should be arguments in favor or against fraud, that is concluding fraud or the negation of fraud. Such conclusions do not exist in a vacuum and must be derived based on rational processes. Arguments can have many components [41], e.g., in major formal approaches to structured argumentation components of arguments are premises or assumptions, rules for derivation, and a conclusion.

In many cases, the design and construction of rules that ultimately lead to useful arguments is likely an incremental process: one can iteratively expand, e.g., on rules that then make up an argument for or against a conclusion. Viewed in a broader sense, arguments might exist only "partially" during the process. This process can be supported by automatic recommendation of possible completions of arguments, to lessen the cognitive load of an engineer, for instance highlighting rules whose bodies cannot be derived using assumptions and suggesting possible additional rules.

In this work, we study the problem of argument completion, and situate our work in the well-known structured argumentation formalism of assumption-based argumentation (ABA) [9,16]. Connected to the general problem of enthymemes [7,8,29], i.e., handling of missing premises of arguments, we in particular focus on the key structure of arguments: they must present full derivations of conclusions (and all parts) based on available assumptions, i.e., arguments have to be a "derivation tree". Such structures can also be found in other structured argumentation formalisms such as ASPIC$^+$ [34].

That is, when completing arguments we in particular require that such completions are actually arguments—satisfying the structural constraint of being derivation trees—and that completions can be automatically computed. This suggests the usage of approaches of declarative problem solving that are both efficient and can handle expressive constraints. Based on recent top-performing systems in computational approaches to ABA and ASPIC$^+$ [30,32,33], we focus on answer set programming (ASP) [10,25,27] for computing completions of partially specified arguments, which offers capabilities of including declarative specification of preferential information, preferring certain completions.

Our main contributions are as follows.

- We formulate argument completion as a computational problem, including constraints such as restricting the number and size of learnable rules and incorporation of preferential reasoning.
- In order to be able to work on a representation of arguments amenable to specification in ASP, we provide an alternative representation of tree-based arguments under mild restrictions.
- We show that the general argument completion problem is NP-hard, which further motivates the use of search algorithms such as ASP solvers.
- We provide a prototype in ASP and empirically show promise both in terms of running times and that utilization of preferences can increase the quality of completed arguments.

More details are available in an online supplement[1].

---

[1] https://gitlab.tugraz.at/krr/aba-completion.

2   Assumption-Based Argumentation

We recall the main background of assumption-based argumentation (ABA) [9]. In ABA, the components are a set of atoms $\mathcal{L}$, a set of assumptions $\mathcal{A} \subseteq \mathcal{L}$ chosen from the set of atoms, and rules of the form $h \leftarrow s_1, \ldots, s_n$, with $h, s_1, \ldots, s_n$ atoms. We use shorthands for the head and body of a rule r: $head(r) = h$ and $body(r) = \{s_1, \ldots, s_n\}$. We focus on flat ABA, which can be represented via requiring that h is not an assumption (assumptions cannot be derived). A contrary function defines what is the contrary of an assumption. We call $(\mathcal{L}, \mathcal{R})$ a deductive system.

Definition 1. *An ABA framework is a tuple $F = (\mathcal{L}, \mathcal{R}, \mathcal{A}, ^-)$, where $(\mathcal{L}, \mathcal{R})$ is a deductive system, $\mathcal{A} \subseteq \mathcal{L}$ a non-empty set of assumptions, and $^-$ a function mapping assumptions $\mathcal{A}$ to atoms $\mathcal{L}$.*

An atom $x \in \mathcal{L}$ is derivable from a set of assumptions $X \subseteq \mathcal{A}$ using rules $\mathcal{R}$, denoted by $X \vdash_{\mathcal{R}} x$, if $x \in X$ or there is a sequence of rules $(r_1, \ldots, r_n)$ such that $head(r_n) = x$ and for each rule r_i we have $r_i \in \mathcal{R}$ and each atom in the body of r_i is derived from rules earlier in the sequence or is in X, i.e., $body(r_i) \subseteq X \cup \bigcup_{j<i} \{head(r_j)\}$. Note that duplicated rules in this sequence can be directly avoided (the later rule can be removed). The deductive closure for an assumption set X w.r.t. rules $\mathcal{R}$ is defined as $Th_{\mathcal{R}}(X) = \{x \in \mathcal{L} \mid X \vdash_{\mathcal{R}} x\}$.

Let $F = (\mathcal{L}, \mathcal{R}, \mathcal{A}, ^-)$ be an ABA framework. An argument A based on F is a finite labeled rooted tree where

- the root is labeled with some atom $c \in \mathcal{L}$,
- each leaf is labeled by an assumption $a \in \mathcal{A}$ or a dedicated symbol $\top \notin \mathcal{L}$,
- each internal node is labeled with $head(r)$ of a rule $r \in \mathcal{R}$ s.t. the set of labels of children of this node is equal to $body(r)$ or $\top$ if the body is empty (and there are exactly $|body(r)|$ many children).

For such an argument A, we denote the conclusion, i.e., the label of the root, by $conc(A) = c$, the set of all atoms (including assumptions) by $atoms(A)$, the assumptions of A by $asm(A)$, and the set of rules occurring in A by $rules(A)$.

Since we will also make use of a different representation of arguments, we recall a related result next.

Proposition 1. *([21,22]). Given an ABA framework $F = (\mathcal{L}, \mathcal{R}, \mathcal{A}, ^-)$ it holds that*

- *if A is an argument in F then $asm(A) \vdash_{rules(A)} conc(A)$ and*
- *if $X \vdash_{\mathcal{R}} c$ there is an argument A' in F with $asm(A') \subseteq X$, $rules(A') \subseteq \mathcal{R}$, and $conc(A') = c$.*

Intuitively, if there is an argument, then one can derive the conclusion of the argument, using the rules in the argument and assumptions in the argument. On the other hand, if c is derivable, using rules $\mathcal{R}$ and assumptions X, then there is an argument based on this derivation. However, the argument might not "need" all assumptions or rules in the derivation (in a sense some assumptions or rules might be redundant).

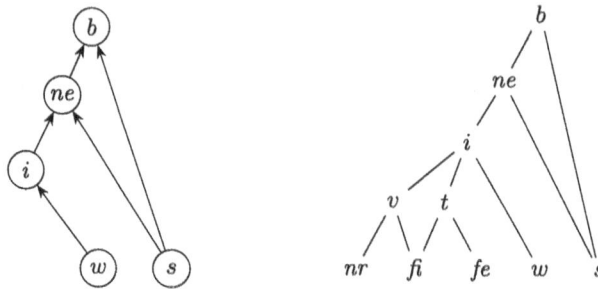

Fig. 1. On the right, an argument is derived in support of protecting against a polarizing social media platform. The dependency graph $G_{S,\mathcal{D}}(V, E)$ of a smaller argument is shown on the left.

Example 1. Let $\mathcal{L} = \{nr, f\!i, fe, w, s, v, t, i, ne, b\}$, which represent statements regarding issues of a social media platform, with the following descriptions: b stands for "platform should be moderated", ne for "defensive action is needed", i for "legal framework is insufficient", t for "threat is foreign and domestic", v for "platform makes democracy vulnerable", and the last five are assumptions with $f\!i$ standing for "false information affects voting", nr for "platform does not support democratic oversight", ex for "foreign powers exploit platform", fe for "foreign powers exploit the platform", w for "laws are inefficient", and s for "democracies should defend themselves". In Fig. 1 (right) an argument with conclusion b is shown, based on all five assumptions and using rules as indicated in the figure, e.g., $v \leftarrow nr, f\!i$. It holds that $\{nr, f\!i, fe, w, s\}$ derives b.

Argumentation semantics [9,20] can be used to determine the statuses of assumptions or arguments. For instance, arguments can be conflicting, i.e., the conclusion of one argument is the contrary of an assumption in another. A set of arguments defends an argument if all attackers of the argument are attacked by the set of arguments. In this work we mainly focus on argument structures.

3   Completing Partial Arguments

In this section we define a notion of partial arguments and completions of such arguments.

While partial arguments could be defined as subarguments, or subgraphs, of a given argument, for our aim of a computational approach involving declarative problem solving approaches, we formulate partial arguments and their completions as sets of atoms, rules, and a conclusion. This has the benefit of being more directly amenable for declarative algorithms, and also eases working with such partial arguments, since the exact tree does not need to be specified (but only its contents).

A simplification we apply is that we assume that an argument contains no two rules with the same head. While in principle arguments may have two different rules with the same head, we think this assumption is not a strong restriction for real-world arguments. Moreover, an argument with two different rules for a head (or more) can be transformed into an argument with only one such rule (by choosing one such rule and replacing subarguments which might lead even to fewer required assumptions). Towards a definition of partial arguments, we first view arguments as triples.

Definition 2. *Let $\mathcal{L}$ be a set of atoms and $\mathcal{R}$ a set of rules over $\mathcal{L}$. A derivation triple is defined as (S, D, c) where $S \subseteq \mathcal{L}$ is a set of atoms (including assumptions), $D \subseteq \mathcal{R}$ is a set of rules over S, i.e., for each $r \in D$ we find that $head(r) \in S$ and $body(r) \subseteq S$, and $c \in S$ is an atom.*

Given an argument it is straightforward to extract (S, D, c): collect all atoms in S, the conclusion in c, and rules in D. The other direction is less straightforward, since not every such triple corresponds to an argument, in a similar vein as in Proposition 1. For instance, one might be able to derive c via rules D using assumptions in S, however there might be atoms in S or rules in D that are unused in the argument.

Example 2. Consider a derivation triple $(S, D, c) = (\{s, w, ne, i, b, a\}, \{(i \leftarrow w), (b \leftarrow ne, s), (ne \leftarrow i, s)\}, b)$ with $\{s, w, a\}$ being assumptions. This derivation triple does not represent an argument since assumption a is unused in the derivation. Analogously, a derivation triple (S, D, c) would not represent an argument if some rule were unused.

For utilizing derivation triples as a representation for arguments, we define conditions on such derivation triples that ensure that they represent arguments. We will make use of an auxiliary definition that can be seen as a dependency graph in a given ABA framework [13].

Definition 3. *Given a set of atoms $\mathcal{L}$ and a set of rules $\mathcal{R}$ over $\mathcal{L}$, the directed dependency graph $G_{\mathcal{L},\mathcal{R}}(V, E)$ is composed of $V = \mathcal{L}$ and $(x, y) \in E$ if and only if there is a rule $r \in \mathcal{R}$ with $x \in body(r)$ and $head(r) = y$.*

Example 3. Consider the argument represented by the derivation triple $(\{s, w, ne, i, b\}, \{(i \leftarrow w), (b \leftarrow ne, s), (ne \leftarrow i, s)\}, b)$, $G_{S,\mathcal{D}}(V, E)$ has $V = \{s, w, ne, i, b\}$ and $E = \{(w, i), (ne, b), (s, b), (i, ne), (s, ne)\}$, as shown on the left of Fig. 1.

Based on the graph $G_{\mathcal{L},\mathcal{R}}$, we can define conditions such that derivation triples correspond directly to arguments.

Definition 4. *Let $F = (\mathcal{L}, \mathcal{R}, \mathcal{A}, ^-)$ be an ABA framework and (S, D, c) be a derivation triple such that $S \subseteq \mathcal{L}$, $D \subseteq \mathcal{R}$ over S, and $c \in S$. We say that (S, D, c) represents an argument if*

- *for each $x \in S$ we find $(S \cap \mathcal{A}) \vdash_D x$,*
- *for each $x \in S$ it holds that there is a path from x to c in $G_{S,D}$, and*
- *for each $r_1, r_2 \in D$ with $r_1 \neq r_2$ we find $head(r_1) \neq head(r_2)$.*

In words, a derivation triple (S, D, c) represents an argument, if the atoms in the argument can be derived using the assumptions and rules in the argument, the conclusion is reachable using the rules as connections in the dependency graph, and finally, no two rules share the same head (see discussion above).

We now show that the above conditions indeed imply that there is an argument based on such a derivation triple.

Theorem 1. *Let $F = (\mathcal{L}, \mathcal{R}, \mathcal{A}, {}^-)$ be an ABA framework, and (S, D, c) be a derivation triple such that $S \subseteq \mathcal{L}$, $D \subseteq \mathcal{R}$ over S and without two rules sharing a head, and $c \in S$. It holds that there is an argument A in F s.t. no two rules share a head in A with $atoms(A) = S$, $rules(A) = D$, and $conc(A) = c$ if and only if (S, D, c) represents an argument.*

Proof. Assume that A is an argument in F without two rules having the same head, with $atoms(A) = S$, $rules(A) = D$, and $conc(A) = c$. It is direct to see that $S \subseteq \mathcal{L}$, $D \subseteq \mathcal{R}$ is over S, and $c \in \mathcal{L}$ (by definition of arguments). Moreover, by previous results [21,22], see Proposition 1, it holds that $(S \cap \mathcal{A}) \vdash_{\mathcal{R}} x$ for each $x \in S$. Since A is an argument, there is a path from each node in the argument (each label) to the conclusion, and likewise in $G_{S,D}$. By assumption, it holds that no two rules share a head (satisfying the third condition in Definition 4).

For the other direction, suppose that (S, D, c) is given as defined above. Consider an arbitrary atom in S. Since each such atom is derivable from the assumptions in S using rules in D, it holds that each atom is either an assumption or the head of a rule in D. By definition, there is at most one such rule (no two rules with the same head). Thus, for each non-assumption there is exactly one rule with this non-assumption as the head.

Consider the following algorithm to construct an argument A: start with a root node with label c. If c is an assumption, then $S = \{c\}$ and $D = \emptyset$, and A is an argument for c. Otherwise, take the rule with c as the head (there is exactly one). Construct nodes for each body element of this rule, and label these nodes with the body elements. Iteratively continue this process for each child node until termination.

We now show that (i) this process terminates with assumptions in S as leaves and (ii) each element in S and D is used in this algorithm, i.e., there is a node in the argument labeled with an $x \in S$ for each element in S, and for each rule $r \in D$ we find an internal node, or root node, corresponding to the rule (a node labeled with the head and children nodes labeled with the body elements).

To see termination, consider an arbitrary path from the root node (labeled with the conclusion c) "downwards", i.e., always from heads to body elements. This path is uniquely determined by D and S (there is exactly one rule per non-assumption). Since for each atom x we find $(S \cap \mathcal{A}) \vdash_D x$, it holds that there is a derivation $(r_1, \ldots, r_n)$ with $head(r_n) = x$ starting from assumptions in $S \cap \mathcal{A}$. If r_i is in this sequence, then all its body elements are derived earlier. In turn, if there is a node in the argument labeled with the head or r_i, then all its children nodes are labeled with assumptions or heads of rules r_j with $j < i$. This holds for each path starting from the root node. Thus, each such path terminates with assumptions in the leaves (and no rule is used twice in a path).

Finally, consider an arbitrary atom $x \in S$. To see that this atom occurs in A, recall that the conclusion c is reachable from x in $G_{S,D}$. This means that there is a path from x to c in this graph. Among such paths, consider an arbitrary one. Then the reverse direction is again uniquely determined by S and D (exactly one rule per non-assumption). Then x must occur in A (by going this path in reverse). The same holds for rules, just note that both the bodies of each rule are derivable and each such element (and the head) is part of A. Then A must have a node and children nodes corresponding to this rule.

It also follows from the proof of this result that in such an argument there is no rule which contains an atom x both in the head and body. Apart from this rule being redundant, such a rule would violate the conditions of argument representation.

Based on the derivation triple definition, we define partial arguments directly as such triples, without checking conditions of representation of arguments (since partial arguments are not arguments in general).

Definition 5. *Let $F = (\mathcal{L}, \mathcal{R}, \mathcal{A},^-)$ be an ABA framework. A partial argument in F is a derivation triple (S, D, c) with $S \subseteq \mathcal{L}$, $D \subseteq \mathcal{R}$ over S s.t. no two rules have the same head, and $c \in S$.*

Example 4. Consider (S, D, b) with $S = \{nr, fi, fe, s, v, t, i, ne, b\}$, with, as before, $\{nr, fi, fe, s\}$ being assumptions. Let D contain the rules $(v \leftarrow nr, fi)$, $(t \leftarrow fi, fe)$, $(ne \leftarrow i)$, $(ne \leftarrow i, s)$, and $(b \leftarrow ne, s)$, see Fig. 2 (left). As also explicated in the figure, this is a partial argument. Compared to the one in Fig. 1 (right), an assumption and a rule are missing. In general, there may not exist a completion of a partial argument to an argument.

Given a partial argument (S, D, c), we say that another triple with the same conclusion (S', D', c) "expands" on the partial argument if $S \subseteq S'$ and $D \subseteq D'$, denoted by $(S, D, c) \sqsubseteq (S', D', c)$. For a set of partial arguments $\mathcal{I}$, this notation extends straightforwardly: $\mathcal{I} \sqsubseteq \mathcal{I}'$ if for each $(S, D, c) \in \mathcal{I}$ there is an $(S', D', c) \in \mathcal{I}'$ s.t. $(S, D, c) \sqsubseteq (S', D', c)$, and vice versa: if $(S', D', c) \in \mathcal{I}'$ then there is an $(S, D, c) \in \mathcal{I}$ with $(S, D, c) \sqsubseteq (S', D', c)$.

Definition 6. *Let $F = (\mathcal{L}, \mathcal{R}, \mathcal{A},^-)$ be an ABA framework and $\mathcal{I}$ be a set of partial arguments in F. A completion $\mathcal{I}^C$ of $\mathcal{I}$ is a set of derivation triples s.t.*

- *$\mathcal{I} \sqsubseteq \mathcal{I}^C$ and*
- *each $(S, D, c) \in \mathcal{I}^C$ represents an argument.*

Note that the derivation triples in $\mathcal{I}^C$ are not restricted to atoms, assumptions, or rules in F. A "completed" argument, represented here as a triple, might use components in F or add different atoms, assumptions, or rules. We say that the components in F are available, while components not in F are learned (or synthesized) by an $(S', D', c) \in \mathcal{I}^C$.

Example 5. Continuing Example 4, one possible completion is given by restoring the rule $i \leftarrow v, t, w$ (previously removed from $\mathcal{I}$), which is now a learned rule. Another way to complete the partial argument is to add an atom, say l, and add two rules: $l \leftarrow v, t, s$ and $i \leftarrow l$. We discuss below ways of preferring completions over others.

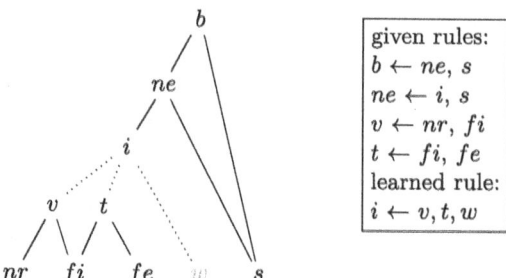

given rules:
$b \leftarrow ne, s$
$ne \leftarrow i, s$
$v \leftarrow nr, fi$
$t \leftarrow fi, fe$
learned rule:
$i \leftarrow v, t, w$

Fig. 2. Partial argument (left), and one possible completion on the right.

Given an arbitrary partial argument, in our general definition, there might not always be a completion that leads to a triple (S, D, c) representing an argument. This can be because every atom in S is already derivable from assumptions in S and rules D. In the latter case either (S, D, c) is already representing an argument or one would need to "remove" parts of S or D to represent an argument, e.g., if some parts do not reach the conclusion (one can view these as arguments with multiple conclusions).

Example 6. Consider the two arguments in Fig. 3. If we combine these two into one triple, with say i as the conclusion, there is no completion, since we cannot add any meaningful rule (all rules going back from i to assumptions are given).

Completing a partial argument might require multiple rules to be learned or, more generally, not having too many restrictions on the completion. Nonetheless, imposing certain restrictions can be useful, and, as we show in the following, can induce NP-hardness in deciding whether such a completion exists. For instance, without specific bounds, a rule might be considered that contains all atoms in the body of this rule. Perhaps such a rule is also redundant. Specifying bounds on

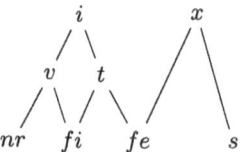

Fig. 3. Two arguments

the rule size and the number of rules can exclude redundant rules, or needlessly large rules.

We consider bounds on the number of learned rules and their bodies in this work. For two given natural numbers $n, k \geq 1$, a learned rule r must have a non-empty body with size at most k: $1 \leq |body(r)| \leq k$. Moreover, the number of learned rules must be at most n. We moreover restrict to non-empty bodies, since otherwise atoms can essentially be seen as facts. Formally, we are given an ABA framework (specifying the current and available components), a partial argument, and two constraints on the number of rules and size of bodies. If we specify these numbers in unary, then the resulting problem is NP-complete (with a non-unary representation, a number is represented compactly and the resulting rules can be large).

Theorem 2. *The problem of deciding whether there is a completion for a partial argument over a given ABA framework, and constraints on the number of learnable rules and their size is NP-hard. The problem is in NP if the number of rules that can be learned and the maximum body size are given in unary.*

Revisiting Example 5, in addition to restricting the learning of components such as rules, prioritizing which rules to learn can be essential. For this purpose we introduce preferential information of the following form.

Suppose we learn a rule of the form $h \leftarrow x_1, \ldots, x_n$. That is, we construct a rule not already known in the given ABA framework. In general these atoms do not need to be related in any particular way for the rule to be learned. With additional information, e.g., that certain atoms in a rule are related, we can construct more informed and meaningful rules.

We formalize relatedness of atoms by $T \subseteq 2^{\mathcal{L}}$, i.e., by a set of sets of atoms. We interpret $S \in T$ so that each atom in S is related to the others in S. With this approach we capture the intuition that multiple atoms appearing in the body of a rule may be connected by a given domain-specific relation. If a rule r is learned with different "topics", i.e., containing atoms from different relations, we assign a cost for each such diverging topic. Define $T(r) = \{S \in T \mid S \cap body(r) \neq \emptyset\}$. Then the cost of a learned rule is $cost(r) = |\{T(r) \mid T(r) \neq \emptyset\}| - 1$. The task is then to find a completion with minimum cost among all possible completions. The cost of a completion is the sum of costs of learned rules.

Example 7. Consider again Example 5. If we group the body of each "original" rule into one relation, e.g., $\{v, t, w\}$ in one relation S, then an optimal solution would not learn a rule like $l \leftarrow v, t, s$ since $\{s\}$ and $\{v, t, w\}$ are different relations.

Since we base our computational approaches to complete arguments in declarative problem solving, we can directly state additional optimization statements, such as prioritizing first minimizing the number of rules and then relatedness as defined above. In Example 5, we would prefer to add a single rule (which is necessary) rather than more than one rule.

Listing 1.1. Module $\pi_{rule\_generation}(n, k)$

```
1   {learnable(1..n)}.
2   {rule(R, Arg)} ← learnable(R), argument(Arg).
3   {rule(R, Arg2)} ← rule(R, Arg), argument(Arg2).
4   {head(R,X)} ← atom(X), learnable(R).
5   {body(R,X)} ← atom(X), learnable(R).
6   {body(R,X)} ← assumption(X), learnable(R).
7   ← #count {X: body(R,X)} > k, learnable(R).
8   ← not body(R,_), learnable(R).
9   ← not head(R,_), learnable(R).
10  ← body(R,X), head(R,X), learnable(R).
11  ← head(R,X), head(R,Y), X != Y, learnable(R).
12  ← rule(R1, Arg), rule(R2, Arg), head(R1, X), head(R2, X), R1 != R2.
```

---

4   Declarative Approach to Compute Completions

We first recall basics in answer set programming (ASP) [27]. A program π is composed of rules r of the form $b_0 \leftarrow b_1, \ldots, b_k, not\, b_{k+1}, \ldots, not\, b_m$, with each b_i being an atom. We say that a rule is positive if $k = m$ and that a rule is a fact if $m = 0$. A literal is an atom b_i or $not\, b_i$. A rule without head b_0 is called a constraint and a shorthand for $a \leftarrow b_1, \ldots, b_k, not\, b_{k+1}, \ldots, not\, b_m, not\, a$ for a fresh a. An atom b_i is $p(t_1, \ldots, t_n)$ with each t_j either a constant or a variable. A program π is ground if π is free of variables. For a non-ground program, let GP be the set of rules obtained by applying all substitutions from the variables to the set of constants appearing in the program. An interpretation I, i.e., a subset of all the ground atoms, satisfies a positive rule $r = h \leftarrow b_1, \ldots, b_k$ iff all positive body elements $b_1, \ldots, b_k$ being in I implies that the head atom is in I. For a program π consisting only of positive rules, let $Cl(\pi)$ be the uniquely determined interpretation I that satisfies all rules in π and no subset of I satisfies all rules in π. Interpretation I is an answer set of a ground program π if $I = Cl(\pi^I)$ where $\pi^I = \{(h \leftarrow b_1, \ldots, b_k) \mid (h \leftarrow b_1, \ldots, b_k, not\, b_{k+1}, \ldots, not\, b_m) \in \pi, \{b_{k+1}, \ldots, b_m\} \cap I = \emptyset\}$ is the reduct, and of a non-ground program π if I is an answer set of GP of π.

We make use of ASP predicates to represent a given ABA F and learnable rules or atoms. All given atoms x are defined as **atom**(x).

A given partial argument a_i with triple (S, D, c) is represented in ASP as **argument**(a_i), **rule**(r, a_i) if $r \in D$, **inarg**(x, a_i) for $x \in S$, **conclusion**(c, a_i), **head**(r, h) if $h = head(r)$, and **body**(r, b) if $b \in body(r)$.

We first describe our ASP encoding for rule generation in Listing 1.1 with parameters n and k. The encoding can generate up to n new rules to complete arguments (Line 1). Each learnable rule is assigned to some or to no argument, and has a body, with one or more body atoms assigned to the rule non-deterministically. Rules from an argument might be used in another (Line 3). Constraints from Lines 7 to 12 enforce an upper bound on the body elements of learned rules, such that each learnable rule has at least one body atom and one different atom for the head, as well as satisfying the condition of one argument not containing two rules with the same head. To complete learnable rules, we use atoms for body elements and non-assumptions for the head.

For potentially using atoms not in the given partial arguments, we use Listing 1.2. Our encoding has a reserve of extra atoms in the pool (Line 1), and non-deterministically chooses atoms to be used in Lines 2 and 3. These atoms may have been used to "fill" learnable rules, which have already been assigned to some argument(s). Module $\pi_{atom\_generation}$ extends the information available about rules, to atoms, by generating the **inarg** predicate in Lines 4 to 7.

Module π_{deriv} in Listing 1.3 ensures that all atoms in an argument are derivable via the rules in argument (Line 4), inspired by [33]. The derivation starts with the assumptions in the argument (Line 1), and derives atoms which are the head of some rule whose body is fully derived already in the argument. This is achieved in Line 3 by marking as "triggered" any rule whose body is fully derived, and in Line 2 by deriving the atoms in the head of such rules.

In Module π_{reach} (Listing 1.4), we ensure that arguments are connected by checking, within each argument, that its conclusion is reachable via the rules in the argument, from every assumption in the argument, and from every atom head of a rule in the argument.

Listing 1.5 encodes preferences. We use a weak constraint for implementing preferences over rules chosen in a completion (Line 3) and the **related**$(rel, atom)$ predicate for representing relations. For each learned rule in the completion, the ASP solver incurs a cost of one for the rule and each relation in the rule, if this rule contains atoms associated with more than one relation.

Listing 1.2. Module $\pi_{atom\_generation}(l, u)$

```
1   pool_atom(l..u).
2   {atom(A)} ← pool_atom(A).
3   {assumption(A)} ← pool_asm(A).
4   inarg(X,Arg) ← rule(R,Arg), head(R,X), learnable(R).
5   inarg(X,Arg) ← rule(R,Arg), body(R,X), learnable(R).
6   inarg(X,Arg) ← rule(R,Arg), head(R,X).
7   inarg(X,Arg) ← rule(R,Arg), body(R,X).
```

Listing 1.3. Module π_{deriv}

```
1  derivable(X,Arg) ← assumption(X), inarg(X, Arg).
2  derivable(X,Arg) ← head(R,X),triggered(R, Arg), rule(R, Arg), inarg(X,
       Arg).
3  triggered(R,Arg) ← rule(R,Arg), derivable(X,Arg) : body(R,X).
4  ← atom(X), inarg(X, Arg), not derivable(X, Arg).
```

Listing 1.4. Module π_{reach}

```
1  start(X, Arg) ← assumption(X), inarg(X, Arg).
2  start(X, Arg) ← head(R,X), not conclusion(X,Arg), inarg(X, Arg), rule(R,
       Arg).
3  reach(X,Y, Arg) ← head(R,Y), body(R,X), rule(R, Arg).
4  reach(X,C, Arg) ← reach(X,D, Arg), body(R,D), head(R,C), rule(R, Arg).
5  ← conclusion(I,Arg),start(X,Arg), not reach(X,I,Arg),inarg(X,Arg),inarg(I,
       Arg).
```

5   Experimental Evaluation

In this section we report on an empirical evaluation of our ASP-based prototype.

Instance Generation. To the best of our knowledge, there is currently no real-world benchmark set for ABA directly amenable to partial arguments. We used ABA frameworks from the International Competition on Computational Models of Argumentation (ICCMA) 2023 [30]. We included instances with 100, 500, and 2000 atoms, containing 10 to 600 assumptions. For each ABA framework, we generate a problem instance suitable for our prototype by first constructing arguments within a 300 s time limit. For subsets of the assumptions of size 1 to 5, we constructed arguments using all of the assumptions in the subset, requiring that they have a unique last derivation (a unique conclusion), and discarding trivial arguments with only one rule. Each instance suitable for our system is generated by randomly picking up to 10 constructed arguments for the respective ABA framework, and uniformly removing a rule with $\frac{1}{2}$ probability. For relatedness, we considered two variants: *i.* by fixing the number of relatedness relations

Listing 1.5. Module π_{pref}

```
1  in_rule(R,X) ← atom(X), 1 body(R,X); head(R,X)}, learnable(R).
2  in_rule(R,X) ← assumption(X), 1 {body(R,X); head(R,X)}, learnable(R).
3  ⇐ related(T1, X), related(T2, Y), T1!=T2, learnable(R), in_rule(R,X),
       in_rule(R,Y). [1@1, R,T1]
```

Table 1. Comparison of random relatedness and rule-based relatedness.

Pref	atoms	#total	Solved	Avg. dist.	TOs	median (s)
Rand. relatedness	100	64	52	8.23	12	2.191
	500	77	35	13.65	42	14.28
	2000	76	19	14.15	57	9.78
Rule-based relatedness	100	64	**55**	7.09	**9**	1.96
	500	77	**46**	15.13	**31**	26.18
	2000	76	**42**	18.88	**34**	23.33

to 10 and randomly assigning body elements to these, and *ii.* by iterating over all derivation rules in the selected arguments, and grouping all unassigned body elements into a fresh relation. Overall, this resulted in 217 instances. The max. number of learnable rules and max. body size are parameters, and in our experiments are set to 20 and 5 respectively.

Evaluation. All experiments were carried out on a Linux 8GB i5 Intel machine, with a 5 min time limit and with clingo 5.6.2 [26]. We compare the performance and quality on the two datasets, one with randomly assigned relatedness relations, and the other with rule-based relatedness. For the quality of each completion of a set of partial arguments, we compare the learned rules to their equivalents (same head) in the originally constructed arguments, and we call the distance of the completion from the originally constructed arguments the sum of the count of atoms appearing in one rule but not the other.

In Table 1 we show the count of solved instances, unsolved instances in terms of timeouts, the average distance from the originally constructed arguments and their median running time. Across all instances we see an improvement in terms of number of solved instances, and a decrease in timeouts when using relatedness assigned based on the derivation rules of the selected arguments from which an instance was generated. We show the average distance separately in Table 2, computed only on the instances solved with the two types of relatedness. On these we see decreased distance overall of completions from the originally selected arguments. Regarding runtime, we see complementary results for the instances based on the 100-atoms ABA frameworks (where most instances are solved with both relatedness assignments), i.e. one relatedness assignment improves runtime over the other.

6   Related Works

Learning concepts generalizing over specific data is a major aim of AI, and it is pursued, e.g., in the form of learning a general function in statistical approaches or a logic program, such as in inductive logic programming (ILP) [15]. In ABA learning [18,19,37,40] the authors use concepts borrowed from ILP to learn

Table 2. Average distance of the completion.

#atoms	100	500	2000
#solved	50	32	18
Avg. dist. (Rand. r.)	7.92	**12.65**	13.50
Avg. dist. (Rule-based r.)	**6**	13.5	**12.72**

an ABA framework that semantically covers a set of given positive examples, and does not cover any of a given set of negative examples. A notion of repair of ABA frameworks was recently proposed [38] which aims to modify an ABA framework to achieve consistency. Argument mining and enthymemes were also recently studied [5] in the context of logical argumentation. In contrast, we focus on completing arguments in ABA, and provide both a declarative approach and foundational properties.

7   Conclusions

We studied the computational problem of completing partial arguments. We provided a characterization of representation of tree-based arguments on sets, and we showed that in general this problem is NP-hard. We presented a prototype of implementing completion in ASP, and an empirical evaluation of this prototype.

For future work, we think that our approach can be fruitfully combined with machine learning approaches so that the result is, e.g., neuro-symbolic. For instance, one can utilize learning approaches to learn preferential information or available rules, and apply our ASP-based implementation. Another direction is to learn how to complete arguments, where our approach could be compiled to act as constraints in learning so that only actual arguments are learned. This related to the notion of shields [2] that restrict learning and to a recently proposed approach [1] using ASP to address and fix learned structures. We think a combination of these techniques with our approach has potential to advance learning in the field of computational argumentation.

Acknowledgments. This research was funded in whole or in part by the Austrian Science Fund (FWF) P35632. For open access purposes, the authors have applied a CC BY public copyright license to any author accepted manuscript version arising from this submission.

References

1. Adam, S., Eiter, T.: ASP-driven emergency planning for norm violations in reinforcement learning. In: Walsh, T., Shah, J., Kolter, Z. (eds.) Proceedings of the AAAI, pp. 14772–14780. AAAI Press (2025)

2. Alshiekh, M., Bloem, R., Ehlers, R., Könighofer, B., Niekum, S., Topcu, U.: Safe reinforcement learning via shielding. In: McIlraith, S.A., Weinberger, K.Q. (eds.) Proceedings of the AAAI, pp. 2669–2678. AAAI Press (2018)
3. Atkinson, K., et al.: Towards artificial argumentation. AI Mag. **38**(3), 25–36 (2017)
4. Baroni, P., Gabbay, D., Giacomin, M., van der Torre, L. (eds.): Handbook of Formal Argumentation. College Publications (2018)
5. Ben-Naim, J., David, V., Hunter, A.: Understanding enthymemes in argument maps: bridging argument mining and logic-based argumentation. CoRR **abs/2408.08648** (2024)
6. Besnard, P., Hunter, A.: A review of argumentation based on deductive arguments. In: Baroni, P., Gabbay, D., Giacomin, M., van der Torre, L. (eds.) Handbook of Formal Argumentation, chap. 9, pp. 437–484. College Publications (2018)
7. Black, E., Hunter, A.: Using enthymemes in an inquiry dialogue system. In: Padgham, L., Parkes, D.C., Müller, J.P., Parsons, S. (eds.) Proceedings of the AAMAS, pp. 437–444. IFAAMAS (2008)
8. Black, E., Hunter, A.: A relevance-theoretic framework for constructing and deconstructing enthymemes. J. Log. Comput. **22**(1), 55–78 (2012)
9. Bondarenko, A., Dung, P.M., Kowalski, R.A., Toni, F.: An abstract, argumentation-theoretic approach to default reasoning. Artif. Intell. **93**, 63–101 (1997)
10. Brewka, G., Eiter, T., Truszczynski, M.: Answer set programming at a glance. Commun. ACM **54**(12), 92–103 (2011)
11. Caminada, M.: Rationality postulates: applying argumentation theory for non-monotonic reasoning. In: Baroni, P., Gabbay, D., Giacomin, M., van der Torre, L. (eds.) Handbook of Formal Argumentation, chap. 15, pp. 771–795. College Publications (2018)
12. Caminada, M., Amgoud, L.: On the evaluation of argumentation formalisms. Artif. Intell. **171**(5–6), 286–310 (2007)
13. Craven, R., Toni, F.: Argument graphs and assumption-based argumentation. Artif. Intell. **233**, 1–59 (2016)
14. Craven, R., Toni, F., Cadar, C., Hadad, A., Williams, M.: Efficient argumentation for medical decision-making. In: Brewka, G., Eiter, T., McIlraith, S.A. (eds.) Proceedings of the KR, pp. 598–602. AAAI Press (2012)
15. Cropper, A., Dumancic, S.: Inductive logic programming at 30: a new introduction. J. Artif. Intell. Res. **74**, 765–850 (2022)
16. Čyras, K., Fan, X., Schulz, C., Toni, F.: Assumption-based argumentation: disputes, explanations, preferences. In: Baroni, P., Gabbay, D., Giacomin, M., van der Torre, L. (eds.) Handbook of Formal Argumentation, chap. 7, pp. 365–408. College Publications (2018)
17. Čyras, K., Oliveira, T., Karamlou, A., Toni, F.: Assumption-based argumentation with preferences and goals for patient-centric reasoning with interacting clinical guidelines. Argument Comput. **12**(2), 149–189 (2021)
18. De Angelis, E., Proietti, M., Toni, F.: ABA learning via ASP. In: Pontelli, E., (eds.) Proceedings 39th International Conference on Logic Programming, ICLP 2023, Imperial College London, UK, 9th July 2023 - 15th July 2023. EPTCS, vol. 385, pp. 1–8 (2023)
19. De Angelis, E., Proietti, M., Toni, F.: Learning brave assumption-based argumentation frameworks via ASP. In: Endriss, U., et al. (eds.) Proceedings of the ECAI, Frontiers in Artificial Intelligence and Applications, vol. 392, pp. 3445–3452. IOS Press (2024)

20. Dung, P.M.: On the acceptability of arguments and its fundamental role in non-monotonic reasoning, logic programming and n-person games. Artif. Intell. **77**(2), 321–358 (1995)
21. Dung, P.M., Kowalski, R.A., Toni, F.: Dialectic proof procedures for assumption-based, admissible argumentation. Artif. Intell. **170**(2), 114–159 (2006)
22. Dung, P.M., Toni, F., Mancarella, P.: Some design guidelines for practical argumentation systems. In: Baroni, P., Cerutti, F., Giacomin, M., Simari, G.R. (eds.) Proceedings of the COMMA, Frontiers in Artificial Intelligence and Applications, vol. 216, pp. 183–194. IOS Press (2010)
23. Gabbay, D., Giacomin, M., Simari, G.R., Thimm, M. (eds.): Handbook of Formal Argumentation, vol. 2. College Publications (2021)
24. García, A.J., Simari, G.R.: Argumentation based on logic programming. In: Baroni, P., Gabbay, D., Giacomin, M., van der Torre, L. (eds.) Handbook of Formal Argumentation, chap. 8, pp. 409–435. College Publications (2018)
25. Gebser, M., Kaminski, R., Kaufmann, B., Schaub, T.: Answer Set Solving in Practice. Synthesis Lectures on Artificial Intelligence and Machine Learning. Morgan & Claypool Publishers (2012)
26. Gebser, M., Kaminski, R., Kaufmann, B., Schaub, T.: Multi-shot ASP solving with clingo. Theory Pract. Log. Program. **19**(1), 27–82 (2019)
27. Gelfond, M., Lifschitz, V.: The stable model semantics for logic programming. In: Proceedings of the ICLP/SLP, pp. 1070–1080. MIT Press (1988)
28. Gordon, T.F., Prakken, H., Walton, D.: The Carneades model of argument and burden of proof. Artif. Intell. **171**(10–15), 875–896 (2007)
29. Hunter, A.: Real arguments are approximate arguments. In: Proceedings of the AAAI, 22–26 July 2007, Vancouver, British Columbia, Canada, pp. 66–71. AAAI Press (2007)
30. Järvisalo, M., Lehtonen, T., Niskanen, A.: ICCMA 2023: 5th international competition on computational models of argumentation. Artif. Intell. **342**, 104311 (2025)
31. Kakas, A.C., Moraitis, P., Spanoudakis, N.I.: GORGIAS: applying argumentation. Argument Comput. **10**(1), 55–81 (2019)
32. Lehtonen, T., Wallner, J.P., Järvisalo, M.: An answer set programming approach to argumentative reasoning in the ASPIC+ framework. In: Calvanese, D., Erdem, E., Thielscher, M. (eds.) Proceedings of the KR, pp. 636–646 (2020)
33. Lehtonen, T., Wallner, J.P., Järvisalo, M.: Declarative algorithms and complexity results for assumption-based argumentation. J. Artif. Intell. Res. **71**, 265–318 (2021)
34. Modgil, S., Prakken, H.: Abstract rule-based argumentation. In: Baroni, P., Gabbay, D., Giacomin, M., van der Torre, L. (eds.) Handbook of Formal Argumentation, chap. 6, pp. 287–364. College Publications (2018)
35. Odekerken, D., Borg, A., Bex, F.: Estimating stability for efficient argument-based inquiry. In: Prakken, H., Bistarelli, S., Santini, F., Taticchi, C. (eds.) Proceedings of the COMMA, Frontiers in Artificial Intelligence and Applications, vol. 326, pp. 307–318. IOS Press (2020)
36. Prakken, H., Sartor, G.: Law and logic: a review from an argumentation perspective. Artif. Intell. **227**, 214–245 (2015)
37. Proietti, M., Toni, F.: Learning assumption-based argumentation frameworks. In: Muggleton, S.H., Tamaddoni-Nezhad, A. (eds.) Proceedings of the ILP, LNCS, vol. 13779, pp. 100–116. Springer (2022)
38. Rapberger, A., Ulbricht, M.: Repairing assumption-based argumentation frameworks. In: Marquis, P., Ortiz, M., Pagnucco, M. (eds.) Proceedings of the KR (2024)

39. Schreiber, G.: Knowledge engineering. In: van Harmelen, F., Lifschitz, V., Porter, B.W. (eds.) Handbook of Knowledge Representation, Foundations of Artificial Intelligence, vol. 3, pp. 929–946. Elsevier (2008)
40. Tirsi, C., Proietti, M., Toni, F.: Abalearn: an automated logic-based learning system for ABA frameworks. In: Basili, R., Lembo, D., Limongelli, C., Orlandini, A. (eds.) Proceedings of the AIxIA, LNCS, vol. 14318, pp. 3–16. Springer (2023)
41. Toulmin, S.E.: The Uses of Argument, Updated Edition. Cambridge University Press (2008)

Constraint Satisfaction
and Optimization

Engineering and Evaluating Multi-objective Pseudo-Boolean Optimizers

Christoph Jabs$^{(\boxtimes)}$ [iD], Jeremias Berg [iD], and Matti Järvisalo [iD]

Department of Computer Science, University of Helsinki, Helsinki, Finland
{christoph.jabs,jeremias.berg,matti.jarvisalo}@helsinki.fi

Abstract. Various real-world settings give rise to combinatorial optimization problems with multiple conflicting objectives, motivating the development of practical approaches to the challenging task of finding Pareto-optimal solutions to declarative models of multi-objective problems. In this work we focus on multi-objective optimization over pseudo-Boolean constraints (MO-PBO) as an extension of propositional clauses and, at the same time, an important class of 0–1 linear constraints. We provide a first-of-kind cross-community evaluation of a selection of recently-proposed approaches applicable to MO-PBO, including first implementations of native MO-PBO algorithms we provide as well as approaches based on integer linear programming techniques and a translation-based approach to MO-MaxSAT, providing insights into the current state-of-the-art approaches to MO-PBO. In terms of algorithmic advances, we engineer MO-PBO solvers by harnessing recent advances in decision procedures for pseudo-Boolean constraints in order to lift multi-objective approaches recently developed for multi-objective optimization under propositional constraints (i.e., MO-MaxSAT) to the realm of MO-PBO. Extending on recent work on certified MO-MaxSAT solving, we also realize certified multi-objective pseudo-Boolean optimization by implementing proof logging for both our native MO-PBO approach and the translation-based MO-MaxSAT approach.

Keywords: Multi-objective optimization · pseudo-Boolean optimization · empirical evaluation · certified optimization

1 Introduction

The declarative approach—from mixed integer linear programming (ILP) [12] to finite-domain constraint optimization [64] and Boolean satisfiability (SAT) [8] based approaches including maximum satisfiability (MaxSAT) [3] together with its extensions to optimization modulo theories [62], and pseudo-Boolean optimization [66]—is key to efficiently solving various NP-hard combinatorial optimization

Work financially supported by Academy of Finland under grants 356046 and 362987. The authors thank the Finnish Computing Competence Infrastructure (FCCI) for computational and data storage resources.

© The Author(s), under exclusive license to Springer Nature Switzerland AG 2026
G. Casini et al. (Eds.): JELIA 2025, LNAI 16093, pp. 115–134, 2026.
https://doi.org/10.1007/978-3-032-04587-4_8

problems arising from real-world settings. Various different algorithmic techniques have been developed for the various declarative paradigms, ranging from linear programming based branch-and-cut algorithms standardly employed in ILP [12] to unsatisfiability-based search via iterative use of decision procedures in logic-based formalisms such as MaxSAT and its extensions [3]. This richness can be considered a virtue, with each paradigm offering its distinct features in terms of the constraint language and algorithmic approaches.

From MaxSAT to ILP, a majority of work on practical algorithms and their implementations towards developing increasingly effective declarative approaches to combinatorial optimization has focused on single-objective optimization problems. As real-world settings often intrinsically involve multiple conflicting objectives [29], beyond a plethora of heuristic approaches to multi-objective optimization [14], there has recently been interest in extending the reach of declarative approaches to enable efficiently solving multi-objective combinatorial optimization problems in various declarative paradigms, including ILP [25,34,42], finite-domain constraint optimization [10,55,67,74], and MaxSAT [15,48,68]. Some approaches address more restrictive settings, being geared to either e.g. bi-objective problems [10,48] or leximax optimization [11], while others do not restrict the number of objectives and in particular enable computing representative Pareto-optimal solutions [15,68] for every non-dominated point in the solution space—a task which is arguable noticeably more challenging than finding a representative optimal solution in the single-objective case.

In this work, we focus on engineering and evaluating practical approaches to solving multi-objective optimization problems expressed as pseudo-Boolean (PB) constraints [66], i.e., linear inequalities with integer coefficients over binary variables. Also known as 0–1 or binary linear constraints, PB constraints constitute on one hand a central fragment of integer programming, and on the other hand a natural generalization of conjunctive normal form clausal propositional constraints employed in SAT and MaxSAT. What makes multi-objective pseudo-Boolean optimization (MO-PBO) particularly interesting from the algorithmic perspective is that, firstly, recent approaches to multi-objective integer-linear programming [25,34,42] are directly applicable, and, secondly—as we will detail in this paper—recent advances in MO-MaxSAT can be harnessed in the context of MO-PBO either (i) by lifting multi-objective MaxSAT solving approaches [15,48,68] to obtain their native MO-PBO counterparts by employing recent advances in PB decision procedures [21,22,33], or (ii) by translating MO-PBO instances to MO-MaxSAT and employing MO-MaxSAT solvers. Contrasting the multi-objective ILP approaches, both of these two approaches allow for realizing—to the best of our knowledge for the first time— certified MO-PBO solving, i.e., integrating proof logging capabilities to MO-PBO solvers for obtaining certificates as guarantees for outputting exactly the sought-after solutions with reasonable overhead. The certificates are achieved by harnessing recent progress in certified MO-MaxSAT [47] and MaxSAT solving [5,6,45,72] via the VERIPB proof format [9,38]. Furthermore, we perform a first-of-kind cross-community evaluation of a wide selection of recently-proposed approaches applicable to MO-PBO, including the native MO-PBO algorithms we propose, the translation-based approach to MO-MaxSAT employing various recently-proposed MO-MaxSAT solvers, and approaches developed for multi-objective ILP solving. The results show that—both ones based on logical reasoning and those relying on classical ILP techniques—the three different approaches each have their role in contributing to the state of the art in MO-PBO solving. We provide open-source implementations of the MO-MaxSAT-based and native MO-PBO approaches, constituting the first certifying solvers for Pareto optimization under pseudo-Boolean constraints. The implementation together with benchmarks used, and empirical data reported on in this paper are available at

https://bitbucket.org/coreo-group/multi-objective-pbo.

2 Multi-objective Pseudo-Boolean Optimization

A literal ℓ is a $\{0, 1\}$-valued Boolean variable x or its negation $\overline{x}$. A normalized pseudo-Boolean (PB) constraint is a 0–1 linear inequality of form $C = (S \geq b)$, where $S = \sum_{i=1}^{k} c_i \ell_i$ is called a PB expression, c_i are positive integers, and b a non-negative integer often called the bound of the constraint. A PB formula is a conjunction of PB constraints $F = (C_1 \wedge C_2 \wedge \cdots \wedge C_N)$, often represented as a set of constraints.

An assignment α assigns a value in $\{0, 1\}$ to each variable x. An assignment α is extended to literals via $\alpha(\overline{x}) = 1 - \alpha(x)$ and further to PB expressions, constraints, and formulas, respectively, via

$$\alpha(S) = \sum_{i=1}^{k} c_i \alpha(\ell_i), \alpha(C) = \begin{cases} 1 \text{ if } \alpha(S) \geq b \\ 0 \text{ otherwise} \end{cases}, \ \alpha(F) = \min\{\alpha(C) \mid C \in F\}.$$

An assignment α for which $\alpha(F) = 1$ *satisfies* F, in which case α is a *solution* to F. When convenient, we view an assignment α as the set of literals α assigns to 1.

We write $r \Rightarrow (\sum_{i=1}^{k} c_i \ell_i \geq b)$ for the reified constraint $b\overline{r} + \sum_{i=1}^{k} c_i \ell_i \geq b$ expressing that the variable r implies the constraint $\sum_{i=1}^{k} c_i \ell_i \geq b$, and respectively $r \Leftarrow (\sum_{i=1}^{k} c_i \ell_i \geq b)$ for $Mr + \sum_{i=1}^{k} c_i \overline{\ell_i} \geq M$ where $M = \sum_{i=1}^{k} c_i - b + 1$ expressing that the constraint implies r.

A multi-objective pseudo-Boolean optimization (MO-PBO) instance consists of a formula F, and a tuple of p linear objective functions $(O_1, \ldots, O_p)$, represented as PB expressions. For two solutions α and β to F, α *dominates* β (in terms of Pareto optimality [29]) if $\alpha(O_i) \leq \beta(O_i)$ for all $i = 1, \ldots, p$, and $\alpha(O_i) < \beta(O_i)$ for some i. A solution α is *Pareto-optimal* if no other solution to F dominates α. We consider the MO-PBO task of finding the *non-dominated set*

$$\{(\alpha(O_1), \ldots, \alpha(O_p)) \mid \alpha \text{ is Pareto-optimal}\},$$

i.e., the objective values of all Pareto-optimal solutions, and typically one solution corresponding to each element in the non-dominated set. Note that this task is slightly different from finding all Pareto-optimal solutions, as there might be multiple solutions corresponding to the same element in the non-dominated set.

3   Relating MO-PBO to MO-MaxSAT and MO-ILP

Closely related to MO-PBO are multi-objective maximum satisfiability (MO-MaxSAT) and multi-objective integer linear programming (MO-ILP). In contrast to MO-PBO, in MO-MaxSAT all constraints are clauses, i.e., at-least-one constraints that have coefficients $c_i = 1$ and bound $b = 1$. MO-ILP differs from MO-PBO in that variables can take any integer values, with constraints taking the form $\sum_{i=1}^{k} c_i x_i \geq b$ with $c_i, b \in \mathbb{Z}$.

3.1   MO-MaxSAT

Employing an MO-MaxSAT algorithm to solve MO-PBO instances requires first encoding the PB constraints as clauses [28,49]. The encoded clausal instance can then be solved with an MO-MaxSAT solver to find the non-dominated set. In terms of practical approaches to MO-MaxSAT solving, Soh et al. [53,68] proposed an MO-MaxSAT algorithm based on enumeration of so-called P-minimal models. More recently, Cortes et al. [15] proposed a lower-bounding algorithm that uses P-minimal as a subroutine, Guerreiro et al. [41] extended on previous work employing minimal correction set enumeration to find Pareto-optimal solutions [54,71], and Jabs et al. [48] proposed BiOptSat, a MaxSAT-based algorithm applicable to bi-objective problems. In our work, we focus on the P-minimal and BiOptSat algorithm and discuss them in more detail in Sect. 4.

3.2   MO-ILP

As (MO-)PBO is a special case of (MO-)ILP, MO-ILP algorithms can be directly applied to solve MO-PBO instances. Various algorithms for MO-ILP have been recently proposed [4,18,25,34–36,42,63,69,70]. The main approaches to MO-ILP can be categorized into two classes: (i) branch-and-bound (B&B) search algorithms [52] and (ii) algorithms that solve a sequence of single-objective scalarizations of the MO problem [18].

Multi-objective B&B algorithms extend upper and lower bounds, used in single-objective B&B for pruning of search nodes, to so-called *upper and lower bound sets* [30]. Furthermore, the branching rules are extended with *objective / Pareto branching* [70], where the search space is split in objective space rather than variable space. Forget et al. [35] present a B&B framework for MO-ILP, which was later on extended with objective branching for any number of objectives [34].

Another approach to MO-ILP solving is based on single-objective scalarizations of the multi-objective problem [18,25]. Typically, optimal solutions to the single-objective scalarizations will be guaranteed to be Pareto-optimal with

Input: $F, (O_1, \ldots, O_p)$
1 $F_W \leftarrow F$ sat, $\alpha \leftarrow \texttt{Oracle}(F_W)$
2 **while** sat **do**
3 | **while** sat **do**
4 | | $F_W \leftarrow F_W \wedge \bigvee_{i=1}^{p} O_i < \alpha(O_i)$
5 | | sat, $\alpha \leftarrow \texttt{Oracle}(F_W \wedge \bigwedge_{i=1}^{p} O_i \leq \alpha(O_i))$
6 | **yield** α as Pareto-optimal
7 | sat, $\alpha \leftarrow \texttt{Oracle}(F_W)$

Algorithm 1. The P-minimal algorithm.

respect to the original problem instance. After finding one such optimal solution, the algorithm will then split the search space into multiple regions, and solve another scalarization for each subregion. Dominguez-Rios et al. [25] improve on previous work in this line by proposing a new strategy of selecting which search region to explore next, and a new strategy of partitioning the search space when a solution is found.

4 Extending MO-MaxSAT Algorithms to PBO

As one of our contributions, we provide an open-source native MO-PBO level implementation of the state-of-the-art MO-MaxSAT algorithms P-minimal [53, 68] and BiOptSat [48]. For this, we phrase the algorithms in terms of MO-PBO and explain how to adapt them to work on PB constraints natively by employing a decision procedure for PB constraints.

4.1 *P*-minimal

The P-minimal algorithm [53, 68] for MO-MaxSAT can be viewed as multi-objective solution-improving search that iteratively queries a constraint oracle for a solution α to the constraints, and then restricts the search space with further constraints that exclude all solutions dominated by α. This continues until the non-dominated set is found.

Algorithm 1 details P-minimal. Here $\texttt{Oracle}(F)$ denotes a query to a constraint oracle for a solution to the formula F. The query returns a Boolean sat indicating whether F has solutions, and one such solution α in the positive case. After initializing the working formula F_W to F and obtaining a solution α of F_W, the main loop of P-minimal (Lines 2–7 of Algorithm 1) iteratively adds a disjunction of constraints (in practice turned into a conjunction via reification, see details in next paragraph) that we call a Pareto dominance cut or PD cut for short, to block all solutions dominated by α to F_W on Line 4. Then it queries the oracle for a solution that dominates α on Line 5 by using temporary constraints that require the next solution to dominate α. When the oracle determines that there are no solutions that dominate α, α is guaranteed to be Pareto-optimal, and the search then continues by dropping the temporary constraints.

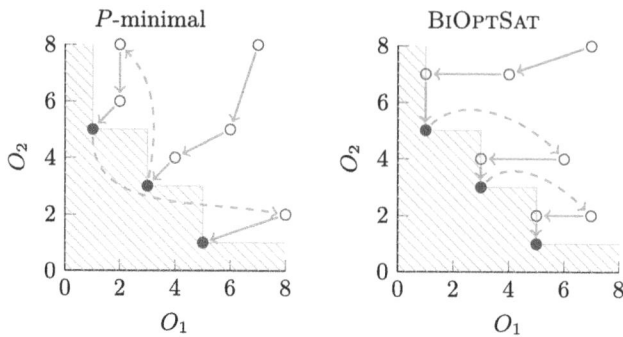

Fig. 1. Illustrations of the search trajectories of the P-minimal and BIOPTSAT algorithms.

Example 1. Let F and (O_1, O_2) constitute an MO-PBO instance with the non-dominated set $\{(1,5),(3,3),(5,1)\}$. Figure 1 illustrates this instance in objective space where the shaded area represents objective values for which no solutions exist. Assume that P-minimal is invoked on this instance and that on Line 1 we obtain α with $O_1(\alpha) = 7$ and $O_2(\alpha) = 8$. P-minimal now introduces a PD cut $(O_1 < 7 \vee O_2 < 8)$ and temporarily forces the next found solution to dominate α, by adding the constraints $O_1 \leq 7$ and $O_2 \leq 8$. By continuing the algorithm, we might find solutions with objective values $(6,5)$, $(4,4)$, and $(3,3)$, as illustrated in Fig. 1 (left). After this, the oracle call on Line 5 returns false, and the temporary constraints are dropped. On Line 7 we might then find a solution with objective values $(2,8)$ (illustrated with a dashed arrow). A possible search trajectory discovering the entire non-dominated set before the algorithm terminates is illustrated on the left in Fig. 1.

In the context of MO-MaxSAT, P-minimal is realized by instantiating `Oracle` as an incremental SAT-solver and encoding bound constraints $(O_i < \alpha(O_i))$ on the objectives as clauses. To lift P-minimal to MO-PBO, we use the pseudo-Boolean conflict-driven conflict learning [60] solver ROUNDINGSAT [21,22,33] as the oracle. The disjunctive constraint $\bigvee_{i=1}^{p} O_i < \alpha(O_i)$ is represented conjunctively as the reified constraints $r_i \Rightarrow (O_i < \alpha(O_i))$ and the clause $\sum_{i=1}^{p} r_i \geq 1$. The temporary constraints are realized via reified constraints and an incremental assumption interface [27,60] offered by ROUNDINGSAT out of the box. All in all, operating natively on the level of MO-PBO significantly simplifies the P-minimal algorithm compared to the case of MO-MaxSAT, as on the MO-PBO level there is no need to resort to (complex) clausal encodings of PB constraints.

4.2 BIOPTSAT

The BIOPTSAT framework [48] (see Algorithm 2) is specific to solving problems with two objectives, and works by enumerating the non-dominated points in increasing order for one objective and in decreasing order for the other. The

Input: $F, (O_1, O_2)$
1 $F_W \leftarrow F$ sat, $\alpha \leftarrow \texttt{Oracle}(F_W)$
2 **while** sat **do**
3 $\quad$ $\alpha \leftarrow \texttt{Minimize}(O_1 \; s.t. \; F_W)$
4 $\quad$ $\alpha \leftarrow \texttt{Minimize}(O_2 \; s.t. \; F_W \wedge O_1 \leq \alpha(O_1))$
5 $\quad$ **yield** α as Pareto-optimal
6 $\quad$ $F_W \leftarrow F_W \wedge O_2 < \alpha(O_2)$
7 $\quad$ sat, $\alpha \leftarrow \texttt{Oracle}(F_W)$

Algorithm 2. The BIOPTSAT framework.

approach first minimizes the first objective (Line 3), and then subsequently minimizes the second objective while fixing the value of the first (Line 4). Thereby, the obtained solution is guaranteed to be Pareto-optimal. The search then repeats after forcing the second objective to improve. This search strategy is also known as the lexicographic method [58,73].

Practical instantiations [48] of BIOPTSAT use solution-improving search for the minimization procedure on Line 4 but differ in how the minimization procedure over the first objective (Line 3) is instantiated. We focus on the variants based on Sat-Unsat (solution-improving search) and OLL [2,44,61] as the ones deemed most effective in previous work on MO-MaxSAT. In the Sat-Unsat variant, the oracle is queried for increasingly better solutions with respect to O_1 by temporarily adding the constraint $O_1 < O_1(\alpha)$ to the oracle, where α is the last-found solution. In contrast, in the OLL variant the oracle is queried for a solution setting all literals in O_1 to false. If such a solution does not exist, the oracle provides an explanation of the inconsistency, which is subsequently resolved by OLL and the objective reformulated. Both BIOPTSAT variants are implemented as described in previous work on solution-improving search and OLL for pseudo-Boolean optimization [1,23].

Example 2. Similarly to Example 1, we detail a possible search trajectory of BIOPTSAT in the Sat-Unsat variant on the right in Fig. 1. In minimizing O_1 BIOPTSAT Sat-Unsat starts by obtaining a solution with objective values $(7,8)$. Next, the oracle is queried again with the additional constraint $O_1 < 7$ added. This process might lead to first finding a solution at $(4,7)$ and then one at $(1,7)$, after which the oracle call with the additional constraint $O_1 < 1$ returns false. BIOPTSAT now continues to minimizing O_2 with the same solution-improving search procedure, while forcing the objective value of O_1 to remain minimal, but adding the constraint $O_1 \leq 1$. Once O_2 cannot be further minimized at $(1,5)$, the solution is returned as Pareto-optimal, the constraints on O_1 are dropped, and the constraint $O_2 < 5$ is added to the oracle. The loop on Line 2 then starts over, and the entire instance is solved as illustrated in the right-hand side of Fig. 1.

5 Certifying Pareto Optimality

Our second contribution concerns certified multi-objective pseudo-Boolean optimization. Proof logging—i.e., writing a machine-checkable proof of the reasoning steps performed by a solver, and afterwards verifying the reasoning steps made by the solver to obtain a guarantee on the correctness of the result produced—has become a readily-available feature in state-of-the-art SAT solvers [16,17,39] and has more recently been extended to single-objective MaxSAT [5,6,45,72] and single-objective PBO solvers [65]. The line of work on proof logging single-objective optimization is mainly based on the pseudo-Boolean VERIPB proof format [9,38]. In addition to a single objective, VERIPB supports certifying that the computed solutions are minimal with respect to a user-specified preorder over solutions. While originally proposed for proof logging symmetry and dominance breaking [9], the preorder in VERIPB has more recently been shown to generalize an objective in the sense of allowing VERIPB to be used to certify the correctness of a discovered non-dominated set in the multi-objective setting, without extending the proof system itself [47].

In this section, we detail how the same proof logging approach proposed for MO-MaxSAT [47] can be used for proof logging MO-PBO solvers, either based on a translation to the MaxSAT paradigm or by natively operating on PB constraints. For the sake of brevity, we will not explain the VERIPB proof system in detail, we refer the interested reader instead to previous work on VERIPB [9, 38], especially in the multi-objective setting [47]. While early work on verifying results from integer programming solvers exists [13,24,43], we are not aware of any work on verifying MO-ILP results.

5.1 Proof Logging for MO-PBO via MO-MaxSAT

Since MO-PBO can be encoded as MO-MaxSAT and solved by existing MO-MaxSAT solvers, a natural approach toward proof-logging MO-PBO is to make use of the existing approaches to creating VERIPB proofs for various MO-MaxSAT algorithms, including P-minimal and BIOPTSAT [47]. However, this requires certifying the translation from an MO-PBO instance $(F, (O_1, \ldots, O_p))$ to a (clausal) MO-MaxSAT instance $(\texttt{As-Clauses}(F), (O_1, \ldots, O_p))$. Intuitively, the translation should guarantee that (i) any solution of F can be extended into a solution of $\texttt{As-Clauses}(F)$, and that (ii) any solution of $\texttt{As-Clauses}(F)$ is a solution of F. In practice, the certification of the translation is integrated into the proof produced by the certifying MO-MaxSAT solver, treating the translation of the PB constraints, in the same way as any other reasoning step of the solver. Together with certificates for the clausal reasoning steps of the MO-MaxSAT solvers described in [47], we end up with a single VERIPB proof that guarantees that at least one solution for each non-dominated point of the original MO-PBO instance has been found.

As a choice for encoding PB constraints to clauses for translating MO-PBO instances to MO-MaxSAT we employ the generalized totalizer encoding [49] as an often-employed encoding in MaxSAT literature. A generalized totalizer encoding can be viewed as a binary tree that has the literals in the PB constraint and their coefficients as leaves. The root of the tree and all internal nodes correspond to a set of auxiliary variables that—informally speaking—count the sum of the coefficients of the literals assigned to 1 at the leafs of the subtree rooted at that node. The PB constraint is enforced by a unit clause over the auxiliary variables at the root node that corresponds to its bound.

In order to certify the derivation of the clauses, we use a procedure originally described for totalizers [72] and later extended to the generalized totalizer encoding [47]. This procedure introduces the semantic definitions of the auxiliary variables at each node as auxiliary PB constraints in the proof and derives the clauses in the encoding from these definitions. However, the semantics in the proof are stricter than the produced encoding. Concretely, in the proof the output variables have semantics encoding *equality* to the PB expression exceeding a certain value, while the clauses in the generalized totalizer encoding only encode an *implication*. In order to avoid issues where a solution found in the MO-MaxSAT solver does not satisfy all constraints in the proof due to these differing semantics, we remove all auxiliary constraints from the VERIPB proof with the help of the derived deletion rule [9, 38] once the clausal encoding for a PB constraint is generated.

5.2   Native Proof Logging for MO-PBO

The native MO-PBO approaches (recall Sect. 4) can also be extended to generate machine-checkable certificates. To do so, we use the VERIPB setup proposed in [47], encoding Pareto dominance as a preorder in the proof. In VERIPB format this preorder for objectives $(O_1, \ldots, O_p)$ is expressed as p constraints $O_i\restriction_\alpha \leq O_i\restriction_\beta$, where $O_i\restriction_\alpha$ is O_i under the assignment α. The formula formed by these constraints is true iff α dominates β or is equal to it. Since VERIPB verifies for redundant constraint that is added to the proof that a *witness* exists which is at least as good with respect to the preorder than any solutions the redundant constraint excludes, by loading the Pareto preorder as defined above, VERIPB ensures that Pareto-optimal solutions can only be excluded from the proof via the explicit solution-exclusion rule [47, Theorem 1].

Certifying a PD cut in the proof after finding the solution α is then done in the same way as in the MO-MaxSAT setting: First, a constraint that excludes all solutions that are dominated by α or have equal objective values (except for α itself) is added to the proof. This constraint is redundant, which can be justified using α as the witness, i.e., for any solution to the instance that does not satisfy this new constraint, α constitutes a solution that is at least as good with respect to Pareto optimality. Next, α is excluded from consideration with the help of the solution logging rule. Lastly, by combining the constraints from the previous steps, the PD cut itself can be derived.

Example 3. Recall the instance in Example 1. Assume that (i) $O_1 = 2x_2 + x_3 + 2x_4 + 3x_5$ and $O_2 = 3x_1 + x_2 + 2x_3 + x_4$, (ii) F includes no other variables, and

Table 1. Example proof for certifying a PD cut.

ID	Pseudo-Boolean Constraint	Comment
	Input constraints and potential previous proof steps	
[a]	$8w_1 + 2\overline{x_2} + \overline{x_3} + 2\overline{x_4} + 3\overline{x_5} \geq 8$	witness: $\{w_1\}$
[b]	$\overline{w_1} + 2x_2 + x_3 + 2x_4 + 3x_5 \geq 1$	witness: $\{\overline{w_1}\}$
[c]	$3w_2 + 3\overline{x_1} + \overline{x_2} + 2\overline{x_3} + \overline{x_4} \geq 3$	witness: $\{w_2\}$
[d]	$5\overline{w_2} + 3x_1 + x_2 + 2x_3 + x_4 \geq 5$	witness: $\{\overline{w_2}\}$
[e]	$5\overline{w_1} + 5\overline{w_2} + x_1 + \overline{x_2} + x_3 + \overline{x_4} + \overline{x_5} \geq 5$	witness: $\alpha \cup \{w_1, w_2\}$
[f]	$\overline{x_1} + x_2 + \overline{x_3} + x_4 + x_5 \geq 1$	Log the solution α
[g]	$\overline{w_1} + \overline{w_2} \geq 1$	PD cut

(iii) P-minimal has found the Pareto-optimal solution $\alpha = \{x_1, \overline{x_2}, x_3, \overline{x_4}, \overline{x_5}\}$ for which $(\alpha(O_1), \alpha(O_2)) = (1, 5)$. Table 1 shows example proof steps required for certifying a PD cut based on α. Steps $[a]$, $[b]$, $[c]$, and $[d]$ introduce new auxiliary variables w_1 and w_2 defined by $w_1 \Leftrightarrow O_1 \geq 1$ and $w_2 \Leftrightarrow O_2 \geq 5$ justified in the proof by witnesses that assign the (otherwise unconstrained) w_i variables the right way. With these definitions, the constraint introduced in step $[e]$ is satisfied only by solutions that are not dominated by or equal to α, and α itself. Lastly, the solution α is ruled out with the solution logging rule (in step $[f]$) and the PD cut (expressed with the w variables) is derived in step $[g]$ and justified by cutting planes reasoning as $([e] + [f])/5$.

By employing the described strategy for certifying PD cuts and a PB oracle which supports proof logging in VERIPB syntax (in our case ROUNDINGSAT), we implement proof logging for the algorithms described in Sect. 4. For proof logging P-minimal, only the PD cuts added to the oracle on Line 4 of Algorithm 1 need to be certified. For BIOPTSAT (Algorithm 2), the minimization on Line 3 is extended to derive the lower bound constraint $O_1 \geq \alpha(O_1)$ in the proof. When using solution-improving search, this constraint is derived by the oracle during the last unsatisfiable query, while for OLL, the proof logging procedure described in [6], adapted for the PB setting, is used. By combining the lower bound constraint $O_1 \geq \alpha(O_1)$ with a PD cut derived from α after Line 4, the constraint that is added to the working formula on Line 6 can be derived in the proof.

6   Empirical Evaluation

We turn to presenting results of a cross-community evaluation of the MaxSAT-translation based approach, native PB-based PBO approach and ILP-based approaches to MO-PBO. The experiments reportted on were run on 2.50-GHz Intel Xeon Gold 6248 machines with 381-GB RAM in RHEL under a per-instance 1-hour time and 32-GB memory limit.

6.1   Solvers

We implemented the PB-based MO-PBO algorithms proposed in Sect. 4 (*P*-minimal, and BIOPTSAT in the Sat-Unsat and OLL variants) in C++, using the PB solver ROUNDINGSAT [21, 22, 32, 33] as the decision oracle. We also implemented proof logging for these algorithms, making use of VERIPB proof logging offered by the ROUNDINGSAT oracle, and extended the MO-MaxSAT solver Scuttle [46] by implementing certificates for the PBO-to-MaxSAT translation (recall Sect. 5), thereby obtaining certificates for the translation-based approach when conjoined with the MO-MaxSAT certificates implemented in Scuttle using its implementations for the *P*-minimal and the bi-objective BIOPTSAT algorithms.

As an additional recent MO-MaxSAT approach for the evaluation, we consider the core-guided approach from [15], which we refer to as lower-bounding (LB). In terms of MO-ILP, we consider the branch-and-bound approach from [34] (employing CPLEX v12.10 with non-trivial challenges in updating to a newer version) and the MultiObjectiveAlgorithms.jl (v1.3.5) [26] implementation of the scalarization-based algorithm [25], employing CPLEX (v20.1) as the ILP solver. Due to intrinsic ILP-specific numerical issues observed in preliminary experiments for the scalarization-based algorithm, we set the following parameters in CPLEX: absolute gap tolerance 10^{-6}, relative gap tolerance 0.0, and integrality tolerance 0.0. It should be noted, however, that even with these tuned parameters, we observed 2 instances where the scalarization-based ILP algorithm reports one more non-dominated point than the PBO and MaxSAT-based implementations of *P*-minimal, which are certified and thereby certifiably correct, underlining the need of proof logging to ensure correctness.

In the runtime comparison, we run all solvers without proof logging, and separately evaluate the proof logging overhead of the certified MO-MaxSAT and MO-PBO implementations.

6.2   Benchmarks and Setup

In our empirical evaluation we use multi-objective PBO benchmarks from seven problem domains: 365 bi-objective instances of learning interpretable decision rules (LIDR) [56] obtained from [48]; 388 bi-objective flying tourist problem (FTP) [59] instance obtained from [15] (after filtering out two empty instance files); 160 knapsack (KS) instances with 3–5 objectives and 100 assignment problem instances with 3 objectives, from [50, 51] encoded as MO-PBO; and 35 bi-objective uncapacitated facility location problem (UFLP) instances from [37]. For further domains, we applied reverse-engineering described in [48] to the single-objective instances in the benchmark set of the Pseudo-Boolean Competition (2005–2024) [57, 65], splitting multi-level objective combinations into individual objectives, keeping only benchmarks where reverse-engineering was succesful on all instances in the benchmark domain. With this process, we obtained 100 bi-objective haplotype inference [40] and 1513 development assurance level (DAL) [7, 19] instances. The DAL instances were filtered based on the LION9 challenge documentation [20] to remove duplicates differing only in the order of

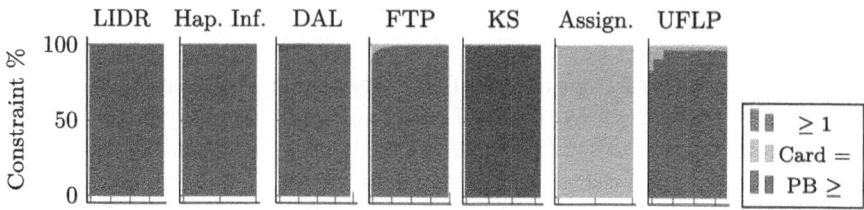

Fig. 2. Distribution of constraint types in the benchmark families.

the objectives and ones turned from maximization to minimization by multiplying the objectives by -1, resulting in 378 distinct DAL instances.

Figure 2 shows the constraint type distribution of each benchmark domain, showing how the types of constraints vary significantly depending on the domain (from clausal at-least-ones through cardinality constraints to more generic PB constraints).

6.3   Results

Table 2 shows the number of solved instances for each solver per benchmark family, separated into multi-objective algorithms for arbitrary number of objectives and algorithm specific for bi-objective problems. All MaxSAT-based approaches (P-minimal, lower-bounding, and BiOptSat) perform well on the LIDR and haplotype inference benchmark instances which are based on fully clausal encodings. The ILP-based approaches perform well on the representatives of classical ILP problems: knapsack, assignment, and uncapacitated facility location. On the real-world MO-PBO instance families DAL and FTP, performance between the three constraint paradigms is not as clear-cut. The performance of the BiOptSat implementations compared to their repective P-minimal counterparts is relatively similar, showing the same trends with respect to the constraint paradigms: with the introduction of non-clausal constraints the PB-based imple-

Table 2. Number of instances solved per benchmark family and solver.

		Multi-objective					Bi-objective		
		MaxSAT		PB	ILP		MaxSAT	PB	
Family	Total	P-min	LB	P-min	B&B	Scalar	BOS-SU	BOS-SU	BOS-OLL
LIDR	365	216	202	162	148	199	**221**	169	179
Hap. Inf.	100	**20**	18	18	0	6	19	17	18
DAL	378	216	197	**251**	154	159		—	
FTP	388	112	122	146	123	**257**	113	145	117
KS	160	62	58	85	114	**151**		—	
Assign.	100	19	20	18	51	**55**		—	
UFLP	35	1	3	12	**30**	29	2	12	2

Table 3. Number of uniquely solved instances and virtual best solver contribution per benchmark family for SCUTTLE P-minimal (MaxSAT), native PBO P-minimal (PBO), and the scalarization-based approach (ILP).

Family	Total	VBS solved	Uniquely solved			VBS contribution		
			MaxSAT	PBO	ILP	MaxSAT	PBO	ILP
LIDR	365	222	**21**	0	6	**200**	10	12
Hap. Inf.	100	20	**2**	0	0	**20**	0	0
DAL	378	260	9	**43**	0	85	**169**	6
FTP	388	258	0	0	**108**	1	115	**141**
KS	160	158	4	1	**64**	7	65	**84**
Assign.	100	59	0	0	**35**	0	10	**45**
UFLP	35	29	0	0	**17**	0	3	**26**

mentations outperform the MaxSAT-based implementations, but fail to fully match the performance of the ILP-based algorithms.

Towards a more fine-grained performance analysis, we select one approach as representative from each paradigm: for MO-MaxSAT SCUTTLE P-minimal, for MO-PBO, the native P-minimal implementation, and for MO-ILP the scalarization-based approach [25]. For the three selected representatives Table 3 shows the number of uniquely solved instances, the number of contributions to the virtual best solver (VBS)—i.e., the number of instances that a given solver solved the fastest out of the selected three, as well as the number of solved instances solved by the VBS. Additionally, Fig. 3 shows a per-instance runtime comparison of the approaches from the three paradigms. The trends visible in Table 2 can be seen again: the MO-MaxSAT-based approach performs best on clausal instances, while the ILP-based approach performs best on classical ILP problems. We observe that the native PBO approach significantly outperforms the others on the DAL domain, contributing to the virtual best solver more than twice as much as MO-MaxSAT approach, whereas the contribution of ILP on the VBS on the DAL domain is very small without any uniquely solved instances. On the FTP domain, even though the ILP approach performs the best, we observe an almost equal VBS contribution from the native PBO approach. The same holds for the knapsack domain. The pairwise runtime comparison in Fig. 3 further corroborates the complementary nature of the three approaches.

Complementary to the runtime performance, the ILP-based approach may suffer from numerical issues as also observed in our experiments. Our first-of-kind certified MO-PBO solvers based on translation to MO-MaxSAT and on the other hand liftings of recent MO-MaxSAT algorithms to natively work on MO-PBO offer guaranteed correctness. We also evaluated the cost of obtaining these certificates: with proof logging enabled, we observed relatively modest average overheads of 25% (for native MO-PBO P-minimal) and 48% (for SCUTTLE P-minimal) compared to running the solvers with proof logging disabled.

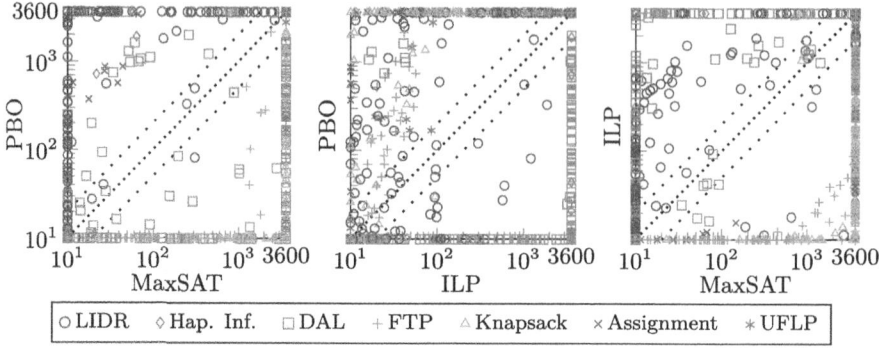

Fig. 3. Per-instance solving time comparisons representative solvers for each paradigm.

7 Conclusions

We engineered first-of-kind certifying algorithms and evaluated a range of approaches for pseudo-Boolean optimization. The results of the cross-community evaluation of the approaches show that MO-ILP, native MO-PBO, and translation-based MO-MaxSAT approaches offer complementary performance. On problems yielding mostly at-most-one constraints translating to MO-MaxSAT is competitive. For instances (with even relatively small number of) more generic PB constraints, it appears beneficial often to employ techniques which natively search on such constraints. For problem settings for which ILP solvers have been classically employed, MO-ILP appears also a good choice. Complementary to the runtime performance, our implementations of MO-PBO solvers based on translation to MO-MaxSAT and on liftings of recent MO-MaxSAT algorithms to natively work on MO-PBO offer guaranteed correctness via proof logging. Empirical runtime overhead from proof logging for these approaches is relatively minor, especially when compared to significant overheads reported for numerically exact ILP solvers in the single objective setting [31].

References

1. Thirty-Fifth AAAI Conference on Artificial Intelligence, AAAI 2021, Thirty-Third Conference on Innovative Applications of Artificial Intelligence, IAAI 2021, The Eleventh Symposium on Educational Advances in Artificial Intelligence, EAAI 2021, Virtual Event, 2–9 February 2021. AAAI Press (2021), https://www.aaai.org/Library/AAAI/aaai21contents.php
2. Andres, B., Kaufmann, B., Matheis, O., Schaub, T.: Unsatisfiability-based optimization in clasp. In: Dovier, A., Costa, V.S. (eds.) Technical Communications of the 28th International Conference on Logic Programming, ICLP 2012, 4–8 September 2012, Budapest, Hungary. LIPIcs, vol. 17, pp. 211–221. Schloss Dagstuhl - Leibniz-Zentrum für Informatik (2012). https://doi.org/10.4230/LIPIcs.ICLP.2012.211, http://drops.dagstuhl.de/opus/portals/extern/index.php?semnr=12008

3. Bacchus, F., Järvisalo, M., Martins, R.: Maximum satisfiability. In: Biere et al. [8], pp. 929–991. https://doi.org/10.3233/FAIA201008
4. Bauß, J., Parragh, S.N., Stiglmayr, M.: On improvements of multi-objective branch and bound. EURO J. Comput. Optim. **12**, 100099 (2024). https://doi.org/10.1016/j.ejco.2024.100099
5. Berg, J., Bogaerts, B., Nordström, J., Oertel, A., Paxian, T., Vandesande, D.: Certifying without loss of generality reasoning in solution-improving maximum satisfiability. In: Shaw, P. (ed.) 30th International Conference on Principles and Practice of Constraint Programming, CP 2024, 2–6 September 2024, Girona, Spain. LIPIcs, vol. 307, pp. 4:1–4:28. Schloss Dagstuhl - Leibniz-Zentrum für Informatik (2024). https://doi.org/10.4230/LIPIcs.CP.2024.4, https://www.dagstuhl.de/dagpub/978-3-95977-336-2
6. Berg, J., Bogaerts, B., Nordström, J., Oertel, A., Vandesande, D.: Certified core-guided MaxSAT solving. In: Pientka, B., Tinelli, C. (eds.) Automated Deduction—CADE 29—29th International Conference on Automated Deduction, Rome, Italy, 1–4 July 2023, Proceedings, LNCS, vol. 14132, pp. 1–22. Springer (2023). https://doi.org/10.1007/978-3-031-38499-8_1
7. Bieber, P., Delmas, R., Seguin, C.: DALculus—theory and tool for development assurance level allocation. In: Flammini, F., Bologna, S., Vittorini, V. (eds.) Computer Safety, Reliability, and Security—30th International Conference, SAFE-COMP 2011, Naples, Italy, 19–22 September 2011, Proceedings. LNCS, vol. 6894, pp. 43–56. Springer (2011). https://doi.org/10.1007/978-3-642-24270-0_4
8. Biere, A., Heule, M., van Maaren, H., Walsh, T. (eds.): Handbook of Satisfiability—Second Edition, Frontiers in Artificial Intelligence and Applications, vol. 336. IOS Press (2021). https://doi.org/10.3233/FAIA336
9. Bogaerts, B., Gocht, S., McCreesh, C., Nordström, J.: Certified dominance and symmetry breaking for combinatorial optimisation. J. Artif. Intell. Res. **77**, 1539–1589 (2023). https://doi.org/10.1613/jair.1.14296
10. Buchet, S., Allouche, D., de Givry, S., Schiex, T.: Bi-objective discrete graphical model optimization. In: Dilkina [24], pp. 136–152. https://doi.org/10.1007/978-3-031-60597-0_10
11. Cabral, M., Janota, M., Manquinho, V.: SAT-based leximax optimisation algorithms. In: Meel, K.S., Strichman, O. (eds.) 25th International Conference on Theory and Applications of Satisfiability Testing, SAT 2022, 2–5 August 2022, Haifa, Israel. LIPIcs, vol. 236, pp. 29:1–29:19. Schloss Dagstuhl - Leibniz-Zentrum für Informatik (2022). https://doi.org/10.4230/LIPIcs.SAT.2022.29, https://www.dagstuhl.de/dagpub/978-3-95977-242-6
12. Chen, D., Batson, R.G., Dang, Y.: Applied Integer Programming: Modeling and Solution. Wiley, December 2009. https://doi.org/10.1002/9781118166000
13. Cheung, K.K.H., Gleixner, A.M., Steffy, D.E.: Verifying integer programming results. In: Eisenbrand, F., Könemann, J. (eds.) Integer Programming and Combinatorial Optimization—19th International Conference, IPCO 2017, Waterloo, ON, Canada, 26–28 June 2017, Proceedings, LNCS, vol. 10328, pp. 148–160. Springer (2017). https://doi.org/10.1007/978-3-319-59250-3_13
14. Coello, C.A.C.: Multi-objective optimization. In: Martí, R., Pardalos, P.M., Resende, M.G.C. (eds.) Handbook of Heuristics., pp. 177–204. Springer (2018). https://doi.org/10.1007/978-3-319-07124-4_17

15. Cortes, J., Lynce, I., Manquinho, V.: New core-guided and hitting set algorithms for multi-objective combinatorial optimization. In: Sankaranarayanan, S., Sharygina, N. (eds.) Tools and Algorithms for the Construction and Analysis of Systems— 29th International Conference, TACAS 2023, Held as Part of the European Joint Conferences on Theory and Practice of Software, ETAPS 2022, Paris, France, 22– 27 April 2023, Proceedings, Part II, LNCS, vol. 13994, pp. 55–73. Springer (2023). https://doi.org/10.1007/978-3-031-30820-8_7

16. Cruz-Filipe, L., Heule, M.J.H., Jr., W.A.H., Kaufmann, M., Schneider-Kamp, P.: Efficient certified RAT verification. In: de Moura, L. (ed.) Automated Deduction— CADE 26—26th International Conference on Automated Deduction, Gothenburg, Sweden, 6–11 August 2017, Proceedings, LNCS, vol. 10395, pp. 220–236. Springer (2017). https://doi.org/10.1007/978-3-319-63046-5_14

17. Cruz-Filipe, L., Marques-Silva, J., Schneider-Kamp, P.: Efficient certified resolution proof checking. In: Legay, A., Margaria, T. (eds.) Tools and Algorithms for the Construction and Analysis of Systems—23rd International Conference, TACAS 2017, Held as Part of the European Joint Conferences on Theory and Practice of Software, ETAPS 2017, Uppsala, Sweden, 22–29 April 2017, Proceedings, Part I, LNCS, vol. 10205, pp. 118–135 (2017). https://doi.org/10.1007/978-3-662-54577-5_7

18. Dächert, K., Klamroth, K.: A linear bound on the number of scalarizations needed to solve discrete tricriteria optimization problems. J. Global Optim. **61**(4), 643–676 (2014). https://doi.org/10.1007/s10898-014-0205-z

19. Delmas, K., Chambert, L., Frazza, C., Seguin, C.: Optimization of development assurance level allocation. In: 2023 IEEE/AIAA 42nd Digital Avionics Systems Conference (DASC), pp. 1–10 (2023). https://doi.org/10.1109/DASC58513.2023.10311260

20. Delmas, R., Seguin, C., Bieber, P.: DALculus optimization benchmarks. https://www.cril.univ-artois.fr/ChallengeLion9/Dalculus.pdf

21. Devriendt, J.: Watched propagation of 0-1 integer linear constraints. In: Simonis, H. (ed.) Principles and Practice of Constraint Programming—26th International Conference, CP 2020, Louvain-la-Neuve, Belgium, 7–11 September 2020, Proceedings, LNCS, vol. 12333, pp. 160–176. Springer (2020). https://doi.org/10.1007/978-3-030-58475-7_10

22. Devriendt, J., Gleixner, A., Nordström, J.: Learn to relax: integrating 0-1 integer linear programming with pseudo-Boolean conflict-driven search. Constraints (4), 26–55 (2021). https://doi.org/10.1007/s10601-020-09318-x

23. Devriendt, J., Gocht, S., Demirovic, E., Nordström, J., Stuckey, P.J.: Cutting to the core of pseudo-boolean optimization: combining core-guided search with cutting planes reasoning. In: Thirty-Fifth AAAI Conference on Artificial Intelligence, AAAI 2021, Thirty-Third Conference on Innovative Applications of Artificial Intelligence, IAAI 2021, The Eleventh Symposium on Educational Advances in Artificial Intelligence, EAAI 2021, Virtual Event, 2–9 February 2021 [1], pp. 3750–3758. https://doi.org/10.1609/aaai.v35i5.16492, https://www.aaai.org/Library/AAAI/aaai21contents.php

24. Dilkina, B. (ed.): Integration of Constraint Programming, Artificial Intelligence, and Operations Research—21st International Conference, CPAIOR 2024, Uppsala, Sweden, 28–31 May 2024, Proceedings, Part I, LNCS, vol. 14742. Springer (2024). https://doi.org/10.1007/978-3-031-60597-0

25. Domínguez-Ríos, M.Á., Chicano, F., Alba, E.: Effective anytime algorithm for multiobjective combinatorial optimization problems. Inf. Sci. **565**, 210–228 (2021). https://doi.org/10.1016/j.ins.2021.02.074
26. Dowson, O.: MultiObjectiveAlgorithms.jl. https://github.com/jump-dev/MultiObjectiveAlgorithms.jl
27. Eén, N., Sörensson, N.: Temporal induction by incremental SAT solving. In: Strichman, O., Biere, A. (eds.) First International Workshop on Bounded Model Checking, BMC@CAV 2003, Boulder, Colorado, USA, 13 July 2003. Electronic Notes in Theoretical Computer Science, vol. 89, pp. 543–560. Elsevier (2003). https://doi.org/10.1016/S1571-0661(05)82542-3, https://www.sciencedirect.com/journal/electronic-notes-in-theoretical-computer-science/vol/89/issue/4
28. Eén, N., Sörensson, N.: Translating pseudo-boolean constraints into SAT. Journal on Satisfiability, Boolean Modeling and Computation **2**, 1–26 (2006). https://doi.org/10.3233/sat190014
29. Ehrgott, M.: Multicriteria Optimization (2. ed.). Springer (2005). https://doi.org/10.1007/3-540-27659-9
30. Ehrgott, M., Gandibleux, X.: Bound sets for biobjective combinatorial optimization problems. Comput. Oper. Res. **34**, 2674–2694 (2007). https://doi.org/10.1016/j.cor.2005.10.003
31. Eifler, L., Gleixner, A.: A computational status update for exact rational mixed integer programming. Math. Program. (4), 1–20 (2022). https://doi.org/10.1007/s10107-021-01749-5
32. Elffers, J., Devriendt, J., Gocht, S., Nordström, J.: RoundingSat: the pseudo-boolean solver powered by proof complexity. https://gitlab.com/MIAOresearch/software/roundingsat
33. Elffers, J., Nordström, J.: Divide and conquer: Towards faster pseudo-boolean solving. In: Lang [54], pp. 1291–1299. https://doi.org/10.24963/ijcai.2018/180, http://www.ijcai.org/proceedings/2018/
34. Forget, N., Gadegaard, S.L., Klamroth, K., Nielsen, L.R., Przybylski, A.: Branch-and-bound and objective branching with three or more objectives. Comput. Oper. Res. **148**, 106012 (2022). https://doi.org/10.1016/j.cor.2022.106012
35. Forget, N., Gadegaard, S.L., Nielsen, L.R.: Warm-starting lower bound set computations for branch-and-bound algorithms for multi objective integer linear programs. Eur. J. Oper. Res. **302**, 909–924 (2022). https://doi.org/10.1016/j.ejor.2022.01.047
36. Gadegaard, S.L., Nielsen, L.R., Ehrgott, M.: Bi-objective branch-and-cut algorithms based on LP relaxation and bound sets. INFORMS J. Comput. **31**, 790–804 (2019). https://doi.org/10.1287/ijoc.2018.0846
37. Gandibleux, X., Contibutors: vOptLib: Library of numerical instances (MOMIP, MOLP, MOIP, MOCO). https://github.com/vOptSolver/vOptLib
38. Gocht, S., Nordström, J.: Certifying parity reasoning efficiently using pseudo-boolean proofs. In: Thirty-Fifth AAAI Conference on Artificial Intelligence, AAAI 2021, Thirty-Third Conference on Innovative Applications of Artificial Intelligence, IAAI 2021, The Eleventh Symposium on Educational Advances in Artificial Intelligence, EAAI 2021, Virtual Event, 2–9 February 2021 [1], pp. 3768–3777. https://doi.org/10.1609/aaai.v35i5.16494, https://www.aaai.org/Library/AAAI/aaai21contents.php

39. Goldberg, E.I., Novikov, Y.: Verification of proofs of unsatisfiability for CNF formulas. In: 2003 Design, Automation and Test in Europe Conference and Exposition (DATE 2003), 3–7 March 2003, Munich, Germany, pp. 10886–10891. IEEE Computer Society (2003), https://doi.ieeecomputersociety.org/10.1109/DATE.2003.10008

40. Graça, A., Lynce, I., Marques-Silva, J., Oliveira, A.L.: Efficient and accurate haplotype inference by combining parsimony and pedigree information. In: Horimoto, K., Nakatsui, M., Popov, N. (eds.) Algebraic and Numeric Biology—4th International Conference, ANB 2010, Hagenberg, Austria, July 31- August 2, 2010, Revised Selected Papers, LNCS, vol. 6479, pp. 38–56. Springer (2010). https://doi.org/10.1007/978-3-642-28067-2_3

41. Guerreiro, A.P., et al.: Exact and approximate determination of the pareto front using minimal correction subsets. Comput. Oper. Res. **153**, 106153 (2023). https://doi.org/10.1016/j.cor.2023.106153

42. Halffmann, P., Schäfer, L.E., Dächert, K., Klamroth, K., Ruzika, S.: Exact algorithms for multiobjective linear optimization problems with integer variables: a state of the art survey. J. Multi-Criteria Decis. Anal. **29**(5–6), 341–363 (2022). https://doi.org/10.1002/mcda.1780, https://onlinelibrary.wiley.com/doi/abs/10.1002/mcda.1780

43. Hoen, A., Oertel, A., Gleixner, A.M., Nordström, J.: Certifying MIP-based presolve reductions for 0-1 integer linear programs. In: Dilkina [24], pp. 310–328. https://doi.org/10.1007/978-3-031-60597-0_20

44. Ignatiev, A., Morgado, A., Marques-Silva, J.: RC2: an efficient MaxSAT solver. J. Satisfiability, Boolean Model. Comput. **11**, 53–64 (2019). https://doi.org/10.3233/SAT190116

45. Ihalainen, H., et al.: Certified MaxSAT preprocessing. In: Benzmüller, C., Heule, M.J.H., Schmidt, R.A. (eds.) Automated Reasoning—12th International Joint Conference, IJCAR 2024, Nancy, France, 3–6 July 2024, Proceedings, Part I, LNCS, vol. 14739, pp. 396–418. Springer (2024). https://doi.org/10.1007/978-3-031-63498-7_24

46. Jabs, C.: Scuttle: a multi-objective MaxSAT solver. https://bitbucket.org/coreo-group/scuttle

47. Jabs, C., Berg, J., Bogaerts, B., Järvisalo, M.: Certifying pareto optimality in multi-objective maximum satisfiability. In: Gurfinkel, A., Heule, M. (eds.) Tools and Algorithms for the Construction and Analysis of Systems—31st International Conference, TACAS 2025, Held as Part of the International Joint Conferences on Theory and Practice of Software, ETAPS 2025, Hamilton, ON, Canada, May 3–8, 2025, Proceedings, Part II, LNCS, vol. 15697, pp. 108–129. Springer (2025). https://doi.org/10.1007/978-3-031-90653-4_6

48. Jabs, C., Berg, J., Niskanen, A., Järvisalo, M.: From single-objective to bi-objective maximum satisfiability solving. J. Artif. Intell. Res. **80**, 1223–1269 (2024). https://doi.org/10.1613/jair.1.15333

49. Joshi, S., Martins, R., Manquinho, V.: Generalized totalizer encoding for pseudo-boolean constraints. In: Pesant, G. (ed.) Principles and Practice of Constraint Programming—21st International Conference, CP 2015, Cork, Ireland, August 31 – September 4, 2015, Proceedings, LNCS, vol. 9255, pp. 200–209. Springer (2015). https://doi.org/10.1007/978-3-319-23219-5_15

50. Kirlik, G.: https://web.archive.org/web/20240517210648/, http://home.ku.edu.tr/~moolibrary/

51. Kirlik, G., Sayin, S.: A new algorithm for generating all nondominated solutions of multiobjective discrete optimization problems. Eur. J. Oper. Res. **232**, 479–488 (2014). https://doi.org/10.1016/j.ejor.2013.08.001

52. Kiziltan, G., Yucaoğlu, E.: An algorithm for multiobjective zero-one linear programming. Manage. Sci. **29**(12), 1444–1453 (1983). https://doi.org/10.1287/mnsc.29.12.1444

53. Koshimura, M., Nabeshima, H., Fujita, H., Hasegawa, R.: Minimal model generation with respect to an atom set. In: Peltier, N., Sofronie-Stokkermans, V. (eds.) Proceedings of the 7th International Workshop on First-Order Theorem Proving, FTP 2009, Oslo, Norway, 6–7 July 2009. CEUR Workshop Proceedings, vol. 556. CEUR-WS.org (2009), https://ceur-ws.org/Vol-556/paper06.pdf

54. Lang, J. (ed.): Proceedings of the Twenty-Seventh International Joint Conference on Artificial Intelligence, IJCAI 2018, 13–19 July 2018, Stockholm, Sweden. ijcai.org (2018), http://www.ijcai.org/proceedings/2018/

55. Malalel, S., Malapert, A., Pelleau, M., Régin, J.C.: MDD archive for boosting the pareto constraint. In: Yap [74], pp. 24:1–24:15. https://doi.org/10.4230/LIPIcs.CP.2023.24, https://www.dagstuhl.de/dagpub/978-3-95977-300-3

56. Malioutov, D., Meel, K.S.: MLIC: a MaxSAT-based framework for learning interpretable classification rules. In: Hooker, J.N. (ed.) Principles and Practice of Constraint Programming—24th International Conference, CP 2018, Lille, France, August 27–31, 2018, Proceedings, LNCS, vol. 11008, pp. 312–327. Springer (2018). https://doi.org/10.1007/978-3-319-98334-9_21

57. Manquinho, V.M., Roussel, O.: The first evaluation of pseudo-boolean solvers (PB'05). J. Satisfiability, Boolean Model. Comput. **2**, 103–143 (2006). https://doi.org/10.3233/sat190018

58. Marler, R., Arora, J.: Survey of multi-objective optimization methods for engineering. Struct. Multidiscip. Optim. **26**, 369–395 (2004). https://doi.org/10.1007/s00158-003-0368-6

59. Marques, R., Russo, L.M.S., Roma, N.: Flying tourist problem: flight time and cost minimization in complex routes. Expert Syst. Appl. **130**, 172–187 (2019). https://doi.org/10.1016/j.eswa.2019.04.024

60. Marques-Silva, J., Lynce, I., Malik, S.: Conflict-driven clause learning SAT solvers. In: Biere et al. [8], pp. 133–182. https://doi.org/10.3233/FAIA200987

61. Morgado, A., Dodaro, C., Marques-Silva, J.: Core-guided MaxSAT with soft cardinality constraints. In: O'Sullivan, B. (ed.) Principles and Practice of Constraint Programming—20th International Conference, CP 2014, Lyon, France, 8–12 September 2014. Proceedings, LNCS, vol. 8656, pp. 564–573. Springer (2014). https://doi.org/10.1007/978-3-319-10428-7_41

62. Nieuwenhuis, R., Oliveras, A.: On SAT modulo theories and optimization problems. In: Biere, A., Gomes, C.P. (eds.) Theory and Applications of Satisfiability Testing—SAT 2006, 9th International Conference, Seattle, WA, USA, 12–15 August 2006, Proceedings, LNCS, vol. 4121, pp. 156–169. Springer (2006). https://doi.org/10.1007/11814948_18

63. Parragh, S.N., Tricoire, F.: Branch-and-bound for bi-objective integer programming. INFORMS J. Comput. **31**, 805–822 (2019). https://doi.org/10.1287/ijoc.2018.0856

64. Rossi, F., van Beek, P., Walsh, T. (eds.): Handbook of Constraint Programming, Foundations of Artificial Intelligence, vol. 2. Elsevier (2006), https://www.sciencedirect.com/science/bookseries/15746526/2

65. Roussel, O.: Pseudo-Boolean Competition 2024. https://www.cril.univ-artois.fr/PB24/

66. Roussel, O., Manquinho, V.: Pseudo-boolean and cardinality constraints. In: Biere et al. [8], pp. 1087–1129. https://doi.org/10.3233/FAIA201012
67. Roussel, S., Polacsek, T., Chan, A.: Assembly line preliminary design optimization for an aircraft. In: Yap [74], pp. 32:1–32:19. https://doi.org/10.4230/LIPIcs.CP.2023.32, https://www.dagstuhl.de/dagpub/978-3-95977-300-3
68. Soh, T., Banbara, M., Tamura, N., Le Berre, D.: Solving multiobjective discrete optimization problems with propositional minimal model generation. In: Beck, J.C. (ed.) Principles and Practice of Constraint Programming—23rd International Conference, CP 2017, Melbourne, VIC, Australia, August 28 – September 1, 2017, Proceedings, LNCS, vol. 10416, pp. 596–614. Springer (2017). https://doi.org/10.1007/978-3-319-66158-2_38
69. Stidsen, T.R., Andersen, K.A.: A hybrid approach for biobjective optimization. Discret. Optim. **28**, 89–114 (2018). https://doi.org/10.1016/j.disopt.2018.02.001
70. Stidsen, T.R., Andersen, K.A., Dammann, B.: A branch and bound algorithm for a class of biobjective mixed integer programs. Manage. Sci. **60**, 1009–1032 (2014). https://doi.org/10.1287/mnsc.2013.1802
71. Terra-Neves, M., Lynce, I., Manquinho, V.: Multi-objective optimization through pareto minimal correction subsets. In: Lang [54], pp. 5379–5383. https://doi.org/10.24963/ijcai.2018/757, http://www.ijcai.org/proceedings/2018/
72. Vandesande, D., Wulf, W.D., Bogaerts, B.: QMaxSATpb: a certified MaxSAT solver. In: Gottlob, G., Inclezan, D., Maratea, M. (eds.) Logic Programming and Nonmonotonic Reasoning—16th International Conference, LPNMR 2022, Genova, Italy, 5–9 September 2022, Proceedings, LNCS, vol. 13416, pp. 429–442. Springer (2022). https://doi.org/10.1007/978-3-031-15707-3_33
73. Wassenhove, L.N.V., Gelders, L.F.: Solving a bicriterion scheduling problem. Eur. J. Oper. Res. **4**(1), 42–48 (1980). https://doi.org/10.1016/0377-2217(80)90038-7
74. Yap, R.H.C. (ed.): 29th International Conference on Principles and Practice of Constraint Programming, CP 2023, August 27–31, 2023, Toronto, Canada, LIPIcs, vol. 280. Schloss Dagstuhl - Leibniz-Zentrum für Informatik (2023), https://www.dagstuhl.de/dagpub/978-3-95977-300-3

Unsupervised Automata Learning via Discrete Optimization

Simon Lutz[1,4]($\boxtimes$), Daniil Kaminskyi[1,4], Florian Wittbold[3], Simon Dierl[1],
Falk Howar[1,2], Barbara König[3], Emmanuel Müller[1], and Daniel Neider[1,4]

[1] TU Dortmund University, Dortmund, Germany
{simon.lutz,daniil.kaminskyi,simon.dierl,falk.howar,
daniel.neider}@tu-dortmund.de,
emmanuel.mueller@cs.tu-dortmund.de
[2] Fraunhofer ISST, Dortmund, Germany
[3] University of Duisburg-Essen, Duisburg, Germany
{florian.wittbold,barbara_koenig}@uni-due.de
[4] Center for Trustworthy Data Science and Security, UA Ruhr, Dortmund, Germany

Abstract. Automata learning is a successful tool for many application domains such as robotics and automatic verification. Typically, automata learning techniques operate in a supervised learning setting (active or passive) where they learn a finite state machine in contexts where additional information, such as labeled system executions, is available. However, other settings, such as learning from unlabeled data - an important aspect in machine learning - remain unexplored. To overcome this limitation, we propose a framework for learning a deterministic finite automaton (DFA) from a given multi-set of unlabeled words. We show that this problem is computationally hard and develop three learning algorithms based on constraint optimization. Moreover, we introduce novel regularization schemes for our optimization problems that improve the overall interpretability of our DFAs. Using a prototype implementation, we demonstrate practical feasibility in the context of unsupervised anomaly detection.

Keywords: Automata Learning · Unsupervised Learning · Discrete Optimization

1 Introduction

In the last decades, the algorithmic learning of finite automata (or automata learning for short) has proven to be a successful tool in many application domains, ranging from pattern and language recognition [16] over robotics [49,50] to automatic verification [20,22,45] and software testing [4]. For reactive system verification, for instance, the goal of automata learning is to provide an appropriate abstraction of the system's input-output relations as a finite-state machine [27].

Traditionally, the literature on automata learning distinguishes two main settings: active and passive learning. In active learning [5], the algorithm (called learner) interacts with a so-called teacher. This teacher has access to a regular language and is able to

© The Author(s), under exclusive license to Springer Nature Switzerland AG 2026
G. Casini et al. (Eds.): JELIA 2025, LNAI 16093, pp. 135–153, 2026.
https://doi.org/10.1007/978-3-032-04587-4_9

answer two types of queries. Membership queries ask whether a specific word is in the target language and equivalence queries ask whether a conjectured automaton is equivalent to the language in question. In passive learning [9,56], the learning algorithm is given a finite set of words which are labeled as positive or negative, i.e., whether they are contained in the regular target language or not, respectively. Then, the objective is typically to learn a minimal automaton that accepts all positive words and rejects all negative ones.

While many advances in active and passive learning have expanded upon these seminal works, other important learning settings remain unexplored. For instance, the field of unsupervised learning is a well-studied aspect in machine learning that, so far, has been ignored in the context of automata learning. However, many important unsupervised learning problems, such as anomaly detection, also arise for automata and reactive systems. Currently, they are addressed via use case specific solutions, which are hard to engineer and difficult to transfer to other settings.

To overcome this gap, this paper proposes a generic approach for unsupervised automata learning based on discrete optimization. Similar to passive learning, we rely on a given, finite set of words but assume that, a priori, no additional information, such as positive or negative labels, is available. While our ideas are applicable to many other unsupervised learning settings on sequential data, in this paper, we focus on a crucial application in unsupervised machine learning: anomaly detection (i.e., identifying patterns in the data that do not conform to expected behavior [14]). This choice is motivated by the many application domains of anomaly detection, including cybersecurity, law enforcement, medicine, and fraud detection, to name but a few.

To be more precise, we aim to learn a DFA from a given finite multi-set S of unlabeled sequences that can distinguish normal from anomalous sequences. To this end, we consider three unsupervised learning settings. In the first setting, we assume two natural numbers $\ell, u \in \mathbb{N}$ with $\ell \leq u \leq |S|$ to be given as input. The task is then to learn a minimal DFA that accepts at least ℓ and at most u sequences from S. Minimality refers to a minimal number of states and is a common requirement in automata learning [9,24,36,41]. The parameters ℓ and u, on the other hand, serve as an estimate for the lower and upper number of anomalies in the data set and are used to prevent degenerate DFAs (i.e., DFAs that accept or reject all sequences). This setting operates under the assumption that normal sequences are drastically different from anomalies, allowing them to be separated by a rather simple pattern. Hence, by looking for an automaton that is as compact as possible, the classification of anomalies is performed automatically.

In the second setting the user does not need to specify both ℓ and u, but only one or the other (say, ℓ). Additionally, the user must fix a size $n \in \mathbb{N}$ of the resulting DFA. The task then is to learn a DFA of size n that accepts the smallest number $k \geq \ell$ of sequences from S. In other words, ℓ serves as a lower bound on the assumed number of anomalies in the given data set. In general, the choice of n should be made carefully in this setting, as too large a number may hinder interpretability while, if n is too small, the resulting DFAs may not be able to separate anomalies from normal sequences.

The last setting is motivated by the assumption that all normal sequences are similar to each other, i.e., have a small edit distance, while the anomalies are vastly different from the normal sequences, resulting in a high edit distance. Under this assumption, the user does not need to specify any bounds, but must still fix a size $n \in \mathbb{N}$ of the resulting DFA. We learn a DFA that minimizes the distance between pairs of sequences classified as normal, while maximizing the distance between pairs of sequences where one is classified as normal and the other as an anomaly.

Our contributions in this paper are fourfold. First, we show that learning a DFA of size n from unlabeled data is NP-complete. This result is in line with the classical learning of DFAs from positive and negative data, which is known to be NP-complete as well [18]. Consequently, the first learning problem lies within the complexity class FNP (i.e., the function problem extension of the decision problems in NP) and the second one lies within the class NPO (i.e., the class of optimization problems whose decision variant lies in NP). The complexity of the third learning problem remains an open problem that we will leave as a part of future work.

Second, we develop three learning algorithms, one for each setting. While in previous work, a DFA was learned by solving a series of constraint satisfaction problems, we reduce learning into a series of constraint optimization problems instead. This allows us to specify an objective function, thus finding not just any solution but one that optimized for additional regularization criteria. The constraint optimization problems can then be solved by highly-optimized mixed-integer programming solvers.

Third, we propose novel regularization terms to enhance the interpretability of the learned DFAs. In particular, we show how to augment our constraint optimization problems to maximize the number of self-loops and parallel edges (see Fig. 1). This approach is orthogonal to the original encoding and can, in principle, also be applied to other constraint-based learning algorithms for finite-state machines.

Fourth, to show the practical feasibility of our three algorithms, we evaluate them empirically on three anomaly detection benchmarks. We examine both the runtime and the anomaly detection performance for different configuration options and uncertainty w.r.t. the anomaly frequency.

Related Work. Automata learning has a long history, dating back to the 1970s [9, 56]. One typically distinguishes between active learning and passive learning.

Active learning was first introduced by Dana Angluin in 1987 [5]. In her work, Angluin showed that the class of regular languages can be learned efficiently by asking queries to a (minimally adequate) teacher. Furthermore, she provided an appropriate learning algorithm - called the L^* algorithm - which approximates the Myhill-Nerode congruence. Since then, various major improvements to and variants of the original algorithm have been proposed [3, 15, 26, 28, 31–33, 38, 39, 48, 51, 57].

Passive learning, on the other hand, was pioneered by Biermann and Feldman [9] and Trakhtenbrot and Barzdin [56]. Given a set of labeled data, a passive learning algorithm seeks to learn a minimal DFA consistent with the data. Algorithms such as Regular Positive Negative Inference (RPNI) [47] and the Blue-fringe algorithm [35] first construct the prefix acceptor – the most precise description of the data – and then generalize it by merging its states while maintaining consistency with the data. In 1987, Gold [18] showed that passive learning is computationally hard (i.e., the corresponding decision problem is NP-complete). Thus, learning algorithms that use constraint solving have become the de facto standard for constraint-based passive learning [19, 24, 40–42].

Besides the traditional active and passive learning of deterministic finite automata, other learning settings have also been investigated. Following the same underlying ideas, various algorithms have been proposed in the literature for learning more expressive state machines such as Mealy Machines with and without timers [12,43,53], I/O automata [2], non-deterministic automata [10,11], alternating automata [6], register automata [1,13,17,30], weighted automata [7,8,23], pushdown automata [29], tree automata [34,46], among others. In the context of incomplete information, Leucker and Neider [36] proposed a variant of Angluin's L^* algorithm for learning from an inexperienced teacher that sometimes may answer "don't know" to a membership query. However, to the best of our knowledge, learning a Deterministic Finite Automaton completely from unlabeled data remains unexplored.

2   Preliminaries

We address the task of learning a deterministic finite automaton from a multi-set of unlabeled sequences ranging over a finite set of symbols.

Following standard notation of automata theory, we refer to a sequence $w = a_1 \ldots a_n$ as a *finite word*. Moreover, we call the nonempty, finite set of *symbols* over which these words can range an *alphabet* Σ. The sequence without any symbols, also referred to as *empty word*, is denoted by ϵ. Furthermore, we denote the set of all words over an alphabet Σ as Σ^*. In the remainder of this paper, we will refer to the multi-set of sequential data $S = \{w_1, \ldots, w_n\}$ as a *sample*. Since a word w can be contained multiple times in a sample S, we denote the number of occurrences of w in S as $S(w)$.

From a given sample, we learn a *deterministic finite automaton (DFA)*. Formally, a DFA is a tuple $A = (Q, \Sigma, q_I, \delta, F)$ where Q is a finite set of states, Σ is a finite set of (input) symbols, $q_I \in Q$ is the *initial state*, $\delta : Q \times \Sigma \to Q$ is the *state-transition function*, and $F \subseteq Q$ is a set of accepting states. The *size* of a DFA is defined to be the number of its states $|Q|$. A *run* on a word $w = a_1 \ldots a_n$ is a sequence of states $q_0 \ldots q_n$ such that $q_0 = q_I$ and $q_i = \delta(q_{i-1}, a_i)$ for $i \in \{1, \ldots, n\}$. We call a run *accepting* if $q_n \in F$, and *rejecting* otherwise. The *language* of a DFA A, denoted $L(A)$, is the set of all words accepted by A.

As mentioned in the introduction, we reduce the task of learning a DFA into a series of *mixed-integer linear programming (MILP)* problems. Let *Var* be a finite set of real variables. An MILP problem consists of two parts, a linear function over the variables, referred to as the *objective function obj*, and a conjunction of *linear constraints Φ* on these variables. The solution to such a MILP problem is an assignment *Var* $\to \mathbb{R}$, referred to as a (feasible) *model*, such that the value of the objective function *obj* is optimal (i.e. minimal/maximal, respectively) while satisfying Φ (i.e., all constraints).

3   Problem Formulation

In this section, we formally introduce our three unsupervised automata learning problems and prove that the first two are computationally hard. As mentioned in the introduction, all three learning settings are assumed to be given a sample S of unlabeled words. The first setup, which we refer to as *Two-Bound DFA Learning*, additionally requires being given two natural numbers $\ell, u \in \mathbb{N}$ with $\ell \leq u \leq |\mathcal{S}|$. While the precise labels of the words in the sample $\mathcal{S}$ are unknown, these numbers provide an estimate of the distribution of positive words in $\mathcal{S}$. Then, the task is to learn a minimal DFA which accepts at least ℓ and at most u words from $\mathcal{S}$. We formally state this problem as:

Problem 1 (Two-Bound DFA Learning Problem).
Given a multi-set of words $\mathcal{S} = \{w_1, \ldots, w_n\}$ and two natural numbers $\ell, u \in \mathbb{N}$ with $\ell \leq u \leq |\mathcal{S}|$, construct a DFA $\mathcal{A}$ which accepts at least ℓ and at most u words from $\mathcal{S}$.

Notice that one may not always find a solution for this problem. For instance, consider the sample $\mathcal{S}$ that only contains the word $'a'$ twice and the bounds $\ell = u = 1$. Being deterministic, every DFA has to either accept both copies of the word $'a'$ or reject them both. Hence, there does not exist a DFA fulfilling the bounds in this case.

Despite this, Problem 1 is decidable. To show decidability, we first represent the sample as a *prefix tree* [25]. A prefix tree for a sample $\mathcal{S}$ is a partial DFA (i.e., some transitions are unspecified) without final states such that, after reading a word $w \in \mathcal{S}$, the DFA is in a unique state q_w. We complete this partial DFA by adding an additional sink state that becomes the target of all unspecified transitions. To decide whether there exists a DFA accepting at least ℓ and at most u words, we iterate over all combinations of final states and check the number of accepted words in each case. Since there is a unique state for each word in $\mathcal{S}$, either one of these DFAs fulfills the bounds or we can conclude that none exists.

However, a DFA constructed this way will generally be unsuitable for applications such as anomaly detection as it suffers from two main issues. On the one hand, by design, it overfits the sample $\mathcal{S}$ and thus poorly generalizes to unseen data. On the other hand, it becomes rather large, hindering interpretability in the sense of Occam's razor. To overcome these issues, we propose an algorithm that constructs a DFA of *minimal size* fulfilling the given bounds (if one exists). By requiring minimality, however, the problem becomes computationally hard. In fact, it can be shown that the problem of whether there exists a DFA with n states for Problem 1 is NP-complete.

Theorem 1. *Given a multi-set of words $\mathcal{S}$, two natural numbers $\ell, u \in \mathbb{N}$ with $\ell \leq u \leq |\mathcal{S}|$, and a natural number n (given in unary), the problem of finding a DFA $\mathcal{A}$ with n states that accepts at least ℓ and at most u words from $\mathcal{S}$ is NP-complete.*

We omit the proof of Theorem 1 at this point and refer interested readers to the full version of the paper [37]. The idea is that we can verify a given solution by simulating all words in $\mathcal{S}$, thus, the problem is in NP. NP-hardness follows by reduction from the NP-complete problem of learning of DFAs from positive and negative data [18].

In this first setup, we require the user to provide a lower and an upper bound on the distribution of positive words in a given sample. However, in practice, this requirement may be too strong. Thus, in the second setup, which we refer to as *Single-Bound DFA Learning*, we reduce the amount of prior knowledge compared to the first case by alleviating the user's burden to specify both ℓ and u. Instead, we assume to be given only one parameter, say ℓ (the case in which u is given is analogous). Now, in contrast to Problem 1, the task to construct a minimal DFA that accepts at least ℓ words from $\mathcal{S}$ always has a trivial solution: the DFA that accepts all words in S only has size 1 and fulfills the bound. However, this DFA underfits the sample S and thus does not capture the underlying structure. To reduce underfitting, we apply a common technique from automata learning and construct a DFA of a fixed size that accepts the smallest number $k \geq l$ of words from the sample. By providing this size as an additional parameter n the user can regularize the trade-off between avoiding underfitting (larger) and interpretability (smaller). We formally state this problem as:

Problem 2 (Single-Bound-Learning-Problem).
Given a multi-set of words $S = \{w_1, \ldots, w_n\}$ and two natural numbers $\ell, n \in \mathbb{N}$ with $\ell \leq |S|$, construct a DFA $\mathcal{A}$ of size n which accepts the smallest number $k \geq l$ of words from S.

This problem is the optimization version of Problem 1, thus, it is also computationally hard. In fact, from Problem 1 being NP-complete, it immediately follows that Problem 2 lies within the complexity class NPO (i.e., the class of optimization problems whose decision variant lies in NP).

The third setup, which we refer to as *Distance-Based DFA Learning*, is motivated by the assumption that for many applications, the pairs of positive (or negative) words are structurally similar, resulting in a low edit distance. In contrast, opposite classifications (i.e., one positive and one negative word) are drastically different, resulting in a high edit distance. In the context of anomaly detection, for instance, deep learning based methods follow this idea and classify new data based on the distance to the training data (e.g., [52]). This assumption allows us to alleviate the user's burden to specify any bounds. Instead, along with the sample S, we only rely on the size $n \in \mathbb{N}$ of the automata as a regularizer (similar to the second setting) and a distance function over words (in our case, the Levenshtein distance). The task is then to construct a DFA of size n such that the distance between all pairs of two accepted (rejected) words is minimized while the distance between pairs of both one accepted and one rejected word is maximized. This dual optimization problem can then be transformed into a plain minimization problem by multiplying the distances to be maximized by -1. This allows us to formally state this problem as:

Problem 3 (Distance-Based-Learning-Problem).
Given a multi-set of words $S = \{w_1, \ldots, w_n\}$ and a natural number $n \in \mathbb{N}$, construct a DFA $\mathcal{A}$ of size n which minimizes the following objective function:

$$\sum_{w_i, w_j \in L(\mathcal{A}) \cap S} dist(w_i, w_j) - \sum_{\substack{w_i \in L(\mathcal{A}) \cap S \\ w_j \notin L(\mathcal{A}) \cap S}} dist(w_i, w_j) \tag{1}$$

where $dist(w_i, w_j)$ denotes the Levenshtein distance between two words w_i and w_j.

While we conjecture that this problem is also computationally hard, we leave a proof of its complexity as part of future work.

4 Learning via Discrete Optimization

In this section, we present our learning algorithms for learning deterministic finite automata from a sample S of unlabeled words. In all three setups, we reduce the tasks to a set of constraint optimization problems and solve them using state-of-the-art mixed-integer programming solvers (in our case, Gurobi [21]).

4.1   Two-Bound DFA Learning

Recall that in the first setup, we are given a sample S and two bounds $\ell, u \in \mathbb{N}$ with $\ell \le u \le |S|$. To learn a minimal DFA that fulfills these bounds, we apply a technique commonly used in automata learning to ensure minimality. The idea is to encode the problem for an automaton of fixed size n such that the encoding has two key properties:

- There exists a feasible model if and only if there exists a DFA of size n fulfilling the bounds on the acceptance.
- This model contains sufficient information to construct such a DFA.

Starting with an automaton of size one and increasing the size whenever there is no feasible model guarantees to produce the minimal solution.

We now describe the MILP model we use to learn a DFA of size n. Since we just check the existence of a suitable DFA in the first setup, we can choose any constant objective function, e.g., $obj = 1$. The set of linear inequalities $\Phi^n_{S,\ell,u} = \Phi^n_{\mathcal{A}} \wedge \Phi_{\mathcal{B}}$ consists of two kinds of constraints: *automata constraints* $\Phi^n_{\mathcal{A}}$, which encode a DFA of size n and the runs on all words from the sample, and *bound constraints* $\Phi_{\mathcal{B}}$ encoding the bounds on the acceptance. Throughout these constraints, we bound the introduced variables to only take on integer values between (and including) 0 and 1, thus simulating boolean variables.

Automata constraints $\Phi^n_{\mathcal{A}}$: The automata constraints are motivated by the SAT encoding of Biermann and Feldman [9]. Without loss of generality, the states of the DFA form the set $Q = \{q_0, \dots, q_{n-1}\}$ where q_0 is the initial state. The alphabet Σ of the DFA is the set of all symbols appearing in the sample S. To encode the transitions of the DFA we introduce variables $\delta_{q,a,q'}$ for $q, q' \in Q$ and $a \in \Sigma$. Intuitively, the variable $\delta_{q,a,q'}$ will be set to 1 if and only if the DFA has a transition from state q to state q' on reading a. Furthermore, we introduce variables f_q for $q \in Q$, which indicate whether a state q is a final state. To encode the runs of the DFA, we start by computing the set of all prefixes in the sample $Pref(S) = \{w \mid ww' \in S \text{ and } w' \in \Sigma^*\}$. We then introduce a third kind of variable: $x_{w,q}$ for all $w \in Pref(S)$ and $q \in Q$. Intuitively, these variables indicate that after reading the prefix w the DFA is in state q.

We now impose constraints on these variables to encode a DFA and its runs. Being deterministic, there must be precisely one transition for each state q and symbol a, which we can model by the following constraint:

$$\sum_{q' \in Q} \delta_{q,a,q'} = 1 \qquad \forall q \in Q, \forall a \in \Sigma \qquad (2)$$

Furthermore, after reading a word w the DFA can only be in one state and after reading the empty word ϵ the DFA is in the initial state, which we defined to be q_0.

$$\sum_{q \in Q} x_{w,q} = 1 \qquad \forall w \in Pref(S) \qquad \text{and} \qquad x_{\epsilon,q_0} = 1 \qquad (3)$$

Moreover, we encode a run based on the following observation: If the DFA is in some state q after reading the word w and there is a transition from q to q' on reading the symbol a, then the DFA is in state q' after reading the word wa. As a constraint in MILP we get:

$$x_{w,q} + \delta_{q,a,q'} - 1 \leq x_{wa,q'} \qquad \forall q, q' \in Q, a \in \Sigma, \forall wa \in \mathit{Pref}(S) \qquad (4)$$

Finally, we define the automata constraints $\Phi_{\mathcal{A}}^n$ to be the conjunction of Eqs. 2 to 4 which concludes the encoding of a DFA of size n and its runs.

Bound constraints Φ_B: To impose constraints on the number of accepted words, we need to track whether a word w is accepted. This is the case if and only if after reading w the DFA is in some state q and this state is final. Intuitively, we could express this case as $x_{w,q} \cdot f_q$, however, this is not linear and thus not a valid MILP constraint. Instead, we exploit the fact that for Boolean variables the multiplication $x_{w,q} \cdot f_q$ is equivalent to the formula $x_{w,q} \wedge f_q$. By introducing fresh variables $\alpha_{w,q}$ for $w \in S$ and $q \in Q$ to store the result, this conjunction can be modeled by the following set of constraints:

$$\alpha_{w,q} \geq x_{w,q} + f_q - 1, \quad \alpha_{w,q} \leq x_{w,q}, \quad \alpha_{w,q} \leq f_q \qquad \forall w \in S, \forall q \in Q \quad (5)$$

Intuitively, the variables $\alpha_{w,q}$ indicate whether a word w is accepted by the DFA (in the state q). Relying on these variables, we can encode the bounds on the acceptance as

$$\sum_{w \in S} \sum_{q \in Q} \alpha_{w,q} \geq \ell \qquad \text{and} \qquad \sum_{w \in S} \sum_{q \in Q} \alpha_{w,q} \leq u \qquad (6)$$

Then the bound constraints Φ_B are defined as the conjunction of the above inequalities.

After introducing the MILP model, we employ it to construct the minimal DFA that fulfills the given bounds on the acceptance. The idea is to check the feasibility of the MILP problem with constant objective function $obj = 1$ and linear inequalities $\Phi_{S,\ell,u}^n$ for increasing n until either a solution is found or we reach $n = |\mathit{Pref}(S)| + 2$. As argued above when proving decidability of Problem 1, the size of the prefix tree is a natural upper bound for the size of the DFA. Therefore, we can conclude that there exists no DFA fulfilling the given bounds on the sample when we exceed this size. In the case where a feasible model exists for some size n, we construct the corresponding DFA from this model based on the variables $\delta_{q,a,q'}$ and f_q. This procedure is described by Algorithm 1. The correctness of this algorithm is established by the following theorem:

Theorem 2. *Given a sample S and two natural numbers $\ell, u \in \mathbb{N}$ with $\ell \leq u \leq |S|$, Algorithm 1 terminates and outputs a minimal DFA $\mathcal{A}_S$ which accepts at least ℓ and at most u words from S, if such a DFA exists.*

We omit proving this theorem here and refer interested readers to the full version of the paper [37].

The idea is to first establish termination and then prove that the MILP problem has a feasible model for some n if and only if there exists a DFA of size n fulfilling the bounds on the acceptance. Then the algorithm learns a minimal DFA by construction.

Algorithm 1. Learning with two bounds

1: **Input:** Sample $\mathcal{S}$, Bounds $\ell, u \in \mathbb{N}$
2: $n \leftarrow 0$
3: **repeat**
4:     $n \leftarrow n + 1$
5:     Construct $\Phi_{\mathcal{S},\ell,u}^n = \Phi_{\mathcal{A}}^n \wedge \Phi_{\mathcal{B}}$ and set $obj = 1$
6:     **if** $obj, \Phi_{\mathcal{S},\ell,u}^n$ has a feasible model (say m) **then**
7:         **return** Construct DFA $\mathcal{A}$ using m
8:     **end if**
9: **until** $n = |Pref(\mathcal{S})| + 2$
10: **return** There exists no DFA fulfilling the given bounds

---

4.2 Single-Bound DFA Learning

In order to not clutter this section, we will only describe the encoding for the case where the lower bound ℓ is given. The case in which the upper bound is given is analogous. We recall that the task is to construct a DFA of a fixed size n that minimizes acceptance above ℓ. As in the first setup, we encode the DFA and the runs on all words in the sample using the same set of variables and automata constraints $\Phi_{\mathcal{A}}^n$ as above. Furthermore, we use the same idea to ensure that the number of accepted words is larger than the lower bound: We introduce variables $\alpha_{w,q}$ and add Constraints 5 and the corresponding inequality of Constraint 6. For the remainder of this section, let Φ_ℓ denote the conjunction of these constraints. In contrast to Two-Bound Learning, we are not satisfied with finding just any DFA, but want to find one that accepts the least number of words while adhering to the lower bound. To achieve this, we use the following objective function:

$$obj = \min \sum_{w \in S} \sum_{q \in Q} \alpha_{w,q} \tag{7}$$

which minimizes the number of accepted words from $\mathcal{S}$. All in all, the resulting Algorithm 2 returns a DFA of size n that minimizes acceptance above the lower bound l.

Theorem 3. *Given a sample S and two natural numbers $\ell, n \in \mathbb{N}$ with $\ell \leq |\mathcal{S}|$, Algorithm 2 terminates and outputs a DFA $\mathcal{A}_{\mathcal{S}}$ of size n that accepts the smallest number $k \geq l$ of words from S.*

We omit the proof of this theorem, which is similar to the proof of Theorem 2.

Algorithm 2. Learning with a single bound

1: **Input:** Sample $\mathcal{S}$, Bound $\ell \in \mathbb{N}$, Size $n \in \mathbb{N}$
2: Construct $\Phi_{\mathcal{S},\ell}^n = \Phi_{\mathcal{A}}^n \wedge \Phi_\ell$
3: Set $obj = \min \sum_{w \in S} \sum_{q \in Q} \alpha_{w,q}$
4: Compute optimal model minimizing obj with respect to $\Phi_{\mathcal{S},\ell}^n$, say m
5: **return** Construct DFA $\mathcal{A}$ using m

Algorithm 3. Learning based on distance

1: **Input:** Sample $\mathcal{S}$, Size $n \in \mathbb{N}$
2: Compute the Levenshtein distance $dist(w_1, w_2)$ for each pair of words $w_1, w_2 \in \mathcal{S}$
3: Construct $\Phi_{\mathcal{A}}^n$
4: Set $obj = \min \sum_{\substack{w_1, w_2 \in \mathcal{S} \\ q_1, q_2 \in Q}} \alpha_{w_1, q_1} \cdot \alpha_{w_2, q_2} \cdot dist(w_1, w_2) - \alpha_{w_1, q_1} \cdot \beta_{w_2, q_2} \cdot dist(w_1, w_2)$
5: Compute optimal model minimizing obj with respect to $\Phi_{\mathcal{A}}^n$, say m
6: **return** Construct DFA $\mathcal{A}$ using m

4.3 Distance-Based DFA Learning

Let us recall the third setup: We are given a sample $\mathcal{S}$, the size $n \in \mathbb{N}$ of the automata, and the Levenshtein distance between samples and want to compute a DFA that minimizes Eq. 1. Analogously to the first two setups, we encode the DFA and the runs on all words in the sample using the same set of variables and automata constraints $\Phi_{\mathcal{A}}^n$ as above. To optimize the distance between pairs of words as described in Problem 3, we need to keep track of which words will be accepted by the automaton and which will be rejected. For this, we introduce variables $\alpha_{w,q}$ and $\beta_{w,q}$, respectively, and add Constraints 5 to track whether a word w is accepted by the DFA as well as $\beta_{w,q} = 1 - \alpha_{w,q}$ for all $w \in \mathcal{S}$ and $q \in Q$, indicating whether a word w is rejected by the automaton. We then define the objective function in the same way as in Problem 3:

$$obj = \min \sum_{w_1, w_2 \in \mathcal{S}} \sum_{q_1, q_2 \in Q} \alpha_{w_1, q_1} \cdot \alpha_{w_2, q_2} \cdot dist(w_1, w_2) - \alpha_{w_1, q_1} \cdot \beta_{w_2, q_2} \cdot dist(w_1, w_2)$$
(8)

Note that for every pair of words w_1 and w_2, the distance $dist(w_1, w_2)$ can be precomputed, thus allowing arbitrary complex distance functions to be used. As above, this MILP model can then be used to construct a DFA of a given size n that minimizes the distance between pairs of accepted words while maximizing the distance between pairs of one accepted and one rejected word (see also Algorithm 3).

Theorem 4. *Given a sample $\mathcal{S}$ and two natural numbers $\ell, n \in \mathbb{N}$ with $\ell \leq |\mathcal{S}|$, Algorithm 3 terminates and outputs a DFA $\mathcal{A}_\mathcal{S}$ of size n which minimizes the following objective function:* $\sum_{w_i, w_j \in L(\mathcal{A})} dist(w_i, w_j) - \sum_{\substack{w_i \in L(\mathcal{A}) \\ w_j \notin L(\mathcal{A})}} dist(w_i, w_j)$

We omit the proof of this theorem which is similar to the proof of Theorem 2.

5 Interpretability

Even though automata are generally regarded as interpretable models [55], they can become unintuitive if there are too many different transitions to different states. Therefore, we introduce heuristics aimed at reducing their complexity and making them more readable for humans. While [55] introduced similar techniques as regularization terms, we adapt them to improve the interpretability of the resulting models, as demonstrated in Fig. 1. Note though, that the model's obtained by different simplification

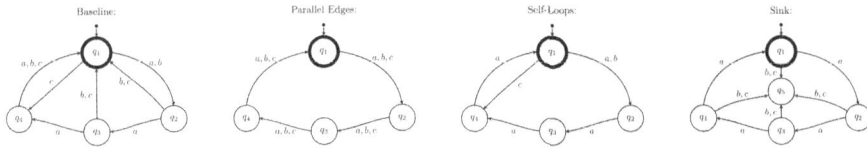

Fig. 1. Depiction of four different DFAs learned with different interpretability heuristics based on the same input dataset.

heuristics need not be equivalent and that thus the modifications may impede or even improve the models accuracy (see Sect. 6). In essence, the following heuristics aim to visually streamline the graphical representation of the resulting model and thus highlight the important structural insights. They are implemented by adding a penalty term to the objective function. For the exact implementation details we refer interested readers to the full version of the paper [37]. Our optimization-based approach is flexible with respect to the heuristics used: as long as a heuristic is expressible as part of the optimization problem, it can be applied. We consider three examples:

- *Sink states*: We favor solutions that have a so-called sink state, which can never be left once it is reached. By our design, all words ending in the sink state are rejected.
- *Self-loops*: By penalizing transitions to other states, we obtain models with a lot of self-loops. By convention, those are omitted in the graphical representation.
- *Parallel edges*: Similar to self-loops, we prefer solutions where there is only one successor state. Thus, the automata will transition to the same state regardless of the next element $a \in \Sigma$.

6 Experimental Evaluation

We implemented a prototype of the three learning algorithms in Python[1] using the industry-strength Gurobi Optimizer [21] as an MILP solver.

We evaluated all three learning settings in the context of anomaly detection on three datasets: a modified version of the ALFRED benchmark set [54] and the two real-world log datasets HDFS [58] and BGL [44], provided by the Loghub system log dataset collection [59]. The exact dataset characteristics are shown in Table 1.

The ALFRED data set contains sequences of action plans, encoded as bit vectors, that achieve one of 7 goals in the ALFRED setting. For each of the pairwise combinations of goals (i.e., 42 class combinations), we created a training and a test set with the elements of the first (normal) class and the elements of the second (anomalous) class in a 9:1 ratio.

The HDFS data set contains system logs for a Hadoop Distributed File System hosted in a private cloud environment. Each entry in the data set represents a sequence of system events, labeled as either normal or anomalous by a set of expert rules. Similarly, BGL is a set of logs collected from a BlueGene/L supercomputer system, containing alert and non-alert messages. To keep the running time within the timeout of two hours, we restricted ourselves to words with a maximum length of 15 and 10, respectively.

---

[1] https://github.com/simonlutz-tudortmund/Interpretable-Anomaly-Detection.

Table 1. Summary of the datasets used.

Dataset	$|S|$	$|\Sigma|$	% anomalies	LB	UB
ALFRED	316–462	9	≈ 0.1	0.09–0.10	0.10–0.11
HDFS	108237	13	0.0585	0.058	0.059
BGL	198192	295	0.1766	0.176	0.177

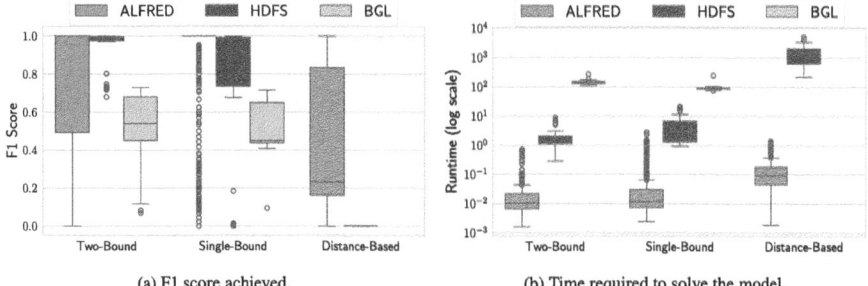

(a) F1 score achieved.   (b) Time required to solve the model.

Fig. 2. Results by three approaches on the selected datasets.

Performance Analysis. In our first experiment, we want to answer the research question asking which learning setting performs the best for detecting anomalies in sequential data. For each of the three datasets, we randomly split the data into training and test set (with a 80:20 ratio) and averaged our results over 50 runs. We examined both the time required to build and solve the model during training (with a two hour timeout) and the F1 score obtained on the test set. We observed that in every experiment the Two-Bound DFA Learning algorithm was able to find a feasible solution of size two. Therefore, for the other two learning settings, we also learned an automaton of size 2. The results of our experiments are displayed in Fig. 2. They show that both the Two-Bound and Single-Bound learning setting were able to achieve high performance on the ALFRED and HDFS datasets. The performance on the BGL dataset is slightly worse, which can be explained by the significantly larger alphabet compared to the length of the words. This means that simple patterns, such as a single letter, are sufficient to differentiate even two normal sequences. These patterns may then be picked up by our algorithms instead of patterns separating normal sequences and anomalies. In terms of running time there seems to be no significant difference between the first two learning settings. However, the results show that the running time of the algorithms heavily depends on the dataset. This is to be expected, as the number of automata constraints $\Phi_{\mathcal{A}}^n$ scales with the number of words (and prefixes) in the sample S, yielding a longer running time. Compared to the first two settings, the Distance-Based learning algorithm performs significantly worse, especially for the HDFS dataset. This can be explained by the fact that the HDFS dataset contains words of different length (ranging from 2 to 15), thus the distance between two words is dominated by their difference in length. The algorithm, by minimizing Eq. 1, will therefore separate words mostly based on their length, neglecting any other differences or patterns.

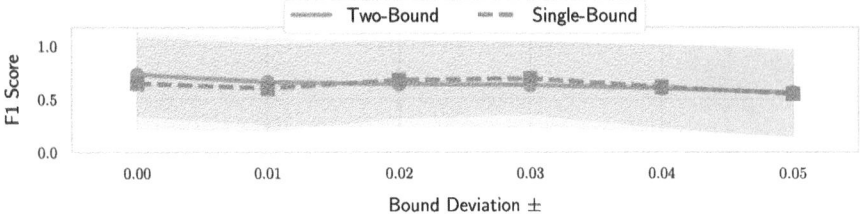

Fig. 3. F1 score for the ALFRED dataset with loosened bounds.

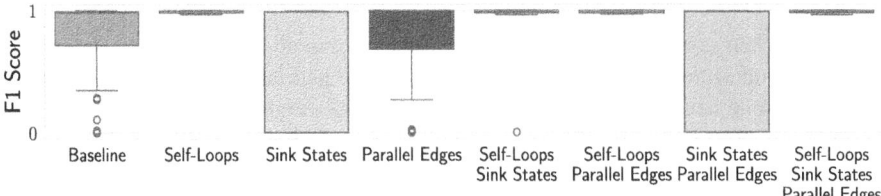

Fig. 4. F1 score for combinations of interpretability heuristics on the HDFS dataset.

Loosened Bounds. For the Two-Bound and Single-Bound learning settings we assume to be given bounds on number of words to be accepted. In this second experiment, we will answer the research questions whether these learning algorithms are robust under imprecise bounds. Focusing on the ALFRED dataset, we analyze the effect of loosening the learning bounds on the F1 score by increasing or decreasing the bounds by a value between 0 and 0.05. The results are displayed in Fig. 3. They show, that the F1 score is highest for the tightest bounds, as expected. Furthermore, the performance of both the Two-Bound and Single-Bound learning algorithm is quite robust to loosening the bounds. The F1 score drops only slightly even for a loosened bound of 0.05, which represents a 50% deviation from the original number of anomalies.

Data Complexity. For all datasets, the Two-Bound setting always found a feasible solution of size two. Since this seemed rather small, we also trained a DFA in the classical passive learning setting (i.e., with labels) on the same datasets. The resulting automata had size four for the ALFRED dataset and size two for the HDFS dataset, while no DFA with up to thirty states could be found for BGL. This shows that even small automata are capable of separating the normal sequences and anomalies.

Influence of Interpretability Heuristics. In this section we investigate the influence of our interpretability heuristics on the algorithm's overall performance. For each possible combination of heuristics, we learned an automaton in the first learning setting on the HDFS dataset with tight bounds. Since any reasonable automaton that includes a sink state has a minimum of three states, we set the minimum number of states of the learned DFAs to three. The results, shown in Fig. 4, indicate that increasing the number of self-loops improves the F1 score. Including more parallel edges does not seem to affect the overall performance, whereas introducing sink states greatly impedes the resulting

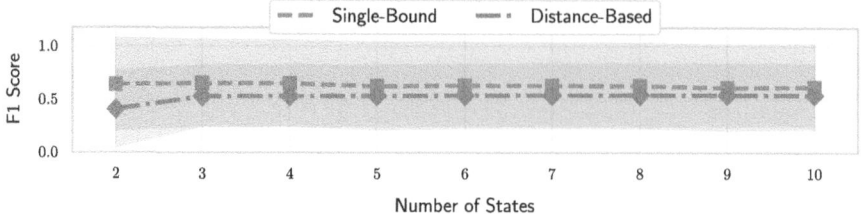

Fig. 5. F1 score for the ALFRED dataset with changing number of states.

F1 score. When combining multiple heuristics, the overall performance behaves the same as in one of the experiments using only a single heuristic. This indicates that the influence of one heuristic on the objective function outweighs the other heuristics. We leave a more thorough evaluation of the interpretability heuristics as part of future work.

Influence of Automaton Size. In the second and third learning setting, we assume the size of the automaton to be given by the user. In this section, we investigate how this influences the overall performance of the learned automata. We conducted experiments with varying sizes (ranging from 2 to 10) on the ALFRED dataset. The results are displayed in Fig. 5. They indicate that increasing the size of the learned automaton does not significantly impact its performance. For the Single-Bound setting the performance remains roughly constant, while for the Distance-Based approach there is only a slight increase in performance between size 2 and 3. This indicates that once a reasonable solution is found the learning algorithm starts to only learn unreachable states when the size is increased. These results may be connected to the complexity of our data and we leave a more thorough investigation as part of future work.

7   Conclusion

This paper has studied the task of learning a deterministic finite automaton from a sample of unlabeled words that could be used to separate normal form anomalous words. We proposed three unsupervised learning settings, studied their properties (e.g., their computational complexity), and developed learning algorithms that utilize off-the-shelf constraint optimization tools. In addition, we have shown how regularization can improve the interpretability of the learned DFAs. Our empirical evaluation has demonstrated practical feasibility in the context of three anomaly detection benchmarks.

We see various promising directions for future research. First, the analysis of the complexity of the third learning setting remains an open problem to be tackled in the future. Second, we plan to develop heuristics that sacrifice the optimality of a solution in favor of computational efficiency. Third, we want to extend our approach to more expressive automata classes, for instance, register automata, to handle data over continuous domains.

Acknowledgements. This work has been financially supported by Deutsche Forschungsgemeinschaft, DFG Project numbers 459419731, 495857894 (STING), and 434592664, and the Research Center Trustworthy Data Science and Security (https://rc-trust.ai), one of the Research Alliance centers within the UA Ruhr (https://uaruhr.de).

References

1. Aarts, F., Heidarian, F., Kuppens, H., Olsen, P., Vaandrager, F.W.: Automata learning through counterexample guided abstraction refinement. In: Giannakopoulou, D., Méry, D. (eds.) FM 2012: Formal Methods - 18th International Symposium, Paris, France, August 27-31, 2012. Proceedings. Lecture Notes in Computer Science, vol. 7436, pp. 10–27. Springer (2012). https://doi.org/10.1007/978-3-642-32759-9_4

2. Aarts, F., Vaandrager, F.W.: Learning I/O automata. In: Gastin, P., Laroussinie, F. (eds.) CONCUR 2010 - Concurrency Theory, 21th International Conference, CONCUR 2010, Paris, France, August 31-September 3, 2010. Proceedings. Lecture Notes in Computer Science, vol. 6269, pp. 71–85. Springer (2010). https://doi.org/10.1007/978-3-642-15375-4_6

3. Aarts, F.D.: Tomte: bridging the gap between active learning and real-world systems. Sl: sn (2014)

4. Aichernig, B.K., Mostowski, W., Mousavi, M.R., Tappler, M., Taromirad, M.: Model learning and model-based testing. In: Machine Learning for Dynamic Software Analysis: Potentials and Limits: International Dagstuhl Seminar 16172, Dagstuhl Castle, Germany, April 24-27, 2016, Revised Papers, pp. 74–100. Springer (2018)

5. Angluin, D.: Learning regular sets from queries and counterexamples. Inf. Comput. **75**(2), 87–106 (1987). https://doi.org/10.1016/0890-5401(87)90052-6

6. Angluin, D., Eisenstat, S., Fisman, D.: Learning regular languages via alternating automata. In: Yang, Q., Wooldridge, M.J. (eds.) Proceedings of the Twenty-Fourth International Joint Conference on Artificial Intelligence, IJCAI 2015, Buenos Aires, Argentina, July 25-31, 2015, pp. 3308–3314. AAAI Press (2015). http://ijcai.org/Abstract/15/466

7. Balle, B., Mohri, M.: Learning weighted automata. In: Maletti, A. (ed.) Algebraic Informatics - 6th International Conference, CAI 2015, Stuttgart, Germany, September 1-4, 2015. Proceedings. Lecture Notes in Computer Science, vol. 9270, pp. 1–21. Springer (2015). https://doi.org/10.1007/978-3-319-23021-4_1

8. Bergadano, F., Varricchio, S.: Learning behaviors of automata from multiplicity and equivalence queries. SIAM J. Comput. **25**(6), 1268–1280 (1996). https://doi.org/10.1137/S009753979326091X

9. Biermann, A.W., Feldman, J.A.: On the synthesis of finite-state machines from samples of their behavior. IEEE Trans. Comput. **21**(6), 592–597 (1972). https://doi.org/10.1109/TC.1972.5009015

10. Björklund, J., Fernau, H., Kasprzik, A.: MAT learning of universal automata. In: Dediu, A., Martín-Vide, C., Truthe, B. (eds.) Language and Automata Theory and Applications - 7th International Conference, LATA 2013, Bilbao, Spain, April 2-5, 2013. Proceedings. Lecture Notes in Computer Science, vol. 7810, pp. 141–152. Springer (2013). https://doi.org/10.1007/978-3-642-37064-9_14

11. Bollig, B., Habermehl, P., Kern, C., Leucker, M.: Angluin-style learning of NFA. In: Boutilier, C. (ed.) IJCAI 2009, Proceedings of the 21st International Joint Conference on Artificial Intelligence, Pasadena, California, USA, July 11-17, 2009, pp. 1004–1009 (2009). http://ijcai.org/Proceedings/09/Papers/170.pdf

12. Bruyère, V., Garhewal, B., Pérez, G.A., Staquet, G., Vaandrager, F.W.: Active learning of mealy machines with timers. CoRR abs/2403.02019 (2024). https://doi.org/10.48550/ARXIV.2403.02019

13. Cassel, S., Howar, F., Jonsson, B., Steffen, B.: Active learning for extended finite state machines. Formal Aspects Comput. **28**(2), 233–263 (2016). https://doi.org/10.1007/S00165-016-0355-5

14. Chandola, V., Banerjee, A., Kumar, V.: Anomaly detection: a survey. ACM Comput. Surv. **41**(3), 15:1–15:58 (2009). https://doi.org/10.1145/1541880.1541882

15. Frohme, M.T.: Active automata learning with adaptive distinguishing sequences. CoRR abs/1902.01139 (2019). http://arxiv.org/abs/1902.01139
16. García, P., Segarra, E., Vidal, E., Galiano, I.: On the use of the morphic generator grammatical inference (MGGI) methodology in automatic speech recognition. Int. J. Pattern Recognit. Artif. Intell. **4**(04), 667–685 (1990)
17. Garhewal, B., Vaandrager, F.W., Howar, F., Schrijvers, T., Lenaerts, T., Smits, R.: Greybox learning of register automata. In: Dongol, B., Troubitsyna, E. (eds.) Integrated Formal Methods - 16th International Conference, IFM 2020, Lugano, Switzerland, November 16-20, 2020, Proceedings. Lecture Notes in Computer Science, vol. 12546, pp. 22–40. Springer (2020). https://doi.org/10.1007/978-3-030-63461-2_2
18. Gold, E.M.: Complexity of automaton identification from given data. Inf. Control **37**(3), 302–320 (1978). https://doi.org/10.1016/S0019-9958(78)90562-4
19. Grinchtein, O., Leucker, M., Piterman, N.: Inferring network invariants automatically. In: Furbach, U., Shankar, N. (eds.) Automated Reasoning, Third International Joint Conference, IJCAR 2006, Seattle, WA, USA, August 17-20, 2006, Proceedings. Lecture Notes in Computer Science, vol. 4130, pp. 483–497. Springer (2006). https://doi.org/10.1007/11814771_40
20. Groce, A., Peled, D., Yannakakis, M.: Adaptive model checking. Logic J. IGPL **14**(5), 729–744 (2006)
21. Gurobi Optimization, LLC: Gurobi Optimizer Reference Manual (2022). https://www.gurobi.com
22. Habermehl, P., Vojnar, T.: Regular model checking using inference of regular languages. Electron. Notes Theoret. Comput. Sci. **138**(3), 21–36 (2005)
23. van Heerdt, G., Kupke, C., Rot, J., Silva, A.: Learning weighted automata over principal ideal domains. In: Goubault-Larrecq, J., König, B. (eds.) Foundations of Software Science and Computation Structures - 23rd International Conference, FOSSACS 2020, Held as Part of the European Joint Conferences on Theory and Practice of Software, ETAPS 2020, Dublin, Ireland, April 25-30, 2020, Proceedings. Lecture Notes in Computer Science, vol. 12077, pp. 602–621. Springer (2020). https://doi.org/10.1007/978-3-030-45231-5_31
24. Heule, M., Verwer, S.: Exact DFA identification using SAT solvers. In: Sempere, J.M., García, P. (eds.) Grammatical Inference: Theoretical Results and Applications, 10th International Colloquium, ICGI 2010, Valencia, Spain, September 13-16, 2010. Proceedings. Lecture Notes in Computer Science, vol. 6339, pp. 66–79. Springer (2010). https://doi.org/10.1007/978-3-642-15488-1_7
25. De la Higuera, C.: Grammatical inference: learning automata and grammars. Cambridge University Press (2010)
26. Howar, F.: Active learning of interface programs. Ph.D. thesis, Dortmund University of Technology (2012). https://hdl.handle.net/2003/29486
27. Hungar, H., Niese, O., Steffen, B.: Domain-specific optimization in automata learning. In: Hunt, W.A., Somenzi, F. (eds.) CAV 2003. LNCS, vol. 2725, pp. 315–327. Springer, Heidelberg (2003). https://doi.org/10.1007/978-3-540-45069-6_31
28. Irfan, M.N., Oriat, C., Groz, R.: Angluin style finite state machine inference with non-optimal counterexamples. In: Proceedings of the First International Workshop on Model Inference In Testing, pp. 11–19. MIIT '10, Association for Computing Machinery, New York, NY, USA (2010). https://doi.org/10.1145/1868044.1868046
29. Isberner, M.: Foundations of active automata learning: an algorithmic perspective. Ph.D. thesis, Technical University Dortmund, Germany (2015). https://hdl.handle.net/2003/34282
30. Isberner, M., Howar, F., Steffen, B.: Learning register automata: from languages to program structures. Mach. Learn. **96**(1–2), 65–98 (2014). https://doi.org/10.1007/S10994-013-5419-7

31. Isberner, M., Howar, F., Steffen, B.: The TTT algorithm: a redundancy-free approach to active automata learning. In: Bonakdarpour, B., Smolka, S.A. (eds.) Runtime Verification - 5th International Conference, RV 2014, Toronto, ON, Canada, September 22-25, 2014. Proceedings. Lecture Notes in Computer Science, vol. 8734, pp. 307–322. Springer (2014). https://doi.org/10.1007/978-3-319-11164-3_26

32. Isberner, M., Steffen, B.: An abstract framework for counterexample analysis in active automata learning. In: Clark, A., Kanazawa, M., Yoshinaka, R. (eds.) Proceedings of the 12th International Conference on Grammatical Inference, ICGI 2014, Kyoto, Japan, September 17-19, 2014. JMLR Workshop and Conference Proceedings, vol. 34, pp. 79–93. JMLR.org (2014). http://proceedings.mlr.press/v34/isberner14a.html

33. Kearns, M.J., Vazirani, U.V.: An Introduction to Computational Learning Theory. MIT Press (1994). https://mitpress.mit.edu/books/introduction-computational-learning-theory

34. Knuutila, T., Steinby, M.: The inference of tree languages from finite samples: an algebraic approach. Theor. Comput. Sci. **129**(2), 337–367 (1994). https://doi.org/10.1016/0304-3975(94)90033-7

35. Lang, K.J., Pearlmutter, B.A., Price, R.A.: Results of the abbadingo one DFA learning competition and a new evidence-driven state merging algorithm. In: Honavar, V.G., Slutzki, G. (eds.) Grammatical Inference, 4th International Colloquium, ICGI-98, Ames, Iowa, USA, July 12-14, 1998, Proceedings. Lecture Notes in Computer Science, vol. 1433, pp. 1–12. Springer (1998). https://doi.org/10.1007/BFB0054059

36. Leucker, M., Neider, D.: Learning minimal deterministic automata from inexperienced teachers. In: Margaria, T., Steffen, B. (eds.) Leveraging Applications of Formal Methods, Verification and Validation. Technologies for Mastering Change - 5th International Symposium, ISoLA 2012, Heraklion, Crete, Greece, October 15-18, 2012, Proceedings, Part I. Lecture Notes in Computer Science, vol. 7609, pp. 524–538. Springer (2012). https://doi.org/10.1007/978-3-642-34026-0_39

37. Lutz, S., et al.: Unsupervised automata learning via discrete optimization (2025). https://arxiv.org/abs/2303.14111

38. Maler, O., Pnueli, A.: On the learnability of infinitary regular sets. Inf. Comput. **118**(2), 316–326 (1995). https://doi.org/10.1006/INCO.1995.1070

39. Merten, M., Howar, F., Steffen, B., Margaria, T.: Automata learning with on-the-fly direct hypothesis construction. In: Hähnle, R., Knoop, J., Margaria, T., Schreiner, D., Steffen, B. (eds.) Leveraging Applications of Formal Methods, Verification, and Validation - International Workshops, SARS 2011 and MLSC 2011, Held Under the Auspices of ISoLA 2011 in Vienna, Austria, October 17-18, 2011. Revised Selected Papers. Communications in Computer and Information Science, vol. 336, pp. 248–260. Springer (2011). https://doi.org/10.1007/978-3-642-34781-8_19

40. Neider, D.: Computing minimal separating DFAs and regular invariants using SAT and SMT solvers. In: Chakraborty, S., Mukund, M. (eds.) Automated Technology for Verification and Analysis - 10th International Symposium, ATVA 2012, Thiruvananthapuram, India, October 3-6, 2012. Proceedings. Lecture Notes in Computer Science, vol. 7561, pp. 354–369. Springer (2012). https://doi.org/10.1007/978-3-642-33386-6_28

41. Neider, D., Gaglione, J., Gavran, I., Topcu, U., Wu, B., Xu, Z.: Advice-guided reinforcement learning in a non-markovian environment. In: Thirty-Fifth AAAI Conference on Artificial Intelligence, AAAI 2021, Thirty-Third Conference on Innovative Applications of Artificial Intelligence, IAAI 2021, The Eleventh Symposium on Educational Advances in Artificial Intelligence, EAAI 2021, Virtual Event, February 2-9, 2021, pp. 9073–9080. AAAI Press (2021). https://ojs.aaai.org/index.php/AAAI/article/view/17096

42. Neider, D., Jansen, N.: Regular model checking using solver technologies and automata learning. In: Brat, G., Rungta, N., Venet, A. (eds.) NASA Formal Methods, 5th International

Symposium, NFM 2013, Moffett Field, CA, USA, May 14-16, 2013. Proceedings. Lecture Notes in Computer Science, vol. 7871, pp. 16–31. Springer (2013). https://doi.org/10.1007/978-3-642-38088-4_2

43. Niese, O.: An integrated approach to testing complex systems. Ph.D. thesis, Technical University of Dortmund, Germany (2003). http://eldorado.uni-dortmund.de:8080/0x81d98002_0x0007b62b

44. Oliner, A., Stearley, J.: What supercomputers say: a study of five system logs. In: 37th Annual IEEE/IFIP International Conference on Dependable Systems and Networks (DSN'07), pp. 575–584 (2007). https://doi.org/10.1109/DSN.2007.103

45. Oliveira, A.L., Silva, J.P.: Efficient algorithms for the inference of minimum size DFAs. Mach. Learn. **44**, 93–119 (2001)

46. Oncina, J., Garcıa, P.: Inference of recognizable tree sets. Tech. rep., Tech. report, Universidad de Alicante, 1993. DSIC-II/47/93 (1993)

47. Oncina, J., Garcia, P., et al.: Inferring regular languages in polynomial update time. Pattern Recognit Image Anal. **1**(49–61), 10–1142 (1992)

48. Petrenko, A., Li, K., Groz, R., Hossen, K., Oriat, C.: Inferring approximated models for systems engineering. In: 15th International IEEE Symposium on High-Assurance Systems Engineering, HASE 2014, Miami Beach, FL, USA, January 9-11, 2014, pp. 249–253. IEEE Computer Society (2014). https://doi.org/10.1109/HASE.2014.46

49. Rieger, A.: Inferring probabilistic automata from sensor data for robot navigation. Univ., Fachbereich Informatik, Lehrstuhl 8 (1995)

50. Rivest, R.L., Schapire, R.E.: Inference of finite automata using homing sequences. In: Proceedings of the Twenty-First Annual ACM Symposium on Theory of Computing, pp. 411–420 (1989)

51. Rivest, R.L., Schapire, R.E.: Inference of finite automata using homing sequences. Inf. Comput. **103**(2), 299–347 (1993). https://doi.org/10.1006/INCO.1993.1021

52. Ruff, L., et al.: Deep one-class classification. In: Dy, J., Krause, A. (eds.) Proceedings of the 35th International Conference on Machine Learning. Proceedings of Machine Learning Research, vol. 80, pp. 4393–4402. PMLR (2018). https://proceedings.mlr.press/v80/ruff18a.html

53. Shahbaz, M., Groz, R.: Inferring mealy machines. In: Cavalcanti, A., Dams, D. (eds.) FM 2009: Formal Methods, Second World Congress, Eindhoven, The Netherlands, November 2-6, 2009. Proceedings. Lecture Notes in Computer Science, vol. 5850, pp. 207–222. Springer (2009). https://doi.org/10.1007/978-3-642-05089-3_14

54. Shridhar, M., et al.: ALFRED: a benchmark for interpreting grounded instructions for everyday tasks. In: 2020 IEEE/CVF Conference on Computer Vision and Pattern Recognition (CVPR), pp. 10737–10746. IEEE, New York, NY, USA (2020). https://doi.org/10.1109/CVPR42600.2020.01075, CVPR 2020

55. Shvo, M., Li, A.C., Icarte, R.T., McIlraith, S.A.: Interpretable sequence classification via discrete optimization. Proc. AAAI Conf. Artif. Intell. **35**(11), 9647–9656 (2021). https://doi.org/10.1609/aaai.v35i11.17161, AAAI 2021

56. Trakhtenbrot, B.A., Barzdin, Y.M.: Finite automata: Behavior and synthesis. Elsevier (1973)

57. Vaandrager, F.W., Garhewal, B., Rot, J., Wißmann, T.: A new approach for active automata learning based on apartness. In: Fisman, D., Rosu, G. (eds.) Tools and Algorithms for the Construction and Analysis of Systems - 28th International Conference, TACAS 2022, Held as Part of the European Joint Conferences on Theory and Practice of Software, ETAPS 2022, Munich, Germany, April 2-7, 2022, Proceedings, Part I. Lecture Notes in Computer Science, vol. 13243, pp. 223–243. Springer (2022). https://doi.org/10.1007/978-3-030-99524-9_12

58. Xu, W., Huang, L., Fox, A., Patterson, D., Jordan, M.I.: Detecting large-scale system problems by mining console logs. In: Proceedings of the ACM SIGOPS 22nd Symposium on Operating Systems Principles, pp. 117–132. SOSP '09, Association for Computing Machinery, New York, NY, USA (2009). https://doi.org/10.1145/1629575.1629587
59. Zhu, J., He, S., He, P., Liu, J., Lyu, M.R.: Loghub: a large collection of system log datasets for AI-driven log analytics. In: 34th IEEE International Symposium on Software Reliability Engineering, ISSRE 2023, Florence, Italy, October 9-12, 2023, pp. 355–366. IEEE (2023). https://doi.org/10.1109/ISSRE59848.2023.00071

Finding Short Tree-Like Unit Refutations in UTVPI Constraint Systems

P. Wojciechowski and K. Subramani[✉]

LDCSEE, West Virginia University, Morgantown, WV, USA
{pwojciec,k.subramani}@mail.wvu.edu

Abstract. In this paper, we investigate unit refutability in Unit Two Variable Per Inequality (UTVPI) Constraint Systems (UCSs). A Unit Two Variable Per Inequality (UTVPI) constraint is a linear relationship of the form: $\pm x_i \pm x_j \leq b_{ij}$, where $b_{ij} \in \mathbb{Z}$. A UCS is a conjunction of such constraints. If it is required that the two variables in a UTVPI constraint have opposite signs, then the constraint is called a difference constraint and a conjunction of such constraints is called a difference constraint system (DCS). When a decision procedure deems a UCS is infeasible, it is important to provide a certificate which attests to the infeasibility of the UCS. Such a certificate is called a negative certificate. Refutations (under an appropriate refutation system) form an important subclass of negative certificates. All problems in the complexity class **P** have succinct negative certificates. We focus on a subclass of refutations called Unit Refutations (UR). The UR refutation system is **incomplete**, in that unsatisfiable UCSs may not have unit refutations. However, they are useful from the perspective of identifying variable domains responsible for system inconsistency. Previous work has examined dag-like unit refutations of UCSs [18]. In this paper, we examine tree-like unit refutations of UCSs.

1 Introduction

This paper is concerned with a restricted refutation system for Unit Two Variable Per Inequality (UTVPI) Constraint Systems (UCSs). A UTVPI constraint is a linear relationship of the form: $\pm x_i \pm x_j \leq b_{ij}$. A UTVPI constraint system (UCS) is a conjunction of UTVPI constraints and can be represented in matrix form as: $\mathbf{A} \cdot \mathbf{x} \leq \mathbf{b}$. Applications of UCSs include domains such as scheduling, array bounds checking [10], abstract interpretation [12], and program verification [3]. Over the years, a number of decision procedures for both the linear and integer feasibility problems in UCSs have been developed [8,10]. This includes procedures which generate certificates that verify their correctness, and those that do not generate such certificates. Decision procedures which do generate such certificates are called certifying [11]. A decision procedure which provides a certificate is both more reliable and trustworthy. Certificates come in two general categories, viz., positive certificates, which verify the correctness of

© The Author(s), under exclusive license to Springer Nature Switzerland AG 2026
G. Casini et al. (Eds.): JELIA 2025, LNAI 16093, pp. 154–167, 2026.
https://doi.org/10.1007/978-3-032-04587-4_10

"yes"-instances, and negative certificates, which verify the correctness of "no"-instances. In this paper, we are interested in a special type of negative certificate called a refutation. More specifically, we are interested in a specific type of refutation called a tree-like unit refutation.

The primary problem concerning refutations is the problem of existence. For unit refutations in UTVPI constraints, this problem was shown to be in **P** [18]. Another important problem is the problem of finding optimal length refutations. We investigate the problem of finding the "shortest" tree-like unit refutations (see Sect. 2). This extends previous work which focused on optimal length dag-like refutations of UCSs [18]. As argued in [15], unit refutations are domain specific refutations, i.e. they prove that a UCS is infeasible with its current set of absolute (one variable) constraints without proving the infeasibility of the underlying system of relative (two variable) constraints. This is a marked difference from unrestricted linear refutations which do not naturally find such refutations.

There are two principal contributions in this paper, viz.,

1. A pseudopolynomial time algorithm for finding a shortest tree-like unit refutation of a UCS (Sect. 4).
2. A 2-approximation algorithm for a shortest tree-like unit refutation of a UCS (Sect. 5).

2 Statement of Problems

In this section, we formally describe the problems under consideration. These definitions can also be found in [18].

We first define difference constraints.

Definition 1. *A constraint of the form* $a_i \cdot x_i + a_j \cdot x_j \leq b_k$ *where* $a_i \neq a_j \in \{1, 0, -1\}$ *and* $b_k \in \mathbb{Z}$ *is called a* **difference constraint**.

Definition 2. *A* **Difference Constraint System (DCS)** *is a conjunction of difference constraints.*

Unit Two Variable Per Inequality (UTVPI) constraints are defined below.

Definition 3. *A constraint of the form* $a_i \cdot x_i + a_j \cdot x_j \leq b_k$ *where* $a_i, a_j \in \{1, 0, -1\}$, a_i *and* a_j *are not both* 0, *and* $b_k \in \mathbb{Z}$ *is called a* **Unit Two Variable Per Inequality (UTVPI)** *constraint.*

In this paper, we are concerned with UTVPI constraints over real-valued variables.

Note that every difference constraint is also a UTVPI constraint. In both UTVPI constraints and difference constraints, the value b_k is called the **defining constant**. Additionally, the terms x_i and $-x_i$ are called **literals**.

Definition 4. *A constraint with only one non-zero coefficient is called an* **absolute constraint**.

Definition 5. *A* **UTVPI Constraint System (UCS)** *is a conjunction of UTVPI constraints.*

Throughout this paper, we use n to refer to the number of variables in a UCS and m to refer to the number of constraints.

Example 1. A UCS with 2 constraints and 2 variables is shown in System (1).

$$x_1 + x_2 \leq 7 \quad x_2 - x_1 \leq -6 \tag{1}$$

A UCS can be represented in matrix form as: $\mathbf{A} \cdot \mathbf{x} \leq \mathbf{b}$. In this representation, $\mathbf{b}$ is called the defining constant vector.

When finding linear refutations (refutations of linear feasibility) of UCSs, we use a single inference rule, viz.,

$$\text{ADD} : \frac{\sum_{i=1}^{n} a_i \cdot x_i \leq b_1 \quad \sum_{i=1}^{n} a'_i \cdot x_i \leq b_2}{\sum_{i=1}^{n} (a_i + a'_i) \cdot x_i \leq b_1 + b_2} \tag{2}$$

We refer to Rule (2) as the **ADD rule**. It is easy to see that Rule (2) is sound since any assignment that satisfies the hypotheses also satisfies the consequent. Additionally, Rule (2) is complete, since every linearly infeasible UCS has a refutation consisting of only applications to the ADD rule [5,12].

Definition 6. *A sequence of applications of the ADD rule that results in a contradiction is known as a linear refutation.*

In this paper, we study a restricted version of the ADD rule, known as the unit-ADD (UADD) rule. In the UADD rule, at least one of the constraints must be an absolute constraint (see Rule 3).

$$\text{UADD} : \frac{a_{i,1} \cdot x_i \leq b_1 \quad \sum_{j=1}^{n} a_{j,2} \cdot x_j \leq b_2}{(a_{i,1} + a_{i,2}) \cdot x_i + \sum_{j \neq i} a_{j,2} \cdot x_j \leq b_1 + b_2} \tag{3}$$

A linear refutation using only the UADD rule is called a unit refutation. The problem of finding such a refutation is called the unit refutability problem (URP).

It is important to note that, unlike the ADD rule, the UADD rule is incomplete. This means that there are UCSs with no linear solutions that do not have a refutation using only the UADD rule.

In this paper, we study tree-like unit refutations.

Definition 7. *A* **tree-like** *refutation is a refutation in which each derived constraint can be used at most once.*

Note that tree-like refutations can reuse the constraints in the original UCS, and constraints can be rederived if necessary. In particular, we focus on tree-like unit refutations.

Definition 8. *A* **tree-like unit** *refutation is a unit refutation in which each derived constraint can be used at most once.*

An alternative structure for refutations is defined as follows:

Definition 9. *A* **dag-like** *refutation is a refutation in which each constraint can be reused, without needing to be rederived.*

An earlier paper focused on dag-like unit refutations [18].

Definition 10. *A* **dag-like unit** *refutation is a unit refutation in which each constraint can be reused, without needing to be rederived.*

Example 2. Let **U** be the UCS in System (4).

$$- x_1 \leq -1 \quad x_1 + x_2 \leq 0 \quad - x_2 + x_3 \leq 1 \quad - x_2 - x_3 \leq 0 \tag{4}$$

A dag-like unit refutation of **U** is shown in Fig. 1.

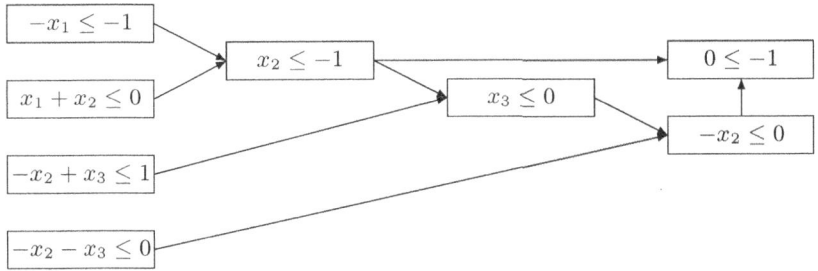

Fig. 1. Dag-like Unit Refutation

Note that the derived constraint $x_2 \leq -1$ is reused. Thus, the refutation in Fig. 1 is not a tree-like unit refutation. However, if we rederive the constraint $x_2 \leq -1$, then we obtain the tree-like unit refutation in Fig. 2.

The focus of this paper is on optimal length refutations, which necessitates the next definition.

Definition 11. *The* **length** *of a refutation is the number of inferences in that refutation.*

Note that the constraint rederivation in a tree-like unit refutation can increase the length of the refutation.

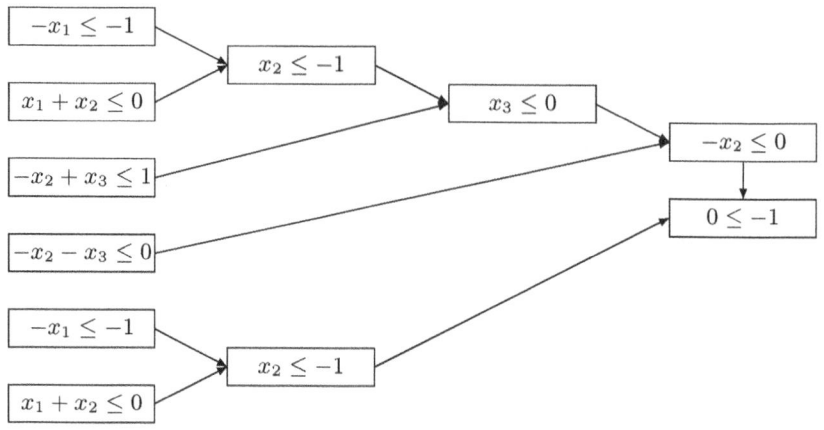

Fig. 2. Tree-like Unit Refutation

Example 3. Note that the Refutation in Fig. 1 has 4 applications of the UADD rule. Thus, it is a refutation of length 4. The refutation in Fig. 2 has 5 applications of the UADD rule. Thus, it is a refutation of length 5. Note that this increase in length comes from rederiving the constraint $x_2 \leq -1$.

We focus on the problem of finding a shortest tree-like unit refutation.

Definition 12. *The Optimum Length Tree-like Unit Refutation (OTLUR) Problem: Given a UCS* **U**, *if* **U** *has a unit refutation, find a tree-like unit refutation of* **U** *with the shortest length.*

2.1 Constraint Network Representation

In [16], we introduced a constraint network representation for UTVPI constraints. It was shown that infeasibility in a UCS could be established by the existence of certain paths in the corresponding constraint network. We describe this constraint network here for the sake of completeness.

Let $\mathbf{U} : \mathbf{A} \cdot \mathbf{x} \leq \mathbf{b}$ denote a UTVPI constraint system and let $\mathbf{X}$ denote the set of all solutions to **U**. Corresponding to this constraint system, we construct the constraint network $\mathbf{G} = \langle \mathbf{V}, \mathbf{E}, \mathbf{b} \rangle$ as follows. For each variable x_i create a node in **V**. For ease of reference, both the variable and its corresponding node are denoted as x_i. Constraints are represented as edges using the following rules:

1. A constraint of the form $x_i - x_j \leq b_{ij}$ is represented as an undirected "gray" edge, $(x_j \overset{b_{ij}}{\blacksquare} x_i)$, or $(x_i \overset{b_{ij}}{\blacksquare} x_j)$, with cost b_{ij}.
2. A constraint of the form $-x_i - x_j \leq b_{ij}$ is represented by an undirected "black" edge, $(x_i \overset{b_{ij}}{\blacksquare} x_j)$, with cost b_{ij}.
3. A constraint of the form $x_i + x_j \leq b_{ij}$ is represented by an undirected "white" edge, $(x_i \overset{b_{ij}}{\square} x_j)$, with cost b_{ij}.

Finally, we add a node x_0 to the network. This node permits the addition of absolute constraints. Each absolute constraint $x_i \leq b_i$ is replaced by a pair of constraints $x_i + x_0 \leq b_i$ and $x_i - x_0 \leq b_i$. The corresponding edges $x_0 \overset{b_i}{\square} x_i$ and $x_0 \overset{b_i}{\blacksquare} x_i$ are added to the constraint network.

We now recall the definitions of paths and cycles from [16].

Definition 13. *A k-path is a sequence of $(k+1)$ nodes, $x_1, x_2, \ldots x_{k+1}$, and k edges $e_1, e_2, \ldots e_k$, such that e_i is the edge corresponding to one of the constraints between x_i and x_{i+1} in* **U**.

Definition 14. *A k-path is considered* valid *if it has the following property: For every i from 2 to k, the coefficients of x_i in the constraints corresponding to the edges e_i and e_{i-1} have opposite signs.*

Summing the UTVPI constraints corresponding to the edges in a valid path results in a UTVPI constraint. Note that this constraint corresponds to an edge between the initial and final vertices on that path. Each valid path has the same type (white, black, or gray) as this edge.

Definition 15. *The* cost *of a path is the sum of the costs of the edges along that path.*

Definition 16. *A cycle is a valid k-path for which $x_1 = x_{k+1}$.*

Example 4. Suppose we have the system of constraints and the corresponding constraint network provided in Fig. 3:

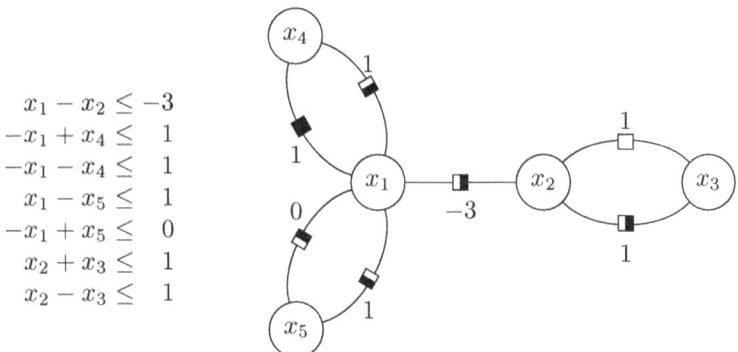

$$
\begin{aligned}
x_1 - x_2 &\leq -3 \\
-x_1 + x_4 &\leq 1 \\
-x_1 - x_4 &\leq 1 \\
x_1 - x_5 &\leq 1 \\
-x_1 + x_5 &\leq 0 \\
x_2 + x_3 &\leq 1 \\
x_2 - x_3 &\leq 1
\end{aligned}
$$

Fig. 3. Example Constraint System and Network (without node x_0)

From Fig. 3, we can see that the 8-path

$$\left(x_1 \overset{-3}{\blacksquare} x_2 \overset{1}{\square} x_3 \overset{1}{\blacksquare} x_2 \overset{-3}{\blacksquare} x_1 \overset{0}{\blacksquare} x_5 \overset{1}{\blacksquare} x_1 \overset{1}{\blacksquare} x_4 \overset{1}{\blacksquare} x_1\right)$$

forms a cycle even though the vertices x_1 and x_2 and the edge $(x_2 \overset{-3}{\square} x_1)$ are used multiple times.

In the remainder of this paper we use gray cycles and tree-like refutations interchangeably. This is due to the following result from [19].

Theorem 1. *A system of UTVPI constraints* **U** *has a tree-like refutation of length l, if and only if, the corresponding constraint network* **G** *has a negative cost gray cycle of length l.*

3   Motivation and Related Work

In this section, we motivate our work, and describe work on related problems. This paper focuses on unit refutations. These refutations are interesting because of the difference between absolute constraints and relative constraints in UCSs. Note that absolute constraints only place bounds on a single variable. This means that it defines the domain of that variable. On the other hand, relative constraints are used to determine the relationship between variables. For this reason, relative constraints do not depend on the variable domains. The differing nature of these constraints means that there is a similar difference between unit refutations and non-unit refutations of UCSs.

A unit refutation must use the absolute constraints present in the input UCS. Thus, a unit refutation of a UCS depends on the domains of the variables in the UCS. On the other hand, unrestricted refutations could utilize only the relative constraints in the input UCS. This means that a non-unit refutation may be domain agnostic. For this reason, studying unit refutations helps in determining the structure of domain specific refutations.

This paper focuses specifically on UCSs. In particular, we focus on the problem of finding short refutations of UCSs. The problem of finding a shortest refutation (not necessarily unit) of a UCS is motivated by a number of applications, including program verification [2,13,14], real-time scheduling [6,7], and incremental shortest paths in weighted networks [4].

Additionally, a specific form of unit refutation, known as unit read-once refutation (UROR), has been studied for DCSs [17]. Refutations of this form have an additional restriction, namely that each constraint is used at most once. The problem of determining if a DCS has a UROR is **NP-complete**, and there exist both parameterized and exact-exponential algorithms for solving this problem [17]. Additionally, the problem of finding a shortest UROR is **NPO-complete**.

Prior work has investigated unit refutations in difference constraints [15] and obtained a number of interesting results. In particular, unit refutations of DCSs can be found in polynomial time. Additionally, the problem of finding the shortest unit refutation of a DCS is **APX-complete** and can be solved in pseudopolynomial time. Note that, while UCSs can be converted to DCSs [12], this conversion doubles both the number of variables and the number of constraints. Through this conversion, structural information about the refutations of the system is lost. In particular, the length of the refutation changes and so does the shape of the refutation (tree-like or dag-like).

Unit refutations have been investigated in UCSs. It was shown in [18] that the problem of determining if a UCS has a unit refutation can be solved in polynomial time. That paper also showed that the problem of finding the shortest unit dag-like refutation of a UCS is **APX-complete** and can be solved in pseudopolynomial time. In this paper, we examine a different type of refutation. This refutation has a different structure which necessitates a different examination.

4   Shortest Tree-Like Unit Refutations

In this section, we provide a pseudopolynomial time algorithm for the OTLUR problem for UCSs. The results in this section are based on results in [18].

We utilize the structure described in [18] to prove upper and lower bounds on the lengths of tree-like unit refutations of UCSs. In the theorems in this section, b_{max} represents the largest defining constant in a UCS.

We first show that the length of a tree-like unit refutation can be exponential in the size of the UCS. Thus, we cannot construct the refutation inference by inference.

Theorem 2. *There exists a UCS with n variables for which the OTLUR has length $((2 \cdot n - 2) \cdot (2 \cdot f(n) + 1) + 1)$ for an arbitrary function $f(n)$.*

Proof. Let **U** be the UCS in System (5):

$$
\begin{aligned}
& x_1 \leq f(n) && -x_1 - x_2 \leq 0 \\
& x_2 - x_3 \leq 0 && \\
& x_{n-1} - x_n \leq -1 && \cdots \\
& x_1 - x_2 \leq 0 && x_{n-1} + x_n \leq 0
\end{aligned}
\tag{5}
$$

Let R be a tree-like unit refutation of **U**. Since $x_1 \leq f(n)$ is the only absolute constraint in **U**, R must use this constraint. In fact, it must be used twice. Note that the constraint $x_{n-1} - x_n \leq -1$ is the only constraint in **U** with a negative right-hand side. Thus, R must use at least $(2 \cdot f(n) + 1)$ copies of this constraint. Otherwise, the right-hand side of the final derived constraint will not be negative. To be able to use the constraint $x_{n-1} - x_n \leq -1$ as part of a unit refutation, we need to derive a constraint of the form $-x_{n-1} \leq b$. To derive this constraint from $x_1 \leq f(n)$, R needs to use the constraints $-x_1 - x_2 \leq 0$ through $x_{n-2} - x_{n-1} \leq 0$. This uses $(n-2)$ applications of the UADD rule, and derives the constraint $-x_{n-1} \leq f(n)$. Applying the UADD rule to this constraint and $x_{n-1} - x_n \leq -1$ results in the constraint $-x_n \leq (f(n) - 1)$. Then, deriving the constraint $x_1 \leq f(n) - 1$ requires using the constraints $x_{n-1} + x_n \leq 0$ through $x_1 - x_2 \leq 0$. This is an additional $(n - 1)$ applications of the UADD rule. In total, deriving the constraint $x_1 \leq (f(n) - 1)$ requires $(2 \cdot n - 2)$ applications of the UADD rule.

Consequently, deriving $-x_1 \leq (-f(n) - 1)$ requires a total of $(2 \cdot n - 2) \cdot (2 \cdot f(n) + 1)$ applications of the UADD rule. To derive the final contradiction, we need to use the constraint $x_1 \leq f(n)$ through an additional use of the UADD rule. Thus, any unit refutation of **U** has length at least $((2 \cdot n - 2) \cdot (2 \cdot f(n) + 1) + 1)$.
□

Note that a similar result was obtained for DCSs in [15]. However, the result in this paper derives a different bound on the length of unit refutations due to the fact that this paper investigates a different constraint system.

Theorem 3. *For each even n, there exists a UCS $\mathbf{U}$ with n variables such that the OTLUR of $\mathbf{U}$ has length $(2 \cdot n^2 \cdot b_{max} + 3 \cdot n)$.*

Proof. Let $\mathbf{U}$ be the UCS in System (6).

$$
\begin{aligned}
x_{\frac{n}{2}-1} &\leq b_{max} & x_1 - x_2 &\leq b_{max} \\
-x_1 - x_2 &\leq b_{max} & x_2 - x_3 &\leq b_{max} \\
&\cdots & x_{\frac{n}{2}-2} - x_{\frac{n}{2}-1} &\leq b_{max} \\
x_{\frac{n}{2}-1} + x_{\frac{n}{2}} &\leq b_{max} & x_{\frac{n}{2}-1} - x_{\frac{n}{2}} &\leq b_{max} \\
x_{\frac{n}{2}} - x_{\frac{n}{2}+1} &\leq 0 & -x_{\frac{n}{2}} - x_{\frac{n}{2}+1} &\leq 0 \\
x_{\frac{n}{2}+1} - x_{\frac{n}{2}+2} &\leq 0 & &\cdots \\
x_{n-2} - x_{n-1} &\leq 0 & x_{n-1} - x_n &\leq 0 \\
x_{n-1} + x_n &\leq -1
\end{aligned}
\tag{6}
$$

Let $\mathbf{G}$ be the constraint network corresponding to $\mathbf{U}$. By construction, the only negative cost gray cycle C' in $\mathbf{G}$ is

$$
(x_{\frac{n}{2}} \overset{0}{\blacksquare} x_{\frac{n}{2}+1} \ldots x_{n-1} \overset{0}{\blacksquare} x_n \overset{-1}{\square} x_{n-1} \overset{0}{\blacksquare} x_{n-1} \ldots x_{\frac{n}{2}+2} \overset{0}{\blacksquare} x_{\frac{n}{2}+1} \overset{0}{\blacksquare} x_{\frac{n}{2}}).
$$

This cycle has n edges and total cost -1.

Additionally by construction, a shortest way to reach a vertex on C using both a white path and a black path are the following two paths p_1 and p_2:

$$
(x_0 \overset{b_{max}}{\square} x_{\frac{n}{2}-1} \overset{b_{max}}{\blacksquare} x_{\frac{n}{2}-2} \ldots x_2 \overset{b_{max}}{\blacksquare} x_1 \overset{}{\blacksquare} x_2 \overset{b_{max}}{\blacksquare} x_3
$$
$$
\ldots x_{\frac{n}{2}-2} \overset{b_{max}}{\blacksquare} x_{\frac{n}{2}-1} \overset{b_{max}}{\square} x_{\frac{n}{2}}).
$$

$$
(x_0 \overset{b_{max}}{\blacksquare} x_{\frac{n}{2}-1} \overset{b_{max}}{\blacksquare} x_{\frac{n}{2}-2} \ldots x_2 \overset{b_{max}}{\blacksquare} x_1 \overset{}{\blacksquare} x_2 \overset{b_{max}}{\blacksquare} x_3
$$
$$
\ldots x_{\frac{n}{2}-2} \overset{b_{max}}{\blacksquare} x_{\frac{n}{2}-1} \overset{b_{max}}{\blacksquare} x_{\frac{n}{2}}).
$$

Each of these paths uses n edges and has a total cost of $n \cdot b_{max}$.

A shortest tree-like refutation C of $\mathbf{U}$ corresponds to the path p_1 followed by $\left\lfloor \frac{b_1 + b_2}{-b_{C'}} + 1 \right\rfloor$ copies of C' followed by the path p_2. Thus, we need $(2 \cdot n \cdot b_{max} + 1)$ copies of C'.

In total C uses $(2 \cdot n^2 \cdot b_{max} + 3 \cdot n)$ edges. Thus, the OTLUR of $\mathbf{U}$ has length $(2 \cdot n^2 \cdot b_{max} + 3 \cdot n)$. □

Theorem 4. *Let $\mathbf{U}$ be a UCS with n variables. The OTLUR of $\mathbf{U}$ has length at most $(8 \cdot n^2 \cdot b_{max} + 6 \cdot n)$.*

Proof. Let $\mathbf{U}$ be a UCS with a unit refutation. Additionally, let $\mathbf{G}$ be the constraint network corresponding to $\mathbf{U}$. From [18], the graph induced by $S^{\square} \cap S^{\blacksquare}$ contains a negative weight gray cycle.

From [18], $\mathbf{U}$ has a unit refutation that corresponds to a white path p_1, a possibly repeated negative cost gray cycle C' and a black path p_2. Recall that each of these uses no vertex more than twice. Thus, p_1, p_2 and C' each have at most $2 \cdot n$ edges.

Since b_{max} is the largest edge weight in $\mathbf{G}$. The weight b_1 of p_1 is at most $2 \cdot n \cdot b_{max}$. Similarly, the weight b_2 of p_2 is at most $2 \cdot n \cdot b_{max}$. Since C' is a negative cost gray cycle, the weight $b_{C'}$ of C' is at most -1.

To make a negative weight gray cycle C through x_0, we need $\left\lceil \frac{b_1 + b_2}{-b_{C'}} + 1 \right\rceil$ copies of C'. Note that

$$\left\lceil \frac{b_1 + b_2}{-b_{C'}} + 1 \right\rceil \leq 4 \cdot n \cdot b_{max} + 1.$$

Thus, the number of edges in C is at most

$$2 \cdot n + 2 \cdot n + 2 \cdot n \cdot (4 \cdot n \cdot b_{max} + 1) = 8 \cdot n^2 \cdot b_{max} + 6 \cdot n.$$

This means that $\mathbf{U}$ has a tree-like unit refutation of length at most $(8 \cdot n^2 \cdot b_{max} + 6 \cdot n)$. Thus, the OTLUR of $\mathbf{U}$ has length at most $(8 \cdot n^2 \cdot b_{max} + 6 \cdot n)$. $\square$

We now present an $O(m \cdot n^2 \cdot ||\mathbf{b}||_{\infty})$ time pseudopolynomial time algorithm for the OTLUR problem for UCSs.

From Theorem 4, an OTLUR of a UCS has length at most $(8 \cdot n^2 \cdot ||\mathbf{b}||_{\infty} + 6 \cdot n)$, it can be found in $O(m \cdot n^2 \cdot ||\mathbf{b}||_{\infty})$ time using the algorithm in [16].

Theorem 5. *An OTLUR of a UCS can be found in $O(m \cdot n^2 \cdot ||\mathbf{b}||_{\infty})$ time.*

Proof. Let $\mathbf{U}$ be a UCS and let $\mathbf{G}$ be the corresponding constraint network. Let l^* denote the length of the OTLUR of $\mathbf{U}$. From Theorem 4, $l^* \leq (8 \cdot n^2 \cdot ||\mathbf{b}||_{\infty} + 6 \cdot n)$. Thus, there is a negative weight gray cycle in $\mathbf{G}$ through x_0 with at most $(8 \cdot n^2 \cdot ||\mathbf{b}||_{\infty} + 6 \cdot n)$ edges. It follows that we can find a shortest negative weight gray cycle through x_0 as follows:

1. After k iterations of the linear feasibility algorithm in [16] (with source x_0), we will find the least weight gray path in $\mathbf{G}$ with at most k edges from x_0 to each vertex.
2. Since $\mathbf{U}$ has a unit refutation of length l^*, $\mathbf{G}$ has a negative weight gray cycle from x_0 to itself of length l^*.
3. After $(8 \cdot n^2 \cdot ||\mathbf{b}||_{\infty} + 6 \cdot n) \geq l^*$ iterations of the linear feasibility algorithm in [16] (with source x_0), we will find a negative weight gray cycle from x_0 to itself.
4. This takes $O(m \cdot n^2 \cdot ||\mathbf{b}||_{\infty})$ time. $\square$

5   Approximability

We now show that the problem of finding the length of an OTLUR for a UCS can be approximated to within a factor of 2 in polynomial time. Our algorithm design makes use of a concept called **simple tree-like unit refutations**.

Definition 17. *A* **simple tree-like unit refutation** R *of a UCS* **U** *corresponds to a negative weight gray cycle* W *that can be divided into: 1. A white path between* v_0 *and some vertex* v_i. *2. A negative weight gray cycle through the vertex* v_i, *possibly repeated. 3. A black path between* v_i *and* v_0.

Lemma 1. *If a UCS* **U** *has a unit refutation, then it has a simple tree-like unit refutation whose length is at most twice the length of the OLTUR.*

Proof. Let R be the OLTUR of **U**. From [18], we know that R corresponds to a negative weight gray cycle through v_0. This walk can be divided into: 1. A white walk w_1 from v_0 to some vertex v_i. 2. A closed gray walk w_2 through the vertex v_i, possibly repeated. 3. A black walk w_3 from v_i to v_0. We now show that for some vertex v_i', none of these paths use a vertex more than twice.

Assume, for the sake of contradiction, that the walk w_1 uses a vertex more than twice. Thus, it contains a gray cycle C' [16]. If this is not a negative weight gray cycle, then we can remove this cycle from w_1 and shorten the corresponding refutation. Thus, C' must have a weight $-b_{C'} < 0$.

Consider the average weight of this cycle $\frac{-b_{C'}}{|C'|}$, and compare it to the average weight of the gray cycle w_2 ($\frac{-b_{w_2}}{|w_2|}$). If the average weight of C' is lower than that of w_2, then we can replace repetitions of w_2 with repetitions of C' until w_2 no longer appears in the walk corresponding to R. Note that this increases the length of the refutation by at most the number of edges in C'. Similarly, if w_2 is more efficient than C' then we can shorten the refutation by replacing C' with another repetition of w_2. In this case, the length of the refutation increases by at most the number of edges in w_2. Thus, w_1 must use each vertex at most twice. We can similarly show that w_2 and w_3 must also use each vertex at most twice.

Each time we eliminate a cycle in the original refutation, the length of the refutation increases by at most the number of edges in a different cycle used in the refutation. The total number of these edges is at most the length of R. Thus, the length of this simple tree-like unit refutation is at most twice the length of R.   □

From Lemma 1, we get the following result.

Theorem 6. *The problem of approximating the length of an OTLUR R of a UCS* **U** *with m constraints over n variables to within a factor of 2 can be solved in $O(n^4)$ time.*

Proof. Let **U** be a UCS with a unit refutation. From Lemma 1, **U** has a shortest simple tree-like unit refutation R. Additionally, R is at most twice the length of the OTLUR of **U**. We show that R can be found in $O(n^4)$ time. R corresponds to a closed walk W that can be divided into: 1. A white path p_1 between v_0 and some vertex v_i. 2. A negative gray cycle C through the vertex v_i, possibly repeated. 3. A black path p_2 between v_i and v_0.

If there exists a white path p_1' from v_0 to v_i that is shorter than p_1 and has fewer edges than p_1, then replacing p_1 with p_1' will result in a shorter refutation. Thus, p_1 must be a shortest path from v_0 to v_i with at most $|p_1|$ edges. A similar argument can be made for C and p_2.

Thus, to find R, then for each vertex v_i and $k \leq n$, we need to find the following: 1. A least weight white path between v_0 and v_i with at most k edges, 2. a least weight gray cycle through v_i with at most k edges, and 3. a least weight black path between v_i and v_0 with at most k edges.

Note that these structures can be found in $O(m \cdot n^2)$ time.

For each combination of v_i, p_1, C, and p_2, the length of the corresponding refutation R' is computed as follows: 1. The path p_1 has weight b_1 and uses $|p_1|$ edges. 2. The path p_2 has weight b_2 and uses $|p_2|$ edges. 3. The cycle C, has weight $-b_C < 0$ and used $|C|$ edges. 4. The overall walk has negative weight if the cycle C is repeated $\left\lceil \frac{b_1+b_2}{b_C} \right\rceil$ times. 5. Thus, the walk uses a total of $(|p_1| + |p_2| + |C| \cdot \left\lceil \frac{b_1+b_2}{b_C} \right\rceil)$ edges. 6. This means that R has length $(|p_1| + |p_2| + |C| \cdot \left\lceil \frac{b_1+b_2}{b_C} \right\rceil) - 1$.

Thus, once v_i, p_1, C, and p_2 are chosen the length of the refutation corresponding to these paths can be found in constant time. Note that for each v_i, there are at most n choices for each of p_1, p_2 and C. Thus, at most n^4 possible walks need to be tested. This can be done in $O(n^4)$ time. $\square$

Theorem 6 establishes that this problem is in **APX**. From [15], the OTLUR problem for DCSs is **APX-hard** under **strict reductions**. Hence, the OTLUR problem is also **APX-hard** for UCSs (under strict reductions), since UCSs subsume difference constraints. It follows that the OTLUR problem for UCSs is **APX-complete**.

Note that in [15], we performed a strict reduction from the Min2SAT problem to the OTLUR problem in DCSs From [1], the Min2SAT problem cannot be approximated to within $(\frac{15}{14} - \epsilon)$ for any $\epsilon > 0$, unless $\mathbf{P} = \mathbf{NP}$. Since our reduction preserves this approximation ratio, an OTLUR of a UCS cannot be approximated to within $(\frac{15}{14} - \epsilon)$ for any $\epsilon > 0$ unless $\mathbf{P} = \mathbf{NP}$.

Observe that the OTLUR problem for UCSs is both **APX-complete** and can be solved with a pseudopolynomial time algorithm. Such problems are unusual. However, there are other problems with similar properties. For example, the 2-dimensional Knapsack problem has a pseudopolynomial time algorithm but no FPTAS [9]. From the **APX-completeness** result and the pseudopolynomial time algorithm, we have the following dichotomy:

1. If $||\mathbf{b}||_\infty$ is polynomial in n and m, then the OTLUR problem for UCSs can be solved in polynomial time.
2. If $||\mathbf{b}||_\infty \geq 2^m \cdot n - 2$, then the OTLUR problem for UCSs is **APX-complete**.

6   Conclusion

In this paper, we investigated tree-like unit refutations of linear feasibility in UTVPI constraints. This work extends work in [15], which focused on difference constraints and work in [18], which investigated dag-like unit refutations of UVTPI constraints. Both difference constraints and UTVPI constraints find wide application in program verification, abstract interpretation and array bounds checking. Our main contribution is the design of a pseudopolynomial time algorithm for the problem of finding an OTLUR of an UCS. We also investigated the approximation complexity this problem.

References

1. Avidor, A., Zwick, U.: Approximating MIN 2-SAT and MIN 3-SAT. Theory Comput. Syst. **38**(3), 329–345 (2005)
2. Cotton, S., Asarin, E., Maler, O., Niebert, P.: Some progress in satisfiability checking for difference logic. In: FORMATS/FTRTFT, pp. 263–276 (2004)
3. Cousot, P., Cousot, R.: Abstract interpretation: a unified lattice model for static analysis of programs by construction or approximation of fixpoints. In: POPL, pp. 238–252 (1977)
4. Demtrescu, C., Italiano, G.F.: A new approach to dynamic all pairs shortest paths. J. ACM **51**(6), 968–992 (2004)
5. Farkas, G.: Über die Theorie der Einfachen Ungleichungen. Journal für die Reine und Angewandte Mathematik **124**(124), 1–27 (1902)
6. Gerber, R., Pugh, W., Saksena, M.: Parametric dispatching of hard real-time tasks. IEEE Trans. Comput. **44**(3), 471–479 (1995)
7. Han, C.C., Lin, K.J.: Job scheduling with temporal distance constraints. Technical Report UIUCDCS-R-89-1560, University of Illinois at Urbana-Champaign, Department of Computer Science (1989)
8. Jaffar, J., Maher, M.J., Stuckey, P.J., Yap, H.C.: Beyond finite domains. In: Proceedings of the Second International Workshop on Principles and Practice of Constraint Programming (1994)
9. Korte, B., Schrader, R.: On the existence of fast approximation schemes. ol mangasarian, rr meyer, and sm robinson (eds.) nonlinear programming (1981)
10. Lahiri, S.K., Musuvathi, M.: An efficient decision procedure for UTVPI constraints. In: Proceedings of the 5th International Workshop on the Frontiers of Combining Systems, September 19-21, Vienna, Austria, pp. 168–183, New York (2005). Springer
11. McConnell, R.M., Mehlhorn, K., Näher, S., Schweitzer, P.: Certifying algorithms. Comput. Sci. Rev. **5**(2), 119–161 (2011)
12. Miné, A.: The octagon abstract domain. High. Order Symbolic Comput. **19**(1), 31–100 (2006)
13. Nieuwenhuis, R., Oliveras, A.: DPLL(T) with exhaustive theory propagation and its application to difference logic. In: CAV, pp. 321–334 (2005)
14. Seshia, S.A., Lahiri, S.K., Bryant, R.E.: A hybrid sat-based decision procedure for separation logic with uninterpreted functions. In: DAC, pp. 425–430 (2003)

15. Subramani, K., Wojciechowski, P.: Unit refutations of difference constraint systems. In: Gal, K., Nowé, A., Nalepa, G.J., Fairstein, R., Radulescu, R. (eds.) ECAI 2023 - 26th European Conference on Artificial Intelligence, September 30 - October 4, 2023, Kraków, Poland - Including 12th Conference on Prestigious Applications of Intelligent Systems (PAIS 2023), vol. 372 of Frontiers in Artificial Intelligence and Applications, pp. 2226–2233. IOS Press (2023)
16. Subramani, K., Wojciechowski, P.J.: A combinatorial certifying algorithm for linear feasibility in UTVPI constraints. Algorithmica $78(1)$, 166–208 (2017)
17. Subramani, K., Wojciechowski, P.: Analyzing unit read-once refutations in difference constraint systems. In: Faber, W., Friedrich, G., Gebser, M., Morak, M. (eds.) JELIA 2021. LNCS (LNAI), vol. 12678, pp. 147–161. Springer, Cham (2021). https://doi.org/10.1007/978-3-030-75775-5_11
18. Wojciechowski, P., Subramani, K.: Dag-like unit refutations in UTVPI constraint systems. In: Nakano, S., Xiao, M. (eds.) WALCOM: Algorithms and Computation - 19th International Conference and Workshops on Algorithms and Computation, WALCOM 2025, Chengdu, China, February 28 - March 2, 2025, Proceedings, volume 15411 of Lecture Notes in Computer Science, pp. 377–392. Springer (2025)
19. Wojciechowski, P.J., Subramani, K., Williamson, M.D.: Polynomial time algorithms for optimal length tree-like refutations of linear infeasibility in UTVPI constraints. Discret. Appl. Math. 305, 272–294 (2021)

Deontic Reasoning

GL-Based Calculi for PCL and Its Deontic Cousin

Agata Ciabattoni[(✉)], Dmitry Rozplokhas[(✉)], and Matteo Tesi[(✉)]

Vienna University of Technology (TU Wien), Vienna, Austria
`matteo.tesi@sns.it`

Abstract. We introduce a natural sequent calculus for preferential conditional logic **PCL** via embeddings into provability logic **GL**, achieving optimal complexity and enabling countermodel extraction. Extending the method to **PCL** with reflexivity and absoluteness – corresponding to Åqvist's deontic system **F** with cautious monotony – we employ hypersequents to capture the **S5** modality; the resulting calculus subsumes the known calculi for the weaker systems **E** and **F** within Åqvist family.

1 Introduction

Conditional logics aim to capture forms of implication, $A \rightsquigarrow B$, that departs from classical implication. These logics support a range of interpretations, including the prototypical ("Typically, if A, then B"), the counterfactual ("If A were the case, then B would be"), and the deontic interpretation ("B is obligatory under condition A," usually written as $\bigcirc(B/A)$).

The most prominent systems for the *prototypical interpretation* are the so-called KLM logics [18]. Within this framework, the logic **P** of preferential reasoning has been particularly influential. **P** (and KLM logics generally) permits only shallow conditionals. An extension of **P** that accommodates nested conditionals is **PCL** (Preferential Conditional Logic), a foundational system for the *counterfactual interpretation* of conditionals. Despite its simple axiomatization, known since the work of Burgess [7], **PCL** lacks an analytic sequent calculus that balances proof-theoretic clarity with optimal complexity. Analytic calculi are characterized by the step-wise decomposition of the formula to be proved, which makes them well-suited for establishing meta-logical properties of the formalized logics and enabling automation. To our knowledge, the only analytic sequent calculus for **PCL** is in [25], which, although complexity-optimal, employs highly combinatorial rules that hinder readability and countermodel construction. Other proposals rely on the more expressive framework of labeled calculi [15, 16, 23], which can handle extensions of **PCL**, through neighbourhood semantics, at the cost of suboptimal computational behavior. Tableaux and resolution calculi have been proposed in [13, 22], but present significant complications: [13] requires intricate blocking conditions to ensure termination, and [22] relies on a non-trivial pre-processing phase.

In this paper, we define a simple and complexity-optimal sequent calculus for **PCL** by establishing and exploiting a connection between **PCL** and Gödel-Löb

© The Author(s), under exclusive license to Springer Nature Switzerland AG 2026
G. Casini et al. (Eds.): JELIA 2025, LNAI 16093, pp. 171–186, 2026.
https://doi.org/10.1007/978-3-032-04587-4_11

logic (**GL**) [26] – the normal modal logic of arithmetic provability. The calculus enables countermodel extraction, producing the small models described in [11], for which the original paper provided only a non-constructive existence proof. The method extends to **PCLTA**, i.e., **PCL** with reflexivity and absoluteness, for which we introduce a new analytic calculus. **PCLTA** is known in the context of the *deontic interpretation* of conditionals as **F+(CM)**, that is Åqvist's dyadic deontic system **F** [1] augmented with the cautious monotonicity axiom (CM) [24].

Our calculi are based on an embedding of **PCL** into normal modal logics, extending that of its shallow counterpart, the KLM logic **P**. The well-known embedding proposed in [6], which maps **P** into **S4**, is not suitable for our purposes, as it gives rise to a different logic of nested conditionals, CT4.[1] Here we (simplify and) extend the correspondence identified in [12] between the conditional operator of **P** and the modality of **GL**, enabling the treatment of nested conditionals via bi-modal logics. We show that **PCL** naturally embeds into a combination of **GL** and **K**, while **F+(CM)** corresponds to a combination of **GL** and **S5**. These embeddings are foundational to our calculi and are formally verified within them. Similarly to previous work on modal interpretation of conditionals, *e.g.*, [5,12], we encode maximality by a unary modal operator $\mathcal{B}et$, which represents the "better" (or preferable) worlds, and is interpreted as the **GL** modality. The resulting sequent calculus for **PCL** is analytic and complexity-optimal. Due to the presence of the **S5** modality,[2] the calculus for **F+(CM)** is formulated within the hypersequent framework, a natural generalization of the sequent format that enables parallel manipulation of multiple sequents [3]. The calculus for **F+(CM)** presented here provides an alternative to the one in [10], which was based on a different semantic interpretation of the logic. Notably, our rules for the dyadic obligation coincide with those of the calculi for the weaker logics **E** and **F** in the Å qvist family [8,9], differing only in the rule for the $\mathcal{B}et$ modality. This alignment reflects the modularity of the Hilbert systems **E**, **F**, and **F+(CM)**, where **F** extends **E** with one additional axiom, and **F+(CM)** further adds (CM).

2   Preliminaries: PCL and F+(CM)

Let $\mathbb{P}$ be the set of propositional atoms. The language of **PCL** is generated by the grammar: $A ::= p \in \mathbb{P} \mid \neg A \mid A \to A \mid A \rightsquigarrow A$, with $\wedge, \vee, \leftrightarrow$ defined as usual. An axiomatization of **PCL** consists of the axioms for classical propositional logic extended with the following axioms and rules:

(CSO) $(A \rightsquigarrow B) \wedge (B \rightsquigarrow A) \to ((A \rightsquigarrow C) \leftrightarrow (B \rightsquigarrow C))$

$$\frac{A \leftrightarrow B}{(A \rightsquigarrow C) \leftrightarrow (B \rightsquigarrow C)}(RCEA)$$

(OR) $(A \rightsquigarrow C) \wedge (B \rightsquigarrow C) \to ((A \vee B) \rightsquigarrow C)$

(ID) $A \rightsquigarrow A$

$$\frac{B_1 \wedge \cdots \wedge B_m \to C}{(A \rightsquigarrow B_1) \wedge \cdots \wedge (A \rightsquigarrow B_m) \to (A \rightsquigarrow C)}(RCK)$$

---

[1] For example, $\neg(\top \rightsquigarrow \bot)$ is valid in CT4 but not in **PCL**.

[2] No cut-free sequent calculus is known for modal **S5**.

(CSO) expresses that conditionally equivalent formulas have the same (conditional) consequences. It is equivalent to the pair of well-known axioms of cautious monotony (CM) $(A \rightsquigarrow B) \wedge (A \rightsquigarrow C) \rightarrow (A \wedge B \rightsquigarrow C)$ and restricted transitivity (RT) $(A \wedge B \rightsquigarrow C) \wedge (A \rightsquigarrow B) \rightarrow (A \rightsquigarrow C)$. (Id) and (OR) are the conditional versions of identity, and of the principle governing disjunctive premises. The rule (RCEA) allows substitution of equivalents in the antecedent, and (RCK) distributes conditionals over classical implication. The semantics of **PCL** is given by the following notion of *preference models* [7].[3]

Definition 1. *A* **PCL** *preference model is a tuple* $\langle W, \{W_w\}_{w \in W}, \{\succeq_w\}_{w \in W}, V \rangle$ *where* W *is a (non-empty) finite set of worlds,* $W_w \subseteq W$ *is a set of worlds accessible from* w, $\succeq_w$ *is a reflexive and transitive binary relation on* W_w, *and* $V : \mathbb{P} \to \mathcal{P}(W)$ *is a valuation function. We write* $v \succ_w u$ *to denote* $v \succeq_w u$ *and* $u \not\succeq_w v$. *The satisfaction w.r.t. such models is defined as follows:*

- $(M, w) \models x$ *if* $w \in V(x)$
- $(M, w) \models A \wedge B$ *if* $(M, w) \models A$ *and* $(M, w) \models B$.
- $(M, w) \models \neg A$ *if* $(M, w) \not\models A$.
- $(M, w) \models A \rightsquigarrow B$ *if for every* $v \in Best_w(\|A\|)$, $(M, v) \models B$,.

where $\|A\| = \{w \mid (M, w) \models A\}$ *and* $Best_w(X) = \{u \in X \mid \forall v \in X, v \not\succ_w u\}$.

We consider a variant of the language extended with the unary operator $\mathcal{B}et$. In the extended language, formulas are evaluated relative to a twice-pointed model (M, u, w), where u is "the point of view" (POV), whose preference relation is used and $w \in W_u$ is the world of evaluation (boolean cases are omitted):

- $(M, u, w) \models x$ *if* $w \in V(x)$.
- $(M, u, w) \models \mathcal{B}et A$ *if for every* $v \in W_u$ *s.t.* $v \succ_u w$, $(M, u, v) \models A$.
- $(M, u, w) \models A \rightsquigarrow B$ *if for every* $v \in Best_w(\|A\|_u)$, $(M, u, v) \models B$.

where $\|A\|_u = \{w \mid (M, u, w) \models A\}$. Notice that for formulas without $\mathcal{B}et$ the evaluation does not depend on the POV, and for such formulas satisfiability w.r.t. two-pointed models is equivalent to satisfiability w.r.t. usual pointed models (since for $(M, w) \models A$, M can be transformed into M' by adding the world u with $W_u = \{w\}$, ensuring $(M', u, w) \models A$).

The logic **F+(CM)** is the extension of **PCL** with reflexivity (i.e. $w \in W_w$) and absoluteness (i.e. $W_{w_1} = W_{w_2}$ and $\succeq_{w_1} = \succeq_{w_2}$ for any $w_1, w_2 \in W$), which arises in the context of normative reasoning [1,24]. Accordingly, an axiomatization of **F+(CM)** can be obtained by extending **PCL** with the following axioms (when referring to **F+(CM)**, we use the notation $\bigcirc(B/A)$ in place of $A \rightsquigarrow B$):

$$(\text{T}) \ A \to \neg \bigcirc (\bot / A)$$

$$(\text{A}_1) \ \bigcirc(B/A) \to \bigcirc(\bigcirc(B/A)/C) \qquad (\text{A}_2) \ \neg\bigcirc(B/A) \to \bigcirc(\neg\bigcirc(B/A)/C)$$

---

[3] Since PCL enjoys the Finite Model Property [7], we limit our analysis to finite models, enabling a simpler truth condition for conditionals [21].

The semantics of **F+(CM)** simplifies that of **PCL** by avoiding accessible worlds and indexed preference relations, thanks to reflexivity and absoluteness. As a result, the satisfability in the extended language does not require POV and can be defined w.r.t. the usual pointed models.

Definition 2. *An* **F+(CM)** *preference model is a tuple* $\langle W, \succeq, V \rangle$, *where W is a (non-empty) finite set of worlds, $\succeq$ is a reflexive and transitive binary relation on W, and $V \colon \mathbb{P} \to \mathcal{P}(W)$ is a valuation function. The satisfaction w.r.t. such models is defined as follows (boolean cases are omitted):*

- $(M, w) \models \mathcal{B}et A$ *if for every* $v \in W$ *s.t.* $v \succ w$, $(M, v) \models A$.
- $(M, w) \models \bigcirc(B/A)$ *if for every* $v \in Best(||A||)$, $(M, v) \models B$.

While **F+(CM)** typically includes an explicit **S5** modality, we omit it here as it can be defined via the conditional as: $\Box A := \bigcirc(\bot/\neg A)$.

3 A Sequent Calculus for PCL Grounded in GL

We uncover and exploit a novel connection between **PCL** and the provability logic **GL** to define **ScPCL**, an analytic sequent calculus for **PCL** which is both simple and complexity-optimal. **ScPCL** extends Gentzen's LK calculus for classical logic with the rules for $\mathcal{B}et$ and for the conditional operator. The axioms and rules of **ScPCL** are displayed in Fig. 1. The intuition behind the modal and conditional rules is as follows:

Rule $\mathcal{B}et$: Due to the finiteness of the models, the $\mathcal{B}et$ modality can be naturally interpreted as the **GL** modality. Indeed, **GL** is sound and complete w.r.t. finite, transitive and irreflexive Kripke frames. Due to transitivity, the truth condition for the $\mathcal{B}et$ modality can be equivalently stated as:

$$(M, u, w) \models \mathcal{B}et A \text{ if } \forall v \in W_u \text{ s.t. } v \succ_u w \text{ and } (M, u, v) \models \mathcal{B}et A, (M, u, v) \models A$$

This rewriting brings to the fore the fixed point property of $\mathcal{B}et$ and leads to the sequent rule below ($\mathcal{B}et A$ is the *diagonal formula*):

$$\frac{\mathcal{B}et A \Rightarrow A}{\Rightarrow \mathcal{B}et A}$$

By adding contexts to the rule, we recover the familiar rule for the **GL** calculus from [27], which we denote as $\mathcal{B}et$ in Fig. 1.

Rule $\rightsquigarrow$: In [12], a correspondence was established between the conditional operator in **P** and the modality $\mathcal{B}et$ of **GL**. The conditional $A \rightsquigarrow B$ in **P** was expressed as $(A \wedge \mathcal{B}et \neg A \to B) \wedge \mathcal{B}et(A \wedge \mathcal{B}et \neg A \to B)$ (denoting the **GL** modality with $\mathcal{B}et$). Here, we simplify this translation –by removing the first conjunct–, and extend it to the nested case. The extension to **PCL**, relies on the small models of [11]. There, a model satisfying any given formula is constructed as a tree-like structure consisting of separate *clusters* of worlds with a certain ordering, each child-cluster is intended to ensure the required evaluation of conditionals in some world of the parent-cluster. Since clusters are finite submodels with a transitive ordering inside, they can be seen as separate **GL**-models, while the tree structure on them can be captured by an independent accessibility relation, which suggests the following translation of the conditional into the bi-modal logic **K+GL**, leading to the $\rightsquigarrow$ rule in Fig. 1: $tr_{\mathbf{PCL}}(A \rightsquigarrow B) = \Box_{\mathbf{K}} \mathcal{B}et\, (A \wedge \mathcal{B}et\neg A \rightarrow B)$. The adequacy of the new embedding is proven at the end of the section.

Example 1. A derivation of cautious monotonicity (CM) in **ScPCL** is:

$$\dfrac{\dfrac{\dfrac{\dfrac{\dfrac{\dots (A \wedge \mathcal{B}et\neg A) \rightarrow B, \neg(A \wedge B), \mathcal{B}et\neg A, A \Rightarrow}{\dots \mathcal{B}et((A \wedge \mathcal{B}et\neg A) \rightarrow B), A, B, \mathcal{B}et\neg(A \wedge B) \Rightarrow C, \mathcal{B}et\neg A}\;_{\mathcal{B}et,\,\mathrm{R}\neg}}{\dots \mathcal{B}et((A \wedge \mathcal{B}et\neg A) \rightarrow B), (A \wedge \mathcal{B}et\neg A) \rightarrow C, A, B, \mathcal{B}et\neg(A \wedge B) \Rightarrow C}\;_{\mathrm{L}\rightarrow}}{\dots \mathcal{B}et((A \wedge \mathcal{B}et\neg A) \rightarrow B), (A \wedge \mathcal{B}et\neg A) \rightarrow C \Rightarrow (A \wedge B \wedge \mathcal{B}et\neg(A \wedge B)) \rightarrow C}\;_{\mathrm{R}\rightarrow,\,\mathrm{L}\wedge}}{\mathcal{B}et((A \wedge \mathcal{B}et\neg A) \rightarrow B), \mathcal{B}et((A \wedge \mathcal{B}et\neg A) \rightarrow C) \Rightarrow \mathcal{B}et((A \wedge B \wedge \mathcal{B}et\neg(A \wedge B)) \rightarrow C)}\;_{\mathcal{B}et}}{A \rightsquigarrow B, A \rightsquigarrow C \Rightarrow A \wedge B \rightsquigarrow C}\;_{\rightsquigarrow}$$

Trivially derivable premises in branching rules are omitted. The topmost sequent is derivable by logical rules. Decomposing a conjunction on the left can also be done using logical rules since $A \wedge B$ abbreviates $\neg(A \rightarrow \neg B)$.

Remark 1. **ScPCL** does not strictly satisfy the subformula property. Nevertheless, there is a finitary restriction on the formulas occurring in derivations. In particular, if $\Rightarrow F$ is the root sequent, then all formulas appearing in the derivation are either subformulas of F or subformulas of $\mathcal{B}et(A \wedge \mathcal{B}et\neg A \rightarrow B)$ for some conditional $A \rightsquigarrow B$ inside F. We call this property *weak subformula property*.

The weak subformula property, together with the specific formulation of the $\mathcal{B}et$ rule, enables to define a notion of complexity for sequents that strictly decreases during bottom-up proof construction.

Definition 3. *The complexity of a sequent $\Gamma \Rightarrow \Delta$ is a triple (d, b, c), where d is the maximal depth of nesting of conditionals in the sequent, b is a number of $\mathcal{B}et$-formulas that appear as subformulas in $\Gamma \cup \Delta$ but do not appear as formulas in Γ, and c the total number of propositional connectives in the sequent.*

Defining a lexicographic ordering on such triples, the complexity of the premises is strictly smaller than the complexity of the conclusion for any rule application.[4] More precisely, in $\rightsquigarrow$ parameter d decreases, in $\mathcal{B}et$ parameter b decreases (if the rule application is not redundant) while parameter d decreases or remains the same, and in every logical rule parameter c decreases while both d and b either decrease or remain the same. Each parameter is polynomially bounded w.r.t. the size of the sequent. Moreover, due to the weak subformula property, the size of any sequent in a derivation is polynomially bounded by the size of the root sequent. Hence the length of any derivation branch –assuming there is no redundant rule applications– is also polynomially bounded in the size

---

[4] Apart from a redundant application of $(\mathcal{B}et)$, which contain $\mathcal{B}etA$ on both sides in the conclusion, and therefore can be closed immediately with the axiom.

of the root sequent. Thus proof search in **ScPCL** attempting all non-redundant rule applications in any arbitrary order can be performed in polynomial space, matching the complexity of **PCL**.

Proposition 1. *Proof search in* **ScPCL** *can be performed in PSPACE.*

We now establish soundness and completeness of **ScPCL** w.r.t. preference semantics of **PCL**. As usual, we can interpret a sequent as a formula: we say that $\Gamma \Rightarrow \Delta$ is valid in **PCL** when $(\bigwedge \Gamma) \to (\bigvee \Delta)$ is valid in **PCL**.

AXIOMS: $p, \Gamma \Rightarrow \Delta, p$ \qquad for $p \in \mathbb{P}$

LOGICAL RULES:

$$\dfrac{A, \Gamma \Rightarrow \Delta}{\Gamma \Rightarrow \Delta, \neg A} R\neg \qquad \dfrac{\Gamma \Rightarrow \Delta, A}{\neg A, \Gamma \Rightarrow \Delta} L\neg \qquad \dfrac{\Gamma, A \Rightarrow \Delta, B}{\Gamma \Rightarrow \Delta, A \to B} L\to \qquad \dfrac{\Gamma \Rightarrow \Delta, A \quad \Gamma, B \Rightarrow \Delta}{\Gamma, A \to B \Rightarrow \Delta} R\to$$

MODAL RULES:

$$\dfrac{\{\mathcal{B}et(A_i \wedge \mathcal{B}et\neg A_i \to B_i)\}_i \Rightarrow \mathcal{B}et(A \wedge \mathcal{B}et\neg A \to B)}{\Gamma, \{A_i \rightsquigarrow B_i\}_i \Rightarrow A \rightsquigarrow B, \Delta} \rightsquigarrow \qquad \dfrac{\Gamma^{b\downarrow}, \Gamma^b, \mathcal{B}etA \Rightarrow A}{\Gamma \Rightarrow \mathcal{B}etA, \Delta} \mathcal{B}et$$

Fig. 1. The calculus ScPCL. $\Gamma^b := \{\mathcal{B}etA \,|\, \mathcal{B}etA \in \Gamma\}$ and $\Gamma^{b\downarrow} := \{A \,|\, \mathcal{B}etA \in \Gamma\}$.

Proposition 2. *If* $\Gamma \Rightarrow \Delta$ *is derivable in* **ScPCL**, *then it is valid in* **PCL**.

Proof. For each rule the validity of premise implies the validity of the conclusion. We only consider the cases of the rules $(\mathcal{B}et)$ and $(\rightsquigarrow)$, other cases being trivial.

Rule $(\mathcal{B}et)$: Suppose towards a contradiction that the conclusion is not valid. Then there is a twice-pointed model (M, u, w) s.t. all the formulas in Γ are true at (M, u, w) while all formulas in Δ and $\mathcal{B}etA$ are false at (M, u, w). The latter implies that the set $X = \{v \in W_u \mid u \succ_u w \text{ and } (M, u, v) \not\models A\}$ is not empty. Then there is some $v \in Best_u(X)$, since $\succ_u$ is a strict preorder on a finite set. (M, u, v) satisfies all formulas in $\Gamma^{b\downarrow}$ and Γ^b due to transitivity of $\succ_u$, it also falsifies A by definition of X and satisfies $\mathcal{B}etA$ since $v \in Best_u(X)$. Thus, (M, u, v) falsifies the premise, leading to a contradiction.

Rule $(\rightsquigarrow)$: Suppose towards a contradiction that the conclusion is not valid. Then there are a model $M = \langle W, \{W_w\}_{w \in W}, \{\leq_w\}_{w \in W}, V \rangle$ and $u, v \in W$ s.t. $(M, u, v) \models A_i \rightsquigarrow B_i$ and $(M, u, v) \not\models A \rightsquigarrow B$. The latter implies that there is $v' \in Best_v(\|A\|_u^M)$ s.t. $v' \notin \|B\|_u^M$. Let us consider an extended model $M' = \langle W \cup \{v'\}, \{W'_w\}_{w \in W'}, \{\succeq'_w\}_{w \in W}, V' \rangle$ that only adds a new world v'' in M with $v' \succ_u v''$ and does not change any other preference relation or valuation:

- $W'_u = W_u \cup \{v''\}$, $W'_{v''} = \emptyset$, $W'_w = W_w$ for any $w \in W \setminus \{u\}$,
- $\succeq'_w = \succeq_w$ for $w \in W \setminus \{u\}$, $\succeq'_{v''}$ is empty and $x \succeq'_u y$ if either $x \succeq_u y$ or $x = y = v''$ or $y = v''$ and $x \succeq_u v$.

$\|C\|_x^{M'} = \|C\|_x^M$ for any $x \in W$ since v'' is never accessible during the evaluation, so $v' \notin \|B\|_u^{M'}$. We observe that $(M', u, v'') \models \mathcal{B}et(A_i \wedge \mathcal{B}et\neg A_i \to B_i)$ for any $1 \leq i \leq n$ since $(M', u, v) \models A_i \rightsquigarrow B_i$. Therefore, by the validity of the premise, we get that v'' satisfies $(M, u, v'') \models \mathcal{B}et(A \wedge \mathcal{B}et\neg A \to B)$. Since $v' \succ'_u v''$ we get $v' \in \|B\|^{M'}$ and thus a contradiction.

The completeness of **ScPCL** is shown by exhibiting a countermodel for any non-derivable sequent. The proof is constructive.

Proposition 3. *If $\Gamma \Rightarrow \Delta$ is valid in* **PCL**, *then it is derivable in* **ScPCL**.

Proof. The proof is by induction on the complexity of $\Gamma \Rightarrow \Delta$. If there is a negated formula or implication in $\Gamma \cup \Delta$, then a logical rule can be applied to it. At least one of the premises is a non-derivable sequent of smaller complexity, so by the inductive hypothesis there will be a countermodel falsifying it, which will also falsify the conclusion.

Now let all formulas in $\Gamma \cup \Delta$ be either a propositional variable, a conditional, or a $\mathcal{B}et$-formula. The premise of each application of $(\rightsquigarrow)$ or $(\mathcal{B}et)$ is an underivable sequent of smaller complexity, so by inductive hypothesis, there exists a twice-pointed model falsifying it. Suppose $(M^{+1}, u^{+1}, v^{+1}), \ldots, (M^{+n}, u^{+n}, v^{+n})$ are all such models for all possible applications of $(\mathcal{B}et)$, and $(M^{-1}, u^{-1}, v^{-1}), \ldots, (M^{-m}, u^{-m}, v^{-m})$ are all such models for all possible applications of $(\rightsquigarrow)$. Denote $I = \{+1, \ldots, +m, -1, \ldots, -m\}$. Let $M^i = \langle W^i, \{W^i_w\}_{w \in W^i}, \{\preceq^i_w\}_{w \in W^i}, V^i \rangle$ for $i \in I$. We will construct our countermodel for $\Gamma \Rightarrow \Delta$ as the disjoint union of all these countermodels obtained inductively, adding one special world w_0 to them. We will not modify the sets of visible worlds W^i_w and orderings $\preceq^i_w$ for any world of any submodel M^i, and select it only for the additional world w_0. Specifically, we consider the model $M = \langle W, \{W_w\}_{w \in W^i}, \{\preceq_w\}_{w \in W^i}, V \rangle$:

- $W = \{w_0\} \sqcup W^{+1} \sqcup \cdots \sqcup W^{+n} \sqcup W^{-1} \sqcup \cdots \sqcup W^{-m}$
- $W_{w_0} = \bigcup_{1 \le i \le m} \{w \in W^{-i} \mid w \succ^{-i}_{u^{-i}} v_i\}$
- $W_w = W^k_w$ for any $w \in W^k$ for $k \in I$
- $x \preceq_{w_0} y$ in either of the following three cases: (1) $x = y = w_0$; (2) $x = w_0$, $y \in W^{+i}$, and $v^{+i} \preceq_{u^{+i}} y$; (3) $x, y \in W^k$ for some $k \in I$ and $x \preceq_{u^k} y$.
- $\preceq_w = \preceq^k_w$ for any $w \in W^k$ for $k \in I$
- $V(p) = \begin{cases} \{w_0\} \sqcup V^{+1}(p) \sqcup \cdots \sqcup V^{+n}(p) \sqcup V^{-1}(p) \sqcup \cdots \sqcup V^{-m}(p), & \text{if } p \in \Gamma \\ V^{+1}(p) \sqcup \cdots \sqcup V^{+n}(p) \sqcup V^{-1}(p) \sqcup \cdots \sqcup V^{-m}(p), & \text{otherwise} \end{cases}$

First, notice that W is finite and all relations $\leq_w$ are reflexive, antisymmetric, and transitive (if the same is assumed for all submodels M^k). Also, it is straightforward to show that for every $u, w \in W^k$ for $k \in I$ $(M, u, w) \models \varphi$ iff $(M^k, u, w) \models \varphi$ (since relations and valuation within submodels did not change and the evaluation of the formula in a submodel does not move outside this submodel). Moreover, for every $w \in W^k$ for $k \in I$ $(M, w_0, w) \models \varphi$ iff $(M^k, u^k, w) \models \varphi$ (since $\preceq_{w_0}$ and $\preceq^k_{u^k}$ coincide on W^k).

We show that (M, w_0, w_0) satisfies (resp. falsifies) all formulas in Γ (resp Δ):

- for atoms due to the definition of V and the fact that the sequent can not be closed by the axiom;
- for $\mathcal{B}et A$ on the left due to presence of both A and $\mathcal{B}et A$ on the left in the premise of any $\mathcal{B}et$ application, which makes A true in v^{+i} and all y such that $v^{+i} \prec_{u^{+i}} y$ (i.e. all $w \in W^{+i}$ s.t. $w_0 \prec w$, due to antisymmetry);

- for $\mathcal{B}etA$ on the right due to possible application of $\mathcal{B}et$ to this formula with A on the right in this premise, implying that A is false in some v^{+i};
- for $A \rightsquigarrow B$ on the left due to presence $\mathcal{B}et(A \wedge \mathcal{B}et\neg A \to B)$ on the left in the premise of any $\rightsquigarrow$ application, which ensures that for every set $U_i = \{w \in W^{-i} \mid w \succ_{u^{-i}}^{-i} v_i\}$ composing W_{w_0}, $Best_{w_0}(||A||_{w_0}^M) \cap U_i = Best_{u^{-i}}(||A||_{u^{-i}}^M) \cap U_i \subseteq ||B||_{u^{-i}}^{M^{-i}} \subseteq ||B||_{w_0}^M$;
- for $A \rightsquigarrow B$ on the right due to possible application of $\rightsquigarrow$ to this formula with $\mathcal{B}et(A \wedge \mathcal{B}et\neg A \to B)$ on the right in this premise, implying there is some world v' such that $v^{-i} \prec_{u^{-i}}^{-i} v'$ (so $v' \in W_{w_0}$) and $v' \in Best_{u^{-i}}(||A||^{M^{-i}}) \setminus ||B||^{M^{-i}} \subseteq Best_{w_0}(||A||^M) \setminus ||B||^M$.

Remark 2. The countermodel constructed in the above proof has the same structure as the small model construction for **PCL** in [11]: starting with a formula that has no $\mathcal{B}et$-modalities, the resulting model will consist of separate chains of worlds, each chain falsifies one conditional in some world of a later chain. While Friedman-Halpern small models are obtained non-constructively via selecting a finite subset of worlds from an arbitrary existing model, our calculus provides a constructive way of obtaining such small models by analyzing failed derivations.

Example 2. Consider the instance of Rational Monotony $(a \rightsquigarrow c) \Rightarrow ((a \wedge b) \rightsquigarrow c), (a \rightsquigarrow \neg b)$. The countermodel provided by the proof above is $W = \{w_0, v_0^{-1}, v_1^{-1}, v_0^{-2}, v_1^{-2}, v_2^{-2}\}$, $V(a) = \{v_1^{-1}, v_1^{-2}, v_2^{-2}\}$, $V(b) = \{v_1^{-1}, v_1^{-2}\}$, $V(c) = \{v_1^{-1}, v_2^{-2}\}$, where $W_{w_0} = \{v_1^{-1}, v_1^{-2}, v_2^{-2}\}$ includes a singleton chain of v_1^{-1} falsifying $(a \rightsquigarrow \neg b)$ and a chain $v_1^{-2} \preceq_{w_0} v_2^{-2}$ falsifying $(a \wedge b \rightsquigarrow c)$.

We use **ScPCL** to show the adequacy of translating **PCL** into **K+GL**, proving that its rules are sound and complete for the **K+GL** semantics of the translated formulas. We recall the bi-relational Kripke model semantics for **K+GL**.

Definition 4. *A* **K+GL***-model is a tuple* $M = \langle W, R_{\mathbf{K}}, R_{\mathbf{GL}}, V \rangle$*, where W is a finite set of worlds, $R_{\mathbf{K}}$ is arbitrary binary relation on W, $R_{\mathbf{GL}}$ is transitive binary relation on W, and V is valuation on W. $\Box_{\mathbf{K}}$ and $\Box_{\mathbf{GL}}$ modalities are evaluated in such models w.r.t. the corresponding relations:*

$$(M, w) \models \Box_{\mathbf{K}} A \quad \text{iff} \quad \forall w' \in W, w R_{\mathbf{K}} w' \Rightarrow (M, w') \models A$$
$$(M, w) \models \Box_{\mathbf{GL}} A \quad \text{iff} \quad \forall w' \in W, w R_{\mathbf{GL}} w' \Rightarrow (M, w') \models A$$

Definition 5. *The translation* $tr_{\mathbf{PCL}}$ *from* **PCL** *into* **K+GL** *is as follows:*

$$tr_{\mathbf{PCL}}(p) = p$$
$$tr_{\mathbf{PCL}}(\neg A) = \neg tr_{\mathbf{PCL}}(A)$$
$$tr_{\mathbf{PCL}}(A \to B) = tr_{\mathbf{PCL}}(A) \to tr_{\mathbf{PCL}}(B)$$
$$tr_{\mathbf{PCL}}(A \rightsquigarrow B) = \Box_{\mathbf{K}} \Box_{\mathbf{GL}}(tr_{\mathbf{PCL}}(A) \wedge \Box_{\mathbf{GL}} \neg tr_{\mathbf{PCL}}(A) \to tr_{\mathbf{PCL}}(B))$$

Lemma 1. *A is valid in* **PCL** *iff* $tr_{\mathbf{PCL}}(A)$ *is valid in* **K+GL***.*

Proof. ($\Leftarrow$): if A valid in **PCL**, by Prop.3 there exists a derivation for $\Rightarrow A$ in **ScPCL**, and we can easily show that if we apply translation $tr_{\textbf{PCL}}$ to every formula in this derivation, each rule application will preserve validity w.r.t. **K+GL**-models (since the rule ($\rightsquigarrow$) after translation of conditionals in the conclusion behaves exactly like the standard sequent rule for $\Box_{\textbf{K}}$-modality).

($\Rightarrow$): if A is not valid, then $\Rightarrow A$ is underivable and we can take a preference countermodel M for A from the proof of Lemma 3 and transform[5] it into a **K+GL**-countermodel for $tr_{\textbf{PCL}}(A)$ by defining $R_{\textbf{K}}(w) = W_w$ and $R_{\textbf{GL}}(w) = \{u \in W \mid u \succ_w w\}$ for each world in M.

As the KLM logic **P** coincides with the Horn fragment of **PCL** the adequacy of $tr_{\textbf{PCL}}$ also justifies the simplification of the translation from **P** into **GL** in [12]: the entailment $\{A_i \rightsquigarrow B_i\}_i \vdash (A \rightsquigarrow B)$ holds in **P** (and, so, in **PCL**) iff

$$\{\Box_{\textbf{K}}\mathcal{B}et(A_i \wedge \mathcal{B}et\neg A_i \rightarrow B_i)\}_i \vdash (\Box_{\textbf{K}}\mathcal{B}et(A \wedge \mathcal{B}et\neg A \rightarrow B))$$

holds in **K+GL**, which in turn holds iff

$$\{\mathcal{B}et(A_i \wedge \mathcal{B}et\neg A_i \rightarrow B_i)\}_i \vdash (\mathcal{B}et\ (A \wedge \mathcal{B}et\neg A \rightarrow B))$$

or, equivalently, it holds in **GL** (since there are no nested conditionals in **P**).

4   Adding Absoluteness: from GL to ÅQvist's F+(CM)

We introduce the calculus **HFcm** for **F+(CM)**, a deontic extension of **PCL** incorporating reflexivity and absoluteness. The rules of **HFcm** are derived by adapting the embedding of **PCL** into **GL** (see Lemma 3). We establish soundness and completeness of the system, with completeness shown relative to derivations that may include cuts. Rather than following the standard approach via cut-elimination (which could be proved similarly to [9]), in Sect. 4.1 we reformulate **HFcm** into a proof-search-oriented calculus. This transformation enables a cut-free completeness result via countermodel extraction from failed proof searches.

Incorporating absoluteness into **PCL** requires a generalization of the standard sequent framework, as no cut-free sequent calculus exists for **S5**. We use hypersequents, arguably the simplest generalization of sequents [2–4].

Definition 6. *A hypersequent is a multiset* $\Gamma_1 \Rightarrow \Pi_1 \mid \ldots \mid \Gamma_n \Rightarrow \Pi_n$ *where, for all* $i = 1, \ldots, n$, $\Gamma_i \Rightarrow \Pi_i$ *is an ordinary sequent, called* component.

A hypersequent version of a sequent rule is obtained by adding a context G, representing a possibly empty hypersequent, to its premises and conclusion. The hypersequent calculus **HFcm** for **F+(CM)** consists of the (group of) rules (I)-(V) described below. **HFcm** includes (I) the *hypersequent version of the classical*

---

[5] This transformation applies only to preference models in which the relations $\succeq_{w_1}$ and $\succeq_{w_2}$ of different worlds coincide on $W_{w_1} \cap W_{w_2}$ (which permits the use of $\succ_w$ in the definition of $R_{\textbf{GL}}$); hence we must rely on a specific kind of countermodel from the completeness proof, rather than an arbitrary one.

sequent calculus LK as in Fig. 1, including the rules of internal weakening and contraction:

$$\frac{G\,|\,A,A,\Gamma \Rightarrow \Delta}{G\,|\,A,\Gamma \Rightarrow \Delta}\,LC \qquad \frac{G\,|\,\Gamma \Rightarrow \Delta,A,A}{G\,|\,\Gamma \Rightarrow \Delta,A}\,RC \qquad \frac{G\,|\,\Gamma \Rightarrow \Delta}{G\,|\,A,\Gamma \Rightarrow \Delta}\,LW \qquad \frac{G\,|\,\Gamma \Rightarrow \Delta}{G\,|\,\Gamma \Rightarrow \Delta,A}\,RW$$

(II) the *hypersequent version of the Bet rule* (for the **GL** modality) from Fig. 1. To manipulate the hypersequent structure, **HFcm** includes the standard external structural rules (III) known as *ext. weakening (EW) and ext. contraction (EC)* below. These behave like weakening and contraction over whole hypersequent components. To capture the **S5** modality, we use (IV) *the rule s5′* below right – a notational variant of the rule for **S5** in [19]:

$$\frac{G}{G\,|\,\Gamma \Rightarrow \Pi}\,EW \qquad \frac{G\,|\,\Gamma \Rightarrow \Pi\,|\,\Gamma \Rightarrow \Pi}{G\,|\,\Gamma \Rightarrow \Pi}\,EC \qquad \frac{G\,|\,\Gamma^{\bigcirc},\Gamma' \Rightarrow \Pi'}{G\,|\,\Gamma \Rightarrow \,|\,\Gamma' \Rightarrow \Pi'}\,s5'$$

$\Gamma^{\bigcirc}$ abbreviates $\{\bigcirc(B/A)\,|\,\bigcirc(B/A) \in \Gamma\}$. (V) *The deontic rules* of **HFcm** are:

$$\frac{G\,|\,\Gamma^{\bigcirc},A,Bet\neg A \Rightarrow B}{G\,|\,\Gamma \Rightarrow \bigcirc(B/A)}\,R\bigcirc \qquad \frac{G\,|\,\Gamma \Rightarrow \Delta,A \qquad G\,|\,\Gamma \Rightarrow \Delta,Bet\neg A \qquad G\,|\,B,\Gamma \Rightarrow \Delta}{G\,|\,\bigcirc(B/A),\Gamma \Rightarrow \Delta}\,L\bigcirc$$

Remark 3. The rules $(R\bigcirc)$ and $(L\bigcirc)$ are as in the calculi [8,9] for Åqvist's systems **E** and **F**. The former calculus replaces the **GL** rule for *Bet* with a **K** rule; the latter uses a rule with no counterpart in normal modal logics. Remark 4 presents equivalent rules for **F+(CM)** derived starting from the rules of **ScPCL**.

In **HFcm** hypersequents are interpreted as follows: $\Gamma_1 \Rightarrow \Delta_1\,|\,\ldots\,|\,\Gamma_n \Rightarrow \Delta_n$ is valid if and only if $\bigvee_{1 \leq i \leq n} \Box(\bigwedge \Gamma_i \rightarrow \bigvee \Delta_i)$ is valid.

Lemma 2. *The calculus* **HFcm** *is sound for* **F+(CM)**.

Proof. We prove, by induction on the height of derivations, that **HFcm** is sound with respect to the semantics in Definition 2. As an illustrative example, we consider the case of the rule R$\bigcirc$. Assume towards a contradiction that $G\,|\,\Gamma \Rightarrow \bigcirc(B/A)$ is not valid. Then there is a world w s.t. w satisfies the formulas in Γ and w falsifies $\bigcirc(B/A)$. Hence, there is a world u, with $u \vDash A$, $u \vDash Bet\neg A$ and $u \nvDash B$. Since formulas $\Gamma^{\bigcirc}$ are satisfied in w, they are also satisfied in u (due to absoluteness), contradicting the validity of the premise $G\,|\,\Gamma^{\bigcirc},A,Bet\neg A \Rightarrow B$.

Proposition 4. *The calculus* **HFcm** *is complete for* **F+(CM)** *with the cut rule:*

$$\frac{G\,|\,\Gamma \Rightarrow \Delta,A \qquad H\,|\,A,\Pi \Rightarrow \Sigma}{G\,|\,H\,|\,\Gamma,\Pi \Rightarrow \Delta,\Sigma}\,Cut$$

Proof. The axioms for **F+(CM)** are provable in **HFcm** and the rules can be simulated, using the cut rule for Modus Ponens. As an example we prove axiom (A_1) in **HFcm**:

$$\frac{G\mid A, \mathcal{B}et\neg A \Rightarrow B, A \quad G\mid A, \mathcal{B}et\neg A \Rightarrow B, \mathcal{B}et\neg A \quad G\mid A, \mathcal{B}et\neg A, B \Rightarrow B}{\dfrac{C, \mathcal{B}et\neg C \Rightarrow \mid \bigcirc(B/A), A, \mathcal{B}et\neg A \Rightarrow B}{\dfrac{\bigcirc(B/A) \Rightarrow \mid C, \mathcal{B}et\neg C \Rightarrow \mid A, \mathcal{B}et\neg A \Rightarrow B}{\dfrac{\bigcirc(B/A) \Rightarrow \mid C, \mathcal{B}et\neg C \Rightarrow \bigcirc(B/A)}{\dfrac{\bigcirc(B/A) \Rightarrow \bigcirc(\bigcirc(B/A)/C)}{\Rightarrow \bigcirc(B/A) \to \bigcirc(\bigcirc(B/A)/C)} \text{ R}\to} \text{ EC, R}\bigcirc, \text{RW}} \text{ EC, R}\bigcirc, \text{RW}} \text{ s5'}} \text{ LO}$$

where G abridges $C, \mathcal{B}et\neg C \Rightarrow$.

We show that replacing $\square_{\mathbf{K}}$ with $\square_{\mathbf{S5}}$ and removing the outermost $\mathcal{B}et$ in the embedding $tr_{\mathbf{PCL}}$ yields an embedding of $\mathbf{F+(CM)}$ into $\mathbf{S5+GL}$. The semantic definition of $\mathbf{S5+GL}$ is identical to that of $\mathbf{K+GL}$ (see Definition 4), except that $R_{\mathbf{K}}$ is replaced with a universal relation $R_{\mathbf{S5}}$.

Definition 7. *The translation $tr_{\mathbf{F}}+(\mathbf{CM})$ from the language of $\mathbf{F+(CM)}$ into the language of $\mathbf{S5+GL}$ is defined as $tr_{\mathbf{PCL}}$ apart from the conditional case:*

$$tr_{\mathbf{F}}+(\mathbf{CM})(\bigcirc(B/A)) = \square_{\mathbf{S5}}(tr_{\mathbf{F}}+(\mathbf{CM})(A) \wedge \mathcal{B}et\neg tr_{\mathbf{F}}+(\mathbf{CM})(A) \to tr_{\mathbf{F}}+(\mathbf{CM})(B))$$

We chose the current translation over the $tr_{\mathbf{PCL}}$-like alternative that retains the outermost $\mathcal{B}et$ in $tr_{\mathbf{F}}+(\mathbf{CM})(\bigcirc(B/A))$, as it simplifies the conditional rule in $\mathbf{HFcm}$ (see Remark 4). Both translations are sound and faithful.

Lemma 3. *A is valid in $\mathbf{F+(CM)}$ iff $tr_{\mathbf{F}}+(\mathbf{CM})(A)$ is valid in $\mathbf{S5+GL}$.*

Proof. The structure of the proof is similar to the one of Lem. 1. ($\Rightarrow$) We need to verify that application of $tr_{\mathbf{F}}+(\mathbf{CM})$ to every rule of $\mathbf{HFcm}$ provides a rule sound w.r.t. $\mathbf{S5+GL}$. This verification coincides with the soundness proof in Lem. 2. ($\Leftarrow$) We argue by contraposition and we transform an arbitrary[6] $\mathbf{F+(CM)}$-countermodel into a $\mathbf{S5+GL}$-countermodel by keeping the set of worlds and the valuation and choosing $R_{\mathbf{GL}}(w) = \{u \in W \mid u \succ w\}$ and universal $R_{\mathbf{S5}}(w)$.

4.1   A Proof-Search Oriented Calculus for F+(CM)

The calculus $\mathbf{HFcm}$ ^{ps} for $\mathbf{F+(CM)}$, in which all rules are invertible, contains the usual rules for boolean connectives in a cumulative form, i.e. in which formulas in the conclusion are copied in the premises, see [17], together with the following rules for the modal and conditional operator:

$$\frac{G\mid \Gamma \Rightarrow \Delta, \bigcirc(B/A)\mid A, \mathcal{B}et\neg A \Rightarrow B}{G\mid \Gamma \Rightarrow \bigcirc(B/A)} \text{R}\bigcirc^{c} \qquad \frac{G\mid \Gamma \Rightarrow \Delta, \mathcal{B}et A\mid \Gamma^{b}, \Gamma^{b\downarrow}, \mathcal{B}et A \Rightarrow A}{G\mid \Gamma \Rightarrow \Delta, \mathcal{B}et A} \text{Bet}$$

$$\frac{G\mid \bigcirc(B/A), \Gamma \Rightarrow \Delta, A \quad G\mid \bigcirc(B/A), \Gamma \Rightarrow \Delta, \mathcal{B}et\neg A \quad G\mid \bigcirc(B/A), B, \Gamma \Rightarrow \Delta}{G\mid \bigcirc(B/A), \Gamma \Rightarrow \Delta} \text{LO}_1^{c}$$

$$\frac{G\mid \bigcirc(B/A), \Gamma \Rightarrow \Delta\mid \Pi \Rightarrow \Sigma, A \quad G\mid \bigcirc(B/A), \Gamma \Rightarrow \Delta\mid \Pi \Rightarrow \Sigma, \mathcal{B}et\neg A \quad G\mid \bigcirc(B/A), \Gamma \Rightarrow \Delta\mid B, \Pi \Rightarrow \Sigma}{G\mid \bigcirc(B/A), \Gamma \Rightarrow \Delta\mid \Pi \Rightarrow \Sigma} \text{LO}_2^{c}$$

---

[6] In $\mathbf{F+(CM)}$, absoluteness ensures consistency between preference relations across worlds, so – unlike in $\mathbf{PCL}$– no special form of countermodel is required.

The rules for the conditional operator absorb the special structural rule $s5$'
(for an overview of the methodology to obtain a proof search oriented calculus -
there called *Kleene variant* - the reader is referred to [20]).

Lemma 4. *Every rule in* **HcFCM**[ps] *is height-preserving invertible and the
rules of weakening and contraction (internal and external) are height-preserving
admissible. The rule $s5'$ is admissible.*

Proof. By induction on the height of the derivation. We present the case of the
rule $s5'$. If $G \mid \Gamma^\bigcirc, \Gamma' \Rightarrow \Pi'$ is an axiom, so is $G \mid \Gamma \Rightarrow \mid \Gamma \Rightarrow \Pi'$. If the last
rule applied is any rule different from $L\bigcirc_1^c$ or $L\bigcirc_2^c$, we invoke the induction
hypothesis and reapply the rule. If the last rule is $L\bigcirc_1^c$, as in

$$\frac{G \mid \Gamma^\bigcirc, \bigcirc(B/A), \Gamma' \Rightarrow \Pi', A \quad G \mid \Gamma^\bigcirc, \bigcirc(B/A), \Gamma' \Rightarrow \Pi', \mathcal{B}et\neg A \quad G \mid \Gamma^\bigcirc, \bigcirc(B/A), B, \Gamma' \Rightarrow \Pi'}{G \mid \Gamma^\bigcirc, \bigcirc(B/A), \Gamma' \Rightarrow \Pi'} L\bigcirc_1^c$$

We proceed as follows:

$$\frac{\dfrac{G \mid \Gamma^\bigcirc, \bigcirc(B/A), \Gamma' \Rightarrow \Pi', A}{G \mid \Gamma^\bigcirc, \bigcirc(B/A) \Rightarrow \mid \Gamma' \Rightarrow \Pi', A} \text{IH} \quad \dfrac{G \mid \Gamma^\bigcirc, \bigcirc(B/A), \Gamma' \Rightarrow \Pi', \mathcal{B}et\neg A}{G \mid \Gamma^\bigcirc, \bigcirc(B/A) \Rightarrow \mid \Gamma' \Rightarrow \Pi', \mathcal{B}et\neg A} \text{IH} \quad \dfrac{G \mid \Gamma^\bigcirc, \bigcirc(B/A), B, \Gamma' \Rightarrow \Pi'}{G \mid \Gamma^\bigcirc, \bigcirc(B/A) \Rightarrow \mid B, \Gamma' \Rightarrow \Pi'} \text{IH}}{G \mid \Gamma^\bigcirc, \bigcirc(B/A) \Rightarrow \mid \Gamma' \Rightarrow \Pi'} L\bigcirc_1^c$$

The case of $L\bigcirc_2^c$ is similar.

We now show that the calculi **HcFCM**[ps] and **HFcm** are equivalent.

Lemma 5. *G is derivable in* **HFcm** *iff G is derivable in* **HcFCM**[ps].

Proof. From right to left, we proceed by induction on the height of the derivation
observing that the rules of **HcFCM**[ps] can be simulated in **HFcm** using the
structural rules and $s5'$. For example, we have:

$$\frac{G \mid \Gamma \Rightarrow \Delta, \bigcirc(B/A) \mid A, \mathcal{B}et\neg A \Rightarrow B}{G \mid \Gamma \Rightarrow \Delta, \bigcirc(B/A)} R\bigcirc^c \quad \mapsto \quad \frac{\dfrac{\dfrac{G \mid \Gamma \Rightarrow \Delta, \bigcirc(B/A) \mid A, \mathcal{B}et\neg A \Rightarrow B}{G \mid \Gamma \Rightarrow \Delta, \bigcirc(B/A) \mid \Rightarrow \bigcirc(B/A)} R\bigcirc}{G \mid \Gamma \Rightarrow \Delta, \bigcirc(B/A) \mid \Gamma \Rightarrow \Delta, \bigcirc(B/A)} \text{LW, RW}}{G \mid \Gamma \Rightarrow \Delta, \bigcirc(B/A)} \text{EC}$$

From left to right, we argue by induction on the height of the derivation in
HFcm using Lemma 4 to simulate the rules of the calculus **HFcm**.

Lemma 6. *If G is derivable in* **HcFCM**[ps]*, there is a derivation of the same
height in which the rule $R\bigcirc^c$ is applied only once to the same formula.*

Proof. If the derivation contains more than one application of rule $(R\bigcirc^c)$ to the
same formula, we have:

$$\frac{H \mid \Gamma_i \Rightarrow \Delta_i, \bigcirc(B/A) \mid A, \mathcal{B}et\neg A, \Theta \Rightarrow B, \Lambda \mid \ldots \mid \Pi, \Gamma_j \Rightarrow \Delta_j, \Sigma, \bigcirc(B/A) \mid A, \mathcal{B}et\neg A \Rightarrow B}{H \mid \Gamma_i \Rightarrow \Delta_i, \bigcirc(B/A) \mid A, \mathcal{B}et\neg A, \Theta \Rightarrow B, \Lambda \mid \ldots \mid \Pi, \Gamma_j \Rightarrow \Delta_j, \Sigma, \bigcirc(B/A)} R\bigcirc^c$$

$$\vdots \mathcal{D}$$

$$\frac{H \mid \Gamma_i \Rightarrow \Delta_i, \bigcirc(B/A) \mid A, \mathcal{B}et\neg A \Rightarrow B \mid \ldots \mid \Gamma_j \Rightarrow \Delta_j, \bigcirc(B/A)}{H \mid \Gamma_i \Rightarrow \Delta_i, \bigcirc(B/A) \mid \ldots \mid \Gamma_j \Rightarrow \Delta_j, \bigcirc(B/A)} R\bigcirc^c$$

The topmost redundant application of rule $(R\bigcirc^c)$ can be replaced by (height-
preserving admissible) contraction and weakening:

$$\frac{H \,|\, \Gamma_i \Rightarrow \Delta_i, \bigcirc(B/A) \,|\, A, \mathcal{B}et\neg A, \Theta \Rightarrow B, \Lambda \,|\, \dots \,|\, \Pi, \Gamma_j \Rightarrow \Delta_j, \Sigma, \bigcirc(B/A) \,|\, A, \mathcal{B}et\neg A \Rightarrow B}{\dfrac{H \,|\, \Gamma_i \Rightarrow \Delta_i, \bigcirc(B/A) \,|\, A, \mathcal{B}et\neg A, \Theta \Rightarrow B, \Lambda \,|\, \dots \,|\, \Pi, \Gamma_j \Rightarrow \Delta_j, \Sigma, \bigcirc(B/A) \,|\, A, \mathcal{B}et\neg A, \Theta \Rightarrow B, \Lambda}{H \,|\, \Gamma_i \Rightarrow \Delta_i, \bigcirc(B/A) \,|\, A, \mathcal{B}et\neg A, \Theta \Rightarrow B, \Lambda \,|\, \dots \,|\, \Pi, \Gamma_j \Rightarrow \Delta_j, \Sigma, \bigcirc(B/A)} \; \text{\tiny EC}} \; \text{\tiny LW,RW}$$

$$\vdots \mathcal{D}$$

$$\frac{H \,|\, \Gamma_i \Rightarrow \Delta_i, \bigcirc(B/A) \,|\, A, \mathcal{B}et\neg A \Rightarrow B \,|\, \dots \,|\, \Gamma_j \Rightarrow \Delta_j, \bigcirc(B/A)}{H \,|\, \Gamma_i \Rightarrow \Delta_i, \bigcirc(B/A) \,|\, \dots \,|\, \Gamma_j \Rightarrow \Delta_j, \bigcirc(B/A)} \; \text{R}\bigcirc^c$$

To prove completeness of **HFcm**^{ps} (and thus also **HFcm**) we reconstruct a countermodel from a failed derivation using the notion of *saturated* hypersequent.

Definition 8. *A hypersequent H is saturated w.r.t. the system* **HcFCM**^{PS} *if it is not an initial sequent and for every component $\Gamma \Rightarrow \Delta$ in H, whenever $\Gamma \Rightarrow \Delta$ contains the principal formulas in the conclusion of a rule (r), then H also contains the formulas introduced by one of the premises of (r) for every rule (r):*

- *(R→) If $\Gamma \Rightarrow \Delta, A \to B \in H$, then $A \in \Gamma$ and $B \in \Delta$.*
- *(L→) If $A \to B, \Gamma \Rightarrow \Delta \in H$, then $A \in \Delta$ or $B \in \Gamma$.*
- *(L$\bigcirc_1$) If $\bigcirc(B/A), \Gamma \Rightarrow \Delta \in H$, then $A \in \Delta$ or $\mathcal{B}et\neg A \in \Delta$ or $B \in \Gamma$.*
- *(L$\bigcirc_2$) If $\bigcirc(B/A), \Gamma \Rightarrow \Delta \in H$ and $\Pi \Rightarrow \Sigma \in H$, then $A \in \Sigma$ or $\mathcal{B}et\neg A \in \Sigma$ or $B \in \Gamma$.*
- *(R$\bigcirc$) If $\Gamma \Rightarrow \Delta, \bigcirc(B/A) \in H$, then $\Pi, A, \mathcal{B}et\neg A \Rightarrow \Sigma, B \in H$ for some Π, Σ.*
- *(Bet) If $\Gamma \Rightarrow \Delta, \mathcal{B}etA \in H$, then $\Pi, \Gamma^b, \Gamma^{b\downarrow}, \mathcal{B}etA \Rightarrow \Sigma, A \in H$ for some Π, Σ.*

Theorem 1. *If $\Rightarrow A$ is valid in* **F+(CM)** *then it is derivable* **HcFCM**^{PS}.

Proof. Assume that $\Rightarrow A$ is not derivable. The proof is in two steps. (**I**) We prove that the search for a proof terminates and that there is a saturated hypersequent. We observe that the number of components generated in any derivation $\mathcal{D}$ of $\Rightarrow A$ can be bounded. By Lemma 6 and the weak subformula property, the number of components introduced by (R$\bigcirc^c$) is bounded by the number of conditionals in A and thus is finite. By the weak subformula property, if there is an infinite bottom-up introduction of components, these are introduced by the rule $\mathcal{B}et$. Hence, since the number of possible sequents occurring in a derivation is finite, there has to be a repetition. In this case, we have met the saturation condition for the rule $\mathcal{B}et$. Thus the number of components is finite. Since we can rule out rule applications for which the saturation condition has already been met (due to the admissibility of contraction), the length of every branch of a putative derivation of $\Rightarrow A$ is bounded and the derivation is finite. Hence if A is not derivable, there is a saturated hypersequent $G^{sat} = \Gamma_1 \Rightarrow \Delta_1 \,|\, \dots \,|\, \Gamma_n \Rightarrow \Delta_n$.

(**II**) We construct a countermodel for A on the basis of G^{sat}. We assign labels to the components $i : \Gamma_i \Rightarrow \Delta_i$ $(i \in \{1, \dots, n\})$ and consider the model: $\mathcal{M} = \langle \{1, \dots, n\}, \preceq, V \rangle$ with $i \in V(p)$ iff $p \in \Gamma_i$ and $i \preceq j$ iff $i = j$ or

$$i : \Gamma_i \Rightarrow \Delta_i, \; j : \Gamma_j \Rightarrow \Delta_j, \; \Gamma^b, \Gamma_i^{b\downarrow} \subseteq \Gamma_j, \text{ and } \mathcal{B}etA \in \Gamma_j \setminus \Gamma_i.$$

We have to check that the model is finite, reflexive and transitive. Finiteness and reflexivity are immediate. Assume that $i \preceq j \preceq u$ for $i \neq j \neq u$, we need to prove that $i \preceq u$. By definition, we get: $\Gamma_i^b, \Gamma_i^{\overline{b\downarrow}} \subseteq \Gamma_j^b, \Gamma_j^{b\downarrow} \subseteq \Gamma_u$. By hypothesis we know that there is $\mathcal{B}etB \in \Gamma_u \setminus \Gamma_j$, therefore $\mathcal{B}etB \notin \Gamma_i$, otherwise we would get $\mathcal{B}etB \in \Gamma_j$, hence a contradiction which yields the desired conclusion.

To complete the proof, we need to establish that:

- For every i, if $B \in \Gamma_i$, then $i \models B$
- For every i, if $B \in \Delta_i$, then $i \not\models B$

This is done by induction on the complexity of B. If B is an atomic formula, the claim stems from the definition of V. If B is a compound formula, the proof follows from the use of the induction hypothesis. We deal with the case in which B is $\mathcal{B}etC$; the other cases are handled similarly. If $\mathcal{B}etC \in \Gamma_i$, suppose $i \preceq j$, then $\Gamma_i^{b\downarrow} \subseteq \Gamma_j$. So we get $C \in \Gamma_j$ and by induction hypothesis we have $j \models C$, hence the desired conclusion. If $\mathcal{B}et \in \Delta_i$, by definition of saturation w.r.t. the rule $\mathcal{B}et$, there is $\Gamma_j \Rightarrow \Delta_j, C$ with $\Gamma_i^b, \Gamma^{b\downarrow} \subseteq \Gamma_j$. Furthermore, $\mathcal{B}etC \in \Gamma_j$, but $\mathcal{B}etC \notin \Gamma_i$, otherwise the hypersequent would be derivable and therefore not saturated. So, by definition, $i \preceq j$ and $j \not\models C$ by induction hypothesis, which entails $i \not\models \mathcal{B}etC$.

As $\Rightarrow A$ is the root of the putative derivation, in the saturated hypersequent there is j s.t. $A \in \Delta_j$ and so $j \not\models A$ which yields the desired conclusion.

Remark 4. $tr_{\mathbf{F}+}(\mathbf{CM})$ could equivalently be defined like $tr_{\mathbf{PCL}}$ (Definition 5), preserving the outermost $\mathcal{B}et$ modality in the clause for the dyadic operator. This yields the alternative version of the rules $(L\bigcirc)$ and $(R\bigcirc)$, closer to those of **ScPCL**:

$$\frac{G \,|\, A \wedge \mathcal{B}et\neg A \to B, \Gamma \Rightarrow \Delta}{G \,|\, \bigcirc(B/A), \Gamma \Rightarrow \Delta} \ (L\bigcirc^*)$$

$$\frac{G \,|\, \Gamma^\bigcirc \Rightarrow \mathcal{B}et(A \wedge \mathcal{B}et\neg A \to B)}{G \,|\, \Gamma \Rightarrow \bigcirc(B/A), \Delta} \ (R\bigcirc^*)$$

The calculus **HFcm*** obtained from **HFcm** by replacing $(L\bigcirc)$ and $(R\bigcirc)$ with their starred versions, is sound and complete w.r.t. **F+(CM)**: soundness can be checked directly analogously the $(\leadsto)$ case in Proposition 2, and completeness holds since $(L\bigcirc)$ and $(R\bigcirc)$ can be simulated in **HFcm*** using $(L\bigcirc^*)$ and $(R\bigcirc^*)$.

Concluding Remark

We have introduced analytic calculi for conditional logics based on the correspondence between the KLM logic **P** and the provability logic **GL**. Specifically, we have considered two extensions of **P**: **PCL**, for counterfactual reasoning, and **F+(CM)**, for deontic reasoning. The approach in this paper could be applied to obtain modular calculi for other extensions of **PCL** [14]. Our calculi are relatively simple and have good meta-logical properties. In particular, we believe that cut-elimination can be proved by adapting Valentini's strategy for **GL** [27] (see also [9]). We leave the investigation of these questions to future work.

Acknowledgements. The work is partially supported by the European Union's Horizon 2020 research and innovation programme under grant agreement No 101034440, the FWF project I 6372-N (Grant-DOI 10.55776/I6372), and the project MSCA IEF No 101152658 "Structures for modal and deontic logics" (REMODEL).

References

1. Åqvist, L.: Deontic logic. In: Gabbay, D., Guenthner, F. (eds.) Handbook of Philosophical Logic, vol. II, pp. 605–714. Springer, Dordrecht (1984)
2. Avron, A.: A constructive analysis of RM. J. Symb. Logic **52**(4), 939–951 (1987)
3. Avron, A.: The method of hypersequents in the proof theory of propositional non-classical logics. In: Logic: From Foundations to Applications, pp. 1–32. OUP, New York (1996)
4. Avron, A.: Hypersequents, logical consequence and intermediate logics for concurrency. Ann. Math. Artif. Intell. **4**, 225–248 (1991)
5. van Benthem, J., Girard, P., Roy, O.: Everything else being equal: a modal logic for ceteris paribus preferences. J. Phil. Logic **38**(1), 83–125 (2009)
6. Boutilier, C.: Conditional logics of normality as modal systems. In: Shrobe, H.E., Dietterich, T.G., Swartout, W.R. (eds.) Proceedings of the 8th National Conference on Artificial Intelligence. Boston, Massachusetts, USA, July 29 - August 3, 1990, 2 Volumes, pp. 594–599. AAAI Press/The MIT Press (1990)
7. Burgess, J.: Quick completeness proofs for some logics of conditionals. Notre Dame J. Formal Logic **22**(3), 76–84 (1981)
8. Ciabattoni, A., Olivetti, N., Parent, X.: Dyadic obligations: proofs and countermodels via hypersequents. In: Aydoğan, R., Criado, N., Lang, J., Sanchez-Anguix, V., Serramia, M. (eds.) PRIMA 2022, pp. 54–71. Springer (2022)
9. Ciabattoni, A., Olivetti, N., Parent, X., Ramanayake, R., Rozplokhas, D.: Analytic proof theory for Aqvist's system F. In: Maranhão, J., Peterson, C., Straßer, C., van der Torre, L. (eds.) DEON 2023, pp. 79–98 (2023)
10. Ciabattoni, A., Tesi, M.: Sequents vs hypersequents for åqvist systems. In: Benzmüller, C., Heule, M.J.H., Schmidt, R.A. (eds.) Automated Reasoning - 12th International Joint Conference, IJCAR. Lecture Notes in Computer Science, vol. 14740, pp. 176–195. Springer (2024)
11. Friedman, N., Halpern, J.Y.: On the complexity of conditional logics. In: Doyle, J., Sandewall, E., Torasso, P. (eds.) Proceedings of the 4th International Conference on Principles of Knowledge Representation and Reasoning (KR'94). Bonn, Germany, May 24-27, 1994, pp. 202–213. Morgan Kaufmann (1994)
12. Giordano, L., Gliozzi, V., Olivetti, N., Pozzato, G.L.: Analytic tableaux calculi for KLM logics of nonmonotonic reasoning. ACM Trans. Comput. Log. **10**(3), 18:1–18:47 (2009)
13. Giordano, L., Gliozzi, V., Olivetti, N., Schwind, C.: Tableau calculus for preference-based conditional logics: PCL and its extensions. ACM Trans. Comput. Logic **10**(3) (2009)
14. Girlando, M.: On the Proof Theory of Conditional Logics. Theses, Aix-Marseille Universite; Helsinki University (2019)
15. Girlando, M., Negri, S., Olivetti, N.: Uniform labelled calculi for preferential conditional logics based on neighbourhood semantics. J. Log. Comput. **31**(3), 947–997 (2021)

16. Girlando, M., Negri, S., Sbardolini, G.: Uniform labelled calculi for conditional and counterfactual logics. In: Iemhoff, R., Moortgat, M., de Queiroz, R.J.G.B. (eds.) WoLLIC 2019. Lecture Notes in Computer Science, vol. 11541, pp. 248–263. Springer (2019)

17. Kleene, S.C.: Introduction to Metamathematics. North Holland, Amsterdam (1952)

18. Kraus, S., Lehmann, D., Magidor, M.: Nonmonotonic reasoning, preferential models and cumulative logics. Artif. Intell. **44**(1–2), 167–207 (1990)

19. Kurokawa, H.: Hypersequent calculi for modal logics extending S4. In: New Frontiers in Artificial Intelligence. LNCS, vol. 8417, pp. 51–68. Springer (2013)

20. Kuznets, R., Lellmann, B.: Grafting hypersequents onto nested sequents. Log. J. IGPL **24**(3), 375–423 (2016)

21. Makinson, D.: Five faces of minimality. Stud. Logica. **52**(3), 339–379 (1993)

22. Nalon, C., Pattinson, D.: A resolution-based calculus for preferential logics. In: Galmiche, D., Schulz, S., Sebastiani, R. (eds.) IJCAR 2018. LNCS (LNAI), vol. 10900, pp. 498–515. Springer, Cham (2018). https://doi.org/10.1007/978-3-319-94205-6_33

23. Negri, S., Olivetti, N.: A sequent calculus for preferential conditional logic based on neighbourhood semantics. In: De Nivelle, H. (ed.) TABLEAUX 2015. LNCS (LNAI), vol. 9323, pp. 115–134. Springer, Cham (2015). https://doi.org/10.1007/978-3-319-24312-2_9

24. Parent, X.: Maximality vs. optimality in dyadic deontic logic. J. Philos. Log. **43**(6), 1101–1128 (2014)

25. Schröder, L., Pattinson, D., Hausmann, D.: Optimal tableaux for conditional logics with cautious monotonicity. In: Coelho, H., Studer, R., Wooldridge, M.J. (eds.) ECAI 2010, Proceedings. Frontiers in Artificial Intelligence and Applications, vol. 215, pp. 707–712. IOS Press (2010)

26. Solovay, R.M.: Provability interpretations of modal logic. Israel J. Math. **25**(3), 287–304 (1976)

27. Valentini, S.: The modal logic of provability: cut-elimination. J. Philos. Logic **12**(4), 471–476 (1983)

deon-$\mathcal{B}$: A Language for Well-Founded Deontic Planning

Davide Soldà$^{(\boxtimes)}$ and Thomas Eiter

Institute of Logic and Computation, TU Wien, Vienna, Austria
{davide.solda,thomas.eiter}@tuwien.ac.at

Abstract. Declarative languages are widely used for reasoning about actions and planning, with semantics and extensions to cater for different needs. We introduce the rule-based action language deon-B, which builds on an extension of the well-founded semantics by incorporating deontic operators, allowing one to reason about obligations, prohibitions, and permissions in a non-monotonic setting. To further enhance its applicability in dynamic environments, we integrate a mechanism for action choice inspired by answer set-based action languages, enabling reasoning about transitions between states and for expressing the evolution of normative goals. Our approach provides a computationally efficient approximation of answer-set-based deontic reasoning while preserving key expressiveness. We evaluate the proposed formalism against well-known deontic challenges such as contrary-to-duty obligations and the distinction between prima facie and actual obligations, demonstrating its ability to capture and resolve normative conflicts within dynamic domains.

1 Introduction

Reasoning about normative concepts such as obligations, prohibitions, and permissions is essential for formalizing legal and ethical reasoning, autonomous systems, and intelligent agents operating under normative constraints [31]. These concepts often account for non-monotonic features such as defeasibility [38,45]. Answer Set Programming (ASP) [11,43] has been used as a framework to model such deontic reasoning, cf. [5,14,34,39,58], allowing for expressive representations of normative rules, in which explicit (strong) and default (weak) negation can be formalized. The latter are useful to model deontic concepts such as *strong and weak permission*, and in a dynamic setting *cancellation* of temporal norms.

However, ASP-based approaches may lack models due to cyclic incomplete information and incur computational challenges [21,24,46,49]. In contrast, well-founded semantics (WFS) [65] yields a single (though partial) model of a logic program that is sound with respect to ASP semantics and polynomial-time computable. On the other hand, WFS has less inference power and does not support explicit negation; simply compiling the latter away as in ASP does not work, as WFS does not adhere to the principle that strong negation entails default negation [4,6]. Fortunately, an extension of WFS for explicit negation (WFSX)

G. Casini et al. (Eds.): JELIA 2025, LNAI 16093, pp. 187–204, 2026.
https://doi.org/10.1007/978-3-032-04587-4_12

is available [4] that provides a fruitful basis for integrating deontic operators, and to make thus well-founded normative reasoning possible. We foster this in our work with the following contributions.

- We introduce well-founded semantics for logic programs with explicit negation and deontic operators, in the vein of deontic ASP [14]. In that, we pay particular attention to the representation of weak permission and show how the WFS-undefined truth value can be leveraged to remain agnostic about normative conflicts when not enough information to resolve them is provided.
- In a further step, we integrate deontic well-founded semantics into an action setting, combining the advantages of well-founded reasoning with action choices typical of planning formalisms, where deontic fluents allow one to capture (temporal) obligations, prohibitions, and permissions while handling deontic challenges effectively. For this we introduce the action language deon-$\mathcal{B}$, which extends the standard action language $\mathcal{B}$ [33] by incorporating deontic fluents and temporal deontic concepts. Equipped with well-founded semantics, the resulting language deon-$\mathcal{B}_{wf}$ provides a framework that allows a planner to make decisions by considering both the evolution of the real (ontic) world and the deontic world over time, and where plan search proceeds with partial information. As a further key feature, we integrate *repeaters* [58] into deon-$\mathcal{B}$, a mechanism that can handle maintenance and achievement obligations [35,37], which must hold continuously until a deadline respectively must be fulfilled at least once before.
- We relate deontic well-founded semantics to deontic ASP in [14] and planning in deon-$\mathcal{B}_{wf}$ to planning in deon-$\mathcal{B}_{asp}$, which is a respective ASP-variant of deon-$\mathcal{B}$ that aligns more with ASP-based action languages [61]. In both cases, the former can be seen as an approximation of the latter that also has lower computational cost. In particular, plans in deon-$\mathcal{B}_{wf}$ amount to secure plans in deon-$\mathcal{B}_{asp}$, which are conformant plans [19,55] that work without complete information about the environment. We stress that this is particularly relevant in dynamic and uncertain environments where (deontic) aspects of the initial state, static laws encoding implicit knowledge, or the effect of actions may be incomplete [9,10].
- We validate our approach by testing it against standard deontic challenges, including *contrary-to-duty* obligations [18,48]—where obligations arise as reparative duties in response to violations—and the handling of temporal *prima facie* and *actual* obligations [15] via the use of repeaters.

By developing a well-founded semantics that accommodates deontic reasoning and integrating it into an action language, we provide a novel approach to modeling normative and dynamic reasoning within a framework that aligns with the computational complexity of classical planning problems.

2   Preliminaries

This section introduces the syntax of logic programs with explicit negation [32], followed by the definition of answer sets and the well-founded semantics for such programs [6]. We use "not" for *default negation* and ¬ for *explicit negation*.

Example 1. Consider $\pi=\{p \leftarrow \text{not } \neg p. \quad \neg p \leftarrow \text{not } p. \quad u \leftarrow p. \quad u \leftarrow \neg p.\}$. Following [6], the well-founded model is $S = \varnothing$, as there is no clear evidence to derive either p or $\neg p$, furthermore, the undefiniteness of p and $\neg p$ propagates to u. Adding p as fact, i.e., $\pi' = \pi \cup \{p\}$, the well-founded model becomes $S' = \{u, p, \text{not } \neg p\}$.

Explicit negation is a well-known key feature In Knowledge representation:

Example 2 ([4]). The statement, "If a driver is unsure that a train is not approaching, they should wait," can be captured as: $wait \leftarrow \text{not } \neg train$.

We asume a signature (set) $\mathcal{P}$ of atoms, and define explicit literals as $\mathcal{L} = \{p, \neg p \mid p \in \mathcal{P}\}$ and default literals as $df\mathcal{L} = \{L, \text{not } L \mid L \in \mathcal{L}\}$.

Definition 1 (Extended Normal Logic Program [32]). *An extended normal logic program π (or simply, a logic program) is a set of rules of the form:*

$$r \; : \; B_0 \leftarrow B_1, \dots B_n, \text{not } B_{n+1}, \dots \text{not } B_m. \qquad n, m \geq 0, \tag{1}$$

where all B_j are explicit literals. We denote by $H(r) = H$ the head and by $B(r) = B^+(r) \cup B^-(r)$ the body of r, where $B^+(r) = \{B_1, \dots, B_n\}$ and $B^-(r) = \{\text{not } B_{n+1}, \dots, \text{not } B_m\}$; if $B(r) = \varnothing$, r is a fact.

We also consider logic programs with function-free first-order literals, where rules are treated as abbreviations for ground instances. As in ASP, we assume safe negation, i.e., each variable in a rule r must occur in $B^+(r)$ [25].

An *interpretation* for $\mathcal{P}$ is any set $I \subseteq df\mathcal{L}$ of default literals; I is consistent if I does not contain both L and not L for the same explicit literal L and satisfies the *coherence principle*, meaning $\neg L \in I$ entails not $L \notin I$ for each explicit literal L, where $\neg \neg L$ stands for L. We call L and $\neg L$ complements to each other. An interpretation is *total*, if for each $p \in \mathcal{P}$, either $p, \neg p \in I$, or $\{\text{not } p, \text{not } \neg p\} \subseteq I$.

For any not -free program π, we denote by $Cn(\pi)$ the $\subseteq$-minimal set of literals s.t., for each rule $r \in \pi$, if $B(r) \subseteq Cn(\pi)$, then $H(r) \in Cn(\pi)$. Note that $Cn(\pi)$ may contain p and $\neg p$, but do not enforce explosion, i.e., $Cn(\pi) = \mathcal{L}$, in this case.

Well-founded semantics was introduced in [64] and extended with explicit negation in [47]. Here, we follow the version based on the reduct operation from [6]; while there the authors considered a para-consistent variant of the well-founded semantics, we limit ourselves to consistent models.

Definition 2. *Let π be a logic program and I a consistent set of explicit literals. The GL-reduct of π modulo I is $\pi^I = \{H(r) \leftarrow B^+(r) \mid B^-(r) \subseteq I \text{ for } r \in \pi\}$.*

We next define semi-normality to aid implementing the coherence principle.

Definition 3 (Semi-normal Program). *The semi-normal version π_s of a program π is given by $\pi_s = \{r_s : H(r) \leftarrow B(r), not \neg H(r) \mid r \in \pi\}$.*

We can now introduce the well-founded semantics as follows:

Definition 4 (WFSX, [4]). *For any logic program π, define the transfinite sequence $\{I_\alpha\}$ by (i) $I_0 = \varnothing$, (ii) $I_{\alpha+1} = Cn(\pi^{Cn(\pi')})$ where $\pi' = \pi_s^{I_\alpha}$, for each successor ordinal $\alpha + 1$, and (iii) $I_\delta = \bigcup_{\alpha<\delta} I_\alpha$ for each limit ordinal δ, and let I_γ be its least fixpoint. If $I_\gamma \subseteq Cn(\pi_s^{I_\gamma})$, then the well-founded model is defined as:*

$$\text{WFMX}(\pi) = I_\gamma \cup not\,(\mathcal{L} \smallsetminus Cn(\pi_s^{I_\gamma})),$$

otherwise, if $I_\gamma \not\subseteq Cn(\pi_s^{I_\gamma})$, π is contradictory and has no well-founded model.

We focus exclusively on non-contradictory well-founded models, which is why the condition $I_\gamma \subseteq Cn(\pi_s^{I_\gamma})$ is included in Definition 4; the latter holds iff no atom p satisfies $\{p, \neg p\} \subseteq I_\gamma$ [4, Theorem 5.3]. To illustrate this, consider the program $\pi = \{p. \neg p.\}$, where $I_\gamma = \{p, \neg p\}$. The semi-normal version of π is given by

$$\pi_s = \{p \leftarrow not\, \neg p. \quad \neg p \leftarrow not\, p.\}$$

which results in $Cn(\pi_s^{I_\gamma}) = \varnothing$, violating the inclusion condition $I_\gamma \subseteq Cn(\pi_s^{I_\gamma})$.

To further demonstrate the role of the semi-normal transformation in defining well-founded models, consider the following example:

Example 3. Let $\pi = \{r0 : q \leftarrow not\, p, \quad r1 : \neg q, \quad r2 : p \leftarrow not\, q\}$. Then we have $\pi_s = \{r0_s : q \leftarrow not\, p, not\, \neg q, \quad r1_s : \neg q \leftarrow not\, q, \quad r2_s : p \leftarrow not\, q, not\, \neg p\}$. We find that $I_1 = \{\neg q\}$ after the first iteration ; However, computing the least fixpoint yields $I_2 = \{\neg q, p\}$ and, therefore, to $\text{WFMX}(\pi) = \{\neg q, p, not\, q\}$. This model is preferred as it adheres to the *coherence principle*, which states that an explicit negation $\neg q$ should entail the corresponding default negation $not\, q$.

We now revisit key relationships between well-founded semantics with explicit negation with respect to well-founded and answer-set semantics.

Theorem 1 (Relation to WFS [4]). *For explicit negation-free logic programs, WFSX coincides with WFS semantics as defined in [65].*

3   Deontic Well-Founded Semantics

We now extend the well-founded semantics introduced in Definition 4, following a similar methodology to that proposed in [14] for defining a deontic answer set semantics. We demonstrate that our well-founded approach provides a computationally efficient approximation of the answer set-based framework from [14], while maintaining sufficient expressiveness to address the deontic challenges discussed therein, which belong to the class of stratified programs.

We introduce two categories of propositions to capture normative concepts: atomic obligations **O**p (meaning "p is obligatory") and atomic prohibitions **F**p

(meaning "p is forbidden"), for any atom $p \in \mathcal{P}$. In many deontic logics, including **KD** [66], prohibitions are commonly defined in terms of obligations, with **F**p often expressed as **O** ¬ p. However, rather than treating **O** and **F** as formal operators, we interpret them as syntactic prefixes that introduce new atoms, "**O**p" and "**F**p," into the signature. Under certain conditions, both **O**p and **F**p may be simultaneously valid, as it happens in some Contrary to Duty scenarios.

Formally, a *deontic atom* is either $p \in \mathcal{P}$ or any of the expressions **O**p or **F**p. The *deontic signature* $d\mathcal{P}$ is defined as $d\mathcal{P} = \mathcal{P} \cup \{\mathbf{O}p, \mathbf{F}p \mid p \in \mathcal{P}\}$. We further denote deontic explicit literals as $d\mathcal{L} = \{p, \neg p \mid p \in d\mathcal{P}\}$. The explicit literals **O**p and ¬**O**p denote "p is obligatory" and "p is explicitly not obligatory," respectively, or equivalently, "¬p is explicitly permitted." As will be discussed and formalized later, permissions can also be inferred in a weaker form using default negation, where default deontic literals are denoted by $df\text{-}d\mathcal{L}$. It is allowed that ¬p is true in the real world and **O**p holds simultaneously, meaning that the obligation is violated; conversely if both p and **O**p holds, we say that the obligation is fulfilled. Lastly, the prohibition **F**p is the dual of the obligation. Its explicit negation, ¬**F**p, conveys that "p is explicitly permitted," whereas a violation occurs when both **F**p and p are true at the same time.

We can now introduce a notion of deontic interpretation, which amounts to a restriction of the possible consistent set of literals, namely if there is a dilemma, i.e., if the obligation for p and the prohibition for p coexist, then we need to derive either p or ¬p to *resolve* the deontic *impasse*.

Definition 5 (Deontic interpretation [14]). *A deontic interpretation is an interpretation I for $d\mathcal{P}$ s.t. for each $p \in \mathcal{P}$, $\{\mathbf{O}p, \mathbf{F}p\} \subseteq I$ implies $\{p, \neg p\} \cap I \neq \varnothing$.*

In ASP the idea behind Definition 5 can be captured by the addition of the following axiom schema (**wD**) in [14]:[1]

$$wD \leftarrow \mathbf{O}p, \mathbf{F}p, \text{not } p, \text{not } \neg p. \qquad \neg\, wD \leftarrow \mathbf{O}p, \mathbf{F}p, \text{not } p, \text{not } \neg p \qquad (\mathbf{wD})$$

The axiom (**wD**) disallows *dilemmas*, such as **O**p, **F**p—simultaneous obligations for (p) and for $(\neg p)$, which remain unresolved without further information on p. However, if we know that p (resp. ¬p) holds, the dilemma is not in place anymore since **O**p (resp. **F**p) has been fulfilled, and **F**p (resp. **O**p) has been violated. Note that in this way, we enriched $d\mathcal{P}$ with a designated atom wD that can be used to detect violations of the (**wD**) axiom.

Definition 6 (deon-WFMX). *The deontic WFMX of a logic program π, denoted deon-WFMX(π), is the WFMX of π, if the latter exists and is a deontic interpretation (cf. Definition 5); otherwise, π has no deontic WFMX.*

We then have the following characterization:

Proposition 1. *For every logic program π, $S = $ deon-WFMX(π) iff $S \cup \{not\ wD, not\ \neg wD\} = $ WFMX($\pi \cup (\mathbf{wD})$) (and exists iff the latter WFMX exists).*

---

[1] [14] expresses (**wD**) by $\perp \leftarrow \mathbf{O}p, \mathbf{F}p, \text{not } p, \text{not } \neg p$, which is beyond our syntax.

Weak Permission. Strong permission is often understood as an exception to a prohibition or as the removal of an obligation to the contrary. In contrast, weak permission arises when there is no derived obligation enforcing the opposite action. However, the (**wD**) axiom permits the coexistence of the obligation of p and its prohibition; we consider such a potential dilemma as a scenario where there is no clear obligation enforcing the opposite action. We show how to express weak permission in such a scenario, following the example presented in [36].

Example 4. In 2019, the NGO vessel *Sea Watch 3* engaged in migrant rescue operations in the Mediterranean Sea. (i) Maritime law mandates that a vessel near a distress site must assist those in need: $r_{(i)}$ = $\mathbf{O}assist \leftarrow distress, proximity$. Further, (ii) Italian law prohibits Sea Watch 3 from performing rescues within the restricted area: $r_{(ii)}$ = $\mathbf{F}assist \leftarrow SeaWatch, migrants, ItalianContiguousZone$.

Maritime law mandates that vessels permitted to refrain from assisting vessels in distress must notify the nearest relevant authorities and avoid the rescue area. Two different interpretations of the permission arise. Scenario (a), where no permission is inferred, is represented as:

$$r_{a1} = \mathbf{O}alertAuthorities \leftarrow \text{not } \mathbf{O}assist, distress, proximity.$$
$$r_{a2} = \mathbf{O}keepClear \leftarrow \text{not } \mathbf{O}assist, distress, proximity.$$

Therefore, in scenario (a) the weak permission for $\neg p$ is expressed by the negation as failure for the obligation of p. Scenario (b), where weak permission can be derived from the conflict, is modeled by adding to r_{a1}, r_{a2} the rules

$$r_{b1} = \mathbf{O}alertAuthorities \leftarrow \mathbf{F}assist, distress, proximity.$$
$$r_{b2} = \mathbf{O}keepClear \leftarrow \mathbf{F}assist, distress, proximity.$$

Note that we model (b) by stating that if you are forbidden (resp., obliged) to do p, then you are weakly permitted to do $\neg p$ (resp., p). As disjunction in rule bodies is not available, we need to have rules ai and bi for $i \in \{1, 2\}$. More in general, the weak permission for p can be expressed as not $\mathbf{F}p$ or $\mathbf{O}p$, and, symmetrically, the weak permission for $\neg p$ as not $\mathbf{O}p$ or $\mathbf{F}p$.[2]

4   Deontic Action Language deon-$\mathcal{B}_{\mathbf{wf}}$

In this section, we introduce an action language that unifies the ontic domain, characterized by fluents describing the state of the world, with deontic fluents that model the evolution of normative concepts such as obligations, prohibitions, and permissions. Following the terminology of [3], our framework captures *state-based norms* by representing punctual obligations as atoms of the form $\mathbf{O}p$, which must be satisfied immediately upon activation. To handle *behavior-based norms*

---

[2] not $\mathbf{F}p$ or $\mathbf{O}p$ is equivalent to as not $\mathbf{F}p$ or ($\mathbf{O}p$ and $\mathbf{F}p$). The former stresses that obligation entails the weak permission, the latter the potential *dilemma* setting.

with deadlines—i.e., norms that are triggered in a given context and require a condition to be achieved or maintained before a deadline is reached—we adapt the concept of *repeaters* from [58]. Repeaters are designated atoms governed by specific inertia laws that propagate over time, producing punctual obligations at each step; they allow us to express both maintenance and achievement obligations, in a way conceptually close to the until operator in [34]. We build upon the action language $\mathcal{B}$ [33], which we extend to incorporate fluents and deontic aspects. We do not explicitly encode *action-based norms*, as our planner is left free to determine which sub-plans may trigger an obligation, given that different sequences of actions may lead to the same normative condition.

Syntax. An *action theory* in deon-$\mathcal{B}$ is formulated over a set $\mathcal{A}$ of *actions* and a set $\mathcal{F}$ of *fluents*, which correspond to the explicit literals describing states of the world. The term *fluent* is used instead of *explicit literal*, as is customary in planning. For example, the condition "the vase is on the table," can be expressed as $on(vase, table)$, and its truth value may change over time. Also for fluents $\neg \neg f$ corresponds to f. We have $\mathcal{F} = ontic\text{-}\mathcal{F} \cup d\text{-}\mathcal{F} \cup \mathbf{R}$, where

- $ontic\text{-}\mathcal{F}$ aligns with $\mathcal{L}$,
- $d\text{-}\mathcal{F}$ denotes $d\mathcal{L} \setminus \mathcal{L}$ from the previous section, and
- $\mathbf{R}$ contains *repeater* expressions $r(D, S, o)$ with sets $D, S \subseteq ontic\text{-}\mathcal{F}$ and $o \in ontic\text{-}\mathcal{F}$ as parameters; intuitively, if some fluent in D (resp. in S) holds, a punctual obligation $\mathbf{O}o$ is yielded (resp. the repeater's propagation is stopped).

To motivate the use of repeaters, as already pinpointed in [58], when modeling temporal norms we encounter a temporal instance of the Ross paradox [52]: for example, if there is an achievement obligation for p before δ, and we know that δ' occurs along the trace after δ, then we might consider it reasonable to have an obligation for p before δ' as well, since the first obligation subsumes it.

However, following this kind of reasoning leads to counter-intuitive consequence, such as that the violation of a single temporal norm would lead to the violation of an undefined number of other subsumed norms. We can avoid such a problem by using repeaters to express

- the achievement obligation of $o \in ontic\text{-}\mathcal{F}$ before $d \in ontic\text{-}\mathcal{F}$, denoted by $\mathbf{A}_d(o)$, as $r(\{o, d\}, \{o, d\}, o)$, and
- the dual maintenance obligation, denoted by $\mathbf{M}_d(o)$, as $r(\varnothing, \{d\}, o)$ or as $r(\varnothing, \varnothing, o)$ whenever $d = \bot$ (which is a logical constant for false).

In this way, we can enforce the principle that a temporal norm is classified as obligatory if it is a necessary condition for fulfillment/violation [63].

A *fluent formula* φ consists of a set of fluents, optionally in the scope of a default negation.

An *action theory* is then a pair (D, Γ) where $D = DL \cup SL \cup E$ is composed of different types of laws that define the behavior of fluents and actions in the system, and Γ describes the starting state of the world:

- *SL* is a set of *static causal laws* which specify relationships between fluent of the form caused(φ, f), meaning that whenever φ holds, f must also hold.
- *DL* is a set of *dynamic causal laws* which describe the effects of actions, expressed as causes(a, f, φ), which states that if action a is executed in a state where φ is true, then f will become true as a result.
- *E* is a set of *executability conditions* which define the circumstances under which an action can be performed, using expressions of the form $exec(a, \varphi)$, indicating that action a is executable whenever φ holds.
- *Γ* is a set of *initial state conditions* of the form init(f), which asserts that fluent f holds in the initial state.

Example 5 (Unknown User Status). We consider a scenario where users in an institutional setting can approve documents based on their roles and qualifications. The system involves users, administrators, and certified approver, and the goal is to ensure that a document gets approved through an appropriate sequence of actions. A user can either be an administrator or not, and an administrator who has attended an approval course automatically counts as a certified approver. Only administrators can promote other users to administrator status, and only certified approver can approve documents. Therefore, the initial state is:

$$init(usr(b)) \quad init(usr(a)), \quad init(adm(a)),$$
$$init(attended(b, app\_crs)), \quad init(doc(d)).$$

Every user is either an administrator or a non-administrator:

$$caused(\{\text{not } adm(X), usr(X)\}, \neg adm(X)).$$
$$caused(\{\text{not } \neg adm(X), usr(X)\}, adm(X)).$$

The count-as relation defining certified approvals is expressed as:

$$caused(adm(X), attended(X, app\_crs), \{cert\_app(X)\}).$$

The action constraints and effects are defined as follows:

$$exec(promote(X, Y), \{adm(X), usr(Y)\}).$$
$$causes(promote(X, Y), adm(Y), \varnothing).$$
$$causes(certify(X, D), app\_doc(D), \{doc(D), \ cert\_app(X)\}).$$

The goal condition is $\Delta = \{app\_doc(d)\}$.

Semantics. We now define transition-based semantics for deon-$\mathcal{B}$. A *state* is an interpretation I over $\mathcal{F}$ such that (i) I is a maximal *consistent* set of default fluents, i.e., for every fluent f, we have $\{f, \neg f\} \not\subseteq I$ and $\neg f \in I$ entails not $f \in I$; and (ii) I is closed under SL according to the well-founded semantics.

Action language $\mathcal{B}$ addresses the frame problem [44] by embedding the commonsense law of inertia for *ontic-$\mathcal{F}$* into its semantics. To properly handle temporal norms, we refine and specialize the inertia law for repeaters **R**, tailoring it to properly handle their behavior following, instead, a logic programming-based definition as done in the action language $\mathcal{K}$ [22].

An action a is *executable* in a state s, if there is some executability condition $exec(a, \phi) \in E$ such that $\phi \subseteq s$. This ensures that actions can only be executed when their preconditions are explicitly satisfied in the given state.

– If action a is executable in state s_i, then the next state s_{i+1} is computed as:

$$\Phi^{\mathrm{wf}}(a, s_i) = s_{i+1} = \mathrm{WFMX}(\pi_{D,\Gamma} \cup \{a\} \cup s_i' \cup (\mathbf{wD})) \smallsetminus s_i' \qquad (2)$$

where $s_i' = \{(\mathrm{not})\ f' \mid (\mathrm{not})\ f \in \mathcal{F} \cap s_i\}$ represents the previous state, and $\pi_{D,\Gamma}$ consists of the following subprograms:

$$
\begin{array}{lll}
\pi_{static} = \{f \leftarrow \phi \mid caused(\phi, f) \in D\} & & (static\ laws)\\
\pi_{inertia} = \{f \leftarrow f', \mathrm{not}\ \neg f \mid f \in ontic\text{-}\mathcal{F}\} & & (inertia\ laws)\\
\pi_{dyn} = \{f \leftarrow \phi, a \mid causes(a, f, \phi) \in D\} & & (dynamic\ effects)\\
\pi_{prop} = \{\mathbf{r} \leftarrow \mathrm{not}\ \neg\mathbf{r}, \mathbf{r}', \mathrm{not}\ S'.\mid\ \mathbf{r} = r(D, S, o) \in \mathbf{R}\}, & (repeater\ propagation)\\
\quad\quad \text{where not } S' = \{\mathrm{not}\ s' \mid s \in S\} & &\\
\pi_{der} = \{\mathbf{O}o \leftarrow r(D, S, o), d.\mid r(D, S, o) \in \mathbf{R}, d \in D\} & & (derivation)\\
\quad\quad \text{where } \mathbf{O} \neg p \text{ stands for } \mathbf{F}p & &
\end{array}
$$

– If a is not executable in s_i, then $\Phi^{\mathrm{wf}}(a, s_i)$ is undefined.

The rules in π_{static}, $\pi_{inertia}$, and π_{dyn} are self explanatory. The rules in π_{prop} and π_{der} govern the repeaters following the framework in [58]: π_{prop} dictates that the repeater persists over time unless some stopping condition in S is satisfied or $\neg r(D, S, o)$ is derived in the next state, which we refer to as the *cancellation* of $r(D, S, o)$. Program π_{der} ensures that whenever the repeater $r(D, S, o)$ is active, the deontic fluent with content o is derived if at least one fluent in D holds.

A *trajectory* is a sequence $\sigma = s_0 a_0 s_1 a_1 \dots s_k$ of alternating states s_i and actions a_i, where each state transition $s_i, a_i, s_{i+1}, 0 \le i < k$, obeys (2) and s_0 is the WFMX of the logic program $\pi_{static} \cup \{f \mid init(f)\} \cup \{(\mathbf{wD})\}$.

A *planning problem* on an action theory $\mathcal{T} = (D, \Gamma)$ is then a triple (D, Γ, Δ), where Δ represents a goal condition expressed as a fluent formula. A sequence of actions $\alpha = a_0, \dots, a_{k-1}$ from a trajectory σ as above is a *plan* for it if $\Delta \subseteq s_n$.

Example 6 (Unknown user status, cont.) The shortest plan under deon-$\mathcal{B}_{\mathrm{wf}}$ is $\alpha = promote(a, b), certify(b, d)$. User b is not initially an admin but has attended the approval course. Since an administrator who has attended the course is a certified approver, promoting b first enables them to approve the document. Under deon-$\mathcal{B}_{\mathrm{asp}}$ the nondeterminism introduces a choice about whether b is initially an administrator ($admin(b)$) or not ($\neg admin(b)$). If b is an administrator, the shortest plan would be: $certify(b, d)$. However, this is an optimistic plan as it relies on one possible instantiation of the nondeterminism.

Regarding the complexity of planning, we obtain the following results:

Theorem 2. *Deciding whether a plan exists for a given planning problem* (D, Γ, Δ) *is PSPACE-complete if fluents are variable-free, while it is EXSPACE-complete when fluents admit variables.*

Theorem 2 aligns with computational complexity results in classical planning [13,50]. Notably, computing the next state once an action is selected can be done in quadratic time [4] when fluents are variable-free, while the problem is complete for exponential time when variables may occur.

5   Relation to Answer Set Semantics

In this section, we discuss the relation of a well-founded approach with respect to an ASP one in both the static and planning settings.

Definition 7. *A consistent interpretation I is an answer set of π if $I = Cn(\pi^I)$.*

While well-founded semantics admits only one model, answer set semantics may yield multiple models; e.g., in Example 1, $\{p, u\}$ and $\{\neg p, u\}$ are answer sets.

We now revisit key relationships between well-founded semantics with explicit negation with respect to answer-set semantics.

Theorem 3 (Relation to ASP [4]). *For explicit-negation-free logic programs, WFSX coincides with WFS semantics as defined in [65]. Furthermore, for every explicit literal L and answer set I of a logic program π, (i) $L \in \mathrm{WFMX}(\pi)$ implies $L \in I$ and (ii) not $L \in \mathrm{WFMX}(\pi)$ implies $L \notin I$.*

In order to derive further results, we introduce the notion of dependency graph, which naturally extends to laws from an action theory.

Definition 8 (Dependency Graph). *The* dependency graph *of a logic program π is the labeled directed graph $DG(\pi) = \langle V, E \rangle$ where we have $V = \mathcal{L}$ and $E = \{(H(r), b, \ell) \mid b \in B^\ell(r), \ r \in \pi, \ \ell \in \{+, -\}\}$.*

A ground atom p depends positively (resp. negatively) on q if every path from p to q contains only arcs labeled + (resp. if there is a path with an arc labeled $-$). A logic program is *locally stratified* if all its ground predicates can be assigned a *rank* such that: (i) no atom depends positively on one of a greater rank, and (ii) no atom depends negatively on one of equal or greater rank [7,17,25]. We extend a folklore correspondence of stratified logic programs to the well-founded with explicit negation settings.

Theorem 4. *If a logic program π is locally stratified, then $\mathrm{WFMX}(\pi)$ exists iff π possesses a unique answer set. Moreover, when both exist, they coincide.*

Stratified programs are beneficial for capturing normative reasoning [53] to guarantee a unique deontic conclusion given a set of ontic and deontic knowledge base; for instance, stratified programs allow to express *count-as* relations [12]; the roles of users in Example 5 can be viewed as such: an admin who has attended an approval course counts as certified user.

Relating our approach to ASP, it is natural to regard any answer set of a logic program π that is a deontic interpretation as in Definition 5 as a *deontic answer set* of π. We then obtain:

Proposition 2. ([14]). *A set S is a deontic answer set of a logic program π iff S is an answer set of the program $\pi \cup (\mathbf{wD})$.*

As a consequence of Theorem 3 and Proposition 1, we know that:

Theorem 5. (Relation to Deontic Answer-sets). *Let π be a logic program. Then for every $L \in \mathcal{L}$ and deontic answer set S of π, (i) $L \in$ deon-WFMX(π) implies $L \in S$ and (ii) not $L \in$ deon-WFMX(π) implies $L \notin S$.*

We can define an ASP version of deon-$\mathcal{B}$, just by modifying the transition relation in Eq. (2) into $\Phi^{\mathrm{asp}}(a, s_i) = s_{i+1} \in \mathrm{ASP}(\pi_{D,\Gamma} \cup \{a\} \cup s_i' \cup (\mathbf{wD})) \smallsetminus s_i'$. Adopting a standard terminology [22], a plan $\alpha = a_0, \ldots, a_{k-1}$ defined analog as for deon-$\mathcal{B}_{\mathrm{wf}}$ above is *optimistic*, and it is called *secure* if it is executable under all possible realization of the (non-)deterministic transition function Φ^{asp}.

An action theory $\mathcal{T} = (D, \Gamma)$ has $DG(\pi_{\mathcal{T}})$ as dependency graph; $\mathcal{T}$ is *odd cycle-free*, if no loop in $DG(\pi_{\mathcal{T}})$ has an odd number of arcs with label $-$.

Proposition 3. *Suppose $\alpha = a_0, \ldots, a_{i-1}$ is a deon-$\mathcal{B}_{\mathrm{wf}}$ plan for a planning problem (D, Γ, Δ). Then α is a deon-$\mathcal{B}_{\mathrm{asp}}$-secure plan iff α is a deon-$\mathcal{B}_{\mathrm{asp}}$-optimistic plan. Furthermore, if (i) D is odd cycle-free and (ii) D is strong negation-free, then α is a deon-$\mathcal{B}_{\mathrm{asp}}$-secure plan.*

We require that the sequence of actions remains executable under well-founded semantics, as the WFSX model may lack sufficient information to satisfy the executability conditions in cases where an answer set does. Furthermore, the odd cycle-free assumption can be weakened to include constraints, which can be encoded by the use of an auxiliary fluent. On the order side, we can weaken the strong negation-free assumption by guaranteeing disjointness of reachable nodes between opposite literals.

We note that conformant planning (and likewise secure planning in deon-$\mathcal{B}_{\mathrm{asp}}$) is EXPSPACE-complete for variable-free fluents [50], and Σ_2^p-hard even for few steps (bounded by a constant) plans in conventional settings [8,13,23,62]. Well-founded planning, instead, is for polynomial-length plans in NP, and for few-step plans feasible in polynomial time.

6   Normative Challenges Addressed by deon-$\mathcal{B}_{\mathrm{wf}}$

We showcase the effectiveness of deon-$\mathcal{B}_{\mathrm{wf}}$ by tackling key challenges in action-based deontic reasoning.

Flexible Handling of Normative Conflicts. An example, adapted from [41,42], helps clarify how the well-founded semantics can be used to apply interpretative principles and still reason about a sound deontic plan when not all the conflicts are solved by those principles. Consider the following two sentences: (i) "Don't eat with your fingers" ($\mathbf{F}w\_f(X)$), and (ii) "If you are served asparagus, eat it with your fingers" ($\neg\mathbf{F}w\_f(a)$). These norms appear to be in conflict. One might resolve it by invoking the *lex specialis* principle, according to which more specific norms override more general ones.

$caused(\{\text{not } overruled(prohibition, X), food(X)\}, \mathbf{F}w\_f(X))$.
$caused(\{\text{not } overruled(permission, X), food(X)\}, \neg\mathbf{F}w\_f(X))$.
$caused(\{\neg\mathbf{F}w\_f(a)\}, overruled(prohibition, w\_f(a)))$.
$caused(\{\mathbf{F}w\_f(a)\}, overruled(permission, w\_f(a)))$.

Therefore, if an explicit permission for $w\_f(a)$ is required as a precondition before eating it with one's fingers, the planner would not suggest eating asparagus in this way, as it can neither derive $\mathbf{F}w\_f(a)$ nor $\neg\mathbf{F}w\_f(a)$. Using ASP semantics, we would have two answer sets: one containing $\mathbf{F}w\_f(a)$ and the other one containing $\neg\mathbf{F}w\_f(a)$, thus not matching the intended behavior.

On the other hand, the conflict can be resolved by explicitly enforcing the *lex specialis* principle - e.g., by dropping the last rule that allows $\mathbf{F}w\_f(a)$ to be overruled. This demonstrates that well-founded semantics for planning is robust enough to handle scenarios where principles like typicality can be enforced, as well as scenarios where the desired behavior is to be agnostic about such a disambiguation. With further information, we may want to enforce the *lex posterior* and *lex superior* principles by using the same encoding template[3].

Contrary to Duty. As discussed in [51], we show how the General Data Protection Regulation (GDPR, Regulation EU 2016/679) provides a compelling scenario for normative reasoning. It establishes guidelines for data protection and imposes obligations on data controllers. We focus on key norms: (i) personal data must be processed lawfully lw (*Art. 5*); (ii) if data is processed unlawfully $\neg lw$, the controller must erase it without delay (*Art. 17.d*, the "right to be forgotten"). We enrich this with the following deontic and factual points, respectively: (iii) in contractual agreements, companies are obligated to retain personal data provided it is lawfully processed until the end of the contract ec; and (iv) some data in such an agreement has been processed unlawfully but not been erased e yet. Note that (iii) features both a deontic and a factual detachment.

The initial conditions and static laws can be modeled as follows:

$init(\mathbf{M}_{\perp}(lf))$. (i) $init(\neg e)$. (iv) $init(\neg lf)$. (iv)
$caused(\{\neg lf\}, \mathbf{M}_e(e))$. (ii)
$caused(\{lf\}, \mathbf{M}_{ec}(\neg e))$. (iii) factual detachment
$caused(\{\mathbf{O}(lf)\}, \mathbf{M}_{ec}(\neg e))$. (iii) deontic detachment

The effect of the erasure action is: $caused(erases, e, \varnothing)$.

---

[3] The former respects time, viz. most recent norms have higher priority over less recent norms, while the latter enforces the hierarchy of authority among normative sources.

The initial state reveals a contrary-to-duty (**CTD**) structure. We show how we can still execute an action while admitting a contrary-to-duty scenario. Specifically, let us consider *erases*. In the initial state, both an obligation and a prohibition on erasure emerge: (a) $\mathbf{O}(e)$, derived from the maintenance obligation $\mathbf{M}_e(e)$ due to $\neg lf$, and (b) $\mathbf{F}(e)$, as a punctual instance of $\mathbf{M}_{ec}(\neg e)$ which is derivable from deontic detachment in (*iii*) by $\mathbf{O}(lf)$, which is a punctual instance of $\mathbf{M}_\top(lf)$. As $\neg e$ holds initially, (a) is violated while (b) is fulfilled. After executing *erases(company)*, (a) is fulfilled, but (b) is violated instead.

This demonstrates how our formalism handles **CTD** scenarios following the (**wD**)-axiom faithfully with respect to the paradigm as proposed in [14].

Prima Facie and Secondary Norms. Normative reasoning often requires distinguishing between *prima facie* obligations—those that hold generally but can be overridden—and *actual* obligations, which remain enforceable after resolving conflicts with other norms [15]. This is conceptually different from **CTD** scenarios, which lack overriding and have both contradictory norms in place. We consider the example from [60]: (*i*) You should not speed; (*ii*) To prevent a possible disaster, you may speed; (*iii*) If you are speeding, then you should speed safely; (*iv*) During certain points an emergency *em* occurs.

According to [54], if a genuine emergency *em* is established, then speeding is permissible under the second rule, effectively canceling the first obligation. Furthermore, if speeding occurs, then the third rule introduces a new obligation: speeding must be done safely, overshadowing the original prohibition.

Only in the absence of an emergency does the prohibition against speeding remain an *actual* obligation—meaning that speeding would be a violation. However, when an emergency arises, the need to prevent disaster outweighs the general prohibition, making speeding an *actual* permission.

Formally, we express this scenario in our formalism as follows:

caused($\{$not $\neg\ \mathbf{M}_\perp(\neg speeding)\}, \mathbf{M}_\perp(\neg speeding)$).   (*i*)

caused($\{em\}, \neg\mathbf{M}_\perp(\neg speeding)$)   (*ii*)

caused($\{speeding\}, \mathbf{O}(speeding\_safely)$).   (*iii*)

caused($\{speeding\_safely\}, speeding$). caused($\{\mathbf{O}(speeding\_safely)\}, \mathbf{O}(speeding)$).

causes($speed\_safely, speeding\_safely, \varnothing$). which is the action effect

Now, consider the plan $\alpha = a_0, speed\_safely, a_2, \ldots$ Under well-founded semantics, the initial state contains a *maintenance obligation* not to speed, $\mathbf{M}_\perp(\neg speed)$, which derives $\mathbf{F}(speed)$ as a punctual prohibition. However, let assume *em* holds in the second state, after executing *speed_safely* the outcome is *speeding_safely*. As by (*ii*) $\{em\}$ causes the cancellation of $\mathbf{M}_\perp(\neg speed)$, no prohibition against speeding is derived at this state. Meanwhile, the obligation to speed safely is detached as a factual consequence of speeding and is fulfilled.

7 Related Work and Conclusion

Well-founded semantics is a well-established non-monotonic reasoning framework, supported by various off-the-shelf tools, and serves as a computationally efficient approximation of answer-set semantics. The latter has been successfully applied in a range of domains [28,30], among them scheduling [1,67], configuration [20], and planning in robotics [16,29,56]. While dynamic answer-set languages for planning have been extensively studied—see [61] for a survey— well-founded semantics as an approximation to answer-set semantics in dynamic environments has received less attention. In this work, we introduced a semantics for a deontic action language in which state transitions following an action execution are computed under well-founded semantics. Our approach seamlessly integrates temporal normative concepts, such as maintenance and achievement obligations, by incorporating the repeater-template mechanism, initially proposed in [58]. We demonstrated how uncertainty in normative conflicts, contrary-to-duty (**CTD**) obligations, temporal defeasibility of obligations can be effectively handled.

Temporal norms have been widely studied from various perspectives [2,40, 59]. A closely related approach to ours is that of [34], which combines temporal and deontic operators within logic programs under the answer-set semantics, sharing several features with our action language deon-$\mathcal{B}_{asp}$. However, a key distinction is the treatment of **CTD** scenarios: while [34] enforces the (**D**)-axiom, which poses challenges in handling dilemmas such as the Gentle Murder paradox. Our framework avoids such issues through the use of the weaker axiom (**wD**) [14].

Outlook. Future work includes implementing our formalism, with applications extending to the monitoring framework introduced in [27,57], ensuring an efficient computation of the deontic consequences from a trace of factual observations to verify normative properties in dynamic systems. Further extensions could be explored, such as considering not only the least partial stable model given by well-founded semantics, but in a similar vein other partial stable models, cf. [26]. We might for instance impose on some fluents *totality* (either p or $\neg p$ is true), increasing the chances to successfully apply the weak-deontic axiom.

Acknowledgments. The project leading to this application has received funding from the European Union's Horizon 2020 research and innovation programme under grant agreement No 101034440.

Furthermore, this research was funded in whole or in part by the Vienna Science and Technology Fund (WWTF) project ICT22-023 and the Austrian Science Fund (FWF) 10.55776/COE12.

References

1. Abels, D., Jordi, J., Ostrowski, M., Schaub, T., Toletti, A., Wanko, P.: Train scheduling with hybrid ASP. In: Proceedings of the 15th International Conference on Logic Programming and Nonmonotonic Reasoning (LPNMR 2019). LNCS, vol. 11481, pp. 3–17. Springer (2019)
2. Ågotnes, T., van der Hoek, W., Rodríguez-Aguilar, J.A., Sierra, C., Wooldridge, M.: A temporal logic of normative systems. In: Makinson, D., Malinowski, J., Wansing, H. (eds.) Towards Mathematical Philosophy: Papers from the Studia Logica conference Trends in Logic IV, pp. 69–106. Springer Netherlands, Dordrecht (2009). https://doi.org/10.1007/978-1-4020-9084-4_5
3. Alechina, N., Dastani, M., Logan, B.: Norm specification and verification in multi-agent systems. J. Appl. Logics **5**(2), 457 (2018)
4. Alferes, J.J., Damasio, C.V., Pereira, L.M.: A logic programming system for non-monotonic reasoning. J. Autom. Reason. **14**, 93–147 (1995)
5. Alferes, J.J., Gonçalves, R., Leite, J.: Equivalence of defeasible normative systems. J. Appl. Non-Classical Logics **23**(1–2), 25–48 (2013)
6. Alferes, J.J.A.: Semantics of logic programs with explicit negation. Universidade NOVA de Lisboa (Portugal) (1993)
7. Apt, K.R., Blair, H.A., Walker, A.: Towards a theory of declarative knowledge. In: Foundations of Deductive Databases and Logic Programming, pp. 89–148. Elsevier (1988)
8. Baral, C., Kreinovich, V., Trejo, R.: Computational complexity of planning and approximate planning in the presence of incompleteness. Artif. Intell. **122**(1–2), 241–267 (2000). https://doi.org/10.1016/S0004-3702(00)00043-6
9. Bertoli, P., Cimatti, A., Roveri, M., Traverso, P.: Strong planning under partial observability. Artif. Intell. **170**(4–5), 337–384 (2006)
10. Bozzano, M., et al.: ROBDT: AI-enhanced digital twin for space exploration robotic assets. In: International Conference on Applied Intelligence and Informatics, pp. 183–198. Springer (2022)
11. Brewka, G., Eiter, T., Truszczyński, M.: Answer set programming at a glance. Commun. ACM **54**(12), 92–103 (2011)
12. Broersen, J., et al.: Deontic logic. Agreement Technol., 171–179 (2013)
13. Bylander, T.: The computational complexity of propositional strips planning. Artif. Intell. **69**(1–2), 165–204 (1994)
14. Cabalar, P., Ciabattoni, A., van der Torre, L.: Deontic equilibrium logic with explicit negation. In: JELIA 2023. LNCS, vol. 14281, pp. 498–514. Springer (2023)
15. Carmo, J., Jones, A.J.: Deontic logic and contrary-to-duties. In: Handbook of Philosophical Logic: Volume 8, pp. 265–343. Springer (2002)
16. Cerexhe, T.J., Gebser, M., Thielscher, M.: Online agent logic programming with oclingo. In: Pham, D.N., Park, S. (eds.) PRICAI 2014. Lecture Notes in Computer Science, vol. 8862, pp. 945–957. Springer (2014). https://doi.org/10.1007/978-3-319-13560-1_82
17. Chandra, A.K., Harel, D.: Horn clause queries and generalizations. J. Logic Program. **2**(1), 1–15 (1985)
18. Chisholm, R.: Contrary-to-duty imperatives and deontic logic. Analysis **24**(2), 33–36 (1963)
19. Cimatti, A., Roveri, M.: Conformant planning via symbolic model checking. J. Artif. Intell. Res. **13**, 305–338 (2000)

20. Comploi-Taupe, R., Francescutto, G., Schenner, G.: Applying incremental answer set solving to product configuration. In: Proceedings of the 26th ACM International Systems and Software Product Line Conference (SPLC 2022), pp. 150–155. ACM (2022). https://doi.org/10.1145/3503229.3547069

21. Dantsin, E., Eiter, T., Gottlob, G., Voronkov, A.: Complexity and expressive power of logic programming. ACM Comput. Surv. (CSUR) **33**(3), 374–425 (2001)

22. Eiter, T., Faber, W., Leone, N., Pfeifer, G., Polleres, A.: Planning under incomplete knowledge. In: International Conference on Computational Logic, pp. 807–821. Springer (2000)

23. Eiter, T., Faber, W., Leone, N., Pfeifer, G., Polleres, A.: A logic programming approach to knowledge-state planning: semantics and complexity. ACM Trans. Comput. Log. **5**(2), 206–263 (2004). https://doi.org/10.1145/976706.976708

24. Eiter, T., Gottlob, G.: On the computational cost of disjunctive logic programming: propositional case. Ann. Math. Artif. Intell. **15**, 289–323 (1995)

25. Eiter, T., Ianni, G., Krennwallner, T.: Answer set programming: a primer. Springer (2009)

26. Eiter, T., Leone, N., Saccà, D.: On the partial semantics for disjunctive deductive databases. Ann. Math. Artif. Intell. **19**(1-2), 59–96 (1997). https://doi.org/10.1023/A:1018947420290

27. Eiter, T., Soldà, D.: Computational aspects of progression for temporal equilibrium logic. In: Larson, K. (ed.) Proceedings of the Thirty-Third International Joint Conference on Artificial Intelligence, IJCAI-24, pp. 3342–3350. International Joint Conferences on Artificial Intelligence Organization (2024). https://doi.org/10.24963/ijcai.2024/370. main Track

28. Erdem, E., Gelfond, M., Leone, N.: Applications of answer set programming. AI Mag. **37**(3), 53–68 (2016). https://doi.org/10.1609/aimag.v37i3.2678

29. Erdem, E., Patoglu, V.: Applications of asp in robotics. KI-Künstliche Intelligenz **32**(2), 143–149 (2018)

30. Falkner, A., Friedrich, G., Schekotihin, K., Taupe, R., Teppan, E.C.: Industrial applications of answer set programming. KI - Künstliche Intelligenz **32**(2), 165–176 (2018). https://doi.org/10.1007/s13218-018-0548-6

31. Gabbay, D., et al.: Handbook of deontic logic and normative systems. College Publications (2021)

32. Gelfond, M., Lifschitz, V.: Logic programs with classical negation. In: Warren, D.H.D., Szeredi, P. (eds.) Logic Programming, Proceedings of the Seventh International Conference, Jerusalem, Israel, pp. 579–597. MIT Press (1990)

33. Gelfond, M., Lifschitz, V.: Action languages. Linköping University Electronic Press (1998)

34. Giordano, L., Martelli, A., Dupré, D.T.: Temporal deontic action logic for the verification of compliance to norms in ASP. In: ICAIL 2013, pp. 53–62. ACM (2013)

35. Governatori, G.: Law, logic and business processes. In: 2010 Third International Workshop on Requirements Engineering and Law, pp. 1–10. IEEE (2010)

36. Governatori, G.: Weak permission is not well-founded, grounded and stable. CoRR **abs/2411.10624** (2024). https://doi.org/10.48550/ARXIV.2411.10624

37. Governatori, G., Hulstijn, J., Riveret, R., Rotolo, A.: Characterising deadlines in temporal modal defeasible logic. In: Advances in Artificial Intelligence, pp. 486–496. Springer (2007)

38. Governatori, G., Olivieri, F., Rotolo, A., Scannapieco, S.: Computing strong and weak permissions in defeasible logic. J. Phil. Logic **42**(6), 799–829 (2013)

39. Hatschka, C., Ciabattoni, A., Eiter, T.: Deontic paradoxes in ASP with weak constraints. In: Proceedings of ICLP 2023. EPTCS, vol. 385, pp. 367–380 (2023)
40. Horty, J.: Deontic Logic and Agency. OUP (2001)
41. Horty, J.F.: Moral dilemmas and nonmonotonic logic. J. Philos. Log. **23**, 35–65 (1994)
42. Joyce, J.: Policy-adaptable methods for resolving normative conflicts through argumentation and graph colouring. arXiv preprint: arXiv:2501.11799 (2025)
43. Lifschitz, V.: Answer Set Programming, vol. 3. Springer Cham (2019)
44. McCarthy, J., Hayes, P.J.: Some philosophical problems from the standpoint of artificial intelligence. In: Readings in artificial intelligence, pp. 431–450. Elsevier (1981)
45. Nute, D.: Defeasible Deontic Logic, vol. 263. Springer Science & Business Media (1997)
46. Peot, M.A., Smith, D.E.: Conditional nonlinear planning. In: Artificial Intelligence Planning Systems, pp. 189–197. Elsevier (1992)
47. Pereira, L.M., Alferes, J.J.: Well founded semantics for logic programs with explicit negation. In: Proceedings of the 10th European Conference on Artificial Intelligence, ECAI '92, pp. 102–106. John Wiley & Sons, Inc., USA (1992)
48. Prakken, H., Sergot, M.: Contrary-to-duty obligations. Stud. Logica. **57**, 91–115 (1996)
49. Przymusinski, T.C.: On the declarative semantics of deductive databases and logic programs. In: Foundations of Deductive Databases and Logic Programming, pp. 193–216. Elsevier (1988)
50. Rintanen, J.: Complexity of planning with partial observability. In: ICAPS, pp. 345–354. AAAI (2004)
51. Robaldo, L., Bartolini, C., Palmirani, M., Rossi, A., Martoni, M., Lenzini, G.: Formalizing GDPR provisions in reified I/O logic: the DAPRECO knowledge base. J. Logic Lang. Inform. **29**, 401–449 (2020)
52. Ross, A.: Imperatives and logic. Philos. Sci. **11**(1), 30–46 (1944)
53. Satoh, K.: PROLEG: practical legal reasoning system. In: Prolog: The Next 50 Years, pp. 277–283. Springer (2023)
54. Sentencing Council: Speeding (revised 2017) (2017). https://www.sentencingcouncil.org.uk/offences/magistrates-court/item/speeding-revised-2017. Accessed 05 Mar 2025
55. Smith, D.E., Weld, D.S.: Conformant Graphplan. In: AAAI/IAAI, pp. 889–896 (1998)
56. Soldà, D., Fabiano, F., Dovier, A.: ECHO: a hierarchical combination of classical and multi-agent epistemic planning problems. J. Log. Comput. **33**(8), 1804–1831 (2023). https://doi.org/10.1093/LOGCOM/EXAD036
57. Soldà, D., Lopez-Miguel, I.D., Bartocci, E., Eiter, T.: Progression for monitoring in temporal ASP. In: ECAI 2023, vol. 372, pp. 2170–2177. IOS Press (2023)
58. Soldà, D., Cabalar, P., Ciabattoni, A., Neufeld, E.: Tackling temporal deontic challenges with equilibrium logic. In: AAMAS (2024)
59. Thomason, R.: Deontic logic as founded on tense logic. In: New Studies in Deontic Logic: Norms, Actions, and the Foundation of Ethics. Reidel Publishing Company (1981)
60. van der Torre, L.W., Tan, Y.H.: An update semantics for prima facie obligations. In: ECAI, pp. 38–42 (1998)
61. Tran, S.C., Pontelli, E., Balduccini, M., Schaub, T.: Answer set planning: a survey. Theory Pract. Logic Program. **23**(1), 226–298 (2023)

62. Turner, H.: Polynomial-length planning spans the polynomial hierarchy. In: Proc. of JELIA, pp. 111–124. Springer (2002)

63. Van Fraassen, B.C.: Values and the heart's command. J. Philos. **70**(1), 5–19 (1973)

64. Van Gelder, A., Ross, K., Schlipf, J.S.: Unfounded sets and well-founded semantics for general logic programs. In: Proceedings of the seventh ACM SIGACT-SIGMOD-SIGART symposium on Principles of database systems, pp. 221–230 (1988)

65. Van Gelder, A., Ross, K.A., Schlipf, J.S.: The well-founded semantics for general logic programs. J. ACM (JACM) **38**(3), 619–649 (1991)

66. von Wright, G.H.: Deontic logics. Am. Philos. Q. **4**(2), 136–143 (1967)

67. Yli-Jyrä, A., Rankooh, M.F., Janhunen, T.: Pruning redundancy in answer set optimization applied to preventive maintenance scheduling. In: Proceedings of the 25th International Symposium on Practical Aspects of Declarative Languages (PADL 2023), pp. 279–294. Springer, Cham (2023)

Dual Scale Detachment

Vincent de Wit[1]([✉]) [iD], Aleks Knoks[2] [iD], and Leendert van der Torre[1] [iD]

[1] Department of Computer Science, University of Luxembourg, Maison du Nombre,
6, Av. de la Fonte, 4365 Esch-sur-Alzette, Luxembourg
vincent.dewit@uni.lu
[2] Institute of Philosophy, University of Luxembourg, Maison des Sciences Humaines,
2, Place de l'Université, 4365 Esch-sur-Alzette, Luxembourg

Abstract. Drawing motivation from the philosophical literature on normative reasons, detachment functions model the way that interaction or competition between reasons determines deontic status of options. This paper presents detachment functions that capture the "dual scale model" of weighing reasons, as outlined in Chris Tucker's recent book "The Weight of Reasons". The dual scale model relaxes an assumption of the standard "single scale model" that much of the informal philosophical literature on reasons relies on, explicitly or implicitly. We define dual scale, single scale, and two further detachment functions, as well as provide a principle-based analysis comparing these systems.

Keywords: balancing scale · detachment functions · principle-based analysis · reasons · weighing · deontic logic

1 Introduction

The philosophical literature that tackles foundational questions about the nature of normativity and the architecture or logical structure of normative domains, such as morality, makes significant use of the notion of normative reasons. Standardly, normative reasons are taken to be facts that obtain in a given normatively sensitive situation, and that either speak in favor of or against the actions that an agent can take in response to the situation [12, p. 17]. For example in some contexts where it is sunny outside, the fact that it is sunny outside can be a reason for choosing the option to go for a walk. Normative reasons are also taken to interact or compete and thereby determine the deontic status of actions (or options) available to the agent, that is, to determine which of these actions are permissible, which obligatory, and which forbidden.

John Horty [7] started a line of research that has been attracting increasing attention in the deontic logic community: How do we bridge the informal literature on reasons in philosophy with the formal literature on deontic logic and normative systems? Horty's own model [7] draws on nonmonotonic logic, default logic, and formal argumentation. However, it also parts ways with the commonplace and mainstream approach in philosophy that conceives of the interaction

G. Casini et al. (Eds.): JELIA 2025, LNAI 16093, pp. 205–219, 2026.
https://doi.org/10.1007/978-3-032-04587-4_13

between reasons relying on the metaphor of normative balancing scales—see e.g. [5, p. 36ff], [6, p. 9–10], [14, p. 726ff] and [18].

In previous work, two of us have proposed a formal framework, called *reason-based detachment*, that models the interaction between reasons as a kind of inference pattern, following the methodology of input/output logic [9]. The framework was later extended to allow formalizing scale-based models and representing the weights of reasons—or normative forces associated with reasons—using numbers [8]. In this paper, we extend this line of research to what we call *dual-scale detachment* which is based on Chris Tucker's "dual scale model" of weighing reasons, as it is presented in his recent book "The Weight of Reasons: A Framework for Ethics" [17]. The dual scale model relaxes an assumption, the single proportion assumption, of the standard "single-scale model" that the informal philosophical literature relies on. Tuckers' book lays this assumption bare, associating reasons with two kinds of weights that play different roles in determining the deontic status of actions. We express Tucker's model as dual-scale detachment and explore its connections to (some of) the detachment functions from [8,9]. Reason-based detachment is not only a general input/output logic methodology to formalize reason-based approaches, but it can also be used to *compare* these approaches. This comparison is based on a principle-based analysis, where a set of relevant principles is first defined, and then, for each approach, it is checked which of the principles are satisfied by the given approach.

This paper thus answers the following two **research questions**: (1) How can we express Tucker's dual scale model in the framework of reason-based detachment? (2) And how does it, once expressed as a detachment function, compare to some benchmark detachment functions we define, drawing on our previous work and ideas from knowledge representation and reasoning?

The framework that we set up here also deals with some limitations of our previous approach, such as capturing the differences between the atomist and holist views about weights of reasons. (Now we follow Tucker's ideas and let the context serve as a shield against the worries associated with additive aggregation of weights.) It is worth noting that the framework set up here is more general, meaning that we had to adapt the principles from [8,9] to the new setting, and that we introduce some new principles, motivated by Tucker's work.

The rest of this paper is structured as follows. In Sect. 2 we introduce the core ideas behind the dual scale model of weighing reasons. In Sect. 3, we formalize it as dual-scale detachment, and in Sect. 4, we define three further kinds of detachment—single-scale, maximum detachment, and uniform detachment—to serve as benchmarks. In Sect. 5, we state the principles, and in Sect. 6 we present our principle-based analysis. In Sect. 7, we discuss related work. In Sect. 8, we summarize and present some of our ideas for future research.

2   The Dual Scale Model

The goal of this section is to give the reader a feel for the dual scale model of weighing reasons—for the details, we refer the reader to the book [17].

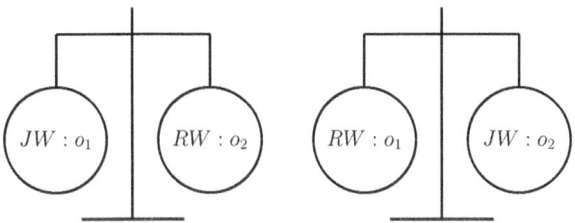

Fig. 1. The dual scale model: Permission scale (left) and commitment scale (right)

One of the core ideas behind the model is that normative reasons have two irreducible kinds of weights, *justifying* and *requiring*, and that these weights play different roles in determining deontic status of the options available to the agent. Only slightly paraphrasing Tucker, we can say that a reason's justifying weight tells us how good the reason is at making acts permissible/okay, while a reason's requiring weight tells us how good the reason is at making permissible acts required/obligatory—see [17, p. 11]. The model is called '*dual* scale' because, unlike the standard (single scale) model, it uses two normative balancing scales in pairwise comparisons of options available to the agent. Thus, consider an abstract toy situation in which the agent is choosing between two (exclusive and exhaustive) options o_1 and o_2, and in which the agent has different reasons speaking in favor of or supporting each of these options. The first scale, called the *permission scale*, determines whether the first option, o_1, is permissible by comparing the aggregate of the *justifying* weight of reasons supporting o_1 to the aggregate of the *requiring* weight of reasons supporting o_2: (sligthly simplifying) if the former is greater than or equal to the latter, then o_1 is permissible, and otherwise it is not. The second scale, called the *commitment scale*, determines whether the first option, o_1, is a commitment by comparing the *requiring* weight of the aggregate of reasons supporting o_1 to the *justifying* weight of the aggregate of reasons supporting o_2: (again, slightly simplifying) if the former is greater than the latter and o_1 is permissible, then o_1 is required, and otherwise it is not. So, justifying weights contribute to making options permissible, whereas requiring weights contribute to making options required. See Fig. 1 for a schematic depiction of the dual scale, as it applies to options o_1 and o_2.

But why would we want to distinguish between justifying and requiring weights of reasons? The short (and incomplete) answer is that it provides one with the resources to explain various intuitions about particular cases and hold onto various sorts of views one might want to hold in moral philosophy. To illustrate, consider a scenario in which the agent is confronted with a choice between either saving their beloved partner (option o_1), or two strangers (option o_2). Almost all of us find it intuitive to say that it is permissible for the agent to choose option o_1. And many of us are attracted to the idea that every person's life is equally (in)valuable—ceteris paribus and when considered from an impersonal point of view. Now, if we hold that reasons have two kinds of weights, then we have a straightforward way to account for both intuitions: in the case at hand, the requiring weight associated with the well-being of the partner is roughly equal to the requiring weights associated with the well-being of each of the two strangers, but, due to the special relationship that the agent has to their partner, the justifying weight of the aggregate of reasons that support o_1 outstrips the requiring weight of the aggregate of reasons that support o_2.[1]

Before leaving this section, it bears emphasis that the dual scale is a model of *pairwise* comparison of options. "The Weight of Reasons" provides additional tools for analyzing more complex scenarios. For example, when a given scenario involves multiple options that are open to the agent, Tucker appeals to "dynamic scale" or, roughly, a tournament of pairwise comparisons between options, with the comparisons taking place on dual scales. We restrict our focus to the dual scale model in this paper, leaving the formalization of other ideas from Tucker's (intricate) book for another day.

3   Dual Scale Detachment

In this section, we express the dual scale model in the framework of [8,9].

As mentioned, the dual scale model of weighing reasons is only one of the elements involved in the assignment of deontic status to options in scenarios. While our formalization focuses on this model, we want it to be sensitive to the other elements and to respect their effects. Because of this, the formalization might strike you as being more complicated than it needs to be, but, we think, it is (slightly) more complicated for good reasons.

Dual scale weighs a set of reasons supporting one option o_1 against a set of reasons supporting another option o_2. So, you might naturally think that the set of reasons that are relevant for the choice between o_1 and o_2 can be defined as the set of reasons supporting o_1 and the set of reasons supporting o_2 i.e. as $R(o_1, o_2) = R(o_1) \cup R(o_2)$. However, Tucker emphasizes that this is not always the case, and we therefore use the more general two place function R. On Tucker's view, it may well happen that something is a reason supporting option o_1 when o_1 is being compared to option o_2, but no longer a reason supporting option o_1 when o_1 is being compared to, for example, option o_3. This is known as *contrastivism about reasons*.

What's more, on Tucker's view, reasons do not exhaust the set of considerations that can be normatively relevant for the assignment of deontic status of options. Following a long tradition in philosophy, he allows for "disablers" and "modifiers" to affect the reasons supporting options before they are compared on the balancing scales: these can, respectively, nullify the weights of reasons or change them. (These contextual factors are also used as a "shield" against standard purported counterexamples to additive aggregation of weights of reasons.) We are not going to explicitly model either disablers or modifiers. Instead, our

---

[1] To be clear, this analysis of the scenario is both very sketchy and very controversial. What's more, it goes against Tucker's own preferred analysis of a similar case—see [17, p. 47ff]. All it's meant to do is to illustrate that distinguishing between two kinds of weights of reasons provides one with additional explanatory tools.

formalization focuses on reasons after the effects of disablers and modifiers have taken place.

With these preliminaries out of the way, we turn to the formalization. We are going to think of reasons as a bipartite graph defined over grounds (or facts) and options (against a background context). In this paper, we leave grounds, options, and contexts abstract, because that is all that we need to do our principle-based analysis. (However, in Sect. 8, we discuss future work in which we structure grounds as propositional formulas with logical connectives, options as complex actions built from atomic actions, and contexts as sets of disablers and modifiers.)

Definition 1 (Reasons). *Let C, O and G be three sets called* contexts, options *and* grounds, *respectively. Let $\mathcal{P}(G \times O)$ stand for the powerset of $G \times O$. A reasons function $R : O \times O \to \mathcal{P}(G \times O)$ associates each pair of options with a set of ground-option pairs, called the* set of reasons *(pertinent to the given pair of options). Let SR be the set of all such functions R. We refer to the elements of C, O, and G using c, o, and g with subscripts.*

Following Tucker, we define the weighting and weighing functions. Note that these are partial functions, in the sense that they are specified for a limited set of reasons, namely, those that are relevant for choices between two options.

The weighting of reasons—or assignment of weights to reasons—is based on the following idea. In the comparison between options o_1 and o_2, a reason for o_1 is also a reason against o_2. However, the metaphorical weight or strength of the positive impact on o_1 may be different from the reverse impact on o_2. We therefore follow Tucker and associate two weights with each reason, calling them justifying and requiring (embedded or final) weights. (The weights are "embedded" or "final" because these are the weights that reasons have after the effects of the modifiers.) The only criteria that we need to impose on the set of weights assigned to reasons is that addition is defined, and that weights can be compared using a binary relation $\geq$. In the following definition, we use real nonnegative numbers, such that each pair of weights is comparable.

Definition 2 (Weighting (of Reasons)). *Let $\mathbb{R}_{\geq 0}$ stand for the nonnegative reals. A weighting function $w : SR \times O \times O \times C \times (G \times O) \to \mathbb{R}_{\geq 0} \times \mathbb{R}_{\geq 0}$ assigns to each pair of options o_1 and o_2 and context c, two weights w_1 and w_2 for every reason $(g, o) = r \in R(o_1, o_2)$ pertinent to the options o_1 and o_2, with the proviso that at least one of w_1 or w_2 is positive. The first weight is called the* justifying *weight, the second weight is called the* requiring *weight: $jw(R, o_1, o_2, c, r) = w_1$ and $rw(R, o_1, o_2, c, r) = w_2$ if and only if $w(R, o_1, o_2, c, r) = (w_1, w_2)$.*

When the choice options, o_1 and o_2, the set of relevant reasons, $R(o_1, o_2)$, and the context, c, are clear from the surrounding text, we may also write $w(r) = (w_1, w_2)$, $jw(r) = w_1$ and $rw(r) = w_2$.

Due to the possible presence of disablers, not all of the reasons in $R(o_1, o_2)$ need to be in force when weighing the options o_1 and o_2. This is why we define the *set of relevant (or non-disabled) reasons* $RR \subseteq R(o_1, o_2)$. This set RR can be thought of as those reasons that are used in the comparison options o_1 and

o_2 by means of the dual scale model. Many of the principles we define in Sect. 5 have to do with varying this set RR.

According to the dual scale model, an option is permissible if the sum of the justifying weights of reasons supporting this option is at least as great as the sum of the requiring weights of the reasons supporting the alternative option. This implies that both options can be permissible, as well as that neither of them are. An option is obligatory when it is permissible and the alternative option is not. This is captured by our next definition. Notice that the three (scale) values it assigns to options correspond to three possible positions of the metaphorical balancing scale: the o_1 pan is lower than the o_2 pan; the o_1 pan is higher than the o_2 pan; and the pans are in balance.

Definition 3 (Additive Dual Scale Weighing (of Options)). *Let V be the set $\{+, -, 0\}$, called (scale) values. An Additive Dual Scale Weighing model is a weighing function $D_w : SR \times O \times O \times \mathcal{P}(G \times O) \times C \to V \times V$ that assigns to each pair of options o_1 and o_2, a subset of reasons $RR \subseteq R(o_1, o_2)$ that are relevant to this pair, a context c, and a weighting function w, a pair of scale values (v_1, v_2) in the following way:*

$$
v_1 = \begin{cases} + & \text{if } \Sigma_{x \in JW_{o_1}} x > \Sigma_{y \in RW_{o_2}} y \\ - & \text{if } \Sigma_{x \in JW_{o_1}} x < \Sigma_{y \in RW_{o_2}} y \\ 0 & \text{otherwise} \end{cases}
$$

$$
v_2 = \begin{cases} + & \text{if } \Sigma_{x \in JW_{o_2}} x > \Sigma_{y \in RW_{o_1}} y \\ - & \text{if } \Sigma_{x \in JW_{o_2}} x < \Sigma_{y \in RW_{o_1}} y \\ 0 & \text{otherwise} \end{cases}
$$

where $JW_o = \{jw((g, o)) \mid (g, o) \in RR\}$, $RW_o = \{rw((g, o)) \mid (g, o) \in RR\}$. When the choice options, the set of relevant reasons, and/or the context are important for the weighting function w we discuss, we write $D_w(R, o_1, o_2, RR, c) = (v_1, v_2)$ or $D_w(R, o_1, o_2, RR, c, v_1, v_2)$. When these are clear from the surrounding text, we may also write $D_w(RR, v_1, v_2)$ or $D_w(RR) = (v_1, v_2)$.

Following Tucker [17], we do not want to reify weights—see e.g. the discussion in Ch. 1. Therefore, in our principle-based analysis we do not refer to the weights explicitly. Instead, we refer to the set of detachment functions that can be defined using all possible weighting functions. Accordingly, our definition of dual scale detachment proceeds in two steps:

Definition 4 (Detachment Functions). *A detachment function $D : SR \times O \times O \times \mathcal{P}(G \times O) \times C \to V \times V$ assigns to each pair of options $(o_1, o_2 \in O)$ a pair of scale values $(v_1, v_2 \in V)$ against the backdrop of a subset of reasons that are relevant to these options $(RR \subseteq R(o_1, o_2))$, and a context $(c \in C)$.*

Definition 5 (Dual Scale Detachment). *Let D be a detachment function. D is a dual scale detachment function if and only if there exists a weighting function w such that $D_w = D$.*

4   Three Kinds of Benchmark Detachments

In this section, we define three further detachment functions which we are then going to compare to dual scale detachment. The first is *single scale detachment*: it corresponds to the standard model of balancing scales in our framework, and it was called *additive balancing* in Knoks et al. [8]. The second one is *uniform detachment*: it is a special case of single scale detachment that assigns all reasons the same weight—cf. "simple counting" in [8]. And the third one is *maximum detachment*: as its name suggests, it relies on the maximality-based approach that is popular in knowledge representation, and it is a generalization of what was called *maximum balancing* in Knoks et al. [8].

In single scale detachment, the justifying and requiring weights of reasons are the same. This means that the two balancing scales mirror each other, effectively turning into one and the same scale.

Definition 6 (Single Scale Detachment). *Let D be a detachment function. Then D is a* single scale detachment function *if and only if there exists a weighting function w such that $D_w = D$ and $jw = rw$.*

In uniform detachment, it's not only that the requiring and justifying weights of reasons are the same. Rather, the (justifying and requiring) weights of all reasons are the same. In fact, this method effectively simply counts and compares the number of reasons supporting each option.

Definition 7 (Uniform Detachment). *Let D be a detachment function. D is a* uniform weight detachment function *if and only if there exists a weighting function w and a weight w_0 such that $D_w = D$, $jw = rw$, and, for each pair of options o_1 and o_2, reason $r \in R(o_1, o_2)$ for this pair, and context c we have $jw(R, o_1, o_2, c, r) = w_0$.*

In maximum detachment, only the reasons with the greatest weights are compared to each other to determine the output. Other than that, the comparison of options works similarly to the way it does in dual scale detachment.

Definition 8 (Maximum Detachment). *Let $Max(S)$ give the maximal element of a finite set of nonnegative real numbers S. A maximum detachment function D_w^M assigns to each pair of options o_1 and o_2, a subset of the reasons $RR \subseteq R(o_1, o_2)$ for this pair, a context c and a weighting function w, two scale values (v_1, v_2) using Max in the following way:*

$$
v_1 = \begin{cases} + & \text{if } Max(JW_{o_1}) > Max(RW_{o_2}) \\ - & \text{if } Max(JW_{o_1}) < Max(RW_{o_2}) \\ 0 & \text{otherwise} \end{cases}
$$

$$
v_2 = \begin{cases} + & \text{if } Max(JW_{o_2}) > Max(RW_{o_1}) \\ - & \text{if } Max(JW_{o_2}) < Max(RW_{o_1}) \\ 0 & \text{otherwise} \end{cases}
$$

A *detachment function D is a* maximum weight detachment function *if and only if there exists a weighting function w such that* $D_w^M = D$.

Our definitions are quite general, in the sense that, for example, grounds can be instantiated with propositional or first-order formulas, options can be instantiated with expressions from an action calculus, and contexts can be instantiated with default weights and modifiers. However, the weighing definition is also quite specific in the sense that we do not assume thresholds (either for individual reasons or for the comparison of the two pans), default values or modifiers in the weighing function. Tucker discusses some of these extensions, we included some of them in our earlier analysis [8], and we will reintroduce them in the journal extension of this paper. From a technical point of view, these extensions would significantly complicate the principles and principle-based analysis. However, we believe that they do not add much to the conceptual analysis of the comparisons that we are interested in in this paper, such as the comparison of dual and single scale.

5   Principles

In this section, we state the principles that we are going to use in our principle-based analysis. These principles describe properties of detachment functions that are not necessarily desirable, but that reveal something about their behavior. The principle-based analysis itself is discussed in Sect. 6.

We present nine principles. The first three restate (some of) the principles formulated in Knoks and van der Torre [9] in the present framework; the next three restate (some of) the principles formulated in Knoks et al. [8]; and the final three principles are new. We reintroduce those principles from [8,9] that provide insights about the detachment functions we have defined above.

The principles are always specified for detachment functions of the form $D(R, o_1, o_2, RR, c) = (v_1, v_2)$. It is important to note that the context c is held fixed, ensuring that the weighting function, on which the detachment function implicitly relies, assigns consistent (embedded) weights to the relevant reasons. This does not mean that the detachment function is restricted to a single context. The definition of detachment functions allows the weighting system to take context into account. Because the weighting function is context sensitive, the weights assigned to the reasons may vary between different contexts. Many principles modify the set of input reasons RR, which makes it unlikely that these principles will hold universally when the context changes, since the weights of the relevant reasons may also vary in those cases.

Our first principle, Groundedness, says that an option can be either permissible or required only if there is at least one reason supporting it.

Principle 1 (Groundedness). *A detachment function D satisfies* Groundedness, Gr, *if and only if*

1. *for every* $(v_1, v_2) \in D(R, o_1, o_2, RR, c)$ *such that* $v_1 = +$ *or* $v_2 = -$ *there exists at least one reason* $(g, o_1) \in RR$, *and*

2. *for every* $(v_1, v_2) \in D(R, o_1, o_2, RR, c)$ *such that* $v_1 = -$ *or* $v_2 = +$ *there exists at least one reason* $(g, o_2) \in RR$.

The principle of Anonymity expresses the idea that grounds (of reasons) can be replaced by other grounds without changing the outcome.

Principle 2 (Anonymity). *A detachment function* D *satisfies* Anonymity, An, *if and only if, for any bijection* $\pi : G \mapsto G$, *we have* $D(R, o_1, o_2, RR, c) = D(R, o_1, o_2, RR^\pi, c)$ *where* $RR^\pi = \{(\pi(g), o) : (g, o) \in RR\}$.

The principle of Unanimity expresses the intuitive idea of a unanimous vote. If all the relevant reasons favor one of the two choice options, then that option should be required.

Principle 3 (Unanimity). *A detachment function* D *satisfies* Unanimity, Ua, *just in case when* RR *is non-empty we have:*

1. *if* $RR = \{(g, o) \in RR \mid o = o_1\}$ *then* $D(R, o_1, o_2, RR, c) = (+, -)$, *and*
2. *if* $RR = \{(g, o) \in RR \mid o = o_2\}$ *then* $D(R, o_1, o_2, RR, c) = (-, +)$.

The next principle, Polarity Monotony, expresses the idea that the valuation of an option can only go from $-$ to 0 to $+$ when reasons that favor that option are added.

Principle 4 (Polarity Monotony). *Let* $- < 0 < +$. *A detachment function* D *satisfies* Polarity Monotony, PoMn, *just in case:*

1. *if* $D(R, o_1, o_2, RR, c) = (v_1, v_2)$ *and* $D(R, o_1, o_2, RR \cup \{(g, o_1)\}, c) = (v_1', v_2')$, *then* $v_1' \geq v_1$ *and* $v_2' \leq v_2$, *and*
2. *if* $D(R, o_1, o_2, RR, c) = (v_1, v_2)$ *and* $D(R, o_1, o_2, RR \cup \{(g, o_2)\}, c) = (v_1', v_2')$ *then* $v_1' \leq v_1$ *and* $v_2' \geq v_2$.

The principle of Union Monotony expresses the following idea: if a detachment function assigns the same scale values to two choice options in two situations involving different reasons, then it also assigns the same scale values to a situation involving all of those different reasons (assuming such a situation exists).

Principle 5 (Union Monotony). *A detachment function* D *satisfies* Union Monotony, UnMn, *just in case if we have (1)* $D(R, o_1, o_2, RR, c) = (v_1, v_2)$ *and (2)* $D(R, o_1, o_2, RR', c) = (v_1, v_2)$, *then we also have (3)* $D(R, o_1, o_2, RR \cup RR', c) = (v_1, v_2)$.

The principle of Sensitivity expresses the following intuitive idea: if we start with a pair of scales that are in balance and add a new reason, then the balance is disturbed.

Principle 6 (Sensitivity). *A detachment function* D *satisfies* Sensitivity, Se, *if and only if for every* $(0, 0) \in D(R, o_1, o_2, RR, c)$, $r \in R(o_1, o_2)$, *and* $(v_1, v_2) \in D(R, o_1, o_2, RR \cup \{r\}, c)$, *we have* $v_1 \neq 0 \vee v_2 \neq 0$.

The principle of Input Symmetry expresses the idea that the order of the choice options is not important.

Principle 7 (Input Symmetry). *A detachment function D satisfies* Input Symmetry, InSym, *if and only if when we have* $D(R, o_1, o_2, RR, c) = (v_1, v_2)$, *then we have* $D(R, o_2, o_1, RR, c) = (v_2, v_1)$.

Input Symmetry is motivated by the overall shape of the framework we work with here, and it expresses a very natural constraint on detachment functions. Our next principle draws its motivation from Tucker's book. As its name suggests, the principle No Dilemmas expresses the thought that a detachment function rules out dilemmas, or cases in which both choice options are associated with negative scale values.

Principle 8 (No Dilemmas). *A detachment function D satisfies* No Dilemmas, *NoDi, if and only if there is no* $(v_1, v_2) \in D(R, o_1, o_2, RR, c)$, *such that* $(v_1, v_2) = (-, -)$.

Our final principle is One Permission which is also new. This principle expresses the intuitive idea that the detachment function allows for only one kind of permission.

Principle 9 (One Permission). *A detachment function D satisfies* One Permission, *OnPe, if and only if there is no* $(v_1, v_2) \in D(R, o_1, o_2, RR, c)$ *such that* $v_1 \neq v_2$ *and* $v_1, v_2 \geq 0$.

6   Analysis

This section presents our principle-based analysis. We analyze the four detachment functions that were defined in Sects. 3 and 4 (dual scale, single scale, uniform detachment, maximum) using the 9 principles from Sect. 5. Table 1 summarizes the results of the analysis. The detachment functions are listed in the upper row; the principles are listed in the left column. A ✓ in a cell means that the principle listed in the left row is satisfied by the detachment function listed in the column. A × in a cell means that the given principle is not satisfied by the given detachment function or that a counterexample exists.

The table shows that dual scale and single scale are distinguished by three principles: Unanimity, No Dilemmas and One Permission. These principles are satisfied by single scale and not satisfied by dual scale. The principle of Unanimity is not satisfied by dual scale detachment because one of the weights may be 0. Therefore, even if there is a unanimous vote for, say, o_1, the output can still be $(0, +)$, if the justifying weight is 0, or $(+, 0)$, if the requiring weight is 0. With single scale this is impossible, since the justifying and requiring weights are always the same. Dual scale detachment does not satisfy No Dilemmas, because it allows for the aggregate requiring weights of reasons supporting each option to outstrip the aggregate justifying weights of reasons supporting each

Table 1. Summary of the principle-based analysis

	Dual Scale	Single Scale	Uniform	Maximum
1.Gr	✓	✓	✓	✓
2.An	×	×	✓	×
3.Ua	×	✓	✓	×
4.PoMn	✓	✓	✓	✓
5.UnMn	×	×	×	✓
6.Se	✓	✓	✓	×
7.InSym	✓	✓	✓	✓
8.NoDi	×	✓	✓	×
9.OnPe	×	✓	✓	×

option. Single scale detachment, by contrast, does not allow for such a possibility, because, with it, the aggregate justifying weights of reasons supporting each option equal the aggregate requiring weights of reasons supporting each option. Thus, whereas dual scale detachment allows for the possibility of dilemmas, single scale detachment avoids dilemmas by design. Tucker discusses this issue in his book too, as an illustration of the greater expressive power of the dual scale model of weighing reasons. And the fact that dual scale detachment does not satisfy One Permission, whereas single scale detachment does, serves as a further illustration.

Uniform detachment satisfies all of the principles, except for Union Monotony. This principle is about combining sets of reasons and assessing whether the output remains the same. What can happen is that both RR and RR' support the same output, e.g. $(+, -)$, but their union $RR \cup RR'$ supports the opposite output due to the fact that there is a considerable overlap (i.e. $RR \cap RR' = \{r = (g, o) \mid o = o_1 \lor o = o_2, r \in RR \lor r \in RR', RR, RR' \subseteq R(o_1, o_2)\} \neq \emptyset$) between the reasons that support o_1 overlap, but not between the reasons that support o_2. Uniform detachment is similar to single scale detachment. The only (revealed) difference between them has to do with the principle of Anonymity, which single scale detachment doesn't satisfy. In single scale detachment—and contrary to uniform detachment—reasons can have different weights. So, it shouldn't come as a surprise that swapping them can lead to changes in the output.

As Table 1 makes clear, maximum detachment does not satisfy No Dilemmas and One Permission. More interestingly, it does not satisfy Sensitivity. This is due to the fact that the addition of a new reason does not necessarily increase the maximum weight amongst all weights—whether justifying or requiring—of the reasons that are already present in RR. So, maximum detachment is not necessarily sensitive to new reasons.

The proofs supporting our principle-based analysis are fairly straightforward. We present two examples here.

Proposition 1 *There is a weighing function such that for the dual scale detachment function D_w there is some R, o_1, o_2, RR, c such that $(v_1, v_2) \in D(R, o_1, o_2, RR, c)$ where $v_1 = -$ and $v_2 = -$.*

Proof We use proof by counterexample; we present a weighing function such that dual scale detachment fails No Dilemmas. Let $r_1 = (g_1, o_1)$ and $r_2 = (g_2, o_2)$. And let $(v_1, v_2) = D_w(R, o_1, o_2, \{r_1, r_2\}, c)$ such that $w(R, o_1, o_2, c, r_1) = (1, 3)$, $w(R, o_1, o_2, c, r_2) = (1, 3)$. Then since $jw(r_1) - rw(r_2) = 1 - 3 = -2$ we have $v_1 = -$ and since $jw(r_2) - rw(r_1) = 1 - 3 = -2$ we have $v_2 = -$, then $D_w(\{r_1, r_2\}) = (-, -)$, which completes the counterexample.

Proposition 2 *Single scale detachment satisfies No Dilemmas.*

Proof Suppose, toward a contradiction, that single scale detachment does not satisfy No Dilemmas. This means that there is some single detachment function D such that, for some o_1, o_2, $RR \subseteq R(o_1, o_2)$, and c, we have $D(R, o_1, o_2, RR, c) = (-, -)$. By Definition 6 (Single Scale), we know that there is some weighting function w such that $D_w(R, o_1, o_2, RR, c) = (-, -)$ and $jw = rw$. By Definition 3 (Additive Dual Scale Weighing), we know, first, that $\Sigma_{(g_1, o_1) \in RR} jw((g_1, o_1)) - \Sigma_{(g_2, o_2) \in RR} rw((g_2, o_2)) < 0$, as well as, second, that $\Sigma_{(g_2, o_2) \in RR} jw((g_2, o_2)) - \Sigma_{(g_1, o_1) \in RR} rw((g_1, o_1)) < 0$. But $jw = rw$ tells us that $\Sigma_{(g_1, o_1) \in RR} jw((g_1, o_1)) = \Sigma_{(g_1, o_1) \in RR} rw((g_1, o_1)) = x$. Similarly, it tells us that $\Sigma_{(g_2, o_2) \in RR} jw((g_2, o_2)) = \Sigma_{(g_2, o_2) \in RR} rw((g_2, o_2)) = y$. So, we have $y < x$ and $x > y$, which is a contradiction.

The dual scale detachment system is the least constrained of the three additive detachment functions. This function allows for multiple deontic status assignments that the other two functions do not allow for, such as $(-, -)$. It also allows to distinguish multiple concepts of permission. If one has no convictions to support the uniform weight or single proportion assumption, then there is no reason not to use the dual scale function.

7   Related Work

In this paper, we build on the reason-based detachment framework proposed by Knoks and van der Torre [9] and further explored by Knoks et al. [8]. There are at least three ways in which this paper goes beyond the earlier papers. First, we have formalized Tucker's dual scale model of weighing reasons in the reason-based detachment framework. Second, we have generalized the framework to allow for two kinds of weights of reasons, which has prompted restating the ideas and principles from the earlier papers in a more general setting. And third, we have incorporated abstract contexts into the definition of detachment functions. While we cannot discuss the issue in detail here, we see this as opening the doors to a more elegant way of dealing with issues surrounding holism about weights of reasons to the way these issues are dealt with in [8].

Thematically, the work we present here is closely related to the formal model(s) of interaction between normative reasons developed by Streit [15, Ch.

3] and Streit et al. [1,16]. Whereas we follow the methodology of input-output logic, Streit et al. [1] make use of formal argumentation theory [4] and, more specifically, weighted argumentation [2,3]. Whereas we focus on the dual scale model, Streit et al. focus on the standard single scale model of weighing reasons. They also model the interaction between disablers, modifiers, and reasons explicitly. Our work also differs from that of Nair [10] who explores issues relating to weights of reasons drawing on probability and confirmation theory; Pandžić and Graff [11] who combine justification logic with numerical representation of strengths of reasons; and Sher [13] whose thinking about weights of reasons draws on tools from decision theory.

Insofar as we follow Tucker and take the balancing metaphor seriously, we part ways with the influential default logic-based model of Horty [7] and the formal work it has inspired.

8   Summary and Future Work

This paper pursued two main goals. The first was to express Tucker's dual scale model of weighing reasons in the framework of reason-based detachment, or to formalize it as a detachment function. The second was to compare it to benchmark detachment functions motivated by our earlier work [8,9]. After sketching the dual scale model in Sect. 2, we presented its formalization in Sect. 3, as well as introduced three further detachment functions in Sect. 4. In Sect. 5, we formulated and discussed 9 principles that detachment functions can satisfy. In Sect. 6, we used these principles to analyze the four detachment functions presented earlier, and, in Sect. 7, we briefly discussed the closest related work.

We envision many promising directions for future research. First, as mentioned, the dual scale is only one component of the broader model of interaction between reasons that is put forward in "The Weight of Reasons". In future work, we plan to formulate and explore detachment functions that would correspond to this broader model, starting with what Tucker calls 'dynamic scale', or (roughly) tournaments of pairwise comparisons between available options that all use dual scale. Relatedly, Tucker discusses a third type of weight, commending weight, which could also be explored in future work.

Regarding weight systems, one could explore combining two or more weight systems and analyzing the effects of their interaction. This approach may lead to the formulation of new principles, and it could have other theoretical implications. Additional interactions with the weight system could also be investigated by considering operations on the context.

In future research, we also propose to structure grounds as propositional formulas with logical connectives, options as complex actions built from atomic actions, and contexts as sets of undercutters and modifiers, following and building on [15, Ch. 3].

The paper in which we introduced reason-based detachment, [9], also presents relational balancing, which can be compared to the functions defined in this paper. In addition, it explores detachment functions that range between total and sparse functions, offering further avenues for study. Finally, additional weighting functions have been defined in the literature based on intervals, additive functions, and so on. A comparison of our formalization of Tucker's dual scale with these other more exotic approaches is left to the journal extension of this paper.

Acknowledgments. This work was supported by the Luxembourg National Research Fund (FNR) through the following three projects: DILLAN (PRIDE19/14268506), EAI (C22/SC/17111440)), and LoDEx (INTER/DFG/23/17415164/LODEX). We thank our three anonymous reviewers for their helpful comments. All mistakes that remain are our own.

References

1. Alcaraz, B., Knoks, A., Streit, D.: Estimating weights of reasons using metaheuristics: a hybrid approach to machine ethics. In: et al., S.D. (ed.) Proceedings of the Seventh AAAI/ACM Conference on AI, Ethics, and Society (AIES-2024), pp. 27–38. ACM Press (2024)
2. Amgoud, L., Doder, D., Vesic, S.: Evaluation of argument strength in attack graphs: foundations and semantics. Artif. Intell. **302**, 1–61 (2022)
3. Amgoud, L., Ben-Naim, J., Doder, D., Vesic, S.: Acceptability semantics for weighted argumentation frameworks. In: Twenty-Sixth International Joint Conference on Artificial Intelligence (IJCAI 2017) (2017)
4. Baroni, P., Gabbay, D., Giacomin, M., van der Torre, L.: Handbook of Formal Argumentation. College Publications, London (2018)
5. Broome, J.: Reasons. In: Wallace, R.J., Smith, M., Scheffler, S., Pettit, P. (eds.) Reason and Value: Essays on the Moral Philosophy of Joseph Raz. Oxford University Press (2004)
6. Dancy, J.: Ethics without Principles. Oxford University Press (2004)
7. Horty, J.: Reasons as Defaults. Oxford University Press (2012)
8. Knoks, A., Shao, M., van der Torre, L., de Wit, V., Yu, L.: A principle-based analysis for numerical balancing. In: Logics for New-Generation Artificial Intelligence (LNGAI2024). College Publications, United Kingdom (2024)
9. Knoks, A., van der Torre, L.: Reason-based detachment. In: Bentzen, B., Liao, B., Liga, D., Markovich, R., Wei, B., Xiong, M., Xu, T. (eds.) Joint Proceedings of the 3rd International Workshop on Logics for New-Generation Artificial Intelligence and the International Workshop on Logic, AI, and Law (LNGAI/LAIL2023, Hangzhou), pp. 49–65. College Publications (2023)
10. Nair, S.: "adding up" reasons: lessons for reductive and nonreductive approaches. Ethics **132**(1), 38–88 (2021)
11. Pandžić, S., Graff, J.: A logic of weighted reasons for explainable inference in AI. In: World Conference on Explainable Artificial Intelligence, pp. 243–267. Springer (2024)
12. Scanlon, T.M.: What We Owe to Each Other. Harvard University Press, Cambridge (1998)
13. Sher, I.: Comparative value and the weight of reasons. Econ. Philos. **35**(1), 103–158 (2019)
14. Snedegar, J.: Reasons for and reasons against. Philos. Stud. **175**(3), 725–43 (2018)

15. Streit, D.: From Metaethics to Machine Decisions: Formal Models of Normative Reasons and their Application in Philosophy and Machine Ethics. Ph.D. thesis, University of Luxembourg (2024)
16. Streit, D., de Wit, V., Knoks, A.: Reasons in weighted argumentation graphs. In: International Workshop on Logic, Rationality and Interaction, pp. 251–9. Springer (2023)
17. Tucker, C.: The Weight of Reasons: A Framework for Ethics. Oxford University Press (2025)
18. Tucker, C.: Weighing reasons. In: Zalta, E.N., Nodelman, U. (eds.) The Stanford Encyclopedia of Philosophy. Metaphysics Research Lab, Stanford University (forthcoming)

Description Logics and Ontological Reasoning

Towards Practicable Defeasible Reasoning for ABoxes

Jonas Haldimann[1,2,(✉)], Magdalena Ortiz[1] (ORCID), and Mantas Šimkus[1] (ORCID)

[1] Institute of Logic and Computation, TU Wien, 1040 Vienna, Austria
jonas@haldimann.de, {magdalena.ortiz,mantas.simkus}@tuwien.ac.at
[2] University of Cape Town and CAIR, Cape Town, South Africa

Abstract. Defeasible reasoning, that is, reasoning with rules that allow for exceptions, has been a longstanding challenge in knowledge representation. The KLM paradigm has been successful for defeasible reasoning in propositional logics, but its application to Description Logics (DLs) has been challenging. Many approaches to terminological reasoning with defeasible inclusions have been proposed, but the reasoning with data (ABoxes in DL jargon) is still largely unexplored. In this paper, we consider defeasible inclusions in the expressive DL $\mathcal{ALCI}$ with closed predicates, but restrict the inclusions in a way that circumvents some of the challenges faced by related approaches. We also consider the data complexity of defeasible reasoning, which, to our knowledge, had not yet been analysed. Unfortunately, our approach is hard for the second level of the polynomial hierarchy, but we identify a restricted fragment that enables tractable reasoning.

1 Introduction

Description Logics (DLs) are a fundamental family of languages for Knowledge Representation and Reasoning (KR) [3] that have been successfully deployed for reasoning in a wide range of domains. Standard DLs can be viewed as subsets of classical first-order logic, which makes them *monotonic*: conclusions derived on the basis of some knowledge cannot be invalidated by acquiring additional facts. But in KR, monotonic logics are rarely enough, and *non-monotonic reasoning (NMR)* has been a core topic of KR since the very early days. One of the key use-cases of NMR is *defeasible reasoning*, i.e., reasoning from rules that may have exceptions. The defeasible reasoning paradigm called KLM, based on the seminal work of Kraus, Lehmann and Magidor [20] is a broad and well-established field [1,22,25]. The KLM approach is compelling: it is based on formal postulates that describe defeasible reasoning in a principled way, and it is not as computationally expensive as other NMR formalisms. Having endured for nearly five decades, it remains a topic of active research [6,11,14,17,19].

Extending this approach from propositional logic to DLs is clearly appealing, but not very easy, and it has received significant attention in the literature [4,7–10,15,26]. The focus of these works has been almost exclusively on inferring defeasible inclusions from TBoxes. Data-centric reasoning services, such as

© The Author(s), under exclusive license to Springer Nature Switzerland AG 2026
G. Casini et al. (Eds.): JELIA 2025, LNAI 16093, pp. 223–239, 2026.
https://doi.org/10.1007/978-3-032-04587-4_14

defeasible instance checking in the presence of ABoxes, have been largely overlooked (see Sect. 5 for details), and, to our knowledge, the data complexity of defeasible inferences about ABox objects has not previously been considered.

Our goal in this paper is to enable defeasible ABox reasoning in expressive DLs. We consider the expressive DL $\mathcal{ALCI}$ with *closed predicates*, which already allows some simple non-monotonic reasoning and which generalizes nominals [13,23]; this is one of the most expressive DLs that can be decided in Exp-Time.[1] We add defeasible inclusions to $\mathcal{ALCI}$ knowledge bases and give them an *exceptionality-based* semantics in the style of *Rational Closure* [21] and the equivalent *system Z* [25]. The classical part of the knowledge base (KB) remains unrestricted, providing the full power of the DL to draw conclusions about both named and unnamed objects, but the defeasible inclusions are syntactically restricted in a way that they can draw inferences only about the ABox individuals.

The result is a simple formalism that allows to draw defeasible inferences about specific objects, and where the combined complexity of these inferences is not higher than for classical reasoning in the underlying DL. Unfortunately, this is not the case for data complexity: we show that credulous and sceptical entailment are both intractable. Simply restricting the DL is not enough to regain tractability, since the propagation of defeasible concepts among neighbouring individuals rules out the existence of a unique preferred model. Nevertheless, we identify a restricted fragment that allows for defeasible instance checking in a time that is polynomial in the size of the ABox.

Existing defeasible semantics for DLs based on rational closure neglect all defeasible information for the unnamed objects implied by the existential axioms. There is no unique consensus of whether role fillers should be typical or not, but in any case, this neglect has been singled out as the culprit of some counterintuitive inferences. To our knowledge, the only adequate solution to this issue so far is limited to the very inexpressive $\mathcal{EL}$ [26]. Our approach fully circumvents the issue of typicality of anonymous objects: since defeasible inferences do not allow inferring new facts about unnamed objects, there is no need to decide how to apply the defeasible inclusions to them. While we do not solve the problem, we do avoid its non-transparent and sometimes counterintuitive aspects. This solution, similar in spirit to the proposal of Baader and Hollunder in one of the very first papers on non-monotonic DLs [2], seems a reasonable compromise: the unnamed objects in an interpretation intuitively describe structures that should be as general as possible, and realistic examples that require defeasible inferences over anonymous objects are not easy to find.

2 Preliminaries

We recall the basic notions behind the expressive DL $\mathcal{ALCI}$ (cf. [3]). Assume countably infinite, mutually disjoint sets N_C, N_R, N_I of *concept names*, *role names*, and *individuals*, respectively. If $r \in N_R$, then r and the expression r^- are

---

[1] Note that closed predicates generalize nominals.

$$\perp^{\mathcal{I}} = \emptyset \qquad\qquad \top^{\mathcal{I}} = \Delta^{\mathcal{I}}$$

$$(\neg C)^{\mathcal{I}} = \Delta^{\mathcal{I}} \setminus C^{\mathcal{I}} \qquad (r^-)^{\mathcal{I}} = \{(e, e') \mid (e', e) \in r^{\mathcal{I}}\}$$

$$(C \sqcap D)^{\mathcal{I}} = C^{\mathcal{I}} \cap D^{\mathcal{I}} \qquad (\exists r.C)^{\mathcal{I}} = \{e \in \Delta^{\mathcal{I}} \mid \exists e' \in \Delta^{\mathcal{I}} : (e, e') \in r^{\mathcal{I}} \text{ and } e' \in C^{\mathcal{I}}\}$$

$$(C \sqcup D)^{\mathcal{I}} = C^{\mathcal{I}} \cup D^{\mathcal{I}} \qquad (\forall r.C)^{\mathcal{I}} = \{e \in \Delta^{\mathcal{I}} \mid \forall e' \in \Delta^{\mathcal{I}} : (e, e') \in r^{\mathcal{I}} \text{ implies } e' \in C^{\mathcal{I}}\}$$

Fig. 1. Interpretation of complex concepts and roles in $\mathcal{ALCI}$.

roles. For a role of the form r^-, let $(r^-)^- = r$. (Complex) concepts are defined inductively as follows: (a) expressions $\top, \perp$ and each $A \in N_C$ are concepts, (b) if C, D are concepts and r is a role, then expressions $\neg C, C \sqcap D, C \sqcup D, \exists r.C$, and $\forall r.C$ are concepts. A *concept inclusion* is an expression of the form $C \sqsubseteq D$, where C, D are concepts. A *TBox* $\mathcal{T}$ is any finite set of concept inclusions. We may use $C \equiv D$ as shorthand for $C \sqsubseteq D$ and $D \sqsubseteq C$. An *assertion* is an expression of the form $A(c), \neg A(c), r(c, d)$, or $\neg r(c, d)$, where A is a concept name, r is a role name, and c, d are individuals. An *ABox* $\mathcal{A}$ is any finite set of assertions.

Note that we allow negated assertions, which will be useful below.

An *interpretation* is a tuple $\mathcal{I} = (\Delta^{\mathcal{I}}, \cdot^{\mathcal{I}})$, where $\Delta^{\mathcal{I}}$ is a non-empty set called *domain* and $\cdot^{\mathcal{I}}$ is a function that maps every $a \in N_I$ to an individual $a^{\mathcal{I}} \in \Delta^{\mathcal{I}}$, every $r \in N_R$ to a set of tuples $r^{\mathcal{I}} \subseteq \Delta^{\mathcal{I}} \times \Delta^{\mathcal{I}}$, and every $C \in N_C$ to a set $C^{\mathcal{I}} \subseteq \Delta^{\mathcal{I}}$. The interpretation function $\cdot^{\mathcal{I}}$ is lifted to all complex concepts using the equations in Fig. 1.

Assume an interpretation $\mathcal{I}$. Given a concept inclusion $C \sqsubseteq D$, we write $\mathcal{I} \models C \sqsubseteq D$, if $C^{\mathcal{I}} \subseteq D^{\mathcal{I}}$. We say $\mathcal{I}$ is a *model* of a TBox $\mathcal{T}$ (in symbols, $\mathcal{I} \models \mathcal{T}$), if $\mathcal{I} \models C \sqsubseteq D$ for all $C \sqsubseteq D \in \mathcal{T}$. Given an assertion $A(c)$, we write $\mathcal{I} \models A(c)$ if $c^{\mathcal{I}} \in A^{\mathcal{I}}$. For an assertion $\neg A(c)$, we write $\mathcal{I} \models \neg A(c)$ if $c^{\mathcal{I}} \notin A^{\mathcal{I}}$. Given an assertion $r(c, d)$, we write $\mathcal{I} \models r(c, d)$ if $(c^{\mathcal{I}}, d^{\mathcal{I}}) \in r^{\mathcal{I}}$. For an assertion $\neg r(c, d)$, we write $\mathcal{I} \models \neg r(c, d)$ if $(c^{\mathcal{I}}, d^{\mathcal{I}}) \notin r^{\mathcal{I}}$. We say $\mathcal{I}$ is a *model* of an ABox $\mathcal{A}$ (in symbols, $\mathcal{I} \models \mathcal{A}$), if $\mathcal{I} \models \alpha$ for all $\alpha \in \mathcal{A}$. We denote by $\Delta_{\mathcal{A}}$ the set of individuals occurring in the assertions in an ABox $\mathcal{A}$.

We recall the extension to DLs with *closed predicates* [13,23]. The intuition of this notion is to declare some predicates as "complete": in the models of a given ABox $\mathcal{A}$, these selected predicates must be interpreted exactly as given in $\mathcal{A}$ and no additional facts can be assumed. For this, assume designated sets $N_C^c \subseteq N_C$ and $N_R^c \subseteq N_R$ of *closed concepts* and *closed roles*, respectively. For an ABox $\mathcal{A}$ and an interpretation $\mathcal{I}$ with $\mathcal{I} \models \mathcal{A}$, we write $\mathcal{I} \models^c \mathcal{A}$, if the following conditions hold: (i) for all $A \in N_C^c$, $d \in A^{\mathcal{I}}$ implies $A(d) \in \mathcal{A}$, (ii) for all $r \in N_R^c$, $(c, d) \in r^{\mathcal{I}}$ implies $r(c, d) \in \mathcal{A}$, (iii) for all individuals d that appear in $\mathcal{A}$, $d^{\mathcal{I}} = d$. Note that the last condition (iii) implies that $\Delta_{\mathcal{A}} \subseteq \Delta^{\mathcal{I}}$ holds whenever $\mathcal{I} \models^c \mathcal{A}$ holds. This is a form of the *standard name assumption (SNA)*.

3 Knowledge Bases with Defeasible Inclusions

In this section, we formally define our DL knowledge bases with *defeasible inclusions* which are concept inclusions that hold for typical, but not necessarily all elements of the domain. Unlike a 'strict' concept inclusion $C \sqsubseteq D$, a defeasible inclusion $C \mathbin{\sqsubset\mkern-10mu\sim} D$ may have exceptions, i.e., in a model $\mathcal{I}$ of $C \mathbin{\sqsubset\mkern-10mu\sim} D$ some elements of $C^{\mathcal{I}}$ may not be in $D^{\mathcal{I}}$; these are considered *exceptional*.

A key design decision in our approach is to make sure that defeasible inclusions apply only to objects that are explicitly named in the knowledge base, and therefore anonymous objects whose existence may be implied by concept inclusions can be treated as non-exceptional. This will be ensured by means of *rooted concepts*, which are concept expressions that are 'guarded' by closed predicates.

Definition 1. *A concept C is* rooted *if one the following is satisfied:*

1. $C \in N_C^c$,
2. C *of the form* $C_1 \sqcap C_2$ *and at least one of* C_1, C_2 *is rooted,*
3. C *of the form* $C_1 \sqcup C_2$ *and both* C_1, C_2 *are rooted, or*
4. C *of the form* $\exists r.D$ *with* $r \in N_R^c$ *or* $r^- \in N_R^c$.

Rooted concepts have the following convenient property:

Proposition 1. *Assume an ABox $\mathcal{A}$ and a rooted concept C. If $\mathcal{I}$ is an interpretation such that $\mathcal{I} \models^c \mathcal{A}$, then $C^{\mathcal{I}} \subseteq \Delta_{\mathcal{A}}$, i.e., $C^{\mathcal{I}}$ is a subset of the individuals that appear in $\mathcal{A}$.*

We can now formally define KBs equipped with defeasible inclusions, which are restricted to have rooted concepts in the antecedents: Proposition 1 will ensure that these inclusions apply only to named objects of the KB.

Definition 2 (Defeasible inclusions and knowledge bases). *A defeasible concept inclusion (DCI) is an expression $C \mathbin{\sqsubset\mkern-10mu\sim} D$, where C, D are concepts and C is rooted. A knowledge base (KB) is a tuple $\mathcal{K} = (\mathcal{T}, \mathcal{D}, \mathcal{A})$, where $\mathcal{T}$ is a TBox, $\mathcal{D}$ is a set of defeasible inclusions, and $\mathcal{A}$ is an ABox.*

Example 1 (adapted from [4]). Consider the knowledge that red blood cells (RBC) usually have a nucleus, but mammalian red blood cells (MRBC) typically do not have a nucleus; and of course mammalian red blood cells are a subclass of red blood cells. c_1, c_2, c_3 are red blood cells and c_3 is additionally a mammalian red blood cell. Furthermore, we assume the beliefs about RBC and $MRBC$ to be complete for c_1, c_2, c_3, i.e., c_1, c_2 are not $MRBC$. This situation can be described by $\mathcal{K} = (\mathcal{T}, \mathcal{D}, \mathcal{A})$ with $\mathcal{A} = \{RBC(c_1), RBC(c_2), RBC(c_3), MRBC(c_3)\}$, $\mathcal{T} = \{MRBC \sqsubseteq RBC, \exists hasNucleus.\top \sqsubseteq EN\}$, and $\mathcal{D} = \{RBC \mathbin{\sqsubset\mkern-10mu\sim} \exists hasNucleus.\top, MRBC \mathbin{\sqsubset\mkern-10mu\sim} \neg\exists hasNucleus.\top\}$ where $MRBC$ and RBC are closed predicates.

We will now define the semantics of a KB $\mathcal{K} = (\mathcal{T}, \mathcal{D}, \mathcal{A})$ as the interpretations $\mathcal{I}$ where $\mathcal{I} \models \mathcal{T}$, $\mathcal{I} \models^c \mathcal{A}$, and $\mathcal{I}$ complies with the defeasible inclusions in $\mathcal{D}$ as much as possible. To properly define the latter, following the definition of system Z, the first step is to define the notion of *tolerance*, which generalizes a similar concept for propositional rules [25].

Definition 3 (Tolerance). *We write* $\mathcal{I}, e \models C \mathrel{\vcenter{\hbox{$\scriptstyle\sqsubset$}}\mkern-2mu\raise1pt\hbox{$\scriptscriptstyle\sim$}} D$, *if* $e \in (\neg C \sqcup D)^{\mathcal{I}}$. *For a set* $\mathcal{D}$ *of defeasible inclusions, we write* $\mathcal{I}, e \models \mathcal{D}$, *if* $\mathcal{I}, e \models C \mathrel{\vcenter{\hbox{$\scriptstyle\sqsubset$}}\mkern-2mu\raise1pt\hbox{$\scriptscriptstyle\sim$}} D$ *for all* $C \mathrel{\vcenter{\hbox{$\scriptstyle\sqsubset$}}\mkern-2mu\raise1pt\hbox{$\scriptscriptstyle\sim$}} D \in \mathcal{D}$. *A defeasible inclusion* $C \mathrel{\vcenter{\hbox{$\scriptstyle\sqsubset$}}\mkern-2mu\raise1pt\hbox{$\scriptscriptstyle\sim$}} D$ *is* tolerated *by a set* $\mathcal{D}$ *of defeasible inclusions and a TBox* $\mathcal{T}$, *if there is an interpretation* $\mathcal{I}$ *and an object* $e \in \Delta^{\mathcal{I}}$ *such that* $\mathcal{I} \models \mathcal{T}$, $e \in (C \sqcap D)^{\mathcal{I}}$ *and* $\mathcal{I}, e \models \mathcal{D}$.

With this notion of tolerance, we can partition sets of defeasible inclusions.

Definition 4 (Tolerance partition). *Assume a finite set* $\mathcal{D}$ *of defeasible inclusions and a TBox* $\mathcal{T}$. *Construct the sequence as follows:*

(i) *Let* $\mathcal{D}^0$ *contain all* $C \mathrel{\vcenter{\hbox{$\scriptstyle\sqsubset$}}\mkern-2mu\raise1pt\hbox{$\scriptscriptstyle\sim$}} D \in \mathcal{D}$ *such that* $C \mathrel{\vcenter{\hbox{$\scriptstyle\sqsubset$}}\mkern-2mu\raise1pt\hbox{$\scriptscriptstyle\sim$}} D$ *is tolerated by* $\mathcal{D}$ *and* $\mathcal{T}$.

(ii) *For all* $\ell > 0$, *let* $\mathcal{D}^{\ell}$ *contain all* $C \mathrel{\vcenter{\hbox{$\scriptstyle\sqsubset$}}\mkern-2mu\raise1pt\hbox{$\scriptscriptstyle\sim$}} D \in \mathcal{D}'_{\ell}$ *such that* $C \mathrel{\vcenter{\hbox{$\scriptstyle\sqsubset$}}\mkern-2mu\raise1pt\hbox{$\scriptscriptstyle\sim$}} D$ *is tolerated by* $\mathcal{D}'_{\ell}$ *and* $\mathcal{T}$, *where* $\mathcal{D}'_{\ell} = \mathcal{D} \backslash (\mathcal{D}^0 \cup \cdots \cup \mathcal{D}^{\ell-1})$.

Let k *be the smallest integer such that* $\mathcal{D}^{k+1} = \emptyset$. *Then* $(\mathcal{D}^0, \ldots, \mathcal{D}^k, \mathcal{D}^{\infty})$ *with* $\mathcal{D}^{\infty} = \mathcal{D}'_{k+1}$ *is called the* tolerance partition *of* $\mathcal{D}$ *(w.r.t.* $\mathcal{T}$*)*.

Tolerance for KBs is the inverse of exceptionality [7] in the sense that a DCI is tolerated by a KB iff it is not exceptional. Hence, the tolerance partition defined here corresponds to the partition of the defeasible beliefs based on exceptionality in [7, p. 159].

Definition 5 (Rank of an object). *Assume a set of* $\mathcal{D}$ *of defeasible inclusions and a TBox* $\mathcal{T}$. *Let* $(\mathcal{D}^0, \ldots, \mathcal{D}^k, \mathcal{D}^{\infty})$ *be the tolerance partition of* $\mathcal{D}$ *w.r.t.* $\mathcal{T}$. *Let* $\mathcal{I}$ *be an interpretation such that* $\mathcal{I} \models \mathcal{D}^{\infty} \cup \mathcal{T}$ *and assume* $e \in \Delta^{\mathcal{I}}$. *We let* $\mathsf{rank}_{\mathcal{D}, \mathcal{T}}(\mathcal{I}, e)$ *be defined as follows. If* $\mathcal{I}, e \models \mathcal{D}$, *then* $\mathsf{rank}_{\mathcal{D}, \mathcal{T}}(\mathcal{I}, e) = 0$. *Otherwise,* $\mathsf{rank}_{\mathcal{D}, \mathcal{T}}(\mathcal{I}, e)$ *is the biggest* $i \in \{1, \ldots, k+1\}$ *such that* $\mathcal{I}, e \not\models \mathcal{D}^{i-1}$.

Intuitively, $\mathsf{rank}_{\mathcal{D}, \mathcal{T}}(\mathcal{I}, e)$ tells us to what extent the defeasible inclusions are satisfied at e in $\mathcal{I}$. If $\mathsf{rank}_{\mathcal{D}, \mathcal{T}}(\mathcal{I}, e) = 0$, then e is non-exceptional and satisfies all inclusions in $\mathcal{D}$. If $\mathsf{rank}_{\mathcal{D}, \mathcal{T}}(\mathcal{I}, e) = k+1$, then e is highly exceptional: it violates some inclusion in $\mathcal{D}^k$, which stores the most specific defeasible inclusions of $\mathcal{D}$.

Note that the rootedness condition guarantees that unnamed objects in the satisfy all the defeasible inclusions. More precisely, we have:

Proposition 2. *Assume a KB* $\mathcal{K} = (\mathcal{T}, \mathcal{D}, \mathcal{A})$, *and interpretation* $\mathcal{I}$ *such that* $\mathcal{I} \models^c \mathcal{A}$. *If* $e \in \Delta^{\mathcal{I}} \backslash \Delta_{\mathcal{A}}$, *then* $\mathsf{rank}_{\mathcal{D}, \mathcal{T}}(\mathcal{I}, e) = 0$.

Based on the above property, we naturally compare two interpretations based on the extent to which they satisfy defeasible inclusions:

Definition 6. *Assume a KB* $\mathcal{K} = (\mathcal{T}, \mathcal{D}, \mathcal{A})$. *Let* $(\mathcal{D}^0, \ldots, \mathcal{D}^k, \mathcal{D}^{\infty})$ *be the tolerance partition of* $\mathcal{D}$ *w.r.t.* $\mathcal{T}$. *An interpretation* $\mathcal{I}$ *is called* $\mathcal{K}$-*admissible, if* $\mathcal{I} \models \mathcal{T}$, $\mathcal{I} \models^c \mathcal{A}$, *and* $\mathcal{I} \models \mathcal{D}^{\infty}$. *Assume a pair* $\mathcal{I}, \mathcal{J}$ *of* $\mathcal{K}$-*admissible interpretations. We write* $\mathcal{I} \prec_{\mathcal{K}} \mathcal{J}$, *if the following holds:*

- $\mathsf{rank}_{\mathcal{D}, \mathcal{T}}(\mathcal{I}, a) \leq \mathsf{rank}_{\mathcal{D}, \mathcal{T}}(\mathcal{J}, a)$ *for all individuals* $a \in \Delta_{\mathcal{A}}$, *and*

- $\mathsf{rank}_{\mathcal{D},\mathcal{T}}(\mathcal{I},a) < \mathsf{rank}_{\mathcal{D},\mathcal{T}}(\mathcal{J},a)$ *for some individual* $a \in \Delta_{\mathcal{A}}$.

A $\mathcal{K}$-*admissible interpretation* $\mathcal{J}$ *is called a* minimal model *of* $\mathcal{K}$, *if there exists no* $\mathcal{K}$-*admissible interpretation* $\mathcal{I}$ *such that* $\mathcal{I} \prec_{\mathcal{K}} \mathcal{J}$.

A KB can have more than one minimal model, even for the lightweight $\mathcal{EL}^{\perp}$.

Example 2. Let $\mathcal{K} = (\mathcal{T}, \mathcal{D}, \mathcal{A})$ with $\mathcal{A} = \{\top(a), A(b), B(c), r(a,b), r(a,c)\}$, $\mathcal{D} = \{\exists r.A \sqsubseteq\!\!\!\sim C, \exists r.B \sqsubseteq\!\!\!\sim D\}$, and $\mathcal{T} = \{C \sqcap D \sqsubseteq \perp\}$. Both $\mathcal{I}$ with $C^{\mathcal{I}} = \{a\}, D^{\mathcal{I}} = \emptyset$ and $\mathcal{I}'$ with $C^{\mathcal{I}'} = \emptyset, D^{\mathcal{I}'} = \{a\}$ are minimal with respect to $\prec$.

Now that we introduced minimal models as semantics for defeasible knowledge bases, we can consider reasoning over minimal models. The two most prominent modes of reasoning are sceptical and credulous entailment. In this paper, we focus on sceptical and credulous entailment of assertions.

Definition 7. *For a KB* $\mathcal{K}$ *and an assertion* α, *we say* $\mathcal{K}$ credulously *(resp.,* sceptically*) entails* α *if* $\mathcal{I} \models \alpha$ *for some (resp., all) minimal models* $\mathcal{I}$ *of* $\mathcal{K}$.

The above two reasoning modes can be easily related as follows:

Proposition 3. *Assume a KB* $\mathcal{K}$ *and an assertion* α. $\mathcal{K}$ *credulously entails* α *iff* $\mathcal{K}$ *does not sceptically entail* $\neg\alpha$, *and (ii)* $\mathcal{K}$ *sceptically entails* α *iff* $\mathcal{K}$ *does not credulously entail* $\neg\alpha$.

Example 3. Consider $\mathcal{K}$ from Example 1. The tolerance partition of $\mathcal{D}$ is $(\mathcal{D}^0, \mathcal{D}^1)$ with $\mathcal{D}^0 = \{RBC \sqsubseteq\!\!\!\sim \exists hasNucleus.\top\}$ and $\mathcal{D}^1 = \{MRBC \sqsubseteq\!\!\!\sim \neg\exists hasNucleus.\top\}$.
Let $\mathcal{I}$ be an interpretation with $\mathcal{I} \models \mathcal{A} \cup \mathcal{T}$ and $\mathcal{I} \models (\exists hasNucleus.\top)(c_1)$, $\mathcal{I} \models (\neg\exists hasNucleus.\top)(c_2), \mathcal{I} \models (\exists hasNucleus.\top)(c_3)$. We have $\mathsf{rank}_{\mathcal{D},\mathcal{T}}(\mathcal{I},c_1) = 0$, since $\mathcal{I}, c_1 \models \mathcal{D}$. We have $\mathsf{rank}_{\mathcal{D},\mathcal{T}}(\mathcal{I},c_2) = 1$, because $\mathcal{I}$ violates an inclusion in $\mathcal{D}^0$ for c_2. For c_3, $\mathcal{I}$ complies with $\mathcal{D}^0$, but because it violates the inclusion in $\mathcal{D}^1$, so we have $\mathsf{rank}_{\mathcal{D},\mathcal{T}}(\mathcal{I},c_3) = 2$. In all minimal models $\mathcal{J}$ of $\mathcal{K}$ we have $c_1^{\mathcal{J}} \in EN^{\mathcal{I}}$, therefore $EN(c_1)$ is sceptically entailed by $\mathcal{K}$.

4   Algorithms and Complexity

In this section, we investigate the complexity of sceptical and credulous entailment of assertions from a given KB, both in terms of combined complexity and data complexity. Recall that for data complexity, when measuring the size of the input instance, all components except the input ABox are assumed to be fixed. We show that both reasoning problems are ExpTime-complete in combined complexity, and thus they are not harder than standard reasoning tasks, e.g., satisfiability of plain $\mathcal{ALCI}$ TBoxes. For data complexity, the two problems are on the second level of the polynomial hierarchy, even if the inclusions use only concepts in $\mathcal{EL}$. Note that standard reasoning is in PTime for $\mathcal{EL}$ and in the first level of the polynomial hierarchy for $\mathcal{ALCI}$. We start by proving Σ_2^P-hardness of credulous entailment.

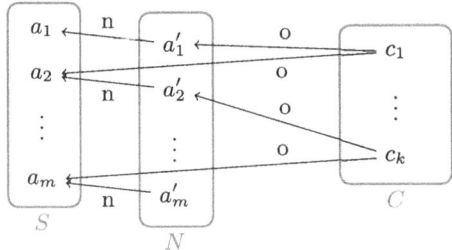

Fig. 2. Illustrating $\mathcal{A}$ from the proof of Proposition 4.

Proposition 4. *In data complexity, credulous entailment of assertions is Σ_2^P-hard.*

Proof. We provide a reduction from credulous entailment of atoms in subset-minimal models of a propositional formula. Assume a formula ϕ. A set I of propositional atoms is called a *minimal model* of ϕ, if I is a model of ϕ, and there exists no $J \subsetneq I$ such that J is a model of ϕ. Given ϕ and an atom g, checking whether $g \in I$ for some minimal model I of ϕ is a Σ_2^P-hard problem [12].

Let ϕ, g be an instance of the above problem; w.l.o.g. we assume ϕ is is a conjunction of k clauses $c_1, \ldots, c_k$ over the propositional atoms $a_1, \ldots, a_m$. Slightly abusing notation, we use the clauses c_j and the propositions a_i as individuals; moreover, we use a_i' for the negation of a_i. Consider the KB $\mathcal{K} = (\mathcal{T}, \mathcal{D}, \mathcal{A})$ with

$$
\begin{aligned}
\mathcal{A} = &\{S(a_1), \ldots, S(a_m)\} \cup \{N(a_1'), \ldots, N(a_m')\} \cup \\
&\{n(a_1', a_1), \ldots, n(a_m', a_m)\} \cup \{C(c_1), \ldots, C(c_k)\} \cup \\
&\{o(c_i, a_j) \mid a_j \text{ occurs in } c_i \text{ positively}\} \cup \\
&\{o(c_i, a_j') \mid a_j \text{ occurs in } c_i \text{ negatively}\} \\
\mathcal{T} = &\{T \sqcap F \sqsubseteq \bot, \quad \exists n.T \sqsubseteq F, \quad \exists n.F \sqsubseteq T, \quad C \sqsubseteq \exists o.T\} \\
\mathcal{D} = &\{S \sqsubset\!\!\!\sim F\}
\end{aligned}
$$

where S, N, C, o, n are closed predicates (used for describing ϕ), the open concepts T and F represent the truth values, and $\mathcal{A}$ is illustrated in Fig. 2.

It is not hard to see that the admissible assignments of $\mathcal{K}$ correspond to the (classical) models of ϕ; see the appendix for details. The more interesting part is to show that g is in a minimal model I of ϕ iff $\mathcal{K}$ credulously entails $T(g)$.

($\Rightarrow$) Assume that there is a subset minimal model I of ϕ with $g \in I$. Consider the DL interpretation $\mathcal{I}$ corresponding to I (see the appendix for details). $\mathcal{I}$ violates the defeasible inclusion in $\mathcal{D}$ for exactly those atoms that are true in I. Since I is subset minimal, there is no admissible model of $\mathcal{K}$ that is smaller than $\mathcal{I}$ wrt. $\prec$; otherwise we could construct a smaller interpretation for ϕ from it. Thus, $\mathcal{I}$ is a minimal model of K with $g \in T^{\mathcal{I}}$ and $\mathcal{K}$ credulously entails $T(g)$.

($\Leftarrow$) Assume that $\mathcal{K}$ credulously entails $\neg T(a)$. Therefore, there is a minimal model $\mathcal{I}$ of $\mathcal{K}$ with $\mathcal{I} \models T(a)$. Consider the propositional interpretation I corresponding to $\mathcal{I}$. $\mathcal{I}$ violates the defeasible inclusion in $\mathcal{D}$ for exactly those atoms that are assigned to true in I. Because $\mathcal{I}$ is minimal among the $\mathcal{K}$-admissible interpretations, there cannot be a model of ϕ that is a subset of I; otherwise we could construct a smaller admissible model of $\mathcal{K}$. Therefore, I is a subset minimal model of ϕ with $g \in I$. $\square$

We now present a procedure to reason about the minimal models of a given KB $\mathcal{K} = (\mathcal{T}, \mathcal{D}, \mathcal{A})$. As we shall see, it yields worst-case optimal upper bounds. The central idea is that, in a minimal model of a KB, defeasible inclusions may be violated only by the individuals that appear in the ABox $\mathcal{A}$.

We recall that a concept C is said to be in *negation normal form (NNF)* if the negation $\neg$ appears in C only in front of concept names only. Every concept can be transformed in polynomial time into an equivalent concept in NNF by "pushing" the negation inside, applying the following rules exhaustively: (a) $\neg \exists r.C \rightsquigarrow \forall r.\neg C$, (b) $\neg \forall r.C \rightsquigarrow \exists r.\neg C$, (c) $\neg \neg C \rightsquigarrow C$, (d) $\neg (C \sqcup D) \rightsquigarrow (\neg C \sqcap \neg D)$, and (e) $\neg (C \sqcap D) \rightsquigarrow (\neg C \sqcup \neg D)$. We use $\sim C$ to denote the concept that is obtained by transforming $\neg C$ into NNF using the above rules.

We define the notion of an (object) *type* w.r.t. a given KB. Intuitively, a type provides a description of an object in an interpretation. Specifically, a type τ is a set of concept expressions that tells us all we need to know regarding the extent to which the defeasible inclusions are satisfied (by a domain object that satisfies all the concepts in τ).

Definition 8 (Types). *Assume a KB $\mathcal{K} = (\mathcal{T}, \mathcal{D}, \mathcal{A})$ and let $(\mathcal{D}^0, \ldots, \mathcal{D}^k, \mathcal{D}^\infty)$ be the tolerance partition of $\mathcal{D}$ w.r.t. $\mathcal{T}$. A $\mathcal{K}$-type τ is any subset-minimal set of concepts such that:*

- $\top \in \tau$, $\bot \notin \tau$
- *if $C \in \tau$, then $\sim C \notin \tau$,*
- *if $C \sqcup D \in \tau$, then $C \in \tau$ or $D \in \tau$,*
- *if $C \sqcap D \in \tau$, then $C \in \tau$ and $D \in \tau$,*
- $\{C, \sim C\} \cap \tau \neq \emptyset$ *and* $\{D, \sim D\} \cap \tau \neq \emptyset$ *for all $C \sqsubseteq D \in \mathcal{T}$ and $C \sqsubThreshold D \in \mathcal{D}$,*
- $\sim C \in \tau$ *or $D \in \tau$ for all $C \sqsubseteq D \in \mathcal{T} \cup \mathcal{D}^\infty$.*

We write $\tau \models C \sqsubThreshold D$, if $\sim C \in \tau$ or $D \in \tau$. For a set $\mathcal{D}$ of defeasible inclusions, we write $\tau \models \mathcal{D}$, if $\tau \models C \sqsubThreshold D$ for all $C \sqsubThreshold D \in \mathcal{D}$.

We next present the notion of a *decoration* for a given KB. Intuitively, we decorate the ABox of the KB by completing it with additional (atomic) assertions and then assigning a type to every individual. The decoration must be coherent: the assigned types and the completed assertions must not contradict the KB.

Definition 9 (Decoration for a KB). *Assume a KB $\mathcal{K} = (\mathcal{T}, \mathcal{D}, \mathcal{A})$ and let $(\mathcal{D}^0, \ldots, \mathcal{D}^k, \mathcal{D}^\infty)$ be the tolerance partition of $\mathcal{D}$ w.r.t. $\mathcal{T}$. An (ABox) completion for $\mathcal{K}$ is any ABox $\mathcal{A}'$ over the same signature as $\mathcal{K}$ such that all individuals that* appear in $\mathcal{A}'$ also appear in $\mathcal{A}$, and no assertions with closed predicates appear in $\mathcal{A}'$. A decoration for $\mathcal{K}$ is a pair $(\mathcal{A}', \delta)$, where $\mathcal{A}'$ is a completion for $\mathcal{K}$ and δ is a function maps every individual c in $\mathcal{A}$ to some $\mathcal{K}$-type $\delta(c)$, such that the following are satisfied:

(a) if $A(c) \in \mathcal{A} \cup \mathcal{A}'$, then $A \in \delta(c)$,
(b) if $r(a, b) \in \mathcal{A} \cup \mathcal{A}'$ and $\forall r.C \in \delta(a)$, then $C \in \delta(b)$,
(c) if $r(a, b) \in \mathcal{A} \cup \mathcal{A}'$ and $\forall r^-.C \in \delta(b)$, then $C \in \delta(a)$.

We will be interested in decorations that can be *realized* in an interpretation that satisfies the strict knowledge of a KB.

Definition 10. *Assume a KB $\mathcal{K} = (\mathcal{T}, \mathcal{D}, \mathcal{A})$ and let $(\mathcal{D}^0, \ldots, \mathcal{D}^k, \mathcal{D}^\infty)$ be the tolerance partition of $\mathcal{D}$ w.r.t. $\mathcal{T}$. We say an interpretation $\mathcal{I}$ is a realization of a decoration $(\mathcal{A}', \delta)$ for $\mathcal{K}$, if the following are satisfied:*

- $\mathcal{I} \models \mathcal{T} \cup \mathcal{D}^\infty$,
- $\mathcal{I} \models^c \mathcal{A} \cup \mathcal{A}'$,
- $a \in (\bigsqcap \delta(a))^\mathcal{I}$ *for all individuals a in $\mathcal{A}$.*

We say $(\mathcal{A}', \delta)$ is realizable w.r.t. $\mathcal{K}$, if it has some realization $\mathcal{I}$.

The next step is to compare decorations in terms of satisfaction of defeasible inclusions.

Definition 11. *Assume a KB $\mathcal{K} = (\mathcal{T}, \mathcal{D}, \mathcal{A})$ and let $(\mathcal{D}^0, \ldots, \mathcal{D}^k, \mathcal{D}^\infty)$ be the tolerance partition of $\mathcal{D}$ w.r.t. $\mathcal{T}$. Given a decoration δ for $\mathcal{A}$ and an individual a from $\mathcal{A}$, we let $\mathsf{rank}_{\mathcal{D}, \mathcal{T}}(\delta, a)$ be defined as follows. If $\tau \models \mathcal{D}$, then $\mathsf{rank}_{\mathcal{D}, \mathcal{T}}(\delta, a) = 0$. Otherwise, $\mathsf{rank}_{\mathcal{D}, \mathcal{T}}(\delta, a)$ is the biggest $i \in \{1, \ldots, k+1\}$ such that $\tau \not\models \mathcal{D}^{i-1}$.*
Given two decorations $(\mathcal{A}_1, \delta_1), (\mathcal{A}_2, \delta_2)$ for $\mathcal{K}$, we write $(\mathcal{A}_1, \delta_1) \prec_\mathcal{K} (\mathcal{A}_2, \delta_2)$, if the following hold:

- $\mathsf{rank}_{\mathcal{D}, \mathcal{T}}(\delta_1, a) \leq \mathsf{rank}_{\mathcal{D}, \mathcal{T}}(\delta_2, a)$ *for all individuals a in $\mathcal{A}$,*
- $\mathsf{rank}_{\mathcal{D}, \mathcal{T}}(\delta_1, a) < \mathsf{rank}_{\mathcal{D}, \mathcal{T}}(\delta_2, a)$ *for some individual a in $\mathcal{A}$.*

Assume a decoration Δ for $\mathcal{K}$. We say Δ is minimal (w.r.t. $\mathcal{K}$), if Δ is realizable w.r.t. $\mathcal{K}$, and there is no decoration Δ' for $\mathcal{K}$ such that $\Delta' \prec_\mathcal{K} \Delta$ and Δ' is realizable w.r.t. $\mathcal{K}$.

We have the following general property:

Proposition 5. *Assume a KB $\mathcal{K} = (\mathcal{T}, \mathcal{D}, \mathcal{A})$ and an assertion α. The following are equivalent:*

1. *There exists a minimal model $\mathcal{I}$ of $\mathcal{K}$ such that $\mathcal{I} \models \alpha$.*
2. *There exists a minimal decoration $(\mathcal{A}', \delta)$ for $\mathcal{K}$ such that $\alpha \in \mathcal{A} \cup \mathcal{A}'$.*

Proof. Assume a KB $\mathcal{K} = (\mathcal{T}, \mathcal{D}, \mathcal{A})$.

($\mathbf{1. \to 2.}$)   Assume $\mathcal{I}$ is a minimal model of $\mathcal{K}$. We show how to construct a decoration $(\mathcal{A}', \delta)$ for $\mathcal{K}$ such that $(\mathcal{A}', \delta)$ is realizable and minimal w.r.t. $\mathcal{K}$. Let N denote the set of individuals that appear in $\mathcal{A}$. Let Σ denote the concept and role names that appear in $\mathcal{K}$. Let $\mathcal{A}_1 = \{A(c) \mid c \in A^{\mathcal{I}} \cap N, A \in \Sigma \backslash N_C^c\}$. Let $\mathcal{A}_1' = \{\neg A(c) \mid c \in N \backslash A^{\mathcal{I}}, A \in \Sigma \backslash N_C^c\}$. Let $\mathcal{A}_2 = \{r(a, b) \mid (a, b) \in r^{\mathcal{I}} \cap N \times N, r \in \Sigma \backslash N_R^c\}$. Let $\mathcal{A}_2' = \{\neg r(a, b) \mid (a, b) \in (N \times N) \backslash r^{\mathcal{I}}, r \in \Sigma \backslash N_R^c\}$. Let $\mathcal{A}' = \mathcal{A}_1 \cup \mathcal{A}_2 \cup \mathcal{A}_1' \cup \mathcal{A}_2'$. For every $a \in N$, let $\delta(a) = \{C \in cl(\mathcal{K}) \mid a \in C^{\mathcal{I}}\}$. Observe that $(\mathcal{A}', \delta)$ is indeed a proper decoration for $\mathcal{K}$. Specifically, since δ is obtained from $\mathcal{I}$, the conditions (a-c) are trivially satisfied. Moreover, the $\mathcal{I}$ immediately witnesses that $(\mathcal{A}', \delta)$ is realizable. Towards a contradiction, suppose $(\mathcal{A}', \delta)$ is not minimal, i.e. there exists some $(\mathcal{A}^*, \delta^*)$ such that (I) $(\mathcal{A}^*, \delta^*)$ is realizable w.r.t. $\mathcal{K}$ and (II) $(\mathcal{A}^*, \delta^*) \prec_{\mathcal{K}} (\mathcal{A}', \delta)$. Let $\mathcal{J}$ be an interpretation that witnesses (II). It is not difficult to verify that $\mathcal{J}$ is $\mathcal{K}$-admissible and $\mathcal{J} \prec_{\mathcal{K}} \mathcal{I}$, which contradicts the assumption that $\mathcal{I}$ is a minimal model of $\mathcal{K}$. Indeed, $\mathcal{J} \prec_{\mathcal{K}} \mathcal{I}$ follows from (II) and the fact that $\mathsf{rank}_{\mathcal{D}, \mathcal{T}}(\delta, a) = \mathsf{rank}_{\mathcal{D}, \mathcal{T}}(\mathcal{I}, a)$ and $\mathsf{rank}_{\mathcal{D}, \mathcal{T}}(\delta^*, a) = \mathsf{rank}_{\mathcal{D}, \mathcal{T}}(\mathcal{J}, a)$ for all individuals $a \in N$.

($\mathbf{2. \to 1.}$)   Assume $(\mathcal{A}', \delta)$ is a minimal realizable decoration for $\mathcal{K}$. Let $\mathcal{J}$ be an interpretation that witnesses realizability of $(\mathcal{A}', \delta)$ w.r.t. $\mathcal{K}$. It is not difficult to verify that $\mathcal{J}$ is a minimal model of $\mathcal{K}$. Indeed, if there exists $\mathcal{I}$ such that $\mathcal{I}$ is $\mathcal{K}$-admissible and $\mathcal{I} \prec_{\mathcal{K}} \mathcal{J}$, then from $\mathcal{I}$ we can construct a decoration $(\mathcal{A}^*, \delta^*)$ such that $(\mathcal{A}^*, \delta^*) \prec_{\mathcal{K}} (\mathcal{A}', \delta)$ and $(\mathcal{A}^*, \delta^*)$ is realizable. The construction of $(\mathcal{A}^*, \delta^*)$ from $\mathcal{I}$ as in the other direction above.   □

The above proposition gives a method to check entailment in minimal models of $\mathcal{K}$ by checking the (non-)existence of minimal realizable decorations. The latter can be effectively done, because each decoration is of relatively small size. Specifically, we have the following result:

Theorem 1. *Credulous and sceptical entailment of assertions is* ExpTime-*complete in combined complexity. In data complexity, credulous and sceptical entailment of assertions is* Σ_2^P-*complete and* Π_2^P-*complete, respectively.*

Proof. We first look at credulous entailment. By Proposition 5, we can focus on the problem of deciding the existence of a minimal realizable decoration $(\mathcal{A}', \delta)$ for $\mathcal{K}$ such that $\alpha \in \mathcal{A} \cup \mathcal{A}'$. An algorithm for this task is as follows:

1. Non-deterministically build a candidate decoration $(\mathcal{A}', \delta)$ for $\mathcal{K}$. Observe that its size (i.e. the space needed to represent it) is polynomial in the size of $\mathcal{K}$. Recall that $\mathcal{A}'$ should use only the individuals that explicitly appear in $\mathcal{A}$, and observe that each type $\delta(a)$ assigned by δ to any individual a is polynomial in size of $\mathcal{K}$.

2. We verify that $\alpha \in \mathcal{A} \cup \mathcal{A}'$ and that the conditions (a-c) in Definition 9 are satisfied. This requires only polynomial time in the size of $\mathcal{K}$.

3. We must check that $(\mathcal{A}', \delta)$ is realizable w.r.t. $\mathcal{K}$. This is feasible in single exponential time in the size of $\mathcal{K}$, and in non-deterministic polynomial time in the case $\mathcal{T}$ and $\mathcal{D}$ are assumed fixed (that is, only $\mathcal{A}$ varies). For the former,

we can simply construct an ordinary $\mathcal{ALCI}$ KB with closed predicates and check for satisfiability. Specifically, for every concept $C \in cl(\mathcal{K})$ we introduce a fresh concept name A_C and add the inclusion $A_C \sqsubseteq C$ to $\mathcal{T}$. Checking whether $(\mathcal{A}', \delta)$ is realizable boils downs to checking the consistency of $\mathcal{K}' = (\mathcal{T} \cup \mathcal{D}^\infty, \mathcal{A} \cup \mathcal{A}' \cup \mathcal{A}^*)$ under the usual DL semantics with closed predicates, where $\mathcal{A}^* = \{A_C(d) \mid d$ is an individual in $\mathcal{A}$ with $C \in \delta(d)\}$. This test is exponential in size of the resulting KB, but it is feasible in non-deterministic polynomial time when the TBox is fixed [13, 23].

4. Finally, we must check that $(\mathcal{A}', \delta)$ is minimal, i.e. check if there is decoration $(\mathcal{A}^*, \delta^*)$ for $\mathcal{K}$ such that $(\mathcal{A}^*, \delta^*) \prec_\mathcal{K} (\mathcal{A}', \delta)$ and $(\mathcal{A}^*, \delta^*)$ is realizable. If it does not exist, then return "yes". To make this check, simply "guess" a decoration $(\mathcal{A}^*, \delta^*)$ and check that $(\mathcal{A}^*, \delta^*) \prec_\mathcal{K} (\mathcal{A}', \delta)$ and that $(\mathcal{A}^*, \delta^*)$ is realizable. The first check is polynomial in $\mathcal{K}$, while the latter test again is since exponential in the size of $\mathcal{K}$ but is it feasible in using an NP oracle when the inclusions of the KB are fixed, i.e. in data complexity.

Overall, we have that there exists a minimal model $\mathcal{I}$ of $\mathcal{K}$ such that $\mathcal{I} \models \alpha$ iff the there is a run of the above procedure that returns "yes". Its run time is single exponential in $\mathcal{K}$. For data complexity, it can be implemented as a non-deterministic polynomial time procedure with an NP oracle, thus yielding the Σ_2^P upper bound.

The EXPTIME lower bound is trivially inherited from classical reasoning in $\mathcal{ALCI}$ [27]. Σ_2^P-hardness of credulous entailment was shown in Proposition 4. To obtain the results for sceptical entailment, we can directly apply Proposition 3, which leads to EXPTIME-completeness in combined complexity and Π_2^P-completeness in data complexity.   □

For applications involving large ABoxes, an inference at the second level of the polynomial hierarchy is out of question. Therefore, we now present a restricted fragment of our formalism that has tractable data complexity. To do this, we define *local* DCIs and KBs.

Definition 12 (Local KBs). *A complex concept C is closed if all concept and role names occurring in it are closed. An ordinary inclusion $C \sqsubseteq D$ or a defeasible inclusion $C \mathbin{\rlap{\raise{0.2ex}{$\sqsubseteq$}}{\lower{0.6ex}{$\sim$}}} D$ is called* local, *if every quantified concept of the form $\exists r.E$ or $\forall r.F$ occurring in C or D is closed. A knowledge base $\mathcal{K} = (\mathcal{T}, \mathcal{D}, \mathcal{A})$ is* local *if every defeasible inclusion in $\mathcal{D}$ and every inclusion in $\mathcal{T}$ is local.*

The intuition of local inclusions is that they can only describe an object and its immediate surroundings. While they can use quantifiers on closed roles and predicates, which can be evaluated by looking up the assertions in the ABox, they cannot be affected by the assignment of open concepts in neighbouring nodes. This will allow us to answer queries about an object without the need to consider the assignments of open concepts for all objects in $\Delta_\mathcal{A}$. Algorithm 1 shows how this locality can be exploited for sceptical inference.

Proposition 6. *For a local knowledge base $\mathcal{K} = (\mathcal{T}, \mathcal{D}, \mathcal{A})$ and a query α, Algorithm 1 returns Yes iff $\mathcal{K}$ sceptically entails α.*

Algorithm 1. Sceptical reasoning from local knowledge bases

Require: local knowledge base $\mathcal{K} = (\mathcal{T}, \mathcal{D}, \mathcal{A})$, assertion α
Ensure: *Yes* if $\mathcal{K}$ sceptically entails α, *No* otherwise
1: $(\mathcal{D}^0, \ldots, \mathcal{D}^k, \mathcal{D}^\infty) \leftarrow$ tolerance partition of $\mathcal{D}$ wrt. $\mathcal{T}$
2: **if** $\mathcal{D}^\infty \cup \mathcal{T} \cup \mathcal{A}$ is inconsistent **then**
3: $\quad$ **return** *Yes* $\qquad\qquad \triangleright$ There is no $\mathcal{K}$-admissible assignment

4: $i_{last} \leftarrow 0$
5: **for** $i \leftarrow k, \ldots, 0$ **do**
6: $\quad \overline{\mathcal{D}^a_{i..k}} \leftarrow \{(\neg C \sqcup D)(a) \mid (C \sqsubseteq D) \in \mathcal{D}_i \cup \cdots \cup \mathcal{D}_k\}$
7: $\quad$ **if** $\overline{\mathcal{D}^a_{i..k}} \cup \mathcal{D}^\infty \cup \mathcal{T} \cup \mathcal{A}$ is inconsistent **then**
8: $\quad\quad i_{last} \leftarrow i + 1$
9: $\quad\quad$ **break**
10: **if** $\overline{\mathcal{D}^a_{i_{last}..k}} \cup \mathcal{D}^\infty \cup \mathcal{T} \cup \mathcal{A} \models \alpha$ $\quad$ **then return** *Yes* $\quad$ **else return** *No*

Algorithm 1 shows that inference from local KBs is tractable in data complexity.

Theorem 2. *Let $\mathcal{K} = (\mathcal{T}, \mathcal{D}, \mathcal{A})$ be a local KB and α be an assertion. Checking whether $\mathcal{K}$ sceptically (or credulously, resp.) entails $C(a)$ is polynomial in data complexity and in P^{NP} in combined complexity.*

Proof. Algorithm 1 gives us an upper bound on the data complexity. The ABox $\mathcal{A}$ is only considered in the satisfiability checks and the entailment check in lines 2, 7, and 10. Because the inclusions in $\mathcal{D}$ and $\mathcal{T}$ are local, the quantified parts in the concepts in $\mathcal{D}, \mathcal{T}$ must be closed and thus can be evaluated by simply looking up whether a certain concept holds in any/all neighbours. Therefore, the quantifiers in $\mathcal{D}, \mathcal{T}$ can be evaluated in polynomial time; after that only the concept assertions for a need to be taken into account. Hence, sceptical inference from local KBs can be decided in polynomial time. Because of Proposition 3, credulous inference from local KBs can also be decided in polynomial time.

For combined complexity, the tolerance partition can be constructed with $O(|\mathcal{D}|^2)$ satisfiability checks. The loop in Lines 5–9 also uses a polynomial number of satisfiability checks, while Lines 2 and 10 require one satisfiability/entailment check each. In total, Algorithm 1 requires a polynomial number of satisfiability checks; thus sceptical inference is in P^{NP}, and with Proposition 3, credulous inference can also be decided in P^{NP}. $\qquad\square$

5   Related Approaches

Extending DLs with defeasible inclusions following the principles of the KLM postulates [20] has received significant attention [4,7–10,15,26], and *rational closure* is the most widely studied semantics [7,9,16,26], largely due to the fact that it does not generally increase the complexity of the underlying logic. Rational closure has been extended to TBoxes in DLs that enjoy the *disjoint model union property (DMUP)* [7,16], but it has been shown that there is no satisfactory extension to DLs that lack it—like the DL we consider here, which has individuals and closed predicates. A refinement called *stable rational closure* has been proposed for logics as rich as $\mathcal{SROIQ}$ [4]. Given a specific ABox, our setting can be reduced to $\mathcal{SROIQ}$ using nominals to express both the ABox assertions and the closed predicates. If we do that, our semantics seems to coincide with the stable rational closure on the examples of Sect. 9 in [4]; a detailed comparison remains to be done. Since our main interest in reasoning about different ABoxes and understanding the data complexity, blurring the line between the ABox and TBox by encoding the former in the latter is not desirable.

All approaches mentioned above share the so-called *quantification neglect* problem, that is, they disregard all defeasible information for concepts appearing nested inside quantification. To our knowledge, this problem has only been solved for the lightweight logic $\mathcal{EL}_\perp$ [26], leaving a large gap in expressiveness to the rich DL considered here. Unfortunately, that approach relies heavily on the existence of universal models. Although it appears very promising for Horn DLs, we do not see how to extend those ideas to expressive DLs and closed predicates.

Our work shares some of the motivation behind $\mathcal{DL}^N$ [5], which overcomes some limitations of rational closure and keeps the complexity in check. The logics are quire different, and our semantics seems stronger, allowing for different possible extensions instead of leaving conflicting inferences unresolved.

6   Discussion and Outlook

In this paper we presented a framework for reasoning with defeasible description logics featuring ABoxes. After showing that the outlined inference is intractable in general, we identify a fragment where queries can be answered in polynomial time in data complexity. The inference presented here is heavily inspired by Rational Closure and the equivalent system Z. This is a natural starting point, many alternatives have been suggested, some of them also based on a tolerance partition, which may avoid the drowning problem, also known as inheritance blocking. A compelling question is how some of these other semantics can be adapted to our framework for tractable reasoning over objects.

Unlike most related works, our approach does not face the issue of quantification neglect: since defeasible inferences are, by definition, applicable only to objects named in the ABox, the question whether roles should range over typical or atypical individuals does not even arise. However, this restriction to rooted concepts is indeed a limitation, and less drastic ways to circumvent the quantification neglect problem are an important issue for further investigation.

For lifting our tractability results to richer fragments and achieving practicable reasoning, a quite different approach may be needed, maybe drawing inspiration from the default inference mechanisms of the prototype-centric $\mathcal{DL}^N$.

We plan to explore whether our approach can serve as a basis for a defeasible version of the Shapes Constraint Language (SHACL), used for validating RDF graphs [18]. Since DLs with closed predicates can capture SHACL specifications [24] and our logic—$\mathcal{ALCI}$ with closed predicate—already covers a significant portion of the standard, this seems promising. In SHACL all data predicates are closed, so our restriction to rooted concepts does not seem so strong. Our approach can be seen as way to find 'most typical' shape assignments under supported semantics, but it would also be interesting to explore how to lift it to the more robust and computationally friendly under well-founded semantics.

Acknowledgments. This work was partially supported by the Austrian Science Fund (FWF) projects PIN8884924 and P30873.

References

1. Adams, E.W.: The Logic of Conditionals: An Application of Probability to Deductive Logic. Synthese Library. Springer, Dordrecht (1975)
2. Baader, F., Hollunder, B.: Embedding defaults into terminological knowledge representation formalisms. J. Autom. Reason. **14**(1), 149–180 (1995). https://doi.org/10.1007/BF00883932
3. Baader, F., Horrocks, I., Lutz, C., Sattler, U.: An Introduction to Description Logic. Cambridge University Press, Cambridge (2017)
4. Bonatti, P.A.: Rational closure for all description logics. Artif. Intell. **274**, 197–223 (2019). https://doi.org/10.1016/J.ARTINT.2019.04.001
5. Bonatti, P.A., Faella, M., Petrova, I.M., Sauro, L.: A new semantics for overriding in description logics. Artif. Intell. **222**, 1–48 (2015). https://doi.org/10.1016/J.ARTINT.2014.12.010

6. Booth, R., Varzinczak, I.: Conditional inference under disjunctive rationality. In: Thirty-Fifth AAAI Conference on Artificial Intelligence, AAAI 2021, Thirty-Third Conference on Innovative Applications of Artificial Intelligence, IAAI 2021, The Eleventh Symposium on Educational Advances in Artificial Intelligence, EAAI 2021, Virtual Event, February 2-9, 2021, pp. 6227–6234. AAAI Press (2021). https://doi.org/10.1609/AAAI.V35I7.16774

7. Britz, K., Casini, G., Meyer, T., Moodley, K., Sattler, U., Varzinczak, I.: Principles of KLM-style defeasible description logics. ACM Trans. Comput. Log. **22**(1), 1:1–1:46 (2021). https://doi.org/10.1145/3420258

8. Casini, G., Meyer, T., Moodley, K., Sattler, U., Varzinczak, I.: Introducing defeasibility into OWL ontologies. In: Arenas, M., et al. (eds.) ISWC 2015. LNCS, vol. 9367, pp. 409–426. Springer, Cham (2015). https://doi.org/10.1007/978-3-319-25010-6_27

9. Casini, G., Straccia, U.: Defeasible inheritance-based description logics. J. Artif. Intell. Res. **48**, 415–473 (2013). https://doi.org/10.1613/JAIR.4062

10. Casini, G., Straccia, U.: A rational entailment for expressive description logics via description logic programs. In: Jembere, E., Gerber, A.J., Viriri, S., Pillay, A. (eds.) SACAIR 2021. CCIS, vol. 1551, pp. 177–191. Springer, Cham (2022). https://doi.org/10.1007/978-3-030-95070-5_12

11. Chama, V., Wang, S., Meyer, T.A., Casini, G.: Defeasible justification for KLM-style logic. In: Giordano, L., Jung, J.C., Ozaki, A. (eds.) Proceedings of the 37th International Workshop on Description Logics (DL 2024), Bergen, Norway, June 18-21, 2024. CEUR Workshop Proceedings, vol. 3739. CEUR-WS.org (2024). https://ceur-ws.org/Vol-3739/paper-3.pdf

12. Eiter, T., Gottlob, G.: On the computational cost of disjunctive logic programming: propositional case. Ann. Math. Artif. Intell. **15**(3–4), 289–323 (1995). https://doi.org/10.1007/BF01536399

13. Franconi, E., Ibáñez-García, Y.A., Seylan, İ: Query answering with dboxes is hard. Electron. Notes Theor. Comput. Sci. **278**, 71–84 (2011). https://doi.org/10.1016/j.entcs.2011.10.007. proceedings of the 7th Workshop on Methods for Modalities (M4M'2011) and the 4th Workshop on Logical Aspects of Multi-Agent Systems (LAMAS'2011)

14. Giordano, L., Gliozzi, V.: Reasoning about exceptions in ontologies: from the lexicographic closure to the skeptical closure. In: Lukasiewicz, T., Peñaloza, R., Turhan, A. (eds.) Proceedings of the Second Workshop on Logics for Reasoning about Preferences, Uncertainty, and Vagueness co-located with the 9th International Joint Conference on Automated Reasoning, PRUV@IJCAR 2018, Oxford, UK, July 19th, 2018. CEUR Workshop Proceedings, vol. 2157. CEUR-WS.org (2018). https://ceur-ws.org/Vol-2157/paper7.pdf

15. Giordano, L., Gliozzi, V.: Reasoning about exceptions in ontologies: from the lexicographic closure to the skeptical closure. Fundam. Informaticae **176**(3–4), 235–269 (2020). https://doi.org/10.3233/FI-2020-1973

16. Giordano, L., Gliozzi, V., Olivetti, N., Pozzato, G.L.: Semantic characterization of rational closure: from propositional logic to description logics. Artif. Intell. **226**, 1–33 (2015). https://doi.org/10.1016/j.artint.2015.05.001

17. Heyninck, J., Kern-Isberner, G., Meyer, T.A., Haldimann, J.P., Beierle, C.: Conditional syntax splitting for non-monotonic inference operators. In: Williams, B., Chen, Y., Neville, J. (eds.) Thirty-Seventh AAAI Conference on Artificial Intelligence, AAAI 2023, Thirty-Fifth Conference on Innovative Applications of Artificial Intelligence, IAAI 2023, Thirteenth Symposium on Educational Advances in Artificial Intelligence, EAAI 2023, Washington, DC, USA, February 7-14, 2023, pp. 6416–6424. AAAI Press (2023). https://doi.org/10.1609/aaai.v37i5.25789

18. Knublauch, H., Kontokostas, D.: Shapes constraint language (SHACL). W3C recommendation, W3C (2017). https://www.w3.org/TR/2017/REC-shacl-20170720/

19. Komo, C., Beierle, C.: Nonmonotonic reasoning from conditional knowledge bases with system W. Ann. Math. Artif. Intell. **90**(1), 107–144 (2021). https://doi.org/10.1007/s10472-021-09777-9

20. Kraus, S., Lehmann, D., Magidor, M.: Nonmonotonic reasoning, preferential models and cumulative logics. Artif. Intell. **44**(1–2), 167–207 (1990)

21. Lehmann, D.: What does a conditional knowledge base entail? In: Brachman, R.J., Levesque, H.J., Reiter, R. (eds.) Proceedings of the 1st International Conference on Principles of Knowledge Representation and Reasoning (KR 1989). Toronto, Canada, May 15-18 1989, pp. 212–222. Morgan Kaufmann (1989)

22. Lehmann, D.: Another perspective on default reasoning. Ann. Math. Artif. Intell. **15**(1), 61–82 (1995). https://doi.org/10.1007/BF01535841

23. Lutz, C., Seylan, I., Wolter, F.: The data complexity of ontology-mediated queries with closed predicates. Logical Methods Comput. Sci. **15**(3), 23 (2019). https://doi.org/10.23638/LMCS-15(3:23)2019

24. Ortiz, M.: A short introduction to SHACL for logicians. In: Hansen, H.H., Scedrov, A., de Queiroz, R.J.G.B. (eds.) Logic, Language, Information, and Computation - 29th International Workshop, WoLLIC 2023, Halifax, NS, Canada, July 11-14, 2023, Proceedings. Lecture Notes in Computer Science, vol. 13923, pp. 19–32. Springer (2023). https://doi.org/10.1007/978-3-031-39784-4_2

25. Pearl, J.: System Z: A natural ordering of defaults with tractable applications to nonmonotonic reasoning. In: Parikh, R. (ed.) Proceedings of the 3rd Conference on Theoretical Aspects of Reasoning about Knowledge, Pacific Grove, CA, USA, March 1990, pp. 121–135. Morgan Kaufmann (1990)

26. Pensel, M., Turhan, A.: Reasoning in the defeasible description logic ϵ - computing standard inferences under rational and relevant semantics. Int. J. Approx. Reason. **103**, 28–70 (2018). https://doi.org/10.1016/J.IJAR.2018.08.005

27. Schild, K.: A correspondence theory for terminological logics: preliminary report. In: Mylopoulos, J., Reiter, R. (eds.) Proc. of the 12th Int. Joint Conf. on Artificial Intelligence (IJCAI 1991), pp. 466–471. Morgan Kaufmann (1991)

Closure-Based Tractable Possibilistic Inference from Partially Ordered DL-Lite Ontologies

Ahmed Laouar$^{(\boxtimes)}$ and Salem Benferhat

CRIL, Univ. Artois & CNRS, UMR 8188, 62300 Lens, France
{laouar,benferhat}@cril.fr

Abstract. Handling partially specified inconsistent information is a major challenge, especially when balancing the richness of query answers with the need to control computational complexity. We address this challenge by proposing an efficient method for computing a consistent and enriched fragment of data, known as a repair, within knowledge bases that rely on a stable terminological component and incorporate partially ordered uncertainty in the data (ABox). Our approach, grounded in possibility theory, avoids exhaustive enumeration of conflicts or justifications by applying a positive deductive closure directly to the partially ordered ABox. This enables repair computation through simple consistency checks over data subsets, ensuring tractability while supporting an extended set of plausible inferences. Beyond this main contribution on efficient repair computation, we briefly introduce a semantic characterisation of repairs that generalises the classical notion of models for consistent knowledge bases. Finally, we present an experimental evaluation against existing possibilistic approaches, demonstrating both practical effectiveness and computational benefits.

Keywords: Inconsistency · Ontologies · Data Repairs · Partial Orders

1 Introduction

Formal ontologies specify the semantics and domain knowledge of datasets, enabling reliable query answering. A knowledge base consists of conceptual knowledge in the ontology (TBox) and factual knowledge in the dataset (ABox). This article focuses on two key issues: inconsistency, where data violate ontological constraints, and uncertainty, where facts have varying reliability. Many works address inconsistency handling in frameworks like propositional logic [21], first-order logic [5], description logics [3,12,22,26], and databases [11,29]. Our work aligns with research [3,13,26] on tractable inconsistency management, especially for large ABoxes. In such settings, inconsistencies stem from ABox assertions contradicting TBox rules. We assume a reliable TBox and focus on efficient reasoning over conflicting ABox data. A common approach to reasoning under

© The Author(s), under exclusive license to Springer Nature Switzerland AG 2026
G. Casini et al. (Eds.): JELIA 2025, LNAI 16093, pp. 240–256, 2026.
https://doi.org/10.1007/978-3-032-04587-4_15

inconsistency is to compute consistent subsets of the ABox, often called repairs, over which queries can be safely evaluated. The ABox Repair (AR) semantics is desirable for its cautious strategy of returning only answers supported by all repairs [26], but it is generally intractable. To address this, the Intersection of ABox Repairs (IAR) semantics [26] offers a natural and tractable alternative by evaluating queries over the intersection of all repairs. However, IAR sacrifices completeness for tractability, potentially missing answers entailed by all repairs but absent from their intersection. The ongoing challenge is to surpass IAR in inferential or expressive power while preserving computational efficiency.

Several levers have been proposed to overcome the limitations of IAR semantics. In this paper, we rely on two main levers. The first lever involves computing the deductive closure of the ABox, which derives all facts entailed by the positive axioms of the TBox. This allows the recovery of conclusions not explicitly present in the ABox. The closure can be applied either before or after repair computation. Applying it beforehand, as in the Intersection of Closed ABox Repairs (ICAR) semantics [26], preserves tractability but may produce questionable conclusions, whereas applying it afterwards, as in the Intersection of Closed Repairs (ICR) semantics [12], yields richer inferences at the expense of tractability.

The second lever involves the widely used strategy of assigning priorities to handle inconsistency. The idea is to resolve conflicts by preferring certain assertions, typically via a total or partial preorder, enabling a more informed selection of consistent subsets. A substantial body of work has explored the use of priorities to guide conflict resolution across diverse settings. These include total orders [9,14], context-dependent or local orders defined only within specific conflicts [10], interval-based or lattice-based preferences [20], and general partial orders [6,7]. While priority relations provide an intuitive way to direct inconsistency handling, they also significantly expand the range of possible semantics, often as extensions of classical, non-prioritised frameworks.

This paper focuses on tractable semantics based on partial preference relations over the ABox, using possibilistic logic. Partially ordered information is managed by extending the partial order into a family of total orders that refine it, each inducing a prioritised consistent repair. Reasoning then aggregates information from these preferred repairs. Within DL-Lite$_\mathcal{R}$, two methods illustrate this approach in possibility theory [17]: the π-repair, which directly intersects repairs from the total extensions [6], and the Cπ-repair, which enriches each repair by computing its deductive closure before intersection [24]. Both are tractable and provide meaningful semantics. Moreover, the closed method is more productive, deriving additional consequences from the knowledge base's logical structure.

In this work, we apply deductive closure at an earlier stage—directly on the initial partially ordered ABox. To enable this, we adapt the classical notion of deductive closure to account for the partial order among assertions. This early enrichment helps identify minimal conflicting elements by isolating less certain assertions and allows for a more efficient implementation of the Cπ-repair semantics through a sequence of consistency checks.

The main contribution of this work is an efficient repair process leveraging the deductive closure of the input ABox. We show possibilistic inference can be applied directly to this enriched ABox, yielding the same repaired ABoxes as previous approaches, without explicitly computing assertion supports. This reduces reasoning to consistency checks over ABox subsets. Additionally, we provide a semantic perspective on possibilistic repairs, outlining a preferential framework with partially ordered interpretations and preferred models. This view supports formal understanding of inference under prioritised inconsistency and will guide future developments. Finally, our experimental evaluation shows computing the deductive closure before generating repairs improves performance over existing methods, validating the practical relevance of our approach.

This paper is organised as follows. Section 2 reviews the DL-Lite$_\mathcal{R}$ language and the Cπ-repair approach. Section 3 introduces the partially preordered closure, characterises $c\pi$-acceptance, and offers a brief semantic perspective. Section 4 presents experimental results, followed by the conclusion. The implementation code, ontology, and datasets are available at https://github.com/ahmedlaouar/py_reasoner/tree/jelia2025.

2 Preliminaries

We briefly recall the basics of the DL-Lite$_\mathcal{R}$ fragment of the DL-Lite description logics [16], and the notions of conflicts and deductive closure. Then, we recall the Closure-Based Partially Ordered Possibilistic Repair (Cπ-repair).

2.1 The DL-Lite$_\mathcal{R}$ Language

A DL-Lite$_\mathcal{R}$ knowledge base is constructed from three mutually disjoint sets: concept names N_C, role names N_R and individual names N_I, as follows:

$$R := P \mid P^- \qquad E := R \mid \neg R \qquad B := A \mid \exists R \qquad C := B \mid \neg B$$

where A is an atomic concept, P is an atomic role and P^- is the inverse of an atomic role. Concepts B and C are called basic and complex concepts, respectively. Roles R and E are called basic and complex roles, respectively. The negation symbol $\neg$ designates complement sets (of concepts and roles), and the existential quantifier symbol $\exists$ denotes existential restriction.

A knowledge base (KB) is a pair $\mathcal{K} = \langle \mathcal{T}, \mathcal{A} \rangle$ where $\mathcal{T}$ is the TBox and $\mathcal{A}$ is the ABox. The TBox is a finite set of inclusion axioms between concepts and roles of the form $B \sqsubseteq C$ and $R \sqsubseteq E$. Axioms with the negation symbol to the right of the inclusion symbol are called negative inclusion axioms, while axioms without the negation symbol are called positive inclusion axioms. The ABox contains a finite set of membership assertions (or ground facts) on atomic concepts and atomic roles of the form $A(a)$ and $P(a, b)$. where a and b are individuals.

The semantics of a DL-Lite$_\mathcal{R}$ KB is given in terms of interpretations. An interpretation $\mathcal{I} = \langle \Delta^\mathcal{I}, \cdot^\mathcal{I} \rangle$ consists of a non-empty domain $\Delta^\mathcal{I}$ and an interpretation function $\cdot^\mathcal{I}$ assigning meaning to concept names, role names, and individual names. We use the standard definitions of satisfaction of axioms and assertions by an interpretation; see [16] for a comprehensive presentation.

An interpretation $\mathcal{I}$ is a model of a KB $\mathcal{K} = \langle \mathcal{T}, \mathcal{A} \rangle$ if it satisfies every axiom in the TBox $\mathcal{T}$ and every assertion in the ABox $\mathcal{A}$. The KB $\mathcal{K}$ is consistent if it admits at least one model; otherwise, it is inconsistent. A TBox $\mathcal{T}$ is incoherent if some concept name is empty in all models of $\mathcal{T}$; otherwise it is coherent. An assertion φ is entailed by a knowledge base $\mathcal{K}$, denoted $\mathcal{K} \models \varphi$, if and only if φ is satisfied by every model of $\mathcal{K}$.

In a DL-Lite$_\mathcal{R}$ KB, the negative inclusion axioms serve to identify conflicts within the ABox [16]. These are inclusion-minimal inconsistent subsets of the ABox, which contradict the TBox in the case of inconsistency.

Definition 1. *Let* $\mathcal{K} = \langle \mathcal{T}, \mathcal{A} \rangle$ *be a DL-Lite$_\mathcal{R}$ KB. A subset of the ABox $\mathcal{C} \subseteq \mathcal{A}$ is a conflict if $\langle \mathcal{T}, \mathcal{C} \rangle$ is inconsistent and $\forall \varphi \in \mathcal{C}$, $\langle \mathcal{T}, \mathcal{C} \setminus \{\varphi\} \rangle$ is consistent.*

The conflict set $\mathsf{Cf}(\mathcal{A})$ contains all the conflicts in $\mathcal{A}$, each consisting of at most two assertions, since in DL-Lite$_\mathcal{R}$ each negative inclusion axiom in the TBox involves at most two concepts or two roles [16].

We use an example built on the set of concept names $\mathsf{N_C} = \{\mathsf{Prof}, \mathsf{FacMember}, \mathsf{FullProf}, \mathsf{Dean}, \mathsf{VisitingProf}, \mathsf{PostDoc}\}$, which represent the basic concepts: professor, faculty member, full professor, dean, visiting professor, and postdoctoral, and the set of individual names $\mathsf{N_I} = \{\mathsf{Bob}, \mathsf{Alice}\}$.

Example 1. Let $\mathcal{K} = \langle \mathcal{T}, \mathcal{A} \rangle$ be a DL-Lite$_\mathcal{R}$ KB where the TBox $\mathcal{T}$ and the ABox $\mathcal{A}$ are given as follows:

$$\mathcal{T} = \begin{cases} 1.\ \mathsf{FullProf} \sqsubseteq \mathsf{Prof} & 3.\ \mathsf{Dean} \sqsubseteq \mathsf{FacMember} & 5.\ \mathsf{Prof} \sqsubseteq \neg\mathsf{PostDoc} \\ 2.\ \mathsf{Prof} \sqsubseteq \mathsf{FacMember} & 4.\ \mathsf{VisitingProf} \sqsubseteq \neg\mathsf{FullProf} \end{cases}$$

$$\mathcal{A} = \begin{cases} \varphi_1 = \mathsf{Dean}(\mathsf{Alice}) & \varphi_3 = \mathsf{Prof}(\mathsf{Bob}) & \varphi_5 = \mathsf{VisitingProf}(\mathsf{Bob}) \\ \varphi_2 = \mathsf{FullProf}(\mathsf{Bob}) & \varphi_4 = \mathsf{PostDoc}(\mathsf{Bob}) \end{cases}$$

One can check that $\mathcal{K}$ is inconsistent. The conflict set of $\mathcal{A}$ is given by $\mathsf{Cf}(\mathcal{A}) = \{\mathcal{C}_1, \mathcal{C}_2, \mathcal{C}_3\}$, such that $\mathcal{C}_1$ contradicts Axiom 4, and $\mathcal{C}_2$ and $\mathcal{C}_3$ contradict Axiom 5. Namely, $\mathcal{C}_1 = \{\mathsf{FullProf}(\mathsf{Bob}), \mathsf{VisitingProf}(\mathsf{Bob})\}$, $\mathcal{C}_2 = \{\mathsf{Prof}(\mathsf{Bob}), \mathsf{PostDoc}(\mathsf{Bob})\}$, and $\mathcal{C}_3 = \{\mathsf{FullProf}(\mathsf{Bob}), \mathsf{PostDoc}(\mathsf{Bob})\}$.

The positive inclusion axioms are used to derive implied facts from the ABox. The deductive closure applies those positive axioms on ABox assertions to return all the assertions that are implicitly or explicitly stated in the ABox [9,16].

Definition 2. *Let* $\mathcal{T}_p$ *denote the set of all positive inclusion axioms of a TBox $\mathcal{T}$. The deductive closure of $\mathcal{A}$ with respect to $\mathcal{T}$ is defined by:*

$$cl(\mathcal{A}) = \{\varphi \mid \langle \mathcal{T}_p, \mathcal{A} \rangle \models \varphi \text{ s.t. } \varphi \text{ is a concept } B(a) \text{ or a role } R(a,b) \text{ assertion}\}$$

where B and R are respectively a concept name and a role name in $\mathcal{T}$, a, b are individuals in $\mathcal{A}$, and $\models$ is the standard DL-Lite$_\mathcal{R}$ inference relation.

The deductive closure bears strong similarities with the notion of the *chase*, which originates in the database community and has also been adapted to DL-Lite$_\mathcal{R}$ [16]. A key difference, however, is that while the *chase* may introduce fresh individuals to complete entailment chains by applying positive TBox axioms to ABox assertions, the deductive closure, as considered here, aims to construct a finite set of entailed assertions restricted to the individuals already present in the ABox. A related notion, referred to as *saturation*, has been employed in the context of quantified ABoxes [2], where existential variables are used instead of introducing fresh individuals, as in the traditional chase.

In our setting, the deductive closure is obtained by exhaustively applying the positive inclusion axioms from $\mathcal{T}$ (e.g., concept and role inclusions) to the assertions in $\mathcal{A}$ until a fixed point is reached, that is, no further assertions can be derived and added. The following example illustrates this process using the ABox from Example 1.

Example 2. Let us continue Example 1 and compute $cl(\mathcal{A})$. The set of positive inclusion axioms of $\mathcal{T}$, denoted by $\mathcal{T}_p$ contains the axioms 1, 2, and 3 of $\mathcal{T}$, namely:

$$\mathcal{T}_p = \{1.\ \mathsf{FullProf} \sqsubseteq \mathsf{Prof} \quad 2.\ \mathsf{Prof} \sqsubseteq \mathsf{FacMember} \quad 3.\ \mathsf{Dean} \sqsubseteq \mathsf{FacMember}\}$$

The deductive closure of $\mathcal{A}$ is $cl(\mathcal{A}) = \mathcal{A} \cup \{\mathsf{FacMember}(\mathsf{Alice}), \mathsf{FacMember}(\mathsf{Bob})\}$. Such that $\mathsf{FacMember}(\mathsf{Alice})$ is obtained from the axiom 3 applied on the assertion $\mathsf{Dean}(\mathsf{Alice})$, and $\mathsf{FacMember}(\mathsf{Bob})$ is obtained by applying one of the axioms 1 or 2 on the assertions $\mathsf{FullProf}(\mathsf{Bob})$ or $\mathsf{Prof}(\mathsf{Bob})$, respectively.

2.2   Partially Ordered Information as a Family of Totally Ordered Possibilistic Repairs

We are interested in partially ordered information, where some data pieces may have incomparable reliability levels. Partial orders are especially useful when it is not feasible to fully compare all information, such as when multiple sources provide data with their own priority criteria [15]. These orders reflect diverse factors like source reliability, specificity, or recency [27,28]. Moreover, combining different total orders often naturally induces a partial order, for example through the Pareto principle [29]. Finally, missing data for some criteria also motivates the use of partial orders, which offer a flexible and realistic way to handle incomparability and uncertainty.

Possibilistic DL-Lite$_\mathcal{R}$. Possibilistic logic is widely used to manage incomplete and uncertain information [4,18,19]. It captures uncertainty by either possibility distributions representing uncertainty in extension, or weighted logics for compact representation. Possibilistic DL-Lite [8] extends standard DL-Lite by assigning weights in the unit interval $]0,1]$ to TBox axioms and ABox assertions, representing their uncertainty degree. Since TBox axioms are fully reliable, weights apply only to ABox assertions. This assignment yields a totally preordered KB, denoted $\mathcal{K}_> = \langle \mathcal{T}, \mathcal{A}_> \rangle$, where:

$$\mathcal{A}_> = \{(\varphi_i, w_i) \mid \varphi \text{ is an assertion and } w_i \in]0,1]\}$$

The possibilistic inference from an inconsistent KB is achieved using an inconsistency degree, denoted $\mathsf{Inc}(\mathcal{A}_>)$. Formally, $\mathsf{Inc}(\mathcal{A}_>) = w_i$ if the sub-base $\{\varphi \mid (\varphi, w_j) \in \mathcal{A}_>, w_j > w_i\}$ is consistent and the sub-base $\{\varphi \mid (\varphi, w_j) \in \mathcal{A}_>, w_j \geq w_i\}$ is inconsistent. The possibilistic repair [9] of $\mathcal{K}_>$ is given by:

$$\mathcal{R}(\mathcal{A}_>) = \{\varphi \mid (\varphi, w_i) \in \mathcal{A}_>, w_i > \mathsf{Inc}(\mathcal{A}_>)\}$$

where the inconsistency degree $\mathsf{Inc}(\mathcal{A}_>)$ is the highest weight assigned to an assertion that makes the ABox inconsistent.

Partially preordered possibilistic DL-Lite$_\mathcal{R}$. In partially preordered possibilistic knowledge bases (KBs), symbolic weights are assigned to ABox assertions from a partially ordered set denoted by $\mathsf{U} = \mathbb{0}, u_1, \ldots, u_n, \mathbb{1}$. This set U is equipped with a strict partial order $\rhd$, forming the uncertainty scale $\mathbb{L} = (\mathsf{U}, \rhd)$. By definition, $\rhd$ is an irreflexive and transitive relation. Some weights may be incomparable; that is, for any two weights $u_i, u_j \in \mathsf{U}$, $u_i \bowtie u_j$ means that neither $u_i \rhd u_j$ nor $u_j \rhd u_i$ holds. The weight $\mathbb{1}$, representing full certainty, is the greatest element of U in the sense that for every $u_i \in \mathsf{U}$, we have $\mathbb{1} \rhd u_i$.

A partially preordered DL-Lite$_\mathcal{R}$ KB is a triple $\mathcal{K}_\rhd = \langle \mathcal{T}, \mathcal{A}_\rhd, \mathbb{L} \rangle$, where a single weight from U is assigned to each assertion:

$$\mathcal{A}_\rhd = \{(\varphi_i, u_i) \mid \varphi \text{ is an assertion and } u_i \in \mathsf{U}\}$$

For simplicity, given two assertions $(\varphi_i, u_i), (\varphi_j, u_j) \in \mathcal{A}_\rhd$, we write $\varphi_i \rhd \varphi_j$ and $\varphi_i \bowtie \varphi_j$ to denote $u_i \rhd u_j$ and $u_i \bowtie u_j$, respectively.

Example 3. Assume the uncertainty scale $\mathbb{L} = (\mathsf{U}, \rhd)$ given by $\mathsf{U} = \{u_1, u_2, u_3, u_4, u_5, \mathbb{1}\}$ and the strict partial order $\rhd$ illustrated by Fig. 1b (solid arrows represent $\rhd$). The weights of $\mathbb{L}$ are assigned to the assertions of $\mathcal{A}_\rhd$, as illustrated by Fig. 1a. The obtained partially preordered ABox is denoted by $\mathcal{A}_\rhd$.

Assertions	Weights
$\varphi_1 = \mathsf{Dean(Alice)}$	u_1
$\varphi_2 = \mathsf{FullProf(Bob)}$	u_2
$\varphi_3 = \mathsf{Prof(Bob)}$	u_3
$\varphi_4 = \mathsf{PostDoc(Bob)}$	u_4
$\varphi_5 = \mathsf{VisitingProf(Bob)}$	u_5

(a) Assertions of $\mathcal{A}_\rhd$

(b) The relation $\rhd$ over U

Fig. 1. The ABox $\mathcal{A}_\rhd$: solid arrows represent strict preference.

A key idea for reasoning with partially ordered information is to extend the partial order into a family of total orders. Each total order preserves the strict relations of the original total order and resolves each incomparability into a strict total preference. Symbolic weights from the uncertainty scale $\mathbb{L}$ are then replaced with numerical values in the interval $]0, 1]$. This family of total orders induces a corresponding family of totally preordered ABoxes, denoted $(\mathcal{A}_{>1}, \ldots, \mathcal{A}_{>m})$, said to be compatible with the partially preordered ABox $\mathcal{A}_{\triangleright}$. Formally:

$$\forall(\varphi_i, w_i), (\varphi_j, w_j) \in \mathcal{A}_{>k}, \text{ if } \varphi_i \triangleright \varphi_j \text{ then } w_i > w_j. \text{ where } w_i, w_j \in]0, 1]$$

The number of numerical values used to replace the symbolic weights from the interval $]0, 1]$ is infinite. However, it suffices to consider only a finite number of extensions—namely, those that induce distinct total orderings. Indeed, if two different distributions of weights over formulas induce the same order, they lead to equivalent repairs and thus can be regarded as indistinguishable in this respect.

After generating all compatible totally preordered ABoxes, one can compute the possibilistic repair $\mathcal{R}(\mathcal{A}_{>i})$ for each of them. This process can be further improved by intersecting the deductive closures of these repairs, rather than the repairs themselves. This yields a more productive (i.e., larger) repair [23]. The procedure for obtaining such a productive repair is as follows:

1. Extend the partial order $\triangleright$ over U to obtain a family of total orders, inducing a set of totally preordered ABoxes $(\mathcal{A}_{>1}, \ldots, \mathcal{A}_{>m})$ compatible with $\mathcal{A}_{\triangleright}$.
2. For each compatible ABox $\mathcal{A}_{>i}$, compute its possibilistic repair $\mathcal{R}(\mathcal{A}_{>i})$.
3. Compute the deductive closure of each repair $cl(\mathcal{R}(\mathcal{A}_{>i}))$.

Definition 3. *The closure-based partially preordered possibilistic repair of $\mathcal{A}_{\triangleright}$, denoted $c\pi(\mathcal{A}_{\triangleright})$, is obtained as follows:*

$$c\pi(\mathcal{A}_{\triangleright}) = \bigcap_{i=1}^{m} \{cl(\mathcal{R}(\mathcal{A}_{>i})) \mid \mathcal{A}_{>i} \text{ is compatible with } \mathcal{A}_{\triangleright}.\}$$

Example 4. We compute the Cπ-repair of the ABox $\mathcal{A}_{\triangleright}$ from Example 1:

$$c\pi(\mathcal{A}_{\triangleright}) = \{\mathsf{Dean(Alice)}, \mathsf{FacMember(Alice)}, \mathsf{Prof(Bob)}, \mathsf{FacMember(Bob)}\}$$

Let $>_1, \ldots, >_m$ be the total order extensions of $\triangleright$. Observe:

- For all $>_i$, $u_1 >_i u_4$ and $u_1 >_i u_5$, so $\mathsf{Dean(Alice)}$ is more certain than the first assertion that makes any $\mathcal{A}_{>i}$ inconsistent, thus $\mathsf{Dean(Alice)} \in \mathcal{R}(\mathcal{A}_{>i})$. In addition, $\mathsf{FacMember(Alice)} \in cl(\mathcal{R}(\mathcal{A}_{>i}))$, so both belong to $c\pi(\mathcal{A}_{\triangleright})$.
- For all $>_i$, $\mathsf{Prof(Bob)} \in \mathcal{R}(\mathcal{A}_{>i})$ or $\mathsf{FullProf(Bob)} \in \mathcal{R}(\mathcal{A}_{>i})$, this is because at least one of $u_2 >_i u_5$ or $u_3 >_i u_4$ holds for any $>_i$. Hence, for all $>_i$, $\mathsf{Prof(Bob)} \in cl(\mathcal{R}(\mathcal{A}_{>i}))$, and $\mathsf{FacMember(Bob)} \in cl(\mathcal{R}(\mathcal{A}_{>i}))$. Therefore, both belong to $c\pi(\mathcal{A}_{\triangleright})$.
- The assertions $\mathsf{FullProf(Bob)}$, $\mathsf{VisitingProf(Bob)}$, and $\mathsf{PostDoc(Bob)}$ are not inferred from $\mathcal{R}(\mathcal{A}_{>i})$ for at least one $>_i$.

The use of closure in Cπ-repair ensures inferring conclusions implicit in all repairs of compatible ABoxes, making it more productive than the unclosed variant [24]. However, extending a partial order into total orders is computationally expensive, as the number of total extensions can grow exponentially.

To address this challenge, we introduce two major improvements. First, we avoid enumerating every total extension of the partial order. Second, we avoid computing the deductive closure for each individual repair. Instead, we perform a single closure operation directly on the initial knowledge base, from which we compute a single repair that fully characterizes the Definition 3.

3 Possibilistic Repairs via Prior Closure of Partial Information: Avoiding Total Enumeration

3.1 How to Deductively Close a Partially Preordered ABox?

As previously introduced, deductive closure can be applied in two ways when reasoning with flat (unordered), totally ordered, or partially ordered ABoxes. One approach, used in the definition of $C\pi$-repair (Definition 3), applies the standard DL-Lite$_\mathcal{R}$ closure to each repair derived from a total order extending the original partial preference. This approach does not require any adaptation of the standard definition of closure, since the repairs are flat (unordered) or totally ordered.

Alternatively, closure can be applied directly to the initial ABox before completing any repairs; this is the approach followed in this article. However, this raises an important question: unlike repairs, the initial ABox is partially ordered, and the standard notion of closure cannot be directly applied. In particular, an assertion may be inferred in multiple ways, each associated with different weights, making it unclear how to assign a single weight to the inferred assertion.

For example, consider the TBox $\mathcal{T}_p = $ Prof $\sqsubseteq$ FacMember, Dean $\sqsubseteq$ FacMember and the ABox $\mathcal{A} = $ (Dean$(jean), u_1)$, (Prof$(jean), u_2)$. Jean is both a professor and a dean, each with an uncertain weight (u_1 or u_2). Since both roles imply being a faculty member, we can infer FacMember(jean) from either assertion. The key question is: what reliability degree should be assigned to this inferred assertion? In standard possibilistic logic under a total order, the natural choice is the maximum of the two degrees, resulting in a unique value. But with only a partial order, selecting a unique degree is not straightforward, complicating reasoning and motivating the need for adapted closure definitions.

In a partially ordered setting, u_1 and u_2 may be incomparable, so no unique maximum applies. Both weights must be retained, each independently supporting the assertion without preference. Thus, the deductive closure of a partially ordered ABox cannot assign a single weight to each assertion. Instead, it yields an extended ABox where inferred assertions may carry sets of weights, reflecting multiple, possibly incomparable justifications. Assigning subsets of the partially ordered set U to assertions defines a new uncertainty scale comparing them. This scale is given by $\mathbb{L}^U = (2^U, \rhd^{\max})$, where the order $\rhd^{\max}$ is defined as follows:

$$\forall \mathcal{X}, \mathcal{Y} \subseteq U, \quad \mathcal{X} \rhd^{\max} \mathcal{Y} \text{ iff } \forall u_j \in \mathcal{Y}, \exists u_i \in \mathcal{X} \text{ such that } u_i \rhd u_j$$

Since $\rhd$ is a strict order relation, one can easily check that $\rhd^{\max}$ is also an irreflexive and transitive order relation between subsets of U.

The following definition introduces the *partially preordered deductive closure* of a partially preordered ABox $\mathcal{A}_{\rhd}$ using the uncertainty scale $\mathbb{L}^{\cup}$.

Definition 4. *Let $\mathcal{T}_p$ denote the set of positive inclusion axioms of $\mathcal{T}$. The partially preordered deductive closure of $\mathcal{A}_{\rhd}$ w.r.t $\mathcal{T}$ is defined as:*

$$cl_{\rhd}(\mathcal{A}_{\rhd}) = \{(\varphi, \mathsf{U}(\varphi)) \mid \varphi \text{ is an assertion and } \mathsf{U}(\varphi) \neq \emptyset\}$$

where, for any assertion φ, $\mathsf{U}(\varphi)$ is the set of weights associated with its derivations, defined as:

$$\mathsf{U}(\varphi) = \{u_i \in \mathsf{U} \mid \exists (\varphi_i, u_i) \in \mathcal{A}_{\rhd} \text{ such that } \langle \mathcal{T}_p, \{\varphi_i\} \rangle \vDash \varphi\}$$

If there is no support for φ in $\mathcal{A}_{\rhd}$, then $\mathsf{U}(\varphi) = \emptyset$.

Note that, to align with the standard closure of Definition 2, each assertion φ is either a concept assertion $B(a)$ or a role assertion $R(a, b)$, where B and R are a concept and a role name in $\mathcal{T}$, and a, b are individuals mentioned in $\mathcal{A}_{\rhd}$. Furthermore, since DL-Lite$_{\mathcal{R}}$ does not allow for conjunction in TBox axioms, the minimal set to derive any assertion contains one assertion at most [24]. Note also that if two assertions φ_i and φ_j are such that $\langle \mathcal{T}_p, \{\varphi_i\} \rangle \vDash \varphi_j$, then all the weights supporting φ_i also support φ_j; that is, $\mathsf{U}(\varphi_i) \subseteq \mathsf{U}(\varphi_j)$.

Example 5. Let us apply the partially preordered closure on $\mathcal{A}_{\rhd}$ from Example 3. The TBox's positive inclusion axioms $\mathcal{T}_p$ are:

$$\mathcal{T}_p = \{1.\ \mathsf{FullProf} \sqsubseteq \mathsf{Prof} \quad 2.\ \mathsf{Prof} \sqsubseteq \mathsf{FacMember} \quad 3.\ \mathsf{Dean} \sqsubseteq \mathsf{FacMember}\}$$

The partially preordered closure of $\mathcal{A}_{\rhd}$ is given by:

$$cl_{\rhd}(\mathcal{A}_{\rhd}) = \left\{ \begin{array}{ll} (\mathsf{Dean}(\mathsf{Alice}), \{u_1\}), & (\mathsf{FullProf}(\mathsf{Bob}), \{u_2\}), \\ (\mathsf{Prof}(\mathsf{Bob}), \{u_2, u_3\}), & (\mathsf{PostDoc}(\mathsf{Bob}), \{u_4\}), \\ (\mathsf{VisitingProf}(\mathsf{Bob}), \{u_5\}), & (\mathsf{FacMember}(\mathsf{Alice}), \{u_1\}), \\ (\mathsf{FacMember}(\mathsf{Bob}), \{u_2, u_3\}) \end{array} \right\}$$

3.2   The Cπ-Acceptance Method

To fully leverage the structure of partially ordered knowledge bases, we propose a new characterisation of Cπ-repair that starts with the partially preordered deductive closure defined in Definition 4. The key idea is the following: an assertion should only be accepted if it is consistent with all the information that is at least as reliable as itself, meaning assertions that are strictly more certain, equally certain, or incomparable. In this framework, each inferred assertion φ is annotated with the set of weights $\mathsf{U}(\varphi)$ it receives through the closure $cl_{\rhd}(\mathcal{A}_{\rhd})$.

Instead of verifying consistency with the entire ABox, we narrow the scope to a relevant subset: those assertions whose weights are not strictly less reliable than any weight in $\mathsf{U}(\varphi)$. In other words, we test whether φ conflicts with what is already known and sufficiently trusted. If such a conflict arises, the assertion must be discarded from the $C\pi$-repair. To make this selection possible, we refine the $\rhd^{\max}$ relation to compare a set of weights $\mathsf{U}(\varphi_i) \subseteq \mathsf{U}$ with a singleton $\{u_j\}$, where $u_j \in \mathsf{U}$. The comparison is defined as follows:

$$\mathsf{U}(\varphi_i) \rhd^{\max} \{u_j\} \iff \exists u_i \in \mathsf{U}(\varphi_i) \text{ such that } u_i \rhd u_j$$

This helps us identify assertions that are strictly less certain than a given assertion $(\varphi_i, \mathsf{U}(\varphi_i)) \in cl_\rhd(\mathcal{A}_\rhd)$ and exclude them from the consistency checking.

Definition 5. *Let $(\varphi_i, \mathsf{U}(\varphi_i))$ be an assertion from $cl_\rhd(\mathcal{A}_\rhd)$. The set of assertions that are strictly less certain than φ_i is defined as:*

$$\mathsf{SLT}(\varphi_i) = \{\varphi_j \mid (\varphi_j, u_j) \in \mathcal{A}_\rhd \text{ and } \mathsf{U}(\varphi_i) \rhd^{\max} \{u_j\}\}$$

The complementary set containing assertions not strictly less certain than φ_i is:

$$\Delta(\varphi_i) = \mathcal{A}_\rhd \setminus \mathsf{SLT}(\varphi_i)$$

We now introduce the crucial notion of $c\pi$-*acceptance*, which plays a key role in characterizing whether an inferred assertion belongs to the $c\pi(\mathcal{A}_\rhd)$, the closed possibilistic repair given by Definition 3.:

Definition 6. *An assertion $(\varphi_i, \mathsf{U}(\varphi_i)) \in cl_\rhd(\mathcal{A}_\rhd)$ is said to be $c\pi$-accepted if and only if the pair $\langle \mathcal{T}, \Delta(\varphi_i) \rangle$ is consistent.*

This definition is fundamental, as it reduces the problem of checking whether an inferred assertion belongs to the intersection of the closures of all repairs to a simple consistency check. Hence, the $C\pi$-repair of a partially preordered ABox $\mathcal{A}_\rhd$ can be computed by applying Definition 6 to all assertions in $cl_\rhd(\mathcal{A}_\rhd)$ and collecting those that are $c\pi$-accepted.

Example 6. Let us now apply the $c\pi$-acceptance characterisation of Definition 6 on the partially preordered closed ABox of Example 5. For each assertion φ_i, we use its set of weights $\mathsf{U}(\varphi_i)$ to exhibit $\Delta(\varphi_i)$, on which a consistency test is performed. The test result is indicated using ($\checkmark$) if successful and ($\times$) otherwise.

$\varphi_1 = \mathsf{Dean}(\mathsf{Alice})$,	$\mathsf{U}(\varphi_1) = \{u_1\}$,	$\Delta(\varphi_1) = \{\varphi_1, \varphi_2, \varphi_3\}$,	$\checkmark$
$\varphi_2 = \mathsf{FullProf}(\mathsf{Bob})$,	$\mathsf{U}(\varphi_2) = \{u_2\}$,	$\Delta(\varphi_2) = \{\varphi_1, \varphi_2, \varphi_3, \varphi_5\}$,	$\times$
$\varphi_3 = \mathsf{Prof}(\mathsf{Bob})$,	$\mathsf{U}(\varphi_3) = \{u_2, u_3\}$,	$\Delta(\varphi_3) = \{\varphi_1, \varphi_2, \varphi_3\}$,	$\checkmark$
$\varphi_4 = \mathsf{PostDoc}(\mathsf{Bob})$,	$\mathsf{U}(\varphi_4) = \{u_4\}$,	$\Delta(\varphi_4) = \{\varphi_1, \varphi_2, \varphi_3, \varphi_4, \varphi_5\}$,	$\times$
$\varphi_5 = \mathsf{VisitingProf}(\mathsf{Bob})$,	$\mathsf{U}(\varphi_5) = \{u_5\}$,	$\Delta(\varphi_5) = \{\varphi_1, \varphi_2, \varphi_3, \varphi_4, \varphi_5\}$,	$\times$
$\varphi_6 = \mathsf{FacMember}(\mathsf{Alice})$,	$\mathsf{U}(\varphi_6) = \{u_1\}$,	$\Delta(\varphi_6) = \{\varphi_1, \varphi_2, \varphi_3\}$,	$\checkmark$
$\varphi_7 = \mathsf{FacMember}(\mathsf{Bob})$,	$\mathsf{U}(\varphi_7) = \{u_2, u_3\}$,	$\Delta(\varphi_7) = \{\varphi_1, \varphi_2, \varphi_3\}$,	$\checkmark$

Successful consistency checks mean $c\pi$-acceptance, one can see that the set of the $c\pi$-accepted assertions is equivalent to $c\pi(\mathcal{A}_\rhd)$ computed in Example 4.

The following proposition shows that, indeed, the repair obtained by checking $c\pi$-acceptance of every assertion in the partially preordered closure of a partially preordered knowledge base is equivalent to the $C\pi$-repair given in Definition 3.

Proposition 1. *An assertion φ is accepted using the $c\pi$-acceptance approach, as per Definition 6, if and only if $\varphi \in c\pi(\mathcal{A}_\rhd)$, as per Definition 3.*

This above proposition offers two major advantages. First, it avoids the need to enumerate all possible extensions of the partially preordered ABox. Second, it eliminates the necessity of computing the closure for each individual repair associated with those extensions. Instead, the closure is computed once, globally, over the initial structure, relying only on the weighted subsets associated with each inferred assertion. Figure 2 illustrates the process of computing the $C\pi$-repair alongside the equivalence with the new characterisation.

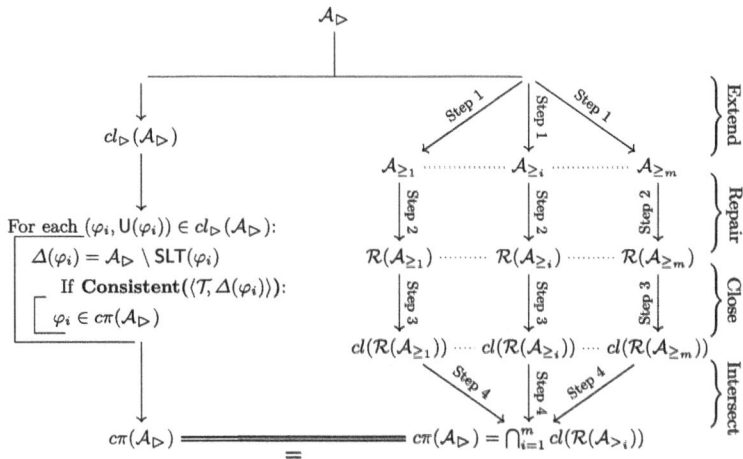

Fig. 2. $c\pi$-acceptance vs. the process of computing the $C\pi$-repair

In DL-Lite$_\mathcal{R}$, consistency checking is performed in AC^0 with respect to data complexity [1,16]. Consistency testing is a crucial task in our approach, as each assertion must be checked for consistency against relevant subsets of the knowledge base. Each individual consistency test is in AC^0. The overall repair computation process, which involves iterating over all assertions and verifying their consistency, remains polynomial and tractable. The following proposition formalises the computation of the complete repair in polynomial time.

Proposition 2. *The computation of the set of assertions $(\varphi, \mathsf{U}(\varphi)) \in cl_\rhd(\mathcal{A}_\rhd)$ that are $c\pi$-accepted is achieved in polynomial time, in accordance with the data complexity of DL-Lite$_\mathcal{R}$.*

Before turning to the experimental evaluation, we briefly outline a possible semantic characterisation of inference under inconsistency and partial priority in ABoxes. This is intended as a preliminary sketch rather than a complete treatment; a more detailed exploration of such semantic foundations is left for future work. Here, we simply introduce the key ingredients that could underlie the semantics of possibilistic repairs.

In the standard setting, where the ABox is consistent and no priority is specified, DL-Lite semantics relies on the classical model/countermodel distinction: an interpretation is a model if it satisfies both the TBox $\mathcal{T}$ and the ABox $\mathcal{A}$, and a countermodel otherwise. This dichotomy can be captured using a binary plausibility scale, where models are assigned value 1 and countermodels 0.

However, when the ABox is inconsistent and equipped with a partial preorder $\leq_{\mathcal{A}}$ (or $\rhd_{\mathcal{A}}$) over its assertions, representing priority or certainty, this binary view becomes inadequate. To account for varying degrees of plausibility, we use again the graded uncertainty scale $\mathcal{U} = \{0, u_1, \ldots, u_n, 1\}$, where 0 represents complete impossibility and 1 represents full plausibility. This approach echoes preferential semantics commonly used in non-monotonic reasoning.

Each interpretation $\mathcal{I}$ is then evaluated based on how it satisfies the TBox and (partially ordered) ABox. If $\mathcal{I} \not\models \mathcal{T}$, or it violates an assertion φ such that weight(φ) $= 1$, it receives 0. If it satisfies both $\mathcal{T}$ and all assertions in $\mathcal{A}$, it receives 1. Otherwise, it receives a set of values $\{u_i \in \mathcal{U} \mid \mathcal{I} \not\models \varphi$ for some $(\varphi, u_i) \in \mathcal{A}\}$, reflecting the uncertainty degrees of the violated assertions.

This gives rise to a partial possibility distribution $\sigma : \Omega \rightarrow 2^{\mathcal{U}}$, where Ω is the set of interpretations. Interpretations are then compared based on the plausibility sets assigned by σ, using a minimality relation (such as the $\rhd^{\max}$ ordering introduced earlier). The preferred interpretations $\mathcal{P}(\mathcal{T}, \mathcal{A})$ are those for which no strictly more plausible interpretation exists, namely interpretations $\mathcal{I}$ such that there is no $\mathcal{I}'$ with $\sigma(\mathcal{I}') > \sigma(\mathcal{I})$. These preferred interpretations, which comply with the TBox and are as consistent as possible with the partially ordered ABox, are then used as the semantic basis for answering queries: a query answer is considered valid if it is satisfied by all preferred interpretations.

4   Experimental Evaluation

We implemented our method in python, using the py_reasoner tool. This tool integrates a PostgreSQL back-end for ABox storage, the RDFLib library to enable efficient access to OWL ontologies in memory, and the Rapid query rewriting engine to rewrite queries related to conflicts and assertion supports.

4.1   Experimental Setting

TBox. We used the latest version of the DBpedia ontology [25], which is populated via mappings from Wikipedia infoboxes. To preserve its original structure, we employed interfacing methods for axiom retrieval and query rewriting restricted to DL-Lite$_{\mathcal{R}}$ axioms. The ontology includes negative inclusion axioms over classes and object properties, consistent with the DL-Lite$_{\mathcal{R}}$ syntax. The TBox contains 34,653 axioms, including 27 explicit negative inclusions, resulting in a total of 614,670 implicit and explicit negative inclusion axioms.

Datasets. We built ABoxes from DBpedia RDF type statements and object relations, supplemented with LHD inferred types from an earlier version of the ontology [25]. The latter includes unclean inferred types, making it well suited for inconsistency experiments. We extracted subsets with progressively increasing ABox and conflict set sizes. Table 1 details the ABoxes used in our evaluation.

Table 1. ABoxes in terms of: size, percentage of assertions in conflicts, number of conflicts, and time to compute the conflict set, size of the deductive closure, time to compute the standard closure, and the partially ordered closure.

ABox ($\mathcal{A}$)	$\#\mathcal{A}$	$\%\mathsf{Cf}(\mathcal{A})$	$\#\mathsf{Cf}(\mathcal{A})$	$\mathsf{Cf}(\mathcal{A})(s)$	$\#cl(\mathcal{A})$	$cl(\mathcal{A})(s)$	$cl_\rhd(\mathcal{A})(s)$
dbr_n1e03_p5e-02	1k	8.3	72	59.29	3833	3.0	2.98
dbr_n1e03_p3e-01	1k	32.7	794	60.05	4716	2.87	3.05
dbr_n1e03_p5e-01	1k	52.4	1643	60.34	5248	3.0	2.94
dbr_n1e04_p5e-02	10k	7.03	1782	62.15	34968	2.73	3.58
dbr_n1e04_p3e-01	10k	32.36	28098	64.95	42691	3.01	3.34
dbr_n1e04_p5e-01	10k	51.56	51495	63.06	49535	3.31	3.3
dbr_n5e04_p5e-02	50k	10.68	25643	69.6	175376	2.88	4.38
dbr_n5e04_p3e-01	50k	33.02	230548	74.6	210992	3.38	6.76
dbr_n5e04_p5e-01	50k	51.79	397370	67.36	238008	3.63	7.07

We defined a partial preorder $\rhd$ over ABox assertions using three criteria. The first two rely on timestamps: derivationTimestamp from DBpedia and wikiTimestamp from Wikidata (via the Wikipedia API), both ordered by recency. The third labels assertions by their source RDF (preferred) or LHD (less preferred). These yield orders $>_\mathsf{dts}$, $>_\mathsf{wts}$, and $>_\mathsf{src}$, such that $\varphi \rhd \varphi'$ if:

$$\varphi >_\mathsf{dts} \varphi' \text{ or } \varphi >_\mathsf{wts} \varphi' \text{ or } \varphi >_\mathsf{src} \varphi' \wedge \neg(\varphi' >_\mathsf{dts} \varphi \text{ or } \varphi' >_\mathsf{wts} \varphi \text{ or } \varphi' >_\mathsf{src} \varphi)$$

The evaluation compares the performance of the new characterisation from Definition 6 with the earlier "dominant supports" method introduced in [24].

4.2   Experimental Results

We implemented the dominant supports characterisation as follows. We first compute the conflict set of the ABox. Then, for each assertion in $cl(\mathcal{A}_\rhd)$ (Definition 2), we compute its support sets, each linear in ABox size. Finally, we check that every conflict has at least one dominant support per assertion.

The new characterisation starts by computing the partially preordered closure, then checks consistency for each assertion with those not strictly less certain. This check can be done in two ways. The first uses a SQL query that detects violations of TBox negative inclusion axioms, ignoring those involving assertions less certain than the one checked. Since SQL involves I/O operations, the second runs in memory using the conflict set, identifying violations where no assertion is strictly less certain. We used the latter for weakly conflicting ABoxes, where the conflict set fits in memory.

Our experiments demonstrate the stable performance of the "$c\pi$-acceptance" method compared to the so-called "dominant supports" method in computing the $C\pi$-repair. Figure 3 [left, middle] plots running times across ABox sizes, grouped by percentage of conflicting assertions. The new method is at least $2\times$ faster on small ABoxes (1k), $10\times$ on medium (10k), and over $40\times$ on large (50k). As both methods process each assertion in the deductive closure, we also plotted repair time against closure size in Fig. 3 [right]. While "dominant supports" slows down with larger closures, the new method remains stable.

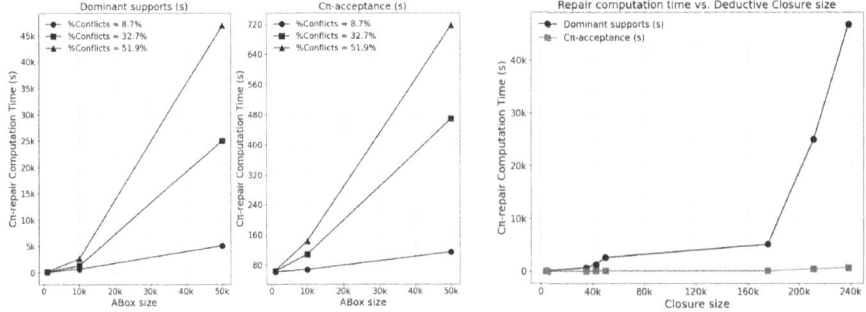

Fig. 3. Comparison of $C\pi$-repair Computation Time using (2) Characterisations.

Discussion. The experimental evaluation highlights the efficiency and scalability of the proposed method. In particular, computing the $C\pi$-repair via the partially preordered closure avoids the exhaustive search over support sets required by the "dominant supports" method. While applying the deductive closure is inherently costly, especially under partial orders, our method mitigates this by limiting consistency checks to relevant assertion subsets. The results show that it scales gracefully with both the ABox size and the closure size, delivering substantial time savings even in large and highly conflicting datasets. This demonstrates the practical advantage of relying on a more targeted and order-aware closure.

5   Conclusion

A natural semantics for handling inconsistent and partially ordered ontologies is to consider the family of total order extensions of the partial order. However, this approach is computationally expensive, as the number of such extensions grows exponentially. In this paper, we tackled the issue of efficiently computing a productive repair for partially preordered DL-Lite$_\mathcal{R}$ ABoxes by introducing a new partially preordered closure operator and by pushing the repair computation to the most basic reasoning task: consistency checking. One of the main strengths of our approach lies in applying deductive closure directly to the initial partially preordered ABox, before any repair computation. Unlike previous approaches, this early application does not introduce unwanted consequences nor degrade the quality of the repairs. On the contrary, it allows us to preserve tractability by reducing the problem to consistency checks over subsets of the closed ABox. This closure-based process yields the same repairs as those obtained by computing and then closing all compatible total order extensions of the ABox, but in a much more efficient manner. We show the efficiency of this method particularly through comparisons with previous approaches that rely on exhaustive searches over the conflict sets of the ABox and the support sets of assertions.

Future work includes extending the closure-based approach and its associated tractability guarantees to more expressive logical languages.

Acknowledgments. This research was supported by the European Union's Horizon research and innovation programme under the MSCA-SE (Marie Skłodowska-Curie Actions Staff Exchange); Call: HORIZON-MSCA-2021-SE-01; Project title: STAR-WARS (STormwAteR and WastewAteR networkS heterogeneous data AI-driven management) [grant agreement 101086252]. A. Laouar's PhD is supported by the ANR project Vivah (Vers une intelligence artificielle à visage humain) [grant number ANR-20-THIA-0004]. This research has also received support from the ANR project EXPIDA (EXplainable and parsimonious Preference models to get the most out of Inconsistent DAtabases), [grant number ANR-22-CE23-0017]. The second author has also received support from the French national project ANR (Agence Nationale de la Recherche) CROQUIS (Collecte, représentation, complétion, fusion et interrogation de données hétérogènes et incertaines de réseaux d'eaux urbains). Finally, we thank the anonymous referees for their valuable feedback on this paper.

References

1. Artale, A., Calvanese, D., Kontchakov, R., Zakharyaschev, M.: The DL-Lite family and relations. J. Artif. Intell. Res. (JAIR) **36**, 1–69 (2009)
2. Baader, F., Koopmann, P., Kriegel, F., Nuradiansyah, A.: Computing optimal repairs of quantified ABoxes wrt static el TBoxes. In: CADE, pp. 309–326 (2021)
3. Baget, J.F., et al.: Inconsistency-tolerant query answering: rationality properties and computational complexity analysis. In: Michael, L., Kakas, A. (eds.) JELIA 2016. LNCS (LNAI), vol. 10021, pp. 64–80. Springer, Cham (2016). https://doi.org/10.1007/978-3-319-48758-8_5
4. Banerjee, M., Dubois, D., Godo, L., Prade, H.: On the relation between possibilistic logic and modal logics of belief and knowledge. J. Appl. Non-Classical Logics **27**(3–4), 206–224 (2017)
5. Baral, C., Kraus, S., Minker, J., Subrahmanian, V.S.: Combining knowledge bases consisting of first-order theories. Comput. Intell. **8**(1), 45–71 (1992)
6. Belabbes, S., Benferhat, S.: Computing a possibility theory repair for partially preordered inconsistent ontologies. IEEE Trans. Fuzzy Syst., 1–10 (2021)
7. Belabbes, S., Benferhat, S., Chomicki, J.: Handling inconsistency in partially preordered ontologies: the Elect method. J. Log. Comput. **31**(5), 1356–1388 (2021)
8. Benferhat, S., Bouraoui, Z.: Min-based possibilistic DL-Lite. J. Log. Comput. **27**(1), 261–297 (2017)

9. Benferhat, S., Bouraoui, Z., Tabia, K.: How to select one preferred Assertional-based repair from inconsistent and prioritized DL-Lite knowledge bases? In: International Joint Conference on Artificial Intelligence (IJCAI), Buenos Aires, Argentina, pp. 1450–1456 (2015)

10. Benferhat, S., Garcia, L.: Handling locally stratified inconsistent knowledge bases. Stud. Logica. **70**(1), 77–104 (2002)

11. Bertossi, L.E.: Database Repairing and Consistent Query Answering. Synthesis Lectures on Data Management Morgan & Claypool Publishers (2011)

12. Bienvenu, M.: On the complexity of consistent query answering in the presence of simple ontologies. In: Proceedings of the AAAI Conference on Artificial Intelligence, vol. 26, pp. 705–711 (2012)

13. Bienvenu, M., Bourgaux, C.: Inconsistency-tolerant querying of description logic knowledge bases. In: Reasoning Web: Logical Foundation of Knowledge Graph Construction and Query Answering, vol. 9885, pp. 156–202. LNCS. Springer (2016)

14. Bienvenu, M., Bourgaux, C., Goasdoué, F.: Querying inconsistent description logic knowledge bases under preferred repair semantics. In: Proceedings of the AAAI Conference on Artificial Intelligence, vol. 28, pp. 996–1002 (2014)

15. Brewka, G.: Preferred subtheories: an extended logical framework for default reasoning. In: IJCAI, Detroit, USA, pp. 1043–1048 (1989)

16. Calvanese, D., De Giacomo, G., Lembo, D., Lenzerini, M., Rosati, R.: Tractable reasoning and efficient query answering in description logics: the DL-Lite family. J. Autom. Reason. **39**(3), 385–429 (2007)

17. Dubois, D., Prade, H.: Possibility Theory: Qualitative and Quantitative Aspects, chap. 6, pp. 169–226. Springer Netherlands, Dordrecht (1998)

18. Dubois, D., Prade, H.: Possibilistic logic - an overview. Comput. Logic **9**, 197–255 (2014)

19. Dubois, D., Prade, H.: A crash course on generalized possibilistic logic. In: Ciucci, D., Pasi, G., Vantaggi, B. (eds.) SUM 2018. LNCS (LNAI), vol. 11142, pp. 3–17. Springer, Cham (2018). https://doi.org/10.1007/978-3-030-00461-3_1

20. Esteva, F., Figallo-Orellano, A., Flaminio, T., Godo, L.: Logics of formal inconsistency based on distributive involutive residuated lattices. J. Log. Comput. **31**(5), 1226–1265 (2021)

21. Finkelstein, A.C., Gabbay, D., Hunter, A., Kramer, J., Nuseibeh, B.: Inconsistency handling in multiperspective specifications. IEEE Trans. Software Eng. **20**(8), 569–578 (1994)

22. Haase, P., van Harmelen, F., Huang, Z., Stuckenschmidt, H., Sure, Y.: A framework for handling inconsistency in changing ontologies. In: Gil, Y., Motta, E., Benjamins, V.R., Musen, M.A. (eds.) ISWC 2005. LNCS, vol. 3729, pp. 353–367. Springer, Heidelberg (2005). https://doi.org/10.1007/11574620_27

23. Laouar, A., Belabbes, S., Benferhat, S.: Tractable closure-based possibilistic repair for partially ordered DL-Lite ontologies. In: European Conference on Logics in Artificial Intelligence, pp. 353–368. Springer (2023)

24. Laouar, A., Belabbes, S., Benferhat, S.: How to tractably compute a productive repair for possibilistic partially ordered dl-liter ontologies? Fuzzy Sets Syst. **510**, 109361 (2025)

25. Lehmann, J., et al.: DBpedia-a large-scale, multilingual knowledge base extracted from Wikipedia. Semantic web **6**(2), 167–195 (2015)

26. Lembo, D., Lenzerini, M., Rosati, R., Ruzzi, M., Savo, D.F.: Inconsistency-tolerant semantics for description logics. In: Hitzler, P., Lukasiewicz, T. (eds.) RR 2010. LNCS, vol. 6333, pp. 103–117. Springer, Heidelberg (2010). https://doi.org/10.1007/978-3-642-15918-3_9

27. Pearl, J.: System Z: a natural ordering of defaults with tractable applications to nonmonotonic reasoning, pp. 201–214. Association for Computing Machinery, New York, NY, USA, 1 edn. (2022)
28. Snow, P.: Diverse confidence levels in a probabilistic semantics for conditional logics. Artif. Intell. **113**(1–2), 269–279 (1999)
29. Staworko, S., Chomicki, J., Marcinkowski, J.: Prioritized repairing and consistent query answering in relational databases. AMAI **64**(2–3), 209–246 (2012)

Higher-order and Non-classical Logics

Strongly First Order Disjunctive Embedded Dependencies in Team Semantics

Pietro Galliani$^{(\boxtimes)}$ (iD)

Università degli Studi dell'Insubria, Via J.H. Dunant, 3, 21100 Varese, Italy
pietro.galliani@uninsubria.it

Abstract. First Order Team Semantics is a generalization of Tarskian Semantics in which formulas are satisfied with respect to sets of assignments. In Team Semantics, it is possible to extend First Order Logic via new types of atoms that describe dependencies between variables; some of these extensions are strictly more expressive than First Order Logic, while others are reducible to it.

Many of the atoms studied in Team Semantics are inspired by Database Theory and belong in particular to the class of Disjunctive Embedded Dependencies, a very general family of dependencies that contains most of the dependencies of practical interest in the study of databases.

In this work, I provide a characterization for the (domain-independent) Disjunctive Embedded Dependencies that fail to increase the expressive power of First-Order Team Semantics when added to it.

Keywords: Team Semantics · Non-Classical Logic · Higher-Order Logic

1 Introduction

First Order Team Semantics [16] is a generalization of Tarski's semantics in which formulas are satisfied by sets of assignments, called *Teams*, rather than by single assignments. This semantics is reducible to Tarskian Semantics and associates the same truth conditions to first order sentences; but, beginning with Väänänen's work on functional dependence atoms [21], Team Semantics was recognized as a natural framework for extending First Order Logic via additional atoms that specify dependencies between the possible values of variables.

Some of the specific logics thus generated, first and foremost Väänänen's Dependence Logic, have been examined in some depth by now; however, many fundamental questions about the collective properties of this family of extensions of First Order Logic remain open.

In particular, some atoms, like for instance functional dependence atoms, when added to First Order Logic (**FO**) bring the expressive power of the resulting formalism all the way up to that of Existential Second Order Logic (**ESO**) [21];

G. Casini et al. (Eds.): JELIA 2025, LNAI 16093, pp. 259–274, 2026.
https://doi.org/10.1007/978-3-032-04587-4_16

others, like inclusion atoms, yield logics whose expressive power is intermediate between **FO** and **ESO** [13]; and others yet, like constancy and nonemptiness atoms, fail to increase the expressive power of **FO** at all [6].

An effective classification of which dependencies (or combinations thereof) belong to these three categories would be quite helpful in clarifying the possibilities of Team Semantics and put some order in the family of the extensions of First Order Logic that can be generated through it, as a first step towards a general-purpose framework that would ideally allow us, given any family of dependencies, to predict at once the characteristics of the logic that they generate.

Some characterizations are known for the dependencies that fail to increase the expressive power of **FO** (that is to say, that are "strongly first order") **and** satisfy certain *closure conditions*; however, no such result is yet known for a family of dependencies that is broad enough to include all (or at least most) the dependencies studied so far in Team Semantics and that is natural enough to be of independent interest.

The main contribution of the present work is a characterization of the strongly first order dependencies in the class of (domain-independent) *Disjunctive Embedded Dependencies* (DEDs), which is well known from Database Theory [17] and indeed contains most dependencies studied so far in Team Semantics.

As a consequence of this characterization, we will also see that a family of domain-independent DEDs, if added collectively to **FO**, increases its expressive power if and only if at least one DED in this family does so individually: in other words, if $\mathbf{D}_1 \ldots \mathbf{D}_n$ are strongly first order domain-independent DEDs then the logic obtained by adding them all to **FO** is still equiexpressive to **FO**.

2   Preliminaries

Notation

We write $\mathfrak{A}$, $\mathfrak{B}$, $\mathfrak{C}$, ..., $\mathfrak{M}$ to indicate first order models, and A, B, C, ... M for their repective domains. Given a relation symbol R, we write $R^{\mathfrak{M}}$ for the interpretation of R in the model $\mathfrak{M}$; and given a constant symbol c, we likewise write $c^{\mathfrak{M}}$ for its interpretation in $\mathfrak{M}$. Where no ambiguity is possible we identify symbols with the relations and elements that they represent, e.g. we write $\mathfrak{M} = (M, R, a)$ for the first order model with domain M such that $R^{\mathfrak{M}} = R \subseteq M^k$ and $a^{\mathfrak{M}} = a \in M$. Given two models $\mathfrak{A}$ and $\mathfrak{B}$, we write $\mathfrak{A} \preceq \mathfrak{B}$ to say that $\mathfrak{B}$ is an elementary extension of $\mathfrak{A}$, and $\mathfrak{A} \equiv \mathfrak{B}$ if $\mathfrak{A}$ and $\mathfrak{B}$ are elementarily equivalent.

Given an assignment s from a set of variables V to a domain A, an element $a \in A$ and a variable $v \in V$, we write $s[a/v]$ for the result of assigning a to v in s. If $\vec{v} = v_1 \ldots v_k$ is a tuple of variables, we will write $s(\vec{v})$ for the tuple of elements $s(v_1) \ldots s(v_k)$. If $\vec{a} = a_1 \ldots a_k$ is a tuple of elements, we write $\text{Rng}(\vec{a}) = \bigcup_{i=1}^k a_i$ for the set of all elements occurring in $\vec{a}$; and we say that a tuple of elements $\vec{b}^{(1)}$ is *disjoint* from a tuple $\vec{b}^{(2)}$ *except on* $\vec{a}$ if $\text{Rng}(\vec{b}^{(1)}) \cap \text{Rng}(\vec{b}^{(2)}) \subseteq \text{Rng}(\vec{a})$. Likewise, we say that a tuple $\vec{b}$ is disjoint from a set A except on a tuple $\vec{a}$ if $\text{Rng}(\vec{b}) \cap A \subseteq \text{Rng}(\vec{a})$. We say that a tuple $\vec{a}$ *lists* (or *is a list of*) a finite set A

if $\vec{a}$ has no repetitions and $\mathrm{Rng}(\vec{a}) = A$. Given a model $\mathfrak{M}$, a first order formula ϕ, and an assignment s whose domain contains the free variables of ϕ, we write $\mathfrak{M} \models_s \phi$ to express that s satisfies ϕ in $\mathfrak{M}$ in the ordinary Tarskian sense.

Given a tuple of elements $\vec{a} = a_1 \ldots a_k \in A^k$, its *identity type* is $\tau(x_1 \ldots x_k) := \bigwedge_{a_i = a_j} (x_i = x_j) \wedge \bigwedge_{a_i \neq a_j} (x_i \neq x_j)$.

Given two extensions L_1 and L_2 of First Order Logic, we write $L_1 \leq L_2$ if every sentence of L_1 is equivalent to some sentence of L_2; $L_1 \equiv L_2$ if $L_1 \leq L_2$ and $L_2 \leq L_1$; and $L_1 < L_2$ if $L_1 \leq L_2$ but $L_2 \not\leq L_1$. **FO** represents First Order Logic itself, and **ESO** represents Existential Second Order Logic.

Team Semantics

We will now recall the basic definitions and properties of Team Semantics.[1]

Definition 2.1 (Team). *Let $\mathfrak{A}$ be a first order model and let $V \subseteq Var$ be a finite set of variables. A team X over $\mathfrak{A}$ with domain $\boldsymbol{Dom}(X) = V$ is a set of assignments $s : V \to A$. Given a team X and a tuple of variables $\vec{v}$, we write $X(\vec{v})$ for the relation $X(\vec{v}) = \{s(\vec{v}) : s \in X\}$; and given two teams X and Y, we write that $X \equiv_V Y$ if $X(\vec{v}) = Y(\vec{v})$ for a list $\vec{v}$ of V.*

Definition 2.2 (Team Semantics). *Let ϕ be a first order formula in negation normal form,[2] let $\mathfrak{M}$ be a model whose signature contains that of ϕ, and let X be a team over $\mathfrak{M}$ whose domain contains the free variables of ϕ. Then ϕ is satisfied by X in $\mathfrak{M}$, and we write $\mathfrak{M} \models_X \phi$, if this follows from the following rules:*

TS-lit: *If ϕ is a literal, $\mathfrak{M} \models_X \phi \Leftrightarrow \forall s \in X$, $M \models_s \phi$ in Tarskian semantics;*

TS-∨: $\mathfrak{M} \models_X \psi_1 \vee \psi_2 \Leftrightarrow \exists X_1, X_2$ *s.t.* $X = X_1 \cup X_2$, $M \models_{X_1} \psi_1$ *and* $M \models_{X_2} \psi_2$;

TS-∧: $M \models_X \psi_1 \wedge \psi_2 \Leftrightarrow \mathfrak{M} \models_X \psi_1$ *and* $M \models_X \psi_2$;

TS-∃: $M \models_X \exists v \psi \Leftrightarrow \exists Y$ *s.t.* $\boldsymbol{Dom}(Y) = \boldsymbol{Dom}(X) \cup \{v\}$, $Y \equiv_{\boldsymbol{Dom}(X) \setminus \{v\}} X$, *and* $M \models_Y \psi$;

TS-∀: $M \models_X \forall v \psi \Leftrightarrow M \models_{X[M/v]} \psi$, *for* $X[M/v] = \{s[m/v] : s \in X, m \in M\}$.

If ϕ is a sentence, we write that $\mathfrak{M} \models \phi$ (in the sense of Team Semantics) if and only if $\mathfrak{M} \models_{\{\varepsilon\}} \phi$, where ε is the empty assignment.

---

[1] We only consider the more common *"lax"* version of this semantics, corresponding to a non-deterministic form of Game-Theoretic Semantics. There also exists a *"strict"* variant which corresponds in a similar way to a deterministic Game-Theoretic Semantics, but since for that variant the property of *locality* fails to hold in general (that is to say, the satisfaction conditions of a formula may depend on variables that are not free in it: see [5] for a more detailed discussion) it is usually preferred to work with the lax form of Team Semantics.

[2] It is common in the study of Team Semantics to require that all expressions are in Negation Normal Form. This is because, in general, there is no obvious interpretation for the negation of a dependency atom. Additionally, in the context of Team Semantics, the contradictory negation $\mathfrak{M} \models_X \sim \phi \Leftrightarrow \mathfrak{M} \not\models_X \phi$ would bring the expressive power of most logics all the way up to full Second Order Logic [19,21].

When working with First Order Logic proper there is no reason to use Team Semantics rather than the simpler Tarskian Semantics:

Proposition 2.3. ([21], *Corollary 3.32) Let $\mathfrak{M}$ be a model, let ϕ be a first order formula in negation normal form over the signature of $\mathfrak{M}$, and let X be a team over $\mathfrak{M}$. Then $\mathfrak{M} \models_X \phi$ if and only if, for all $s \in X$, $\mathfrak{M} \models_s \phi$ in the usual Tarskian sense. In particular, if ϕ is a first order sentence in negation normal form, $\mathfrak{M} \models \phi$ in Team Semantics if and only if $\mathfrak{M} \models \phi$ in Tarskian Semantics.*

However, Team Semantics allows one to augment First Order Logic in new ways, for example via new *dependence atoms* such as Functional Dependence Atoms [21], Inclusion Atoms [5,13], Independence Atoms [14] or Anonymity Atoms [22]:[3]

TS-func: $\mathfrak{M} \models_X =(\vec{v}; \vec{w}) \Leftrightarrow \forall s, s' \in X$, if $s(\vec{v}) = s'(\vec{v})$ then $s(\vec{w}) = s'(\vec{w})$;
TS-inc: $M \models_X \vec{v} \subseteq \vec{w} \Leftrightarrow X(\vec{v}) \subseteq X(\vec{w})$;
TS-ind: $M \models_X \vec{v} \perp \vec{w} \Leftrightarrow X(\vec{v}\vec{w}) = X(\vec{v}) \times X(\vec{w})$;
TS-anon: $M \models_X \vec{v} \Upsilon \vec{w} \Leftrightarrow \forall s \in X \ \exists s' \in X$ s.t. $s(\vec{v}) = s'(\vec{v})$ but $s(\vec{w}) \neq s'(\vec{w})$.

The logics obtained by adding them to First Order Logic are called respectively Dependence Logic, Inclusion Logic, Independence Logic and Anonymity Logic. In order to study the family of all logics that are obtainable in such a way, it is convenient to use the following notion of *generalized dependency* [20]:

Definition 2.4 (Generalized Dependency). *Let R be a k-ary relation symbol and let $\mathbf{D}$ be a class, closed under isomorphisms, of models over the signature $\{R\}$. Then $\mathbf{D}$ is a k-ary generalized dependency and $\mathbf{FO}(\mathbf{D})$ is the logic obtained by adding to First Order Logic the atoms $\mathbf{D}\vec{v}$ for all k-tuples of variables $\vec{v}$, with the satisfaction conditions*

TS-D: $\mathfrak{M} \models_X \mathbf{D}\vec{v} \Leftrightarrow (M, X(\vec{v})) \in \mathbf{D}$

where $(M, X(\vec{v}))$ is the model with domain M in which R is interpreted as $X(\vec{v})$.

If $\mathcal{D}$ is a family of generalized dependencies, we write $\mathbf{FO}(\mathcal{D})$ for the logic obtained by adding to First Order Logic the atoms corresponding to all $\mathbf{D} \in \mathcal{D}$.

The atoms mentioned above can all be modeled as families of generalized dependencies: for example, Dependence Logic is obtained by adding to First Order Logic all atoms corresponding to generalized dependencies of the form

$$\mathbf{Dep}_{n,m} = \{(M, R) : (M, R) \models \forall \vec{x}\vec{y}\vec{z}(R\vec{x}\vec{y} \wedge R\vec{x}\vec{z} \rightarrow \vec{y} = \vec{z})\} \tag{1}$$

where $n, m \in \mathbb{N}$, $\vec{x}$ has arity n, $\vec{y}$ and $\vec{z}$ have arity m, and as usual $\vec{y} = \vec{z}$ is a shorthand for $\bigwedge_{i=1}^{m} y_i = z_i$. Inclusion atoms, independence atoms and anonymity atoms can be likewise represented via first order sentences as in (1). Thus, they are *first order* dependencies in the following sense:

---

[3] These atoms could be defined so that they can apply to tuples of terms and not only to tuples of variables. Since here we always operate in logics at least as expressive as First Order Logic and we are not restricting existential quantification, for simplicity's sake we limit ourselves to tuples of variables.

Definition 2.5 (First Order Generalized Dependency). *A generalized dependency* **D** *is first order if there exists a first order sentence* **D**(R) *such that* **D** $= \{(M, R) : (M, R) \models \mathbf{D}(R)\}$. *If so, with a slight abuse of notation we identify* **D** *with the sentence* **D**(R).

Definition 2.4 is, however, arguably *too* general. Indeed, it admits "dependencies" like $\mathbf{E} = \{(M, R) : |M| \text{ is even}\}$, whose corresponding satisfaction condition does not ask anything of $X(\vec{v})$ but instead says that the *model* has an even number of elements. This is unreasonable: intuitively, a dependence atom $\mathbf{D}\vec{v}$ should say something about the possible values of $\vec{v}$. This can be formalized as follows:[4]

Definition 2.6 (Domain-Independent Generalized Dependencies). *A k-ary dependency* **D** *is* domain-independent *if, for all domains of discourse M, N and all k-ary relations $R \subseteq M^k \cap N^k$, $(M, R) \in \mathbf{D}$ if and only if $(N, R) \in \mathbf{D}$.*

It is easy to see that, aside from the pathological "dependency" **E** mentioned above, all examples of dependencies that we saw so far are domain-independent.

What can we say, in general, about the properties of a logic of the form **FO**$(\mathcal{D})$? Clearly, it is always the case that **FO** $\leq$ **FO**$(\mathcal{D})$; and if **D** $\in \mathcal{D}$ is not first order then **FO** $<$ **FO**$(\mathcal{D})$, because the **FO**$(\mathcal{D})$ sentence

$$\forall \vec{v}(\neg R\vec{v} \vee (R\vec{v} \wedge \mathbf{D}\vec{v})) \tag{2}$$

defines the class **D**, which by hypothesis is not first-order definable.

However, the converse is not true. As we saw, functional dependence atoms are first order; and yet, (Functional) Dependence Logic is as expressive as Existential Second Order Logic [21]. Inclusion Logic, Independence Logic and Anonymity Logic are likewise more expressive than First Order Logic; but whereas Independence Logic is also as expressive as Existential Second Order Logic [14], Anonymity Logic is equivalent to Inclusion Logic (see Propositions 4.6.3. and 4.6.4. of [4], in which anonymity is called 'non-dependence') and both are only as expressive as the positive fragment of Greatest Fixpoint Logic [13].

Definition 2.7 (Definability of a dependency). *Let $\mathcal{D}$ be a family of dependencies, and let* **E** *be a k-ary dependency. Then* **E** *is definable in* **FO**$(\mathcal{D})$ *if there exist a tuple of k variables $\vec{v} = v_1 \ldots v_k$ and a formula $\phi(\vec{v}) \in$ **FO**$(\mathcal{D})$ over the empty signature such that $\mathfrak{M} \models_X \mathbf{E}\vec{v} \Leftrightarrow \mathfrak{M} \models_X \phi(\vec{v})$ for all $\mathfrak{M}$ and X.*

Proposition 2.8. *Let $\mathcal{D}$ and $\mathcal{E}$ be families of generalized dependencies. If every* **E** $\in \mathcal{E}$ *is definable in* **FO**$(\mathcal{D})$ *then* **FO**$(\mathcal{E}) \leq$ **FO**$(\mathcal{D}) \equiv$ **FO**$(\mathcal{D}, \mathcal{E})$.

It is sometimes useful to "restrict" a team to the assignments that satisfy individually some first order formula, like we did in (2):

Definition 2.9 ($\theta \hookrightarrow \phi$). *Let θ be a first order formula and let ϕ be a* **FO**$(\mathcal{D})$ *formula for some collection $\mathcal{D}$ of generalized dependencies. Then we write $\theta \hookrightarrow \phi$ for the* **FO**$(\mathcal{D})$ *formula $\theta' \vee (\theta \wedge \phi)$, where θ' is the first order formula in Negation Normal Form that is equivalent to $\neg\theta$.*

---

[4] This notion first appeared in [18], in which it is called "Universe Independence".

Proposition 2.10. *For all models* $\mathfrak{M}$, *teams* X, *families of generalized dependencies* $\mathcal{D}$, *first order formulas* θ *and* $\mathbf{FO}(\mathcal{D})$ *formulas* ϕ, $\mathfrak{M} \models_X \theta \hookrightarrow \phi \Leftrightarrow \mathfrak{M} \models_{X_{|\theta}} \phi$ *for* $X_{|\theta} = \{s \in X : \mathfrak{M} \models_s \theta$ *in Tarski semantics*$\}$.

Finally we mention an extra connective that can be added to Team Semantics: the *global disjunction* $\sqcup$ such that $\mathfrak{M} \models_X \psi_1 \sqcup \psi_2$ if and only if $\mathfrak{M} \models_X \psi_1$ or $\mathfrak{M} \models_X \psi_2$. $\mathbf{FO}(\mathcal{D}, \sqcup)$ represents the logic obtained by adding $\sqcup$ to $\mathbf{FO}(\mathcal{D})$.

Strongly First Order Dependencies

A special case of functional dependency is the "constancy dependency" $=(\emptyset; \vec{w})$, usually written $=(\vec{w})$, for which $\mathfrak{M} \models_X =(\vec{w}) \Leftrightarrow \forall s, s' \in X, s(\vec{w}) = s'(\vec{w})$:

Proposition 2.11 ([5], §3.2). *Let* $=(\cdot)$ *be the family of all constancy dependencies of all arities. Then* $\mathbf{FO}(=(\cdot)) \equiv \mathbf{FO}$.

Which other dependencies likewise fail to increase the expressive power of $\mathbf{FO}$? In [6] the class of the *upwards closed dependencies* (i.e., those such that $(M, R) \in \mathbf{D}, R \subseteq S \subseteq M^k \Rightarrow (M, S) \in \mathbf{D}$) was introduced and the following result was shown:

Theorem 2.12 ([6], **Theorem 21**). *Let* $\mathcal{D}^\uparrow$ *be the family of all first order upwards closed dependencies and let* $=(\cdot)$ *be the family of all constancy dependencies. Then* $\mathbf{FO}(\mathcal{D}^\uparrow, =(\cdot)) \equiv \mathbf{FO}$.

Thus, first order upwards closed dependencies and constancy dependencies are "safe" for $\mathbf{FO}$ in the sense of [10]. The *non-emptiness atoms* $\mathbf{NE} = \{(M, R) : R \neq \emptyset\}$, for which $\mathfrak{M} \models_X \mathbf{NE}(\vec{v}) \Leftrightarrow X(\vec{v}) \neq \emptyset$, belong in $\mathcal{D}^\uparrow$ and will be useful in this work.

Definition 2.13 (Strongly First Order Dependencies [7]). *A dependency* $\mathbf{D}$, *or a family of dependencies* $\mathcal{D}$, *is strongly first order if* $\mathbf{FO}(\mathbf{D}) \equiv \mathbf{FO}$ *(respectively* $\mathbf{FO}(\mathcal{D}) \equiv \mathbf{FO}$*)*.

Theorem 2.14 ([7], **Corollary 8**). *Let* $\mathcal{D}^1$ *be the family of all unary first order dependencies. Then* $\mathbf{FO}(\mathcal{D}^1) \equiv \mathbf{FO}$.

Upwards closed dependencies and unary dependencies are somewhat uncommonly encountered when working with Team Semantics. Instead, the class of *downwards closed dependencies* (i.e. those such that $(M, R) \in \mathbf{D}, S \subseteq R \Rightarrow (M, S) \in \mathbf{D}$) is of special importance, because functional dependencies—the very first ones studied in Team Semantics—are in it; and in [8], it was shown that a domain-independent[5] downwards closed dependency is strongly first order if and only if it is definable in $\mathbf{FO}(=(\cdot))$. This entirely answered the question of which dependencies are strongly first order for a fairly general class of dependencies, which however fails to include many dependencies of interest.

In [9], a similar approach was adapted for characterizing strongly first order dependencies that satisfy a more general – if somewhat technical - closure property. That paper also contains the following result, which we will need:

---

[5] This result actually uses a weaker, more technical condition than domain-independence called *relativizability*.

Theorem 2.15 ([9], Proposition 14). *If* $\mathbf{FO}(\mathcal{D}) \equiv \mathbf{FO}$ *then* $\mathbf{FO}(\mathcal{D}, \sqcup) \equiv \mathbf{FO}$.

In [11], it was then shown that if a domain-independent $\mathbf{D}$ is *union-closed*, in the sense that $(M, R_i) \in \mathbf{D} \ \forall i \in I \Rightarrow (M, \bigcup_i R_i) \in \mathbf{D}$, then it is strongly first-order if and only if it is definable in $\mathbf{FO}(=(\cdot), \mathbf{NE}, \sqcup)$. Examples of union-closed dependencies are the inclusion and anonymity dependencies mentioned before.

Finally, in [12] a characterization was found for the domain-independent dependencies that are *doubly strongly first order* in the sense that $\mathbf{FO}(\mathbf{D}, \sim \mathbf{D}) \equiv \mathbf{FO}$, where $\sim \mathbf{D} = \{(M, R) : (M, R) \notin \mathbf{D}\}$. This can be seen as studying the safety of $\mathbf{D}$ with respect to a richer base language, in which it is also possible to deny dependencies (i.e. the contradictory negation of Team Logic is available in the language, but only for dependence atoms).

Disjunctive Embedded Dependencies

One of the concerns of Database Theory is the specification and analysis of dependencies between entries of relational databases [1–3]. Many such dependencies, like the functional and inclusion dependencies seen above, have been studied in this context, and the following notion of *disjunctive embedded dependency* has been found to suffice for many practically relevant scenarios:

Definition 2.16 (Disjunctive Embedded Dependencies). *Let* R *be a k-ary relational symbol. A (unirelational)[6] Disjunctive Embedded Dependency (or DED) over the vocabulary $\{R\}$ is a first order sentence of the form*

$$\forall \vec{x} \left(\phi(\vec{x}) \rightarrow \bigvee_i \exists \vec{y}^{(i)} \psi_i(\vec{x}, \vec{y}^{(i)}) \right) \tag{3}$$

where ϕ and all ψ_i are conjunctions of relational and identity atoms.

Functional dependencies, inclusion dependencies, independence atoms, and nonemptiness atoms are all DEDs, since the sentences $\forall \vec{x}\vec{y}\vec{z}((R\vec{x}\vec{y} \wedge R\vec{x}\vec{z}) \rightarrow \vec{y} = \vec{z})$, $\forall \vec{x}\vec{y}(R\vec{x}\vec{y} \rightarrow \exists \vec{z}(R\vec{z}\vec{x}))$, $\forall \vec{x}\vec{y}\vec{z}\vec{w}((R\vec{x}\vec{y} \wedge R\vec{z}\vec{w}) \rightarrow R\vec{x}\vec{w})$ and $\forall x(x = x \rightarrow \exists \vec{y}R\vec{y})$ are of the required form. In fact, since they do not require a disjunction in the consequent they belong to the more restricted class of (non-disjunctive) *embedded dependencies*, which suffices already for many purposes:

---

[6] In Database Theory a dependency may involve multiple relations corresponding to different tables; in Team Semantics, however, we only have one relation to work with. There exists a version of Team Semantics, called *Polyteam Semantics* [15], in which satisfaction is defined with respect to tuples of teams: that would allow us to work with multirelational DEDs, but in the present work we will not do so. A multirelational DED, at any rate, is always equivalent to a unirelational DED over the Cartesian product of its relations: for example, $\forall x_1 x_2 (R x_1 x_2 \wedge S x_2 x_1 \rightarrow \exists y S y y)$ is equivalent to $\forall x_1 x_2 z_1 z_2 z_3 z_4 (U x_1 x_2 z_3 z_4 \wedge U z_1 z_2 x_2 x_1 \rightarrow \exists w_1 w_2 y U w_1 w_2 y y)$ whenever $U = R \times S$ (or, at any rate, the projection of U over the first two columns corresponds to R and its projection over the other two corresponds to S).

> *Embedded dependencies turn out to be sufficiently expressive to capture virtually all other classes of dependencies studied in the literature.* [2]

Anonymity atoms, however, are not DEDs: for example, they do not satisfy Proposition 2.18 below. The even more general class $\text{DED}^{\neq}$ allows inequality literals $z \neq w$ inside of (3), and would contain them; but in this work we will limit ourselves to the inequality-free case.

Proposition 2.17. *Let $\mathbf{D}(R)$ be a DED. Then $\mathbf{D}$ is preserved by unions of chains, in the sense that if $(R_n)_{n \in \mathbb{N}}$ is a family of relations over A s.t.*

1. $(A, R_n) \in \mathbf{D}$ *for all $n \in \mathbb{N}$;*
2. $R_n \subseteq R_{n+1}$ *for all $n \in \mathbb{N}$*

then $(A, \bigcup_{n \in \mathbb{N}} R_n) \in \mathbf{D}$.

Proposition 2.18. *Let $\mathbf{D}(R)$ be a DED, and let (A, R) and (B, S) be such that*

1. (A, R) *is a substructure of (B, S);*
2. *There is a homomorphism $\mathfrak{h} : (B, S) \to (A, R)$ that is the identity over A;*
3. $(B, S) \in \mathbf{D}$.

Then $(A, R) \in \mathbf{D}$.

Proof. Suppose that $\mathbf{D}(R)$ is of the form of Equation (3), and take any tuple $\vec{a}$ such that $(A, R) \models \phi(\vec{a})$. Since ϕ is a conjunction of atoms and (A, R) is a substructure of (B, S), it must be the case that $(B, S) \models \phi(\vec{a})$; and since $(B, S) \models \mathbf{D}(S)$, there exists some i and some tuple $\vec{b}$ of elements of B such that $(B, S) \models \psi_i(\vec{a}, \vec{b})$. Now, $\mathfrak{h}(\vec{a}) = \vec{a}$ and ψ_i is a conjunction of atoms, so for $\vec{c} = \mathfrak{h}(\vec{b})$ we have that $(A, R) \models \psi_i(\vec{a}, \vec{c})$; therefore, $(A, R) \models \bigvee_i \exists \vec{y}^{(i)} \psi_i(\vec{a}, \vec{y}^{(i)})$. □

One particular consequence of the above result will be useful to us in this work:

Corollary 2.19. *Let $\mathbf{D}$ be a domain-independent DED, let R be any relation over some A, let $B \supseteq A$, and let $\vec{b}_1^{(1)} \ldots \vec{b}_n^{(1)}, \vec{b}_1^{(2)} \ldots \vec{b}_n^{(2)}, \ldots \in B^k \backslash A^k$ be k-tuples of elements of B such that, for $\vec{a}$ listing the elements of $A \cap \bigcup_{i=1}^n \text{Rng}(\vec{b}_i^{(1)})$,*

1. *Every $\vec{b}_i^{(q)}$ is disjoint from A except on $\vec{a}$;*
2. *Whenever $q \neq q'$, $\vec{b}_1^{(q)} \ldots \vec{b}_n^{(q)}$ and $\vec{b}_1^{(q')} \ldots \vec{b}_n^{(q')}$ are disjoint except on $\vec{a}$;*
3. *For all $q \in \mathbb{N}$, the identity type of $\vec{b}_1^{(q)} \ldots \vec{b}_n^{(q)} \vec{a}$ is the same.*

Suppose furthermore that $(B, S) \in \mathbf{D}$ for some S with $R \subseteq S \subseteq R \cup \bigcup_{q \in \mathbb{N}} \{\vec{b}_1^{(q)}, \ldots, \vec{b}_n^{(q)}\}$ and that $\{\vec{b}_1^{(q)}, \ldots, \vec{b}_n^{(q)} : q \in Q\} \subseteq S$ for some nonempty $Q \subseteq \mathbb{N}$. Then $(B, R \cup \{\vec{b}_1^{(q)} \ldots \vec{b}_n^{(q)} : q \in Q\}) \in \mathbf{D}$ as well.

3   Strongly First Order DEDs

Some Properties

The next two propositions are proven as in ([11], Lemma 1 and Proposition 3):

Proposition 3.1. *Let* $\mathbf{D}(R)$ *be a strongly first order, k-ary DED. Then there cannot exist an infinite chain of k-ary relations* $R_1 \subseteq S_1 \subseteq R_2 \subseteq S_2 \subseteq \ldots$ *over some domain M such that* $(M, R_n) \in \mathbf{D}$ *and* $(M, S_n) \notin \mathbf{D}$ *for all $n \in \mathbb{N}$.*

Proposition 3.2. *Let* $\mathbf{D}(R)$ *be a domain-independent, strongly first order DED, let* $(A_1, R_1) \in \mathbf{D}$ *and let* $(A_1, R_1) \preceq (A_2, R_2)$ *(that is, (A_2, R_2) is an elementary extension of (A_1, R_1)). Then* $(A_2, S_1) \in \mathbf{D}$ *for all S_1 with* $R_1 \subseteq S_1 \subseteq R_2$.

Then by a straightforward application of compactness we get the following:

Corollary 3.3. *Let* $\mathbf{D}$ *be a k-ary, domain-independent, strongly first order DED, let* $(A, R) \in \mathbf{D}$ *and let* $\vec{a}$ *be a tuple of elements of A and* $(\vec{a}^{(i)})_{i \in \mathbb{N}}$ *be a sequence of k-tuples over A such that*

1. $\vec{a}^{(i)} \in R$ *for all $i \in \mathbb{N}$;*
2. *If $i \neq j$, $\vec{a}^{(i)}$ and $\vec{a}^{(j)}$ are disjoint apart from $\vec{a}$;*
3. *The identity types of $\vec{a}^{(i)}\vec{a}$ are the same for all $i \in \mathbb{N}$.*

Furthermore , let $B \supseteq A$, *and let* $(\vec{b}^{(i)})_{i \in \mathbb{N}}$ *be a sequence of k-tuples over B s.t.*

1. *Every $\vec{b}^{(i)}$ is disjoint from A except on $\vec{a}$;*
2. *If $i \neq j$, $\vec{b}^{(i)}$ and $\vec{b}^{(j)}$ are disjoint except on $\vec{a}$;*
3. *The identity types of the $\vec{b}^{(i)}\vec{a}$ are all equal to the identity types of the $\vec{a}^{(i)}\vec{a}$.*

Then $(B, R \cup \{\vec{b}^{(i)} : i \in \mathbb{N}\}) \in \mathbf{D}$.

Proposition 3.4. *Let* $\mathbf{D}$ *be a k-ary domain-independent dependency. Suppose that there exist a domain* $B = A \cup \bigcup_{i \in \mathbb{N}} B_i$, *where all B_i are disjoint from each other and from A, and relations* $R \subseteq A^k$, $Q_i, T_i \subseteq (A \cup B_i)^k \setminus A^k$ *such that*

1. *For all $i, j \in \mathbb{N}$, there is an isomorphism* $\mathfrak{f}_{i,j} : (A \cup B_i, R \cup Q_i, R \cup T_i) \to (A \cup B_j, R \cup Q_j, R \cup T_j)$ *such that* $\mathfrak{f}_{i,j}(a) = a$ *for all $a \in A$;*
2. *for all $I, J \subseteq \mathbb{N}$ and for* $R_{I,J} = R \cup \bigcup_{i \in I} Q_i \cup \bigcup_{j \in J} T_j$ *we have that*

$$(B, R_{I,J}) \in \mathbf{D} \text{ if and only if } I \cap J = \emptyset.$$

Then $\mathbf{D}$ *is not strongly first order.*

Proof. Without loss of generality, we can assume that $B \cap \mathbb{N} = \emptyset$. For any $\ell \in \mathbb{N}$, $\ell > 1$, let $\mathfrak{M}_\ell$ be a model with domain $B \cup \{1 \ldots \ell\}$, with a unary predicate N with $N^{\mathfrak{M}_\ell} = \{1 \ldots \ell\}$, with two constants $\mathbf{1}$ and $\mathbf{end}$ with $\mathbf{1}^{\mathfrak{M}_\ell} = 1$ and $\mathbf{end}^{\mathfrak{M}_\ell} = \ell$, with a binary relation E such that $E^{\mathfrak{M}_\ell} = \{(i, i+1) : i \in 1 \ldots \ell - 1\}$ and with two $(k+1)$-ary relations Q, T with $Q^{\mathfrak{M}_\ell} = \{(i, \vec{a}) : i \in 1 \ldots \ell, \vec{a} \in R \cup Q_i\}$ and $T^{\mathfrak{M}_\ell} = \{(i, \vec{a}) : i \in 1 \ldots \ell, \vec{a} \in R \cup T_i\}$. Then the **FO(D)** sentence

$$\forall n \forall n'((N(n) \land N(n')) \hookrightarrow \exists v \exists v'((n = \mathbf{1} \hookrightarrow v = \mathbf{1}) \land (n = \mathbf{end} \hookrightarrow v \neq \mathbf{1}) \land$$
$$(E(n, n') \hookrightarrow ((v = \mathbf{1} \hookrightarrow v' \neq \mathbf{1}) \land (v \neq \mathbf{1} \hookrightarrow v' = \mathbf{1}))) \land$$
$$\forall \vec{z}(((v = \mathbf{1} \land Qn\vec{z}) \lor (v \neq \mathbf{1} \land Tn\vec{z})) \hookrightarrow \mathbf{D}\vec{z}) \land$$
$$\forall \vec{w}(((v' = \mathbf{1} \land Qn'\vec{w}) \lor (v' \neq \mathbf{1} \land Tn'\vec{w})) \hookrightarrow \mathbf{D}\vec{w}) \land$$
$$(n = n' \hookrightarrow v = v')))$$

is true in $\mathfrak{M}_\ell$ if and only if ℓ is even.[7] A standard back-and-forth argument shows that no first order sentence can be true in $\mathfrak{M}_\ell$ if and only if ℓ is even; thus, **FO(D)** must be more expressive than **FO**, i.e. **D** is not strongly first order.   □

The Characterization

The following notions of U-sentences and U-embeddings are from [11], in which they were used to characterize strongly first order union-closed dependencies:

Definition 3.5 (U-sentences, $\Rightarrow_U$). *Let R be a k-ary relation symbol and let $\vec{a}$ be a tuple of constant symbols. Then a first order sentence over the signature $\{R, \vec{a}\}$ is a U-sentence if and only if it is of the form $\exists \vec{x}(\eta(\vec{x}) \land \forall \vec{y}(R\vec{y} \to \theta(\vec{x}, \vec{y})))$, where $\vec{x}$ and $\vec{y}$ are disjoint tuples of variables without repetitions, $\eta(x)$ is a conjunction of first order literals over the signature $\{R, \vec{a}\}$ in which R occurs only positively, and $\theta(\vec{x}, \vec{y})$ is a first order formula over the signature $\{\vec{a}\}$ (i.e. in which R does not appear). Given two models $\mathfrak{A}$ and $\mathfrak{B}$ with the same signature, we will write $\mathfrak{A} \Rightarrow_U \mathfrak{B}$ if, for every U-sentence ϕ, $\mathfrak{A} \models \phi \Rightarrow \mathfrak{B} \models \phi$.*

Proposition 3.6. *Let $\phi = \exists \vec{x}(\eta(\vec{x}) \land \forall \vec{y}(R\vec{y} \to \theta(\vec{x}, \vec{y})))$ be a U-sentence. Then there exists a $\mathbf{FO}(=(\cdot), \mathbf{NE})$ formula $\phi'(\vec{y})$ over the empty signature, with free variables in $\vec{y}$, such that $\mathfrak{M} \models_X \phi'(\vec{y}) \Leftrightarrow (M, X(\vec{y})) \models \phi$ for all $\mathfrak{M}$ and X.*

Proof. Take $\phi'(\vec{y}) := \exists \vec{x}(=(\vec{x}) \land \eta'(\vec{x}) \land \theta(\vec{x}, \vec{y}))$, where η' is obtained from η by replacing every atom $R\vec{z}$ (for $\vec{z} \subseteq \vec{x}$) with $\vec{z} = \vec{z} \lor (\mathbf{NE}(\vec{z}) \land \vec{z} = \vec{y})$.   □

Definition 3.7 (U-embedding). *A structure (A, R) is said to be U-embedded in a structure (B, S) if*

1. (A, R) is a substructure of (B, S);

---

[7] This is inspired by the Dependence Logic sentence to express even cardinality found in [21], §4.1: in brief, for each $n \in 1 \ldots \ell$ we choose an index v that is either 1 or not so, and the dependence statements ensure that we cannot associate both 1 and a different value for the same n; whenever some value n is associated with 1, its successor cannot be so; the index 1 must be associated with 1, and the last element ℓ cannot be so.

2. *For every finite tuple of parameters $\vec{a}$ in A and every first order formula $\theta(\vec{y}, \vec{z})$ over the empty signature, $(A, R) \models \forall \vec{y}(R\vec{y} \rightarrow \theta(\vec{y}, \vec{a})) \Rightarrow (B, S) \models \forall \vec{y}(S\vec{y} \rightarrow \theta(\vec{y}, \vec{a}))$. a structure (A, R) is isomorphic to some structure (A', R') which is U-embedded in (B, S), we say that the isomorphism $\iota : (A, R) \rightarrow (A', R')$ is a U-embedding of (A, R) into (B, S).*

The next proposition is proved as in the first part of Proposition 5 of [11]:

Proposition 3.8. *Let $\mathfrak{A} = (A, R)$ and let $\mathfrak{B} = (B, S)$, where R and S are k-ary relations and A is countably infinite, and suppose that $\mathfrak{A} \Rightarrow_U \mathfrak{B}$. Then there exist an elementary extension $\mathfrak{B}' \succeq \mathfrak{B}$ and a U-embedding $\iota : \mathfrak{A} \rightarrow \mathfrak{B}'$.*

Corollary 3.9. *Let $\mathfrak{A} = (A, R)$ and let $\mathfrak{B} = (B, S)$, where R and S are k-ary relations and A is countably infinite, and suppose that $\mathfrak{A} \Rightarrow_U \mathfrak{B}$. Then there exists a countably infinite structure $(B_0, S_0) \equiv (B, S)$ and a U-embedding $\iota : (A, R) \rightarrow (B_0, S_0)$.*

Proof. Follows from Proposition 3.8 via the Löwenheim-Skolem Theorem.   □

Lemma 3.10. *Let (A, R) be countably infinite and U-embedded in (B, S), and let $\vec{b} \in (S \backslash R)^k$. Also, let $\vec{a}$ list some finite C such that $A \cap \mathrm{Rng}(\vec{b}) \subseteq C \subseteq A$, and let $\tau(\vec{x}, \vec{y})$ be the identity type of $\vec{b}\vec{a}$. Then there are infinitely many $\vec{a}^{(1)}, \vec{a}^{(2)}, \ldots$ in R such that*

1. *All tuples $\vec{a}^{(q)}$ satisfy $\tau(\vec{a}^{(q)}, \vec{a})$;*
2. *If $q \neq q'$ then $\mathrm{Rng}(\vec{a}^{(q)}) \cap \mathrm{Rng}(\vec{a}^{(q')}) \subseteq \mathrm{Rng}(\vec{a})$.*

Proof. Suppose that this is not the case: then there exist in (A, R) a finite number of tuples $\vec{a}^{(1)} \ldots \vec{a}^{(q)}$ such that all $\vec{d} \in R$ that satisfy $\tau(\vec{d}, \vec{a})$, intersect one of them somewhere other than in $\vec{a}$. So, if $\vec{c}$ lists $\bigcup_{j=1}^{q} \mathrm{Rng}(\vec{a}^{(j)}) \backslash \mathrm{Rng}(\vec{a})$, $(A, R) \models \forall \vec{y}(R\vec{y} \rightarrow (\tau(\vec{y}, \vec{a}) \rightarrow \vec{y} \cap \vec{c} \neq \emptyset))$ where $\vec{y} \cap \vec{c} \neq \emptyset$ is a shorthand for $\bigvee_{i,j} y_i = c_j$. Then, by the definition of U-embedding, $(B, S) \models \forall \vec{y}(S\vec{y} \rightarrow (\tau(\vec{y}, \vec{a}) \rightarrow \vec{y} \cap \vec{c} \neq \emptyset))$; and this is impossible, because $\vec{b}$ is disjoint from A except on $\vec{a}$.   □

Proposition 3.11. *Let (A, R) be countably infinite and U-embedded in (B, S), let $t \in \mathbb{N}$, let $\vec{b}_1, \ldots, \vec{b}_t \in S \backslash R$, and suppose that $(A, R) \in \mathbf{D}$ where $\mathbf{D}$ is a domain-independent, strongly first order DED. Then $(B, R \cup \{\vec{b}_1 \ldots \vec{b}_t\}) \in \mathbf{D}$.*

Proof. Suppose that this is not the case. Then let $\vec{a}$ list $A \cap \bigcup_{i=1}^{t} \mathrm{Rng}(\vec{b}_i)$, and for each $i = 1 \ldots t$ let $\tau_i(\vec{z}, \vec{w})$ be the identity type of $\vec{b}_i \vec{a}$. Because of Lemma 3.10, R contains infinitely many copies of each $\vec{b}_i$, all satisfying the same identity types with $\vec{a}$ and disjoint from any other copy of the same $\vec{b}_i$ except over $\vec{a}$. Now, for all $q \in \mathbb{N}$, let B_q be a isomorphic, disjoint copy of $B \backslash A$, and let us identify B_1 with $B \backslash A$ itself; and for every q, let $(\vec{b}_1^{(q)} \ldots \vec{b}_t^{(q)})$ be the copy of $(\vec{b}_1 \ldots \vec{b}_t)$ in $A \cup B_q$. Finally, let $C = A \cup \bigcup_q B_q$.

By Corollary 3.3, $(C, R \cup \{\vec{b}_i^{(q)} : q \in \mathbb{N}\}) \in \mathbf{D}$ for all $i \in 1 \ldots t$.

On the other hand, it cannot be that, for $R' = R \cup \{\vec{b}_1^{(q)}, \ldots, \vec{b}_t^{(q)} : q \in \mathbb{N}\}$, $(C, R') \in \mathbf{D}$: indeed, otherwise by Corollary 2.19 we would have that $(C, R \cup \{\vec{b}_1^{(1)}, \ldots, \vec{b}_t^{(1)}\}) \in \mathbf{D}$ and so by domain independence $(B, R \cup \{b_1, \ldots, b_t\}) \in \mathbf{D}$.

Therefore, there must exist a minimal $r \in 2 \ldots t$ such that, for $R' = R \cup \{\vec{b}_1^{(q)}, \ldots, \vec{b}_r^{(q)} : q \in \mathbb{N}\}$, $(C, R') \notin \mathbf{D}$. Then let $\mathfrak{g} : \mathbb{N} \times \mathbb{N} \to \mathbb{N}$ be any bijection from $\mathbb{N} \times \mathbb{N}$ to $\mathbb{N}$ and, for all $n \in \mathbb{N}$, let $Q_n = \{\vec{b}_1^{\mathfrak{g}(n,q')}, \ldots, \vec{b}_{r-1}^{\mathfrak{g}(n,q')} : q' \in \mathbb{N}\}$ and $T_n = \{\vec{b}_r^{\mathfrak{g}(n,q')} : q' \in \mathbb{N}\}$. Let us see if we can apply Proposition 3.4.

By construction, it is clear there exist isomorphisms

$$\mathfrak{f}_{n,n'} : (A \cup \bigcup_{q' \in \mathbb{N}} B_{\mathfrak{g}(n,q')}, Q_n, T_n) \to (A \cup \bigcup_{q' \in \mathbb{N}} B_{\mathfrak{g}(n',q')}, Q_{n'}, T_{n'})$$

that keep A fixed pointwise. Now let $R_{I,J} = R \cup \bigcup_{i \in I} Q_i \cup \bigcup_{j \in J} T_j$ for $I, J \subseteq \mathbb{N}$.

- If $I \cap J \neq \emptyset$ then $(C, R_{I,J}) \notin \mathbf{D}$: otherwise, since $Q_i \cup T_i \subseteq R_{I,J}$ for some i, by Corollary 2.19 $(C, R \cup Q_i \cup T_i) \in \mathbf{D}$, which is impossible because this is isomorphic to $(C, R \cup \{\vec{b}_1^q, \ldots, \vec{b}_r^q : q \in \mathbb{N}\})$.
- If $I \cap J = \emptyset$ then $(C, R_{I,J}) \in \mathbf{D}$. Indeed, consider $R_I = R \cup \bigcup_{i \in I} Q_i$. $\bigcup_{i \in I} Q_i$ is a countably infinite set of copies of $b_1 \ldots b_{r-1}$, disjoint from each other and from A outside of $\vec{a}$; therefore, because of the minimality of r we have that $(C, R_I) \in \mathbf{D}$. Now let $A' = A \cup \bigcup \{B_{\mathfrak{g}(n,q')} : n \in I, q' \in \mathbb{N}\}$. By the domain independence of $\mathbf{D}$, $(A', R_I) \in \mathbf{D}$; and by construction and by the fact that $I \cap J = \emptyset$, all tuples in $\bigcup_{j \in J} T_j$ are disjoint from A' except on $\vec{a}$.

  Since $R_I \supseteq R$, R_I contains already infinitely many copies of $\vec{b}_r$ disjoint from each other apart from $\vec{a}$; and so, by Corollary 3.3, $(C, R_{I,J}) \in \mathbf{D}$.

Thus, it is not possible for $\mathbf{D}$ to be strongly first order, which contradicts our hypothesis; and therefore, it must be the case that $(B, R \cup \{\vec{b}_1 \ldots \vec{b}_t\}) \in \mathbf{D}$. $\square$

Corollary 3.12. *Let $\mathbf{D}$ be a domain-independent, strongly first order DED, and suppose that $(A, R) \in \mathbf{D}$ is countably infinite and that $(A, R) \Rightarrow_U (B, S)$. Then $(B, S) \in \mathbf{D}$.*

Proof. Suppose that this is not the case. Then by Corollary 3.9 there is a countable model $(B_0, S_0) \equiv (B, S)$ and a U-embedding ι of (A, R) into $(B_0, S_0) \notin \mathbf{D}$. Let (A_0, R_0) be the image of (A, R) along ι, and let $(\vec{b}_j)_{j \in \mathbb{N}}$ enumerate $S_0 \backslash R_0$. Since $\mathbf{D}$ is domain-independent, we have that $(B_0, R_0) \in \mathbf{D}$; and since by Proposition 2.17 $\mathbf{D}$ is closed by unions of chains and $(B_0, S_0) \notin \mathbf{D}$, there exists some $t \in \mathbb{N}$ such that $(B_0, R_0 \cup \{\vec{b}_1 \ldots \vec{b}_t\}) \notin \mathbf{D}$. This contradicts Proposition 3.11. $\square$

Proposition 3.13. *Let $\mathbf{D}$ be a domain-independent, strongly first order DED and suppose that $(A, R) \in \mathbf{D}$. Then there exists a U-sentence ϕ such that*

- *$(A, R) \models \phi$;*
- *$\phi \models \mathbf{D}(R)$.*

Proof. If (A, R) is finite then it is easy to find a U-sentence that fixes R up to isomorphism (just list all tuples in R and state that the relation contains precisely them) and that therefore, by the domain independence of **D**, entails **D**(R). Otherwise, by Löwenheim-Skolem we can assume that (A, R) is countably infinite. Now let $(B_i, S_i)_{i \in I}$ list all countable models such that $(B_i, S_i) \notin$ **D**. For all $i \in I$, it cannot be the case that $(A, R) \Rightarrow_U (B_i, S_i)$: otherwise, by Corollary 3.12 we would have that $(B_i, S_i) \in$ **D** as well. So there exists some U-sentence $\phi_i(R)$ such that $(A, R) \models \phi_i(R)$ but $(B_i, S_i) \not\models \phi_i(S_i)$. Now consider the theory $\{\phi_i(R) : i \in I\} \cup \{\neg$**D**$(R)\}$. This theory is unsatisfiable: if it had a model, by Löwenheim-Skolem it should have a countable model—i.e. some (B_i, S_i), which cannot be true because $(B_i, S_i) \not\models \phi_i(S_i)$. Thus, by compactness, there must exist some finite subtheory of it that is already unsatisfiable. Therefore, for some finite subset I_0 of I we have that $(A, R) \models \bigwedge_{i \in I_0} \phi_i(R)$ and that $\bigwedge_{i \in I_0} \phi_i(R) \models$ **D**(R); and since U-sentences are closed by conjunction, the result follows. $\square$

Proposition 3.14. *Let* **D** *be a strongly first order, domain-independent DED. Then* **D**(R) *is logically equivalent to a finite disjunction of U-sentences.*

Proof. Let $(A_i, R_i)_{i \in I}$ list all countable models such that $(A_i, R_i) \in$ **D**. Then, by Proposition 3.13, for every i there exists some U-sentence $\phi_i(R)$ such that $(A_i, R_i) \models \phi_i(R_i)$ and $\phi_i(R) \models$ **D**(R). Now consider the theory $\{\neg\phi_i(R) : i \in I\} \cup \{$**D**$(R)\}$: this theory is unsatisfiable, because if it had a model it would need to have a countable model—i.e. one of the (A_i, R_i). So there is a finite subset $I_0 \subseteq I$ such that **D**$(R) \models \bigvee_{i \in I_0} \phi_i$, and so **D**$(R)$ is equivalent to $\bigvee_{i \in I_0} \phi_i$. $\square$

Theorem 3.15. *Let* **D** *be a domain-independent DED. Then the following are equivalent:*

1. **D** *is strongly first order;*
2. **D** *is logically equivalent to a finite disjunction of U-sentences;*
3. **D** *is definable in* **FO**$(=(\cdot), $**NE**$, \sqcup)$.[8]

Proof. **1.** →**2.** This is Proposition 3.14.
 2. →**3.** Let **D**$(R) = \bigvee_{i=1}^n \phi_i$ be a disjunction of U-sentences.
 For every i, let $\phi_i'(\vec{y})$ be the translation of ϕ_i in **FO**$(= (\cdot), $**NE**$)$ as per Proposition 3.6. Then **D**(R) is definable by the **FO**$(= (\cdot), $**NE**$, \sqcup)$ formula $\phi'(\vec{y}) = \bigsqcup_{i=1}^n \phi_i'(\vec{y})$: indeed, $\mathfrak{M} \models_X$ **D**$\vec{y}$ if and only if $(M, X(\vec{y})) \in$ **D**, that is if and only if $(M, X(\vec{y})) \models \phi_i$ for some $i = 1 \ldots n$, that is if and only if $\mathfrak{M} \models_X \phi_i'(\vec{y})$ for some such i, that is if and only if $\mathfrak{M} \models_X \phi'(\vec{y})$.

---

[8] Recall that definability—in the sense of Definition 2.7—means that any atom **D**$\vec{v}$ is equivalent to some formula in **FO**$(=(\cdot), $**NE**$, \sqcup)$. Instead, in this paper we write $L_1 \equiv L_2$ if every *sentence* (not necessarily every formula!) of L_1 is equivalent to some sentence of L_2 and vice versa, so that in particular **FO**$(\mathcal{D}) \equiv$ **FO** if and only if $\mathcal{D}$ is strongly first order. These two notions are quite distinct.

3. →**1.** Suppose that $\mathbf{D}$ is definable in $\mathbf{FO}(=(\cdot), \mathbf{NE}, \sqcup)$. Then, by Proposition 2.8, $\mathbf{FO}(\mathbf{D}) \leq \mathbf{FO}(=(\cdot), \mathbf{NE}, \sqcup)$. By Theorem 2.12, $\mathbf{FO}(=(\cdot), \mathbf{NE}) \equiv \mathbf{FO}$; so, by Theorem 2.15, $\mathbf{FO}(=(\cdot), \mathbf{NE}, \sqcup) \equiv \mathbf{FO}$, and therefore $\mathbf{FO} \leq \mathbf{FO}(\mathbf{D}) \leq \mathbf{FO}(=(\cdot), \mathbf{NE}, \sqcup) \equiv \mathbf{FO}$ and thus $\mathbf{FO}(\mathbf{D}) \equiv \mathbf{FO}$.

$\square$

Corollary 3.16. *Let* $\mathcal{D}$ *be a family of domain-independent DEDs. Then* $\mathbf{FO}(\mathcal{D}) \equiv \mathbf{FO}$ *if and only if every* $\mathbf{D} \in \mathcal{D}$, *taken individually, is strongly first order.*

Proof. If $\mathbf{FO}(\mathcal{D}) \equiv \mathbf{FO}$ then every $\mathbf{D} \in \mathcal{D}$ must be strongly first order, because $\mathbf{FO} \leq \mathbf{FO}(\mathbf{D}) \leq \mathbf{FO}(\mathcal{D}) \equiv \mathbf{FO}$. Conversely, suppose that every $\mathbf{D} \in \mathcal{D}$ is strongly first order, and therefore by Theorem 3.15 is definable in $\mathbf{FO}(=(\cdot), \mathbf{NE}, \sqcup)$: then $\mathbf{FO} \leq \mathbf{FO}(\mathcal{D}) \leq \mathbf{FO}(=(\cdot), \mathbf{NE}, \sqcup) \equiv \mathbf{FO}$, and so $\mathbf{FO}(\mathcal{D}) \equiv \mathbf{FO}$.

$\square$

4   Conclusions and Further Work

In this work, we were able to characterize which dependencies are 'safe' to add to First Order Logic with Team Semantics for a very general class of dependencies that captures most dependencies of interest to Database Theory (and nearly all the dependencies that have been studied so far in Team Semantics).

This almost entirely solves the problem of which "reasonable" dependencies are strongly first order; generalizing the characterization from the class DED to the class DED$^{\neq}$ would further broaden the scope of this result, but since Proposition 2.18 fails to hold for this larger class it seems that some additional ideas would be required.

Another direction worth pursuing at this point might be to try to characterize the classes of dependencies $\mathcal{D}$ for which $\mathbf{FO}(\mathcal{D})$ is as expressive as existential second order logic (as is the case for functional dependence atoms) or for which the model checking problem $\mathbf{FO}(\mathcal{D})$ is in PTIME for finite models (as is the case for inclusion atoms). This last question could also have interesting implications in descriptive complexity theory.

Acknowledgments. I thank the anonymous reviewers for their helpful comments and suggestions.

References

1. Abiteboul, S., Hull, R., Vianu, V.: Foundations of Databases. Addison-Wesley (1995)
2. Deutsch, A.: FOL modeling of integrity constraints (dependencies). In: Liu, L., Özsu, M.T. (eds.) Encyclopedia of Database Systems, pp. 1155–1161. Springer US, Boston, MA (2009). https://doi.org/10.1007/978-0-387-39940-9_980

3. Deutsch, A., Tannen, V.: Optimization properties for classes of conjunctive regular path queries. In: Ghelli, G., Grahne, G. (eds.) Database Programming Languages, pp. 21–39. Springer, Berlin, Heidelberg (2002). https://doi.org/10.1007/3-540-46093-4_2

4. Galliani, P.: The Dynamics of Imperfect Information. Ph.D. thesis, University of Amsterdam (2012). http://dare.uva.nl/record/425951

5. Galliani, P.: Inclusion and exclusion dependencies in team semantics: on some logics of imperfect information. Ann. Pure Appl. Logic **163**(1), 68 – 84 (2012). https://doi.org/10.1016/j.apal.2011.08.005

6. Galliani, P.: Upwards closed dependencies in team semantics. Inf. Comput. **245**, 124–135 (2015). https://doi.org/10.1016/j.ic.2015.06.008

7. Galliani, P.: On strongly first-order dependencies. In: Dependence Logic, pp. 53–71. Springer, Cham (2016). https://doi.org/10.1007/978-3-319-31803-5_4

8. Galliani, P.: Characterizing downwards closed, strongly first-order, relativizable dependencies. J. Symbol. Logic **84**(3), 1136–1167 (2019). https://doi.org/10.1017/jsl.2019.12

9. Galliani, P.: Characterizing strongly first order dependencies: The non-jumping relativizable case. Electron. Proc. Theor. Comput. Sci. **305**, 66–82 (2019). https://doi.org/10.4204/eptcs.305.5

10. Galliani, P.: Safe dependency atoms and possibility operators in team semantics. Inf. Comput., 104593 (2020)

11. Galliani, P.: Strongly first order, domain independent dependencies: the union-closed case. In: International Workshop on Logic, Language, Information, and Computation, pp. 263–279. Springer, Cham (2022). https://doi.org/10.1007/978-3-031-15298-6_17

12. Galliani, P.: Doubly strongly first-order dependencies. J. Logic Comput., exae056 (2025). https://doi.org/10.1093/logcom/exae056

13. Galliani, P., Hella, L.: Inclusion logic and fixed point logic. In: Rocca, S.R.D. (ed.) Computer Science Logic 2013 (CSL 2013). Leibniz International Proceedings in Informatics (LIPIcs), vol. 23, pp. 281–295. Schloss Dagstuhl–Leibniz-Zentrum fuer Informatik, Dagstuhl, Germany (2013). https://doi.org/10.4230/LIPIcs.CSL.2013.281

14. Grädel, E., Väänänen, J.: Dependence and independence. Stud. Logica. **101**(2), 399–410 (2013). https://doi.org/10.1007/s11225-013-9479-2

15. Hannula, M., Kontinen, J., Virtema, J.: Polyteam semantics. J. Log. Comput. **30**(8), 1541–1566 (2020)

16. Hodges, W.: Compositional semantics for a language of imperfect information. J. Interest Group Pure Appl. Logics **5**(4), 539–563 (1997). https://doi.org/10.1093/jigpal/5.4.539

17. Kanellakis, P.C.: Elements of relational database theory. In: van Leeuwen, J. (ed.) Formal Models and Semantics, pp. 1073–1156. Handbook of Theoretical Computer Science, Elsevier, Amsterdam (1990). https://doi.org/10.1016/B978-0-444-88074-1.50022-6

18. Kontinen, J., Kuusisto, A., Virtema, J.: Decidability of predicate logics with team semantics. In: 41st International Symposium on Mathematical Foundations of Computer Science (MFCS 2016). Leibniz International Proceedings in Informatics (LIPIcs), vol. 58, pp. 60:1–60:14 (2016). https://doi.org/10.4230/LIPIcs.MFCS.2016.60

19. Kontinen, J., Nurmi, V.: Team logic and second-order logic. Fund. Inform. **106**(2–4), 259–272 (2011). https://doi.org/10.3233/FI-2011-386

20. Kuusisto, A.: Defining a double team semantics for generalized quantifiers (extended version) (2013). https://trepo.tuni.fi/handle/10024/68064, manuscript
21. Väänänen, J.: Dependence Logic. Cambridge University Press (2007). https://doi.org/10.1017/CBO9780511611193
22. Väänänen, J.: An atom's worth of anonymity. Logic J. IGPL **31**(6), 1078–1083 (2022). https://doi.org/10.1093/jigpal/jzac074

A Kripke Semantics for Intuitionistic Łukasiewicz Logic with Weak Excluded Middle

Andrew Lewis-Smith[1] and Zhiguang Zhao[2]($\boxtimes$)

[1] Middlesex University, London, UK
[2] Taishan University, Tai'an, China
zhaozhiguang23@gmail.com

Abstract. We provide a generalisation of Kripke semantics for an extension of intuitionistic Łukasiewicz logic (**LLi**) with weak excluded middle (**LLi$_{\mathbf{WEM}}$**). This analogises the situation with intuitionistic logic (**IL**) extended by weak excluded middle (**WEM**). This paper extends the insights of [8] regarding **LLi** to **LLi$_{\mathbf{WEM}}$**.

Keywords: substructural logic · Kripke semantics · intermediate logic

1 Introduction

Hajek's basic logic (**BL**) and its constructive variant generalised basic logic (**GBL**) occupy a central place in contemporary research on fuzzy and substructural logics. **BL** is primarily studied algebraically. This is only natural: the logic is strongly algebraizable [10] and is the logic of t-norms [12]. But the papers of Jipsen and Montagna [7] and Bova and Montagna [2] suggest an alternative view of the situation. We can employ algebraic embedding results via poset products to construct generalisations of Kripke semantics appropriate to extensions of **GBL** [8], [11] and [3]. This situates systems like **GBL** and **BL** as substructural variants of constructive and intermediate logics, whose relational semantics are canonical (and serve as the springboard for model-theoretic investigations in classical modal logic).

Presently, we study intuitionistic Łukasiewicz logic (**LLi**) with Jankov's axiom or weak excluded middle (**WEM**), hereon **LLi$_{\mathbf{WEM}}$**. The semantics we devise for **LLi$_{\mathbf{WEM}}$** extends that of [3] and [8], but is a significant departure from these latter. The present structures are defined over partially-ordered frames with a greatest element, hence our designation 'Jankov-Jipsen-Bova-Montagna structure' or JBM-structure.[1] However, unlike the semantics for **LLi** and **BL**, the present semantics requires that the top-node be 'crisp', distinct from other,

---

[1] We have decided, for reasons of parsimony and euphony, to write 'JBM' instead of 'JJBM'. We hope the reader will appreciate our attempt to reduce terminological and acronym bloat.

© The Author(s), under exclusive license to Springer Nature Switzerland AG 2026
G. Casini et al. (Eds.): JELIA 2025, LNAI 16093, pp. 275–289, 2026.
https://doi.org/10.1007/978-3-032-04587-4_17

fuzzy-valued nodes (i.e., valued in **MV**-chains). Therefore, the completeness proof for this system is quite specific – not given in earlier results by Jipsen and Montagna or Bova and Montagna or in [8]; to our knowledge, these particular algebras have not been characterised in the earlier literature and therefore the present paper bears independent interest. In addition, the semantics presented here is a restriction of that given in our earlier papers – the restriction of the top node to the Booleans is essential to procure soundness and completeness.

In addition to our project of extracting Kripke semantics for fuzzy logics – particularly substructural analogues of intermediate logics – We anticipate that the semantics and logic given here can be used to in a form analogous to that of Jankov logic for answer set programming [14–16], and similarly as a basis for exploration regarding fuzzy analogues of *Medvedev degrees* [13], well-known to computability theorists. In both cases, Jankov's system characterises certain notions of computation. We intend to explore and extend these connections to the fuzzy case in future work.

The structure of the paper is as with [8] and [3]. Section 2 gives **LLi$_{\mathbf{WEM}}$**'s natural deduction system,[2] followed by suitable definitions of algebras, validity, and our relational semantics. We show how our semantics can specialise to the classic semantics for Jankov logic, and then prove **LLi$_{\mathbf{WEM}}$** sound and complete for our semantics.

2   Proof Theory for LLi$_{\mathbf{WEM}}$

We consider briefly the proof theory of **LLi$_{\mathbf{WEM}}$**. We present the Hilbert-style and natural deduction renderings for the sake of clarity, but also to serve our later exposition and results (in particular our completeness proof).

The formulas of **LLi$_{\mathbf{WEM}}$** are inductively defined from atomic formulas, including $\bot$, and the binary connectives $\psi \wedge \chi$, $\psi \vee \chi$, $\psi \otimes \chi$ and $\psi \to \chi$. We will refer to this language as $\mathcal{L}_\otimes$, since it extends the language $\mathcal{L}$ of Jankov logic **JL** (see Note 1) with a second form of conjunction, $\psi \otimes \chi$.

Figure 1 gives a natural deduction system for **LLi$_{\mathbf{WEM}}$**. When we write a sequent $\Gamma \vdash \phi$ we are always assuming Γ to be a finite sequence of formulas. Note that we have the structural rules of weakening and exchange, but not contraction. Hence, the number of occurrences of a formula in Γ matters, and one could think of the contexts Γ as multisets. In particular, the rule $\to$-I removes one occurrence of ϕ from the context Γ, ϕ, concluding $\phi \to \psi$ from the smaller context Γ. This makes **LLi$_{\mathbf{WEM}}$** a form of Affine logic. **LLi$_{\mathbf{WEM}}$** indeed has a *resource sensitive* deduction theorem. The connective $\to$ internalises the consequence relation $\vdash$, and $\otimes$ internalises the comma in the sequent:

Proposition 1. *The following hold in any calculus with rules* $Ax, \to I, \to E,$ $\otimes I, \otimes E$ *(and so for* **LLi$_{\mathbf{WEM}}$***:*

1. $\Gamma, \psi \vdash \chi$ iff $\Gamma \vdash \psi \to \chi$.

---

[2] In future work, these will be adapted into labelled calculi by importing insights from the semantics given here (and in earlier papers).

$$\frac{}{\phi \vdash \phi} \text{ Ax} \qquad \frac{\Gamma \vdash \psi}{\Gamma, \phi \vdash \psi} \text{ W} \qquad \frac{\Gamma, \phi, \psi, \Delta \vdash \chi}{\Gamma, \psi, \phi, \Delta \vdash \chi} \text{ Ex}$$

$$\frac{\Gamma, \phi \vdash \psi}{\Gamma \vdash \phi \to \psi} \to \text{I} \qquad \frac{\Gamma \vdash \phi \to \psi \qquad \Delta \vdash \phi}{\Gamma, \Delta \vdash \psi} \to \text{E}$$

$$\frac{\Gamma \vdash \phi \qquad \Delta \vdash \psi}{\Gamma, \Delta \vdash \phi \otimes \psi} \otimes \text{I} \qquad \frac{\Gamma, \phi, \psi \vdash \chi \qquad \Delta \vdash \phi \otimes \psi}{\Gamma, \Delta \vdash \chi} \otimes \text{E}$$

$$\frac{\Gamma \vdash \phi \qquad \Gamma \vdash \psi}{\Gamma \vdash \phi \wedge \psi} \wedge \text{I} \qquad \frac{\Gamma \vdash \phi_1 \wedge \phi_2}{\Gamma \vdash \phi_i} \wedge \text{E}$$

$$\frac{\Gamma \vdash \phi_i}{\Gamma \vdash \phi_1 \vee \phi_2} \vee \text{I} \qquad \frac{\Gamma \vdash \phi \vee \psi \qquad \Delta, \phi \vdash \chi \qquad \Delta, \psi \vdash \chi}{\Gamma, \Delta \vdash \chi} \vee \text{E}$$

$$\frac{\Gamma, \phi, \phi \to \psi \vdash \chi}{\Gamma, \psi, \psi \to \phi \vdash \chi} \text{ DIV} \qquad \frac{\Gamma \vdash \bot}{\Gamma \vdash \phi} \bot \text{ E}$$

$$\frac{}{\Gamma \vdash \neg\phi \vee \neg\neg\phi} \text{ WEM}$$

Fig. 1. Intuitionistic Łukasiewicz logic with WEM

2. $\Gamma, \phi, \psi \vdash \chi$ iff $\Gamma, \phi \otimes \psi \vdash \chi$.

Proof. As in [8].

Below, we present the Hilbert system **GBL$_{\text{WEM}}$**. This is simply **GBL**, or **GBL** with exchange, weakening, and ex-falso quodlibet (see [2,7,8]), with **WEM**.

(A1) $\phi \to \phi$
(A2) $(\phi \to \psi) \to ((\psi \to \chi) \to (\phi \to \chi))$
(A3) $(\phi \otimes \psi) \to (\psi \otimes \phi)$
(A4) $(\phi \otimes \psi) \to \psi$
(A5) $(\phi \to (\psi \to \chi)) \to ((\phi \otimes \psi) \to \chi)$
(A6) $((\phi \otimes \psi) \to \chi)) \to (\phi \to (\psi \to \chi))$
(A7) $(\phi \otimes (\phi \to \psi)) \to (\phi \wedge \psi)$
(A8) $(\phi \wedge \psi) \to (\phi \otimes (\phi \to \psi))$
(A9) $(\phi \wedge \psi) \to (\psi \wedge \phi)$
(A10) $\phi \to (\phi \vee \psi)$
(A11) $\psi \to (\phi \vee \psi)$
(A12) $((\phi \to \psi) \wedge (\chi \to \psi)) \to ((\phi \vee \chi) \to \psi)$
(A13) $\bot \to \phi$
(A14) $\neg\phi \vee \neg\neg\phi$
(R1) $\phi, \phi \to \psi \vdash_{\text{GBL}_{\text{WEM}}} \psi$

When we wish to stress the precise system in which a sequent $\Gamma \vdash \phi$ is derivable we use the system as a subscript of the provability sign, e.g. $\Gamma \vdash_{\text{GBL}_{\text{WEM}}} \phi$.

Proposition 2. *The natural deduction system* **LLi**$_{\mathbf{WEM}}$ *(Fig. 1) has the same derivable formulas as the Hilbert-style system* **GBL**$_{\mathbf{WEM}}$:

$$\psi_1, \ldots, \psi_n \vdash_{\mathbf{GBL_{WEM}}} \phi \quad \textit{iff} \quad \vdash_{\mathbf{LLi_{WEM}}} \psi_1 \to \cdots \to \psi_n \to \phi$$

Proof. As in the proof of Proposition 1.5 in [8]. Left-to-right follows by induction on the structure of the natural deduction proof once one shows each instance of a natural deduction rule translates to a theorem of **GBL**$_{\mathbf{WEM}}$. We amend the provability ordering from [8] for the present system:

$$\phi \le \psi \text{ iff } \vdash_{\mathbf{GBL_{WEM}}} \phi \to \psi$$

Since **GBL**$_{\mathbf{WEM}}$ results from **GBL** by adding $(A14)$, all other cases are as in [8], except $(A14)$, which simply says the provability relation is directed. For the right to left direction of the 'iff', this follows by induction on the **GBL**$_{\mathbf{WEM}}$ derivation of $\psi_1 \to \cdots \to \psi_n \to \phi$ once we show that each of the axioms of **GBL**$_{\mathbf{WEM}}$ are theorems of **LLi**$_{\mathbf{WEM}}$. The only case left to verify then is $(A14)$. But this is an axiom in the natural deduction calculus **LLi**$_{\mathbf{WEM}}$, hence always provable in that calculus.   □

Note 1. Jankov's logic **JL** (alias **WEM** [5] or **KC** [4]) results from **LLi**$_{\mathbf{WEM}}$ by adjoining the structural rule of contraction.[3]

2.1   GBL and MV-Algebras

We situate the algebraic semantics characterising **LLi**$_{\mathbf{WEM}}$ in terms of the somewhat larger theory of residuated lattices.

Definition 1. $\mathcal{A} = \langle A, \wedge, \vee, \otimes, 1, \to \rangle$ *is called a* commutative residuated lattice *if*

- $\langle A, \wedge, \vee, \otimes, 1 \rangle$ *is a commutative lattice-ordered monoid.*
- $x \otimes y \le z$ *iff* $x \le y \to z$.

Definition 2 (GBL$_{\mathbf{WEM}}$**-algebras).** *A* **GBL**-*algebra* $\mathcal{A}$ *is a commutative residuated lattice which satisfies the* divisibility property: *if* $x \le y$ *then* $y \otimes (y \to x) = x$; *bounded from below, i.e. there is an element* $\bot \in A$ *such that* $\bot \le x$ *for all* $x \in A$; *integral in that* 1 *is the top element of the lattice, i.e.* $x \le 1$ *for all* $x \in A$. *In this case we also denote* 1 *by* $\top$. *A* **GBL**$_{\mathbf{WEM}}$-*algebra is a* **GBL**-*algebra that also satisfies* weak excluded middle *(WEM), in that* $\neg x \vee \neg\neg x = \top$ *for all* $x \in A$. *Finally, we note the condition of the divisibility property is equivalent to requiring that the residuated lattice satisfy the equation* $x \otimes (x \to y) = y \otimes (y \to x)$.

---

[3] Jankov's system is known under different names in the literature. We do not favour any of these, and instead opt for our own.

Definition 3 (MV-algebra and MV-chain). *A* **GBL**-*algebra* $\mathcal{A}$ *is called an* **MV**-*algebra if the negation map* $(\neg x = x \to \bot)$ *is an involution, i.e.* $(x \to \bot) \to \bot = x$, *for all* x, *and is pre-linear:* $(x \to y) \vee (y \to x)$. *An* **MV**-*algebra is an* **MV**-*chain if its underlying order is a linear order.*

MV-algebras provide an algebraic semantics for classical Łukasiewicz logic.

3   Valid Sequents in LLi$_{\text{WEM}}$

Definition 4 (Denotation functions). *Given a* **GBL**-*algebra* $\mathcal{A}$, *and a mapping (which is called an assignment) from propositional variables to elements of* $\mathcal{A}$:

$$p \mapsto \llbracket p \rrbracket \in \mathcal{A}$$

We thus refer to the denotation of a variable p *as* $\llbracket p \rrbracket_{\text{GBL}}$. *We can extend that mapping to all formulas in the language of* L *in a straightforward way:*

$$\llbracket \phi \otimes \psi \rrbracket_{\text{GBL}} := \llbracket \phi \rrbracket_{\text{GBL}} \otimes \llbracket \psi \rrbracket_{\text{GBL}}$$
$$\llbracket \phi \wedge \psi \rrbracket_{\text{GBL}} := \llbracket \phi \rrbracket_{\text{GBL}} \wedge \llbracket \psi \rrbracket_{\text{GBL}}$$
$$\llbracket \phi \vee \psi \rrbracket_{\text{GBL}} := \llbracket \phi \rrbracket_{\text{GBL}} \vee \llbracket \psi \rrbracket_{\text{GBL}}$$
$$\llbracket \phi \to \psi \rrbracket_{\text{GBL}} := \llbracket \phi \rrbracket_{\text{GBL}} \to \llbracket \psi \rrbracket_{\text{GBL}}$$

Definition 5 (Validity). *A sequent* $\phi_1, \ldots, \phi_n \vdash_{\text{LLi}_{\text{WEM}}} \psi$ *is valid in an* **GBL**$_{\text{WEM}}$-*algebra* $\mathcal{A}$, *if* $\llbracket \phi_1 \rrbracket \otimes \ldots \otimes \llbracket \phi_n \rrbracket \leq \llbracket \psi \rrbracket$ *holds for all assignments in* $\mathcal{A}$. *A sequent is valid if it is valid in all* **GBL**$_{\text{WEM}}$-*algebras. We can write this:* $\Gamma \models_{\text{GBL}_{\text{WEM}}} \phi$. *In the case where* ϕ *is valid in all* **GBL**$_{\text{WEM}}$-*algebras, we write* $\models_{\text{GBL}_{\text{WEM}}} \phi$.

The valid sequents, in the sense above, are precisely the ones provable in generalised basic logic with (**WEM**). The proof is straightforwardly similar to that given in [10] for basic logic:

Proposition 3. *A sequent* $\Gamma \vdash \psi$ *is* **GBL**$_{\text{WEM}}$-*valid iff it is provable in* **GBL**$_{\text{WEM}}$.

4   Kripke Semantics for LLi$_{\text{WEM}}$

Note 2. The Kripke semantics for **GBL**$_{\text{WEM}}$ that we propose is a variant of our semantics introduced in [8]. We first need to define a particular class of functions from the set of worlds W to (possibly different) MV-chains.

Definition 6 (Sloping functions). *Let* $\mathcal{W} = \langle W, \succeq \rangle$ *be a partial order with a greatest element* $w\prime$, *and* $\{\mathcal{A}_w\}_{w \in W}$ *be a* W-*indexed family of* **MV**-*chains with almost disjoint domains except that they share the top element* $\top$ *and the bottom element* $\bot$ *in common, and* $\mathcal{A}_{w\prime} = \{\bot, \top\}_{\text{BA}}$ *be the Boolean algebra of two elements (noting that all Boolean algebras are MV-chains, but not vice versa;*

in the present case, the Boolean algebra of two elements coincides with MV-chain of two elements). A function $f \colon W \to \bigcup_{w \in W} A_w$ is said to be a sloping function for **GBL$_{\text{WEM}}$** *(hereon sloping function, or sloping) if $f(w) \in A_w$ for all $w \in W$ and $f(w) > \bot$ implies $\forall v \succ w (f(v) = \top)$. We also stipulate that if $w\prime$ is greatest element in the partial order of worlds $\langle W, \succeq \rangle$ then either $f(w\prime) = \bot$ or $f(w\prime) = \top$, i.e. the greatest element is mapped to the Booleans $\{\bot, \top\}_{\text{BA}}$ or $\{\bot, \top\}$.*

Lemma 1. *If $f, g \colon W \to \bigcup_{w \in W} A_w$ are sloping, then so are the following functions:*

$$(f \wedge g)(w) := f(w) \wedge_{A_w} g(w)$$
$$(f \vee g)(w) := f(w) \vee_{A_w} g(w)$$
$$(f \otimes g)(w) := f(w) \otimes_{A_w} g(w)$$

Proof. As in [8]. Let f, g be sloping functions. Let us consider each case:

- $f \wedge g$. Assume $(f \wedge g)(w) > \bot$, then both $f(w) > \bot$ and $g(w) > \bot$. But since f, g are sloping functions, we have $\forall v \succ w (f(v) = \top)$ and $\forall v \succ w (g(v) = \top)$, so $\forall v \succ w ((f \wedge g)(v) = \top)$.
- $f \vee g$. Assume $(f \vee g)(w) > \bot$, then $f(w) > \bot$ or $g(w) > \bot$. But since f, g are sloping functions, we have $\forall v \succ w (f(v) = \top)$ or $\forall v \succ w (g(v) = \top)$, so $\forall v \succ w ((f \vee g)(v) = \top)$.
- $f \otimes g$. Assume $(f \wedge g)(w) > \bot$, then both $f(w) > \bot$ and $g(w) > \bot$. But since f, g are sloping functions, we have $\forall v \succ w (f(v) = \top)$ and $\forall v \succ w (g(v) = \top)$, so $\forall v \succ w ((f \otimes g)(v) = \top)$.   □

Definition 7. *Let $\lfloor \cdot \rfloor$ be the usual "floor" operation an MV-chain $\mathcal{A}$, corresponding to the case distinction*

$$\lfloor x \rfloor := \begin{cases} \top & \text{if } x = \top \\ \bot & \text{if } x < \top \end{cases}$$

which is known as the "Monteiro-Baaz Δ-operator". Given a (not necessarily sloping) function $f \colon W \to \bigcup_{w \in W} A_w$ and a $w \in W$, let us write $\lfloor \inf \rfloor_{v \succeq w}$ for the following construction:

$$\lfloor \inf \rfloor_{v \succeq w} f(v) := \min \{ f(w), \inf_{v \succ w} \lfloor f(v) \rfloor \}$$

where $\inf_{v \succ w} \lfloor f(v) \rfloor$ is the infimum of the set $\{ \lfloor f(v) \rfloor : v \succ w \} \subseteq \{\bot, \top\}$.

Lemma 2. *This definition of $\inf_{v \succeq w}$ can also be equivalently written as*

$$\lfloor \inf \rfloor_{v \succeq w} f(v) := \begin{cases} f(w) & \text{if } \forall v \succ w (f(v) = \top) \\ \bot & \text{if } \exists v \succ w (f(v) < \top) \end{cases}$$

and for any $f \colon W \to \bigcup_{w \in W} A_w$ the function $\lambda w . \lfloor \inf \rfloor_{v \succeq w} f(v)$ is a sloping function.

Proof. First let us show that this is an equivalent definition. Consider two cases:

Case 1. $\forall v \succ w(f(v) = \top)$. In this case $\inf_{v \succ w} \lfloor f(v) \rfloor = \top$ and hence

$$\lfloor \mathbf{inf} \rfloor_{v \succeq w} f(v) = \min\{f(w), \top\} = f(w)$$

Case 2. $\exists v \succ w(f(v) < \top)$. In this case $\inf_{v \succ w} \lfloor f(v) \rfloor = \bot$

$$\lfloor \mathbf{inf} \rfloor_{v \succeq w} f(v) = \min\{f(w), \bot\} = \bot$$

In order to see that $\lambda w. \lfloor \mathbf{inf} \rfloor_{v \succeq w} f(v)$ is a sloping function, assume that for some w we have $\lfloor \mathbf{inf} \rfloor_{v \succeq w} f(v) > \bot$, and let $w' \succ w$. By definition we have that $\forall v \succ w(f(v) = \top)$, and hence $f(w') = \top$ and $\forall v \succ w'(f(v) = \top)$, which implies $\lfloor \mathbf{inf} \rfloor_{v \succeq w'} f(v) = \top$.   □

Definition 8. *Let* $\mathcal{W} = \langle W, \succeq \rangle$ *be a poset with a greatest element w⊢, and* $\{\mathcal{A}_w\}_{w \in W}$ *be a W-indexed family of MV-chains as described in Definition 6. A Jankov-Jipsen-Bova-Montagna structure for* $\{\mathcal{A}_w\}_{w \in W}$ *(or JBM-structure) is a pair* $\mathcal{M} = \langle \mathcal{W}, \Vdash^{\mathrm{JBM}} \rangle$ *where* $\Vdash^{\mathrm{JBM}}$ *is an infix operator (on worlds and propositional variables) taking values in* $\bigcup_{w \in W} \mathcal{A}_w$, *i.e.* $(w \Vdash^{\mathrm{JBM}} p) \in \mathcal{A}_w$, *such that for any propositional variable* p *the function* $\lambda w.(w \Vdash^{\mathrm{JBM}} p) \colon W \to \bigcup_{w \in W} \mathcal{A}_w$ *is a sloping function.*

Example 1. *Diamond-shaped structure). Let* $\mathcal{M} = \langle \mathcal{W}, \Vdash^{\mathrm{JBM}} \rangle$ *be such that* $W = \{w_0, w_1, w_2, w_3\}$, *with* $w_0 \preceq w_1, w_0 \preceq w_2, w_1 \preceq w_3, w_2 \preceq w_3$ *and thus* $w_0 \preceq w_3$ *by transitivity. We set* $\mathcal{A}_{w_3}$ *to be the two-valued* **MV**-*algebra and* $\mathcal{A}_{w_0}, \mathcal{A}_{w_1}, \mathcal{A}_{w_2}$ *to be the standard* **MV**-*chain with domain* $[0, 1]$ *where* $0 = \bot$ *and* $1 = \top$. *Now let us define the function* $\lambda w.(w \Vdash^{\mathrm{JBM}} p) \colon W \to \bigcup_{w \in W} \mathcal{A}_w$ *for each propositional variable* p *as follows:*
$(w_0 \Vdash^{\mathrm{JBM}} p) = \bot$, $(w_1 \Vdash^{\mathrm{JBM}} p) = 0.5$, $(w_2 \Vdash^{\mathrm{JBM}} p) = 0.2$, *and* $(w_3 \Vdash^{\mathrm{JBM}} p) = \top$. *It is easy to see that* $\lambda w.(w \Vdash^{\mathrm{JBM}} p)$ *is a sloping function for each variable* p, *therefore* $\mathcal{M} = \langle \mathcal{W}, \Vdash^{\mathrm{JBM}} \rangle$ *is a JBM-structure.*

Definition 9 (JBM Kripke Semantics for $\mathcal{L}_\otimes$). *Given a JBM-structure*

$$\mathcal{M} = \langle \mathcal{W}, \Vdash^{\mathrm{JBM}} \rangle$$

the valuation function $w \Vdash^{\mathrm{JBM}} p$ *on propositional variables* p *can be extended to all* $\mathcal{L}_\otimes$-*formulas as:*

$$
\begin{aligned}
w \Vdash^{\mathrm{JBM}} \top \quad &:= \top \\
w \Vdash^{\mathrm{JBM}} \bot \quad &:= \bot \\
w \Vdash^{\mathrm{JBM}} \phi \wedge \psi \ &:= (w \Vdash^{\mathrm{JBM}} \phi) \wedge_{\mathcal{A}_w} (w \Vdash^{\mathrm{JBM}} \psi) \\
w \Vdash^{\mathrm{JBM}} \phi \vee \psi \ &:= (w \Vdash^{\mathrm{JBM}} \phi) \vee_{\mathcal{A}_w} (w \Vdash^{\mathrm{JBM}} \psi) \\
w \Vdash^{\mathrm{JBM}} \phi \otimes \psi \ &:= (w \Vdash^{\mathrm{JBM}} \phi) \otimes_{\mathcal{A}_w} (w \Vdash^{\mathrm{JBM}} \psi) \\
w \Vdash^{\mathrm{JBM}} \phi \to \psi \ &:= \lfloor \mathbf{inf} \rfloor_{v \succeq w} ((v \Vdash^{\mathrm{JBM}} \phi) \to_{\mathcal{A}_v} (v \Vdash^{\mathrm{JBM}} \psi))
\end{aligned}
$$

Lemma 3. *For any* ϕ, *the function* $\lambda w.(w \Vdash^{\mathrm{JBM}} \phi) \colon W \to \bigcup_{w \in W} \mathcal{A}_w$ *is sloping.*

Proof. By induction on ϕ. The cases for $\vee, \wedge, \otimes$ follow directly from Definition 9. The case for $\rightarrow$ follows from Lemma 2.   □

We can now generalise the monotonicity property of Jankov's logic (under the partially-ordered Kripke frames with greatest element) to $\mathbf{LLi_{wEM}}$:

Corollary 1 (Monotonicity). *The following (generalised) monotonicity property holds for all $\mathcal{L}_\otimes$-formulas ϕ, i.e.*

$$if\ w \preceq v then(w \Vdash^{JBM} \phi) \leq (v \Vdash^{JBM} \phi)$$

Proof This follows from the observation that the valuations are sloping functions, which are in turn monotone functions.   □

5   Validity Under JBM Structures

Definition 10. *Let $\Gamma = \psi_1, \ldots, \psi_n$. Consider the following definitions:*

- *A sequent $\Gamma \vdash \phi$ holds in a JBM-structure $\mathcal{M}$ (written $\Gamma \Vdash^{JBM}_{\mathcal{M}} \phi$) if for all $w \in W$,*

$$(w \Vdash^{JBM} \psi_1 \otimes \ldots \otimes \psi_n) \leq (w \Vdash^{JBM} \phi)$$

Otherwise, we say that the sequent fails $\mathcal{M}$ (written $\Gamma \nVdash^{JBM}_{\mathcal{M}} \phi$) and this means:

$$\exists w \in W : (w \Vdash^{JBM} \psi_1 \otimes \ldots \otimes \psi_n) > (w \Vdash^{JBM} \phi)$$

- *A sequent $\Gamma \vdash \phi$ is said to be valid under the JBM Kripke semantics for $\mathcal{L}_\otimes$ (written $\Gamma \Vdash^{JBM} \phi$) if $\Gamma \Vdash^{JBM}_{\mathcal{M}} \phi$ for all JBM-structures $\mathcal{M}$.*

6   JBMs and Jankov-Kripke Structures

Note 3. Jankov-Bova-Montagna structures generalise Jankov-Kripke structures (JK-structures for short), i.e. Kripke structures where the frame is a poset with greatest element.[4] This is because Kripke structures merely require the valuations $(w \Vdash^{JBM} p) \in \{\bot, \top\}$, i.e. in the Boolean algebra of two-elements. Therefore, any Jankov-Kripke structure can be seen as a JBM-structure, by defining

$$w \Vdash^{JBM} \phi = \begin{cases} \top\ \text{if} w \Vdash^{JK} \phi \\ \bot\ \text{if} w \nVdash^{JK} \phi \end{cases}$$

Note 4. Recall that $\mathcal{L} \subset \mathcal{L}_\otimes$ (with $\mathcal{L}$ referring to the language of **JL**), so any $\mathcal{L}$-formula is also an $\mathcal{L}_\otimes$-formula.

---

[4] We do not provide the definition here, which can be found in standard textbooks e.g. [9].

Theorem 1. *For any Jankov-Kripke structure* $\mathcal{JK} = \langle \mathcal{W}, \Vdash^{JK} \rangle$ *and* $\mathcal{L}$*-formula* ϕ*, we have* $\forall w$*:*

$$w \Vdash^{JK} \phi \quad \text{iff} \quad (w \Vdash^{JBM} \phi) = \top$$

Proof. By induction on the complexity of the formula ϕ. The base case follows by definition.

Induction step: We consider the important case. Suppose the result holds for all sub-formulas of ϕ:

$\rightarrow$ **Case.** $\phi = \psi \rightarrow \chi$. We use the fact that when restricted to Jankov-Kripke structures, $(v \Vdash^{JBM} \psi) \in \{\top, \bot\}$ and $(v \Vdash^{JBM} \chi) \in \{\top, \bot\}$, and hence

(i) $\forall v \succeq w(((v \Vdash^{JBM} \psi) = \top) \rightarrow ((v \Vdash^{JBM} \chi) = \top)) \Leftrightarrow \forall v \succeq w((v \Vdash^{JBM} \psi) \rightarrow (v \Vdash^{JBM} \chi)) = \top$

(ii) $\forall v \succeq w(((v \Vdash^{JBM} \psi) \rightarrow (v \Vdash^{JBM} \chi)) = \top) \Leftrightarrow \inf_{v \succeq w}((v \Vdash^{JBM} \psi) \rightarrow (v \Vdash^{JBM} \chi)) = \top$, i.e. the $\lfloor \inf \rfloor_{v \succeq w}$ translates directly into a universally quantifed expression, i.e. it is (again) a standard $\inf_{v \succeq w}$ operation (on a set).

Therefore:

$$
\begin{aligned}
w \Vdash^{JK} \psi \rightarrow \chi &\equiv \forall v \succeq w((v \Vdash^{JK} \psi) \rightarrow (v \Vdash^{JK} \chi)) \\
&\overset{(\text{IH})}{\Leftrightarrow} \forall v \succeq w((v \Vdash^{JBM} \psi) = \top \rightarrow (v \Vdash^{JBM} \chi) = \top) \\
&\overset{(6)}{\Leftrightarrow} \forall v \succeq w((v \Vdash^{JBM} \psi) \rightarrow (v \Vdash^{JBM} \chi) = \top) \\
&\overset{(6)}{\Leftrightarrow} \lfloor \inf \rfloor_{v \succeq w}((v \Vdash^{JBM} \psi) \rightarrow (v \Vdash^{JBM} \chi)) = \top \\
&\equiv (w \Vdash^{JBM} \psi \rightarrow \chi) = \top
\end{aligned}
$$

Thus ends the proof. □

We also note the following:

Proposition 4. *The JBM-structures generalise the present JK-structures.*

Proof. Trivial. □

7 Soundness

We now prove the soundness of the Kripke semantics for **LLi$_{WEM}$**.

Theorem 2 (Soundness). *If* $\Gamma \vdash_{\text{LLi}_{WEM}} \phi$ *then* $\Gamma \Vdash^{JBM} \phi$.

Proof By induction on the derivation of $\Gamma \vdash \phi$. Assume $\Gamma = \psi_1, \ldots, \psi_n$ and let $\otimes \Gamma := \psi_1 \otimes \ldots \otimes \psi_n$. Fix a JBM-structure $\mathcal{M} = \langle \mathcal{W}, \Vdash^{JBM} \rangle$ with $\mathcal{W} = \langle W, \succeq \rangle$, and let $w \in W$. We exhibit only one case, as the rest of the proof is analogous to that of [8].

(WEM) $\Gamma \vdash \neg\phi \vee \neg\neg\phi$. By Definition 10, we need to show:

$$w \Vdash^{JBM} (\otimes \Gamma) \overset{(\text{L.10})}{\leq} (w \Vdash^{JBM} (\phi \rightarrow \bot) \vee ((\phi \rightarrow \bot) \rightarrow \bot)) = \top$$

which is equivalent to:

$$w \Vdash^{\mathrm{JBM}} (\otimes \Gamma) \leq \max\{(w \Vdash^{\mathrm{JBM}} (\phi \to \bot), w \Vdash^{\mathrm{JBM}} ((\phi \to \bot) \to \bot))\} = \top$$

where the right of the inequality means: Either $(w \Vdash^{\mathrm{JBM}} (\phi \to \bot)) = \top$ or $(w \Vdash^{\mathrm{JBM}} (\phi \to \bot) \to \bot) = \top$. Here we break into cases.

Case 1. $(w \Vdash^{\mathrm{JBM}} (\phi \to \bot)) = \top$. We have:

$$
\begin{aligned}
&(w \Vdash^{\mathrm{JBM}} (\phi \to \bot)) = \top \\
\equiv\ &\lfloor \mathbf{inf} \rfloor_{v \succeq w}((v \Vdash^{\mathrm{JBM}} \phi) \to_{\mathcal{A}_v} (v \Vdash^{\mathrm{JBM}} \bot)) = \top \\
\Leftrightarrow\ &\forall v : v \succeq w((v \Vdash^{\mathrm{JBM}} \phi) = (v \Vdash^{\mathrm{JBM}} \bot))
\end{aligned}
$$

Case 2. $(w \Vdash^{\mathrm{JBM}} (\phi \to \bot) \to \bot) = \top$. We have:

$$
\begin{aligned}
&(w \Vdash^{\mathrm{JBM}} (\phi \to \bot) \to \bot)) = \top \\
\equiv\ &\lfloor \mathbf{inf} \rfloor_{v \succeq w}((v \Vdash^{\mathrm{JBM}} \phi \to \bot) \to_{\mathcal{A}_v} (v \Vdash^{\mathrm{JBM}} \bot)) = \top \\
\Leftrightarrow\ &\forall v \succeq w((v \Vdash^{\mathrm{JBM}} \phi \to \bot) = (v \Vdash^{\mathrm{JBM}} \bot)) \\
\Leftrightarrow\ &\forall v \succeq w, \exists u \succ v(((u \Vdash^{\mathrm{JBM}} \phi) \to_{\mathcal{A}_u} (u \Vdash^{\mathrm{JBM}} \bot)) < \top) \vee (((v \Vdash^{\mathrm{JBM}} \phi) \to_{\mathcal{A}_v} (v \Vdash^{\mathrm{JBM}} \bot)) = \bot) \\
\Leftrightarrow\ &\forall v \succeq w, \exists u \succ v((u \Vdash^{\mathrm{JBM}} \phi) > \bot) \vee ((v \Vdash^{\mathrm{JBM}} \phi) = \top)
\end{aligned}
$$

These latter cases show that we must then prove:

$$\forall v \succeq w((v \Vdash^{\mathrm{JBM}} \phi) = (v \Vdash^{\mathrm{JBM}} \bot)) \vee \forall v \succeq w, \exists u \succ v((u \Vdash^{\mathrm{JBM}} \phi) > \bot) \vee ((v \Vdash^{\mathrm{JBM}} \phi) = \top) \quad (1)$$

If $\forall v \succeq w(v \Vdash^{\mathrm{JBM}} \phi = v \Vdash^{\mathrm{JBM}} \bot)$ does not hold, then there is a point $v \succeq w$ with $(v \Vdash^{\mathrm{JBM}} \phi) > \bot$. Then the top node $w\prime$ is such that $(w\prime \Vdash^{\mathrm{JBM}} \phi) > \bot$, therefore by the crispness of the top node, we have that $(w\prime \Vdash^{\mathrm{JBM}} \phi) = \top$. Then for any $v \succeq w$, if v is the top node, then $(v \Vdash^{\mathrm{JBM}} \phi) = \top$; otherwise, there is a $u = w\prime \succ v$ such that $(u \Vdash^{\mathrm{JBM}} \phi) = \top > \bot$. $\square$

8   JBM's, Poset Products, Completeness

A *poset product* (cf. [2] and [7]) is defined over a poset $\mathcal{W} = \langle W, \preceq \rangle$ as the algebra $\mathbf{A}_{\mathcal{W}}$ of signature $\mathcal{L}_{\otimes}$ whose elements are sloping functions $f \colon W \to \bigcup_{w \in W} \mathcal{A}_w$ and operations are defined as below:

$$
\begin{aligned}
(\bot)(w) \quad &:= \bot \\
(f_1 \wedge f_2)(w) \quad &:= f_1(w) \wedge_{\mathcal{A}_w} f_2(w) \\
(f_1 \vee f_2)(w) \quad &:= f_1(w) \vee_{\mathcal{A}_w} f_2(w) \\
(f_1 \otimes f_2)(w) \quad &:= f_1(w) \otimes_{\mathcal{A}_w} f_2(w) \\
(f_1 \to f_2)(w) \quad &:= \begin{cases} f_1(w) \to_{\mathcal{A}_w} f_2(w) & \text{if } \forall v \succ w(f_1(v) \leq f_2(v)) \\ \bot & \text{otherwise.} \end{cases}
\end{aligned}
$$

Since f_1 and f_2 are sloping functions, we have that

$$\forall v \succ w(f_1(v) \leq f_2(v)) \quad \Leftrightarrow \quad \forall v \succ w((f_1(v) \to_{\mathcal{A}_v} f_2(v)) = \top)$$

Therefore, this last clause of the definition can be simplified to

$$(f_1 \to f_2)(w) := \lfloor \mathbf{inf} \rfloor_{v \succeq w}(f_1(v) \to_{\mathcal{A}_v} f_2(v))$$

Definition 11 (Poset Product semantics for $\mathcal{L}_\otimes$). *Let* $\mathcal{W} = \langle W, \preceq \rangle$ *be a fixed partially-ordered set with a greatest element, and* $\mathbf{A}_\mathcal{W}$ *be the poset product described above. Given* $h : Atoms \to \mathbf{A}_\mathcal{W}$ *an assignment of atomic formulas to elements of* $\mathbf{A}_\mathcal{W}$*, any formula* ϕ *can be mapped to an element* $[\![\phi]\!]_h \in \mathbf{A}_\mathcal{W}$ *as follows:*

$$
\begin{aligned}
[\![p]\!]_h &:= h(p) \quad (for\,atomic\,formulas\,p)\\
[\![\bot]\!]_h &:= \bot\\
[\![\phi \wedge \psi]\!]_h &:= [\![\phi]\!]_h \wedge [\![\psi]\!]_h\\
[\![\phi \vee \psi]\!]_h &:= [\![\phi]\!]_h \vee [\![\psi]\!]_h\\
[\![\phi \otimes \psi]\!]_h &:= [\![\phi]\!]_h \otimes [\![\psi]\!]_h\\
[\![\phi \to \psi]\!]_h &:= [\![\phi]\!]_h \to [\![\psi]\!]_h
\end{aligned}
$$

A formula ϕ *is said to be* valid *in* $\mathbf{A}_\mathcal{W}$ *under* h *if for every* $w \in W$, $[\![\phi]\!]_h^{\mathbf{A}_\mathcal{W}}(w) = \top$. *A formula* ϕ *is valid in* $\mathbf{A}_\mathcal{W}$ *if it is valid in* $\mathbf{A}_\mathcal{W}$ *under* h *for any possible mapping* $h \colon Atoms \to \mathbf{A}_\mathcal{W}$.

The next proposition we prove directly, as it is not contained in any of the cited works from earlier.

Proposition 5. *Let* $\mathcal{W} = \langle W, \preceq \rangle$ *be a partially-ordered set with greatest element* $w\prime$, *and* $\{\mathcal{A}_w : w \in W\}$ *an indexed collection of* **MV***-chains, with the restriction* $\{\mathcal{A}_{w\prime} : w\prime \in W\}$ *being the two-element* **MV***-chain. Then the poset product of this collection is a* **GBL$_{\mathbf{WEM}}$***-algebra:*

$$
\mathbf{A}_\mathcal{W} = \prod_{w \in \langle W, \preceq \rangle} \mathcal{A}_w.
$$

Proof. First, the poset products of MV-chains are **GBL**-algebras; see [7, Proposition 3.2]. As **GBL$_{\mathbf{WEM}}$**-algebras are **GBL**-algebras, we only need to show that the product $\mathbf{A}_\mathcal{W}$ satisfies **WEM**: We must show, where f is a sloping function in $\mathbf{A}_\mathcal{W}$, that $\neg f \vee \neg\neg f = \top$. This gives, as in the soundness proof above, two cases: either $\neg f = \top$ or $\neg\neg f = \top$. We consider each case in turn.

Case 1. $\neg f = \top$. This is the same as $f \to \bot = \top$. This holds iff for all $w > v$, including the maximal element $w\prime$, $f(w\prime) \leq \bot(w\prime)$. But this can only hold iff $f(w\prime) = \bot$.

Case 2. $\neg\neg f = \top$. This is the same as $(f \to \bot) \to \bot = \top$. This holds iff $(f \to \bot)(w\prime) = \bot$, which holds iff $f(w\prime) \to \bot(w\prime) = \bot$ iff $f(w\prime) = \top$.

Since $f(w\prime) \in \{\bot, \top\}$, the two cases above are sufficient. $\square$

To obtain the embedding for completeness, by [11] we show that the subdirectly irreducibles of the variety under consideration embed in the intended poset product. Unfortunately, one cannot embed the more general class of algebras in this way.[5]

In what follows we give some necessary definitions for the completeness proof:

Definition 12 (Variety). *A class of algebras of the same signature is a variety if it is closed under taking homomorphic images, subalgebras and products.*

Definition 13 (Subdirect Product, Subdirect Embedding). *[6] An algebra $\mathcal{A}$ is a subdirect product of an indexed family $(\mathcal{A}_i)_i \in I$ of algebras if*

   i $\mathcal{A}$ is a subalgebra of $\prod_{i \in I} \mathcal{A}_i$ (the embedding $\mathcal{A} \to \prod_{i \in I} \mathcal{A}_i$ is called the subdirect embedding) and
   ii $\pi_i(\mathcal{A}) = \mathcal{A}_i$ for each $i \in I$, where $\pi_i : \prod_{i \in I} \mathcal{A}_i \to \mathcal{A}_i$ is the projection map to the i-coordinate.

Definition 14 (Subdirectly irreducible algebra). *[6] An algebra $\mathcal{A}$ is subdirectly irreducible if for every subdirect embedding $\alpha : \mathcal{A} \to \prod_{i \in I} \mathcal{A}_i$ there is an $i \in I$ such that $\pi_i \circ \alpha : \mathcal{A} \to \mathcal{A}_i$ is an isomorphism.*

Definition 15 (Simple residuated lattice). *A residuated lattice $\mathcal{A}$ is simple iff $\mathcal{A}$ has only two deductive filters $F \subseteq A$, i.e. the trivial filter $\{1\}$ and the improper filter A.*

Lemma 4. *Simple* **GBL***-algebras are totally-ordered MV-algebras.*

Proof. Let $\mathcal{A}$ be a simple **GBL**-algebra. Then by definition there is only one non-trivial deductive filter . The proof of Lemma 3.8 in [1] shows that the minimum non-trivial deductive filter of $\mathcal{A}$ forms an integral GMV-algebra, and hence $\mathcal{A}$ is an integral and commutative GMV-algebra. But since $\mathcal{A}$ is also bounded, it forms an MV-algebra (see e.g. [1] Definition 2.3). Since $\mathcal{A}$ is simple it is subdirectly irreducible, and all subdirectly irreducible MV-algebras are totally-ordered. □

Proposition 6. *Let* **S** *be the class of subdirectly irreducible members of the variety* **V** *of* **GBL$_{\mathbf{WEM}}$***-algebras. Then every member of* **S** *can be embedded inside a poset product $\prod_{w \in \langle W, \preceq \rangle} \mathcal{A}_w$, whose factors $\mathcal{A}_w$ are MV-chains and whose poset has a greatest element $w\prime$ such that $\mathcal{A}_{w\prime} = \{\bot, \top\}$.*

Proof. The strategy for this argument comes from [11] Sect. 3.2 and Lemma 5.2(2), pages 107 and 114 respectively.[6] The general idea is that, to procure completeness, we look at a subset of a variety of residuated lattices that generates

---

[5] To illustrate why this cannot be the case: Let **2** be the Boolean Algebra $\{\bot, \top\}$ and let **2** × **2** be the direct product of these. Recall that every direct product is a poset product, where the ordering relation on the indexing poset is the equality relation. Then **2** × **2** is a **GBL$_{\mathbf{WEM}}$**-algebra, but is not embeddable into any poset product indexed by a poset with greatest element whose corresponding factor is **2**. Thanks to Wesley Fussner for this illuminating example.

[6] We thank Wesley Fussner for discussion of this embedding result. The argument is due to him (derived principally from his paper [11]), presented with some minor corrections and added details.

whole variety, i.e. the 'subdirect irreducibles' for that class. Then we show that these irreducibles can be embedded within the poset product of MV-chains whose poset has a greatest element, $w\prime$, such that $\mathcal{A}_{w\prime} = \{\bot, \top\}$.

First of all, each subdirectly irreducible **GBL**-algebra **A** can be embedded into a poset product of MV-chains; in particular, if **A** has a maximal deductive filter, then the poset product has a the top node of the form $\mathbf{A}/G$ [7, Corollary 5.4].

So, let **V** be the variety of **GBL$_{\mathbf{WEM}}$**-algebras and let **S** be the subdirect irreducible members of **V**. If **A** is in **S**, then the set $G = \{x : \neg x = \bot\}$ is a non-trivial deductive filter (for the definition, see [11] Sect. 2.2 page 101). Suppose H is any other non-trivial deductive filter, take x be in H. By WEM, $\neg x \vee \neg\neg x = \top$. Since **A** is subdirectly irreducible and commutative, **A** is also weakly commutative in the sense of [1]; by applying Proposition 22 of [1], we obtain that $\top$ is a join-irreducible element. This implies that $\neg x = \top$ or $\neg\neg x = \top$. If $\neg x = \top$, then $\neg\neg x = \bot$; if $\neg\neg x = \top$, then $\neg x = \neg\neg\neg x = \bot$. Thus either $x \in G$ or $\neg x \in G$. Now if $\neg x$ is in G, then by definition $\neg\neg x = \bot$ and since $x \leq \neg\neg x$, we have $x = \bot$. This contradicts the assumption that H is non-trivial, so we must have that $x \in G$. Hence G is the largest non-trivial deductive filter of **A**.

Forming the quotient algebra (of **A**) by the maximal deductive filter G, we obtain $\mathbf{A}/G$. This is a simple algebra by [6] Theorem 8.9 in II.8: the maximal deductive filter G corresponds to the maximal congruence in the congruence lattice given by the interval $[\theta_G, \nabla]$, where θ is a congruence on **A**. Now, since simple **GBL**-algebras are totally ordered MV-algebras by Lemma 4, we thus have that $\mathbf{A}/G$ is a simple MV-algebra that satisfies WEM. This implies that $\mathbf{A}/G$ is the 2-element Boolean algebra $\{\bot, \top\}$ as desired.   □

Note 5. We conclude this section by observing that given a poset product $\mathbf{A}_{\mathcal{W}}$ over a poset $\mathcal{W} = \langle W, \succeq \rangle$ with a greatest element and a mapping $h\colon Atoms \to \mathbf{A}_{\mathcal{W}}$ of atomic formulas to elements of $\mathbf{A}_{\mathcal{W}}$, we can obtain a JBM-structure $\mathcal{M}^{\mathbf{A}_{\mathcal{W}}} = \langle \mathcal{W}, \Vdash_h^{\mathrm{JBM}} \rangle$, by taking

$$(w \Vdash_h^{\mathrm{JBM}} p) := h(p)(w)$$

recalling that $h(p)\colon W \to \bigcup_{w \in W} \mathcal{A}_w$ is a sloping function.

Proposition 7. *Let $\mathbf{A}_{\mathcal{W}}$ be the poset product over a poset $\mathcal{W} = \langle W, \succeq \rangle$ with greatest elements, and $h\colon Atoms \to \mathbf{A}_{\mathcal{W}}$ be a fixed mapping of atomic formulas to elements of $\mathcal{W}$. Let $\mathcal{M}^{\mathbf{A}_{\mathcal{W}}}$ be the JBM-structure defined above. Then, for any formula ϕ,*

$$(w \Vdash_h^{\mathrm{JBM}} \phi) = \llbracket \phi \rrbracket_h^{\mathbf{A}_{\mathcal{W}}}(w).$$

Proof. By induction on the complexity of ϕ.   □

As expected, we can always map an interpretation of $\mathcal{L}_{\otimes}$-formulas in the poset product $\mathbf{A}_{\mathcal{W}}$ into a general Kripke semantics (on the Kripke frame $\mathcal{W}$) for $\mathcal{L}_{\otimes}$-formulas.

Now we can derive completeness of $\mathbf{LLi_{WEM}}$ for the semantics presented above.

Theorem 3. *If $\Gamma \Vdash^{\mathrm{JBM}} \phi$, then $\Gamma \vdash_{\mathbf{LLi_{WEM}}} \phi$.*

Proof. Let $\Gamma \equiv \psi_1, \ldots, \psi_n$. Suppose $\Gamma \nvdash_{\mathbf{LLi_{WEM}}} \phi$. By Proposition 2 it follows that $\nvdash_{\mathbf{GBL_{WEM}}} \psi_1 \to \ldots \to \psi_n \to \phi$. By the algebraic completeness result for $\mathbf{GBL_{WEM}}$ algebras with respect to the proof system $\mathbf{GBL_{WEM}}$ (cf. Section 3), it follows that for some $\mathbf{GBL_{WEM}}$ algebra $\mathcal{G}$ and some mapping $h : Atom \to G$ from propositional variables to elements of $\mathcal{G}$, we have $[\![\psi_1 \to \ldots \to \psi_n \to \phi]\!]_h^{\mathcal{G}} \neq \top$. By Proposition 5 there exists a poset $\mathcal{W} = \langle W, \succeq \rangle$ with maximal element (denoted w') and an assignment $h' : Atom \to \mathbf{A}_{\mathcal{W}}$ of atomic formulas to elements of the poset product $\mathbf{A}_{\mathcal{W}}$, such that for some $w \in W$, $[\![\psi_1 \to \ldots \to \psi_n \to \phi]\!]_{h'}^{\mathbf{A}_{\mathcal{W}}}(w) \neq \top$. By Proposition 7, we have a JBM-structure $\mathcal{M}^{\mathbf{A}_{\mathcal{W}}}$ such that for some $w \in W$, $(w \Vdash_{h'}^{\mathrm{JBM}} \psi_1 \to \ldots \to \psi_n \to \phi) \neq \top$, and hence $(w \Vdash_{h'}^{\mathrm{JBM}} \psi_1 \otimes \ldots \otimes \psi_n) \not\preceq (w \Vdash^{\mathrm{JBM}} \phi)$ and $\psi_1, \ldots, \psi_n \nVdash^{\mathrm{JBM}} \phi$. $\square$

Acknowledgement. The research of Zhiguang Zhao is supported by Shandong Provincial Natural Science Foundation, China (project number: ZR2023QF021).

References

1. Jipsen, P., Montagna, F.: The blok-ferreirim theorem for normal GBL-algebras and its application. Algebra Univers. **60**, 381–404 (2009)
2. Bova, S., Montagna, F.: The consequence relation in the logic of commutative GBL-algebras is PSPACE-complete. Theoret. Comput. Sci. **410**(12), 1143–1158 (2009)
3. Lewis-Smith, A.: A Kripke semantics for Hajek's BL. Electron. Proc. Theor. Comput. Sci. **381**, 20–31 (2023)
4. Gabbay, D., Maksimova, L.: Interpolation and Definability: modal and intuitionistic logics. Oxford University Press UK (2005)
5. Jankov, V.A.: The Calculus of the Weak Law of Excluded Middle. Izv. Akad. Nauk SSSR Math. USSR - Izvestija Ser. Mat. Tom 32 (1968), No. 5 Vol. 2 (1968), No. 5
6. Burris, S., Sankappanavar, H.: A course in universal algebra. American Math. Mon. **91** (1981)
7. Jipsen, P., Montagna, F.: Embedding theorems for classes of GBL-algebras. J. Pure Appl. Algebra **214**(9), 1559–1575 (2010)
8. Lewis-Smith, A., Oliva, P., Robinson, E.: Kripke Semantics for Intuitionistic Łukasiewicz Logic. Stud. Logica. **410**(12), 313–339 (2021)
9. Priest, G.: An Introduction to Non-Classical Logic: From If to Is. 2nd edn. Cambridge University Press (2008)
10. Hájek, P.: Metamathematics of Fuzzy Logics. Kluwer Academic Publishers (1998)
11. Fussner, W.: Poset Products as relational models. Stud. Logica. **110**, 95–120 (2022)
12. Cignoli, R., Esteva, F., Godo, L., Torrens, A.: Basic Fuzzy Logic is the logic of continuous t-norms and their residua. Soft. Comput. **4**, 106–112 (2000)
13. Terwijn, S.: Constructive logic and the medvedev lattice. Notre Dame J. Formal Logic **47**, 73–82 (2006)

14. Lifschitz, V., Pearce, D., Valverde, A.: Strongly equivalent logic programs. ACM Trans. Comput. Logic (TOCL) **2**(4), 526–541 (2001)
15. Gelfond, M., Lifschitz, V.: The stable model semantics for logic programming. In: Logic programming, Proceedings of the Fifth International Conference and Symposium, Volume 2, Eds. Robert A. Kowalski and Kenneth A. Bowen, Series in logic programming, The MIT Press, Cambridge, Mass., and London, 1070–1080 (1988)
16. Pearce, D.: A new logical characterisation of stable models and answer sets. Non-Monotonic Extensions of Logic Programming. Ed. J. Dix, L. M. Pereira and T. C. Przymusinski, 57-70 (1997)

From Modal Ockham Algebras to Modal Berman Variety: Relational Semantics and Kripke-Completeness

Yiheng Wang[✉][ID]

Institute of Logic and Cognition, Sun Yat-sen University, Guangzhou 510275, China
ianwang747@gmail.com

Abstract. This paper investigates the sequential logics for modal Ockham algebras, which are Ockham algebras with normal modal operators $\Box, \Diamond$ satisfying interaction axioms. Relational semantics are established for this logic, and discrete duality is shown using star semantics. We then obtain the Kripke-completeness for this logic and some common modal extensions by the canonical model method. Furthermore, we extend existing results, which are based on modal Ockham algebra, to each modal Berman variety.

Keywords: modal Ockham algebra · modal Berman variety · Kripke-completeness · discrete duality · star frame

1 Introduction

Ockham algebra was introduced by Berman [4] and named after the medieval logician William of Ockham by Urquhart [32]. An Ockham algebra $(A, \wedge, \vee, \sim, 0, 1)$ is a bounded distributive lattice with an *Ockham negation* $\sim$ i.e. satisfying (o1) $\sim 0 = 1$, (o2) $\sim 1 = 0$, (o3) $\sim(a \wedge b) = \sim a \vee \sim b$, and (o4) $\sim(a \vee b) = \sim a \wedge \sim b$ for any $a, b \in A$. It can also be obtained from the quasi-Boolean algebra[1] (cf. [5,29]) by removing the double negation law $\sim\sim a = a$ for any $a \in A$. The variety of all Ockham algebras $\mathbf{O}$ is important since many well-known classes of algebras are its subvariety. To illustrate this, Berman [4] introduced the notion of *Berman variety*: A Berman variety $\mathbf{K}_{\kappa,\lambda}$ is a subvariety of $\mathbf{O}$ that satisfies the following condition[2]: for any $a \in A$, $(\sim_{\kappa,\lambda}) \sim^{2\kappa+\lambda}a = \sim^{\lambda}a$ where $\kappa \geq 1$, $\lambda \geq 0$. Blyth and Varlet [7, p. 8] related different Berman varieties by an inclusion order: $\mathbf{K}_{\kappa,\lambda} \subseteq \mathbf{K}_{\kappa',\lambda'}$ if and only if $\kappa \mid \kappa'$ and $\lambda \leq \lambda'$ where $\mid$ is the divisibility relation. Clearly, the smallest Berman variety $\mathbf{K}_{1,0}$ is exactly the variety of all quasi-Boolean algebras. Many algebraic studies related to Ockham algebras and Berman variety can be found in the literature [7,8,19,20,22,25,32].

Some Berman varieties, particularly the variety of quasi-Boolean algebras endowed with modal operations, have been explored in the context of applying

---

[1] Also known as De Morgan algebra (cf. [21]).
[2] Let $\sim^0 a = a$ and $\sim^{n+1}a = \sim^n\sim a$ where $n \geq 0$.

G. Casini et al. (Eds.): JELIA 2025, LNAI 16093, pp. 290–305, 2026.
https://doi.org/10.1007/978-3-032-04587-4_18

rough set theory to knowledge representation within AI. We provide a brief overview of these connections. Pawlak's rough set theory [28] is founded on the so-called *approximation space* (W, R) such that W is a non-empty set and R is an equivalence relation modeling the *indiscernibility* on W. Let $[w]_R = \{v \in U : wRv\}$ be the equivalence class of any $w \in W$ under R. Then for any $X \subseteq W$, *lower* and *upper* approximations are defined as $L(X) = \{x \in X : [w]_R \subseteq X\}$ and $U(X) = \{x \in X : [w]_R \cap X \neq \varnothing\}$. The resulting pair $(L(X), U(X))$ is called a *rough set* in (W, R). Further operations can be defined on the collection of all rough sets of (W, R) (cf. [23]):[3]

$$(L(X), U(X)) \sqcap (L(Y), U(Y)) = (L(X) \cap L(Y), U(X) \cap U(Y))$$

$$(L(X), U(X)) \sqcup (L(Y), U(Y)) = (L(X) \cup L(Y), U(X) \cup U(Y))$$
$$- (L(X), U(X)) = (L(\overline{X}), U(\overline{X}))$$

An *approximation space algebra* $((L(X), U(X)), \sqcap, \sqcup, -, (W, W), (\varnothing, \varnothing))$ induced by these operations was shown to be a quasi-Boolean algebra (cf. [1,2]). Subsequent research has extensively investigated modal extensions of quasi-Boolean algebras through logical and algebraic frameworks to capture richer aspects of rough sets (cf. e.g. [1,3,31,34]). Since the variety of all quasi-Boolean algebras is the smallest Berman variety, studies of modal Ockham algebra (modal Berman variety) shall generalize the study of rough set algebra.

This paper studies the logics of Ockham algebras (Berman variety) enriched with normal modal operators $\square, \Diamond$ (cf. Definition 1 and 8). Such structures can be traced back to Dunn's [16] work on *positive modal logic* K_+. The algebraic counterpart of K_+ is the *positive modal algebra*. A positive modal algebra $(A, \wedge, \vee, \square, \Diamond, 0, 1)$ is a bounded distributive lattice further satisfying $(n_\square)$, $(n_\Diamond)$, $(k_\square)$, $(k_\Diamond)$, $(i_\square)$, and $(i_\Diamond)$ in Definition 1 below. $(i_\square)$ and $(i_\Diamond)$ are called *interaction axioms*, they are essential in establishing classical-like relational semantics. Relational semantics of positive modal logics were developed in, e.g. [9,10]. Following this research line, modal Ockham algebras (Berman variety) can be regarded as enriching positive modal algebras with an additional operation $\sim$, and this paper focuses on establishing their relational semantics with Kripke-completeness.

There are already many systematic studies on logic with non-classical negations using relational structures (cf. e.g. [13,14,33]). Dunn [15,17] summarized two treatments of non-classical negations: *star semantics* and perp semantics[4]. This paper shall focus on star semantics. A *star frame* defined in [15] is a 3-tuple $(W, \leq, g)$[5] where $(W, \leq)$ is a poset and g is an antitone function on $(W, \leq)$. Examples using such structures are the De Morgan frame studied in [11,18,21][6].

---

[3] Throughout this paper, standard set-theoretical operations $\cap$ (intersection), $\cup$ (union), and $\overline{(\cdot)}$ (complement) are employed.

[4] Famous examples are Routley star [30] and intuitionistic negation, respectively.

[5] Note that in [15] and other literature, the Routley star $*$ are used instead of g. However, throughout this paper, we shall always use g to denote such a function since we follow Rasiowa's tradition.

[6] A *De Morgan frame* $(W, \leq, g)$ is a star frame further satisfying that g is an involution i.e. $g(g(w)) = w$ for any $w \in W$. Usually, a binary relation R is added to it for the study of relational semantics of some modal extensions.

According to Dunn [15], the definition of star frame originated from the representation theorem of quasi-Boolean algebra by Białynicki-Birula and Rasiowa [5,29]. However, in Białynicki-Birula and Rasiowa's work, the frame counterpart of quasi-Boolean algebra is the so-called *involutive frame* (W, g), where W is non-empty and g is an involution on W. Clearly, an involutive frame can be obtained from a De Morgan frame by dropping the partial order. This suggests a simpler approach to use star semantics. Some recent results have echoed this idea. In [24], the Kripke-completeness for logics of quasi-Boolean algebra with normal modal operators was shown using the involutive frame rather than the De Morgan frame. In [26], a relational structure for the logic of Ockham algebra is shown by weakening g to a mere function. Completeness w.r.t. such frames is claimed in the same paper without too much detail. Inspired by these works, we shall deal with more general logics from modal Ockham algebra to Berman variety using simpler star frames.

The contribution and organization of this paper are as follows. This paper continues all these research lines by adding a binary relation R to (W, g) where g is a mere function, just like in [26]. We call the resulting frame (W, g, R) an OML-frame (cf. Definition 4) in Sect. 2. Using the canonical model method, we then show the Kripke-completeness for logics of modal Ockham algebras w.r.t. such structures in Sect. 3. We further extend these results to logics of the modal Berman variety of each κ, λ by adding more conditions to the OML-frame (cf. Definition 9) in Sect. 4. Some common modal extensions are also shown to be Kripke-complete by canonicity. Discrete dualities are also presented in Sect. 2 and 4. We give some concluding remarks in Sect. 5.

2   Sequential Logic for Modal Ockham Algebras

In this section, we introduce the sequential logic for Ockham algebra with modal operators. Then, we present relational semantics with discrete duality.

2.1   Sequential Logic

Definition 1. *An algebra structure* $(A, \wedge, \vee, \sim, \Box, \Diamond, 0, 1)$ *is called a* modal Ockham algebra *(MO for short) where* $(A, \wedge, \vee, \sim, 0, 1)$ *is an Ockham algebra, and* $\Box, \Diamond$ *are unary operations on* A *satisfying the following conditions: for any* $a, b \in A$,

$$(\text{n}_\Box)\ \Box 1 = 1 \quad (\text{n}_\Diamond)\ \Diamond 0 = 0 \quad (\text{k}_\Box)\ \Box(a \wedge b) = \Box a \wedge \Box b \quad (\text{k}_\Diamond)\ \Diamond(a \vee b) = \Diamond a \vee \Diamond b$$

$$(\text{i}_\Box)\ \Box(a \vee b) \leq \Box a \vee \Diamond b \quad (\text{i}_\Diamond)\ \Box a \wedge \Diamond b \leq \Diamond(a \wedge b)$$

Let **MO** be the variety of all MOs. The order $\leq$ on A is the lattice order.

Fact 1. *The following holds for any MO: for any* $a, b \in A$, *(1) If* $a \leq b$, *then* $\sim b \leq \sim a$; *(2) If* $a \leq b$, *then* $\Diamond a \leq \Diamond b$ *and* $\Box a \leq \Box b$; *(3)* $\Box a \vee \Box b \leq \Box(a \vee b)$ *and* $\Diamond(a \wedge b) \leq \Diamond a \wedge \Diamond b$.

Definition 2. *The set of all formulas $\mathscr{F}$ is defined inductively as follows:*

$$\mathscr{F} \ni \alpha ::= p \mid \perp \mid \alpha_1 \wedge \alpha_2 \mid \alpha_1 \vee \alpha_2 \mid \sim\!\alpha \mid \Box\alpha \mid \Diamond\alpha$$

where $p \in \mathbf{Var} = \{p_i : i < \omega\}$, a denumerable set of propositional variables. Let $\top := \sim\!\perp$. Formulas in $\mathbf{Var} \cup \{\perp\}$ are called *atomic*. The *complexity* of any formula α is defined in the usual way. A *substitution* is an endomorphism $\sigma : \mathscr{F} \to \mathscr{F}$. Since there is no implication-like operation in Ockham algebra (Berman variety), the traditional Hilbert-like axiomatization system is not available here. Thus, we use basic sequents (essentially consequence pairs) to represent axioms. We call such kinds of logic *sequential logic*. A *basic sequent* is an expression of the form $\alpha \Rightarrow \beta$ where $\alpha, \beta \in \mathscr{F}^7$. Let s, t etc. denote any basic sequents, and $\mathcal{BS}$ denote the *set of all basic sequents*. Now, we are ready to define the sequential logic of **MO**.

Definition 3. *An* Ockham modal logic *(OML for short) L is a set of basic sequents such that the following conditions hold:*

(1) L contains all instances of the following axiom schemata:

$$(\text{ID}) \; \alpha \Rightarrow \alpha \quad (\top) \; \alpha \Rightarrow \top \quad (\perp) \; \perp \Rightarrow \alpha \quad (\perp_\sim) \; \sim\!\!\sim\!\perp \Rightarrow \perp$$

$$(\text{DM1}) \; \sim\!(\alpha \wedge \beta) \Rightarrow \sim\!\alpha \vee \sim\!\beta \quad (\text{DM2}) \; \sim\!\alpha \wedge \sim\!\beta \Rightarrow \sim\!(\alpha \vee \beta)$$

$$(\text{DIS}) \; \alpha \wedge (\beta \vee \gamma) \Rightarrow (\alpha \wedge \beta) \vee (\alpha \wedge \gamma) \quad (\text{N}_\Box) \; \top \Rightarrow \Box\top \quad (\text{N}_\Diamond) \; \Diamond\perp \Rightarrow \perp$$

$$(\text{K}_\Box) \; \Box\alpha \wedge \Box\beta \Rightarrow \Box(\alpha \wedge \beta) \quad (\text{K}_\Diamond) \; \Diamond(\alpha \vee \beta) \Rightarrow \Diamond\alpha \vee \Diamond\beta$$

$$(\text{I}_\Box) \; \Box(\alpha \vee \beta) \Rightarrow \Box\alpha \vee \Diamond\beta \quad (\text{I}_\Diamond) \; \Box\alpha \wedge \Diamond\beta \Rightarrow \Diamond(\alpha \wedge \beta)$$

(2) L is closed under the following rules: for $i \in \{1, 2\}$,

$$\frac{\alpha_i \Rightarrow \beta}{\alpha_1 \wedge \alpha_2 \Rightarrow \beta}(\wedge\text{L}) \quad \frac{\alpha \Rightarrow \beta_1 \quad \alpha \Rightarrow \beta_2}{\alpha \Rightarrow \beta_1 \wedge \beta_2}(\wedge\text{R}) \quad \frac{\alpha_1 \Rightarrow \beta \quad \alpha_2 \Rightarrow \beta}{\alpha_1 \vee \alpha_2 \Rightarrow \beta}(\vee\text{L}) \quad \frac{\alpha \Rightarrow \beta_i}{\alpha \Rightarrow \beta_1 \vee \beta_2}(\vee\text{R})$$

$$\frac{\alpha \Rightarrow \beta}{\sim\!\beta \Rightarrow \sim\!\alpha}(\text{CP}) \quad \frac{\alpha \Rightarrow \beta}{\Box\alpha \Rightarrow \Box\beta}(\text{M}_\Box) \quad \frac{\alpha \Rightarrow \beta}{\Diamond\alpha \Rightarrow \Diamond\beta}(\text{M}_\Diamond) \quad \frac{\alpha \Rightarrow \gamma \quad \gamma \Rightarrow \beta}{\alpha \Rightarrow \beta}(\text{CUT})$$

(3) L is closed under uniform substitution: if $\alpha \Rightarrow \beta \in L$, then $\sigma(\alpha) \Rightarrow \sigma(\beta) \in L$ for any substitution σ.

A basic sequent $s = \alpha \Rightarrow \beta$ is *derivable in L* (denoted by $\vdash_L s$) if $s \in L^8$. For any set of formulas Γ, let $\bigwedge\Gamma$ and $\bigvee\Gamma$ be the conjunction and disjunction of all formulas in Γ, respectively. In particular, $\bigwedge\varnothing = \top$ and $\bigvee\varnothing = \perp$. A formula α is *derivable from Γ in L* (denoted by $\Gamma \vdash_L \alpha$) if there exists a finite subset $\Theta \subseteq \Gamma$ such that $\vdash \bigwedge\Theta \Rightarrow \alpha$. In particular, we write $\vdash_L \alpha$ if $\vdash_L \top \Rightarrow \alpha$. A basic sequent rule with premisses $s_1, \ldots, s_n$ and conclusion s_0 is *admissible* in L if $\vdash_L s_0$ whenever $\vdash_L s_i$ for each $1 \leq i \leq n$. We write $\vdash_L \alpha \Leftrightarrow \beta$ if $\vdash_L \alpha \Rightarrow \beta$ and $\vdash_L \beta \Rightarrow \alpha$. Let $\{L_i : i \in I\}$ be a family of OMLs, then clearly $\bigcap_{i \in I} L_i$ is an OML. Let the *minimal OML* be denoted as $\mathsf{OK} = \bigcap\{L : L \text{ is an OML}\}$. For every set of basic sequents $\mathcal{S}$ and any OML L, let $L \oplus \mathcal{S} = \bigcap\{\mathsf{J} : \mathsf{J} \text{ is an OML and } L \cup \mathcal{S} \subseteq \mathsf{J}\}$, i.e., the smallest OML containing $L \cup \mathcal{S}$. An OML L is *consistent* if there exists a basic sequent s such that $s \notin L$ i.e. $L \neq \mathcal{BS}$.

---

[7] Note that a basic sequent is different from a sequent in sequent calculus, the latter one is usually composed of multisets.

[8] The subscript $_L$ in $\vdash_L s$ shall be omitted if it is clear from the context.

Lemma 1. *The following holds in any OML:*

(1) $\vdash \sim\!\perp \Leftrightarrow \top$ *and* $\vdash \sim\!\top \Leftrightarrow \perp$.
(2) $\vdash \sim\!(\alpha \wedge \beta) \Leftrightarrow \sim\!\alpha \vee \sim\!\beta$ *and* $\vdash \sim\!\alpha \wedge \sim\!\beta \Leftrightarrow \sim\!(\alpha \vee \beta)$.
(3) $\vdash \Box\top \Leftrightarrow \top$ *and* $\vdash \Diamond\!\perp \Leftrightarrow \perp$.
(4) $\vdash \Box(\alpha \wedge \beta) \Leftrightarrow \Box\alpha \wedge \Box\beta$ *and* $\vdash \Diamond(\alpha \vee \beta) \Leftrightarrow \Diamond\alpha \vee \Diamond\beta$.

Proof. For (1), it follows from $(\perp)$, $(\top)$, and $(\perp_\sim)$. For (2), it follows from rules for $\wedge, \vee$ and axioms (DM1) and (DM2). For (3), it follows from $(\perp)$, $(\top)$, $(N_\Box)$, and $(N_\Diamond)$. For (4), we only prove the former. By $(\wedge L)$ on $\vdash \alpha \Rightarrow \alpha, \vdash \alpha \wedge \beta \Rightarrow \alpha$. By $(M_\Box)$, $\vdash \Box(\alpha \wedge \beta) \Rightarrow \Box\alpha$. Similarly one has $\vdash \Box(\alpha \wedge \beta) \Rightarrow \Box\beta$. By $(\wedge R)$, $\vdash \Box(\alpha \wedge \beta) \Rightarrow \Box\alpha \wedge \Box\beta$. The other direction follows from $(K_\Box)$.   □

Lemma 2. *The following rules are admissible in any OML: for* $i \in \{1,2\}$,

$$\frac{\alpha_1 \Rightarrow \beta_1 \quad \alpha_2 \Rightarrow \beta_2}{\alpha_1 \wedge \alpha_2 \Rightarrow \beta_1 \wedge \beta_2}(\wedge) \qquad \frac{\alpha_1 \Rightarrow \beta_1 \quad \alpha_2 \Rightarrow \beta_2}{\alpha_1 \vee \alpha_2 \Rightarrow \beta_1 \vee \beta_2}(\vee) \qquad \frac{\sim\!\alpha_i \Rightarrow \beta}{\sim\!(\alpha_1 \vee \alpha_2) \Rightarrow \beta}(\sim\!\vee L)$$

$$\frac{\alpha \Rightarrow \sim\!\beta_1 \quad \alpha \Rightarrow \sim\!\beta_2}{\alpha \Rightarrow \sim\!(\beta_1 \vee \beta_2)}(\sim\!\vee R) \qquad \frac{\sim\!\alpha_1 \Rightarrow \beta \quad \sim\!\alpha_2 \Rightarrow \beta}{\sim\!(\alpha_1 \wedge \alpha_2) \Rightarrow \beta}(\sim\!\wedge L) \qquad \frac{\alpha \Rightarrow \sim\!\beta_i}{\alpha \Rightarrow \sim\!(\beta_1 \wedge \beta_2)}(\sim\!\wedge R)$$

Proof. We only show the proof of $(\sim\!\vee L)$. By $(\wedge L)$ on $\vdash \sim\!\alpha_i \Rightarrow \beta, \vdash \sim\!\alpha_1 \wedge \sim\!\alpha_2 \Rightarrow \beta$. By (CUT) on $\vdash \sim\!\alpha_1 \wedge \sim\!\alpha_2 \Rightarrow \beta$ and Lemma 1 (2), $\vdash \sim\!(\alpha_1 \vee \alpha_2) \Rightarrow \beta$.   □

Let $\mathfrak{A} = (A, \wedge, \vee, \sim, \Box, \Diamond, 0, 1)$ be a MO. An *assignment* in $\mathfrak{A}$ is a homomorphism $\theta : \mathscr{F} \to A$. A basic sequent $s = \alpha \Rightarrow \beta$ is *valid* in $\mathfrak{A}$ (denoted by $\mathfrak{A} \models s$) if $\theta(\alpha) \leq \theta(\beta)$ for any assignment θ. A basic sequent s is *valid* in a class of algebras $\mathbf{C}$ (denoted by $\mathbf{C} \models s$) if it is valid in every algebra of that class. Let $\mathsf{Th}(\mathbf{C}) = \{s \in \mathcal{BS} : \mathbf{C} \models s\}$ be the *sequential theory of a class of MOs* $\mathbf{C}$. For any set of basic sequents $\mathcal{S}$, let $\mathsf{Alg}(\mathcal{S})$ be the variety of all MOs that validate all basic sequents in $\mathcal{S}$. By $(M_\Box)$, $(M_\Diamond)$, (CP), and Lemma 2 $(\wedge)$ and $(\vee)$, $\Leftrightarrow$ is a congruence relation on $\mathscr{F}$. Then, by the TarskiLindenbaum construction (cf. e.g. [6, Chapter 5]), one has the following algebraic characterization:

Fact 2. *For any OML L, $L = \mathsf{Th}(\mathsf{Alg}(L))$.*

2.2   Relational Semantics

In this subsection, we shall present the relational semantics of OML and prove the discrete duality (cf. [27]). The frame for OML is simply obtained by adding a function g to a frame in classical modal logic.

Definition 4. *An* Ockham modal logic frame *(OML-frame for short) is a 3-tuple* $\mathfrak{F} = (W, g, R)$ *such that[9]:*

(1) W *is a non-empty set of points.*
(2) $g : W \to W$ *is a function on* W.
(3) R *is a binary relation on* W.

For any $w \in W$, we call $R(w) = \{u \in W : wRu\}$ the *set of w-successors.* For any $X \subseteq W$, let $R(X) = \bigcup_{w \in X} R(w)$ and $g(X) = \{g(w) : w \in X\}$. For any relation R, let $R^1 = R$ and $(w, u) \in R^n$ iff $(w, u) \in R^{n-1} \circ R$. For any set W, let 2^W be the powerset of W. For any OML-frame $\mathfrak{F} = (W, g, R)$, we define the following operations on 2^W: for any $X \subseteq W$,

$$\sim_g(X) = \{w \in W : g(w) \notin X\}$$

$$\Box_R(X) = \{w \in W : R(w) \subseteq X\} \quad \Diamond_R(X) = \{w \in W : R(w) \cap X \neq \varnothing\}$$

Let $\mathfrak{F}$ be any OML-frame, we call $\mathfrak{F}^+ = (2^W, \cap, \cup, \sim_g, \Box_R, \Diamond_R, \varnothing, W)$ its *dual*.

Definition 5. *An* Ockham modal logic model *(OML-model for short) is a 4-tuple* $\mathfrak{M} = (W, g, R, V)$ *such that:*

(1) $\mathfrak{F} = (W, g, R)$ *is an OML-frame.*
(2) $V : \mathbf{Var} \to 2^W$ *is function which is called a* valuation.

By homomorphically extending the valuation V, on obtains the *truth set* of $V(\alpha)$ for any formula α in $\mathfrak{M}$ defined inductively as follows:

$$V(\bot) = \varnothing \quad V(\alpha \wedge \beta) = V(\alpha) \cap V(\beta) \quad V(\alpha \vee \beta) = V(\alpha) \cup V(\beta)$$

$$V(\sim\alpha) = \sim_g V(\alpha) \quad V(\Box\alpha) = \Box_R V(\alpha) \quad V(\Diamond\alpha) = \Diamond_R V(\alpha)$$

Then the *satisfaction relation* of any formula α at point w in $\mathfrak{M}$ (denoted by $\mathfrak{M}, w \models \alpha$) is defined as $\mathfrak{M}, w \models \alpha$ iff $w \in V(\alpha)$. A formula α is *valid in* $\mathfrak{M}$ (denoted by $\mathfrak{M} \models \alpha$) if $\mathfrak{M}, w \models \alpha$ for any $w \in W$. Then clearly $\mathfrak{M} \models \alpha$ if and only if $V(\alpha) = W$. A formula α is *valid in a frame* $\mathfrak{F}$ (denoted by $\mathfrak{F} \models \alpha$) if it is true in every model based on $\mathfrak{F}$. A formula α is *valid in a class of frames* $\mathcal{K}$ (denoted by $\mathcal{K} \models \alpha$) if $\mathfrak{F} \models \alpha$ for any $\mathfrak{F} \in \mathcal{K}$. For a set of formulas Γ, one has $\mathfrak{M}, w \models \Gamma$ if $\mathfrak{M}, w \models \alpha$ for any $\alpha \in \Gamma$. Other definitions concerning the validity of Γ shall follow from the definition of $\mathfrak{M}, w \models \Gamma$ naturally.

For any basic sequent $\alpha \Rightarrow \beta$, we write $\mathfrak{M}, w \models \alpha \Rightarrow \beta$ if $\mathfrak{M}, w \models \alpha$ implies $\mathfrak{M}, w \models \beta$ i.e. $\mathfrak{M}, w \not\models \alpha$ or $\mathfrak{M}, w \models \beta$. The validity of any (set of) basic sequents shall be defined naturally following the above definitions. The *sequential theory of a class of frames* $\mathcal{K}$ is defined as the set $\mathsf{Th}(\mathcal{K}) = \{s \in \mathcal{BS} : \mathcal{K} \models s\}$. Conversely, for any set of basic sequents $\mathcal{S}$, let $\mathsf{Fr}(\mathcal{S}) = \{\mathfrak{F} : \mathfrak{F} \models \mathcal{S}\}$ be the set of frames that validate $\mathcal{S}$. An OML L is *Kripke-complete* if $L = \mathsf{Th}(\mathsf{Fr}(L))$.

Now, we turn to the discrete duality between the variety of MOs and the class of all OML-frames. For any MO $\mathfrak{A} = (A, \wedge, \vee, \sim, \Box, \Diamond, 0, 1)$, let $PF(A)$ be the set of all prime filters in A. For any $B \subseteq A$, let $\Box^{-1}(B) = \{a \in A : \Box a \in B\}$ and

---

[9] An OML-frame without R i.e. (W, g) was also given and called "star frame" in [26]. Note that such a star frame is different from Dunn's star frame defined in [15].

$\Diamond^{-1}(B) = \{a \in A : \Diamond a \in B\}$. Then we define a function $g_A : PF(A) \to PF(A)$ and a relation $R_A \subseteq PF(A) \times PF(A)$ as follows: for any $F, G \in PF(A)$,

$$g_A(F) = \{a \in A : \sim a \notin F\} \quad (F, G) \in R_A \text{ iff } \Box^{-1}(F) \subseteq G \subseteq \Diamond^{-1}(F)$$

We call $\mathfrak{A}_+ = (PF(A), g_A, R_A)$ the *dual* of $\mathfrak{A}$. For any $F \in PF(A)$, observe that $\Box^{-1}(F)$ is a filter and $\Diamond^{-1}(F)$ is an ideal.

Lemma 3. *The following hold for any OML-frame $\mathfrak{F}$ and MO $\mathfrak{A}$: (1) $\mathfrak{F}^+$ is a modal Ockham algebra; (2) $\mathfrak{A}_+$ is an OML-frame.*

Proof. (1) Clearly the $\langle \cap, \cup, \varnothing, W \rangle$-reduct of $\mathfrak{F}^+$ is a bounded distributive lattice with $\subseteq$ being its ordering. Since g is a function on W, $\sim_g(W) = \varnothing$ and $\sim_g(\varnothing) = W$, thus (o1) and (o2) hold. For any $X, Y \subseteq W$, $\sim_g(X \cap Y) = \{w : g(w) \notin X \cap Y\}$ and $\sim_g(X) \cup \sim_g(Y) = \{w : g(w) \notin X \text{ or } g(w) \notin Y\}$. Clearly $g(w) \notin X \cap Y$ iff $g(w) \in \overline{X \cap Y} = \overline{X} \cup \overline{Y}$ iff $g(w) \notin X$ or $g(w) \notin Y$. Thus $\sim_g(X \cap Y) = \sim_g(X) \cup \sim_g(Y)$. Similarly, one has $\sim_g(X \cup Y) = \sim_g(X) \cap \sim_g(Y)$. Thus, (o3) and (o4) hold. For the modal axioms, we only show the $\Box$ cases. For $(n_\Box)$, since $R(w) \subseteq W$ for any $w \in W$, $\Box_R(W) = W$. For $(k_\Box)$, since $R(w) \subseteq X \cap Y$ iff $R(w) \subseteq X$ and $R(w) \subseteq Y$, $\Box_R(X \cap Y) = \Box_R(X) \cap \Box_R(Y)$ for any $X, Y \subseteq W$. For $(i_\Box)$, suppose any $w \notin \Box_R(X) \cup \Diamond_R(Y)$. Then $w \notin \Box_R(X)$ and $w \notin \Diamond_R(Y)$. Thus there is a $u \in R(w)$, $u \notin X$ and $u \notin Y$. Then $w \notin \Box_R(X \cup Y)$.

(2) We show that the function g_A is well-defined i.e., for any $F \in PF(A)$, $g_A(F) \in PF(A)$. Suppose $a \in g_A(F)$ and $a \leq b$ i.e. $a \wedge b = a$. Then $\sim a = \sim(a \wedge b) = \sim a \vee \sim b \notin F$. Then $\sim b \notin F$ and $b \in g_A(F)$. Suppose $a, b \in g_A(F)$, then $\sim a, \sim b \notin F$. Since F is a prime filter, $\sim a \vee \sim b = \sim(a \wedge b) \notin F$. Then $a \wedge b \in g_A(F)$. Suppose $a \vee b \in g_A(F)$, then $\sim(a \vee b) = \sim a \wedge \sim b \notin F$. Further suppose $a \notin g_A(F)$ and $b \notin g_A(F)$. Then $\sim a \in F$ and $\sim b \in F$. Then $\sim a \wedge \sim b \in F$, which results in a contradiction. Therefore, $g_A(F)$ is a prime filter. For R_A, it can be easily verified that R_A is a binary relation on $PF(A)$. $\square$

Lemma 4. *Let $F \in PF(A)$, then (1) $\Box a \in F$ if and only if for any $G \in PF(A)$, FR_AG implies $a \in G$; (2) $\Diamond a \in F$ if and only if there exists a $G \in PF(A)$ such that FR_AG and $a \in G$.*

Proof. (1) The only-if-part is easy to check. Conversely, suppose $\Box a \notin F$. Let E be the ideal generated by $\{a\} \cup \overline{\Diamond^{-1}(F)}$. Suppose $c \in \Box^{-1}(F) \cap E$, then $\Box c \in F$. Note that $\overline{\Diamond^{-1}(F)}$ is an ideal. Then $c \leq a \vee b$ for some $b \in \overline{\Diamond^{-1}(F)}$ or $c = a$ or $c \in \overline{\Diamond^{-1}(F)}$. For $c \leq a \vee b$, by Definition 1 $(i_\Box)$ and Fact 1 (2), $\Box c \leq \Box(a \vee b) \leq \Box a \vee \Diamond b$. Since $\Box a, \Diamond b \notin F$, $\Box a \vee \Diamond b \notin F$ for F is a prime filter. Then $\Box c \notin F$, which results in a contradiction. For $c = a$, then $\Box a \in F$, which results in a contradiction. For $c \in \overline{\Diamond^{-1}(F)}$, then $\Diamond c \notin F$ and $\Box c \in F$. Then $\Box a \vee \Diamond c \notin F$. By Definition 1 $(i_\Box)$, $\Box(a \vee c) \leq \Box a \vee \Diamond c$. Then $\Box(a \vee c) \notin F$. Since $\Box a \vee \Box c \leq \Box(a \vee c)$, $\Box a \vee \Box c \notin F$. However, since $\Box c \leq \Box a \vee \Box c$ and $\Box c \in F$, $\Box a \vee \Box c \in F$, which results in a contradiction. Thus $\Box^{-1}(F) \cap E = \varnothing$. Note that $\Box^{-1}(F)$ is a filter. By the Prime Filter Theorem for Distributive Lattice (cf. e.g. [12, pp. 235–236]), there is a prime filter $G \supseteq \Box^{-1}(F)$ such that $G \cap E = \varnothing$.

Then for any $b \notin \Diamond^{-1}(F)$, $a \vee b \notin G$ and thus $a, b \notin G$. Therefore, there is a $G \in P\Gamma(A)$ such that $\Box^{-1}(F) \subseteq G \subseteq \Diamond^{-1}(F)$ and $a \notin G$.

(2) The if-part is easy to check. Conversely, suppose $\Diamond a \in F$. Let E be the filter generated by $\Box^{-1}(F) \cup \{a\}$. Then for any $c \in E$, $a \wedge b \leq c$ for some $b \in \Box^{-1}(F)$ or $c = a$ or $c \in \Box^{-1}(F)$. For $a \wedge b \leq c$, by Definition 1 $(i_\Diamond)$ and Fact 1 (2), $\Box b \wedge \Diamond a \leq \Diamond(a \wedge b) \leq \Diamond c$. Since $\Box b, \Diamond a \in F$, $\Diamond c \in F$ and $c \in \Diamond^{-1}(F)$. Thus $E \subseteq \Diamond^{-1}(F)$. For $c = a$, clearly $c \in \Diamond^{-1}(F)$. For $c \in \Box^{-1}(F)$, one has $\Box c, \Diamond a \in F$. By Definition 1 $(i_\Diamond)$ and Fact 1 (2) and (3), $\Box c \wedge \Diamond a \leq \Diamond(a \wedge c) \leq \Diamond c$. Thus $\Diamond c \in F$ and $c \in \Diamond^{-1}(F)$. Note that $\Diamond^{-1}(F)$ is an ideal. Then by the Prime Filter Theorem for Distributive Lattice, there is a prime filter $G \supseteq E \supseteq \Box^{-1}(F) \cup \{a\}$ such that $G \subseteq \Diamond^{-1}(F)$ and $a \in G$. □

Theorem 1 (Discrete Duality). *Let $\mathfrak{A}$ and $\mathfrak{F}$ be MO and OML-frame, respectively. Let functions $h : A \to 2^{PF(A)}$ and $k : W \to PF(2^W)$ be defined as follows: for any $a \in A$ and $w \in W$, $h(a) = \{F \in PF(A) : a \in F\}$ and $k(w) = \{X \in 2^W : w \in X\}$. Then, the following conditions hold: (1) h is an embedding from $\mathfrak{A}$ to $(\mathfrak{A}_+)^+ = (2^{PF(A)}, \cap, \cup, \sim_{g_A}, \Box_{R_A}, \Diamond_{R_A}, \varnothing, PF(A))$ i.e. h is an injective modal Ockham algebra homomorphism; (2) k is an embedding from $\mathfrak{F}$ to $(\mathfrak{F}^+)_+ = (PF(2^W), g_{2^W}, R_{2^W})$ i.e. k is injective, $k(g(w)) = g_{2^W}(k(w))$, and wRu iff $k(w)R_{2^W}k(u)$.*

Proof (1) Suppose $a \neq b$, then $a \not\leq b$ or $b \not\leq a$. By the Prime Filter Theorem, there is a prime filter F that contains exactly one of a and b in either case. Thus, $h(a) \neq h(b)$ and h is injective. It remains to show that h is a homomorphism. Clearly one has $h(a \wedge b) = h(a) \cap h(b)$, $h(a \vee b) = h(a) \cup h(b)$, $h(0) = \varnothing$, and $h(1) = PF(A)$. Suppose any $F \in h(\sim a)$, then $\sim a \in F$. Then $a \notin g_A(F)$ and $g_A(F) \notin h(a)$. Therefore $F \in \sim_{g_A}(h(a))$ and $h(\sim a) \subseteq \sim_{g_A}(h(a))$. The converse direction can be treated similarly. For $h(\Box a) = \Box_{R_A} h(a)$ and $h(\Diamond a) = \Diamond_{R_A} h(a)$, they follow from Lemma 4 (1) and (2).

(2) It is easy to check that $k(w) \in PF(2^W)$ for each $w \in W$. If $w \neq n$, then clearly $k(w) \neq k(n)$ and thus k is injective. Suppose any $X \in k(g(w))$, then $g(w) \in X$. Then $w \notin \sim_g(X)$ i.e. $\sim_g(X) \notin k(w)$. Note that $g_{2^W}(k(w)) = \{Y \in 2^W : \sim_g(Y) \notin k(w)\}$. Thus $X \in g_{2^W}(k(w))$ and $k(g(w)) \subseteq g_{2^W}(k(w))$. The converse direction can be treated similarly, thus $k(g(w)) = g_{2^W}(k(w))$. Suppose wRu for any $w, u \in W$. Further suppose any $X \in \Box_R^{-1}(k(w))$, then $\Box_R(X) \in k(w)$ i.e. $w \in \Box_R(X)$. Then $R(w) \subseteq X$. Since $u \in R(w)$, $u \in X$ and thus $X \in k(u)$. Then $\Box_R^{-1}(k(w)) \subseteq k(u)$. Suppose any $X \in k(u)$, then $u \in X$. Since $u \in R(w)$, one has $R(w) \cap X \neq \varnothing$. Then $w \in \Diamond_R(X)$ i.e. $\Diamond_R(X) \in k(w)$. Then $k(u) \subseteq \Diamond_R^{-1}(k(w))$. Therefore, one has wRu implies $k(w)R_{2^W}k(u)$. Conversely, suppose that $k(w)R_{2^W}k(u)$. Clearly, $w \in \Box_R(R(w))$, then $\Box_R(R(w)) \in k(w)$. Thus $R(w) \in \Box_R^{-1}(k(w))$. Since $k(w)R_{2^W}k(u)$ i.e. $\Box_R^{-1}(k(w)) \subseteq k(u)$. Then $R(w) \in k(u)$ i.e. $u \in R(w)$. Therefore, $k(w)R_{2^W}k(u)$ iff wRu. □

3   Kripke-Completeness and Canonicity

In this section, we use the canonical model method to show the Kripke-completeness of some OMLs. We start with the definitions of the prime theory (cf. [9]).

Definition 6. *A set of formulas Γ is a* prime theory *if the following conditions are satisfied:*

(1) Γ is a theory *of an OML L: Γ is closed under the consequence relation $\vdash_L$ i.e. $\Gamma = \{\alpha \in \mathscr{F} : \Gamma \vdash_L \alpha\}$.*
(2) Γ is consistent: *$\bot \notin \Gamma$.*
(3) Γ is prime: *if $\alpha \vee \beta \in \Gamma$, then $\alpha \in \Gamma$ or $\beta \in \Gamma$.*

Let $PT(L)$ denote the set of all prime theories of L. Let $\square^{-1}(\Gamma) = \{\alpha : \square\alpha \in \Gamma\}$ and $\lozenge^{-1}(\Gamma) = \{\alpha : \lozenge\alpha \in \Gamma\}$. A *dual theory* of an OML L is a set of formulas $\Sigma = \{\alpha : \ \vdash \alpha \Rightarrow \bigvee \Delta\}$ where $\Delta \subseteq \Sigma$ is a finite subset of Σ.

Fact 3. *For any prime theory Γ and dual theory Σ, the followings hold:*

(1) $\alpha \wedge \beta \in \Gamma$ if and only if $\alpha \in \Gamma$ and $\beta \in \Gamma$.
(2) $\alpha \vee \beta \in \Gamma$ if and only if $\alpha \in \Gamma$ or $\beta \in \Gamma$.
(3) $\alpha \vee \beta \in \Sigma$ if and only if $\alpha \in \Sigma$ and $\beta \in \Sigma$.
(4) $\square^{-1}(\Gamma)$ is a theory and $\overline{\lozenge^{-1}(\Gamma)} = \mathscr{F} \backslash \lozenge^{-1}(\Gamma)$ is a dual theory.
(5) For any theory Γ and dual theory Σ, if $\Gamma \cap \Sigma = \varnothing$, then there is a prime theory $\Gamma' \supseteq \Gamma$ such that $\Gamma' \cap \Sigma = \varnothing$.

Definition 7. *Let L be an OML, the* canonical model *of L is the 4-tuple $\mathfrak{M}^L = (W^L, g^L, R^L, V^L)$ defined as follows: for any $\Gamma, \Theta \in PT(L)$,*

(1) $W^L = PT(L)$.
(2) $g^L(\Gamma) = \{\alpha \in \mathscr{F} : \sim\alpha \notin \Gamma\}$.
(3) $\Gamma R^L \Theta$ if and only if $\square^{-1}(\Gamma) \subseteq \Theta \subseteq \lozenge^{-1}(\Gamma)$.
*(4) $V^L(p) = \{\Gamma \in W^L : p \in \Gamma\}$ for any $p \in$ **Var**.*

The 3-tuple $\mathfrak{M}^L = (W^L, g^L, R^L)$ is the canonical frame *of L.*

Lemma 5. *For any $\Gamma, \Theta \in PT(L)$, (1) $\sim\alpha \in \Gamma$ if and only if $\alpha \notin g^L(\Gamma)$; (2) $g^L : W^L \to W^L$ is a function on W^L.*

Proof. (1) follows from the definition of g^L. For (2), it suffices to show that $g^L(\Gamma)$ is a prime theory. By Lemma 1 (1), $\sim\bot \in \Gamma$, then $\bot \notin g^L(\Gamma)$ i.e. $g^L(\Gamma)$ is consistent. Suppose any $g^L(\Gamma) \vdash \beta$ i.e. $\vdash \bigwedge_{1 \le i \le n} \alpha_i \Rightarrow \beta$ for a finite subset $\Sigma = \{\alpha_i\} \subseteq g^L(\Gamma)$. For each i, $\sim\alpha_i \notin \Gamma$. By Fact 3 (2), $\bigvee \sim\alpha_i \notin \Gamma$. By Lemma 1 (2) and (CUT), $\sim \bigwedge_{1 \le i \le n} \alpha_i \notin \Gamma$ and thus $\bigwedge_{1 \le i \le n} \alpha_i \in g^L(\Gamma)$. By (CP), $\vdash \sim\beta \Rightarrow \sim \bigwedge_{1 \le i \le n} \alpha_i$. Then $\sim\beta \notin \Gamma$ i.e. $\beta \in g^L(\Gamma)$. Therefore, $g^L(\Gamma)$ is closed under the consequence relation $\vdash_L$. Further suppose $\alpha, \beta \in g^L(\Gamma)$. Then $\sim\alpha, \sim\beta \notin \Gamma$. By Fact 3 (1), $\sim\alpha\wedge\sim\beta \notin \Gamma$ i.e. $\sim(\alpha\vee\beta) \notin \Gamma$. Then $\alpha\vee\beta \in g^L(\Gamma)$. $\square$

By Lemma 5, the canonical frame $\mathfrak{F}^L$ is an OML-frame, and the canonical model $\mathfrak{M}^L$ is an OML-model.

Lemma 6. *For any $\Gamma \in PT(L)$, the followings hold: (1) $\square\alpha \in \Gamma$ if and only if $\alpha \in \Theta$ for all $\Theta \in R^L(\Gamma)$; (2) $\lozenge\alpha \in \Gamma$ if and only if $\alpha \in \Theta$ for some $\Theta \in R^L(\Gamma)$.*

Proof. The proofs are similar to the Lemma 4, we only provide outlines here.

(1) The proof for the only-if-part is easy. Suppose $\square\alpha \notin \Gamma$. Let Σ be the dual theory generated by $\{\alpha\} \cup \overline{\lozenge^{-1}(\Gamma)}$. Suppose $\gamma \in \square^{-1}(\Gamma) \cap \Sigma$, then $\square\gamma \in \Gamma$. Then $\vdash \gamma \Rightarrow \alpha \vee \beta$ for some $\beta \in \overline{\lozenge^{-1}(\Gamma)}$ or $\gamma = \alpha$ or $\gamma \in \overline{\lozenge^{-1}(F)}$. For $\vdash \gamma \Rightarrow \alpha \vee \beta$, by $(I_\square)$ and $(M_\square)$, $\vdash \square\gamma \Rightarrow \square(\alpha \vee \beta)$ and $\vdash \square(\alpha \vee \beta) \Rightarrow \square\alpha \vee \lozenge\beta$. By (CUT), $\vdash \square\gamma \Rightarrow \square\alpha \vee \lozenge\beta$. Since $\square\alpha, \lozenge\beta \notin \Gamma$, by Fact 3 (2), $\square\alpha \vee \lozenge\beta \notin \Gamma$. Then $\square\gamma \notin \Gamma$, which results in a contradiction. Similarly, one has $\square^{-1}(\Gamma) \cap \Sigma = \varnothing$ in all other cases, . By Fact 3 (4), $\square^{-1}(\Gamma)$ is a theory. Thus by Fact 3 (5), there is a prime theory $\Theta \supseteq \square^{-1}(\Gamma)$ such that $\Theta \cap \Sigma = \varnothing$. Then for any $\alpha \notin \lozenge^{-1}(\Gamma)$, $\alpha \vee \beta \notin \Theta$ and thus $\beta \notin \Theta$.

(2) The proof for the if-part is easy. Conversely, suppose $\lozenge\alpha \in \Gamma$. Let Σ be the theory generated by $\square^{-1}(\Gamma) \cup \{\alpha\}$. Then for any $\gamma \in \Sigma$, $\vdash \alpha \wedge \beta \Rightarrow \gamma$ for some $\beta \in \square^{-1}(\Gamma)$ or $\gamma = \alpha$ or $\gamma \in \square^{-1}(\Gamma)$. For $\vdash \alpha \wedge \beta \Rightarrow \gamma$, by $(I_\lozenge)$ and $(M_\lozenge)$, $\vdash \square\beta \wedge \lozenge\alpha \Rightarrow \lozenge(\alpha \wedge \beta)$ and $\vdash \lozenge(\alpha \wedge \beta) \Rightarrow \lozenge\gamma$. By (CUT), $\vdash \square\beta \wedge \lozenge\alpha \Rightarrow \lozenge\gamma$. Since $\square\beta, \lozenge\alpha \in \Gamma$, $\lozenge\gamma \in \Gamma$ and $\gamma \in \lozenge^{-1}(\Gamma)$. Similarly, one has $\Sigma \subseteq \lozenge^{-1}(\Gamma)$ in all other cases. Then $\Sigma \cap \overline{\lozenge^{-1}(\Gamma)} = \varnothing$ where $\overline{\lozenge^{-1}(\Gamma)}$ is a dual theory. Then by Fact 3 (5), there is a prime theory $\Theta \supseteq \square^{-1}(\Gamma)$ s.t. $\Theta \subseteq \lozenge^{-1}(\Gamma)$ and $\alpha \in \Theta$. $\square$

Lemma 7 (Truth Lemma). *For any formula* $\alpha \in \mathscr{F}$, $\mathfrak{M}^L, \Gamma \models \alpha$ *iff* $\alpha \in \Gamma$.

Proof. The proof proceeds by induction on the complexity of α. We only show proofs of the following cases. For $\alpha = \sim\beta$, suppose $\mathfrak{M}^L, \Gamma \models \sim\beta$, then $\mathfrak{M}^L, g^L(\Gamma) \not\models \beta$. By the induction hypothesis, $\beta \notin g^L(\Gamma)$. By Lemma 5 (1), $\sim\beta \in \Gamma$. The converse direction can be treated similarly. For $\alpha = \square\beta$, suppose $\square\beta \in \Gamma$ and $\Gamma R^L \Theta$. Then by Definition 7 (3), $\beta \in \Theta$. By the induction hypothesis, $\mathfrak{M}^L, \Theta \models \beta$. Then $\mathfrak{M}^L, \Gamma \models \square\beta$. Conversely, suppose $\square\beta \notin \Gamma$. By Lemma 6 (1), there is a $\Theta \in R^L(\Gamma)$ such that $\beta \notin \Theta$. By the induction hypothesis, $\mathfrak{M}^L, \Theta \not\models \beta$ and thus $\mathfrak{M}^L, \Gamma \not\models \square\beta$. By Lemma 6 (2), the proof for the $\lozenge$ case is similar. $\square$

Theorem 2. (Canonical Model Theorem). *For any basic sequent* $\alpha \Rightarrow \beta$ *and any OML L,* $\alpha \Rightarrow \beta \in L$ *if and only if* $\mathfrak{M}^L \models \alpha \Rightarrow \beta$.

Proof. Suppose $\alpha \Rightarrow \beta \in L$ i.e. $\vdash \alpha \Rightarrow \beta$ and $\mathfrak{M}^L, \Gamma \models \alpha$. By Lemma 7, $\alpha \in \Gamma$. Since Γ is a prime theory, $\beta \in \Gamma$ and thus by Lemma 7, $\mathfrak{M}^L, \Gamma \models \beta$ for any Γ. Thus $\mathfrak{M}^L \models \alpha \Rightarrow \beta$. Conversely, suppose $\alpha \Rightarrow \beta \notin L$ i.e. $\not\vdash \alpha \Rightarrow \beta$. By Zorn's Lemma, one can easily show that there is a prime theory Γ such that $\alpha \in \Gamma$ and $\beta \notin \Gamma$. By Lemma 7, $\mathfrak{M}^L, \Gamma \models \alpha$ and $\mathfrak{M}^L, \Gamma \not\models \beta$. Thus $\mathfrak{M}^L, \Gamma \not\models \alpha \Rightarrow \beta$. $\square$

Now, we are ready to introduce the notion of *canonicity*. An OML L is *canonical* if $\mathfrak{F}^L \models L$. A set of basic sequents $\mathcal{S}$ is *canonical* if for any OML L, $\mathcal{S} \subseteq L$ implies L is canonical.

Lemma 8. *If an OML L is canonical, then L is Kripke-complete.*

Proof. The soundness can be shown regularly. For completeness, suppose L is canonical, then $\mathfrak{F}^L \models L$. Further suppose $\not\vdash \alpha \Rightarrow \beta$. By Theorem 2, $\mathfrak{M}^L \not\models \alpha \Rightarrow \beta$. Then L is Kripke-complete. $\square$

Corollary 1. OK *is canonical and thus Kripke-complete.*

We further show the Kripke-completeness of some common modal extensions of OK, which are listed in the following Table 1: for $n \geq 1$,

Table 1. Some extensions of OK

Modal Axioms	Basic Sequents	Logics
$(EM_\Box^n)$	$\top \Rightarrow \Box^n p \vee \sim\Box^n p$	$EM^n = OK \oplus (EM_\Box^n) \oplus (EM_\Diamond^n)$
$(EM_\Diamond^n)$	$\Diamond^n p \wedge \sim\Diamond^n p \Rightarrow \bot$	
$(LC_\Box^n)$	$\Box^n p \wedge \sim\Box^n p \Rightarrow \bot$	$LC^n = OK \oplus (LC_\Box^n) \oplus (LC_\Diamond^n)$
$(LC_\Diamond^n)$	$\top \Rightarrow \Diamond^n p \vee \sim\Diamond^n p$	
$(D_\Box)$	$\top \Rightarrow \sim\Box\bot$	$OD = OK \oplus (D_\Box) \oplus (D_\Diamond)$
$(D_\Diamond)$	$\top \Rightarrow \Diamond\top$	
$(T_\Box)$	$\Box p \Rightarrow p$	$OT = OK \oplus (T_\Box) \oplus (T_\Diamond)$
$(T_\Diamond)$	$p \Rightarrow \Diamond p$	
$(4_\Box)$	$\Box p \Rightarrow \Box\Box p$	$O4 = OK \oplus (4_\Box) \oplus (4_\Diamond)$
$(4_\Diamond)$	$\Diamond\Diamond p \Rightarrow \Diamond p$	
$(B_\Box)$	$p \Rightarrow \Box\Diamond p$	$OB = OK \oplus (B_\Box) \oplus (B_\Diamond)$
$(B_\Diamond)$	$\Diamond\Box p \Rightarrow p$	
$(5_\Box)$	$\Diamond p \Rightarrow \Box\Diamond p$	$O5 = OK \oplus (5_\Box) \oplus (5_\Diamond)$
$(5_\Diamond)$	$\Diamond\Box p \Rightarrow \Box p$	

Lemma 9. *For any OML-frame* $\mathfrak{F} = (W, g, R)$, *the following correspondence results hold: for* $n \geq 1$ *and any* $w, u, v \in W$[10],

(1) $\mathfrak{F} \models (EM_\Box^n) \wedge (EM_\Diamond^n)$ *if and only if* $wR^n u$ *implies* $g(w)R^n u$.
(2) $\mathfrak{F} \models (LC_\Box^n) \wedge (LC_\Diamond^n)$ *if and only if* $g(w)R^n u$ *implies* $wR^n u$.
(3) $\mathfrak{F} \models (D_\Box) \wedge (D_\Diamond)$ *if and only if* $R(w) \neq \varnothing$.
(4) $\mathfrak{F} \models (T_\Box) \wedge (T_\Diamond)$ *if and only if* wRw.
(5) $\mathfrak{F} \models (4_\Box) \wedge (4_\Diamond)$ *if and only if* wRu *and* uRv *implies* wRv.
(6) $\mathfrak{F} \models (B_\Box) \wedge (B_\Diamond)$ *if and only if* wRu *implies* uRw.
(7) $\mathfrak{F} \models (5_\Box) \wedge (5_\Diamond)$ *if and only if* wRu *and* wRv *implies* uRv *or* vRu.

Proof. We only show the proof for (2), others are similar or easy to check. Suppose $g(w)R^n u$ but not $wR^n u$. Let $V(p) = W \backslash \{u\}$ and $\mathfrak{M} = (\mathfrak{F}, V)$. Then $\mathfrak{M}, w \models \Box^n p$ and $\mathfrak{M}, g(w) \not\models \Box^n p$. Thus $\mathfrak{M}, w \models \Box^n p \wedge \sim\Box^n p$ and $\mathfrak{M}, w \not\models (LC_\Box^n)$. Let $V'(p) = \{u\}$ and $\mathfrak{M}' = (\mathfrak{F}, V')$. Then $\mathfrak{M}', w \not\models \Diamond^n p$ and $\mathfrak{M}', w \not\models \sim\Diamond^n p$. Thus $\mathfrak{M}', w \not\models (LC_\Diamond^n)$. Conversely, suppose $g(w)R^n u$ implies $wR^n u$. For $(LC_\Box^n)$, let $\mathfrak{M}$ be any OML-model based on $\mathfrak{F}$. Suppose $\mathfrak{M}, w \models \Box^n p \wedge \sim\Box^n p$, then for any

---

[10] Here $\mathfrak{F} \models (EM_\Box^n) \wedge (EM_\Diamond^n)$ means $\mathfrak{F} \models (EM_\Box^n)$ and $\mathfrak{F} \models (EM_\Diamond^n)$, and similarly for the other axioms.

$v \in R^n(w)$, $\mathfrak{M}, v \models p$ and there is a $v' \in R^n(g(w))$ such that $\mathfrak{M}, v' \not\models p$. However, $v' \in R^n(w)$ and $\mathfrak{M}, v' \models p$, which results in a contradiction. For $(LC^n_\Diamond)$, let $\mathfrak{M}'$ be any OML-model based on $\mathfrak{F}$. Suppose $\mathfrak{M}, w \not\models \Diamond^n p \vee \sim\Diamond^n p$, then for any $v \in R^n(w)$, $\mathfrak{M}, v \not\models p$ and there is a $v' \in R^n(g(w))$ such that $\mathfrak{M}, v' \models p$. Similarly, by the assumption, one has $\mathfrak{M}, v' \not\models p$, which also results in a contradiction. Thus $\mathfrak{F} \models (LC^n_\Box)$ and $\mathfrak{F} \models (LC^n_\Diamond)$. □

Theorem 3. *Logics* EM^n, LC^n, OD, OT, $\mathsf{O4}$, OB, *and* $\mathsf{O5}$ *where* $n \geq 1$ *are Kripke-complete.*

Proof. We only show the proof for LC^n. By Lemma 8, it suffices to show that $(LC^n_\Box)$ and $(LC^n_\Diamond)$ are canonical. Let $(LC^n_\Box)$ and $(LC^n_\Diamond)$ belong to any OML L, we show that $g^L(\Gamma)(R^L)^n\Theta$ implies $\Gamma(R^L)^n\Theta$. Suppose for any $\Gamma, \Theta \in PT(L)$, $g^L(\Gamma)(R^L)^n\Theta$ and any $\Box^n\alpha \in \Gamma$ i.e. $\alpha \in \Box^{-1^n}(\Gamma)$. Since $\Box^n\alpha \wedge \sim\Box^n\alpha \notin \Gamma$, by Fact 3 (1), $\sim\Box^n\alpha \notin \Gamma$ By Lemma 5 (1), $\Box^n\alpha \in g^L(\Gamma)$. Since $g^L(\Gamma)(R^L)^n\Theta$, $\alpha \in \Theta$. Further suppose $\alpha \notin \Diamond^{-1^n}(\Gamma)$ i.e. $\Diamond^n\alpha \notin \Gamma$. Since $\Diamond^n\alpha \vee \sim\Diamond^n\alpha \in \Gamma$, by Fact 3 (2), $\sim\Diamond^n\alpha \in \Gamma$. By Lemma 5 (1), $\Diamond^n\alpha \notin g^L(\Gamma)$. Since $g^L(\Gamma)(R^L)^n\Theta$, $\alpha \notin \Theta$. Therefore, $\Gamma(R^L)^n\Theta$. □

4   From Modal Ockham Algebra to Modal Berman Variety

In this section, we extend our results from previous sections to the modal Berman variety. Recall that a *Berman variety* is the subvariety of the variety of all Ockham algebras satisfying a condition of the form: for $\kappa \geq 1, \lambda \geq 0$,

$$(\sim_{\kappa,\lambda}) \quad \sim^{2\kappa+\lambda}a = \sim^\lambda a$$

Clearly, $2\kappa + \lambda$ is odd (even) if and only if λ is odd (even).

Definition 8. *For* $\kappa \geq 1, \lambda \geq 0$, *the* modal Berman variety $\mathbf{MK}_{\kappa,\lambda}$ *is the subvariety of modal Ockham algebras that further satisfies the condition* $(\sim_{\kappa,\lambda})$. *A* Berman variety modal logic *(BML for short)* $L_{\kappa,\lambda}$ *for each* $\kappa \geq 1, \lambda \geq 0$ *is obtained from an OML L (cf. Definition 3) by adding the following axioms:*

$$(N1) \; \sim^{2\kappa+\lambda}\alpha \Rightarrow \sim^\lambda\alpha \quad (N2) \; \sim^\lambda\alpha \Rightarrow \sim^{2\kappa+\lambda}\alpha$$

For each $L_{\kappa,\lambda}$ where $\kappa \geq 1$ and $\lambda \geq 0$, let $\mathsf{BK}_{\kappa,\lambda}$ be the *minimal BML*. Now, we extend the relational semantics for OML to any BML $L_{\kappa,\lambda}$.

Definition 9. *For any* $\kappa \geq 1, \lambda \geq 0$, *a* Berman variety modal logic frame *(BML-frame for short)* $\mathfrak{F} = (W, g, R)$ *is an OML-frame (cf. Definition 4) further satisfying the following condition: for any* $w \in W$,

$$(g_{\kappa,\lambda}) \quad g^{2\kappa+\lambda}(w) = g^\lambda(w)$$

For any $B \subseteq A$ where $(A, \sim)$ is an Ockham algebra, let $\sim(B) = \{\sim a : a \in B\}$. The definitions of $\mathfrak{F}^+$, $\mathfrak{A}_+$, model, satisfaction relation, validity, etc., are the same as those of the Ockham modal logic.

Example 1. As we have mentioned in the introduction, the variety of all quasi-Boolean algebras is the smallest Berman variety $\mathbf{K}_{1,0}$. Then similarly one obtains the smallest modal Berman variety $\mathbf{MK}_{1,0}$. The BML-frame for its logic $L_{1,0}$ shall be defined as an OML-frame further satisfying $g(g(w)) = w$ i.e. g is an involution on W. Relational semantics for $L_{1,0}$ was systematically studied recently in [24]. Since g is an involution (a bijection) in the BML-frame of $L_{1,0}$, one has $w \in X$ iff $g(w) \in g(X)$ for any $w \in W$ and $X \subseteq W^{11}$. Then $\sim_g(X) = \overline{g(X)} = g(\overline{X})$ in the BML-frame of $L_{1,0}$. Relevant discussions can be found in the representation theorem of quasi-Boolean algebra [5, 29].

Lemma 10. *Let (W, g, R) and $(A, \sim)$ be any BML-frame and member of Berman variety, then the following conditions hold: for any $w \in W$, $X \subseteq W$, $B \subseteq A$, $\kappa \geq 1$ and $n, \lambda \geq 0$,*

(1) If $w \in X$, then $g(w) \in g(X)$ but not conversely.
(2) $a \in B$ if and only if $\sim a \in \sim(B)$.
(3) If $w \in \sim_g^n(X)$, then $g(w) \notin \sim_g^{n-1}(X)$ and $g^2(w) \in \sim_g^{n-2}(X)$.
(4) If $g^n(w) \in X$, then $g^{n-1}(w) \notin \sim_g(X)$ and $g^{n-2}(w) \in \sim_g^2(X)$.
(5) If $w \in \sim_g^{2\kappa+\lambda}(X)$, then $g^\lambda(w) \notin X$ $(g^\lambda(w) \in X)$ if λ is odd (even).
(6) If $a \in g_A^n(F)$, then $\sim a \notin g_A^{n-1}(F)$ and $\sim^2 a \in g_A^{n-2}(F)$.
(7) If $\sim^n a \in F$, then $\sim^{n-1}a \notin g_A(F)$ and $\sim^{n-2}a \in g_A^2(F)$.
(8) If $a \in g_A^{2\kappa+\lambda}(F)$, then $\sim^\lambda a \notin F$ $(\sim^\lambda a \in F)$ if λ is odd (even).

Proof. Items (1) and (2) are easy to check. For (3), suppose $w \in \sim_g^{2\kappa+\lambda}(X)$. By the definition of $\sim_g$, $g(w) \notin \sim_g^{2\kappa+\lambda-1}(X)$. Then $g^2(w) \in \sim_g^{2\kappa+\lambda-2}(X)$. The proof of (4) is similar to (3). For (5), suppose $w \in \sim_g^{2\kappa+\lambda}(X)$. By 2κ times application of (3), $g^{2\kappa}(w) \in \sim_g^\lambda(X)$. If λ is odd, then by λ times application of (3), $g^{2\kappa+\lambda}(w) \notin X$. By Definition 9 $(g_{\kappa,\lambda})$, $g^\lambda(w) \notin X$. The proof is similar when λ is even. Proofs for (6)-(8) are similar to (3)-(5). □

Now, we show that the discrete duality results still hold for the modal Berman variety and its relational structure.

Lemma 11. *The following hold for any BML-frame $\mathfrak{F}$ and $\mathfrak{A} \in \mathbf{MK}_{\kappa,\lambda}$ for each $\kappa \geq 1$ and $\lambda \geq 0$: (1) $\mathfrak{F}^+$ is a member of modal Berman variety; (2) $\mathfrak{A}_+$ is an BML-frame.*

Proof. (1) By Lemma 3 (1), it suffices to show that $\sim_g^{2\kappa+\lambda}(X) = \sim_g^\lambda(X)$ for any $X \subseteq W$. Suppose any $w \in \sim_g^{2\kappa+\lambda}(X)$. By Lemma 10 (5), $g^\lambda(w) \notin X$ $(g^\lambda(w) \in X)$ if λ is odd (even). If λ is odd, $g^{\lambda-1}(w) \in \sim_g(X)$. By $\lambda - 1$ times application of Lemma 10 (4), one has $w \in \sim_g^\lambda(X)$. Otherwise, let λ be even, then by λ times application of Lemma 10 (4), one has $w \in \sim_g^\lambda(X)$. Conversely, suppose any $w \in \sim_g^\lambda(X)$. By λ times application of Lemma 10 (3), one has $g^\lambda(w) \notin X$ $(g^\lambda(w) \in X)$ if λ is odd (even). By Definition 9 $(g_{\kappa,\lambda})$, one has $g^{2\kappa+\lambda}(w) \notin X$

---

[11] Note that this property doesn't hold generally in any BML-frame, only the if-part i.e. $w \in X$ implies $g(w) \in g(X)$ always holds (cf. Lemma 10 (1)).

$(g^{2\kappa+\lambda}(w) \in X)$ if λ is odd (even). If λ is odd, $g^{2\kappa+\lambda-1}(w) \in \sim_g X$. By $\lambda - 1$ times application of Lemma 10 (4), one has $w \in \sim_g^{2\kappa+\lambda}(X)$. The proof is similar when λ is even.

(2) By Lemma 3 (2), it suffices to show that for any $F \in PF(A)$, $g_A^{2\kappa+\lambda}(F) = g_A^\lambda(F)$. Suppose any $a \in g_A^{2\kappa+\lambda}(F)$, by Lemma 10 (8), $\sim^\lambda a \notin F$ ($\sim^\lambda a \in F$) if λ is odd (even). If λ is odd, $\sim^{\lambda-1}a \in g_A(F)$. By $\lambda - 1$ times applications of Lemma 10 (7), $a \in g_A^\lambda(F)$. Otherwise, let λ be even. By λ times applications of Lemma 10 (7), $a \in g_A^\lambda(F)$. The converse direction can be treated similarly. □

Theorem 4 (Discrete Duality). *Let $\mathfrak{F}$ be any BML-frame and $\mathfrak{A} \in \mathbf{MK}_{\kappa,\lambda}$ for each $\kappa \geq 1$ and $\lambda \geq 0$. Let functions $h : A \to 2^{PF(A)}$ and $k : W \to PF(2^W)$ be defined as in Theorem 1. Then (1) h is an embedding from $\mathfrak{A}$ to $(\mathfrak{A}_+)^+$; (2) k is an embedding from $\mathfrak{F}$ to $(\mathfrak{F}^+)_+$.*

Proof. The proof is quite similar to Theorem 1. □

For Kripke-completeness, we adopt the same canonical model method adopted in the previous section. For any BML $L_{\kappa,\lambda}$ where $\kappa \geq 1$ and $\lambda \geq 0$, the *canonical model* of $L_{\kappa,\lambda}$ is defined exactly the same as in Definition 7. By proofs similar to Lemma 11 (2), one can show that $g^{L^{2\kappa+\lambda}}(\Gamma) = g^{L^\lambda}(\Gamma)$. Thus for any BML $L_{\kappa,\lambda}$, its canonical frame $\mathfrak{F}^{L_{\kappa,\lambda}}$ is a BML-frame. Further, one can check that Lemma 5, 6, 7, 8, 9, and Theorem 2 still hold for any BML $L_{\kappa,\lambda}$. Let $\mathsf{BEM}_{\kappa,\lambda}^n = \mathsf{EM}^n \oplus (N1) \oplus (N2)$, $\mathsf{BLC}_{\kappa,\lambda}^n = \mathsf{LC}^n \oplus (N1) \oplus (N2)$, and $\mathsf{BD}_{\kappa,\lambda}$, $\mathsf{BT}_{\kappa,\lambda}$, $\mathsf{B4}_{\kappa,\lambda}$, $\mathsf{BB}_{\kappa,\lambda}$, $\mathsf{B5}_{\kappa,\lambda}$ be obtained similarly. Then one can generalize the conclusions in Theorem 3 to have the following completeness results:

Theorem 5. *For each $\kappa, n \geq 1$ and $\lambda \geq 0$, logics $\mathsf{BK}_{\kappa,\lambda}$, $\mathsf{BEM}_{\kappa,\lambda}^n$, $\mathsf{BLC}_{\kappa,\lambda}^n$, $\mathsf{BD}_{\kappa,\lambda}$, $\mathsf{BT}_{\kappa,\lambda}$, $\mathsf{B4}_{\kappa,\lambda}$, $\mathsf{BB}_{\kappa,\lambda}$, and $\mathsf{B5}_{\kappa,\lambda}$ are Kripke-complete.*

5 Concluding Remarks

This paper develops relational semantics for sequential logics of modal Ockham algebras. We define the OML-frame and show the Kripke-completeness of some OMLs with discrete duality results. Furthermore, we extend these results to each modal Berman variety by adding more conditions to the OML-frame. Based on this paper, many future works are worth exploring. Using tools and techniques from classical modal logic, we can study the model theory of these logics e.g., the finite model property in lattices of these logics, correspondence theory, elementarity and canonicity. Furthermore, connectives $\square$ and $\lozenge$ are barely interrelated except for the interaction axioms, this is also the case in positive modal logic. However, it is possible that $\square$ and $\lozenge$ can have more connections, at least in some Berman varieties. For example, in the variety of (modal) quasi-Boolean algebras, $\square$ and $\lozenge$ can be duals like in classical modal logic (cf. e.g. [24]). If one adds some extent of interconnections between $\square$ and $\lozenge$, then surely the definitions of OML/BML-frame are to be changed. Generalizing the rough set theoretical semantics and representation of quasi-Boolean algebra to modal Ockham algebra and modal Berman variety is also an interesting question.

Acknowledgments. Thanks are given to anonymous reviewers for their helpful comments on this paper. This work was supported by the Chinese National Funding of Social Sciences (Grant no. 18ZDA033).

References

1. Banerjee, M., Chakraborty, M.K.: Rough algebra. Bull. Pol. Acad. Sci. **41**(4), 293–297 (1993)
2. Banerjee, M., Chakraborty, M.K.: Rough consequence and rough algebra. In: Rough Sets, Fuzzy Sets and Knowledge Discovery: Proceedings of the International Workshop on Rough Sets and Knowledge Discovery (RSKD'93), pp. 196–207. Springer (1994)
3. Banerjee, M., Chakraborty, M.K.: Rough sets through algebraic logic. Fund. Inform. **28**(3–4), 211–221 (1996)
4. Berman, J.: Distributive lattices with an additional unary operation. Aequationes Math. **16**, 165–171 (1977)
5. Białynicki-Birula, A., Rasiowa, H.: On the representation of quasi-Boolean algebras. Bull. Pol. Acad. Sci. Cl. III **5**(3), 259–261 (1957)
6. Blackburn, P., De Rijke, M., Venema, Y.: Modal Logic, vol. 53. Cambridge University Press, Cambridge (2001)
7. Blyth, T.S., Varlet, J.C.: Ockham Algebras. Oxford Science Publications (1994)
8. Blyth, T., Noor, A., Varlet, J.: Ockham algebras with de Morgan skeletons. J. Algebra **117**(1), 165–178 (1988)
9. Celani, S., Jansana, R.: A new semantics for positive modal logic. Notre Dame J. Formal Logic **38**(1), 1–18 (1997)
10. Celani, S., Jansana, R.: Priestley duality, a Sahlqvist theorem and a Goldblatt-Thomason theorem for positive modal logic. Log. J. IGPL **7**(6), 683–715 (1999)
11. Celani, S.A.: Classical modal De Morgan algebras. Stud. Logica. **98**(1), 251–266 (2011)
12. Davey, B.A., Priestley, H.A.: Introduction to Lattices and Order. Cambridge University Press, Cambridge (2002)
13. Došen, K.: Negation in the light of modal logic. In: What is Negation? Springer (1999)
14. Dunn, J.M.: Gaggle theory: an abstraction of Galois connections and residuation, with applications to negation, implication, and various logical operators. In: European Workshop on Logics in Artificial Intelligence, pp. 31–51. Springer (1990)
15. Dunn, J.M.: Star and perp: two treatments of negation. Philos. Perspect. **7**, 331–357 (1993)
16. Dunn, J.M.: Positive modal logic. Stud. Logica. **55**(2), 301–317 (1995)
17. Dunn, J.M., Zhou, C.: Negation in the context of gaggle theory. Stud. Logica. **80**, 235–264 (2005)
18. Dzik, W., Orlowska, E., van Alten, C.: Relational representation theorems for general lattices with negations. In: Schmidt, R.A. (ed.) RelMiCS 2006. LNCS, vol. 4136, pp. 162–176. Springer, Heidelberg (2006). https://doi.org/10.1007/11828563_11
19. Fang, J.: Contributions to the Theory of Ockham Algebras. Ph.D. thesis, University of St Andrews (1992)
20. Fang, J.: Distributive lattices with unary operations. Science Press (2011)

21. Figallo, A.V., Pelaitay, G.: Tense operators on De Morgan algebras. Logic J. IGPL **22**(2), 255–267 (2014)
22. Garcia, P., Esteva, F.: On Ockham algebras: congruence lattices and subdirectly irreducible algebras. Stud. Logica. **55**, 319–346 (1995)
23. Iwinski, T.B.: Algebraic approach to rough sets. Bull. Acad. Pol. Sci. **35**, 673–683 (1987)
24. Ma, M., Guo, J.: Kripke-completeness and sequent calculus for quasi-Boolean modal logic. Stud. Logica. 1–30 (2024)
25. Ma, M., Lin, Y.: Countably many weakenings of Belnap-Dunn logic. Stud. Logica. **108**(2), 163–198 (2020)
26. Odintsov, S., Wansing, H.: Routley star and hyperintensionality. J. Philos. Log. **50**(1), 33–56 (2021)
27. Orłowska, E., Radzikowska, A., Rewitzky, I.: Dualities for Structures of Applied Logics. College Publications (2015)
28. Pawlak, Z.: Rough sets. Int. J. Comput. Inf. Sci. **11**, 341–356 (1982)
29. Rasiowa, H.: An Algebraic Approach to Non-classical Logics, Studies in logic and the foundations of mathematics, vol. 78. PWN-Polish Scientific Publishers, Warszawa (1974)
30. Routley, R., Routley, V.: The semantics of first degree entailment. Noûs pp. 335–359 (1972)
31. Saha, A., Sen, J., Chakraborty, M.K.: Algebraic structures in the vicinity of pre-rough algebra and their logics I. Inf. Sci. **282**, 296–320 (2014)
32. Urquhart, A.: Distributive lattices with a dual homomorphic operation. Stud. Logica. **38**, 201–209 (1979)
33. Vakarelov, D.: Theory of Negation in Certain Logical Systems: Algebraic and Semantic Approach. Ph.D. thesis, University of Warsaw (1977)
34. Wang, Y., Lin, Z., Ma, M.: Decidability of topological quasi-Boolean algebras. J. Appl. Non-Classical Logics **34**(2–3), 269–293 (2024)

Logic Programming and Answer Set Programming

Lazy Atom Discovery
in Compilation-Based ASP Solving

Andrea Cuteri(ID), Giuseppe Mazzotta(✉)(ID), and Francesco Ricca(ID)

University of Calabria, Rende, Italy
{andrea.cuteri,giuseppe.mazzotta,francesco.ricca}@unical.it

Abstract. State-of-the-art Answer Set Programming (ASP) systems
that adopt the Ground&Solve approach are limited by the grounding
bottleneck. This issue arises whenever the grounding produces a large
propositional program that cannot be handled efficiently during solving.
The grounding bottleneck can be mitigated through compilation-based
ASP solving, which avoids generating propositional rules for selected
"problematic" subprograms. However, compilation-based ASP systems
generate in advance the propositional atoms required for solving the
problem. As a consequence, as soon as a large number of propositional
atoms is required, also this approach exhibits overhead. In this paper a
novel compilation-based technique is presented that overcomes this limitation by discovering propositional atoms *lazily*, i.e., during the solving
process. Empirical results confirm the effectiveness of the approach.

Keywords: ASP · Grounding Bottleneck · Compiled Propagators

1 Introduction

Answer Set Programming (ASP) [10,42] is a well-established logic-based formalism founded on the stable model semantics [34,42] which has been widely
applied across diverse domains in both academia and industry [31,35]. Nowadays, ASP has found extensive applications in a variety of fields, including Planning [58], Scheduling [13,23,24,26,43], Robotics [33], Natural Language Processing [21,51,57,63], and Databases [3,29,48], among many others [31].

The success of ASP can be attributed to two key factors. First, ASP offers
a highly expressive language that allows hard combinatorial problems to be
modeled in a very compact and natural way [22]. Second, efficient systems [41]
make ASP applicable to real-world problems [31,35] and industrial contexts [6,
25,37,52,56].

Standard ASP systems, such as CLINGO [38] and DLV [1], are based on the
well-known Ground&Solve approach [44]. In this approach, a solution to (i.e.,
an answer set of) an ASP program is computed in two stages. First, the input
program is transformed into its propositional counterpart by a grounding procedure (i.e., variables are substituted with constants appearing in the program).
Then, answer sets are computed using a CDCL-like algorithm [49].

G. Casini et al. (Eds.): JELIA 2025, LNAI 16093, pp. 309–326, 2026.
https://doi.org/10.1007/978-3-032-04587-4_19

Although effective in numerous scenarios, this approach faces a significant limitation known as the *grounding bottleneck* [41]. In many practical cases [12, 53], the grounding stage consumes all computational resources, preventing the solving process from even beginning.

In the last few years substantial research has been dedicated at facing the grounding bottleneck, leading to the development of several techniques, such as hybrid formalisms [5,38,53,59], lazy grounding systems [9,45,47,54,61], complexity-driven program rewritings [8], and compilation approaches [17,19, 20,27,50].

Among such techniques, compilation-based approaches address the problem by compiling non-ground rules into specialized procedures, known as propagators, that simulate rule inferences during the solving process. As a result, ground rules are never materialized, but their inferences are still taken into account during the solving process by rule-specific propagators. These techniques have proven effective in mitigating the grounding bottleneck and have led to significant performance improvements compared to alternative systems when evaluating both grounding-intensive and solving-intensive benchmark problems [27,28,50]. However, recent studies have shown that such systems suffer when the atoms needed to solve the problem increases [27]. This is due to the fact that compilation-based ASP systems, such as PROASP [27,28], generate in advance the propositional atoms required for solving the problem. As a consequence, whenever the problem instance at hand requires to build a large number of propositional atoms, compilation-based systems exhibit overhead [28].

In this paper, we present a novel compilation-based technique that overcomes this limitation by postponing the identification of propositional atoms to the solving phase. For this reason, we refer to the technique as *lazy atom discovery*, highlighting that new atoms are generated within the compiled propagators only when they need to be assigned a truth value during solving, rather than at its outset. Note that, PROASP pre-generates propositional atoms to ensure efficient solver–propagator interaction without altering the internal data structures of the solver. Nonetheless, we identify a class of subprograms that supports lazy atom discovery while maintaining compatibility with the solver architecture. To this end, we introduce the concept of lazy program split, built on properties of the Fitting operator [36], which characterizes subprograms whose evaluation can be entirely postponed. In particular, we develop novel compilation algorithms that translate program splits into specialized propagators, which discover atoms and evaluate rules incrementally by applying the Fitting operator to partial interpretations. Finally, we present an efficient implementation of these techniques on top of the compilation-based system PROASP [27,28]. Empirical results confirm that the proposed techniques enhance the solver's memory and time efficiency, particularly on benchmarks that are unsuitable for previous approaches.

2   Preliminaries

We now review the ASP language, focusing on the concepts relevant to this work. A comprehensive description can be found in the existing literature. [10,11,39].

ASP Syntax. A term can either be a variable or a constant. A variable is a string starting with upper case letter, while a constant is a number or a string starting with lowercase letter. An atom is an expression of the form $p(t_1, \ldots, t_n)$ where p is a predicate of arity $n \geq 0$ and $t_1, \ldots, t_n$ are terms. A literal is either an atom a or its negation $\sim a$, where $\sim$ represents negation as failure. Given a literal $l = a$ (resp. $\sim a$), $\bar{l}$ denotes the complement of l that is $\sim a$ (resp. a); while *terms*(l) denotes the set of terms appearing in literal l. A literal l is *ground* if it does not contain any variable. A literal of the form a is said to be positive, otherwise it is negative. For a set of literals S, S^+ (resp. S^-) denotes the set of positive (resp. negative) literals appearing in S. A rule is an expression of the form $h \leftarrow l_1, \ldots, l_n$ where h is an atom referred to as *head* that can be also omitted, and $l_1, \ldots, l_n$, with $n > 0$, is a conjunction of literals referred to as *body*. Given a rule r, $B(r)$ is the set of literals appearing in the body of r while $H(r)$ is the set of atoms appearing in the head of r. A rule r is a constraint if $H(r) = \emptyset$; or it is a fact if $B(r) = \emptyset$. Moreover, r is *safe* if each variable appearing in r appears also in $B(r)^+$. A *program* Π is a set of safe rules. Given an ASP expression ϵ (a program, a rule etc.), $pred(\epsilon)$ and $vars(\epsilon)$ denotes respectively the set of predicates and variables appearing in ϵ. Given a rule r, $head(r) \subseteq pred(r)$ is the set of predicates appearing in $H(r)$. This notation extends also to programs, and so $head(\Pi)$ is the set of predicates appearing in the head of some rules in Π. Given a program Π, the *Herbrand Universe* U_Π is the set of constants occurring in Π, while the *Herbrand base* B_Π is the set of ground atoms that can be obtained from predicates of Π and constants in U_Π. A variable substitution $\sigma : V \mapsto U_\Pi$ is a function mapping a set of variables V to constants in U_Π. The application of a substitution σ to an ASP expression ϵ, denoted by $\sigma(\epsilon)$, is the expression obtained from ϵ by substituting variables of ϵ with the constants they are mapped to. A substitution $\sigma : vars(\epsilon) \mapsto U_\Pi$ is a well-formed substitution for ϵ. Let r be a rule, and $\sigma : vars(r) \mapsto U_\Pi$, then $\sigma(r)$ is a ground instantiation of r. The grounding of program Π, $ground(\Pi)$, is the union of all ground instantiations of rules in Π. The *dependency graph* of program Π is the labeled graph $G_\Pi = \langle V, E \rangle$, where V is the set of predicates appearing in Π and E contains a positive (resp. negative) edge from p to q if there exists a rule $r \in \Pi$ such that p appears in $B(r)^+$ (resp. p appears in $B(r)^-$) and $q \in head(r)$. Program Π is said to be *stratified* if there exist no loop in G_Π involving negative edges; *tight* if G_Π does not contain positive loops [32]. We focus on tight ASP programs, as this class is sufficiently expressive for our purposes while remaining amenable to modelling many complex problems [12], and corresponds to the class supported by PROASP [27,28].

Stable Model Semantics. Given a program Π, an interpretation I is a set of literals over atoms in B_Π. A literal l is true w.r.t. I (i.e., $I \models l$) if $l \in I$; false (i.e. $I \not\models l$) if $\bar{l} \in I$; undefined otherwise. A conjunction of literals $Conj$ is true w.r.t. I (i.e., $I \models Conj$) if $I \models l$ for each l in $Conj$; false (i.e. $I \not\models Conj$) if there exists l in $Conj$ such that $I \not\models l$; undefined otherwise. An interpretation I is total if for each atom $a \in B_\Pi$, $a \in I$ or $\sim a \in I$. An interpretation I is consistent if it does not exist $l \in I$ such that $\bar{l} \in I$. An atom $a \in B_\Pi$ is supported in Π

w.r.t. I if there exists $r \in ground(\Pi)$ such that $H(r) = a$ and $I \models B(r)$. Given a rule $r \in ground(\Pi)$, then r is satisfied w.r.t. I if $I \models H(r)$ or $I \not\models B(r)$. A total and consistent interpretation I is a *model* of Π if all rules in $ground(\Pi)$ are satisfied. Let I be a model of Π, then I is a *supported model* if each positive literal in I is supported in Π w.r.t. I. Let I be a model then we denote by Π^I the Gelfond-Lifschitz reduct [42] which is obtained from Π by (i) removing all those rules in $ground(\Pi)$ having in the body at least one false negative literal w.r.t. I; and (ii) removing negative literals from the body of the remaining rules. Then, I is a *stable model* (or an *answer set*) of Π if I is a $\subset$-minimal model of Π^I. For a program Π, $AS(\Pi)$ denotes the set of answer set of Π. For the class of programs considered in this paper (i.e., tight programs) supported models coincide with answer sets.

Example 1. Let Π_1 and Π_2 be the following program:

$$\Pi_1 = \left\{ \begin{array}{ll} a \leftarrow \sim na & b \leftarrow a \\ na \leftarrow \sim a & c \leftarrow na \end{array} \right. \qquad \Pi_2 = \left\{ \begin{array}{ll} a \leftarrow \sim na & b \leftarrow a, c \\ na \leftarrow \sim a & c \leftarrow a, b \end{array} \right.$$

Π_1 is tight and its answer sets are $M_1 = \{a, \sim na, b, \sim c\}$ and $M_2 = \{\sim a, na, \sim b, c\}$ that are the supported models of Π_1. Conversely, Π_2 is not tight and its answer sets are $N_1 = \{a, \sim na, \sim b, \sim c\}$ and $N_2 = \{\sim a, na, \sim b, \sim c\}$. Here, supported models of Π_2 are N_1, N_2, and $N_3 = \{a, \sim na, b, c\}$, but N_3 is not answer sets.

2.1   CDCL Evaluation

Standard ASP systems [1,38] compute stable models of a program Π in two stages. First, a grounder module computes $ground(\Pi)$, and then a solver module computes answer sets of Π by implementing an extension of the CDCL (Conflict Driven Clause Learning) with *propagators* specific for ASP [44]. CDCL is based on a *choose-propagate-learn* pattern that builds a stable model incrementally starting from an empty interpretation I. At each step the algorithm heuristically chooses a literal that is added to I, and propagates this choice. Propagations are typically computed by procedures, namely propagators, that implement specific rule inferences. Among propagators, we distinguish between *eager* and *post* propagators. The former are employed to infer deterministic consequences of the current choice, while the latter are designed to efficiently prune the search space based on a set of derived consequences. Post propagators are typically applied when eager propagators yield no further derivation. During propagation, if the interpretation I becomes inconsistent, then the *learn* phase starts by analyzing conflicting literals (i.e., $l \in I$ and $\bar{l} \in I$). In particular, this can be done since each literal has an associated "reason" that, roughly, is the set of literals that implied its truth. If consistency can be restored, then the process back-jumps to the choices that led to the conflict and continues the search. On the other hand, if consistency cannot be restored, then the algorithm stops since program Π has no models. Finally, as soon as I is total and consistent then I is an answer set of Π. Modern solvers, such as CLINGO [38] and DLV2 [1], transform ground rules into clauses by applying the well-known Clark's completion [16].

By means of this transformation, the solver is able to compute supported models by leveraging unit propagation of program clauses. As pointed out in the previous section, for tight programs this is sufficient to compute answer sets. However, such a translation can be avoided, as has been done in DLV [46], by equipping the solver with propagators implementing the Fitting operator [36], which guarantees that rules of a logic program are satisfied and true atoms are also supported w.r.t. a candidate answer set. More precisely, given a program Π and a (partial) interpretation I, the Fitting operator Φ_Π is defined as [36]:

- $\Phi_\Pi(I) = T_\Pi(I) \cup \overline{\gamma_\Pi(I)}$
- $T_\Pi(I) = \{H(r) \mid r \in ground(\Pi) \wedge I \models B(r)\}$
- $\gamma_\Pi(I) = \{a \in B_\Pi \mid \forall r \in ground(\Pi) \ s.t. \ H(r) = a, I \not\models B(r)\}$.

Example 2. Let $\Pi = \{a \leftarrow; b \leftarrow; c \leftarrow a, b; d \leftarrow \sim a, \sim b\}$. Let $I = \{a, b\}$ be an interpretation. Then for the fact $a \leftarrow$ (resp. $b \leftarrow$) the empty body is true w.r.t. I and so a (resp. b) is derived by $T_\Pi(I)$. On the other hand, for the rule $c \leftarrow a, b$ the body is also true w.r.t. I and so c is derived as well. For the atom d the only rule having d in the head is $d \leftarrow \sim a, \sim b$. Here the body is false w.r.t. I and so d is derived by $\gamma_\Pi(I)$. Thus $\Phi_\Pi(I) = T_\Pi(I) \cup \overline{\gamma_\Pi(I)} = \{a, b, c, \sim d\}$.

2.2 Compilation-Based ASP Solving

Here we recall how the compilation-based ASP solver PROASP works.

Compilation Stage. PROASP is a compilation-based ASP solver that compiles a tight logic program Π into an hybrid ad-hoc solver where a subset of the rules is grounded while the remaining are simulated by rule-specific eager propagators. More precisely, at compilation stage PROASP applies a sequence of rewriting steps that build two programs, namely Π_{prop} and Π_{gen}. Program Π_{prop}, referred to as *propagator program*, consists of rules and constraints able to simulate inferences of rules in Π that will not be grounded. Thus, by compiling these rules into ad-hoc eager propagators, we obtain the *Propagator* module, which is responsible for efficiently computing inferences of such rules during solving. Conversely, the program Π_{gen}, referred to as *generator program*, contains rules to be grounded and rules defining the domain of predicates appearing in Π_{prop}. Thus, the compilation of rules in Π_{gen} originates the *Generator* module, which generates ground atoms over predicates in Π_{prop} and the instantiations of rules that are not compiled into propagators. Then, *Generator* and *Propagator* modules are integrated with a SAT solver to obtain an ad-hoc solver for Π, namely PROASP *solver*.

Solving Stage. Given a program instance F, that is a set of facts, the PROASP solver for Π can be used to compute an answer set of $\Pi \cup F$, if any. The answer set computation is performed in two steps. First, the generator module takes as input F and generates the set of ground atoms that are relevant for the computation of answer sets of $\Pi \cup F$ and ground instantiations of rules that should be grounded. Then, ground rules are transformed into clauses via Clark's completion [16]; generated atoms become propositional variables; and *Glucose* starts the CDCL. During CDCL, *Glucose* derives deterministic consequences from clauses obtained from the subset of rules that has been instantiated by the generator. Whereas, for remaining rules *Glucose* relies on the *Propagator* module to derive such inferences. By proceeding in this way, as soon as a total and consistent interpretation is computed then it is an answer set of $\Pi \cup F$.

3   Lazy Program Splits

The generation phase of the compilation-based solvers can generate a large number of atoms before starting the solving phase. In some cases this could be a bottleneck as highlighted in [27]. To this end, we introduce the notion of a *lazy program split*, which identifies subprograms that can be evaluated within a propagator using the Fitting operator, without requiring full knowledge of all atoms in the solver (i.e., skipping generation phase for such program split).

Definition 1 (Lazy Program Split). *Given a program Π, and $L \subseteq \Pi$, then L is a lazy program split for Π if L is stratified, and $head(L) \cap head(\Pi \setminus L) = \emptyset$.*

Intuitively, stratification of lazy program split is required to ensure that only deterministic inferences can be generated from L. While, the second condition guarantees that rules in L do not affect the standard compilation pipeline for rules in $\Pi \setminus L$. In this way, the solver can operate without requiring full knowledge of the propositional atoms that appear in the heads of rules within a lazily split program. Note that Definition 1 does not require that the program Π is stratified. Moreover, since L may depend on/from non-stratified subprograms of Π, the evaluation of L cannot be delegated to a grounder before/after the answer set computation. Instead, we can leverage the following properties to simulate L with an ad-hoc propagator that implements the Fitting operator.

Theorem 1. *Let Π be a program, $L \subseteq \Pi$ be a lazy program split, and I be an interpretation over B_Π. Then for each $M \in AS(\Pi)$, $I \subseteq M$ iff $I \cup \Phi_L(I) \subseteq M$.*

Proof. Let $M \in AS(\Pi)$ and $I' = I \cup \Phi_L(I)$. If $I' \subseteq M$ then it trivially follows that $I \subseteq I' \subseteq M$. On the other hand, if $I \subseteq M$ then we show for each $l \in \Phi_L(I)$, $l \in M$. Let $l \in \Phi_L(I)$, then, by construction, we know that either $l \in T_L(I)$ or $l \in \overline{\gamma_L(I)}$. If $l \in T_L(I)$ then there exists $r \in ground(L) \subseteq ground(\Pi)$ such that $H(r) = l$ and $I \models B(r)$. Thus, if $\bar{l} \in M$ then r is violated and so M would not be an answer set of Π. Otherwise $l \in \overline{\gamma_L(I)}$. This means that $l = {\sim}a$, and for each $r \in ground(L)$ such that $H(r) = a$, $I \not\models B(r)$. From Definition 1, $pred(a)$ does not appear in the head of any rule of $\Pi \setminus L$, and so if $\bar{l} = a \in M$ then a is not supported in Π w.r.t. M and M is not an answer set. Thus, $I' \subseteq M$.   □

Theorem 1 ensures that the application of the Fitting operator to a lazy program split L preserves the answer sets of program Π. Thus, whenever $I \cup \Phi_L(I)$ is inconsistent then I cannot be extended to an answer set of Π.

Observation 1 *Let Π be a program, $L \subseteq \Pi$ be a lazy program split, and I be an interpretation over B_Π. $I \cup \Phi_L(I)$ is inconsistent if and only if then there is no $M \in AS(\Pi)$ such that $I \subseteq M$.*

Example 3. Let Π_1 be the program from Example 1, then $L = \{b \leftarrow a;\ c \leftarrow na\}$ is a lazy program split of Π_1. For $I = \{a, \sim na\}$, the Fitting operator extends I to the answer set M_1 of Π_1. More precisely, $M_1 = I \cup \Phi_L(I) = \{a, \sim na, b, \sim c\}$, where $T_L(I) = \{b\}$ and $\gamma_L(I) = \{c\}$. On the other hand, for $I = \{na, \sim a, b\}$ the Fitting operator leads to an inconsistent interpretation $I \cup \Phi_L(I) = \{na, \sim a, b, c, \sim b\}$, where $T_L(I) = \{c\}$ and $\gamma_L(I) = \{b\}$. Here, $I \cup \Phi_L(I)$ is not contained neither in M_1 nor in M_2.

4   Compilation of Fitting's Operator

Given a program Π and a lazy split $L \subseteq \Pi$, we show how to compile post-propagators that simulate the Fitting operator on L, so that rules in $ground(L)$ can be excluded from $ground(\Pi)$ and evaluated entirely by a compiled propagator embedded in the solver. As a result, atoms in the head of $ground(L)$ become unknown to the solver, and, by applying the Fitting operator, atoms in $ground(L)$ can be lazily discovered during solving. More in detail, given a (partial) interpretation I, the Fitting operator is defined as $\Phi_L(I) = T_L(I) \cup \gamma_L(I)$. Thus, we propose to compile L into two ad-hoc post-propagators, namely *Consequence* and *Support*. The *Consequence* propagator computes inferences coming from $T_L(I)$; whereas, the *Support* propagator computes atoms in $\gamma_L(I)$. The Fitting operator applied to L is, thus, obtained by inferring all atoms derived by *Consequence* as true and all atoms derived by *Support* as false.

To present our technique we adopt the pseudo-code notation convention proposed by [28]. In the algorithms, the code enclosed between « » is printed by the compiler as it is, whereas the code enclosed in ⟦ ⟧$_i$ is first substituted with its run-time value and then printed. As an example, given a rule r such that $H(r) = b(X)$, line 18 of Algorithm 1 prints the instruction $h = \sigma(b(X))$.

Compilation of Consequence. The *Consequence* propagator computes inferences coming from $T_L(I)$ by evaluating rules in L in a bottom-up fashion. To this end, Algorithm 1 compiles each $r \in L$ into a bottom-up evaluation procedure that builds ground instantiations of $B(r)$ that are true w.r.t. I, and derives $H(r)$ as true. At the beginning, the code that initializes σ_0 with an empty substitution (line 3) is printed; then, the body of r is reordered (line 4) to obtain a list of literals B in which positive literals precede negative ones. To process the body of r, Algorithm 1 prints a nested block that contains either a conditional statement or a for-loop for each literal $L_i \in B$, with $1 \leq i \leq n$. In detail, if L_i is positive, the instructions for computing the variable substitutions Σ_i are generated. These substitutions extend the previous one, σ_{i-1}, by mapping the variables in L_i to possible constants (line 8). Next, the code is generated to identify substitutions $\sigma_i \in \Sigma_i$ for which $\sigma_i(L_i)$ is true w.r.t. I (i.e., $\sigma_i(L_i) \in I$), and to iterate over them (line 10). Once all positive literals are processed, we know that all variables

---

Algorithm 1 Compile Consequence for r

Input : A rule r of program L
1 **begin**
2     $\ll D = \emptyset \gg$
3     $\ll \sigma_0 = \epsilon \gg$
4     $B = orderConsequence(B(r))$
5   **for all** $i \in 1, \ldots, |B|$ **do**
6        $lit = B[i]$
7   **if** $lit \in B(r)^+$ **then**
8           $\ll \Sigma_i = \{\sigma' \mid \{D(\sigma_{i-1}) \cup \; [\![terms(lit)]\!]_i \} \rightarrow U_\Pi \wedge \sigma' \supseteq \sigma_i\} \gg$
9           $\ll T_i = \{\sigma_i \mid \sigma_i \in \Sigma_i \wedge \sigma_i(\; [\![lit]\!]_i) \in I\} \gg$
10         $\ll$**For** $\sigma_i \in T_i \gg$
11         $openLiteralScope()$
12         $\ll \quad l_i = \sigma_i(\; [\![lit]\!]_i) \gg$

13   **else**
14           $\ll \sigma_i = \sigma_{i-1} \gg$
15           $\ll l_i = \sigma_i(\; [\![lit]\!]_i) \gg$
16           $\ll$**if** $l_i \in I \gg$
17         $openLiteralScope()$

18     $\ll \quad\quad\quad h = \sigma_{[|B|]_i}(\; [\![H(r)]\!]_i) \gg$
19     $\ll \quad\quad\quad R = \sigma_{[|B|]_i}(\; [\![B(r)]\!]_i) \gg$
20     $\ll \quad\quad\quad D = D \cup \{h\} \gg$
21   **for all** i **in** $1, \ldots, |B|$ **do**
22        $closeLiteralScope()$

---

are mapped to some constants (from rules safety). Thus, when L_i is negative the algorithm can print the code that: sets $\sigma_i = \sigma_{i-1}$; computes l_i by applying the substitution σ_i to L_i (i.e., $\sigma_i(L_i)$); and, checks whether l_i is true w.r.t. I (see lines 14-16). Subsequently, the compiler prints the code that: computes h as the application of σ_n to $H(r)$ (line 18); sets $\sigma_n(B(r))$ as its "reason" of the derivation (line 19); and, derives h (line 20) as true. Note that this can be safely done because the procedure generated so far executes the inner-most block if and only if: σ_n is a well-formed substitution for r and $I \models \sigma_n(B(r))$, with $n = |B|$. For completeness, the role of $openLiteralScope()$ and $closeLiteralScope()$ is to ensure that blocks of code are properly nested. For example an implementation C++ would require to open and close brackets for delimiting blocks of code.

Compilation of Support. The *Support* propagator computes atoms in $\gamma_L(I)$ by evaluating rules in L top-down. For a given atom a, it searches for a rule $r' \in ground(L)$ such that $H(r') = a$ and $B(r')$ is not false w.r.t. I. If no such r' exists then a is inferred as false (i.e., it is not supported). To this end, Algorithm 2 compiles each $r \in L$ into a top-down evaluation starting from a ground atom a.

Algorithm 2 Compile Support for r

Input: A rule r of program L

1 **begin**
2 $\quad$ «if pred(a) = $[\![\text{pred(h)}]\!]_i$»
3 $\quad$ «σ_0: $[\![terms(h)]\!]_i \to U_\Pi \wedge \sigma_0([\![h]\!]_i) = a$»
4 $\quad$ $B = orderSupport(B(r))$
5 $\quad$ **for all** $i \in 1, \ldots, |B|$ **do**
6 $\quad\quad$ $lit = B[i]$
7 $\quad\quad$ **if** $lit \in B(r)^+$ **then**
8 $\quad\quad\quad$ «$\Sigma_i = \{\sigma' : \{D(\sigma_{i-1}) \cup [\![terms(lit)]\!]_i\} \to U_\Pi \wedge \sigma' \supseteq \sigma_{i-1}\}$»
9 $\quad\quad\quad$ «$T = \{\sigma_i \mid \sigma_i \in \Sigma_i \wedge \sigma_i([\![lit]\!]_i) \in I\}$»
10 $\quad\quad\quad$ «$F = \{\sigma_i \mid \sigma_i \in \Sigma_i \wedge \overline{\sigma_i([\![lit]\!]_i)} \in I\}$»
11 $\quad\quad\quad$ «$U = \Sigma_i \setminus (T \cup F)$»
12 $\quad\quad\quad$ «$R = R \cup \{\overline{\sigma_i([\![lit]\!]_i)} \mid \sigma_i \in F\}$»
13 $\quad\quad\quad$ «For $\sigma_i \in T \cup U$»
14 $\quad\quad\quad$ $openLiteralScope()$
15 $\quad\quad\quad$ « $l_i = \sigma_i([\![lit]\!]_i)$»
16 $\quad\quad$ **else**
17 $\quad\quad\quad$ «$\sigma_i = \sigma_{i-1}$»
18 $\quad\quad\quad$ «$l_i = \sigma_i([\![lit]\!]_i)$»
19 $\quad\quad\quad$ «if $\overline{l_i} \in I$»
20 $\quad\quad\quad$ « $R = R \cup \{\overline{l_i}\}$»
21 $\quad\quad\quad$ «else»
22 $\quad\quad\quad$ $openLiteralScope()$
23 $\quad$ « $return \perp$»
24 $\quad$ **for all** j in $1, \ldots, |B_e|$ **do**
25 $\quad\quad$ $closeLiteralScope()$
26 $\quad$ «$return \top$»

Algorithm 2 starts by printing the code that matches $H(r)$ with a via a variable substitution. More precisely, if a and $H(r)$ have the same predicate then such matching exists via the substitution σ_0 that maps the i-th variable of $H(r)$ to the i-th constant of a (lines 2–3). Then, analogously to Algorithm 1, the body of r is ordered in the list B (line 4) in such a way that positive literals in $B(r)$ precede negative ones; and for each $L_i \in B$ a nested block is printed to search for ground instantiations of L_i that are not false w.r.t. I. Let $B = L_1, \ldots, L_n$. If L_i is positive, a nested block is generated to compute the set Σ_i of substitutions that extend σ_{i-1} by mapping variables in L_i to constants from U_Π (line 8). Then, Σ_i is partitioned into three disjoint sets T, F and U that will contain, respectively, variable substitutions $\sigma_i \in \Sigma_i$ such that $\sigma_i(L_i)$ is true, false or undefined w.r.t. I (lines 9-11). Here, for each $\sigma_i \in F$, $\overline{\sigma_i(L_i)}$ is stored R which denotes the "reason" for a to be derived as false (line 12). Then, a for loop iterating over substitutions $\sigma_i \in T \cup U$ (line 13) is opened to continue processing the body.

Once positive literals are processed, analogously to the previous case, each variable of a negative literal L_i is mapped to a constant by previous substitution σ_{i-1}. Thus, Algorithm 2 generates a block of code that initializes σ_i as σ_{i-1} and sets $l_i = \sigma_i(L_i)$. Then, it checks whether l_i is false w.r.t. I. If so, $\overline{l_i}$ is added to the reason R (and the inner blocks are skipped). Otherwise, since l_i may support a, the code goes into an else block properly closing the nested scopes (lines 18–22).

By construction, the innermost block of the compiled code is reached if and only if σ_n, with $n = |B|$, is a well-formed substitution for r and $\sigma_n(B(r))$ is not false w.r.t. I. Thus, in line 23, a return statement returning $\perp$ is printed which means that a cannot be derived by γ_L since can be supported by a instantiation of r (line 23). Eventually, all the nested block are closed and a statement returning $\top$ is printed (line 26), denoting that no instantiations of r can support a.

The support propagator is obtained by calling the sub procedures generated by Algorithm 2 for each $r \in L$, and infers a as false if all of these return $\top$.

5   Implementation and Experiments

This section outlines the main updates to PROASP and evaluates it against state-of-the-art Ground&Solve and compilation-based methods.

5.1   Implementation Details

Techniques proposed in Sect. 4 have been implemented on top of the PROASP system [28], by accommodating lazy atom discovery. In particular, the solver skips the generation phase for the lazy program split L, and an additional propagator generated by the algorithms described in Sect. 4 is embedded in the solver as post-propagator. It is worth observing that the solver must be aware of the atoms at the interface between itself and the new propagator. However, according to Definition 1, predicates in $head(L)$ do not appear in the heads of rules in $\Pi \setminus L$, meaning that the generator phase would omit rules defining these predicates. To resolve this, we extend the generator phase to derive the domains of predicates in $head(L)$ based on the bodies of rules in $\Pi \setminus L$. This is achieved by augmenting the generator program of PROASP [27] with additional rules. All the technical details of this extension are provided for reasons of space in the Appendix, which also contains a full example of the compiler's output.

5.2   Experiments

Benchmarks. In our evaluation, we considered benchmarks from the literature presenting a large number of propositional atoms [15,60], and synthetic benchmarks used to assess the scalability of compilation-based systems [27]. Concerning benchmarks with grounding issues, we considered the House Reconfiguration Problem [60] (HRP) and Log Generation (LG) [15]. More precisely, HRP consists of finding an assignment of things, belonging to some people, to cabinets and cabinets to rooms such that specific constraints are satisfied. In this benchmark, instances are very heterogeneous and vary in terms of number of cabinets, rooms and things to be assigned. On the other hand, LG consists of generating event logs whose traces are compliant with DECLARE specifications [55]. Thus, instances of such benchmarks may vary according to the length of event log traces, number of activities, or number of DECLARE constraints. In particular, we focused on the generation of a single trace and we considered large instances of increasing size (up to 100 activities, 6 constraints, and 1000 as trace length) so that even generating a single trace is nontrivial. Then, we included in our evaluation Synth1 and Synth2 benchmarks by [27] which pointed out strengths and significant challenges for compilation-based system. For each benchmark we manually selected, following the methodology by [28], the lazy program split that generates the largest number of atoms in the PROASP solver, which limits PROASP performance as highlighted in [27].

Compared Methods. In this comparison, we include state-of-the-art Ground& Solve systems as well as compilation-based solver in different configurations. More precisely, we consider: (*i*) the ASP system CLINGO [38] v. 5.6.2; (*ii*) the ASP solver WASP [2] v. d87f3f0 equipped with GRINGO [40] as grounder; and (*iii*) six versions of PROASP obtained by blending grounding, compilation, and lazy atom discovery. More precisely, PROASP-GR denotes the compiled PROASP where all rules are grounded; PROASP-CP denotes the compiled PROASP where no rules are grounded; PROASP-HY denotes the compiled PROASP where only some rules are grounded; and, for each the previous versions, we consider a variant with lazy atom discovery which avoids materialization of atoms for a given lazy program split, namely PROASP-GR-L, PROASP-CP-L, and PROASP-HY-L.

Hardware Setup. All experiments were executed on an Intel(R) Xeon(R) CPU E5-4610 v2 @ 2.30GHz running Debian Linux (3.16.0-4-amd64), with memory and CPU time (i.e. user+system) limited to 12GB and 1200 s. Each system was limited to run on a single core. Benchmarks and executables are available at [18]. The source code of the PROASP system is available at https://github.com/MazzottaG/ProASP

Results. Obtained results are reported in Figs. 1 and 2. More precisely, cactus plots report either execution time or memory consumption for all the compared systems for a given benchmark. In a cactus plot, instances are sorted by memory (resp. time), and a point (i, j) of the plot indicates that a system solved the i-th instance with a memory (resp. time) limit of j gigabytes (resp. seconds).

Benchmarks with Lots of Atoms. As expected, for HRP, PROASP-CP and PROASP-HY incur substantial overhead in memory and execution time (Figs. 1a and 1b) due to the large number of symbols generated upfront, which also hinders solving performance. This issue is effectively addressed by PROASP-CP-L and PROASP-HY-L, which improve performance of PROASP. Nonetheless, for HRP,

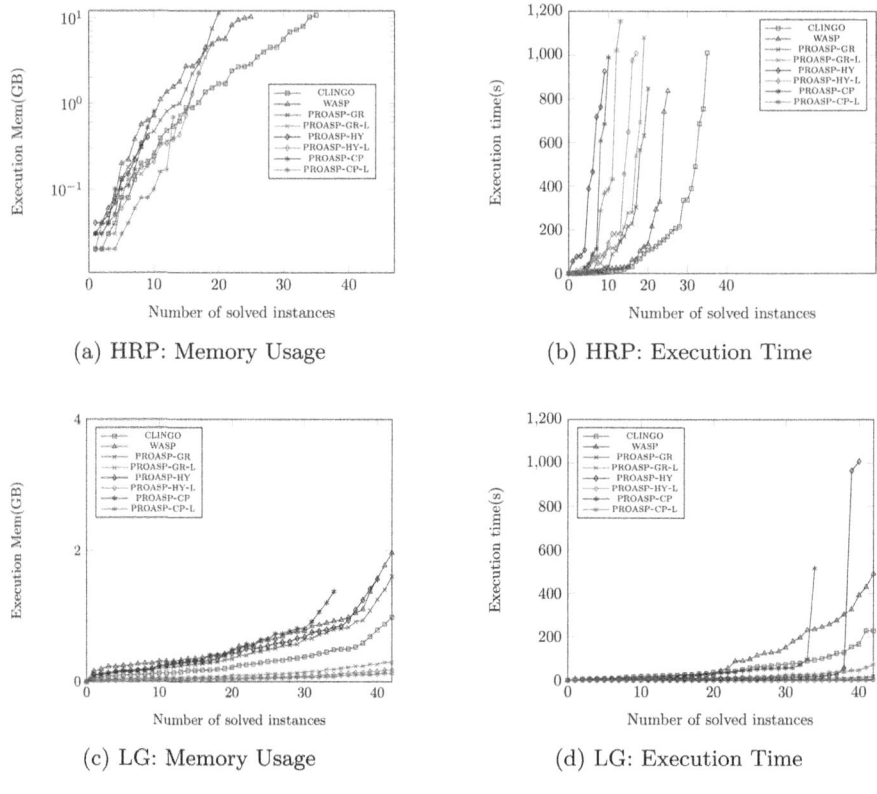

(a) HRP: Memory Usage

(b) HRP: Execution Time

(c) LG: Memory Usage

(d) LG: Execution Time

Fig. 1. Grounding intensive benchmarks

Ground&Solve systems remain preferable, with CLINGO delivering the best performance, since many instances can be fully grounded. Concerning the LG benchmark (see Fig. 1c) compiled solvers are more effective (see Fig. 1d). Moreover, the proposed techniques have a clearer impact, with PROASP-CP-L, PROASP-GR-L, and PROASP-HY-L achieving the best performance overall.

Benchmarks for Compilation-Based Systems. Experiments conducted by [27] highlighted strengths and limitations of compiled systems. Thus, this benchmark allows for fairly assessing the improvement introduced by the proposed techniques.

In Synth2, CLINGO, WASP, and PROASP-GR are clearly impacted by the grounding bottleneck. As expected, PROASP-CP, which grounds no rules, helps alleviate this issue. Nonetheless, Synth2 is handled more effectively by PROASP-CP-L and PROASP-GR-L which also avoid the generation of atoms present due to a number of rules performing projections (see Figs. 2a and 2b).

In Synth1, where the main issue is the sheer number of atoms to be generated by the original versions of PROASP, PROASP-GR-L and PROASP-CP-L are easily the best performing approaches (see Fig. 2c and 2d).

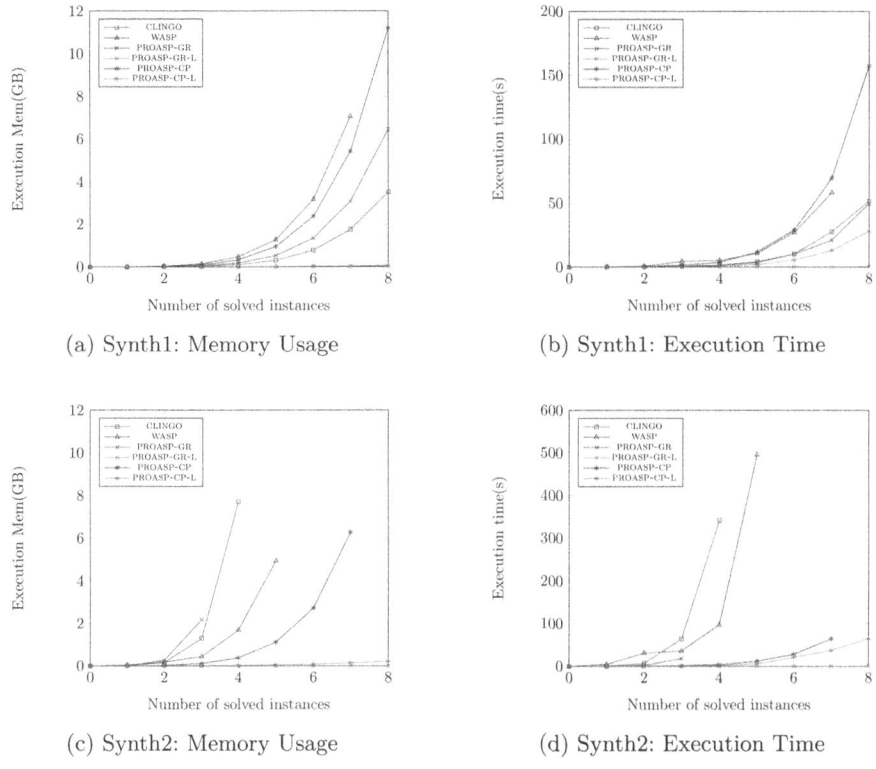

(a) Synth1: Memory Usage

(b) Synth1: Execution Time

(c) Synth2: Memory Usage

(d) Synth2: Execution Time

Fig. 2. Synthetic benchmarks

All in all, the proposed techniques overcome the limitations of PROASP and enhance performance also in scenarios where PROASP was already effective.

6   Related Work

The grounding bottleneck inspired a large body of literature leading to the proposals, ranging from hybrid formalisms [5,38,53,59] to compilation-based approaches [17,19,20,27,50]. More in detail, hybrid formalisms, such as Constraints Answer Set Programming (CASP) [4,5,14,53,59], ASP Modulo Theories [38], and HEX programs [30], are aimed at connecting ASP systems with external sources of computation, thus shifting the problem out of the ASP systems realm.

Lazy grounding systems [9,45,47,54,61], do not materialize ground rules until their body is satisfied during solving. Albeit promising, these systems still do not match the performance of state-of-the-art systems [62]. The techniques proposed in this paper shift the evaluation of program splits during solving but, differently from lazy grounding systems, no ground rules are materialized.

Complexity-driven program rewritings [7,8] address the issue by encoding the original program into different formalisms, such as propositional epistemic logic programs, or into disjunctive programs, generating smaller ground programs. Such techniques are orthogonal to compilation and could be combined.

This paper builds on compilation-based approaches [19,20,27,50], which mitigate the grounding bottleneck by translating non-ground rules into specialized procedures that simulate inferences without fully grounding the program [27,28,50]. These methods are extended here with lazy atom generation.

7   Conclusions

State-of-the-art systems are affected by the *Grounding Bottleneck* problem, which might limit the applicability of ASP. Recently, compilation-based ASP solvers have proven effective in addressing this issue. Nevertheless, existing compilation-based systems still require the upfront materialization of ground atoms, which can be detrimental in certain cases, as noted by [27]. In this paper, we introduced a compilation-based technique that avoids the generation of all ground atoms in advance. We implemented these techniques in PROASP, with empirical results showing substantial performance gains.

As far as future work is concerned, we plan to extend our techniques beyond tight programs, e.g., by supporting the well-founded operator.

Acknowledgments. This work was supported by the Italian Ministry of Industrial Development (MISE) under project EI-TWIN n. F/310168/05/X56 CUP B29J24000680005; and by the Italian Ministry of Research (MUR) under projects: PNRR FAIR - Spoke 9 - WP 9.1 CUP H23C22000860006, Tech4You CUP H23C22000370006, and PRIN PINPOINT CUP H23C22000280006.

References

1. Alviano, M., et al.: The ASP system DLV2. In: Balduccini, M., Janhunen, T. (eds.) Logic Programming and Nonmonotonic Reasoning, pp. 215–221. Springer International Publishing, Cham (2017). https://doi.org/10.1007/978-3-319-61660-5_19

2. Alviano, M., Dodaro, C., Leone, N., Ricca, F.: Advances in WASP. In: Calimeri, F., Ianni, G., Truszczynski, M. (eds.) LPNMR 2015. LNCS (LNAI), vol. 9345, pp. 40–54. Springer, Cham (2015). https://doi.org/10.1007/978-3-319-23264-5_5

3. Arenas, M., Bertossi, L.E., Chomicki, J.: Consistent query answers in inconsistent databases. In: PODS '99: Proceedings of the Eighteenth ACM SIGMOD-SIGACT-SIGART Symposium on Principles of Database Systems, pp. 68–79. ACM Press (1999)

4. Aziz, R.A., Chu, G., Stuckey, P.J.: Stable model semantics for founded bounds. Theory Pract. Log. Program. **13**(4–5), 517–532 (2013)

5. Balduccini, M., Lierler, Y.: Constraint answer set solver EZCSP and why integration schemas matter. Theory Pract. Log. Program. **17**(4), 462–515 (2017)
6. Barbara, V., et al.: Neuro-symbolic AI for compliance checking of electrical control panels. Theory Pract. Log. Program. **23**(4), 748–764 (2023)
7. Beiser, A., Hecher, M., Unalan, K., Woltran, S.: Bypassing the ASP bottleneck: Hybrid grounding by splitting and rewriting. In: IJCAI, pp. 3250–3258. ijcai.org (2024)
8. Besin, V., Hecher, M., Woltran, S.: Body-decoupled grounding via solving: a novel approach on the ASP bottleneck. In: IJCAI, pp. 2546–2552. ijcai.org (2022)
9. Bomanson, J., Janhunen, T., Weinzierl, A.: Enhancing lazy grounding with lazy normalization in answer-set programming. In: Proceedings of the AAAI Conference on Artificial Intelligence, pp. 2694–2702. AAAI Press (2019)
10. Brewka, G., Eiter, T., Truszczynski, M.: Answer set programming at a glance. Commun. ACM **54**(12), 92–103 (2011)
11. Calimeri, F., Faber, W., Gebser, M., Ianni, G., Kaminski, R., Krennwallner, T., Leone, N., Maratea, M., Ricca, F., Schaub, T.: Asp-core-2 input language format. Theory Pract. Log. Program. **20**(2), 294–309 (2020)
12. Calimeri, F., Gebser, M., Maratea, M., Ricca, F.: Design and results of the fifth answer set programming competition. Artif. Intell. **231**, 151–181 (2016)
13. Cardellini, M., et al.: Rescheduling rehabilitation sessions with answer set programming. J. Log. Comput. **33**(4), 837–863 (2023)
14. Cat, B.D., Denecker, M., Bruynooghe, M., Stuckey, P.J.: Lazy model expansion: interleaving grounding with search. J. Artif. Intell. Res. **52**, 235–286 (2015)
15. Chiariello, F., Maggi, F.M., Patrizi, F.: ASP-based declarative process mining, pp. 5539–5547. AAAI Press (2022). https://doi.org/10.1609/AAAI.V36I5.20493
16. Clark, K.L.: Negation as failure. In: Logic and Data Bases, pp. 293–322. Advances in Data Base Theory, Plenum Press, New York (1977)
17. Cuteri, A., Mazzotta, G., Ricca, F.: Compilation-based techniques for evaluating normal logic programs under the well-founded semantics. In: Dovier, A., Formisano, A. (eds.) Proceedings of the 38th Italian Conference on Computational Logic, Udine, Italy, June 21-23, 2023. CEUR Workshop Proceedings, vol. 3428 (2023). https://ceur-ws.org/Vol-3428/paper11.pdf
18. Cuteri, A., Mazzotta, G., Ricca, F.: Benchmarks (2025). https://osf.io/nxhpr/?view_only=c5d9b4b1ecf04e44beac10517c13301b
19. Cuteri, B., Dodaro, C., Ricca, F., Schüller, P.: Partial compilation of ASP programs. Theory Pract. Log. Program. **19**(5–6), 857–873 (2019). https://doi.org/10.1017/S1471068419000231
20. Cuteri, B., Dodaro, C., Ricca, F., Schüller, P.: Overcoming the grounding bottleneck due to constraints in ASP solving: constraints become propagators. In: IJCAI, pp. 1688–1694. ijcai.org (2020)
21. Cuteri, B., Reale, K., Ricca, F.: A logic-based question answering system for cultural heritage. In: Calimeri, F., Leone, N., Manna, M. (eds.) JELIA 2019. LNCS (LNAI), vol. 11468, pp. 526–541. Springer, Cham (2019). https://doi.org/10.1007/978-3-030-19570-0_35
22. Dantsin, E., Eiter, T., Gottlob, G., Voronkov, A.: Complexity and expressive power of logic programming. ACM Comput. Surv. **33**(3), 374–425 (2001)
23. Dodaro, C., Galatà, G., Khan, M.K., Maratea, M., Porro, I.: An ASP-based solution for operating room scheduling with beds management. In: Fodor, P., Montali, M., Calvanese, D., Roman, D. (eds.) RuleML+RR 2019. LNCS, vol. 11784, pp. 67–81. Springer, Cham (2019). https://doi.org/10.1007/978-3-030-31095-0_5

24. Dodaro, C., Galatà, G., Maratea, M., Porro, I.: Operating room scheduling via answer set programming. In: Ghidini, C., Magnini, B., Passerini, A., Traverso, P. (eds.) AI*IA 2018. LNCS (LNAI), vol. 11298, pp. 445–459. Springer, Cham (2018). https://doi.org/10.1007/978-3-030-03840-3_33

25. Dodaro, C., Leone, N., Nardi, B., Ricca, F.: Allotment problem in travel industry: a solution based on ASP. In: ten Cate, B., Mileo, A. (eds.) RR 2015. LNCS, vol. 9209, pp. 77–92. Springer, Cham (2015). https://doi.org/10.1007/978-3-319-22002-4_7

26. Dodaro, C., Maratea, M.: Nurse scheduling via answer set programming. In: Balduccini, M., Janhunen, T. (eds.) LPNMR 2017. LNCS (LNAI), vol. 10377, pp. 301–307. Springer, Cham (2017). https://doi.org/10.1007/978-3-319-61660-5_27

27. Dodaro, C., Mazzotta, G., Ricca, F.: Compilation of tight ASP programs. Front. Artif. Intell. Appl. **372**, 557–564. IOS Press (2023). https://doi.org/10.3233/FAIA230316

28. Dodaro, C., Mazzotta, G., Ricca, F.: Blending grounding and compilation for efficient ASP solving. In: Proceedings of the 21st International Conference on Principles of Knowledge Representation and Reasoning, KR (2024)

29. Eiter, T., Fink, M., Greco, G., Lembo, D.: Repair localization for query answering from inconsistent databases. ACM Trans. Database Syst. **33**(2), 10:1–10:51 (2008)

30. Eiter, T., Redl, C., Schüller, P.: Problem solving using the HEX family. In: Computational Models of Rationality, pp. 150–174. College Publications (2016)

31. Erdem, E., Gelfond, M., Leone, N.: Applications of answer set programming. AI Mag. **37**(3), 53–68 (2016)

32. Erdem, E., Lifschitz, V.: Tight logic programs. Theory Pract. Log. Program. **3**(4–5), 499–518 (2003)

33. Erdem, E., Patoglu, V.: Applications of ASP in robotics. Künstliche Intell. **32**(2–3), 143–149 (2018)

34. Faber, W., Pfeifer, G., Leone, N.: Semantics and complexity of recursive aggregates in answer set programming. Artif. Intell. **175**(1), 278–298 (2011)

35. Falkner, A.A., Friedrich, G., Schekotihin, K., Taupe, R., Teppan, E.C.: Industrial applications of answer set programming. Künstliche Intell. **32**(2–3), 165–176 (2018)

36. Fitting, M.: A deterministic prolog fixpoint semantics. J. Log. Program. **2**(2), 111–118 (1985). https://doi.org/10.1016/0743-1066(85)90014-7

37. Francescutto, G., Schekotihin, K., El-Kholany, M.M.S.: Solving a multi-resource partial-ordering flexible variant of the job-shop scheduling problem with hybrid ASP. In: Faber, W., Friedrich, G., Gebser, M., Morak, M. (eds.) JELIA 2021. LNCS (LNAI), vol. 12678, pp. 313–328. Springer, Cham (2021). https://doi.org/10.1007/978-3-030-75775-5_21

38. Gebser, M., Kaminski, R., Kaufmann, B., Ostrowski, M., Schaub, T., Wanko, P.: Theory solving made easy with clingo 5. OASICS, vol. 52, pp. 2:1–2:15. Schloss Dagstuhl (2016)

39. Gebser, M., Kaminski, R., Kaufmann, B., Schaub, T.: Answer Set Solving in Practice. Synthesis Lectures on Artificial Intelligence and Machine Learning, Morgan & Claypool Publishers (2012). https://doi.org/10.2200/S00457ED1V01Y201211AIM019

40. Gebser, M., Kaminski, R., König, A., Schaub, T.: Advances in *gringo* series 3. In: Delgrande, J.P., Faber, W. (eds.) LPNMR 2011. LNCS (LNAI), vol. 6645, pp. 345–351. Springer, Heidelberg (2011). https://doi.org/10.1007/978-3-642-20895-9_39

41. Gebser, M., Leone, N., Maratea, M., Perri, S., Ricca, F., Schaub, T.: Evaluation techniques and systems for answer set programming: a survey. In: IJCAI, pp. 5450–5456. ijcai.org (2018)

42. Gelfond, M., Lifschitz, V.: Classical negation in logic programs and disjunctive databases. New Genr. Comput. **9**(3/4), 365–386 (1991)
43. Grasso, G., Iiritano, S., Leone, N., Lio, V., Ricca, F., Scalise, F.: An ASP-based system for team-building in the Gioia-Tauro seaport. In: Carro, M., Peña, R. (eds.) PADL 2010. LNCS, vol. 5937, pp. 40–42. Springer, Heidelberg (2010). https://doi.org/10.1007/978-3-642-11503-5_5
44. Kaufmann, B., Leone, N., Perri, S., Schaub, T.: Grounding and solving in answer set programming. AI Mag. **37**(3), 25–32 (2016)
45. Lefèvre, C., Nicolas, P.: The first version of a new ASP solver: ASPeRiX. In: Erdem, E., Lin, F., Schaub, T. (eds.) LPNMR 2009. LNCS (LNAI), vol. 5753, pp. 522–527. Springer, Heidelberg (2009). https://doi.org/10.1007/978-3-642-04238-6_52
46. Leone, N., et al.: The DLV system for knowledge representation and reasoning. ACM Trans. Comput. Log. **7**(3), 499–562 (2006)
47. Lierler, Y., Robbins, J.: DualGrounder: lazy instantiation via clingo multi-shot framework. In: Faber, W., Friedrich, G., Gebser, M., Morak, M. (eds.) JELIA 2021. LNCS (LNAI), vol. 12678, pp. 435–441. Springer, Cham (2021). https://doi.org/10.1007/978-3-030-75775-5_29
48. Manna, M., Ricca, F., Terracina, G.: Taming primary key violations to query large inconsistent data via ASP. Theory Pract. Log. Program. **15**(4–5), 696–710 (2015)
49. Marques-Silva, J., Lynce, I., Malik, S.: Conflict-driven clause learning SAT solvers. Front. Artif. Intell. Appl. **336**, 133–182. IOS Press (2021)
50. Mazzotta, G., Ricca, F., Dodaro, C.: Compilation of aggregates in ASP systems. In: The Thirty-Sixth AAAI Conference on Artificial Intelligence (AAAI-22), pp. 5834–5841. AAAI Press (2022)
51. Mitra, A., Clark, P., Tafjord, O., Baral, C.: Declarative question answering over knowledge bases containing natural language text with answer set programming. pp. 3003–3010. AAAI Press (2019)
52. Müller, L., Wanko, P., Haubelt, C., Schaub, T.: Investigating methods for ASPmT-based design space exploration in evolutionary product design. Int. J. Parallel Program. **52**(1), 59–92 (2024)
53. Ostrowski, M., Schaub, T.: ASP modulo CSP: the clingcon system. Theory Pract. Log. Program. **12**(4–5), 485–503 (2012)
54. Palù, A.D., Dovier, A., Pontelli, E., Rossi, G.: GASP: answer set programming with lazy grounding. Fundam. Informaticae **96**(3), 297–322 (2009)
55. Pesic, M., Schonenberg, H., van der Aalst, W.M.P.: DECLARE: full support for loosely-structured processes. In: IEEE International Enterprise Distributed Object Computing Conference (EDOC), pp. 287–300 (2007)
56. Rajaratnam, D., Schaub, T., Wanko, P., Chen, K., Liu, S., Son, T.C.: Solving an industrial-scale warehouse delivery problem with answer set programming modulo difference constraints. Algorithms **16**(4), 216 (2023)
57. Schüller, P.: Modeling variations of first-order horn abduction in answer set programming. Fundam. Informaticae **149**(1–2), 159–207 (2016)
58. Son, T.C., Pontelli, E., Balduccini, M., Schaub, T.: Answer set planning: a survey. Theory Pract. Log. Program. **23**(1), 226–298 (2023)
59. Susman, B., Lierler, Y.: SMT-based constraint answer set solver EZSMT (system description). OASIcs, vol. 52, pp. 1:1–1:15. Schloss Dagstuhl (2016)
60. Taupe, R., Weinzierl, A., Friedrich, G.: Conflict generalisation in ASP: learning correct and effective non-ground constraints. Theory Pract. Log. Program. **20**(5), 799–814 (2020). https://doi.org/10.1017/S1471068420000368

61. Weinzierl, A.: Blending lazy-grounding and CDNL search for answer-set solving. In: Balduccini, M., Janhunen, T. (eds.) LPNMR 2017. LNCS (LNAI), vol. 10377, pp. 191–204. Springer, Cham (2017). https://doi.org/10.1007/978-3-319-61660-5_17
62. Weinzierl, A., Taupe, R., Friedrich, G.: Advancing lazy-grounding ASP solving techniques - restarts, phase saving, heuristics, and more. Theory Pract. Log. Program. **20**(5), 609–624 (2020)
63. Yang, Z., Ishay, A., Lee, J.: Coupling large language models with logic programming for robust and general reasoning from text. pp. 5186–5219. Association for Computational Linguistics (2023)

Encoding Action Reversibility In Planning Using Quantified ASP and Bule

Wolfgang Faber⬤ and Michael Morak$^{(\boxtimes)}$⬤

University of Klagenfurt, Klagenfurt, Austria
{wolfgang.faber,michael.morak}@aau.at

Abstract. Action reversibility in planning deals with the question whether the consequences of a given action can be undone so that the state of the environment returns to what it was before the action was applied. This problem is known to be PSPACE-complete in general. In this paper, we evaluate two PSPACE-complete logic programming languages, namely: Quantified Answer Set Programming (QASP) that extends Answer Set Programming (ASP) with quantified atoms; and Bule, a logic programming language that extends Quantified Boolean Formulas (QBFs) with Datalog-like rules in order to separate the problem domain and problem instance. We give two novel encodings for the problem of action reversibility and perform experiments to see how the solvers for these two languages compare to established methods.

1 Introduction

Automated Planning is a field of research that traditionally deals with the problem of generating sequences of actions, called plans, that transform a given initial state of the environment to some goal state [21,22]. An action, simply put, is a modifier that acts upon and changes the environment. An interesting problem in this field is the question whether an action can be reversed by subsequently applying other actions, thus undoing the effects that the action had on the environment. This problem has been investigated on and off throughout the years [10,13], and has recently received renewed interest [6,15,27–29].

Action reversibility is an important problem with regard to several aspects. Intuitively, actions whose effects cannot be reversed might lead to dead-end states, that is, states from which the goal state can no longer be reached. Early detection of the possibility of dead-end states is beneficial in the plan generation process [25]. Reasoning in more complex structures is even more prone to dead-ends [7]. An example is the concept of Agent Planning Programs [11], which represent networks of planning tasks where the goal state of one task is an initial state of some other task. Another aspect is online planning, where we can observe that applying reversible actions is safe and hence explicitly providing information about safe states of the environment could be avoided [9]. Another, although not very obvious, benefit of action reversibility is in plan optimization. If the effects of an action are later reversed by a sequence of other actions in

© The Author(s), under exclusive license to Springer Nature Switzerland AG 2026
G. Casini et al. (Eds.): JELIA 2025, LNAI 16093, pp. 327–342, 2026.
https://doi.org/10.1007/978-3-032-04587-4_20

a plan, these actions might be removed from the plan, potentially shortening it significantly. It has been shown that under given circumstances, pairs of inverse actions, which are a special case of action reversibility, can be removed from plans [8].

A general framework for action reversibility that has recently been introduced [28] offers a broad definition of the term, and generalises several existing notions of reversibility, like "undoability" [10], or the concept of "reverse plans" [13]. The concept of reversibility in this general framework directly incorporates the set of states in which a given action is reversible. This notion is called S-reversibility where S is a set of states where an action must be reversible. This is then extended to ϕ-reversibility, where the set of states is characterized by a formula ϕ in terms of propositional logic. These notions are then further refined to universal reversibility (referring to the set of all states) and to reversibility w.r.t. some planning task Π (where the action must be reversible in all reachable states w.r.t. the initial state specified in Π). These last two versions match the notion of "undoability" proposed in the literature [10]. Furthermore, the notions can be further restricted to require that some action is reversible by a single "reverse plan" that does not depend on the state in which the action under consideration is applied. For single actions, this matches the concept of the "reverse plan" proposed in the mid-2000s [13].

The complexity analysis of Morak et al. [28] indicates that some of these problems can be addressed by means of Answer Set Programming (ASP) and Epistemic Logic Programs (ELPs). An experimental evaluation of these two languages to compute reverse plans has recently been carried out [15]. Another implementation, using a recently proposed language extension for ASP, namely, ASP with Quantifiers [1], abbreviated as ASP(Q), was also proposed by the same authors [16] and work has started to compile a reasonably broad benchmark set for action reversibility [29].

Contributions. In this paper, we use the `plasp` tool [12] to translate PDDL domains into ASP facts and then encode the action reversibility problem using two recently proposed logic-based languages:

- The language of *Quantified ASP (QASP)* [17] that extends ASP with quantified atoms in a similar way to how quantified boolean formulas (QBFs) extend propositional (SAT) formulas with quantification. Interestingly, the initial work presenting QASP does so with the aim to solve planning problems using this new ASP-based quantified language.
- The SAT and QBF programming language *Bule* [23] that extends SAT and QBF modelling with the ability to write non-ground rule-like constructs that are then grounded and translated into a SAT or QBF formula.

Both of these languages match the well-known PSPACE complexity of deciding STRIPS planning problems [3] and hence seem well-suited to encode reversibility tasks. Due to the explicit use of quantification, the encodings in the above two formalisms are arguably more intuitive than the established ASP and ELP encodings. They also allow for more flexibility regarding modification towards other forms of reversibility (like the non-uniform variants) which, under standard complexity-theoretic assumptions, seem unlikely to be directly solvable using ASP or ELP encodings.

Finally, we perform some preliminary experiments on an established set of benchmarks to compare existing approaches with the new encodings.

2   Preliminaries

2.1   STRIPS Planning

Let $\mathcal{F}$ be a set of *facts*, that is, propositional variables describing the environment, which can either be true or false. Then, a subset $s \subseteq \mathcal{F}$ is called a *state*, which intuitively represents a set of facts considered to be true. An action is a tuple $a = \langle pre(a), add(a), del(a) \rangle$, where $pre(a) \subseteq \mathcal{F}$ is the set of *preconditions* of a, and $add(a) \subseteq \mathcal{F}$ and $del(a) \subseteq \mathcal{F}$ are the add and delete effects of a, respectively. W.l.o.g., we assume actions to be well-formed, that is, $add(a) \cap del(a) = \emptyset$ and $pre(a) \cap add(a) = \emptyset$. An action a is *applicable* in a state s iff $pre(a) \subseteq s$. The result of applying an action a in a state s, given that a is applicable in s, is the state $a[s] = (s \setminus del(a)) \cup add(a)$. A sequence of actions $\pi = \langle a_1, \ldots, a_n \rangle$ is applicable in a state s_0 iff there is a sequence of states $\langle s_1, \ldots, s_n \rangle$ such that, for $0 < i \leq n$, it holds that a_i is applicable in s_{i-1} and $a_i[s_{i-1}] = s_i$. Applying the action sequence π on s_0 is denoted $\pi[s_0]$, with $\pi[s_0] = s_n$. The *length* of action sequence π is denoted $|\pi|$.

A *STRIPS planning task* $\Pi = \langle \mathcal{F}, \mathcal{A}, s_0, G \rangle$ is a four-element tuple consisting of a set of *facts* $\mathcal{F} = \{f_1, \ldots, f_n\}$, a set of *actions* $\mathcal{A} = \{a_1, \ldots, a_m\}$, an *starting state* $s_0 \subseteq \mathcal{F}$, and a *goal* $G \subseteq \mathcal{F}$. A state $s \subseteq \mathcal{F}$ is a *goal state (for Π)* iff $G \subseteq s$. An action sequence π is called a *plan* iff $\pi[s_0] \supseteq G$. We further define several relevant notions w.r.t. a planning task Π. A state s is *reachable from state s'* iff there exists an applicable action sequence π such that $\pi[s'] = s$. A state $s \in 2^{\mathcal{F}}$ is simply called *reachable* iff it is reachable from the starting state s_0. The set of all reachable states in Π is denoted by $\mathcal{R}_\Pi$. An action a is *reachable* iff there is some state $s \in \mathcal{R}_\Pi$ such that a is applicable in s.

Deciding whether a STRIPS planning task has a plan is known to be PSPACE-complete in general and it is NP-complete if the length of the plan is polynomially bounded [3].

2.2   Reversibility of Actions

We now review the notion of uniform reversibility, which is a subclass of action reversibility as explained in detail by Morak et al. [28]. Intuitively, we call an action reversible if there is a way to undo all the effects that this action caused, and we call an action *uniformly reversible* if its effects can be undone by a single sequence of actions irrespective of the state where the action was applied.

While this intuition is fairly straightforward, when formally defining this concept, we also need to take several other factors into account—in particular, the set of possible states where an action is considered plays an important role [28].

Definition 1. *Let $\mathcal{F}$ be a set of facts, $\mathcal{A}$ be a set of actions, $S \subseteq 2^{\mathcal{F}}$ be a set of states, and $a \in \mathcal{A}$ be an action. We call a S-reversible iff for each state $s \in S$ wherein a is applicable, there exists a sequence of actions $\pi = \langle a_1, \ldots, a_n \rangle \in \mathcal{A}^n$ such that π is applicable in $a[s]$ and $\pi[a[s]] = s$.*

The notion of reversibility in the most general sense does not depend on a concrete STRIPS planning task, but only on a set of possible actions and states w.r.t. a set of facts. Note that the set of states S is an explicit part of the notion of S-reversibility. At this point, it is also worth noting that when S is the set of reachable states in a planning task Π, our notion of reversibility coincides with the notion of "undoability" as defined by Daum et al. [10], and our notion of *reversibility* coincides with their notion of "universal undoability". The above general definition simply requires that there is a way to reverse an action for each state. However, it is often convenient to have a single reverse plan that works irrespective of the starting state. This leads to the more restrictive notion of *uniform reversibility*.

Definition 2. *Let $\mathcal{F}$, $\mathcal{A}$, S, and a be as in Definition 1. We call a uniformly S-reversible iff there exists a sequence of actions $\pi = \langle a_1, \ldots, a_n \rangle \in \mathcal{A}^n$ such that for each $s \in S$ wherein a is applicable it holds that π is applicable in $a[s]$ and $\pi[a[s]] = s$.*

The notion of uniform reversibility naturally gives rise to the notion of the reverse plan. We say that some action a has an *S-reverse plan* π iff a is uniformly S-reversible using the sequence of actions π. We may drop the set S and simply refer to *reverse plans* and *reversibility* if S is clear from the context or not relevant. When S is the set of all possible states, we refer to these notions as *universal reverse plans* and *universal reversibility*, respectively. S is often given via a propositional formula ϕ, where S is the set of models of ϕ. This gives rise to the notions of *ϕ-reversibility* and *ϕ-reverse plans*, defined analogously to the above. It is interesting to note that this definition of the reverse plan based on uniform reversibility now coincides with the same notion as defined by Eiter, Erdem, and Faber [13]. Note, however, that in that paper the authors use a much more general planning language.

Even if the length of the reverse plan is polynomially bounded, the problem of deciding whether an action is uniformly (ϕ-)reversible is intractable. In particular, deciding whether an action is universally uniformly reversible (resp. uniformly ϕ-reversible) by a polynomial length reverse plan is NP-complete (resp. in Σ_2^{P1}) [28].

2.3   Answer Set Programming (ASP)

We assume the reader is familiar with ASP and will only give a very brief overview of the core language. We will also make use of some advanced con-

---

[1] Note that a tight lower bound for this case is as-of-yet unknown. The problem was shown hard for UNIQUESAT, which generalizes NP, and there are hints that it might not be complete for one of the standard complexity classes in the polynomial hierarchy [28].

structs like choice rules, arithmetic, and simple aggregates, which can, however, be translated into the core language. For the full syntax and semantics, we refer to standard literature [2, 18, 24], and, in our case, the ASP-Core-2 input language format [5].

Briefly, *ASP programs* consist of sets of *rules* of the form

$$a_1 \mid \cdots \mid a_n \leftarrow b_1, \ldots, b_\ell, \neg b_{\ell+1}, \ldots, \neg b_m.$$

In these rules, all a_i and b_i are *atoms* of the form $p(t_1, \ldots, t_n)$, where p is a predicate and $t_1, \ldots, t_n$ are terms, that is, either variables or constants. The domain of constants in an ASP program P is given implicitly by the set of all constants that appear in it. Generally, before evaluating an ASP program, variables are removed by a process called *grounding*, that is, for every rule, each variable is replaced by all possible combination of constants, and appropriate ground copies of the rule are added to the resulting program $ground(P)$. In practice, several optimizations have been implemented in state-of-the-art grounders that try to minimize the size of the grounding.

The result of a (ground) ASP program P is calculated as follows [20]. An *interpretation* I (i.e. a set of ground atoms appearing in P) is called a *model* of P iff it satisfies all the rules in P in the sense of classical logic. It is further called an *answer set* of P iff there is no proper subset $I' \subset I$ that is a model of the so-called reduct P^I of P w.r.t. I. P^I is defined as the set of rules obtained from P where all negated atoms on the right-hand side of the rules are evaluated over I and replaced by $\top$ or $\bot$ accordingly. The main decision problem for ASP is deciding whether a program has at least one answer set (i.e. whether it is satisfiable). This has been shown to be Σ_2^P-complete [14].

2.4 Quantified Answer Set Programming (QASP)

An extension of ASP with quantified atoms, called QASP has been proposed recently [17], providing a formalism reminiscent of quantified Boolean formulas (QBFs), but based on ASP. A *QASP program* is of the form

$$Q_1 X_1 Q_2 X_2 \cdots Q_n X_n P$$

where P is an ASP program, and for each *quantifier level* $i \in \{1, \ldots, n\}$, $Q_i \in \{\exists, \forall\}$ and X_i is a set of atoms from P. Atoms in X_i are, therefore, (existentially or universally) *quantified at level* i.

The intuitive reading of a QASP program $\exists X_1 \forall X_2 P$ is that there exists a subset $Y_1 \subseteq X_1$ of atoms such that for all subsets $Y_2 \subseteq X_2$ there exists an answer set M of P such that exactly the atoms Y_1 out of X_1 and Y_2 out of X_2 are true in M.

Formally, this is done via a recursive definition, where the function $fixcons(Y, X)$ represents a set of ASP constraints that enforce that the atoms Y need to be true and all other atoms in X false: $fixcons(Y, X) = \{\bot \leftarrow \neg x \mid x \in Y\} \cup \{\bot \leftarrow x \mid x \in X \setminus Y\}$. Then satisfiability of a QASP program is defined as follows:

- $\exists X\, P$ is satisfiable if $P \cup \textit{fixcons}(Y, X)$ has at least one answer set for some $Y \subseteq X$.
- $\forall X\, P$ is satisfiable if $P \cup \textit{fixcons}(Y, X)$ has at least one answer set for each $Y \subseteq X$.
- $\exists X\, \mathcal{Q}P$ is satisfiable if $\mathcal{Q}(P \cup \textit{fixcons}(Y, X))$ has at least one answer set for some $Y \subseteq X$.
- $\forall X\, \mathcal{Q}P$ is satisfiable if $\mathcal{Q}(P \cup \textit{fixcons}(Y, X))$ has at least one answer set for each $Y \subseteq X$.

In general, deciding satisfiability for a QASP program is known to be PSPACE-complete [17, Theorem 5.2].

2.5   The Bule Language

The *Bule* modelling language [23] was created to solve problems in PSPACE and is based on quantified Boolean formulas (QBFs) enhanced with a non-ground, rule-like syntax that allows for Datalog-inspired problem encodings that separate the problem domain and concrete problem instance, called intensional and extensional programs, respectively. To this end, the set of predicate symbols is divided into extensional and intensional predicates. Atoms formed by these predicates are called extensional and intensional atoms, respectively.

Extensional programs consist of rules of the form

$$L_1, \ldots, L_k :: H,$$

where H is an extensional atom and L_i $(0 < i \leqslant k)$ are extensional (non-ground) literals, where atoms are defined as in ASP. Variables must appear in at least one non-negated literal on the left-hand side of the rule.

Intensional programs consist of rules of the form

$$L_1, \ldots, L_k :: Q[T]H$$

or

$$L_1, \ldots, L_k :: C_1, \ldots C_n,$$

where H is an intensional atom, $Q \in \{\exists, \forall\}$ and T is a non-negative integer. Each C_i $(0 < i \leqslant n)$ is a *conditional literal* of the form $M_1, \ldots, M_m : B$, where $M_1, \ldots, M_m$ are extensional literals and B is an intensional literal. The first type of rule serves as a variable declaration for existentially or universally quantified variables at some level T. The second type of rule generates clauses.

A Bule program $P = (P_{ext}, P_{int})$ consists of an extensional and an intensional program, containing only the respective types of rules. Note that P_{ext} therefore only contains extensional rules, which are in fact plain positive Datalog rules (when viewing :: as $\rightarrow$). Hence, given a set of ground facts $\mathcal{D}$, let $P_{ext}(\mathcal{D})$ be the unique minimal model of the logical theory $P_{ext} \cup \mathcal{D}$, i.e. its Datalog extension.

The semantics of a Bule program executed on a set of input ground facts $\mathcal{D}$ is now defined via a QBF formula $\exists \mathbf{x}_1 \forall \mathbf{y}_1 \ldots \exists \mathbf{x}_n.\phi$, generated as follows:

Let θ be a homomorphism mapping variables to constants. For each such homomorphism θ, whenever $\theta(L_i) \subseteq P_{ext}(\mathcal{D})$ for each $0 < i \leqslant k$ in a rule $L_1, \ldots, L_k :: Q[T]H$, variable $\theta(H) \in \mathbf{x}_T$ if $Q = \exists$ or $\theta(H) \in \mathbf{y}_T$ if $Q = \forall$.

Furthermore, for each homomorphism θ, whenever $\theta(L_i) \subseteq P_{ext}(\mathcal{D})$ for each $0 < i \leqslant k$ in a rule $L_1, \ldots, L_k :: C_1, \ldots C_n$ the QBF formula ϕ contains the clause

$$\bigvee_{0 < i \leqslant n} \bigvee_{\ell \in \hat{C}_i} \ell,$$

where

$$\hat{C}_i = \bigcup_{\substack{\theta' \\ \forall j, 0 < j \leqslant m: \\ \theta'(\theta(M_j)) \subseteq P_{ext}(\mathcal{D})}} \theta'(\theta(B)),$$

that is, the set of ground literals obtained from B for each homomorphism θ' extending θ and mapping all M_j to the extensional program $P_{ext(\mathcal{D})}$.

Intuitively, first the (positive) extensional program part is evaluated. Based on the ground facts so derived, each ground instance of a variable declaration rule generates an appropriately quantified boolean variable. Each ground instance of the body $L_1, \ldots, L_k$ of a clause generating rule generates a QBF clause consisting of one literal for each ground instance of each conditional literal $C_1, \ldots, C_n$.

3   Reversibility in Quantified ASP

In this section, we propose an encoding for uniform universal reversibility of STRIPS actions using the QASP formalism. It makes use of the *plasp* translator, which transforms planning tasks given in the widely-used PDDL language into ASP databases. We start with a brief review of the syntax of this tool.

3.1   The *plasp* Format

The system *plasp*, described by Dimopoulos et al. [12], transforms PDDL domains and problems into facts. Together with suitable programs, plans can then be computed by ASP solvers—and hence also by ELP solvers, since ELPs are a superset of ASP programs. Given a STRIPS domain with facts $\mathcal{F}$ and actions $\mathcal{A}$, the following relevant facts and rules will be created by *plasp*:

```
variable(variable("f")). for all f ∈ F
action(action("a")). for all a ∈ A
precondition(action("a"),variable("f"),value(variable("f"),true))
    :- action(action("a")). for each a ∈ A and f ∈ pre(a)
postcondition(action("a"),_,variable("f"),value(variable("f"),true))
    :- action(action("a")). for each a ∈ A and f ∈ add(a)
postcondition(action("a"),_,variable("f"),value(variable("f"),false))
    :- action(action("a")). for each a ∈ A and f ∈ del(a)
```

In addition, a predicate `contains` encodes all possible values for a given variable (for STRIPS: values true or false).

3.2   The QASP Encoding

Our novel QASP encoding takes a time horizon as input, in the form `horizon(n)`, contains facts `time(i)` for each $0 \leqslant i \leqslant n$, and uses the *plasp*-generated database as input facts. We will now sketch the core ideas in our encoding. It is based on an existing ASP encoding for the uniform reversibility task [15] and re-uses the core idea of encoding planning, which itself is based on the *sequential-horizon* encoding for STRIPS planning, which is supplied as part of *plasp*[2].

The encoding makes use of the following main predicates (in addition to several auxiliary predicates, as well as those imported from *plasp*):

- `chosen/1` encodes the action to be tested for reversibility.
- `holds/3` encodes that some fact (or variable, as they are called in *plasp* parlance) is set to a certain value at a given time step.
- `occurs/2` encodes the candidate reverse plan, saying which action occurs at which time step.

With the meaning of our main predicates defined, we describe the main parts of our QASP encoding. Uniform reversibility requires that there exists a sequence of actions that reverses the chosen action for all relevant starting states. With the quantifiers present in QASP, we are able to model this intuitively: the `occurs/2` atoms will be existentially quantified, while the `holds/3` atoms (at time point 0, representing the starting state) will be universally quantified. Hence, our QASP instance will be satisfiable if there is an action that is uniformly reversible.

In order to later compare our encoding against existing encodings for ASP and several extensions, we first guess an action that we want to check reversibility for:

```
_exists(1, chosen(A)) :- action(action(A)).
{ chosen(A) } :- action(action(A)).
:- #count{A:chosen(A)} != 1.
```

Note the `_exists/2` predicate, which is a special built-in predicate of the QASP language that needs to contain a number i and an atom a, specifies that atom a is existentially quantified at level i. Similarly, universally quantified atoms are specified using the special `_forall/2` predicate in the same way.

The next step then is to guess a potential reverse plan, that is, a sequence of actions that should reverse the chosen action above. This is done by guessing an action for each time point via the `occurs/2` predicate. Again, these atoms are existentially quantified. Note that the first action is always taken to be the chosen action.

```
occurs(A, 1) :- chosen(A).
_exists(1, occurs(A, T)) :- action(action(A)), time(T), T > 1.
{occurs(A, T)} :- action(action(A)), time(T), T > 1.
:- #count{A:occurs(A, T)}!=1,time(T), T > 1.
```

---

[2] See https://github.com/potassco/plasp/tree/master/encodings.

So far, our encoding guesses a potential reverse plan. We must now check that for all possible starting states, the reverse plan actually works. Hence, we need to choose a starting state and check that the plan works in this starting state. In order to check this for every possible choice of starting state, the holds/3 atoms at time point 0 are universally quantified via the special _forall/2 predicate. If the considered starting state is inconsistent, we derive fail.

```
_forall(2, holds(V,Val,0)) :- contains(variable(V),value(variable(V),Val)).
{holds(V,Val,0)} :- contains(variable(V),value(variable(V),Val)).
fail :- #count{Val:holds(V,Val,0)} != 1, variable(variable(V)).
```

We further ensure that the starting state satisfies the preconditions of the chosen action which we would like to revert:

```
fail :- not holds(V, Val, 0), chosen(A),
        precondition(action(A), variable(V), value(variable(V), Val)).
```

We now model the execution of the chosen reverse plan on the given starting state. Facts that are changed by some action (modelled via the caused predicate) change in the next state, while all other facts do not.

```
caused(V, Val, T) :- occurs(A, T),
    postcondition(action(A), E, variable(V), value(variable(V), Val)).
modified(V, T) :- caused(V, _, T).
holds(V, Val, T) :- caused(V, Val, T).
holds(V, Val, T) :- holds(V, Val, T - 1), not modified(V, T), time(T).
```

All the actions are now executed and the final state is established. In order to verify that the reverse plan actually works, we now only need to check two conditions: (1) that the reverse plan was actually applicable, and (2) that the final state equals the starting state. This is done by the following three constraints:

```
:- not fail, occurs(A, T), precondition(action(A), variable(V),
    value(variable(V), Val)), not holds(V, Val, T - 1).
:- not fail, holds(V, Val, 0), not holds(V, Val, H+1), horizon(H).
:- not fail, holds(V, Val, H+1), not holds(V, Val, 0), horizon(H).
```

Note that in case that fail holds (which means that the starting state is invalid), none of these constraints apply and therefore the QASP program is always satisfiable. This completes the encoding.

3.3 Correctness

Correctness follows by construction and via the semantics of QASP. Note that the advanced ASP constructs in the above encoding can be viewed as "syntactic sugar" and are compiled away, so as to yield a classical ASP program [5]. In practice, this is done during the grounding step, that is, when all variables are replaced with relevant constants. This is also the first step that the QASP solver performs in our experiments in Sect. 5.

Theorem 1. *Given a STRIPS planning task $\Pi = \langle \mathcal{F}, \mathcal{A}, s_0, G \rangle$ and, the QASP encoding in this section, when applied to Π, is satisfiable if and only if there is an action a that is universally uniformly reversible.*

Proof (Idea). The rule guessing the `occurs` predicate then guesses a sequence of actions to revert the action a which is applied first. The rules deriving the `holds` predicate at time point 0, together with the universal quantification, ensure that for each state an answer set exists, given the following rules and constraints:

The `holds` and `caused` rules execute action a and the sequence of actions, keeping track of which value each fact has after each step (represented by time points T). Hence any answer set keeps track of all facts that hold at each time step after each action is executed. Finally, in order to satisfy the three constraints, the sequence of actions contained in the `occurs` predicate must (1) satisfy all of the action's preconditions at each time step, respectively, and (2) must reach the starting state at the last time step.

Rewriting all advanced ASP constructs used to plain ASP [5] and using the semantics of QASP [17], we have that the our QASP program for Π is satisfiable if and only if there exists an assignment to the (existentially quantified) `occurs` atoms, such that for all assignments to the (universally quantified) `holds` atoms at time point 0, the following holds: either the guessed starting state is invalid (and `fail` is derived in the relevant answer set), or the sequence of actions contained in the `chosen` atoms returns to the starting state after applying the chosen action in the first time step, establishing our claim.   □

4   Reversibility in Bule

For the Bule encoding, we first ground the *plasp* output described in Sect. 3.1 using the ASP grounder *gringo*, and then apply some minor syntactic modifications. This transforms the *plasp* output into the Bule syntax as follows, for STRIPS facts $\mathcal{F}$ and actions $\mathcal{A}$:

```
#ground variable[variable[f]]. for all f ∈ F
#ground action[action[a]]. for all a ∈ A
#ground precondition[action[a],variable[f],value[true]].
    for each a ∈ A and f ∈ pre(a)
#ground postcondition[action[a],_,variable[f],value[true]].
    for each a ∈ A and f ∈ add(a)
#ground postcondition[action[a],_,variable[f],value[false]].
    for each a ∈ A and f ∈ del(a)
```

Again, additionally the predicate `contains` encodes all possible values for a given variable (for STRIPS: values true or false). The reversibility encoding is based on a planning encoding given in [23]. Time steps are defined using

```
#ground time[0..n+1].
#ground horizon[n].
```

The main reversibility problem is set up stating that there exists an action to be reversed followed by a reverse plan. At each time step (starting from 1) exactly one action has to occur.

```
action[A], time[T], T > 0 :: #exists[0] occurs(A, T).
time[T], T > 0 :: action[A]:occurs(A, T).
action[A], action[B], time[T], T > 0, A < B :: ~occurs(A,T) | ~occurs(B,T).
```

Now we state that for each starting state the sequence of actions determined above needs to be a reversal.

```
contains[V,Val] :: #forall[1] holds(V, Val, 0).
```

Then we identify inconsistent starting states and starting states in which the chosen action is not applicable, since these should not be considered for checking the reversal condition.

```
contains[V, V1], contains[V, V2], V1 < V2 ::
  holds(V, V1, 0) & holds(V, V2, 0) -> invvar(V).
contains[V, V1], contains[V, V2], V1 < V2 ::
  ~holds(V, V1, 0) & ~holds(V, V2, 0) -> invvar(V).
contains[V, V1], contains[V, V2], V1 != V2 ::
  invvar(V) & holds(V, V1, 0) -> holds(V, V2, 0).
contains[V, V1], contains[V, V2], V1 != V2 ::
  invvar(V) & ~holds(V, V1, 0) -> ~holds(V, V2, 0).
precondition[A, V, Val] :: occurs(A, 1) & ~holds(V, Val, 0) -> invprec(V).
variable[V], action[A] ::
  invprec(V) & occurs(A, 1) -> precondition[A, V, Val]: ~holds(V, Val, 0).
```

These conditions are fused into a single variable `invalid`.

```
invalid -> invalidvar | invalidprec.
invalidvar -> invalid.
invalidprec -> invalid.
variable[V] :: invvar(V) -> invalidvar.
invalidvar -> variable[V]:invvar(V).
variable[V] :: invprec(V) -> invalidprec.
invalidprec -> variable[V]:invprec(V).
```

Eventually, actions are applied, and if any precondition is unmet or an invalid state occurs or the plan is not a reversal, `noplan` will hold.

```
postcondition[A,_,V,_],time[T],T>0 :: occurs(A,T) -> mod(V,T).
variable[V], time[T], T > 0 ::
  mod(V,T) -> postcondition[A,_,V,_] : occurs(A,T).
postcondition[A,_,V,Val], time[T], T > 0 :: occurs(A,T) -> holds(V,Val,T).
contains[V,Val], time[T], time[T-1] ::
  holds(V,Val,T-1) & ~mod(V,T) -> holds(V,Val,T).
contains[V,V1], contains[V,V2], time[T], T > 0, V1 < V2 ::
  holds(V,V1,T) & holds(V,V2,T) -> noplan.
contains[V,V1], contains[V,V2], time[T], T > 0, V1 < V2 ::
  ~holds(V,V1,T) & ~holds(V,V2,T) -> noplan.
```

```
precondition[A,V,Val], time[T], time[T-1] ::
  occurs(A,T) & ~holds(V,Val,T-1) -> noplan.
contains[V,Val],horizon[H]:: holds(V,Val,0) & ~holds(V,Val,H+1) -> noplan.
contains[V,Val],horizon[H]:: ~holds(V,Val,0) & holds(V,Val,H+1) -> noplan.
```

Finally require the starting state to be irrelevant or the plan to be a reversal.

```
invalid | ~noplan.
```

Correctness of this encoding follows from correctness of the planning encoding in [23], the added quantifier pattern and relevance, applicability, and reversal conditions. If the Bule encoding is satisfiable, then the action occurring in step 1 is universally uniformly reversible (and only then).

5   Experimental Evaluation

We have conducted preliminary experiments on universal uniform reversibility with our encodings, and compared them with existing ASP-based encodings [15,16]. We benchmark the well-known ASP solver clingo [19], version 5.7.1, as well as an extension for ELPs built on top of clingo, called eclingo [4], version 1.2.0. For QASP, we use the qasp2qbf converter [17] paired with the depqbf QBF solver [26] in their most recent versions as of May 28, 2025. We have obtained an as-yet-unpublished prototype implementation for ASP(Q) from Francesco Ricca, called qasp version 0.1.2. Finally, we use the bule solver for the Bule QBF programming language, available from https://github.com/vale1410/bule. All our benchmark files, including generator scripts, are available at https://seafile.aau.at/d/4a465ed4a3c942869fb8/.

The domains of our generated benchmarks are reused from [15] where, by construction, there only exists one reversible action per planning task which has a unique reverse plan whose length is the number of facts in the planning task. We have analyzed runtime and memory consumption of two problems: (a) finding the single reversible action and its unique reverse plan of size i (by setting the constant horizon to i), and (b) showing that no reverse plan of length i-1 exists for any action (by setting the constant horizon to i-1). We compare our encoding, described in the previous sections, to the "general" ASP and ELP encodings presented by Faber, Morak, and Chrpa [15]. We omit the "simple" ASP and ELP encodings presented therein, since they make use of a complexity-theoretic shortcut, which cannot be exploited with our general encodings. Hence, to get comparative benchmarks, all five encodings that we benchmark here are able to solve the exact same problem: uniform S-reversibility. All benchmarks were run on a Linux computer with a 2.3 GHz AMD EPYC 7601 CPU with 8 (virtualized) cores and 500 GB RAM. We have set a timeout of 20 min and a memory limit of 16GB.

The results for problem (a) are plotted in Fig. 1, requiring that solvers output all models that they find (i.e. after finding the first and only model containing

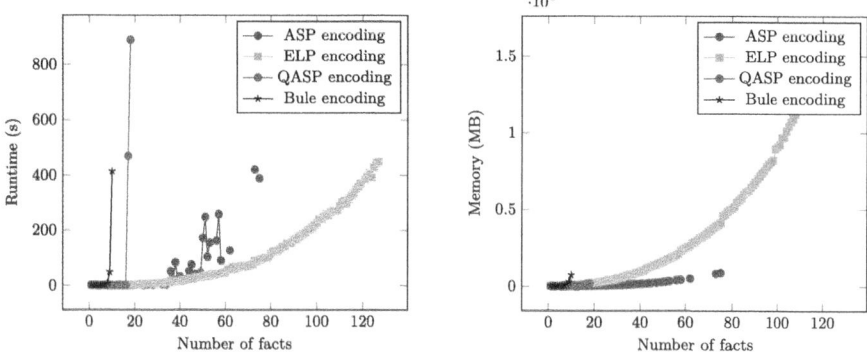

Fig. 1. Finding the unique reverse plan (plan length equals number of facts).

a reverse plan, they have to prove that this is also the last model). We reproduce and verify existing results [15], but observe that `eclingo` has improved substantially since the original benchmarks from 2021 and is now able to beat the saturation-based ASP encoding and solve all 125 instances, whereas the ASP encoding starts to struggle with timeouts above size 60. However, the latter is still much more memory efficient. Regarding our new encodings, both tools suffer from timeouts, with the Bule encoding solving 10 instances and QASP less than 20. We also tested an existing ASP(Q) encoding [16] which produced the same results as in 2022: only seven out of 125 instances could be solved. Hence we did not include these data points in our figures.

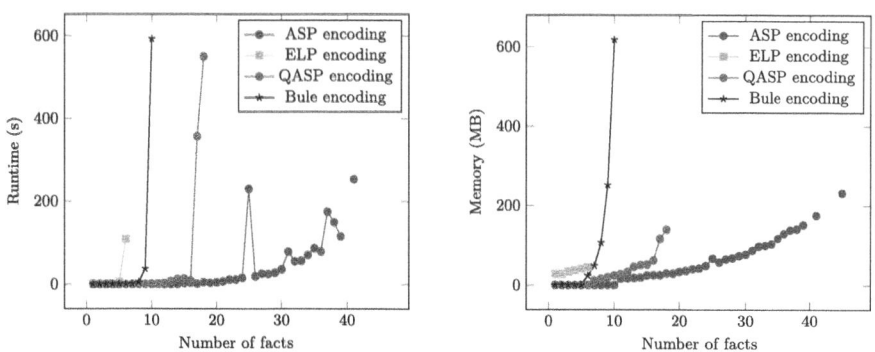

Fig. 2. Establishing irreversibility (i.e. non-existence of a reverse plan).

The results for problem (b) are plotted in Fig. 2. Interestingly, compared to (a), here, both our Bule and QASP encodings were able to beat the ELP encoding significantly, which performed the worst. This is surprising since the new version of `eclingo` offered dramatically increased performance for problem (a), but this was not observed for problem (b). Overall, the ASP encoding in this case performed best by a significant margin. However, none of our encodings were able to solve more than 45 instances within the time and memory limits.

6   Conclusions

In this paper, we proposed two new encodings for the problem of deciding uniform reversibility for actions in STRIPS planning as defined by Morak et al. [28], using the Bule QBF programming language [23] and the language of Quantified ASP (QASP) [17]. These make use of the PDDL-to-ASP translation tool *plasp* [12] and we compare these new encodings and associated solving tools with existing encodings and solvers, namely, Answer Set Programming (ASP), its extension with epistemic operators, called Epistemic Logic Programs (ELPs), and ASP with Quantifiers (ASP(Q)), proposed in previous works [15,16].

We observe that both Bule (based on QBF formulas) and QASP (based on ASP) offer a rich language that directly incorporates quantifiers. This allows for intuitive encodings of the reversibility problem when compared to plain ASP or ELPs. However, this expressive power comes at a cost to solving performance, where plain ASP dominates. Interestingly, however, for ELPs, the performance for identifying uniformly reversible actions was competitive to plain ASP, but for the converse problem (i.e. proving that no such action exists) the ELP solver *eclingo* offered the worst performance of our four competitors. This is despite us observing a marked increase in performance of *eclingo* compared to its 2021 version [15]. We also observed that the richer languages of QASP and Bule make modelling problems easier due to the ability to explicitly quantify over atoms, which is a trade-off to be considered when choosing the language for encoding problems.

For future work, we plan to further optimize our encodings and compare and extend them also with other existing solutions and techniques proposed in the literature. It would be interesting to see how the encodings perform when compared to a procedural implementation of the algorithms proposed for reversibility checking by [28]. We would also like to compare our approach to existing tools *RevPlan*[3] (implementing techniques of Eiter et al. [13]) and *undoability* (implementing techniques of Daum et al. [10]). Furthermore, we aim to explore how our techniques can be extended to planning languages more expressive than STRIPS. We envision various avenues for that, one is to deal with "lifted representations" (going beyond propositional atoms), another one is to allow for non-deterministic action effects or exogenous events, for which ASP and ELP seem to be well-suited.

Acknowledgements. The list of authors is alphabetically ordered. This work was partially supported by the Austrian Science Fund (FWF) under grant numbers 10.55776/PIN8782623 and 10.55776/COE12.

---

[3] http://www.kr.tuwien.ac.at/research/systems/revplan/index.html.

References

1. Amendola, G., Ricca, F., Truszczynski, M.: Beyond NP: quantifying over answer sets. Theory Pract. Log. Program. **19**(5–6), 705–721 (2019). https://doi.org/10.1017/S1471068419000140

2. Brewka, G., Eiter, T., Truszczynski, M.: Answer set programming at a glance. Commun. ACM **54**(12), 92–103 (2011). https://doi.org/10.1145/2043174.2043195

3. Bylander, T.: The computational complexity of propositional STRIPS planning. Artif. Intell. **69**(1–2), 165–204 (1994). https://doi.org/10.1016/0004-3702(94)90081-7

4. Cabalar, P., Fandinno, J., Garea, J., Romero, J., Schaub, T.: eclingoâĂŕ: a solver for epistemic logic programs. Theory Pract. Log. Program. **20**(6), 834–847 (2020). https://doi.org/10.1017/S1471068420000228

5. Calimeri, F., et al.: Asp-core-2 input language format. Theory Pract. Log. Program. **20**(2), 294–309 (2020). https://doi.org/10.1017/S1471068419000450

6. Chrpa, L., Faber, W., Morak, M.: Universal and uniform action reversibility. In: Proceedings of the KR, pp. 651–654 (2021). https://doi.org/10.24963/kr.2021/63

7. Chrpa, L., Lipovetzky, N., Sardiña, S.: Handling non-local dead-ends in agent planning programs. In: Proceedings of the IJCAI, pp. 971–978 (2017). https://doi.org/10.24963/ijcai.2017/135

8. Chrpa, L., McCluskey, T.L., Osborne, H.: Optimizing plans through analysis of action dependencies and independencies. In: Proceedings of the ICAPS (2012). http://www.aaai.org/ocs/index.php/ICAPS/ICAPS12/paper/view/4712

9. Cserna, B., Doyle, W.J., Ramsdell, J.S., Ruml, W.: Avoiding dead ends in real-time heuristic search. In: Proceedings of the Thirty-Second AAAI Conference on Artificial Intelligence, (AAAI-18), pp. 1306–1313 (2018)

10. Daum, J., Torralba, Á., Hoffmann, J., Haslum, P., Weber, I.: Practical undoability checking via contingent planning. In: Proceedings of the ICAPS, pp. 106–114 (2016)

11. De Giacomo, G., Gerevini, A.E., Patrizi, F., Saetti, A., Sardiña, S.: Agent planning programs. Artif. Intell. **231**, 64–106 (2016). https://doi.org/10.1016/j.artint.2015.10.001

12. Dimopoulos, Y., Gebser, M., Lühne, P., Romero, J., Schaub, T.: plasp 3: towards effective ASP planning. TPLP **19**(3), 477–504 (2019). https://doi.org/10.1017/S1471068418000583

13. Eiter, T., Erdem, E., Faber, W.: Undoing the effects of action sequences. J. Appl. Logic **6**(3), 380–415 (2008). https://doi.org/10.1016/j.jal.2007.05.002

14. Eiter, T., Gottlob, G.: On the computational cost of disjunctive logic programming: propositional case. Ann. Math. Artif. Intell. **15**(3–4), 289–323 (1995). https://doi.org/10.1007/BF01536399

15. Faber, W., Morak, M., Chrpa, L.: Determining action reversibility in STRIPS using answer set and epistemic logic programming. TPLP **21**(5), 646–662 (2021). https://doi.org/10.1017/S1471068421000429

16. Faber, W., Morak, M., Chrpa, L.: Determining action reversibility in STRIPS using answer set programming with quantifiers. In: Proceedings of the PADL, pp. 42–56 (2022). https://doi.org/10.1007/978-3-030-94479-7_4

17. Fandinno, J., Laferrière, F., Romero, J., Schaub, T., Son, T.C.: Planning with incomplete information in quantified answer set programming. Theory Pract. Log. Program. **21**(5), 663–679 (2021). https://doi.org/10.1017/S1471068421000259

18. Gebser, M., Kaminski, R., Kaufmann, B., Schaub, T.: Answer Set Solving in Practice. Synthesis Lectures on Artificial Intelligence and Machine Learning, Morgan & Claypool Publishers (2012). https://doi.org/10.2200/S00457ED1V01Y201211AIM019

19. Gebser, M., Kaminski, R., Kaufmann, B., Schaub, T.: Multi-shot ASP solving with clingo. Theory Pract. Log. Program. **19**(1), 27–82 (2019)

20. Gelfond, M., Lifschitz, V.: Classical negation in logic programs and disjunctive databases. New Gener. Comput. **9**(3/4), 365–386 (1991). https://doi.org/10.1007/BF03037169

21. Ghallab, M., Nau, D.S., Traverso, P.: Automated planning - theory and practice. Elsevier (2004)

22. Ghallab, M., Nau, D.S., Traverso, P.: Automated Planning and Acting. Cambridge University Press (2016). http://www.cambridge.org/de/academic/subjects/computer-science/artificial-intelligence-and-natural-language-processing/automated-planning-and-acting?format=HB

23. Jung, J.C., Mayer-Eichberger, V., Saffidine, A.: QBF programming with the modeling language bule. In: Proceedings of the SAT. LIPIcs, vol. 236, pp. 31:1–31:14. Schloss Dagstuhl - Leibniz-Zentrum für Informatik (2022). https://doi.org/10.4230/LIPICS.SAT.2022.31

24. Lifschitz, V.: Answer Set Programming. Springer (2019). https://doi.org/10.1007/978-3-030-24658-7

25. Lipovetzky, N., Muise, C.J., Geffner, H.: Traps, invariants, and dead-ends. In: Proceedings of the ICAPS, pp. 211–215 (2016). http://www.aaai.org/ocs/index.php/ICAPS/ICAPS16/paper/view/13190

26. Lonsing, F., Egly, U.: DepQBF 6.0: a search-based QBF solver beyond traditional QCDCL. In: Proceedings of the CADE. LNCS, vol. 10395, pp. 371–384. Springer, Cham (2017). https://doi.org/10.1007/978-3-319-63046-5_23

27. Med, J., Chrpa, L., Morak, M., Faber, W.: Weak and strong reversibility of non-deterministic actions: universality and uniformity. In: Proceedings of the ICAPS, pp. 369–377. AAAI Press (2024). https://doi.org/10.1609/ICAPS.V34I1.31496

28. Morak, M., Chrpa, L., Faber, W., Fišer, D.: On the reversibility of actions in planning. In: Proceedings of the KR, pp. 652–661 (2020). https://doi.org/10.24963/kr.2020/65

29. Schwartz, T., Boockmann, J.H., Martin, L.: Towards the evaluation of action reversibility in STRIPS using domain generators. In: Proceedings of the FoIKS. LNCS, vol. 13388, pp. 226–236. Springer, Cham (2022). https://doi.org/10.1007/978-3-031-11321-5_13

DIRT: a Literature-Based Benchmark Suite for Grounders

Lucas Van Laer[1]([⊠])[ID], Simon Vandevelde[1][ID], and Joost Vennekens[2][ID]

[1] KU Leuven, De Nayer Campus, Dept. of Computer Science,
Flanders Make – DTAI-FET Belgium Leuven.AI – KU Leuven institute for AI,
B-3000 Leuven, Belgium
{lucas.vanlaer,s.vandevelde}@kuleuven.be
[2] Vrije Universiteit Brussel, Brussels, Belgium
joost.vennekens@vub.be

Abstract. In this paper, we survey literature on grounding in Answer Set Programming (ASP) and related fields, analyse the common benchmarks used for this purpose, and introduce a new grounding benchmark called DIRT. In ASP, reasoning engines typically rely on a "ground-and-solve" approach, in which a high-level description of a problem domain (e.g., an Answer Set Program) is first transformed into a low-level description (e.g., aspif) in order to solve. This process, better known as grounding, has a significant effect on the overall speed of the reasoning engine. For this reason, literature contains numerous works dedicated to optimizing various aspects of the grounding process. However, each paper tends to measure their improvements on distinct benchmarks, making a direct comparison between works often difficult. We argue that this is caused by a lack of standardized benchmarks for grounding, and substantiate this claim through a survey of grounding literature. Based on this survey, we have distilled the Dataset for Instantiating in Reasoning Tools (DIRT) as a specialized grounding benchmark. We provide encodings for ASP and ASP-like formats, and present their baseline performance on this problem set. In this way, our benchmark suite can help identify bottlenecks in state-of-the-art grounders, and can serve as a standardized dataset for future works on grounding.

Keywords: Knowledge Representation and Reasoning · Grounding · Benchmark

1 Introduction

In the development of efficient software systems, benchmarking is often crucial, e.g., to identify problems, to weigh different alternatives against each other, or to determine how a new approach compares to the existing state-of-the-art. This has also been the case for logical reasoning engines, where the development of SAT solvers has, for more than two decades, been driven by the yearly SAT competitions [19]. For a number of years, a similar competition was also held for the

G. Casini et al. (Eds.): JELIA 2025, LNAI 16093, pp. 343–356, 2026.
https://doi.org/10.1007/978-3-032-04587-4_21

more expressive language of Answer Set Programming (ASP) [5]. A number of editions of the ASP Competition included a "model and solve" track, which also allowed systems to compete that were similar in spirit to ASP systems, without necessarily adhering to the specific ASP syntax, such as the IDP reasoning engine [13] for the FO(·) language [10].

Benchmarking such ASP and "ASP-like" systems is more complex than benchmarking SAT solvers because of their more expressive first-order input language. Typically, these systems have a "ground-and-solve" architecture, in which a *grounder* first eliminates the first-order variables and then passes the resulting ground theory to a *solver* to perform the actual reasoning task. The currently most well-known example is the *clingo* [16] system, which combines the grounder *gringo* [18] with the solver *clasp* [17].

When it comes to these two steps, the solving step has generally gotten more attention in the relevant literature. Similarly, ASP Competitions tended to contain mostly "solving-heavy" problems, for which grounding was fairly straightforward. We believe that this has led to a situation in which there is currently no good set of benchmarks available to guide the development of more efficient grounders. In particular, to the best of our knowledge, there is no benchmark suite that has the following properties:

- The benchmarks are focused on grounding rather than solving.
- The benchmarks cover a wide range of different input patterns, so that they can provide a comprehensive picture of the strengths and weaknesses of different approaches.
- Each benchmark on its own is relatively small and focused, so that actionable insights can be derived from a poor performance on a specific benchmark.

The goal of DIRT is to fill that gap. We start with a structured literature review, surveying the current literature on grounding. On the one hand, this survey further substantiates our claim that no benchmark suite with the above properties already exists. On the other hand, we also use this survey to catalogue individual benchmarks that have been used in the literature. Based on this, we construct our own proposed set of benchmarks. We then apply the benchmarks to evaluate and compare the grounders of a number of ASP(-like) systems, in order to demonstrate that useful insights can indeed be drawn from these experimental results. Crucially, we don't limit ourselves to only pure ASP systems but have chosen similar *ASP-like* systems, which have different input languages and complementary features.

2   Structured Literature Review

We begin with a structured literature review of the current literature on grounding in ASP(-like) systems, i.e. systems that perform model generation for first-order languages with rich knowledge representation features such as aggregates, non-monotonicity, etc. For this, we followed the methodology of Kitchenham [21], a common methodology for systematic reviews. In short, this involves creating a search query to cast out as broad a net as possible, and manually filtering irrelevant articles afterwards in two rounds. To minimize errors, the articles are reviewed by two people independently in both rounds, with the results cross-validated afterwards to reach the final selection.

2.1   Methodology

As our goal is to find research that concerns the experimental evaluations of the grounding component of ASP-like systems, we decided on the following inclusion criteria for literature:

– Articles written in English.
– Articles about grounding of Answer Set Programming or Logic Programming.
– Articles with an experiments section or similar.

We exclude an article if it matched any of the following criteria:

– Articles which are not published or peer-reviewed.
– Posters, presentations, demo papers and PhD consortium papers.

As a first step, we queried various digital libraries. Based on the above in-/exclusion criteria and a preliminary set of articles, we decided on Query 1.1 .

Listing 1.1. Digital library query

```
(''grounder'' OR ''instantiator'')
  AND (''answer set programming'' OR ''logic programming
    '')
  AND (''experiments'' OR ''evaluation'')
```

This query consists of three parts. The first part restricts the selection of articles to those about grounding. More specifically, we looked for articles that mention a grounder or instantiator, as these two are sometimes used interchangeably. The second conjunct removes articles where the term **''grounder''** is used in a different context than ours, such as in 3D visual grounding or philosophy. The final conjunct tries to further restricts the selection to those articles that specifically contain experimental results. Using this query, we queried the following digital libraries:

– ACM Digital Library, 257 results
– Springer Link, 238 results
– Science Direct, 56 results
– IEEE Xplore, 27 results

Querying ACM Digital Library and Springer Link was done via the online interface, as it allows exporting query results. Science Direct did not appear to support exact text matching, so we exported the results of the query and filtered them ourselves using a Python script and the Elsevier full text API. For IEEE

Xplore, we had to slightly modify the query to ensure that the full text was searched and not only metadata. In total, querying these four libraries resulted in 578 articles (428 without duplicates).

As a next step, the first and second author manually reviewed these articles independently and cross-validated their results, as advised in [21, p32]. We reviewed in two rounds, filtering first on the title and abstract, and then on the full text. Importantly, we erred on the side of caution in the first round, and included all papers on which consensus could not be reached, resulting in 96 articles. After reading the full texts, 50 relevant articles remained after the second round.

We then applied "backward snowballing" [29] on these articles, which involved looking up the articles in their reference lists through the Crossref database [2]. This resulted in another 559 citations, of which 24 were deemed relevant after review, leading to a total of 74 selected articles.

2.2 Review Results

We will now discuss the results of our review. To begin, we categorized each of the 74 articles according to 11 categories[1]. The classical category consists of articles that discuss grounding methods in a traditional ground-and-solve architecture. Some examples include the description of gringo [18] and experiments on parallel grounding of ASP programs [24]. Within this category, we also distinguish three subcategories that focus on specific kinds of applications: game, planning and defeasible logic. For example, in the game category we include the work by Schiffel [27], which describes translation from Game Description Logic to ASP for general game playing. Similarly, we also distinguish articles that focus on planning problems (such as [26]) and on performing reasoning tasks for defeasible logic (such as [25]).

Next, we have categories that aim to modify the grounding process, such as lazy grounding. Here, grounding and solving are interleaved in multiple steps, so that only the required part of the grounding for each solving step is constructed. This is demonstrated by, among others, the ASPeRiX system [22] and the GASP system [11]. A more extreme approach is to try to avoid grounding altogether, as done by the articles in our circumvention category. For example, the method by Balduccini et al. circumvents the grounding of parts of an ASP program by integrating SLDNF resolution from Prolog in the ASP solving process [3].

Rather than focusing on the grounding process itself, several articles also consider optimizations before or after grounding. In pre-ground optimizations, we categorize papers which focus on optimizing the non-ground input *before* grounding. For instance, the lpopt [4] system decomposes large rules into smaller ones to reduce the size of the eventual grounding. On the other hand, [20] presents work on eliminating redundant rules *after* grounding, as part of the post-ground optimization category.

---

[1] The full list of articles and their classification can be found in our online repository: https://zenodo.org/records/15592332.

In `incremental grounding`, we group systems that reuse results from previous calls of a reasoning engine. For instance, [8] adds multi-shot reasoning to DLV2 using a form of incremental grounding. Somewhat similarly, `external` groups articles that present grounding tasks in which the value of a certain symbol is computed by an external source, such as [7].

Finally, besides the aforementioned papers on new grounding methods, we also found a number of articles that `benchmark` existing systems or introduce new benchmarks. Among others, this category contains all works on the ASP Competition. In Table 1, we show the number of articles in each of the above categories. Note that articles may belong to multiple categories at once.

Table 1. Number of articles in each category

Class	number of articles
classical	16
lazy grounding	13
pre-ground optimizations	12
benchmark	11
incremental grounding	9
circumvention	8
external	3
game	2
post-ground optimizations	1
defeasible logic	1
planning	1

As a next step, we extracted the names of the benchmarks that were used in each of the articles. This could either be names of individual benchmarks (e.g., "map coloring") or names of a benchmark set (e.g., "second ASP competition"). After removing the duplicates, this resulted in 184 benchmarks in total. Of these, 133 benchmarks appeared only in a single article and 19 (including the "sixth ASP competition" and "second ASP competition" benchmark sets) appeared in two articles. For the benchmarks that appeared in ≥ 3 articles, Table 2 shows how these articles were divided across the different categories. The `game`, `planning` and `defeasible logic` categories contain no such benchmarks and are therefore omitted from the table.

3   Grounding Benchmark

Based on the results of our review, we now define a new suite of benchmarks titled "Dataset for Instantiating in Reasoning Tools" (DIRT). Recall that our goal here is to have benchmarks that satify the following properties:

Table 2. For each benchmark b that appears in ≥ 3 articles, the number of articles in each category in which b appears.

	classical	circum.	lazy	pre	incr.	post	bench.	ext.
Graph colouring	10	6	2	2	-	-	-	-
Reachability	2	3	2	1	1	-	-	1
Hanoi towers	4	2	1	1	2	-	-	-
N-queens	4	1	1	1	1	1	-	-
Hamiltonian Path	6	-	1	1	-	-	-	-
Stable marriage	-	3	2	2	-	-	1	-
Ramsey number	7	-	-	-	-	-	-	-
Timetabling	6	-	-	-	-	-	-	-
Packing problem	-	2	2	-	1	-	1	-
Sudoku	3	-	-	-	1	-	1	-
Schurman number	2	2	-	-	-	1	-	-
Sokoban	1	1	1	-	2	-	-	-
Latin square	2	-	-	1	-	-	1	-
Blocked N-queens	3	-	-	1	-	-	-	-
Strategic companies	3	-	1	-	-	-	-	-
Incremental scheduling	-	-	3	1	-	-	-	-
Hamiltonian Cycle	1	1	-	1	-	-	-	-
Permutation pattern matching	1	-	1	1	-	-	-	-
Weighted sequence problem	1	-	1	1	-	-	-	-
Food	3	-	-	-	-	-	-	-
blocksworld	1	-	-	1	1	-	-	-
Partner units problem	-	-	3	-	-	-	-	-
Non-partition-removal-coloring	-	1	1	1	-	-	-	-
Labyrinth	-	1	1	1	-	-	-	-
Ricochet Robots	-	-	1	1	1	-	-	-
cutedge	-	3	-	-	-	-	-	-
Natural Language Understanding	-	1	-	1	-	-	1	-
1st ASP Comp	-	-	-	2	-	-	1	-
3rd ASP Comp	-	-	-	1	-	-	2	-
4th ASP Comp	-	-	-	1	-	-	2	-
Pacman	-	-	-	-	3	-	-	-
Content Caching	-	-	-	-	3	-	-	-
Photo-voltaic System	-	-	-	-	3	-	-	-

- Grounding (and not just solving) is a potential bottleneck. Based on this criterion, we typically exclude, for instance, the NP-problems of the ASP Competitions, which have solving as a bottleneck long before grounding becomes challenging.
- The problem specification is small and focused, so that potential issues with grounder efficiency can easily be linked to specific formulas. This motivates to exclude, e.g., planning problems, which typically have a rather large specification in which it would be difficult to pinpoint specific issues.

A final practical consideration is that the benchmarks and its instance should of course still be available, which historically has not always been the case. For instance, we found numerous papers link to the ASPARAGUS system, which is unfortunately no longer available. However, this motivated us to publish a mirror of our dataset at Zenodo[2].

We evaluated the benchmarks found in the survey according to the aforementioned criteria, which led to the following set of benchmarks:

- Graph colouring [1]
- Stable marriage [1]
- Permutation pattern matching [1]
- Reachability [1]
- Packing problem [15]
- Quasi group [15]
- Ramsey numbers [15]
- N-queens [15]
- Non-partition-removal-coloring [15]
- Hamiltonian path [6]
- Common item and complete sets [28]
- Triangle graph [28]

In most cases, we include the same instances as in the referenced paper. However, there were two exceptions. For graph colouring, the ASP Competition 2013 instances had a density of 10%, meaning the graph contained 10% of all possible edges, which made them very hard to solve for sizes that were still trivial to ground. We therefore generated our own random instances with a much lower density (between 1% to 0.1%), which are still solvable at sizes for which grounding becomes challenging (2500 to 10000 nodes). Second, the ASP Competition 2013 used reachability as a benchmark for query answering rather than answer set generation. Consequently, the provided instances were so big that none of the considered system could fully ground them. To avoid hitting our memory limits, we generated graphs with fewer nodes (100–4500 nodes) and a density between 0.1% and 0.05%.

We further extended this set of benchmarks by including a number of different benchmark variations on the Triangle graph proposed in [28]. Essentially, all of these benchmarks share the formula

---

[2] https://zenodo.org/records/15592332.

$$edge(X,Y), edge(Y,Z), edge(Z,X)$$

that identifies triangles in a graph. This is an interesting benchmark because the size of the full grounding of the formula is $O(n^3)$, with n the number of nodes, which very quickly becomes intractable. However, if the graph is given, then there is no need to compute this entire grounding so a clever grounder will avoid this. Building further on this idea, we can consider a number of different contexts in which it might be interesting to see whether a grounder can avoid the $O(n^3)$ blow-up:

- `TriangleGraphFindAll`: Given a graph, find all triangles in this graph.
- `TriangleGraphContainsAll`: Given a graph and a ternary predicate p, check that p holds for all triangles in the graph.
- `TriangleGraphCheck`: Given a graph and a ternary predicate p, check whether p contains precisely all triangles in the graph.
- `TriangleGraphConstructGraph`: Given a ternary predicate p with arguments of type *node*, construct a graph g, such that p are precisely the triangles in g.
- `TriangleGraphSubset`: Given a graph g and a set of nodes s of g, find a set of triangles in the graph that contain at least all nodes in s.
- `TriangleGraphConstructAtleast`: Given a graph g, construct a ternary predicate p such that it contains at least all triangles in g.

In total, our benchmark suite contains 18 benchmarks, each meeting our aforementioned goals. Furthermore, our benchmark suite should be usable to compare different systems, which do not all have exactly the same input language. Therefore, for each benchmark, we include encodings in a number of different input languages, namely FO($\cdot$), ManyWorlds, and ASP-Core-2. For the sake of fair comparison, we have generally tried to make the different encodings as similar to each other as possible. However, there is one exception: unlike ASP-Core-2, both the FO($\cdot$) and ManyWorlds language allow the use of functions. For instance, in FO($\cdot$), one can write either the unary function $radius(circle) = 1$ or the binary predicate $radius(circle, 1)$, while ASP only allows the latter. For a number of benchmarks, this had a severe impact on the grounding times of the systems that allow both representations. We therefore also included a variant `BenchmarkAlt` for some `Benchmarks`, in which functions were used. An up to date version of our benchmark suite can be found on our online repository[3].

4   Experimental Setup

While the main contribution of this paper is the DIRT benchmark suite itself, we also validate this benchmark suite by using it to evaluate and compare a number of state-of-the-art reasoning systems, in the hope of identifying a number of interesting observations. Because "real" ASP-solvers (i.e., those that use an ASP language such as ASP-Core-2 as their input) are often benchmarked against each

---

[3] https://gitlab.com/EAVISE/sli/DIRT.

other, we have chosen to include a number of less studied reasoning engines in our comparison as well, partially also guided by practical considerations in obtaining the relevant encodings of our benchmark. The selection of reasoning engines to include is of course somewhat arbitrary, but by making the benchmarks and experimental results publicly available, we ensure that it is easy to benchmark other reasoning engines as well.

In our experiments, we chose to include the following reasoning engines:

- clingo [16] is a state-of-the-art ASP solver, with an impressive track record in the ASP Competition.
- IDP3 [13] is an ASP-like system, which uses the FO(·) language, a rich extension of classical first-order logic, as its input. In the Third ASP Competition, it was shown to be competitive with clingo on certain benchmarks [9].
- IDP-Z3 [10] is the successor of the IDP3 system. It used the Z3 SMT-solver [23] as a back-end, allowing it to ground to a more expressive format (e.g., including real-values constants) than its predecessor, which grounded to SAT.
- SLI [28] is a recent FO(·) system which also grounds to Z3, using bit vectors as an efficient implementation technique for its grounder.
- ManyWorlds [14] is a combinatorial programming language with a solver with the same name.

For each benchmark instance, we asked each reasoning engine to compute a single answer set. All experiments were run on an Intel Xeon Silver 4210R CPU with a time-out of 10 min and max memory usage of 16GB.

We measure the run time that elapses before the solving starts, which we refer to as the `pre-solve` time. While the bulk of this should be actual grounding time, operations such as parsing and initialisation are also included. As not all systems allow accurately separating time spent on these steps from time spent on grounding, we chose to include them together to ensure a fair comparison.

While all reasoning engines are able to report their grounding time and solving time separately, some of them have a monolithic design that does not allow to run the grounding phase separately. In other words, for these systems, we always have to run the entire task of both grounding and finding one answer set. When these systems encounter a time-out or memory-out, we unfortunately have no way of telling whether this happened during its grounding phase or during the solving. To ensure a level playing field, we therefore adopt the approach that we run all systems with the task of finding one answer set. If the system has a time-out or memory-out at any time, we simply record it as such. If the system returns an answer set, we record only the time it reports for grounding and ignore whatever time was spent solving. In addition, this way of benchmarking also ensures that we have a fair comparison between clingo and the other systems: if we would just use the grounder gringo on its own, it would write its output to a file, causing time to be lost in I/O operations. When running Clingo in its entirety, the grounding is passed in-memory between the grounder and solver, similar to how this is done in the monolithic systems.

In addition to the run time, we also measure memory usage by means of the maximum resident set size (rss) of the process as reported by the operating system.

5   Benchmark Results

Table 3 contains averages and standard deviations for pre-solve time and max rss together with the total number of time-/memouts for each benchmark. To begin, these results show some interesting global tendencies. For instance, we observe that the IDP-Z3 system appears to perform worst overall, often performing one or even two orders of magnitude worse than the fastest systems and not being able to complete 71% of all instances. We also observe that, for `Reachability`, `Non-partition-removal-coloring`, and `TriangleGraphSubset`, only IDP3 and clingo perform well. We suspect this is due to their support for propagation at the non-ground level.

Recall that we included a number of variants of the `TriangleGraph` benchmark to identify which systems were able to avoid cubic blow-up in specific contexts. Interestingly, none of the reasoning engines were able to avoid it for `TGConstructGraph`. IDP-Z3 performed poorly on all `TG` benchmarks, hitting either timeouts or memouts. clingo is able to avoid the blow-up on everything except `TGConstructAtleast` and `TGConstructGraph`. Similarly, ManyWorlds fails on `TGConstructGraph` and `TGSubset`, while SLI also fails on `TGFindAll`. This shows that the different variants indeed capture interesting differences in the computational behaviour across different contexts.

IDP3's results for `TGConstructGraph` are unexpected, since its grounder uses symbolic propagation before grounding [12]. In other words, we would have expected the propagator to be able to propagate all the edges, thus trivializing grounding. However, further analysis of the IDP3 system shows that this symbolic propagation of the edges only happens when the triangles are defined using Clark's completion.

Not a single reasoning engine was able to ground the instances of the packing problem benchmark, as they either ran out of time or memory. This confirms the findings of [15], where completely grounding these instances was not possible while compiling the main constraint of the problem showed better success. By contrast, `PackingProblemAlt` results in a trivial grounding for all supported systems.

Only SLI and clingo were able to ground any `StableMarriage` instances. On average, clingo was an order of magnitude faster than SLI, but timed out in 2 instances, while SLI solved all instances. Both IDP3 and IDP-Z3 ran out of time, while ManyWorlds ran out of memory. Interestingly, not a single reasoning engine was able to find a solution in the alternative versions of stable marriage. Further analysis of SLI showed that grounding was feasible, but that solving caused a timeout.

In the results of the graph colouring benchmark SLI outperforms all other reasoning engines in both timing and memory. IDP3 outperformed both clingo and

ManyWorlds, while the latter two performed 2 orders of magnitude worse. For reachability, only clingo and IDP3 were able to ground and solve all instances. IDP3 also used significantly more memory than clingo for instances with many edges.

Table 3. Average results of all benchmarks.The number of instances for each benchmark is shown in brackets. Benchmarks where no reasoning engine could solve a single instance where left out.`TriangleGraph` benchmarks have been shortened to TG and then the variant name.`Non-partition-removal-coloring` has been shortened to NPRC.

CommonItem (160)	IDP-Z3	IDP3	SLI	ManyWorlds	clingo
presolve (s)	$352_{\pm 106}$	$124_{\pm 102}$	$\mathbf{1.43}_{\pm 0.755}$	$4.05_{\pm 2.16}$	$3.02_{\pm 1.67}$
max rss (MB)	$841_{\pm 87.7}$	$590_{\pm 282}$	$\mathbf{210}_{\pm 99.5}$	$570_{\pm 290}$	$441_{\pm 212}$
timeouts/memouts	150/0	0/0	0/0	0/0	0/0
CompleteSets (160)					
presolve (s)	$461_{\pm 62.4}$	$200_{\pm 165}$	$\mathbf{1.59}_{\pm 0.795}$	$4.46_{\pm 2.18}$	$3.46_{\pm 1.72}$
max rss (MB)	$891_{\pm 83.6}$	$655_{\pm 305}$	$\mathbf{230}_{\pm 104}$	$631_{\pm 303}$	$477_{\pm 222}$
timeouts/memouts	153/0	3/0	0/0	0/0	0/0
GraphColouring (50)					
presolve (s)	$467_{\pm 30.0}$	$9.09_{\pm 7.89}$	$\mathbf{2.56}_{\pm 2.21}$	$88.0_{\pm 63.9}$	$111_{\pm 95.0}$
max rss (MB)	$13560_{\pm 975}$	$1207_{\pm 993}$	$\mathbf{324}_{\pm 248}$	$6052_{\pm 3789}$	$3232_{\pm 2281}$
timeouts/memouts	3/41	0/0	0/0	0/17	0/0
N-queens (7)					
presolve (s)	$0.265_{\pm 0.0665}$	$0.149_{\pm 0.0193}$	$\mathbf{0.0288}_{\pm 0.00179}$	$0.109_{\pm 0.0331}$	$0.520_{\pm 0.416}$
max rss (MB)	$89.0_{\pm 5.92}$	$35.9_{\pm 3.31}$	$49.1_{\pm 3.63}$	$\mathbf{18.5}_{\pm 2.71}$	$24.5_{\pm 2.78}$
timeouts/memouts	0/0	0/0	0/0	0/0	0/0
NPRC (110)					
presolve (s)	Na	$10.3_{\pm 18.8}$	$9.57_{\pm 21.4}$	$15.9_{\pm 35.9}$	$\mathbf{2.95}_{\pm 5.50}$
max rss (MB)	Na	$955_{\pm 1682}$	$2081_{\pm 4391}$	$1433_{\pm 3062}$	$\mathbf{346}_{\pm 590}$
timeouts/memouts	0/110	0/0	0/20	0/30	0/0
PPM (200)					
presolve (s)	$2.88_{\pm 3.71}$	$0.993_{\pm 0.970}$	$\mathbf{0.139}_{\pm 0.188}$	$0.746_{\pm 1.05}$	$15.0_{\pm 27.0}$
max rss (MB)	$238_{\pm 247}$	$477_{\pm 452}$	$140_{\pm 173}$	$\mathbf{126}_{\pm 159}$	$1499_{\pm 2646}$
timeouts/memouts	0/0	78/74	0/0	0/0	0/20
PackingProblemAlt (50)					
presolve (s)	$0.512_{\pm 0.234}$	$0.257_{\pm 0.0826}$	$\mathbf{0.0445}_{\pm 0.0132}$	$0.127_{\pm 0.0378}$	Na
max rss (MB)	$103_{\pm 17.4}$	$57.3_{\pm 16.6}$	$45.9_{\pm 3.63}$	$\mathbf{20.2}_{\pm 5.16}$	Na
timeouts/memouts	0/0	0/0	0/0	0/0	Na
QuasiGroup (100)					
presolve (s)	Na	$150_{\pm 143}$	$\mathbf{24.2}_{\pm 0.242}$	$117_{\pm 3.07}$	$80.4_{\pm 75.9}$
max rss (MB)	Na	$\mathbf{5701}_{\pm 5236}$	$8055_{\pm 0.293}$	$5953_{\pm 301}$	$6894_{\pm 6328}$
timeouts/memouts	30/70	0/90	0/95	0/96	0/90
RamseyNumbers (15)					
presolve (s)	$437_{\pm 142}$	$32.3_{\pm 51.2}$	$56.2_{\pm 67.0}$	$86.3_{\pm 34.0}$	$\mathbf{5.05}_{\pm 7.98}$
max rss (MB)	$3335_{\pm 1059}$	$641_{\pm 963}$	$4333_{\pm 5456}$	$3521_{\pm 1454}$	$\mathbf{498}_{\pm 753}$
timeouts/memouts	13/0	0/0	0/1	0/12	0/0
Reachability (50)					
presolve (s)	Na	$0.113_{\pm 0.00694}$	$160_{\pm 218}$	$67.3_{\pm 5.45}$	$\mathbf{0.0154}_{\pm 0.0167}$
max rss (MB)	Na	$718_{\pm 1192}$	$6080_{\pm 4051}$	$4439_{\pm 222}$	$\mathbf{21.0}_{\pm 1.08}$
timeouts/memouts	28/22	0/0	11/24	0/48	0/0
TGCheck (28)					
presolve (s)	$62.9_{\pm 72.4}$	$0.896_{\pm 1.68}$	$0.404_{\pm 0.851}$	$0.924_{\pm 2.06}$	$\mathbf{0.292}_{\pm 0.626}$
max rss (MB)	$1060_{\pm 1142}$	$42.4_{\pm 40.6}$	$68.0_{\pm 85.8}$	$123_{\pm 242}$	$\mathbf{40.0}_{\pm 43.2}$
timeouts/memouts	0/24	0/0	0/0	0/0	0/0
TGConstructAtleast (14)					
presolve (s)	$30.5_{\pm 42.9}$	$0.630_{\pm 1.34}$	$\mathbf{0.110}_{\pm 0.110}$	$0.860_{\pm 1.85}$	$10.8_{\pm 16.9}$
max rss (MB)	$1010_{\pm 1327}$	$\mathbf{82.2}_{\pm 127}$	$540_{\pm 988}$	$103_{\pm 202}$	$2829_{\pm 4413}$
timeouts/memouts	0/12	0/0	0/2	0/0	0/11
TGConstructGraph (14)					
presolve (s)	$87.6_{\pm 124}$	$\mathbf{5.97}_{\pm 8.26}$	$43.5_{\pm 67.4}$	$8.62_{\pm 12.1}$	$33.7_{\pm 53.9}$
max rss (MB)	$3496_{\pm 4838}$	$703_{\pm 957}$	$5638_{\pm 8125}$	$\mathbf{560}_{\pm 776}$	$2570_{\pm 4035}$
timeouts/memouts	0/12	0/12	0/11	0/12	0/11
TGContainsAll (14)					
presolve (s)	$33.4_{\pm 47.1}$	$\mathbf{0.455}_{\pm 0.888}$	$0.840_{\pm 1.86}$	$1.88_{\pm 4.25}$	$0.582_{\pm 1.30}$
max rss (MB)	$1061_{\pm 1401}$	$62.7_{\pm 84.6}$	$111_{\pm 183}$	$238_{\pm 490}$	$\mathbf{50.5}_{\pm 68.5}$
timeouts/memouts	0/12	0/0	0/0	0/0	0/0
TGFindAll (14)					
presolve (s)	Na	$\mathbf{0.208}_{\pm 0.252}$	$3.18_{\pm 4.47}$	$0.930_{\pm 2.10}$	$0.333_{\pm 0.755}$
max rss (MB)	Na	$\mathbf{39.5}_{\pm 33.6}$	$1699_{\pm 2352}$	$103_{\pm 202}$	$49.2_{\pm 62.0}$
timeouts/memouts	1/12	0/0	0/12	0/0	0/0
TGSubset (14)					
presolve (s)	$93.2_{\pm 131}$	$1.79_{\pm 3.95}$	$6.41_{\pm 9.02}$	$11.0_{\pm 15.5}$	$\mathbf{0.442}_{\pm 1.01}$
max rss (MB)	$5834_{\pm 8131}$	$166_{\pm 304}$	$1696_{\pm 2347}$	$1390_{\pm 1945}$	$\mathbf{45.7}_{\pm 54.5}$
timeouts/memouts	0/12	0/0	0/12	0/12	0/0
StableMarriage (50)					
presolve (s)	Na	Na	$114_{\pm 58.4}$	Na	$\mathbf{24.5}_{\pm 13.1}$
max rss (MB)	Na	Na	$12948_{\pm 2443}$	Na	$\mathbf{1620}_{\pm 838}$
timeouts/memouts	50/0	50/0	0/0	0/50	2/0

6   Conclusion

Benchmarking is a crucial technique to identify bottlenecks in systems and to facilitate comparisons between multiple approaches. In existing literature on grounding in ASP(-like approaches), we find that most works tend to use distinct benchmarks to measure their performance, thus hindering a clear comparison between them. In this paper, we set out to create a specialized grounding benchmark suite. After reviewing existing literature, we carefully selected problem benchmarks based on a list of criteria to ensure their usefulness in our context. Together, they form our new DIRT benchmark suite. We also provide encodings in ASP and ASP-like languages, and show the performance of the clingo, IDP-Z3, SLI, ManyWorlds and IDP3 reasoning tools. This showed us interesting results, such as odd behaviour in certain benchmarks, which can be used as a basis to further fine-tune the grounding algorithms.

The results of the benchmark suite also show that some benchmarks, such as Hamiltonian path, are interesting grounding wise but are incredibly difficult to solve. Unfortunately, as some reasoning systems did not allow for properly separating grounding from solving, our method of benchmarking required instances to be both groundable *and solvable* within time and memory limits. As such, some benchmarks had to be omitted from the results. As part of our future work, we therefore plan on further researching how we can accurately benchmark the grounding step by itself. We would also like to invite other researchers working on ASP(-like) reasoning engines to supply encodings for the DIRT benchmark suite to expand the comparison.

Acknowledgements. This research received funding from the Flemish Government under the "Onderzoeksprogramma Artificiële Intelligentie (AI) Vlaanderen" programme.We would also like to thank Bart Bogaerts and Jo Devriendt.

References

1. Alviano, M., et al.: The fourth answer set programming competition: preliminary report. In: Cabalar, P., Son, T.C. (eds.) LPNMR 2013. LNCS (LNAI), vol. 8148, pp. 42–53. Springer, Heidelberg (2013). https://doi.org/10.1007/978-3-642-40564-8_5
2. Association, P.I.L.: Crossref rest api (2025). https://www.crossref.org/documentation/retrieve-metadata/rest-api/
3. Balduccini, M., Lierler, Y., Schüller, P.: Prolog and ASP inference under one roof. In: Cabalar, P., Son, T.C. (eds.) LPNMR 2013. LNCS (LNAI), vol. 8148, pp. 148–160. Springer, Heidelberg (2013). https://doi.org/10.1007/978-3-642-40564-8_15
4. Bichler, M., Morak, M., Woltran, S.: lpopt: A rule optimization tool for answer set programming. In: Hermenegildo, M.V., Lopez-Garcia, P. (eds.) LOPSTR 2016. LNCS, vol. 10184, pp. 114–130. Springer, Cham (2017). https://doi.org/10.1007/978-3-319-63139-4_7
5. Brewka, G., Eiter, T., Truszczyński, M.: Answer set programming at a glance. Commun. ACM **54**(12), 92–103 (2011). https://doi.org/10.1145/2043174.2043195

6. Calimeri, F., Perri, S., Ricca, F.: Experimenting with parallelism for the instantiation of ASP programs. J. Algorithms **63**(13), 34–54 (2008). https://doi.org/10.1016/j.jalgor.2008.02.003, place: USA Publisher: Academic Press Inc

7. Calimeri, F., Fuscà, D., Perri, S., Zangari, J.: External computations and interoperability in the new DLV grounder. In: Esposito, F., Basili, R., Ferilli, S., Lisi, F.A. (eds.) AI*IA 2017 Advances in Artificial Intelligence, pp. 172–185. Springer International Publishing, Cham (2017)

8. Calimeri, F., Ianni, G., Pacenza, F., Perri, S., Zangari, J.: ASP-based Multishot reasoning via DLV2 with incremental grounding. In: Proceedings of the 24th International Symposium on Principles and Practice of Declarative Programming. PPDP '22, Association for Computing Machinery, New York, NY, USA (2022).https://doi.org/10.1145/3551357.3551371, https://doi.org/10.1145/3551357.3551371, event-place: Tbilisi, Georgia

9. Calimeri, F., et al.: The third answer set programming competition: preliminary report of the system competition track. In: Delgrande, J.P., Faber, W. (eds.) Logic Programming and Nonmonotonic Reasoning, pp. 388–403. LPNMR'11, Springer Berlin Heidelberg, Berlin, Heidelberg (2011).https://doi.org/10.1007/978-3-642-20895-9_46, https://dl.acm.org/doi/10.5555/2010192.2010246, event-place: Vancouver, Canada

10. Carbonnelle, P., Vandevelde, S., Vennekens, J., Denecker, M.: Idp-z3: a reasoning engine for fo (.) (2022)

11. Dal Palù, A., Dovier, A., Pontelli, E., Rossi, G.: Gasp: answer set programming with lazy grounding. Fund. Inform. **96**(3), 297–322 (2009)

12. De Cat, B., Denecker, M., Stuckey, P.: Lazy model expansion by incremental grounding. Dovier, Agostino (Editor), Schloss Dagstuhl - Leibniz-Zentrum fuer Informatik (2012)

13. De Cat, B., Jansen, J., Janssens, G.: Idp3: combining symbolic and ground reasoning for model generation (2013)

14. Devriendt, J.: Manyworlds: combinatorial programming with functions (2024)

15. Dodaro, C., Mazzotta, G., Ricca, F.: Blending grounding and compilation for efficient ASP solving. In: Proceedings of the 21st International Conference on Principles of Knowledge Representation and Reasoning. KR '24 (2024).https://doi.org/10.24963/kr.2024/30, https://doi.org/10.24963/kr.2024/30, place: Hanoi, Vietnam

16. Gebser, M., Kaminski, R., Kaufmann, B., Schaub, T.: Multi-shot ASP solving with clingo. Theory Pract. Logic Program. **19**(1), 27–82 (2019). https://doi.org/10.1017/S1471068418000054, place: Cambridge, UK Publisher: Cambridge University Press

17. Gebser, M., Kaufmann, B., Schaub, T.: Conflict-driven answer set solving: from theory to practice. Artif. Intell. **187**, 52–89 (2012)

18. Gebser, M., Schaub, T., Thiele, S.: GrinGo: a new grounder for answer set programming. In: Proceedings of the 9th International Conference on Logic Programming and Nonmonotonic Reasoning. pp. 266–271. LPNMR'07, Springer-Verlag, Berlin, Heidelberg (2007). https://dl.acm.org/doi/10.5555/1758481.1758508, event-place: Tempe, AZ, USA

19. Heule, M.J.H., Iser, M., Järvisalo, M., Suda, M. (eds.): Proceedings of SAT competition 2024: solver, benchmark and proof checker descriptions, department of computer science report Series B, vol. B-2024-1. Department of Computer Science, University of Helsinki, Helsinki (2024). https://helda.helsinki.fi/handle/10138/584822

20. Janhunen, T.: Removing redundancy from answer set programs. In: Proceedings of the 24th International Conference on Logic Programming, pp. 729–733.

ICLP '08, Springer-Verlag, Berlin, Heidelberg (2008). https://doi.org/10.1007/978-3-540-89982-2_66, event-place: Udine, Italy

21. Kitchenham, B.: Procedures for performing systematic reviews. Keele, UK, Keele University **33**(2004), 1–26 (2004)

22. Lefèvre, C., Bjøatrix, C., Stéphan, I., Garcia, L.: Asperix, a first-order forward chaining approach for answer set computing. Theory Pract. Logic Program. **17**(3), 266–310 (2017)

23. Moura, L.D., Bjørner, N.: Z3: an efficient SMT solver. In: Proceedings of the Theory and Practice of Software, 14th International Conference on Tools and Algorithms for the Construction and Analysis of Systems, pp. 337–340. Springer-Verlag, Budapest, Hungary (2008)

24. PERRI, S., RICCA, F., SIRIANNI, M.: Parallel instantiation of ASP programs: techniques and experiments. Theor. Pract. Logic Program. **13**(2),pp. 253–278 (2013), place: Cambridge, UK Publisher: Cambridge University Press

25. Rohaninezhad, M., Arif, S.M., Noah, S.A.M.: A grounder for SPINdle defeasible logic reasoner. Expert Syst. Appl. **42**(20),pp. 7098–7109 (2015). https://doi.org/10.1016/j.eswa.2015.04.065,https://www.sciencedirect.com/science/article/pii/S0957417415003073

26. Scala, E., Vallati, M.: Exploiting classical planning grounding in hybrid pddl+ planning engines. In: 2020 IEEE 32nd International Conference on Tools with Artificial Intelligence (ICTAI), pp. 85–92 (2020).https://doi.org/10.1109/ICTAI50040.2020.00024, iSSN: 2375-0197

27. Schiffel, S.: Grounding GDL game descriptions. In: Cazenave, T., Winands, M.H.M., Edelkamp, S., Schiffel, S., Thielscher, M., Togelius, J. (eds.) CGW/GIGA -2016. CCIS, vol. 705, pp. 152–164. Springer, Cham (2017). https://doi.org/10.1007/978-3-319-57969-6_11

28. Van Laer, L., Vandevelde, S., Vennekens, J.: Efficiently grounding FOL using bit vectors. In: Logic Programming and Nonmonotonic Reasoning: 17th International Conference, pp. 167–173. Springer-Verlag (2024). https://doi.org/10.1007/978-3-031-74209-5_13

29. Wohlin, C.: Guidelines for snowballing in systematic literature studies and a replication in software engineering. In: Proceedings of the 18th International Conference on Evaluation and Assessment in Software Engineering. EASE '14, Association for Computing Machinery, New York, NY, USA (2014).https://doi.org/10.1145/2601248.2601268, https://doi.org/10.1145/2601248.2601268

An Experiment with Anthem: Semantic Equivalence of Tiling Programs

Vladimir Lifschitz^(✉)

University of Texas at Austin,Austin, USA
lifschitzv@gmail.com

Abstract. ANTHEM is a proof assistant designed for verifying several conditions that play an important role in answer set programming. In this note we show that ANTHEM can help us verify equivalence of logic programming solutions to the same problem that have been independently developed by different programmers.

1 Introduction

ANTHEM (https://potassco.org/anthem/) is a proof assistant designed for verifying a number of conditions that play an important role in answer set programming (ASP). One of these conditions is *external equivalence* of ASP programs. External equivalence means, informally speaking, that the programs exhibit the same external behavior for all permissible inputs. The word "external" refers to the idea that two programs with the same output predicates may be equivalent even if their auxiliary ("private") predicates are different. This can be made precise by defining equivalence with respect to a "user guide," which is a formal expression specifying the set of permissible inputs and the set of output predicates [2].

The article mentioned above motivates studying the external equivalence relation by the fact that improving a correct but inefficient ASP encoding amounts to replacing a program by another program that is equivalent to it with respect to a user guide. ANTHEM does not tell us how to improve a program, but it can help us verify that two versions of a program have the same functionality as far as their output predicates are concerned.

Michael Gelfond has observed (personal communication) that verifying external equivalence can be used also for another purpose: for investigating the relationship between independently developed ASP encodings of the same domain. As an experiment, we investigate here the relationship between two encodings written by students for a class taught at the University of Texas in 2005. The assignment was to solve a tiling puzzle: covering the 8×8 square by twentyâĂŞone 3×1 tiles and a single 1×1 tile [1]. The puzzle has 1424 solutions, as can be demonstrated by running the answer set solver CLINGO (https://potassco.org/clingo/) on either encoding.

To make the question more interesting, we generalize the problem as follows:

G. Casini et al. (Eds.): JELIA 2025, LNAI 16093, pp. 357–363, 2026.
https://doi.org/10.1007/978-3-032-04587-4_22

Given a positive integern, find all covers of the $n \times n$ square by 3×1 tiles and a single 1×1 tile.

Such a cover exists whenever n is different from 2 and is not a multiple of 3 (Krzysztof Apt, personal communication).

The programs written by students have been generalized accordingly. (That was straightforward: it was enough to replace 8 in the programs by n, and 6 by n-2.) The programs have been also edited to make them more concise, and adapted to the syntactic restrictions required by ANTHEM.

Listing 1.1. Program A

```
 1   % T = 1: a 1x1 tile.
 2   % T = 2: a horizontal 3x1 tile with the
 3   % leftmost square at (X,Y).
 4   % T = 3: a vertical 3x1 tile with the
 5   % topmost square at (X,Y).
 6
 7   {place(X,Y,T)} :- X = 1..n, Y = 1..n, T = 1..3.
 8
 9   :- place(X,Y,T1), place(X,Y,T2), T1 != T2.
10   :- place(X,Y,1), place(X1,Y1,1), X != X1.
11   :- place(X,Y,1), place(X1,Y1,1), Y != Y1.
12
13   % filled(X,Y) means that (X,Y) is covered by
14   % one of the tiles.
15   filled(X,Y) :- place(X,Y,1).
16   filled(X+I,Y) :- place(X,Y,2), I = 0..2.
17   filled(X,Y+I) :- place(X,Y,3), I = 0..2.
18
19   :- not filled(X,Y), X = 1..n, Y = 1..n.
20   :- place(X,Y,2), X > n-2.
21   :- place(X,Y,3), Y > n-2.
22   :- place(X,Y,2), place(X+I,Y,T), I = 1..2.
23   :- place(X,Y,3), place(X,Y+I,T), I = 1..2.
24   :- place(X,Y,2), place(X+I,Y-J,3),
25       I = 1..2, J = 1..2.
26   :- place(X,Y,3), place(X-I,Y+J,2),
27       I = 1..2, J = 1..2.
```

2   Two Encodings

The programs, shown in Listings 1.1 and 1.2, are designed in accordance with the same general principles, common in applications of ASP to search problems. A solution is represented by a set of ground atoms that are formed using "output predicates" of the program. Both programs include choice rules that describe "potential solutions." They include also constraints, which weed out potential solutions that are not fully satisfactory, and define auxiliary predicates, which are used to express the constraints.[1]

Listing 1.2. Program B

```
1    % h(R,C) means that there is a tile
2    % at (R,C), (R,C+1), (R,C+2).
3    % v(R,C) means that there is a tile
4    % at (R,C), (R+1,C), (R+2,C).
5
6    {h(1..n,1..n-2)}.
7    {v(1..n-2,1..n)}.
8
9    square(1..n,1..n).
10
11   % covered(R,C) means that (R,C) is covered
12   % by a 3x1 tile.
13   covered(R,C+I) :- h(R,C), I = 0..2.
14   covered(R+I,C) :- v(R,C), I = 0..2.
15
16   :- square(R1,C1), square(R2,C2),
17      not covered(R1,C1), not covered(R2,C2),
18      R1 != R2.
19
20   :- square(R1,C1), square(R2,C2),
21      not covered(R1,C1), not covered(R2,C2),
22      C1 != C2.
23
24   :- h(R,C), h(R,C+(1..2)).
25   :- v(R,C), v(R+(1..2),C).
26   :- h(R,C), v(R-(0..2),C+(0..2)).
```

But the two programs have different output predicates.

In Program A, the output predicate is **place/3**. Its last argument shows whether the tile is 1×1 or 3×1, and, in the latter case, whether it is placed horizontally or vertically. The other two arguments are the coordinates of the "head" of the tile. The choice rule in Line 7 allows us to choose the number of tiles and their positions arbitrarily, as long as the head of every tile is within the $n \times n$ square. The constraint in Line 19, expressing that the entire square is covered, uses the auxiliary predicate **filled/2**, which is defined in Lines 15–17.

In Program B, on the other hand, two output predicates describe the positions of 3×1 tiles placed horizontally (**h/2**) and vertically (**v/2**), and there is no

---

[1] This perspective on the structure of search programs is useful for writing them, but the search algorithms implemented in answer set solvers do not involve generating all potential solutions—their number can be astronomical. These algorithms are similar to those used in the design of satisfiability solvers.

symbol for the position of the 1×1 tile. Instead of the constraint expressing that the entire square is covered, in Listing 1.2 we see a pair of constraints requiring that 3×1 tiles miss at most one position in the $n \times n$ square (Lines 16–22).[2] The auxiliary predicate `covered/2`, defined in Lines 13 and 14, is slightly different from `filled/2` from Program A: `filled(R,C)` means that the position in row R and column C is covered by one of the 3×1 tiles.

The programs differ also by the way they order the arguments denoting the coordinates of a position: the row number R in Program B corresponds to the Y-coordinate in Program A, and the column number C corresponds to the X-coordinate. Thus the atom `h(5,6)` in the output of Program B corresponds to `place(6,5,2)` in the output of Program A.

3   Combining Output Predicates

Because of the difference between their output predicates, Programs A and B are not externally equivalent in the sense of the theory behind ANTHEM. They are only equivalent in the weaker sense discussed by Pearce and Valverde [5], who observe that two knowledge descriptions can be semantically equivalent even if they are expressed in different languages or vocabularies.

But we can make these programs externally equivalent if we extend Program A by definitions of `h/2` and `v/2` (Listing 1.3), and extend Program B by a definition of `place/3` (Listing 1.4). Adding these rules makes the programs equivalent with respect to the user guide that classifies n as a placeholder for an integer, and the symbols `h/2`, `v/2`, `place/3` as output predicates (Listing 1.5).

This claim can be verified by ANTHEM as described in the next section.

Listing 1.3. Rules to be added to Program A

```
1   h(R,C) :- place(C,R,2).
2   v(R,C) :- place(C,R,3).
```

Listing 1.4. Rules to be added to Program B

```
1   place(X,Y,1) :- square(Y,X), not covered(Y,X).
2   place(X,Y,2) :- h(Y,X).
3   place(X,Y,3) :- v(Y,X).
```

Listing 1.5. User guide for the extended programs

```
1   input: n -> integer.
2   output: h/2.
3   output: v/2.
4   output: place/3.
```

---

[2] The original program employed the `#count` aggregate to express this condition more concisely. The versions of ANTHEM available at the time of this writing are not applicable to aggregate expressions.

4   Operation of Anthem

ANTHEM has been designed and implemented by researchers at the University of Potsdam, the University of Nebraska Omaha, and the University of Texas at Austin. It verifies a claim about external equivalence of programs by reducing it to proving certain formulas in a first-order theory and invoking the theorem prover VAMPIRE [4] to find a proof. Formulas are written in a language with terms of two sorts, *general* and its subsort *integer*. General variables are similar to variables in ASP programs; their domain includes both integers and symbolic constants. Integer variables are distinguished from general variables by the symbol $ as their last character. The syntax of the language does not allow general variables in the scope of an arithmetic operation.

The user can help VAMPIRE organize search by providing a *proof outline*—a list of first-order sentences ("lemmas") to be proved consecutively before attempting to prove the main goal. Some lemmas are used in only one half of the proof of equivalence, "forward" (left-to-right) or "backward" (right-to-left).

The output of ANTHEM describes each reasoning task given to VAMPIRE by listing the axioms and the conjecture that VAMPIRE is instructed to derive from them. The user of ANTHEM usually approaches a verification task by checking first whether VAMPIRE can succeed within reasonable time—say, 5 minutes—without help. For nontrivial tasks, this first attempt usually fails. The next step is to find a lemma that can be derived by VAMPIRE from the axioms without help and that is likely to facilitate achieving the goal when added to the list of axioms. Several steps of this kind may be required. Some lemmas can be stated more concisely using explicitly defined predicates, and such definitions can be included in the proof outlines along with the statements of lemmas.

The proof outline used in the verification of the equivalence claim from Sect. 3 is shown in Listing 1.6. Given this proof outline, the ANTHEM-VAMPIRE team, invoked with 6 cores on a machine running Ubuntu 20.04.6, 8 Intel(R) Xeon(R) E3-1271 CPUs, 16 GB RAM, terminated within 326 s.

Listing 1.6. Proof outline

```
 1    definition:  forall  I$  J$  (filled2(I$,J$) <->
 2       place(I$,J$,2)  or  place(I$-1,J$,2)
 3       or  place(I$-2,J$,2)).
 4
 5    definition:  forall  I$  J$  (filled3(I$,J$) <->
 6       place(I$,J$,3)  or  place(I$,J$-1,3)
 7       or  place(I$,J$-2,3)).
 8
 9    lemma(forward):
10    filled2(I$,J$) ->
11       h(J$,I$)  or  h(J$,I$-1)  or  h(J$,I$-2).
12
13    lemma(forward):  filled2(I$,J$) -> covered(J$,I$).
14
```

```
15   lemma(forward):
16   filled3(I$,J$) ->
17     v(J$,I$) or v(J$-1,I$) or v(J$-2,I$).
18
19   lemma(forward): filled3(I$,J$) -> covered(J$,I$).
20
21   lemma(forward):
22   filled(I$,J$) ->
23     place(I$,J$,1)
24     or filled2(I$,J$) or filled3(I$,J$).
25
26   lemma(forward):
27   square(I$,J$) ->
28     place(I$,J$,1)
29     or filled2(I$,J$) or filled3(I$,J$).
30
31   lemma(forward):
32   square(I$,J$) -> place(I$,J$,1) or covered(J$,I$).
33
34   lemma(backward): not(h(R,C) and v(R,C)).
35
36   lemma(backward):
37   not(h(R$,C$) and h(R$,C$+I$) and 1 <= I$ <= 2).
38
39   lemma(backward):
40   not(h(R$,C$) and v(R$,C$+I$) and 0 <= I$ <= 2).
41
42   lemma(backward):
43   not(v(R$,C$) and h(R$+I$,C$) and 0 <= I$ <= 2).
44
45   lemma(backward):
46   not(v(R$,C$) and h(R$+I$,C$-J$)
47     and 0 <= J$ <= 2 and 1 <= I$ <= 2).
48
49   lemma(backward):
50   square(I$,J$) ->
51     place(I$,J$,1)
52     or filled2(I$,J$) or filled3(I$,J$).
53
54   lemma(backward): filled2(I$,J$) -> filled(I$,J$).
55
56   lemma(backward): filled3(I$,J$) -> filled(I$,J$).
```

5   Conclusion

Programs A and B describe the same domain in the same dialect of answer set programming, and they represent the input in the same way. But the output is represented in them by different predicates. After extending each encoding by rules defining the output predicates of the other we obtained a pair of programs that are equivalent with respect to the user guide in which the output predicates of A and B are combined.

The proof outline required for completing verification in the example above includes a large number of lemmas. Inventing these lemmas in the process of interaction with ANTHEM involved a long series of experiments; it was challenging and time consuming. This example can serve as a benchmark for evaluating future versions of ANTHEM and VAMPIRE. Making the number of lemmas smaller without increase in runtime will be a sign of progress.

Acknowledgements. Many thanks to Michael Gelfond, who suggested to me the possibility of using ANTHEM for comparing alternative encodings of the same domain, to Zachary Hansen for sharing with me the best available version of ANTHEM, to Pedro Cabalar, Jorge Fandinno, Martin Gebser, Roland Kaminski and anonymous referees for comments on drafts of this note, and to Krzysztof Apt and Tobias Stolzmann for useful discussions related to its topic.

References

1. Dijkstra, E.W.: Seemingly on a problem transmitted by Bengt Jonsson (1989). https://www.cs.utexas.edu/~EWD/ewd10xx/EWD1039.PDF
2. Fandinno, J., Hansen, Z., Lierler, Y., Lifschitz, V., Temple, N.: External behavior of a logic program and verification of refactoring. Theor. Pract. Logic Prog. (2023)
3. Gomes, C., Kautz, H., Sabharwal, A., Selman, B.: Satisfiability solvers. In: van Harmelen, F., Lifschitz, V., Porter, B. (eds.) Handbook of Knowledge Representation, pp. 89–134. Elsevier (2008)
4. Kovaćs, L., Voronkov, A.: First-order theorem proving and Vampire. In: International Conference on Computer Aided Verification, pp. 1—-35 (2013)
5. Pearce, D., Valverde, A.: Synonymous theories and knowledge representations in answer set programming. J. Comput. Syst. Sci. **78**, 86–104 (2012)

Generalizing the Syntax of Terms in Mini-GRINGO

Vladimir Lifschitz$^{(\boxtimes)}$

University of Texas at Austin, Austin, USA
lifschitzv@gmail.com

Abstract. In answer set programming, a program verification task can be sometimes accomplished by transforming rules into first-order sentences so that the task is reduced to reasoning in classical logic, and invoking a resolution theorem prover. The proof assistant ANTHEM, which implements this idea, allows us to reason about programs written in mini-GRINGO—a subset of the input language of the grounder GRINGO. The goal of this paper is to extend the syntax of terms permitted in that subset. First, instead of the specific choice of arithmetic functions made in earlier publications on mini-GRINGO, we approach integer arithmetic in an abstract way, so that different choices are allowed for different dialects of the language. Second, symbolic constants can be used now as function symbols. This generalization preserves the main property of the more limited form of the language established in earlier work: mini-GRINGO rules can be faithfully represented by first-order sentences.

1 Introduction

In answer set programming (ASP), a program verification task can be sometimes accomplished by transforming rules into first-order sentences so that the task is reduced to reasoning in classical logic, and invoking a resolution theorem prover. The proof assistant ANTHEM,[1] which implements this idea, allows us to reason about programs written in mini-GRINGO—a subset of the input language of the ASP grounder GRINGO.

The semantics of mini-GRINGO is defined in terms of the operator τ, which transforms a mini-GRINGO program into a "propositional theory"—a set of propositional formulas. Stable models (answer sets) of a propositional theory are defined by Paolo Ferraris [8]. Stable models of a mini-GRINGO program Π are defined as stable models of $\tau(\Pi)$ [14, Section 3].

If a program Π contains variables, then the set $\tau(\Pi)$ is infinite and thus cannot be directly used in computational procedures. ANTHEM relies instead on the operator τ^* [14, Section 6], which transforms a program into a finite set of first-order sentences. The target language of τ^* is two-sorted. There are *general* variables, which are similar to variables in mini-GRINGO programs: the set of values of a general variable includes both symbolic constants and (symbols for)

---

[1] https://potassco.org/anthem/.

© The Author(s), under exclusive license to Springer Nature Switzerland AG 2026
G. Casini et al. (Eds.): JELIA 2025, LNAI 16093, pp. 364–377, 2026.
https://doi.org/10.1007/978-3-032-04587-4_23

integers. The other sort is *integer*, a subsort of *general*. The need to distinguish between general terms and integer terms when we represent rules by formulas is related to the difference between the treatment of function symbols in logic programming and in first-order logic. In an ASP program, the rule

```
foo(london + paris).
```

is syntactically correct, even though adding symbolic constants is not defined. (The stable model of this one-rule program is empty.) In first-order logic, on the other hand, functions represented by function symbols are required to be total. In the target language of τ^*, the expression $t_1 + t_2$ is an integer term if both t_1 and t_2 are integer terms. But if at least one of them is a general term then $t_1 + t_2$ is syntactically incorrect.

The claim that the translation τ^* faithfully represents the meaning of mini-GRINGO programs can be made precise using infinitary propositional formulas. Two-sorted first-order sentences can be transformed into infinitary propositional formulas by the process of grounding—replacing quantifiers by infinite conjunctions and disjunctions. For any mini-GRINGO program Π, the result of grounding $\tau^*(\Pi)$ is satisfied by the same HT-interpretations as $\tau(\Pi)$ [14, Proposition 3]. In other words, the result of grounding $\tau^*(\Pi)$ is strongly equivalent [11, 15] to $\tau(\Pi)$. It follows that both sets of formulas have the same stable models.

Some recent publications [5, 10, 13] extend mini-GRINGO by additional constructs found in many ASP programs—conditional literals and aggregates—and show how to extend the definition of τ^* to rules containing these constructs. The goal of this paper is to extend mini-GRINGO and τ^* in a different way: we extend the class of terms permitted in the language.

According to the Potassco User Guide, the input language of GRINGO includes symbols for 12 arithmetic functions on integers: addition, subtraction, unary minus, multiplication, integer division, modulo, exponentiation, absolute value, and four bitwise operations [9, Section 3.1.7]. The authors of the original publication on mini-GRINGO [14] chose to include the first six of these functions in the language and to disregard the other six. Including all twelve would not be difficult, but the technical results of the paper, strictly speaking, would need to be proved for the extended language anew. We address this difficulty by showing that integer arithmetic of mini-GRINGO can be described in an abstract way that covers many "dialects" of the language. In the definition proposed below, the set of arithmetic functions is a parameter. This is useful, in particular, because integer arithmetic is sometimes treated in different ways in different versions of Potassco software. In Version 6, the result of integer division will be understood as the quotient rounded toward negative infinity, whereas earlier versions round toward zero.[2]

In addition, the new version of mini-GRINGO allows symbolic constants to be used as uninterpreted function symbols [9, Section 3.1.1]. Such use of symbolic constants is common in answer set programming. For example, the blocks world

---

[2] Roland Kaminski, personal communication (May 5, 2025).

planning program in the Potassco User Guide [9, Section 5.3] expresses that block b1 is initially on the table by the rule

```
init(on(b1,table)).
```

Here on is an uninterpreted function symbol.

The main result of this paper shows that mini-GRINGO rules generalized as described above can be faithfully represented by first-order sentences: we define τ^* for the new version of the language in such a way that the result of grounding $\tau^*(\Pi)$ is strongly equivalent to $\tau(\Pi)$.

The syntax and semantics of extended mini-GRINGO are described in Sect. 2. The translation τ^* for the new version of the language is defined in Sect. 3. The main result is stated in Sect. 4, and a proof outline is presented in Sect. 5. Section 6 describes the direction of future work.

2   Mini-GRINGO

2.1   Syntax of Terms

We assume that

- two disjoint sets of symbols are selected: *basic symbols* and *variables*; the latter is countably infinite;
- two disjoint sets of basic symbols are selected: *symbolic constants* and *numerals*; a 1–1 correspondence $n \mapsto \overline{n}$ between the set $\mathbf{Z}$ of integers and the set of numerals is selected;
- a set of *arithmetic function symbols* is selected, disjoint from the set of basic symbols and the set of variables; for every arithmetic function symbol f, a function $\hat{f}$ is selected that maps a subset of $\mathbf{Z}^k$ to $\mathbf{Z}$, where the *arity* k of f is a positive integer.

EXAMPLE. Symbolic constants are strings of letters, digits and underscores that begin with a lowercase letter. Variables are strings of letters, digits and underscores that begin with a upppercase letter. Numerals are (i) 0, (ii) strings of digits that begin with a digit different from 0, and (iii) - followed by a string of type (ii). Basic symbols are symbolic constants, numerals, inf *and* sup *. Arithmetic function symbols are*

$$+ \quad \times \quad /$$

and the corresponding functions $\hat{f}$ are addition, multiplication and integer division (floor of the quotient).

Mini-GRINGO terms are defined recursively:

- all basic symbols and variables are terms;
- if c is a symbolic constant and $\mathbf{t}$ is a non-empty tuple of terms, then $c(\mathbf{t})$ is a term;
- if f is an arithmetic function symbol of arity k, and $\mathbf{t}$ is a k-tuple of terms, then $f(\mathbf{t})$ is a term;

- if t_1 and t_2 are terms then $t_1 \mathbin{..} t_2$ is a term.

*EXAMPLE, CONTINUED. Abbreviations for mini-*GRINGO *terms:*

$$-t \ is \ (-1) \times t$$
$$t_1 - t_2 \ is \ t_1 + (-t_2)$$
$$t_1 \setminus t_2 \ is \ t_1 - t_2 \times (t_1 / t_2)$$

A mini-GRINGO term (or any other syntactic expression) is *ground* if it does not contain variables. A ground mini-GRINGO term is *precomputed* if it contains neither arithmetic function symbols nor the interval symbol. We assume that a total order on precomputed mini-GRINGO terms is selected such that numerals are contiguous (every term between two numerals is a numeral), and, for all integers m and n, $\overline{m} \leq \overline{n}$ iff $m \leq n$.

EXAMPLE, CONTINUED. inf *is smaller than numerals, which in turn are smaller than symbolic constants, which are smaller than complex terms, which are smaller than* sup. *Symbolic constants are ordered lexicographically. Complex terms are ordered both structurally and lexicographically, as described in the last clause of the definition of term ordering in the ASP-Core-2 document* [1, *Section 3*].

2.2 Syntax of Programs

An *atom* is an expression of the form $c(\mathbf{t})$, where c is a symbolic constant and $\mathbf{t}$ is a tuple of mini-GRINGO terms (possibly empty, in which case the parentheses can be dropped). An atom $c(\mathbf{t})$ is *precomputed* if all members of $\mathbf{t}$ are precomputed mini-GRINGO terms. A *literal* is an atom possibly preceded by one or two occurrences of *not*.

Comparisons are expressions of the forms $t_1 \leq t_2$ and $t_1 \neq t_2$, where t_1 and t_2 are mini-GRINGO terms. Abbreviations:

$$t_1 \geq t_2 \ stands for \ t_2 \leq t_1,$$
$$t_1 = t_2 \ stands for \ t_1 \leq t_2 \wedge t_1 \geq t_2,$$
$$t_1 < t_2 \ stands for \ t_1 \leq t_2 \wedge t_1 \neq t_2,$$
$$t_1 > t_2 \ stands for \ t_1 \geq t_2 \wedge t_1 \neq t_2.$$

A *rule* is an expression of the form

$$H \leftarrow B_1 \wedge \cdots \wedge B_n \tag{1}$$

$(n \geq 0)$, where

- the head H is either an atom (then (1) is a *basic rule*), or an atom in braces (then (1) is a *choice rule*), or empty (then (1) is a *constraint*), and
- each member B_i of the body is a literal or a comparison.

A *mini-*GRINGO *program* is a finite set of rules.

2.3   Semantics of Terms

The set $[t]$ of *values* of a ground mini-GRINGO term t is defined recursively:

- if t is a basic symbol then $[t]$ is $\{t\}$;
- if t is $c(t_1, \ldots, t_k)$, where c is a symbolic constant, then $[t]$ is the set of terms of the form $c(s_1, \ldots, s_k)$, where $s_i \in [t_i]$ $(i = 1, \ldots, k)$;
- if t is $f(t_1, \ldots, t_k)$, where f is an arithmetic function symbol, then $[t]$ is the set of numerals of the form $\overline{\hat{f}(n_1, \ldots, n_k)}$, where $n_1, \ldots, n_k$ is a tuple in the domain of $\hat{f}$ such that $\overline{n_i} \in [t_i]$ $(i = 1, \ldots, k)$;
- if t is $t_1 \mathbin{..} t_2$ then $[t]$ is the set of numerals $\overline{n}$ for all integers n such that, for some integers n_1, n_2,

$$\overline{n_1} \in [t_1], \quad \overline{n_2} \in [t_2], \quad n_1 \leq n \leq n_2.$$

It is clear that values of a ground mini-GRINGO term are precomputed mini-GRINGO terms, and that $[t]$ is the singleton $\{t\}$ whenever t is precomputed.

EXAMPLE, CONTINUED.

$$[2 + 2] = \{4\}, \quad [(1 \mathbin{..} 2) \times 2] = \{2, 4\}, \quad [2 / 0] = [\mathtt{london} + \mathtt{paris}] = \emptyset.$$

For any ground mini-GRINGO terms $t_1 \ldots, t_k$, by $[t_1, \ldots, t_k]$ we denote the set of tuples $s_1, \ldots, s_k$ of terms such that $s_1 \in [t_1], \ldots, s_k \in [t_k]$.

2.4   Semantics of Programs

The translation τ, defined below, transforms literals, comparisons and rules into propositional combinations of precomputed atoms. For any ground atom $c(\mathbf{t})$,

- $\tau(c(\mathbf{t}))$ is $\bigvee_{\mathbf{s} \in [\mathbf{t}]} c(\mathbf{s})$,
- $\tau(not\ c(\mathbf{t}))$ is $\bigvee_{\mathbf{s} \in [\mathbf{t}]} \neg c(\mathbf{s})$, and
- $\tau(not\ not\ c(\mathbf{t}))$ is $\bigvee_{\mathbf{s} \in [\mathbf{t}]} \neg\neg c(\mathbf{s})$.

For any ground comparison $t_1 \prec t_2$, $\tau(t_1 \prec t_2)$ is

$\top$("true"), if there exist s_1 in $[t_1]$ and s_2 in $[t_2]$ such that $s_1 \prec s_2$;
$\bot$("false"), otherwise.

EXAMPLE, CONTINUED.

$$\tau(\mathtt{foo}((1 \mathbin{..} 2) \times 2)) = \mathtt{foo}(2) \vee \mathtt{foo}(4),$$
$$\tau(\mathtt{foo}(\mathtt{london} + \mathtt{paris})) = \bot,$$
$$\tau(\mathtt{london} \leq \mathtt{paris}) = \top.$$

If *Body* is a conjunction $B_1 \wedge B_2 \wedge \cdots$ of ground literals and ground comparisons then $\tau(Body)$ stands for the conjunction $\tau(B_1) \wedge \tau(B_2) \wedge \cdots$.

If R is a ground basic rule $c(\mathbf{t}) \leftarrow Body$ then $\tau(R)$ is the propositional formula

$$\tau(Body) \rightarrow \bigwedge_{\mathbf{s}\in[\mathbf{t}]} c(\mathbf{s}).$$

If R is a ground choice rule $\{c(\mathbf{t})\} \leftarrow Body$ then $\tau(R)$ is the propositional formula

$$\tau(Body) \rightarrow \bigwedge_{\mathbf{s}\in[\mathbf{t}]} (c(\mathbf{s}) \vee \neg c(\mathbf{s})).$$

If R is a ground constraint $\leftarrow Body$ then $\tau(R)$ is $\neg\tau(Body)$.

An *instance* of a rule is a ground rule obtained from it by substituting precomputed mini-GRINGO terms for variables. For any program Π, $\tau(\Pi)$ is the set of the propositional formulas $\tau(R)$ for all instances R of the rules of Π.

A set of precomputed atoms is a *stable model* of a program Π if it is a stable model of $\tau(\Pi)$.

3   Representing Terms and Programs by Formulas

3.1   Signature σ_0

An arithmetic function symbol f of arity k is *total* if the domain of $\hat{f}$ is the entire set $\mathbf{Z}^k$, and *partial* otherwise.

By σ_0 we denote the two-sorted signature that consists of

(i)   the sort *general* and its subsort *integer*;
(ii) all numerals as object constants of sort *integer*;
(iii) all basic symbols other than numerals as object constants of sort *general*;
(iv) expressions $c\backslash k$, where c is a symbolic constant and k is a positive integer, as function constants of arity k, with both arguments and value of sort *general*;
(v)   all total arithmetic function symbols as function constants with both arguments and value of sort *integer*;
(vi) expressions c/k, where c is a symbolic constant and k is a nonnegative integer, as predicate constants of arity k, with arguments of sort *general*;
(vii) the symbol $\leq$ as a binary predicate constant with both arguments of sort *general*.

(Partial arithmetic function symbols are not included, because they do not represent total functions even in application to integers.)

EXAMPLE, CONTINUED. Object constants of sort general *are symbolic constants,* inf *and* sup. *Function constants of group (v) are* + *and* × *(but not* /*).*

We identify general variables with variables of mini-GRINGO.

3.2 Signature σ_0^- and the Standard Interpretation

By σ_0^- we denote the signature obtained from σ_0 by removing the predicate symbols c/k. The *standard interpretation* S of σ_0^- is defined as follows:

- its domain of the sort *general* is the set of all precomputed mini-GRINGO terms;
- its domain of the sort *integer* is the set of all numerals;
- if r is a basic symbol then $r^S = r$;
- for every function constant $c\backslash k$ and precomputed mini-GRINGO terms $t_1, \ldots, t_k$,
$$(c\backslash k)^S(t_1, \ldots, t_k) = c(t_1, \ldots, t_k);$$

- for every total arithmetic function symbol f and integers $n_1, \ldots, n_k$, where k is the arity of f,
$$f^S(\overline{n_1}, \ldots, \overline{n_k}) = \overline{\hat{f}(n_1, \ldots, n_k)};$$

- $\leq^S$ is the order on precomputed mini-GRINGO terms specified in the definition of mini-GRINGO (Sect. 2.1).

A ground term over σ_0 is *precomputed* if it does not contain arithmetic function symbols. It is clear that the map $r \mapsto r^S$ is a 1–1 correspondence between precomputed terms over σ_0 and precomputed mini-GRINGO terms; r^S can be obtained from r by replacing each function symbol $c\backslash k$ with c.

The set of sentences over σ_0^- that are satisfied by the standard interpretation is denoted by *Std*.

EXAMPLE, CONTINUED. The formula

$$\exists X \neg \exists N (N = X), \tag{2}$$

where X is a general variable and N is an integer variable, belongs to Std: take X to be inf. *By Lagrange's four-square theorem, the formula*

$$\forall N(N \geq 0 \rightarrow \exists \, IJKL(N = I \times I + J \times J + K \times K + L \times L)),$$

where N, I, J, K, L are integer variables, belongs to Std as well.

Formula (2) is a sentence over the signature σ_0^- in every possible dialect of mini-GRINGO. But it does not necessarily belong to *Std* in dialects other than our running example, because the general framework of Sect. 2.1 allows the set of basic symbols to contain nothing other than numerals.

3.3 Representing Mini-GRINGO Terms by Formulas

Assume that for every partial arithmetic function symbol f we chose a formula

$$V_f(N_1, \ldots, N_{k+1})$$

over σ_0^-, where k is the arity of f, and $N_1,\dots,N_{k+1}$ are integer variables, with all free variables explicitly shown, which describes the function $\hat{f}$ in the following sense: for any integers $n_1,\dots,n_{k+1}$,

$$V_f(\overline{n_1},\dots,\overline{n_{k+1}}) \in Std \text{ iff } \hat{f}(n_1,\dots,n_k) = n_{k+1}. \tag{3}$$

EXAMPLE, CONTINUED. The formula

$$(0 \le N_1 - N_2 \times N_3 < N_2) \vee (0 \ge N_1 - N_2 \times N_3 > N_2)$$

can be chosen as V_f. Indeed, the formula

$$(0 \le \overline{n_1} - \overline{n_2} \times \overline{n_3} < \overline{n_2}) \vee (0 \ge \overline{n_1} - \overline{n_2} \times \overline{n_3} > \overline{n_2})$$

is satisfied by the standard interpretation iff

$$0 \le n_1 - n_2 \times n_3 < n_2 \tag{4}$$

or

$$0 \ge n_1 - n_2 \times n_3 > n_2. \tag{5}$$

Condition (4) is equivalent to the condition

$$n_2 > 0 \, and \, 0 \le n_1/n_2 - n_3 < 1$$

and consequently to

$$n_2 > 0 \, and \, n_3 \le n_1/n_2 < n_3 + 1.$$

Similarly, condition (5) is equivalent to the condition

$$n_2 < 0 \, and \, 0 \le n_1/n_2 - n_3 < 1$$

and consequently to

$$n_2 < 0 \, and \, n_3 \le n_1/n_2 < n_3 + 1.$$

For a mini-GRINGO term t and a general variable X that does not occur in t, $val_t(X)$ is the formula over σ_0 defined recursively:

- if t is a basic symbol or a variable then $val_t(X)$ is $X = t$;
- if t is $c(t_1,\dots,t_k)$, where c is a symbolic constant, then $val_t(X)$ is

$$\exists X_1\dots X_k(val_{t_1}(X_1) \wedge \dots \wedge val_{t_k}(X_k) \wedge X = (c\backslash k)(X_1,\dots,X_k)),$$

where $X_1,\dots,X_k$ are general variables that do not occur in t;
- if t is $f(t_1,\dots,t_k)$, where f is a total arithmetic function symbol, then $val_t(X)$ is

$$\exists N_1\dots N_k(val_{t_1}(N_1) \wedge \dots \wedge val_{t_k}(N_k) \wedge X = f(N_1,\dots,N_k)),$$

where $N_1,\dots,N_k$ are integer variables that do not occur in t;

- if t is $f(t_1, \ldots, t_k)$, where f is a partial arithmetic function symbol, then $val_t(X)$ is

$$\exists N_1 \ldots N_k N_{k+1}(val_{t_1}(N_1) \wedge \cdots \wedge val_{t_k}(N_k) \wedge N_{k+1} = X \wedge \\ V_f(N_1, \ldots, N_{k+1})),$$

where $N_1, \ldots, N_{k+1}$ are integer variables that do not occur in t;
- if t is $t_1 \mathbin{..} t_2$ then $val_t(X)$ is

$$\exists N_1 N_2(val_{t_1}(N_1) \wedge val_{t_2}(N_2) \wedge N_1 \leq X \leq N_2),$$

where N_1, N_2 are integer variables that do not occur in t.

The formula $val_t(X)$ expresses that X is a value of t, as defined in Sect. 2.3 for ground t; this is made precise in Lemma 3 (Sect. 5). It is clear that the free variables of this formula are X and the variables occurring in t.

EXAMPLE, CONTINUED. The formula $val_{c(Y)}(X)$ is

$$\exists X_1(X_1 = Y \wedge X = (c/1)(X_1)).$$

The formula $val_{Y+Z}(X)$ is

$$\exists N_1 N_2(N_1 = Y \wedge N_2 = Z \wedge X = N_1 + N_2).$$

The formula $val_{Y/Z}(X)$ is

$$\exists N_1 N_2 N_3(N_1 = Y \wedge N_2 = Z \wedge N_3 = X \\ \wedge ((0 \leq N_1 - N_2 \times N_3 < N_2) \vee (0 \geq N_1 - N_2 \times N_3 > N_2))).$$

3.4   Representing Programs by Formulas

The translation τ^B, defined below, produces a formula that characterizes the meaning of an expression in the body of a rule; this is made precise in Lemma 4 (Sect. 5). This translation transforms

- $c(t_1, \ldots, t_k)$ into

$$\exists X_1 \cdots X_k(val_{t_1}(X_1) \wedge \cdots \wedge val_{t_k}(X_k) \wedge (c/k)(X_1, \ldots, X_k));$$

- $not\ c(t_1, \ldots, t_k)$ into

$$\exists X_1 \cdots X_k(val_{t_1}(X_1) \wedge \cdots \wedge val_{t_k}(X_k) \wedge \neg(c/k)(X_1, \ldots, X_k));$$

- $not\ not\ c(t_1, \ldots, t_k)$ into

$$\exists X_1 \cdots X_k(val_{t_1}(X_1) \wedge \cdots \wedge val_{t_k}(X_k) \wedge \neg\neg(c/k)(X_1, \ldots, X_k));$$

- $t_1 \prec t_2$ into $\exists X_1 X_2(val_{t_1}(X_1) \wedge val_{t_2}(X_2) \wedge X_1 \prec X_2)$;

where each X_i is a general variable.

If *Body* is a conjunction $B_1 \wedge B_2 \wedge \cdots$ of literals and comparisons then $\tau^B(Body)$ stands for the conjunction $\tau^B(B_1) \wedge \tau^B(B_2) \wedge \cdots$.

The translation τ^* converts a basic rule

$$c(t_1, \ldots, t_k) \leftarrow Body$$

of a program Π into the formula

$$\widetilde{\forall}(val_{t_1}(X_1) \wedge \cdots \wedge val_{t_k}(X_k) \wedge \tau^B(Body) \rightarrow (c/k)(X_1, \ldots, X_k)),$$

where $X_1, \ldots, X_k$ are alphabetically first general variables that do not occur in Π, and $\widetilde{\forall}$ denotes universal closure. A choice rule

$$\{c(t_1, \ldots, t_k)\} \leftarrow Body$$

is converted into

$$\widetilde{\forall}(val_{t_1}(X_1) \wedge \cdots \wedge val_{t_k}(X_k) \wedge \tau^B(Body) \wedge \neg\neg(c/k)(X_1, \ldots, X_k)$$
$$\rightarrow (c/k)(X_1, \ldots, X_k)),$$

and a constraint $\leftarrow Body$ becomes $\widetilde{\forall}\neg\tau^B(Body)$.

By $\tau^*(\Pi)$ we denote the set of sentences $\tau^*(R)$ for all rules R of Π.

4   Relationship Between Π and $\tau^*(\Pi)$

The relationship between Π and $\tau^*(\Pi)$ can be described using the grounding translation gr, which transforms sentences over σ_0 into infinitary propositional combinations of precomputed atoms. This translation is defined recursively:

- if F is $(c/k)(r_1, \ldots, r_k)$ then $gr(F)$ is $c(r_1^S, \ldots, r_k^S)$;
- if F is $r_1 \prec r_2$, where $\prec$ is $=$ or $\leq$, then $gr(F)$ is $\top$ if $r_1^S \prec r_2^S$, and $\bot$ otherwise;
- $gr(\bot)$ is $\bot$;
- $gr(F \odot G)$ is $gr(F) \odot gr(G)$ for every binary connective $\odot$;
- $gr(\forall X\, F(X))$ is the conjunction of the formulas $gr(F(r))$ over all precomputed terms r over σ_0 if X is a general variable, and over all numerals r if X is an integer variable;
- $gr(\exists X\, F(X))$ is the disjunction of the formulas $gr(F(r))$ over all precomputed terms r over σ_0 if X is a general variable, and over all numerals r if X is an integer variable.

(There is no clause for negation here because we treat $\neg F$ as shorthand for $F \rightarrow \bot$.)

Miroslaw Truszczynski [16] extended the stable model semantics of propositional theories proposed by Paolo Ferraris [8] to the infinitary case. Sets $\mathcal{H}_1$, $\mathcal{H}_2$ of infinitary formulas are *strongly equivalent* if, for every set $\mathcal{H}$ of infinitary formulas, the sets $\mathcal{H}_1 \cup \mathcal{H}$ and $\mathcal{H}_2 \cup \mathcal{H}$ have the same stable models [11, Section 3.1].

Strong equivalence of infinitary formulas can be characterized as equivalence in the deductive system denoted by HT^∞ [11, Corollary 2].[3]

Theorem. *For any mini-*GRINGO *program* Π, $gr(\tau^*(\Pi))$ *is strongly equivalent to* $\tau(\Pi)$.

Corollary. *For any mini-*GRINGO *program* Π, $gr(\tau^*(\Pi))$ *has the same stable models as* Π.

5   Proof Outline

Lemma 1. *For any formula* $F(X)$ *over* σ_0^- *that has no free variables other than* X,

(a) *if* X *is a general variable then*
   - *the sentence* $\forall X\, F(X)$ *belongs to* Std *iff for every precomputed term* r *over* σ_0 *the sentence* $F(r)$ *belongs to* Std;
   - *the sentence* $\exists X\, F(X)$ *belongs to* Std *iff for at least one precomputed term* r *over* σ_0 *the sentence* $F(r)$ *belongs to* Std;
(b) *if* X *is an integer variable then*
   - *the sentence* $\forall X\, F(X)$ *belongs to* Std *iff for every integer* n *the sentence* $F(\overline{n})$ *belongs to* Std;
   - *the sentence* $\exists X\, F(X)$ *belongs to* Std *iff for a least one integer* n *the sentence* $F(\overline{n})$ *belongs to* Std.

Proof. Recall that a sentence belongs to *Std* iff it is satisfied by the standard interpretation S. (a) The domain of the sort *general* in S is the set of precomputed terms of mini-GRINGO, and every element of this domain is r^S for some precomputed term r over σ_0. (b) The domain of the sort *integer* in S is the set of numerals, and every element of this domain is $\overline{n}$ for some integer n.

Lemma 2. *For any sentence* F *over* σ_0^-, $gr(F)$ *is strongly equivalent to* $\top$ *if* $F \in Std$, *and to* $\bot$ *otherwise.*

The proof is by induction on the size of F, using Lemma 1.

Lemma 3. *Let* $t(\mathbf{Z})$ *be a mini-*GRINGO *term, where* $\mathbf{Z}$ *is a list of variables that contains every variable occurring in* $t(\mathbf{Z})$, *and let* $F(\mathbf{Z}, X)$ *stand for the formula* $val_{t(\mathbf{Z})}(X)$. *For any list* $\mathbf{q}$ *of precomputed terms over* σ_0 *of the same length as* $\mathbf{Z}$ *and any precomputed term* r *over* σ_0 , *the formula* $gr(F(\mathbf{q}, r))$ *is strongly equivalent to* $\top$ *if* $r^S \in [t(\mathbf{q}^S)]$, *and to* $\bot$ *otherwise.*

Proof by induction on t. There are several cases to consider, depending on whether $t(\mathbf{Z})$ is a basic symbol (Case 1); a variable (Case 2); $c(t_1(\mathbf{Z}), \ldots, t_k(\mathbf{Z}))$,

---

[3] This system is an infinitary version of the logic of here-and-there—the three-valued logic, intermediate between intuitionistic and classical, introduced by Arend Heyting [12], which plays an important role in the theory of stable models.

where c is a symbolic constant (Case 3); $f(t_1(\mathbf{Z}), \ldots, t_k(\mathbf{Z}))$, where f is an arithmetic function symbol (Case 4); $t_1(\mathbf{q}) \ldots t_2(\mathbf{q})$ (Case 5). We consider here Case 4 as the most interesting. In this case, $t(\mathbf{q}^S)$ is $f(t_1(\mathbf{q}^S), \ldots, t_k(\mathbf{q}^S))$; $[t(\mathbf{q}^S)]$ is the set of numerals $\hat{f}(n_1, \ldots, n_k)$, where $n_1, \ldots, n_k$ is a tuple in the domain of $\hat{f}$ such that, for all i, $\overline{n_i} \in [t_i(\mathbf{q}^S)]$. The induction hypothesis is that for any precomputed terms $r_1, \ldots, r_k$ over σ_0, $gr(F_i(\mathbf{q}, r_i))$ is strongly equivalent to $\top$ if $r_i^S \in [t_i(\mathbf{q})]$, and to $\bot$ otherwise $(i = 1, \ldots, k)$.

Case 4.1: f is total. The formula $F(\mathbf{Z}, X)$ is

$$\exists N_1 \ldots N_k(F_1(\mathbf{Z}, N_1) \wedge \cdots \wedge F_k(\mathbf{Z}, N_k) \wedge X = f(N_1, \ldots, N_k)),$$

where $F_i(\mathbf{Z}, X_i)$ is $val_{t(\mathbf{Z})}(X_i)$, so that $F(\mathbf{q}, r)$ is

$$\exists N_1 \ldots N_k(F_1(\mathbf{q}, N_1) \wedge \cdots \wedge F_k(\mathbf{q}, N_k) \wedge r = f(N_1, \ldots, N_k)).$$

The formula $gr(F(\mathbf{q}, r))$ is the disjunction of the conjunctions

$$gr(F_1(\mathbf{q}, \overline{n_1})) \wedge \cdots \wedge gr(F_k(\mathbf{q}, \overline{n_k})) \wedge G_{n_1 \cdots n_k} \tag{6}$$

where $n_1, \ldots, n_k$ is an arbitrary tuple of integers, and $G_{n_1 \cdots n_k}$ stands for $\top$ if

$$r^S = \overline{\hat{f}(n_1, \ldots, n_k)}, \tag{7}$$

and for $\bot$ otherwise. Since r is precomputed, condition (7) can be rewritten as $r = \overline{\hat{f}(n_1, \ldots, n_k)}$. *Case 4.1.1:* r is a numeral $\overline{n}$ for some integer n. Then $gr(F(\mathbf{q}, r))$ is strongly equivalent to the disjunction of the formulas

$$gr(F_1(\mathbf{q}, \overline{n_1})) \wedge \cdots \wedge gr(F_k(\mathbf{q}, \overline{n_k})),$$

where $n_1, \ldots, n_k$ is an arbitrary tuple of integers such that

$$\hat{f}(n_1, \ldots, n_k) = n. \tag{8}$$

By the induction hypothesis, this conjunction is srongly equivalent to $\top$ if

$$\overline{n_1} \in [t_1(\mathbf{q}^S)], \quad \ldots, \quad \overline{n_k} \in [t_k(\mathbf{q}^S)], \tag{9}$$

and to $\bot$ otherwise. By (8), condition (9) is equivalent to $\overline{n} \in [t(\mathbf{q})]$. *Case 4.1.2:* r is not a numeral. Then $r^S \notin [t(\mathbf{q})]$, and all disjunctive terms (6) of $gr(F(\mathbf{q}, r))$ are strongly equivalent to $\bot$.

Case 4.2: f is partial. The formula $F(\mathbf{Z}, X)$ is

$$\exists N_1 \ldots N_{k+1}(F_1(\mathbf{Z}, N_1) \wedge \cdots \wedge F_k(\mathbf{Z}, N_k) \wedge N_{k+1} = X \wedge V_f(N_1, \ldots, N_{k+1})),$$

where $F_i(\mathbf{Z}, X_i)$ is $val_{t(\mathbf{Z})}(X_i)$, so that $F(\mathbf{q}, r)$ is

$$\exists N_1 \ldots N_{k+1}(F_1(\mathbf{q}, N_1) \wedge \cdots \wedge F_k(\mathbf{q}, N_k) \wedge N_{k+1} = r \wedge V_f(N_1, \ldots, N_{k+1})).$$

The formula $gr(F(\mathbf{q}, r))$ is the disjunction of the conjunctions

$$gr(F_1(\mathbf{q}, \overline{n_1})) \wedge \cdots \wedge gr(F_k(\mathbf{q}, \overline{n_k})) \wedge G_{n_{k+1}} \wedge gr(V_f(\overline{n}_1, \ldots, \overline{n}_{k+1})) \qquad (10)$$

where $n_1, \ldots, n_{k+1}$ is an arbitrary tuple of integers, and G_n stands for $\top$ if r is $\overline{n}$ and for $\bot$ otherwise. *Case 4.2.1:* r is a numeral n. By Lemma 2, it follows that $gr(F(\mathbf{q}, r))$ is strongly equivalent to the disjunction of the conjunctions

$$gr(F_1(\mathbf{q}, \overline{n_1})) \wedge \cdots \wedge gr(F_k(\mathbf{q}, \overline{n_k}))$$

where $n_1, \ldots, n_k$ is an arbitrary tuple of integers satisfying the condition

$$V_f(\overline{n}_1, \ldots, \overline{n}_k, n) \text{ belongs to } \textit{Std}.$$

By (3), this condition is equivalent to (8), and we can reason as in Case 4.1.1. *Case 4.2.2:* r is not a numeral. Then $r^S \notin [t(\mathbf{q})]$; all disjunctive terms (10) of $gr(F(\mathbf{q}, r))$ are strongly equivalent to $\bot$, because the conjunctive term $G_{n_{k+1}}$ in each of them is $\bot$.

Lemma 4. *Let $Body(\mathbf{Z})$ be a conjunction of literals and comparisons, where $\mathbf{Z}$ is the list of all its variables, and let $F(\mathbf{Z})$ stand for the formula $\tau^B(Body(\mathbf{Z}))$. For any list $\mathbf{q}$ of precomputed terms over σ_0 of the same length as $\mathbf{Z}$, the formula $gr(F(\mathbf{q}))$ is strongly equivalent to $\tau(Body(\mathbf{q}^S))$.*

The proof uses Lemma 3.

In the proof of the theorem, it is sufficient to consider the case when the program consists of a single rule R. The proof uses Lemmas 3 and 4 and distinguishes between three cases, depending on whether R is a basic rule, a choice rule, or a constraint.

6   Future Work

In published research on the original version of mini-GRINGO, the possibility of relating τ^* to τ is the basis of results on using τ^* for program verification [2, Theorem 3], [3, Section 7], [4, Theorems 1 and 2], [6, Theorem 2], [7, Theorem 3]. The result of this paper will allow us to extend this work to generalized mini-GRINGO and to extend the class of programs that can be verified by ANTHEM.

Acknowledgements. Thanks to Jorge Fandinno, Zachary Hansen and Yuliya Lierler for comments on a draft of this paper.

References

1. Calimeri, F.: ASP-Core-2 input language format. Theory Pract. Logic Program. **20**, 294–309 (2020)
2. Fandinno, J., Hansen, Z., Lierler, Y.: Axiomatization of aggregates in answer set programming. In: Proceedings of the AAAI Conference on Artificial Intelligence (2022)

3. Fandinno, J., Hansen, Z., Lierler, Y., Lifschitz, V., Temple, N.: External behavior of a logic program and verification of refactoring. Theory Pract. Logic Program. (2023)
4. Fandinno, J., Lifschitz, V.: On Heuer's procedure for verifying strong equivalence. In: Proceedings of European Conference on Logics in Artificial Intelligence (2023)
5. Fandinno, J., Lifschitz, V.: Deductive systems for logic programs with counting: preliminary report. In: Proceedings of International Conference on Logic Programming and Nonmonotonic Reasoning (LPNMR) (2024)
6. Fandinno, J., Lifschitz, V., Lühne, P., Schaub, T.: Verifying tight logic programs with Anthem and Vampire. Theory Pract. Logic Program. **20** (2020)
7. Fandinno, J., Lifschitz, V., Temple, N.: Locally tight programs. Theory Pract. Logic Program. (2024)
8. Ferraris, P.: Answer sets for propositional theories. In: Proceedings of International Conference on Logic Programming and Nonmonotonic Reasoning (LPNMR), pp. 119–131 (2005)
9. Gebser, M., et al.: Potassco User Guide (2019). https://github.com/potassco/guide/releases/
10. Hansen, Z., Lierler, Y.: Sm-based semantics for answer set programs containing conditional literals and arithmetic. In: Erdem, E., Vidal, G. (eds.) Practical Aspects of Declarative Languages - 27th International Symposium, PADL 2025, Denver, CO, USA, January 20-21, 2025, Proceedings. Lecture Notes in Computer Science, vol. 15537, pp. 71–87. Springer (2025)
11. Harrison, A., Lifschitz, V., Pearce, D., Valverde, A.: Infinitary equilibrium logic and strongly equivalent logic programs. Artif. Intell. **246**, 22–33 (2017)
12. Heyting, A.: Die formalen Regeln der intuitionistischen Logik. Sitzungsberichte der Preussischen Akademie von Wissenschaften. Physikalisch-mathematische Klasse, pp. 42–56 (1930)
13. Lifschitz, V.: Strong equivalence of logic programs with counting. Theory Pract. Logic Program. **22** (2022)
14. Lifschitz, V., Lühne, P., Schaub, T.: Verifying strong equivalence of programs in the input language of gringo. In: Proceedings of the 15th International Conference on Logic Programming and Non-monotonic Reasoning (2019)
15. Lifschitz, V., Pearce, D., Valverde, A.: Strongly equivalent logic programs. ACM Trans. Comput. Log. **2**, 526–541 (2001)
16. Truszczynski, M.: Connecting first-order ASP and the logic FO(ID) through reducts. In: Erdem, E., Lee, J., Lierler, Y., Pearce, D. (eds.) Correct Reasoning: Essays on Logic-Based AI in Honor of Vladimir Lifschitz, pp. 543–559. Springer (2012)

Author Index

The manufacturer's authorised representative in the EU is Springer
Nature Customer Service Centre GmbH, Europaplatz 3, 69115 Heidelberg,
Germany. If you have any concerns regarding our products, please
contact ProductSafety@springernature.com

Printed and bound by CPI Group (UK) Ltd, Croydon, CR0 4YY
28/04/2026
02098527-0005